SPORTS LAW AND REGULATION

Edited by

Joseph Gordon Hylton

and

Paul M. Anderson

National Sports Law Institute

4951130

Library of Congress Cataloging-in-Publication Data

Sports law and regulation / edited by Joseph Gordon Hylton
and Paul M. Anderson.
    p. cm.
  ISBN 0-87462-006-6 (pbk.)
  1. Sports—Law and legislation—United States. I. Hylton,
J. Gordon (Joseph Gordon), 1952- II. Anderson, Paul M.
(Paul Martin), 1969-
KF3989 .S677 1999
344.73'099—dc21
  99-6783

MARQUETTE UNIVERSITY PRESS
MILWAUKEE

The Association of Jesuit University Presses

MARQUETTE
UNIVERSITY
PRESS

Contents

INTRODUCTION

Sports fans some times imagine that there was once a golden age where the playing field and the court room existed on parallel planes which never intersected. However, the historical record makes it quite clear that there was no such age. Since the beginning of American professional sports in the mid-nineteenth century, players, owners, and fans have repeatedly made recourse to the legal system to enforce their rights.

In 1880, owner Arthur Soden of the National League Boston Red Caps withheld part of the salary of outfielder Charley Jones, ostensively for lackadaisical play. Rather than accept the penalty, Jones filed suit in his native Cincinnati, recovered a judgment against his team, and then attached its assets the next time the Red Caps played in the Queen City.[1] When competitors to the first major sports league, the National Baseball League, emerged—as they did on a fairly regular basis in the nineteenth century team owners were never reluctant to go to court in search of ruling binding players to their existing teams.[2]

Nor were early legal actions restricted to the player-owner relations. In the mid-1880s, the owners of the Detroit Wolverines brought suit against a farmer named Deppart and pursued the action all the way to the Michigan Supreme Court. For a fee, Deppart had allowed baseball fans to watch Wolverine games from the roof of his barn which was adjacent to the team's ballpark.[3] Fans also were willing to take teams to court, particularly when a fan was injured by a batted ball or another spectator.[4] And while professional sports leagues have generally escaped direct governmental regulation, state prohibitions on Sunday baseball were a regular feature of the nineteenth century sporting world.[5] Boxing, of course, has been subject to strict state control almost from its inception as a public, commercial spectator sport.[6]

Although sport and law have been intertwined from the outset, the serious study of sports law is of recent origin. Until the 1970s, the conventional wisdom had it that while various aspects of "the law" applied to sports, they did so in the same way that they did to other industries and other types of human activities. Consequently, it was frequently asserted that there was no such thing as "sports law" per se.

However, during the 1970s the law of sport began to be taken more seriously as a distinct legal specialty. The Sports Lawyers Association was organized in 1974, reflecting the fact that a growing body of lawyers devoted all or substantial portions of their law practices to sports law. In 1977, the American Bar Association began a Forum on the Entertainment and Sports Industries. In the law schools the number of sports law classes grew steadily, and in 1981, the Association of American Law Schools created a section on law and sports. The first important legal treatise devoted to sports law also appeared during the 1970s, most notably Lionel Sobel's PROFESSIONAL SPORTS & THE LAW (1977) and John C. Weistart and Cym H. Lowell's extraordinarily comprehensive THE LAW OF SPORTS (1979).

A number of factors help explain these sudden developments. First of all, the sports industry exploded in terms of both size and profitability. As a result of a growing public fascination with a wide array of sports and the accompanying growth in sports broadcasting, money poured into the coffers of professional, collegiate, and olympic sports. Overall revenues increased dramatically in the 1970s, and, predictably, the greater economic stakes inspired a greater volume of sports-related litigation. The increase in litigation was fueled in large part by the growing militancy of athletes and players associations/ unions who were intent on insuring that participants shared in the growing revenues. Additionally, American courts which had once taken a hands-off approach to many aspects of the management of sports now showed a willingness to entertain legal challenges to even the most entrenched of sports industry practices.

As a result, sports law became an integral part of the American sporting experience. Although to the chagrin of traditional-minded sports fans, since the 1970s, legal issues have regularly competed with the previous days ball games for space on the first page of the sports section. To be an informed sports fan, one had to know at least something about sports law.

Perhaps most important for the development of the field of sports law was the growing awareness of unique quality of the legal problems associated with sports industry. While there was no National Sports Act to preempt and define the field (as the National Labor Relations Act did for labor law), the special problems of sports produced a body of legal results that frequently seemed at odds with the general application of legal rules and statutes. Nowhere was this more true than in the application of the federal antitrust laws to sports, but the distinctive features of sports law were not limited to antitrust. In areas as varied as taxation, contracts, and intellectual property, the special problems of the sports industry made it possible to talk of a distinct "sports law" which crossed traditional doctrinal boundaries but could be talked about as a coherent whole.

However, the most dramatic expansion of sports law as a field occurred in the 1980s and 1990s. Public interest in sports remained on the upswing, and the on-the-field world of professional sports was routinely interrupted by strikes, lockouts, franchise relocations, disputes over property rights, and by a seemingly endless stream of litigation involving owners, players, fans, and broadcasters. Academic interest in sports law kept pace, and by the 1990s, a majority of American law schools offered at least one course in sports law, and professors of sports law had a number of different casebooks from which to choose.[7] Today, two law schools—Marquette and Tulane—offer extensive sports law programs within the bounds of a traditional J.D. curriculum. In addition, a number of scholarly journals devoted solely to sports law have appeared.[8]

Since its organization in 1989, the National Sports Law Institute of Marquette University has played a significant role in the development of the field of sports law. Its journal, the MARQUETTE SPORTS LAW JOURNAL, was the first scholarly journal in the United States devoted exclusively to the law of sports. For a decade, path-breaking articles addressing a panoply of issues from the world of sports have appeared within its covers. Bridging the gap between the academy and the world of law practice, the JOURNAL has been an important participant in the past decade's debates over sports law and sports policy.

The essays in this collection all originally appeared in the MARQUETTE SPORTS LAW JOURNAL. Collectively, they serve as an introduction to the field of sports law for all students of the sports industry with or without formal legal training. Designed for both classroom use and the general reader, SPORTS LAW AND REGULATION also provides a general history of the law of sports in the closing decades of the twentieth century and a guide to where it is headed in the next.

Joseph Gordon Hylton

[1] *Baseball Chronology - CBS SportsLine, September, 1880,* <http://
    cbs.cportsline.com/u/baseball/bol/chronology/1880
    SEPTEMBER.html>
[2] The competitor "major" baseball leagues that appeared during the National
    League's first quarter century were the National/International Associa-
    tion (1877-81); the American Association (1881-1891); the Union
    Association (1884); the Players League (1890), and, of course, the
    American League (1901-03). (Note: The International/National Asso-
    ciation of 1877-91 should not to be confused with the National League's
    predecessor National Association which operated from 1871-75.)
    Reported cases involving the validity of contracts of players switching
    teams include: Allegheny Base Ball Club v. Bennett, 14 F. 257 (W.D. Pa.
    1882); Metropolitan Exhibition Co. v. Ewing, 42 F. 198 (S.D.N.Y.
    1890); Metropolitan Exhibition Co. v. Ward, 9 N.Y.S. 779 (N.Y.Sup.Ct.
    1890); Philadelphia Ball Club v. Lajoie, 202 Pa. 210, 51 A. 973 (1902).
[3] Detroit Base-Ball Club v. Deppart, 61 Mich. 63, 27 N.W. 856 (1886).
[4] Negligence-*Duty of Baseball Club to Spectator,* 24 Mich. Law Rev. 76
    (1925).
[5] See for example, Ex parte Roguemore, 60 Tex. Crim. 282, 131 S.W. 1101
    (Tex. Crim. App. 1910).
[6] *See* April Anderson, *The Punch that Landed: The Professional Boxing Safety
    Act of 1996,* 9 MARQ. SPORTS L.J. 191, (1998); STEVEN A. RIESS, SPORT IN
    INDUSTRIAL AMERICA: 1850-1920, 145-149 (1995); ELLIOTT J. GORN &
    WARREN GOLDSTEIN, A BRIEF HISTORY OF AMERICAN SPORTS 114-129
    (1993).
[7] These include MICHAEL J. COZZILLIO & MARK S. LEVINSTEIN, SPORTS LAW:
    CASES AND MATERIALS (1997), MATTHEW C. MCKINNON, ET AL., SPORTS
    LAW (1996), WALTER C. CHAMPION, JR., FUNDAMENTALS OF SPORTS LAW
    (1990), RAY YASSER, ET AL., SPORTS LAW: CASES AND MATERIALS (3RD ED.
    1997), PAUL C. WEILER & GARY R. ROBERTS, SPORTS AND THE LAW: TEXT,
    CASES, PROBLEMS (2ND ED. 1998), and ROBERT M. JARVIS & PHYLLIS
    COLEMAN, SPORTS LAW: CASES AND MATERIALS (1999).
[8] These include the MARQUETTE SPORTS LAW JOURNAL, the SPORTS LAWYERS
    JOURNAL, the SETON HALL JOURNAL OF SPORT LAW, and the recently
    established VIRGINIA JOURNAL OF SPORTS AND THE LAW.

ACKNOWLEDGEMENTS

The essays produced in this book were originally published in the MARQUETTE SPORTS LAW JOURNAL, a publication of Marquette University which holds the copyright to their contents. Appreciation is extended to the students who have served on the staff of the JOURNAL since its founding in 1990. Special thanks are due to Ante Z. Udovicic, Marquette Law '98, who performed the initial formatting and editing of most of the articles that appear in this book. Our greatest debt, however, is to Professor Andrew Tallon of the Marquette University Press whose support made this project possible.

Joseph Gordon Hylton
Paul M. Anderson

PART I

SPORTS FRANCHISE ISSUES

SQUEEZE PLAY:
THE GAME OF OWNERS, CITIES, LEAGUES AND CONGRESS*

John Wunderli

The geographic volatility of professional sports teams has been the source of much controversy in recent decades. When teams do move, as when the Raiders left Oakland for Los Angeles (only to later return), when the Rams left Los Angeles for St. Louis, and when the Browns moved from Cleveland to Baltimore (and became the Ravens), fans in the departed city reportedly felt something akin to a death in the family and began to clamor for some sort of government intervention to right the wrong perpetrated upon them. Similarly, when National Hockey League teams departed from Winnipeg and Quebec to Phoenix and Denver, many Canadians viewed it as a national disaster.

More often than not, however, it is not the actual relocation of a team, but the threatened relocation that affects the sports fan. In recent years, this has taken the form of existing teams, particularly those in smaller markets, publicly proclaiming that unless a new stadium or arena is constructed at public expense, the team will be "forced" to relocate to a more hospitable environment.

In this essay, John Wunderli examines the economic background of the franchise relocation phenomenon and explains the inadequacy of antitrust law to deal with this problem. In the end, Wunderli endorses formal congressional intervention into the marketplace to insure that the supply of major league sports franchises not be too narrowly restricted by existing major league sports leagues.

* From Volume 5, Number 1, Fall 1994, pp. 83-121.

I. Introduction

In the next ten years, twelve stadium leases will expire between NFL or Major League Baseball franchises and their host community.[1] In the next twenty years, twenty-eight (28) stadium leases will expire.[2] The impending expiration of a lease will often signal the commencement of a game — an invitational sponsored by the affected franchise owner — called "So you really want a professional sports franchise?" ("Squeeze Play" for short). The players in this game are the owner, the league, the cities competing to acquire the franchise, and the city fighting to retain the franchise. At the end of the game, one city *may* win, the league may or may not win, one or more cities will lose, and the owner will almost certainly win.

The 1982-85 lease expiration season provided some interesting contests. In 1982 Al Davis moved the Raiders from Oakland to Los Angeles, leaving the city of Oakland and the county of Alameda to pay $1.5 million a year until the year 2004 to service the debt on the Oakland-Alameda Coliseum.[3] Oakland lost, Los Angeles won, the NFL lost, and Al Davis won.[4]

In December of 1984, Philadelphia Eagles owner Leonard Tose announced that he was going to move the Eagles to Phoenix.[5] In response, the city of Philadelphia offered Tose: 1) rent deferment for ten years, 2) stadium renovations, including the construction of luxury boxes, 3) a new practice facility, and 4) promotion of the team.[6] Tose accepted Philadelphia's offer and the Eagles remained in Veteran's Stadium. The city of Philadelphia "won," Phoenix lost, and Tose definitely won.

Within months, Robert Irsay threatened to move the Colts from Baltimore to Indianapolis, in spite of the recent $24 million in stadium improvements.[7] Baltimore responded by offering: 1) a $15 million loan at 8%, 2) $6 million in cash for a new training facility, and 3) guaranteed ticket sales of 43,000 per game for the 1984-85 season. [8] However, Baltimore apparently was not up to the task, as Indianapolis "won" the Colts with an offer of: 1) a new 61,300 seat capacity domed stadium, 2) modest rent, 3) a $5 million training facility, and 4) guaranteed ticket sales of 45,000/game for three seasons.[9] Baltimore lost, Indianapolis won, Irsay won, and the league had a team move from the 14th largest market to the 34th.[10]

Shortly thereafter, the Saints and the Cardinals threatened to move from New Orleans and St. Louis, respectively. Baltimore and Phoenix, both recent losers, threw their hats in the ring to compete for the Saints.[11] Also playing the game at this time was Jacksonville, with a standing offer of an 82,000 seat stadium, new training facilities, sky boxes, and a guarantee worth $125.8 million.[12] New Orleans fought off all challengers, but at a price of a new training facility, tax abatements, bond issues, and other public subsidies which were estimated at one time to "drain[ ] the public coffers by $6 million in operating deficits and $10 million in annual bond payments."[13] Phoenix and Baltimore lost again; and owner Tom Benson won. However, Phoenix later managed a victory at St. Louis' expense when the Cardinals relocated. William Bidwell also won, and the NFL watched as a team went from the 12th largest market to the 26th.

Table 1 illustrates the pervasiveness of this game.[14] It contains a compilation of the win/loss records of the cities who either won or lost a professional baseball, football, basketball, or hockey franchise during the 1971-1982 seasons. A city gets a win if it acquires a franchise by relocation or expansion, and gets a loss if it loses a franchise by relocation or dissolution. The table only deals with events which result in franchise creation, movement, and demise, and not with the competitions which result in the status quo. Although not all of the contest outcomes represented by the standings had the impact of a Raiders relocation, it remains particularly striking that fifty-eight cities were involved in the major league professional sports franchise game in just a twelve-year period.

TABLE I

Win/Loss Records of Cities Who Played the Professional Sports Franchise Creation, Movement, and Demise Game During the 1971-1982 Seasons

CITY	W	L	%	CITY	W	L	%
Rutherford, NJ	2	0	1.000	Phoenix	1	1	.500
Seattle	2	0	1.000	Indianapolis	1	1	.500
Portland	1	0	1.000	Toronto	1	1	.500
Foxboro	1	0	1.000	Birmingham	1	1	.500
Arlington, TX	1	0	1.000	Cincinnati	1	1	.500
Nassau County	1	0	1.000	Winnipeg	1	1	.500
San Francisco	1	0	1.000	San Diego	3	4	.429

Orchard Park	1	0	1.000	Los Angeles	2	3	.400
Hartford	1	0	1.000	Dallas	1	2	.333
Landover, MD	1	0	1.000	New Orleans	1	2	.333
San Antonio	1	0	1.000	Washington, DC	1	2	.333
Pontiac, MI	1	0	1.000	Vancouver	1	2	.333
Tampa Bay	1	0	1.000	Ottawa	1	2	.333
Rutgers, NJ	1	0	1.000	Detroit	1	2	.333
Anaheim	1	0	1.000	Baltimore	1	3	.250
Salt Lake	2	1	.667	Cincinnati	0	1	.000
Kansas City	2	1	.667	Pittsburgh	0	1	.000
Calgary	2	1	.667	Miami	0	1	.000
Minneapolis	2	1	.667	Philadelphia	0	1	.000
Buffalo	2	2	.500	Charlotte	0	1	.000
Cleveland	2	2	.500	Chicago	0	1	.000
Denver	2	2	.500	St. Paul	0	1	.000
Memphis	1	1	.500	Hollywood, FL	0	1	.000
Norfolk	1	1	.500	Louisville	0	1	.000
Houston	1	1	.500	Commach, L.I.	0	1	.000
Atlanta	1	1	.500	Bloomington	0	1	.000
Cherry Hill, NJ	1	1	.500	Boston	0	2	.000
St. Louis	1	1	.500	New York	0	2	.000
				Oakland	0	2	.000

Perhaps even more striking than the number of cities involved in this game is the amount of money at stake. In 1984, it was estimated that in twenty years more than $6 billion dollars were spent to build or refurbish stadiums to attract or retain professional baseball and football teams alone.[15]

The initial question to be addressed is whether or not this competition between cities and the subsequent transfer of wealth from a city to a franchise owner presents a problem that needs to be solved. The cities obviously see some benefit in having a professional sports franchise within its walls, and are willing to pay to have this benefit up to its perceived value. The cities are, in effect, consumers of professional sports franchises. A lease agreement between a franchise and a public stadium more accurately represents a city's rental of a franchise than a franchise's rental of a stadium.

This competition between cities for franchises would not be troubling if a fixed number of franchises spontaneously dropped from the sky and had to locate somewhere. In that case, we could justifiably rely on competition to efficiently allocate the franchises to the cities who will benefit the most from them. Of course, the cities with franchises would still be troubled if a team subsequently moved. This should not be of great concern, however, since it is not hard to imagine that after the initial allocation of teams, a city without one will emerge, obtaining better utility from a franchise than a city which already has one. Teams should locate in cities that value them the most. Nonetheless, this very scenario involving a team changing cities has been the main focus of concern in the courts and in Congress.

The troubling aspect of this competition among cities is that there is no magical fixed number of franchises to be allocated among our cities. Imagine if a firm created a communications system or product which could interconnect citizens within a city and between cities. Imagine also that the system was cost effective in all cities with a population of one million or above. If this firm was the only firm offering this product, we could expect: 1) that the firm would not produce a product for every city over one million; 2) that cities over one million would compete against one another for the available products, ultimately paying more than the social cost of the product; and 3) the excess profit would go from the taxpayer to the controlling firm. This would be troubling.

Similarly troubling, the owners of professional sports franchises, acting collectively in leagues, decide how many franchises to "rent" to the cities. If economic theory is at all reliable, this means that the owners can be expected to not offer franchises at their social cost, but rather at a price significantly above — a monopoly price. This will result in a misallocation of resources. Consider the following:

> [M]any of the families in Louisiana would find it tough to afford even the guided tour of the Superdome, even though the people of Louisiana subsidize the Superdome to the tune of $3 million to $5 million per year . . . Meanwhile, the people of New Orleans, many of whom are poor, pay the highest city sales tax in the United States (9%), send their children to what may be the poorest public schools in North America, and face cuts in public transportation and city services.[16]

This quote illustrates the allocative decisions that cities must make. A monopoly price charged for the Saints distorts the allocation of resources.[17] It is this dynamic which should concern us and lead us to reevaluate the rules of the game.

This article will look at questions surrounding the rules of the game between team owners and cities. Of particular concern are these questions: (1) Who should make the rules of this game?; and (2) What should the rules be? It will of course be necessary to try to identify what the rules currently are, and who is making them. In addressing these questions, we need to analyze what the "players"[18] want, or in other words, what outcomes are considered to be victories.

II. The Players

A. The Owners and the League

An owner must be considered a businessman first. As such, he[19] wins by maximizing profits, measured by the margin between costs and revenues. Of course, this margin is widened by either increasing revenues or decreasing costs.

A franchise's direct revenues, or receipts, are basically a function of two variables: 1) the population size of the metropolitan area, and 2) the team's winning percentage.[20] For our purposes, our analysis is focused on what an owner wants from a city, so the critical variable affecting club receipts is the city's population size. Scully estimated that "each one million in population is worth $2.9 million in club revenues, holding the quality of the club constant."[21] So we would expect that an owner would prefer his team to be in a high population area, and would only move his team to a smaller statistical area if the lost revenues due to the move were at least compensated for by a decrease in costs.

Decreased costs come in the form of public subsidies. These include the following; 1) reduced rent for the use of public stadia, 2) construction of new facilities at public expense,[22] and 3) tax abatements for privately owned facilities. Not surprisingly, these are the most common demands owners make on cities.[23]

In a world of franchise free agency, we would expect teams to be located in the highest population areas. Since owners derive revenue from the population base of a city, they will require more from smaller cities and less from large cities. At the same time, it seems intuitive that a larger city would have more resources to devote to a professional sports team than a smaller city. So why are the Colts in Indianapolis and the Cardinals in Phoenix?

First, consider the effect of revenue sharing. Revenue sharing insulates the owner from the adverse effects of moving from a high population city to a low population city. Since the receipts affected by the population size are spread among all the teams in the league, a team will only have to internalize a small fraction of the lost revenues due to the drop in population caused by the move. The extent to which a league shares revenues is the extent to which all cities compete on a level playing field to rent a franchise. Since an owner need not consider population size, the winning city will simply be the one which offers more subsidies, or a greater reduction in costs.[24]

Once cities are on a level playing field, there is still an intuition that the larger cities should be able to offer more than the smaller cities. There are two possible responses to this intuition. First, while a larger city may have greater revenues available to it due to a larger tax base, this does not necessarily mean that the larger city has more funds to devote to professional sports. With larger city revenues come greater demands for those revenues. A large city may have social, infrastructure, and educational demands that smaller cities do not. The point is that a large city will not necessarily have greater discretionary funds to devote to professional sports than a smaller city.

Second, we must consider the marquee effect of a major league team. A smaller city may be willing to spend more to be considered a "big league city" than a larger, established city. Other reasons for wanting a franchise will be discussed in the next section as we take a closer look at the cities. For now, we must keep in mind that factors exist which disrupt any natural stability of teams gravitating to the largest cities and staying there.

These dynamics present interesting issues for a league. On one hand, the moves of the Colts and Cardinals should cause the NFL some concern, since both moves represented a loss in population and presumably a loss in revenue to be shared among the owners. On the other hand, the league is no more than the owners themselves, and it is this very threat of relocation which allows each owner to extract greater public subsidies from their host city. It is not hard to believe that the public subsidies received as a result of the relocation threat more than make up for the lost revenue of a couple of moves. However, the league still has reason to be concerned if too many owners make good on their threats.

Major League Baseball has less revenue sharing and more group control over its members. We might expect that MLB would be relatively stable, which it has been in recent years. Baseball owners must consider the population base of a potential new city more so than football owners. Nevertheless, as the demographics of the nation change, it is to be expected that new metropolitan areas will emerge to compete on equal footing with an area in which a baseball team is currently located. And although relatively stable, MLB still maintains the threat of relocation in the form of the Suncoast Dome in Tampa/St. Petersburg.[25] The new and open Suncoast Dome, as well as the recent NFL relocations, serve as a reminder to the cities that the franchise stability of Major League Baseball is due more to cities like Chicago building new Comiskey Parks than any benevolence of the league.

History suggests that no sports league has made a strong effort to prevent its franchises from moving. For example, between 1950 and 1982, eleven relocations occurred in baseball, forty in basketball, fourteen in hockey, and thirteen in football.[26] The few times in which a league rejected a bid to relocate was directed at "mavericks" of the league, such as Charlie Finley, Bill Veeck, and Al Davis. Furthermore, Finley's and Veeck's teams were eventually allowed to move after they no longer owned the team.[27]

Although moves from high population areas to low population areas might be a concern, a greater concern to any league is owners moving from low population to high population areas. An open high population area represents an exploitable area for the entire league, either as an expansion opportunity or as an open and visible "Suncoast Dome" threat. Owners, acting as a league, do not like to see someone else appropriating an exploitable area to themselves, as did the Raiders and the Clippers. In either case, however, a team relocation can mean substantial direct benefits to the moving owner at the expense of lost potential revenues to the league as a whole.

The main point is that it is not at all clear, at any given time, whether a league would favor a move of one of its franchises or not. A move could mean moderate lost revenues to the league. However, a league is a collection of owners, each concerned with his own opportunities to maximize profits by pursuing increased revenue sources or decreased costs. Most owners would want to be able to capitalize on future lucrative offers themselves, or at least maintain a viable threat so as to extract further concessions from their current host community. Therefore, even if the owners could prevent any individual owner from moving, we would expect leagues to continue to be very liberal in granting permission.

B. The Cities

Contrary to the artificial world which was constructed earlier by Table 1 and the accompanying discussion, in which a city wins when it has a professional sports franchise and loses when it does not, cities win in the real world by maximizing the quality of life of its citizens. A city must make many allocative decisions towards this end. Professional sports is one of many uses to which a city can devote its resources. As a tool for increasing the quality of life, a professional sports franchise must be measured against social, infrastructure, health, and education needs. This section addresses why a city wants, or should want, a professional sports franchise.

Cities can be viewed in one of two ways, or a mixture of both, with respect to professional sports. They can be seen as investors or consumers. As investors, cities get into the business of professional sports to get a financial return or, in other words, to reap direct and indirect economic benefits. As a consumer, cities rent franchises as a means to obtain certain intangible benefits, to be used as a unifying mechanism, to generate civic pride, to give prestige to the city, or as an educational tool. Let us not also forget that a city is renting a team to provide another entertainment outlet for its citizens.

Whether or not a professional sports team is a good financial investment for cities is a questionable proposition. It is clear that for a sports team to be a good investment, the economic benefits must exceed the costs. The costs to a city of having a franchise take many forms. There are stadium construction costs and annual deficits associated with reduced rental charges. "Costs, however, may take forms other than operational expenditures and bonded indebtedness. Opportunity costs of land use and foregone tax revenues are not analyzed. Costs for additional police protection, traffic control, and sanitation rarely are calculated."[28] While it may be difficult, a reasonably accurate number could be obtained, the result of which would represent the actual financial cost of a franchise. It is more difficult to measure the economic benefits.

Johnson defines economic benefits, direct and indirect, as follows:

> Direct economic benefits take the form of rental income, tax revenues, franchise expenditures in the community, and increased jobs. Indirect economic benefits include the additional business generated by fans and participants in related industries such as food, hotel, and transportation; the increased convention business a city attracts as a result of a team's presence; and the additional jobs produced by the secondary effects of a team's presence.[29]

The direct and indirect economic benefits together represent the "economic impact" of a franchise. The estimates of the economic impact of various teams on their respective cities shows a considerable range of potential economic activity.

It is estimated that the Packers economic impact is $20-25 million; the Pirates, $21 million; the Raiders (in Oakland), $36 million in direct benefits and $100 million in indirect benefits; the Jets, $33 million; and the Colts, $30 million.[30] Other estimates, however, have the Raiders (in Oakland) worth $36 million in direct benefits and $180 million in indirect benefits (or overall economic activity).[31] Still others estimate the Raiders impact in Oakland at $75 million total; and the Colts, $35 million.[32] And others claim the Colts impact is $21 million; while the Pirates generate $37 million in economic activity.[33]

This range of estimates can be attributed to "alternative assumptions . . . when researchers differ in skill or in predisposition."[34] The measurement of indirect economic benefits is highly speculative. First, a multiplier must be chosen to estimate the impact of every new dollar spent on the economy. The multiplier chosen can vary, depending on how self-contained the area economy is, or how much "leakage" of economic activity there is out to other areas. "Generally, the smaller the community the smaller the multiplier because these areas have greater difficulty containing all spending than do larger areas."[35] Multipliers range from 1.2 in a study of the Pittsburgh Pirates, to 3.2 in a team-financed study on the impact of Chicago baseball.[36] Even more distressing than the range of multipliers is the implicit assumption that the use of a multiplier makes; the assumption is:

> that all first-round spending attributable to team or stadium activities is net new spending for the local area . . . . Spending on sports may merely redistribute preexisting local spending. What if the dollar spent at the stadium or the adjacent restaurant is merely one dollar less spent on entertainment elsewhere in the city?[37]

The concern with this assumption is that a team only produces a positive impact on the economy if it is attracting recreational spending from outside of the studied economy.

Another issue associated with estimating the economic impact of professional sports is the type of jobs created. Most of the jobs created by teams are seasonal, low-wage, and part-time.[38] This means that the presence of a team in a city could actually reduce the city's share of regional income if the surrounding communities are "higher wage."[39]

Perhaps we should step back from the world of economic impacts and consider the direct costs and revenues of the stadia. In 1974, Benjamin Okner published a widely cited study of twenty baseball or football stadia.[40] He concluded that the average stadium covers only

60% of total costs, and noticed a tendency toward greater public subsidization. The difference between the cost and the direct revenue on a stadium must be made up by other revenues that the city government makes as a result of the franchise's presence. In other words, the economic impact of the team must be translated into an increase in tax revenues (or other revenue source, such as public transit) under the same tax levels or rate structure, or the franchise must be considered either a bad investment or an expense.

Gray gives an example of a hypothetical city which invests $100 million in a sports stadium.[41] He assumes that the opportunity cost is five percent, so the city would require a $5 million annual return on its investment plus additional revenue to cover its annual operating and maintenance costs (which he assumes are $1 million).

> If the city could recover $4 million of this $6 million through new tax and other revenues, such as increased sales taxes, entertainment taxes, income taxes, and transit use generated because of the presence of the franchise, the city could still recover its opportunity cost by charging the franchise tenant as low as $2 million in annual rental fees.[42]

It must be assumed that by "new tax and other revenues," Gray does not mean that the city could raise the tax levels or create new taxes and have that count as a return to an investment. The additional revenues must be the result of real economic growth. Real economic growth is measured in the subjective world of economic impact projections, which brings us full circle.

To summarize this discussion of the economic impact of professional sports, the factors to look for are: 1) the extent a team attracts spending from outside of the area paying the costs of the team; 2) the extent the team deflects residents of the area from spending elsewhere; 3) the creation of jobs — look for whether they are permanent, temporary, seasonal, full-time, or part-time; and, 4) the additional tax revenue generated by the above three factors, holding tax levels constant.

The question of whether a sports franchise is "worth it" financially to a community is unanswerable in the abstract, and is very difficult, if not impossible, even in any specific case. What is clear is that money is commonly transferred from cities to sports teams in exchange for perceived economic and intangible benefits. There is reason to be skeptical of claims that professional sports produce net positive financial returns to a city, although this may be true in some cases. But in light of the strong position of the owners in this game, it is not hard to imagine that any financial gains which will come to a city as a result of a franchise will be captured and appropriated to the team itself somehow. It seems more realistic to view cities as consumers of the intangible benefits of having a professional sports franchise.

As a result, we must look at these intangible benefits which the cities are purchasing. Commonly cited intangible benefits include a boost to civic pride, a unifying force, and prestige. If civic pride is meant to refer to the lift the city gets through experiencing vicarious victory, then this element appears to be a wash. If a city benefits from victory, it should be acknowledged that it is harmed by loss. In which case, the affect on civic pride must be considered neutral.

However, a professional sports team can be a unifying force whether the team wins or loses. Whether a city is rejoicing together or commiserating together, there is value in the fact that the city is doing something together. It is important for communities to look for ways to bind its citizens together. Communities will benefit from any mechanism which encourages individuals to transcend cultural, religious, racial, political, or economic divisions. Sport is central enough to the experience of the vast majority of people to be a useful tool to break down the barriers which divide citizens. However, it must be strongly noted that a professional sports team does not automatically have a unifying effect by virtue of being a professional sports team. In fact, the same power a sports team has to unify, it has to divide, if it is perceived as only for a particular race, economic class, or culture. Prestige is perhaps the most likely, and at the same time least appealing, reason for a city to acquire a major league sports franchise. There are two main problems with pursuing or subsidizing a major league team for the prestige it brings the city. First, prestige is merely a function of perceptions which could quickly change. One day the city is a "major league" city, the next day it is a minor league city for having a bad team, and the next day it is a stupid city for spending so many taxpayer dollars just so people will think the city is major league. Second, any prestige that comes from having a major league franchise will be lost, and more so, if the franchise leaves. "It's almost worse for a city's image to lose a major league team than to have never had one at all."[43]

If the only thing a major league sports team had to offer a city was prestige, then the competition among cities to acquire teams would not be of concern, as it would be no concern if the teams magically dropped from the sky. The competition would be as entertaining a spectacle as the sports themselves, perhaps more so. A cynic would feel this way about watching cities compete against each other today, musing at the folly of the cities handing over large amounts of money to snake oil salesmen in pursuit of illusory fame and riches. However, to those who believe that a sports team can be a very positive element in a community, the fact that two cities compete against each other for a sports team when each is equally able to support a team is less amusing, especially when the team owner is the one inviting the competition, setting the rules, and profiting at the cities' expense.

A professional sports team should be a tool to be used to improve the quality of life of the members of a community. A sports team can be a very effective educational and communicative tool. The intangibles of a sports franchise can be good or bad, but sports is definitely a powerful medium. It may sound trite, but it is nevertheless true, that a sporting contest has metaphorical qualities which lends itself to shared observation, evaluation, and discussion. It also has romantic qualities which frame idealistic thoughts and memories.[44] Professional sports can also bring to the fore pettiness, greed, divisiveness, and an exaggerated emphasis on athletic victories.[45] A sports franchise is a powerful tool that a city can use to improve the quality of life of its citizens.

III. The Rules of the Game

There needs to be rules to this game involving the cities, owners, and leagues. Determinations need to made concerning which cities should have franchises, and under what conditions a franchise should be able to move from one city to another. The rules are first concerned with who should have the authority to make the necessary determinations: the owners, the leagues, the cities, Congress, the market, or some combination? Second, the rules must concern what those determinations should be, given different circumstances.

Basically, there are two working rules of the game: (1) teams cannot agree not to "compete;" and (2) cities cannot "take" teams. In the world of law, this refers to the law of antitrust and eminent domain. This article will take the rule against the taking of teams as given and focus on the rules within the framework of antitrust. Next, this article will look to proposed changes or additions to the rules in the form of federal legislation from mandatory lease terms to mandatory expansion. Finally, this article will propose what the rules should be.

A. Antitrust

Antitrust law and concepts can be both complicated and elusive, so before we dive into the specific cases which concern our issues, it will be helpful to identify the overarching themes and goals of antitrust. The source of antitrust law which we will be focusing on is Section 1 and 2 of the Sherman Act, which condemns 1) every contract, combination, and conspiracy in restraint of trade and 2) monopolization, combinations and conspiracies to monopolize, and attempts to monopolize.[46] The Sherman Act stands as a far and deep reaching rule regulating the game of American business and economic organization. The question is whether it can reach our specific game.

Generally, the body of antitrust "common law" which has emerged from the Sherman Act can be said to have two goals: 1) to achieve an efficient allocation of society's resources, and 2) to prevent large concentrations of economic, and thus political, power. The antitrust laws rely on consumer preferences to determine what is an optimal allocation of resources. In other words, individual consumers choose to allocate their personal resources among various products at given prices based on individual preferences. These preferences are not questioned, but rather are by definition, optimal. The aggregation of individual consumer choices provides our societal allocation.

In order for consumer preferences to result in an optimal allocation, the consumers must be choosing between products offered at their social cost. If a consumer is faced with a choice between two products, such as sports and education, and one product is not offered at its social cost, then the resulting consumer allocation will not be optimal; a product offered at other than social cost is said to create an allocative distortion.

This is where the concept of competition comes in for antitrust purposes. Competition is the mechanism used by antitrust law to assure that products are offered to consumers at a price which equals the social cost to produce the product. Perfect competition in an industry will result in that industry's product being offered to the consumer at social cost. The antithesis of a perfectly competitive industry is a monopolized industry, characterized by reduced output and prices above social costs. Antitrust law demands competition by condemning the practices which move away from perfect competition and towards monopoly. "[A]ntitrust supplements or, perhaps, defines, the rules of the game by which competition takes place."[47]

The focus on competition defines both the reach and the limitations of antitrust law to achieve the ultimate goal of optimal and efficient allocation of resources. Competition may not be sustainable or desirable in an industry, such as one that will lead to a natural monopoly.[48] In such a case, absent any wrongdoing, the industry is beyond the reach of the antitrust rules, and other rules must be brought to bear on the industry to insure that the product's price approximates what we would expect under competition. Consider the following assessment by Areeda and Kaplow:

> [A]n otherwise perfectly competitive system will not always achieve an efficient result. . . . [P]roduction at least cost will sometimes be possible only at a scale of production where a few firms or even a single firm can satisfy the entire demand. In that event competition will not be sustainable, price will probably exceed the competitive price, and competitive efficiency will be lost. Proper regulation could theoretically restore pricing efficiency. This is one explanation of government regulation of public utilities.[49]

So it appears from the outset that antitrust law may not have all the necessary rules of the game.

The above analysis both frames the issues and reveals the conclusion of this article: If a) the cities are treated as consumers, making allocative decisions between, for example, professional sports and education; and b) the product which the league offers to the cities as consumers is viewed as the rental of a professional sports franchise, and c) each professional sport is a natural monopoly[50], we would expect 1) that the number of franchises available to the cities would be less than optimal; 2) the price of the franchises to the cities would be above social costs, with monopoly profits going to the league members; 3) the effect of low output and high cost will result in a distortion in the cities' allocation of resources[51]; 4) the antitrust laws will not be able to solve the real problem of sub-optimal allocation of resources; and, therefore, 5) external regulation by the federal government is necessary, and 6) this regulation should take the form of setting a "price" for a city to rent a franchise, at which price one should be made available to them.

We will return to evaluate the effect of our assumptions and predictions, but for now, we must return to earth and take a look at the cases which have sparked such lively discussion among courts, academics, leagues, city councils, and sports fans.

B. Raiders I

In 1978, the lease between the Raiders and the Oakland Coliseum expired.[52] That same year, Carroll Rosenbloom decided to move the Rams from the Los Angeles Coliseum (Coliseum) to Anaheim.[53] This left the Coliseum in search of a new tenant and Al Davis, owner of the Raiders, in an enviable bargaining position. After Oakland officials refused to meet Davis' demands, he decided to move his Raiders to Los Angeles, and so notified the NFL on March 3, 1980.[54] One week later, acting under the recently amended Rule 4.3 of Article IV of the NFL Constitution, which requires three-quarters approval for any team to relocate[55] to a different city, the NFL voted 22-0 against Al Davis' proposed move.[56] Two years later, a Los Angeles jury agreed with the Los Angeles Coliseum and Al Davis that this was a violation of § 1 of the Sherman Act.[57] The Ninth Circuit was then asked to decide whether the jury could be allowed to reach that conclusion. The court held that the jury could find that Rule 4.3 violated § 1 of the Sherman Act under the circumstances.

In order to find a § 1 violation, an agreement between two or more separate entities must first be shown. After an agreement is shown, the court will decide whether the type of agreement conforms to a paradigmatic fact pattern which can confidently be condemned as anticompetitive without further analysis ("per se" treatment), or whether a more involved analysis is required to determine what effect the agreement has on competition ("rule of reason" analysis). Per se treatment is usually reserved for cases in which horizontal competitors (separate firms offering the same or similar products to the same group of consumers) agree to fix prices,[58] divide markets,[59] or not deal with a competitor or supplier.[60] A rule of reason analysis is for the non-obvious cases and requires a balancing of pro- and anti-competitive effects of the agreement in a relevant geographic and product market, as well as a look to any possible less restrictive alternatives.

The *Raiders* court held that; (1) NFL teams were separate entities for § 1 purposes, (2) that "per se" treatment was inappropriate, and (3) that pursuant to a rule of reason analysis, a jury could find that competition for NFL football was diminished in southern California as a result of the operation of Rule 4.3 on the Raiders proposed move. Therefore, Rule 4.3 violated § 1 of the Sherman Act in this case.

The claim against the NFL was that the individual teams agreed, through the mechanism of Rule 4.3, to prevent the Raiders from moving into the Rams territory and competing against them. On the surface, this looks like an agreement among competitors to divide the market and not compete with each other within those market divisions. Such an agreement seems like a candidate for per se treatment. Yet the court recognized the unique character of the sports industry, and it was confusing enough to not condemn the NFL so quickly.[61]

1. Single Entity Issue

Much of the difficulty of applying the antitrust laws in the sports industry stems from the various levels of competition that exist among the teams in a given league. The central difference between an individual sports team and a typical individual firm of production is 1) a sports team cannot produce a marketable product without other sports teams, and as a result, 2) it is not a rational economic goal of any sports team to "compete" so well as to put the other teams out of business.[62] Neale concludes from this that all teams which cooperate to produce a single "World Champion" should be considered as divisions of a single economic firm.[63]

I f teams were viewed merely as divisions of a single firm, then they would be incapable of conspiring under § 1 of the Sherman Act. This idea frightened the district court enough to cite it as the first reason to not view leagues as single entities.[64] The second reason was that "other organizations have been found to violate § 1 though their product . . . requires the same kind of cooperation from the organization's members."[65] Given the examples used by the Ninth Circuit in agreement, this statement is clearly wrong.[66] The majority seemed to be concerned not with the level of cooperation required to create the product, but rather with who makes the policy decisions.[67] The third reason given by the district court and accepted by the Ninth Circuit was that the teams are separate business entities whose products have an independent value.[68]

What seems to be driving this case and others which treat teams as separate entities is the observation that "clubs do compete with one another off the field as well as on to acquire players, coaches, and management personnel [and] . . . where two teams operate in close proximity, there is also competition for fan support, local television and local radio revenues, and media space."[69] The court wants to be able to force teams to continue to compete in these spheres and wants to keep § 1 as a vehicle to do so.

The *Raiders* majority, therefore, would have all league agreements pass a rule of reason analysis in order to have the blessing of antitrust.

Roberts, on the other hand, argues that all league agreements should be immune from § 1 liability.[70] However, the dissent in *Raiders* would carve out a functional immunity for "downstream" outputs, i.e. getting the football product to the fans, but would maintain § 1 scrutiny in the sphere of "upstream" inputs, i.e. players, coaches, and investors.

The dissent's argument has appeal because it appears to address a concern that players would be exploited without § 1 forcing teams to compete for them, while at the same time granting the league some relief. However, with respect to the players, it is not at all clear that they 1) should be a concern of antitrust or 2) need § 1 to protect them from exploitation.[71] With respect to granting the league some relief, the world of the dissent is not clear enough to be helpful. The dissent constructs a functional test where the league is immune from § 1 attack in instances in which "member clubs must coordinate intraleague policy and practice if the joint product is to result."[72] It is not even clear that the present case would meet this functional test. One might rightly ask why it is necessary for a league to keep the Raiders in Oakland, or control any team movement for that matter, in order to produce their product.

2. Rule of Reason Analysis

The consequence of treating teams as separate entities in this case is that a jury must now determine whether on balance the application of Rule 4.3 harmed competition. The court allowed the jury to define the relevant product market as NFL football and the relevant geographic market as southern California. The consequence of this market definition is that the NFL loses. It would be difficult once the market was defined as NFL football in southern California to find anything procompetitive about Rule 4.3 to balance against even the most minor anticompetitive effect.

If the geographic market was enlarged to the U.S., or even just to California, the effect on competition would be a wash. The competition lost in Los Angeles between the Raiders and the Rams if the Raiders are prevented from moving would be offset by the competition lost in the Bay Area between the Raiders and the Giants if the Raiders are allowed to move. Similarly, if the product market were enlarged to include other forms of entertainment, the NFL could at least argue that the "intrabrand" competition lost between the teams is offset by the increased ability of the NFL to compete "interbrand."

Given the court's blessing on the relevant market, the comments about less restrictive alternatives available to the league to meet its goals seem meaningless. The court talked about how the league could flesh out Rule 4.3 by adding some objective criteria which need to be met in order to prevent a move. However, a different rule would not change the competitive effects in the southern California NFL football market.

If at the heart of *Raiders* is the question of who gets to decide when a team can move, the league or an individual owner, then the case will have a very limited affect on the cities. A city that wants to acquire a team would prefer, given a choice between the two, that an individual owner be able to move at will. On the other hand, a city with a team would prefer the owner to have to at least jump through a hoop before moving. If the *Raiders* court contributed a valuable observation it was that cities with teams should not place too much faith in any league to look out for the cities' interest.[73] Even if the league did begin to prevent team transfers, this would merely represent a win for the cities with teams and a loss for those who want teams. *Raiders* does, however, show signs of reaching beyond a simple power struggle between one owner and other owners.

An interesting, yet defective, market definition was advanced by the Los Angeles Coliseum. The Coliseum argued that the relevant product market was the market of "stadia offering their facilities to NFL teams"[74] in the U.S. The defect lies not in the definition of the market, but in the Coliseum's contention that Rule 4.3 restrains competition among stadia within this market. Roberts correctly points out that 1) Rule 4.3 in no way prevents or lessens competition among stadia to house NFL teams, and 2) the NFL's interest is for stadia competition to be as vigorous as possible.[75] Nevertheless, the *Raiders* court accepted this market definition as possible grounds for § 1 liability. This is significant because this market analysis can be applied to *all* team movements prevented by the league, regardless of whether the team is moving into another team's territory. In other words, the restraint applicable to stadia does not rely on the fact that the Raiders were prevented from competing with the Rams.

C. Piazza v. MLB

On August 6, 1992, Vincent Piazza and other investors ("Investors"), executed a Letter of Intent with Robert Lurie, owner of the San Francisco Giants, to purchase the Giants baseball team for $115 million.[76] The Investors intended to move the Giants to the Suncoast Dome, located in St. Petersburg. The league refused to approve the sale and move, and the Giants were subsequently sold for $100 million to a San Francisco group which kept the Giants in San Francisco. The Investors claim 1) that the league's actions "have placed direct and indirect restraints on the purchase, sale, transfer, and relocation of Major League Baseball teams and on competition in the purchase, sale, transfer and relocation of such teams. . . "[77]

The issue of interest for our concerns is how the court defined the relevant market.[78] The Investors claim that the relevant product market is the market for existing baseball teams. It initially appears that the Investors made the same defective argument as the one made by the Coliseum in *Raiders*: that the league restrained competition among potential investors who wish to purchase a team. This is the characterization of the market which the court first seems to create and accept.[79] However, at the end of the opinion the market analysis becomes sharper. The court notes that a market may be defined as "any grouping of sales whose sellers, if unified by a hypothetical cartel or merger, could raise prices significantly above the competitive level."[80] The court then defines the market in this case:

> [T]his market has the following components: (1) the product being sold is an ownership interest in professional baseball teams; (2) the sellers are team owners; and (3) the buyers are those who would like to become team owners. . . . [I]t would not be unreasonable also to infer that if the team owners combined, they could increase the price of teams considerably and control the conditions of sale.[81]

This definition suggests not that the league is restraining competition among potential owners, which it would have no interest in doing, but rather that the league could restrain competition among the teams. This is a much more defensible market definition.

The other difference in market definition between the *Piazza* case and the *Raiders* case is that the Coliseum in *Raiders* argued that the relevant product was stadia services, which it was selling, while the Investors in *Piazza* argued that the relevant product was the teams themselves, which they were purchasing.

D. Relevance of Raiders and Piazza to the Cities

Regardless of the incorrect application of the Coliseum's market definition in *Raiders*, a potentially viable § 1 argument from either case could be made by a city which was denied a team in favor of franchise free agency. For example, if a city and an owner have come to terms on a deal which would move a team into the city, and the move is prevented by the league, the city could argue that the teams are 1) collectively restraining competition among themselves to purchase the services of the cities (in the form of stadia, for example) *or* 2) restraining competition among themselves in the provision of sports franchises to the cities. In the first case, the claim would be that the teams are agreeing to act as a monopsonist, similar to agreeing not to compete in the purchase of "upstream" inputs such as players. In the second case, the effect would be similar to price fixing: under a free market, i.e. franchise free agency, one owner might be willing to offer his franchise for $2 million in public subsidies, but without franchise free agency, the league could disallow the move, "increase the price of teams considerably and control the conditions of sale."[82]

The argument for franchise free agency can certainly be defended in terms of allocative efficiency. If teams act as independent profit maximizers, they will locate in the cities which offer them the best mixture of population and public subsidy — where the teams will be valued the most. If confronted with a choice between having the Raiders in Oakland or in Los Angeles, it is clear they should be in Los Angeles. Presumably, the Raiders would either reach more people in Los Angeles, or the Raiders had some other value greater to Los Angeles than to Oakland. The league, however, instead of allowing free movement of teams, would rather keep Los Angeles open, either as a threat which all teams could use against their respective cities, or as means to extract a large fee from a prospective owner through expansion, similar to how Major League Baseball is using the Suncoast Dome.

Al Davis personally does not present a compelling story: when he bought into this industry, he contracted with his fellow owners to abide by certain rules; instead, he "stole" a money making opportunity from the league. This has led some commentators to conclude that the league should be allowed to prevent this result.[83] Yet, however offensive Al Davis' move is to our sense of contractual obligations, the antitrust laws should not be concerned with protecting the league's opportunities for profit. Rather, antitrust law should be concerned with insuring that the rules for making profit lead to an efficient allocation of resources. Therefore, the themes of § 1 antitrust analysis suggest that there should be franchise free agency.

This conclusion, however, reveals an apparent limitation of § 1 of the Sherman Act in the world of cities and professional sports leagues.

This analysis takes place in a world of a limited number of teams, where cities compete for those teams and the "best" cities win. In such a world, franchise free agency would probably be the best rule of the game. Cities without teams would have a fair chance to get one if they wanted one badly enough. Although cities with teams would prefer a world where the team is forced to stay, at least under franchise free agency if the city lost a team it would have a fair chance of getting another one. The problem, however, is that the number of teams is artificially limited by the owners themselves, which causes all cities to make sub-optimal allocative decisions with respect to professional sports. The question then is whether antitrust is up to the task of increasing the output of professional sports teams.

E. Mid-South Grizzlies

In 1975, the Grizzlies, a professional football team located in Memphis, applied for membership into the NFL after the league they were in, the WFL, disbanded.[84] They were denied membership by the NFL, so they sued, claiming that the NFL teams violated §§ 1 and 2 of the Sherman Act. The court dismissed the Grizzlies' claim on the NFL's motion for summary judgement.

The opinion appears to mix § 1 and § 2 issues in its discussion of the case. The court briefly noted that the requisite conspiracy requirement of § 1 was not in dispute. Apparently it was accepted by all parties that the teams were distinct entities capable of competing for antitrust purposes. Yet quickly after jumping over the conspiracy hurdle, the court spends quite a bit of time discussing the NFL's monopoly position, created by congressional fiat[85], which has a distinct § 2 feel to it.

Eventually, however, the court returned to the § 1 question, which requires a definition of a relevant market. The market identified by the Grizzlies was major league professional football in the United States. The court viewed the relevant competition to be for "ticket buyers, for local broadcast revenue, and for sale of the concession items like food and beverages and team paraphernalia."[86] In other words, the court viewed the potential competition between teams in the same way that Al Davis argued and won in *Raiders*. The Grizzlies lost in this case because there would be no other team within a 280 mile radius to compete with, so their existence or non-existence as a team had no effect on competition.

Yet what about the competition between teams that does not rely on geographic proximity? The Grizzlies began to argue on appeal that teams also compete for players and coaches. The court, however, rejected this contention by stating:

> First, the Grizzlies exclusion from the league in no way restrained them from competing for players by forming a competitive league. Second, they fail to explain how, if their exclusion from the league reduced competition for team personnel, that reduction caused an injury to the Grizzlies' business or property.[87]

At the heart of this case is the notion that the Grizzlies represented individuals who wanted to share a monopoly position with other co-investors, not compete against them. The court was confident that not allowing the Grizzlies into the NFL would not harm competition.

The court also dismissed the Grizzlies § 2 claim without much analysis. This case reveals the limitations of § 2 of the Sherman Act. A violation of § 2 requires both a showing of monopoly power *and* either a misuse of that power or that the power was wrongly acquired. If a firm has a monopoly position either by legislative grant, superior business skill, or by being the only firm in a natural monopoly industry, § 2 cannot reach the firm, even if the firm is reducing output and charging prices above the competitive level as a result of its monopoly position. It was clear that the NFL had monopoly power. But it was also clear to the court that the NFL has a monopoly position by legislative fiat. The court was not about to use the antitrust laws to take away power granted by Congress.[88]

Suppose that instead of the Grizzlies, it was the city of Memphis which was attempting to argue for the Grizzlies' admission to the NFL. Suppose also that Memphis could not lure another NFL team away for $3 million a year, the amount Memphis was willing to pay for an NFL football team, but the Grizzlies would be willing to set up shop for $2.5 million. The city might argue under § 1 that the NFL teams compete in the provision of sports franchises to cities, and the addition of the Grizzlies would create more competition, as evidenced by the Grizzlies willingness to provide NFL football for a mere $2.5 million. This basic market conception was formulated above from *Raiders* and *Piazza*, but towards the end of existing franchise free agency, not to create a new franchise. There is at least one problem with cities using § 1 in this context. The fact that no team will move to Memphis for $3 million a year is not the result of an agreement among the teams not to compete, rather it is the result of an agreement not to expand by accepting anyone else into the club.[89] The addition of the Grizzlies in Memphis is not going to increase competition among the teams to provide football to cities.

However, a team without a city could argue that its presence would increase the competition among teams to provide football, since theoretically that team would be competing against all others to play in the other teams' cities. For example, a team without a city could compete against the Saints to play in New Orleans for less in public subsidies. This may make for a valid "essential facilities" argument, which the Grizzlies court rejected because the doctrine "is predicated on the assumption that admission of the excluded applicant would result in additional competition, in an economic rather than athletic sense."[90] To carry this argument to its conclusion would create a world where anyone who wants to can say they own an NFL team, demand a part of the TV and gate revenues, and then compete against an established team to take over their city. I do not think a court will be willing to take the antitrust laws this far.[91]

Suppose that instead of using § 1, the city of Memphis took a § 2 approach. They might argue that the NFL is a monopoly, and even if it acquired its monopoly legally, it is misusing its power by leaving Memphis open as a "Suncoast Dome city," i.e. an attractive area which could support a franchise, but is being used by the teams as a relocation threat. This argument would most likely fail because in essence the claim is that the league is limiting output in order to raise prices, exactly what we would expect from a monopolist. Acting like a monopolist, without more, is not illegal if the monopoly power was acquired legally. If the real problem is that cities are being overcharged for franchises because of the monopoly position of leagues, then antitrust law is not going to be large enough to solve the problem, even though this is precisely the concern of antitrust. There must be other rules.

IV. Proposed Rules of the Game

There are two rule themes proposed in the world of contract. The first theme, proposed by Shropshire, concerns the payment of damages when a team relocates without league approval, and operates within the relationship of team to league.[92] The second theme, proposed by Beisner, concerns mandatory lease terms, and operates within the relationship of team to city.[93] Both proposals have their merits, yet neither addresses the underlying dynamics which create the problems they are trying to solve.

Shropshire argues that teams should be seen as having a fiduciary relationship towards the league, i.e. each team owes a duty to the other teams as a partner would have toward other partners in a partnership. The significance of this fiduciary duty is to allow for compensatory and punitive damages for breach of contract in the event a team usurps a league developed opportunity — e.g., moves to a "Suncoast Dome site." Essentially, Shropshire's concern is to not allow a single owner to steal from the league. But presumably if a team is required to fully compensate the league for the league's loss, and the team still finds a move profitable, then the move should be O.K.

Shropshire claims to be concerned with an economically efficient allocation of resources, as he cites this idea as one important goal of contract remedies.[94] Yet if we conceive of punitive damages as representing a payment above what would fully compensate the league, it would seem that franchise moves would never deter franchises from moving. If we are concerned with an efficient allocation of resources, punitive damages should only be employed to compensate for the probability of not getting caught.[95] To the extent that Shropshire views punitive damages merely as a means to have owners internalize the full costs of a move, his argument has merit as a way to further refine the franchise free agency landscape. However, having the owners internalize the full costs of their actions requires a redefinition of compensatory damages, not the addition of punitive damages.

If Shropshire is suggesting the use of punitive damages above true compensatory damages as a means for the league to control franchise movement for its own benefit, then his argument is simply that relocation decisions should be made by the league, not the market. This could be good or bad for a city, depending on whether the city does or does not already have a franchise, and depending on how benevolent the league feels towards protecting the city's interests. As we have noted and will continue to note, the league has little reason or incentive to watch after the city's interests.

To protect the cities' interests, Beisner argues that Congress should mandate certain stadium lease terms to correct for the unequal bargaining power between cities and teams caused by the reduced supply of teams.[96] Beisner argues that every stadium lease should include "a notification provision, set mandatory minimums for owner contribution and length of lease, and, upon relocation, require a franchise owner to reimburse the local municipality for any investment in remodeling."[97] Basically, the length of the lease and other team commitments would be indexed to the amount of public subsidies from the municipality. This is an interesting idea. The effect would be similar to the cities collectively price fixing. Unfortunately, this does not have the effect of cities collectively agreeing not to compete. If the problem is caused by an artificially reduced supply of teams, then mandating team concessions in one area will merely shift the competition for teams to another area. Cities will still find ways to lure teams away, and the leagues will still use this reality to extract public subsidies from sources other than stadium leases. Beisner's proposal is thoughtful, but it does not solve the problem — it just changes the landscape.

A. Congressional Proposals

The Raiders litigation caused a number of congressmen to propose rule changes to the relocation game. The overriding concern of this wave of proposed legislation, with limited exceptions, was how to best keep teams from moving. It should come as no surprise that most of the congressmen sponsoring the bills on this topic were representing communities who already had professional sports teams.

S enator DeConcini and Representative Stark introduced bills which would grant all sports leagues immunity from antitrust.[98] In other words, DeConcini's and Stark's proposed rule change was to eliminate the rules. These bills are either motivated by the sincere, yet naive, belief that a collection of team owners are the best people to watch out for the cities' interests, or by the hope of moving from Congress into a commissioner's office. All of the other bills recognize that there must be some external source for the rules of this game, whether antitrust plays a part or not.

Bills proposed by Senators Gorton, Eagleton, Specter, and Representative Dellums would require that certain objective criteria be met before a team could expand.[99] For example, Specter's and Dellums' bills would make it unlawful for a team to relocate unless one of three per se situations are met: 1) if there is a material breach of the lease by the stadium operator, 2) if the stadium is inadequate, or 3) if a team has experienced net losses for three consecutive years.[100] Gorton and Eagleton identify a set of objective factors to be taken into account when approving a team relocation.[101]

The major difference between Gorton's and Eagleton's bills lies in who makes the determination whether a relocation is appropriate and what standard must be met in making that determination. Eagleton's bill would have the leagues decide relocation issues by granting the leagues antitrust immunity if they make findings concerning the objective factors enumerated in the bill. The league will then be allowed to prevent any relocation or allow any "reasonable and appropriate" relocation after a consideration of these factors. Gorton's bill, on the other hand, would create a Professional Sports Franchise Arbitration Board to review any proposed relocation to determine if the relocation is "necessary and appropriate."

The "necessary and appropriate" threshold in the Gorton bill, coupled with external federal review, would make it almost impossible to relocate a franchise. While a rule of this sort would create stability, this should not be the only or even primary goal of federal legislation. Locking franchises into where they are is great for the cities with franchises, but bad not only for the cities without franchises, but bad also for the leagues. The teams would lose all of their bargaining strength, with only a select few cities reaping the rewards. An evaluation of the initial draft of Gorton's bill was that "[It] is very important legislation. But some modifications have to be made so we do not continue to deprive newly developing areas, areas where there are an abundance of fans and an abundance of interest that would require and support a franchise."[102]

At this point in the evaluation of the proposed rule changes one gets the feeling that no one wants to address the real source of the problem: less than optimal supply of franchises due to league monopoly power.[103] Congress needs to make rules which will increase the supply of teams. There are two ways Congress can approach this problem. It can either mandate expansion by the leagues, i.e. tell the leagues that they must create X new teams by year Y; or it can reduce the barriers to entry in the league, i.e. set a "price" which if paid would allow a team to enter the league. Mandating expansion, while helpful, would provide only a temporary and limited answer to the problem, and would be cumbersome to implement. Reducing the barriers to league entry would be the best rule change Congress could adopt. Both of these options will now be considered in more detail.

B. The Case for Expansion

Senator Gorton realized that creating a system which would make it more difficult for teams to relocate would not be a good rule change, standing alone. "For the 'have-nots,' the status quo, which gives cities without a franchise at least the chance to entice a team away from another city, is preferable to a regulatory scheme designed solely to encourage stability."[104] For this reason, Gorton proposed in his bill[105] to mandate expansion in the National Football League and in Major League Baseball. This has been a controversial idea, but not without its supporters.[106]

The first hurdle for a mandatory expansion rule is to justify congressional intervention in the first place. Gorton made a compelling argument. After noting that "legislators . . . realize that professional sports teams are important community assets, economically and pshychologically,"[107] Gorton asks:

> Why should Congress intervene to help state and local officials who evidently will not help themselves by negotiating secure leases or delaying the expenditure of public funds until a team is committed to locate in the community?. . .
>
> First, due to the enormous discrepancy between the demand for professional sports teams and the supply, particularly in football and baseball, it is extremely difficult for any local officials to make meaningful demands on a team in negotiating a lease. For every city cautious enough to require a pledge of security, there is another city willing to forego that security to win a franchise. In short, in a seller's market, buyers make few demands.[108]
>
> Second, the fact that the market is so heavily tilted in favor of team owners is in large measure attributable to a series of congressional manipulations of the free market. . . . These actions and this omission have permitted the leagues to control the supply of the product in the marketplace virtually free from any competitive pressure to respond to market demand. . . .
>
> It is hardly sound or balanced public policy to manipulate the free market for the benefit of the league and owners and then to turn our backs on the cities which become the victims of that manipulation. . . .[109]

Gorton's basic argument is that Congress helped create this monster, so Congress should help contain it.

Even if Congress was not in any way responsible for the leagues' monopoly power, this factor would not be a reason for Congress to not intervene and regulate the sports industry. Neale argues that "each professional sport is a natural monopoly."[110] In other words, "there appears to be a strong tendency toward a single league, and this for one good reason: only a single league can produce that most useful of all products, the World Champion. . . . [And] one large league can provide any quantity of output as cheaply as two or more smaller firms. . . . [T]here is a likelihood that the first league in the sport — like the first utility in a city — will become a monopoly."[111]

Johnson cites Lowell and Weistart to rebut the argument that sports franchises are analogous to public utilities. Lowell and Weistart argue that sports franchises are not like public utilities because they lack "the presence of an activity affecting the basic public need for food, shelter, and sanitation."[112] It is difficult to argue with the observed difference between sports and public utilities, but this observation is missing the point. Although sports plays a strong role in the American way of life and could be viewed as a public trust, it is not these characteristics which make sports like public utilities. Instead, sports are like public utilities in that they are both natural monopolies, and if left unregulated would be fertile ground for individuals to extract excess profits at the expense of the public welfare.

If leagues hold their powerful positions because the sports industry is a natural monopoly, then they will be able to act like monopolists without existing antitrust law able to do anything about these actions. The only way to have the leagues offer their products at a price which approximates a competitive level is through external regulation.[113]

Of course, the leagues do not like mandatory expansion because it would weaken the owners' privileged position. Perhaps the value of the current owners' investment will be diminished, but so what? "By some estimates, 95% of the value of a franchise is economic rent that is the result of team monopoly and monopsony advantage imparted by legislation."[114] Regardless of how the owners acquired a monopoly position[115], the owners should not feel entitled to reap the benefits of a monopoly position indefinitely. Investors must always bear the risk that the government will come to its senses and do what is in the public interest.

Other criticisms have been leveled against mandatory expansion. For example, the Justice Department, at the time Gorton's bill was on the table, believed that there was no justification for mandatory expansion.[116]

> In a free market system, firms—not regulators or legislators—are generally considered the best judges of how and where their products are marketed. Congress does not mandate that steel manufacturers, for example, must open new plants in specific cities according to a specific schedule. The assessment of demand and the amount of athletic and managerial talent available to satisfy this demand are best left to the judgement of the NFL and Major League Baseball.[117]

The comparison of sports leagues to steel manufacturers reveals the flaw in the Justice Department's argument. First, if the steel industry is competitive, there would be no reason for Congress to mandate that steel manufacturers open new plants. But even if the industry is monopolized and the antitrust laws continue to be ineffective in reaching the steel industry, as they were in 1920,[118] a city could unilaterally subsidize or start up a steel plant located within its boundaries to meet the city's steel needs, and that plant could independently produce steel. A city cannot unilaterally create a major league baseball team which could independently produce baseball for the city. This dilemma is another twist caused by the unique nature of sports leagues. The arguments as to why sports leagues are unique, do not fit neatly into antitrust analysis, and should not be governed by antitrust law. These arguments are then why the federal government needs to set rules specifically governing sports leagues. If left alone, the leagues will certainly be able to assess the demand for sports franchises, as claimed by the Justice Department, but this does not mean that the leagues will meet the demand — quite the contrary.

Mandatory expansion, however, is a cumbersome way for the federal government to regulate the sports industry. The government would have to decide how many teams a league could support, then a decision will need to be made concerning which cities should get a team. Senator DeConcini, who proposed that leagues should be immune from antitrust,[119] argued that "Congress should not be in the business of selecting cities . . . [but] should create a legal climate in which leagues can follow their best business judgment."[120] DeConcini has a good point about Congress creating a legal climate if included in this climate is an opportunity for cities to follow their best judgement. In other words, Congress should create a level playing field for all participants. This is why the best rule Congress could give the professional sports industry is to reduce the barriers to entry, and let the chips fall where they may.

C. Reduced Barriers to Entry

If there were a "price" set for participation in the major league sports industry, then cities would be free to make an allocative decision about whether a sports franchise is worth that price to the city. We could trust this decision the way we trust any consumer decision to lead to the most efficient allocation of resources. Cities without franchises could get one if they wanted one, and cities with franchises could not be extorted by threats of relocation, since a city could replace a lost franchise. It appears to be the only solution which does not distinctly advantage the 'haves' over the 'have-nots', or vice versa.[121] Even though this may be a good solution to a tough problem, few have been willing to support reducing the barriers to league entry, nor has it been given much serious study.[122] Two questions must be answered concerning reduced barriers to entry before it can be embraced: first, what is the buy-in "price," and second, what affect will this have on the sports themselves.

The question about the price to be paid for league entry is meant to address the concern many have about the economic viability of expansion. Johnson suggests that the "price" to join a major league should include 1) minimum population requirements, 2) adequate playing facilities, and 3) a minimal level of financial solvency.[123] He also suggests that cities in which a franchise fails financially could be required to wait five years or longer before reentry into the league. Once entry requirements are met, Johnson advises that a two-year waiting period take effect for the new team to organize its front office, to promote the team, to prepare the playing facilities, and to allow the league time to adjust its schedule.

The requirements for entry should approximate the population and stadium capacity of the community with the smallest media market currently in the league. Consider that in 1993, the Cincinnati Reds were operating profitably in the 30th largest media market, and without incorporating any smaller markets it would be possible for Major League Baseball to expand to thirty-six teams, and additionally, another six are within 14% of Cincinnati.[124] We could take Cincinnati's average annual gate receipts over the last five years and use this figure as a "price" — guaranteed ticket sales of X amount at at least Y price level. If any team fails to meet this requirement in two consecutive years, then the team may be voted out of the league. In this manner, a city in a higher media market than thirtieth could acquire a team, with a good chance that the population alone would keep the team in the league. At the same time, a smaller city could still acquire a franchise if it was willing to subsidize the team in the amount necessary to cover the guaranteed ticket sales requirement. If a team were in danger of not meeting the quota, tickets could be bought up by the local chamber of commerce or by the local government if either thought the team was worth the cost. The communities could make rational decisions concerning the worth of sports teams and at the same time the leagues could be left alone to make any marketing, relocative, or internal allocative decisions as they see fit, while at the same time protecting themselves from free riders. Reducing the barriers to entry sounds attractive.

Those not yet convinced, or those who have something to lose, will still argue that expansion will hurt the quality of the game product in two ways which will affect the demand for professional sports: 1) it will reduce the quality of player talent, and 2) it will saturate the market. In considering both arguments, the reader should first reflect on the success of the NCAA in basketball and football. Every year millions of fans await anxiously as the NCAA basketball tournament selection committee whittles the college basketball field down to sixty-four teams, none of which could beat the Dallas Mavericks. Neither the number of teams in a league nor the absolute skill level of the players can be shown to be related to fan interest.

Neale asserts that as a league expands, the quality of the product is affected by two contrary tendencies: "diminishing quality returns" and the "input-enthusiasm effect."[125] As less skilled players are drawn into the sport, the demand function may contract, leading to a reduction in revenue per game seat. "However, we know by introspection that the reduction will be small since the appeal of a seat depends mostly on the uncertainty of the outcome and on the weather."[126] But any reduction in demand due to diminishing quality returns will be counteracted by the input-enthusiasm effect. As leagues expand into new areas, public attention will be drawn more to the particular sport and more private concentration will be put into a development of the skills of the sport. "In other words, the larger the scale of operations, the higher the quality of inputs and of products. . . . Larger scale, therefore, does not necessarily increase costs more than revenue."[127]

Bill James, baseball expert and rotisserie guru, estimates that there is sufficient talent for sixty major league baseball teams.[128] Both Larry MacPhail in 1951 and George Will in 1990 suggest that baseball would be better organized if there were expansion to six major leagues instead of two.[129] The bottom line is that expansion should be embraced, not feared. Reduced barriers to entry will not lead to the downfall of professional sports, but it *will* change the rules of the game.

V. Conclusion

Our cities see in professional sports an opportunity to improve the quality of life of its citizens. A sports team can be used to unite and even educate a community, or it can give a city prestige. For whatever reasons, more cities want and can support major league sports teams than teams are made available. Team owners, acting as individual leagues, restrict the amount of teams available to be "rented" by the cities. This allows individual team owners to extract excess profits from the cities, which results in a sub-optimal allocation of resources. The only way to correct this situation is for Congress to reduce the barriers to entry into professional sports leagues. The fact that a community like Tampa/St. Pete could build a baseball stadium in the 24th largest U.S. market and have twenty-eight self-interested owners decide whether they can participate in the national pastime is an embarrassment. Perhaps, when the Piazza litigation fails to get the Giants transferred to Tampa/St. Pete, a few congressmen will take notice of the real problem between cities and professional sports: the sports output is controlled by a select few individuals with little incentive to allow a city like St. Pete to play with them. Professional sports is truly the tail that wags the dog.

Notes

1. *See* Arthur T. Johnson, *The Sports Franchise Relocation Issue and Public Policy Response, in* Government and Sport 229, (Arthur T. Johnson et. al. eds., 1985) (for the lease expiration dates for Major League Baseball); Glenn M. Wong, *Of Franchise Relocation, Expansian and Competition in Professional Team Sports: The Ultimate Political Football,* 9 Seton Hall Legis. J. 7, 46 (1985) (for the lease expiration dates for the NFL).
2. Wong, *supra* note 1, at 46.
3. *Id.* at 30.
4. This contest will be discussed in more detail, infra notes 52-73, and accompanying text.
5. Wong, *supra* note 1, at 33.
6. *Id.* at 35; *See also* Daniel S. York, *The Professional Sports Community Protection Act: Congress' Best Response to Raiders?,* 38 Hastings L.J. 345, 352 (1987).
7. John Beisner, *Sports Franchise Relocation: Competitive Markets and Taxpayer Protection,* 6 Yale L. & Pol'y Rev. 429, 430-431 (1988).
8. Wong, *supra* note 1, at 40.
9. *Id.*
10. Based on the 1980 rank of Standard Metropolitan Statistical Areas.
11. Wong, *supra* note 1, at 36.
12. Beisner, *supra* note 7, at 431.
13. Wong, *supra* note 1, at 45.
14. The information for these league standings is taken from a table in Wong, *supra* note 1, at 27.

15. Wong, *supra* note 1, at 39.

16. JAY J. COAKLEY, SPORT IN SOCIETY: ISSUES AND CONTROVERSIES 62 (1990).

17. This will be treated more in depth, *infra* note 51.

18. By "players," I mean those involved in the franchise acquisition game: cities, owners, leagues, and the federal government.

19. For convenience, I am not going to use gender neutral language.

20. GERALD W. SCULLY, THE BUSINESS OF MAJOR LEAGUE BASEBALL 119 (1989).

21. *Id.*

22. The construction of new practice facilities and improvements to existing facilities could also be seen as affecting the revenue side by improving a team's winning percentage, but for simplicity we can conceptualize all public subsidies as decreasing the franchise's cost. This conceptualization makes it easier to analyze things like the affect of revenue sharing on owner incentives.

23. Johnson, *supra* note 1, at 219. Johnson notes that about 25 cities were confronted with demands for increased public subsidies between 1980 and 1985.

24. NFL commissioner Pete Rozelle claimed that revenue sharing actually contributed to forestall opportunistic behavior before the Senate Committee on Commerce, Science, and Transportation in 1985. He argued that revenue sharing leads to less income disparity between teams and thus lessens the incentives for a team to relocate. John A. Gray, *Section 1 of the Sherman Act and Control Over NFL Franchise Relocations: The Problem of Opportunistic Behavior*, 25 AM. BUS. L.J. 123, 132 n.29 (1987). I fail to see the logic in this argument. In the same address to the Committee, Rozelle listed the St. Louis Cardinals as one of the teams which was stable because of revenue sharing. I suppose the Arizona Cardinals are now more stable because of revenue sharing.

25. Major League Baseball may be in danger of losing their best asset as the *Piazza* case (Piazza v. Major League Baseball, 831 F. Supp. 420 (E.D. Pa. 1993)) goes to trial. This is an antitrust suit brought by investors who had agreed to buy the Giants and move them to Tampa/St. Pete, but the owners voted to prevent the sale. The investors won the first round by defeating a motion for summary judgement on the grounds that baseball is immune from antitrust. This case will be discussed later in more detail.

26. Johnson, *supra* note 1, at 232.

27. ANDREW ZIMBALIST, BASEBALL AND BILLIONS 125 (1992).

28. Johnson, *supra* note 1, at 224.

29. *Id.* at 222-23.

30. *Id.* at 223.

31. Gray, *supra* note 24, at 130.

32. York, *supra* note 6, at 354-355.

33. Beisner, *supra* note 7, at 433 n.24.

34. Robert A. Badde & Richard F. Dye, *Sports Stadiums and Area Development: A Critical Review*, 2 Econ. Dev. Q. 265, 270 (1988).
35. Mark S. Rosentraub & David Swindell, *"Just Say No?" The Economic and Political Realities of a Small City's Investment in Minor League Baseball*, 5 Econ. Dev. Q. 152, 156 (1991).
36. Baade & Dye, *supra* note 34, at 270.
37. *Id.* at 270-71.
38. *Id.*
39. Zimbalist, *supra* note 27, at 137.
40. Benjamin A. Okner, *Subsidies of Stadiums and Arenas, in* Government and the Sports Business (Roger Noll, ed., 1974).
41. Gray, *supra* note 24, at 131.
42. *Id.*
43. Baade & Dye, *supra* note 34, at 272, *quoting* Merlin E. Dewing, Chairman of a Minnesota task force to revitalize the economy.
44. Perhaps professional sports are romantic in another sense. CNN reported a study which found that cities with major league baseball teams have a 28% lower divorce rate when compared to cities seeking a baseball team. CNN television broadcast, Apr. 12, 1994. I can certainly attest to the boost my marriage receives from those quiet evenings with my wife, Keith Olberman, and Baseball Tonight; or from the intimate discussions with my wife over whether we should parlay Frank Thomas into a blockbuster rotisserie trade.
45. For a complete discussion on all the potential sociological harms of sports, *see generally* Coakley, *supra* note 16.
46. 15 U.S.C. §§ 1-2 (1937). The statute says "every" contract . . . but this is not taken literally, much like how the strike zone rule is not taken literally. In fact, applying the Sherman Act is a lot like applying the strike zone, except the strike zone rule at least has clear bright line boundaries on paper. For example, a fastball thigh high in the middle of the plate is an easy call, but start looking at curve balls at the corners just above belt high and things get complicated. As we shall see, antitrust has a similar feel. We can only be glad that umpires have not developed a "per se" and "rule of reason" analysis in calling games.
47. Phillip Areeda & Louis Kaplow, Antitrust Analysis: Problems, Text, Cases 12 (1988).
48. A natural monopoly is where a single firm can satisfy the demand in an industry at a point where its long run average total cost curve is declining; in other words, where one firm can meet demand at less cost than two or more firms. Walter C. Neale, *The Peculiar Economics of Professional Sports: A Contribution to the Theory of the Firm In Sporting Competition and in Market Competition*, 78 Q. J. Econ. 1 (1964).
49. Areeda & Kaplow, *supra* note 47, at 12.
50. *See generally* Neale, *supra* note 48.

51. Imagine that two cities are faced with an allocative decision in a two
     product world. In this case imagine that instead of guns and butter, the
     products were professional sports and education. Assume that the com-
     petitive price of one unit of professional sports (a franchise) is $5 million
     and the monopoly price is $10 million. Assume also that one city would
     be willing to pay $7 million for one sports unit and the other city would
     be willing to pay $12 million. At a competitive price, both cities would
     pay $5 million for a franchise and the rest of their respective budgets
     would go to education. At a monopoly price, one city will pay $10 million
     for a franchise, while the other would not get a franchise and the whole
     budget would go to education. In the first case, the monopoly price paid
     by the city means that $5 million which would go to education under a
     competitive price will now go to the owner of the franchise. This result
     sounds concerning, but is not the primary economic concern. The
     primary concern is that the second city would have been willing to pay the
     competitive price for a franchise and was denied that opportunity. In
     other words, the city was denied the opportunity to pay for a franchise,
     and as a result, more resources were devoted to education than would be
     optimal.
This sounds like an odd conclusion. However, the discomfort with this
     conclusion is caused not by the effect of competition, but by the allocative
     priorities set by the cities. For example, if a city's total budget is $10
     million and it is willing to pay up to $5 million for sports vs. education,
     we might justifiably be concerned, not with competition, but with a
     system that relies on consumer preference to allocate resources. However,
     if a city's total budget is $200 million, it is not hard to credit a city's
     determination that after $195 million was allocated to education, the
     marginal value to the city of a sports franchise for $5 million is greater than
     an additional $5 million in education.
52. Los Angeles Memorial Coliseum Comm'n v. NFL, 726 F.2d 1381,
     1385 (9th Cir. 1984).
53. *Id.* at 1384.
54. *Id.* at 1385.
55. Roberts suggests that to say a team is relocating is misdirecting the
     analysis since what is at issue is not the location of the "team", but rather
     the location of eight home games. Gary R. Roberts, *The Evolving
     Confusion of Professional Sports Antitrust, The Rule of Reason, and the
     Doctrine of Ancillary Restraints*, 61 S. Cal. L. Rev. 945, 948 n.11 (1988).
     Whatever the merit of this distinction may be, I will continue to employ
     the convention of referring to the team as relocating.
56. *Los Angeles Memorial Coliseum Comm'n*, 726 F.2d at 1385.
57. *Id.* at 1386.
58. United States v. Addyston Pipe & Steel Co., 85 F. 271 (6th Cir. 1898),
     aff'd, 175 U.S. 211 (1899).
59. United States v. Topco Assoc., 405 U.S. 596 (1972).

60. Eastern States Lumber Ass'n. v. United States, 234 U.S. 600 (1914).

61. Instead, it seems the court chose to confuse the NFL, other sports leagues, academics, and law students in the same way the sports industry seems to have baffled it.

62. These two dynamics are described in a more detailed and humorous way as "The Louis-Schmelling Paradox," and "The Inverted Joint Product or the Product Joint." *See* Neale, *supra* note 48, at 2.

63. *Id.*; *See also* Roberts, *supra* note 55.

64. *Los Angeles Memorial Coliseum Comm'n*, 726 F.2d at 1388.

65. *Id.*

66. The court cited *United States v. Sealy, Inc.*, 388 U.S. 350 (1967), and *United States v. Topco Assoc.*, 405 U.S. 596 (1972). Both cases involved legally separate, horizontal competitors who collectively formed an association, which allocated territories to its members. In both cases an individual firm could offer its products to consumers, mattresses or a food product line, without the assistance of the other competitors. However, the defendants in *Topco*, a case given per se treatment, had a slightly better position. In that case, individual grocery stores agreed to jointly create a food product line in order to compete with the national supermarket chains. As a part of this effort, the stores agreed not to use the joint product line to compete against one another. *Topco* is a disfavored case, however, because the per se treatment neglected to consider the positive effect on interbrand competition.
    This becomes relevant in the Raiders case when the product market is defined as NFL football and not the entertainment in general. The NFL wants to argue that even if Rule 4.3 restrains competition among NFL teams, the rule helps the league compete better with other forms of entertainment. The *Topco* defendants lost with a more compelling argument.

67. The court determined that "NFL policies are not set by one individual or parent corporation, but by the separate teams acting jointly." *Los Angeles Memorial Coliseum Comm'n*, 726 F.2d at 1389. Other similar statements lead one to believe that whether the court was right or wrong on this point, it would not have reached a different result even if it had the benefit of *Copperweld Corp. v. Independence Tube Corp.*, 467 U.S. 752 (1984). It appears that the Ninth Circuit had already determined that a parent corporation and a subsidiary could not conspire under § 1: "[T]his circuit has found the threshold requirement of concerted activity missing among multiple corporations operated as a single entity when corporate policies are set by one individual or by a parent corporation." *Los Angeles Memorial Coliseum Comm'n*, 726 F.2d at 1388.

68. The Ninth Circuit backed up this conclusory and question begging reason by stating that 1) the teams are all independently owned, and 2) although the teams share revenue, they do not share profit or loss. *Los*

Angeles Memorial Coliseum Comm'n, 726 F.2d at 1389-1390. It is not clear why these observations are important.

69. *Id.* at 1390.

70. Roberts, *supra* note 55.

71. I believe a league's product output and price will be determined independent of the cost of the players input, since I maintain that player payroll has the quality of a fixed cost. If this is true, the exploitation of a player will not affect the allocative decisions of a consumer, but rather merely concerns the distribution of wealth between players and owners. This is why I also believe that the best way to protect the players' interests is through the mechanism of labor law.

72. *Los Angeles Memorial Coliseum Comm'n*, 726 F.2d at 1409.

73. "The NFL's professed interest in ensuring that cities and other local governments secure a return on their investments in stadia . . . may not be as important as it would have us believe because the League has in the past allowed teams to threaten a transfer to another location in order to give the team leverage in lease negotiations." *Id.* at 1397. The leagues collectively do not have a very good track record when it comes to voting against transfers. *See* ZIMBALIST, *supra* note 27.

74. *Los Angeles Memorial Coliseum Comm'n*, 726 F.2d at 1393.

75. Roberts, *supra* note 55.

76. *Piazza*, 831 F.Supp at 422.

77. *Id.* at 429 n.13.

78. This case is potentially much more significant for Major League Baseball since the court spends a good deal of thought and energy virtually eliminating MLB's antitrust exemption. However, I will not address baseball's antitrust exemption for four reasons: first, the exemption does not need more commentary; second, it is almost uniformly considered an anomaly, with no good reasons supporting its existence; third, I want to focus on how the antitrust laws can affect cities and professional leagues generally; and fourth, I do not believe that antitrust is large enough to solve the real problems between leagues and cities, so baseball's exemption is of minor significance.

79. *Id.* at 430.

80. *Id.* at 439, quoting PHILIP E. AREEDA & HERBERT HOVENKAMP, ANTITRUST LAW 518.1b (Supp. 1991).

81. *Piazza*, 831 F.Supp. at 439.

82. *Id.*

83. *See* John C. Weistart, *League Control of Market Opportunities: A Perspective on Competition and Cooperation in the Sports Industry*, 1984 DUKE L.J. 1013 (1984).

84. Mid-South Grizzlies v. NFL, 720 F.2d 772, 776 (3rd Cir. 1983).

85. The court cites two statutes that contributed to the NFL's monopoly position. The first allowed sports leagues an antitrust exemption with respect to the sale of broadcast rights in 1961. 15 U.S.C. § 1291 (1961).

The second, an amendment to § 1291, allowed the NFL and AFL to merge. *Id., amended by* Pub. L. 89-800 (1966). One of the issues in this case is whether this amendment mandated expansion since it allowed the merger agreement "if such agreement increases rather than decreases the number of professional football clubs so operating." *Id.* The court held that this language did not mandate expansion. *Mid-South Grizzlies,* 720 F. 2d at 776.

86. *Mid-South Grizzlies,* 720 F.2d at 787.

87. *Id.*

88. At a point in the opinion when the court is confusing § 1 with § 2, it says, "It would take a court bolder than this to claim that the congressionally authorized acquisition of market power, even market power amounting to monopoly power, was unlawful under Section 1 of the Sherman Act." *Id.* at 784.

89. The court cited a 1973 study by the Stanford Research Institute which identified thirteen viable locations for new franchises, in addition to Memphis: Mexico City; Birmingham, Alabama; Seattle, Washington; Nassau County, New York; Anaheim, California; Chicago, Illinois; Phoenix, Arizona; Honolulu, Hawaii; Tampa, Florida; the Tidewater area of Virginia; Charlotte-Greensboro, North Carolina; Indianapolis, Indiana; and Orlando, Florida. As already discussed, Anaheim, Phoenix, and Indianapolis acquired NFL teams by luring away existing teams, Seattle, Tampa, and now Charlotte acquired NFL teams by expansion. *Id.*

90. *Mid-South Grizzlies,* 720 F.2d at 787.

91. This also takes the city of Memphis out of the argument, so I will leave this argument to some colorful investor types and their lawyers to use to try to break into a sports league.

92. Kenneth L. Shropshire, *Opportunistic Sports Franchise Relocations: Can Punitive Damages in Actions Based Upon Contract Strike a Balance?*, 22 Loy. L.A. L. Rev. 569 (1989).

93. Beisner, *supra* note 7, at 432.

94. Shropshire, *supra* note 92, at 593.

95. Shavell, Law and Economics class at Yale Law School, Fall of 1993. The probability of a team not getting caught relocating without permission is obviously zero.

96. Beisner, *supra* note 7, at 432.

97. *Id.*

98. S. 298, 99th Cong., 1st Sess., 131 Cong. Rec. S.682-83 (daily ed. Jan. 24, 1985) (DeConcini); H.R. 6467, 97th Cong., 2d Sess. (1982) (Stark).

99. S. 287, 99th Cong., 1st Sess., 131 Cong. Rec. S.6631 (daily ed. Jan. 24, 1985) (Gorton); S. 259, 99th Cong., 1st Sess. § 5(a)-(b) (1985) (Eagleton); S. 172, 99th Cong., 1st Sess., 131 Cong. Rec. S.282 (daily ed. Jan. 3, 1985) (Specter); H.R. 785, 99th Cong., 1st Sess., § 4(c) (1985) (Dellums).

100.York, *supra* note 6. Specter's proposal allows for a shorter time period of team losses if the losses "endanger the continued profitability of the team." *Id.* at 358-59.
101.Gorton's bill identifies nine objective factors, including: "stadium adequacy; past fan support; public financial support, including the construction of facilities; net operating losses; and the degree to which the team has negotiated in good faith with local officials regarding the current situation." *Id.* at 363.

Eagleton's bill identifies twelve factors which must be considered before a relocation is permitted: 1) the comparative adequacy of the team's current stadium or arena; 2) the comparative adequacy of facilities related to the stadium or arena, including transportation, vending, or retail facilities; 3) the desire or ability of the stadium or arena operator or local government to remedy any inadequacies in the facility, or to provide other arrangements or incentives to make it reasonable and appropriate for the team to remain in the area; 4) the extent to which the team has directly or indirectly received public financial support through facilities construction or special tax treatment, and the extent to which debt on such support remains outstanding; 5) the effects of the relocation on any contract or agreement entered into by the team; 6) the extent to which the team's ownership or management has contributed to any circumstance that might demonstrate that relocation is necessary; 7) the comparative operating revenue in the previous three seasons; 8) any net operating losses by the team in the previous three seasons; 9) team fan support, demonstrated by attendance, ticket sales, or other factors; 10) the number of professional and college teams playing the same sport in the current and proposed locations; 11) any bona fide offer to purchase the team at fair market value and keep it in the same location; 12) the extent to which the team has engaged in good faith negotiations aimed at keeping the team in its current stadium or arena or another facility in the area. *Id.* at 366; S. 259, § 6(b), *supra* note 99.

102.Wong, *supra* note 1, at 62, *quoting* Senator Lautenberg at the Professional Sports Team Protection Act Hearings on S.2505 before the Senate Comm. on Commerce, Science, and Transportation (1984).
103.The congressional proposals are like adopting the two point conversion and penalizing missed field goals in order to create more touchdowns. If football really needs more touchdowns, deepen the end zone.
104.Senator Slade Gorton, *Professional Sports Franchise Relocation: Introductory Views From the Hill*, 9 SETON HALL LEGIS. J. 1, 5 (1985).
105.S.287.
106.The bill introduced by Sen. Eagleton, S.259, was killed when then Sen. Al Gore and Sen. Charles Mathias threatened a filibuster and demanded mandatory NFL expansion in exchange for releasing the bill. York, *supra* note 6, at 371. It is certainly no coincidence that Sen. Mathias is from Maryland, and Sen. Gorton's bill specified that one of the expansion NFL

franchises be located in Baltimore. Nor is it a coincidence that Sen. Gore is from Tennessee, a state which could not get the Grizzlies into the league through the current rules of antitrust.

107.Gorton, *supra* note 104, at 2.

108.Gorton noted that "in the past 20 years, state and local governments have spent over $6 billion building or renovating stadiums." *Id.*

109.*Id.* at 2-3.

110.Neale, *supra* note 48, at 4.

111.*Id.* at 6, 8.

112.Johnson, *supra* note 1, at 234.

113."Expansion to thirty-five or forty [baseball] teams by the end of the century would mean that more cities have their demand for a team satisfied, a more equitable relationship would develop between existing teams and host cities, and there would be a greater number of MLB players. This outcome sounds like something economists call a welfare maximizing solution. But economists never claimed that welfare maximization was a property of unregulated monopolies." ZIMBALIST, *supra* note 27, at 146.

114.Baade & Dye, *supra* note 34, at 265 (referring to an estimate made by Gerald Scully, sports economist).

115.It at least appears clear that each of the four major leagues — baseball, football, basketball, and hockey — do have monopoly positions, without the prospect of any serious competition.

116.Gray, *supra* note 24, at 158.

117.*Id., quoting* the Justice Department's position during the Hearings on Professional Sports Antitrust Legislation, Senate Comm. on the Judiciary, 99th Cong., 1st Sess. (1985).

118.*See* United States v. United States Steel Corp., 251 U.S. 417 (1920). US Steel brought 180 independent firms under one umbrella, controlling 80-95% of domestic production of steel. The court refused to break up US Steel because "the law does not make mere size an offence or the existence of unexerted power an offence." *Id.* at 451.

119.S.298.

120.York, *supra* note 6, at 370.

121.All of the cities would be better off under this proposal except those cities who currently have franchises only for the prestige value. Those cities will lose because the value of the franchise to them will be diluted, similar to a person who buys a car $30,000 over cost only to display his wealth to the neighbors, and then the same car starts selling at cost and half the block buys one. Similarly, the owners who bought into the sports industry to take advantage of its monopoly position will lose, but neither of these losses should cause much concern.

122.Johnson, *supra* note 1, at 239.

123.*Id.*

124.ZIMBALIST, *supra* note 27, at 145.

125. Neale, *supra* note 48, at 8.
126. *Id.* at 8 n.7.
127. *Id.* at 9.
128. ZIMBALIST, *supra* note 27, at 143.
129. *Id.* I imagine they both envision the "leagues" as one league, existing under the umbrella of Major League Baseball. *See* Neale, *supra* note 48, at 6.

FAIR OR FOUL?
THE SURVIVAL OF SMALL-MARKET TEAMS IN MAJOR LEAGUE BASEBALL*

Kevin E. Martens

In the essay that follows, Kevin Martens examines the problem of franchise relocation from the perspective of the "small-market" team in major league baseball. Although baseball has been the most geographically stable of the four major team sports with no team relocation since 1972, rumors of impending franchise shifts have been a continuing part of the baseball landscape. Martens' essay pays particular attention to the legal consequences of various proposals designed to shore-up the prospects of the smaller market teams.

I. INTRODUCTION

"Remember what happened in 1965." That statement can be heard in any discussion regarding the importance of constructing a new baseball facility in my hometown of Milwaukee, Wisconsin. Local business and civic leaders understand the significance of 1965 to baseball fans in Milwaukee. To his credit, Bud Selig, the owner of the Milwaukee Brewers and Major League Baseball's current acting commissioner, has not used the painful memory of 1965 to gain public support for his most recent stadium proposal.[1] Nevertheless, many baseball fans in Milwaukee fear that what happened in 1965 will soon reoccur unless team revenues are

*From Volume 4, Number 2, Spring 1994, pp. 323-374.

increased by the construction of a new stadium with luxury boxes.[2] Most Milwaukeeans remember that 1965 was the year that the Milwaukee Braves left Milwaukee for Atlanta.[3] Furthermore, they also understand that, if economic circumstances force the Brewers to abandon the city, Major League Baseball will, in all likelihood, vanish from the city for good.

The Braves franchise, which had originally moved to Milwaukee from Boston in 1953, initially prospered in its new locale.[4] From 1953 to 1957, attendance averaged over two million fans a year, with a high of 2.22 million fans in 1957, when the team claimed its first World Series crown.[5] After 1957, however, the team's attendance began to decline as its on-the-field performance soured.[6] Thus, when the Braves' lease of municipally-owned County Stadium expired after the 1965 season, a "window of opportunity" existed for the team's new owners (led by Ray Bartholome), who claimed that the team was losing money, to relocate.[7] Bartholome, lured by an attractive television deal, moved the franchise to Atlanta.[8] The community would not lose the Braves without a fight; however, local efforts (led by Senator William Proxmire) to enjoin the team from leaving Milwaukee failed in 1966.[9]

I was only two years old when Major League Baseball returned to Milwaukee in 1970 after a five-year hiatus.[10] To this day, I am amazed by the number of former Milwaukee Braves fans in Milwaukee who still follow the franchise in Atlanta and prefer the style of play in the senior circuit over that of the American League.[11] Paradoxically, many of these individuals are also the most loyal supporters of the Brewers, frequenting games both in Milwaukee and at the team's spring training facility in Chandler, Arizona. As someone who grew up with the Brewer franchise, I often wondered how these "old-timers" could remain loyal to the Braves, especially when it was clear to me that the Braves had greedily "abandoned" Milwaukee and its fans for what its owners perceived as greener pastures elsewhere.[12]

Now, however, after listening to the debates raging over the new baseball stadium proposal for Milwaukee, I have gained some insight into the perspective of these "old-timers." Despite their divided loyalties, they have an appreciation for the presence of Major League Baseball in Milwaukee that is generally lacking in most younger baseball fans who have never experienced the hardship of losing a professional baseball franchise.[13] While growing up, I remember the danger of discussing the Braves with more senior baseball enthusiasts, knowing that it would precipitate a lecture about the "good old days" and a reminder of how lucky I was to have a Major League Baseball team in my hometown. I also recall that, when attendance waned at Brewer games late in the season, these "old-timers" would quickly remind the community that a failure to support our local nine would force the team to move to a more "appreciative" locale.

At the time, however, most baseball fans in Milwaukee viewed such proclamations with a combination of disdain and bemusement. After all, the circumstances involving the Braves' move to Atlanta were much different than those involving the Brewers franchise. The Brewers, unlike the Braves, were *committed* to Milwaukee. The franchise was brought to the city from Seattle in 1970 by a local group formed for the specific purpose of bringing Major League Baseball back to Milwaukee.[14] The Brewers' on-the-field performance would soon culminate in the franchise's first division title in 1981 and a World Series appearance in 1982. Furthermore, attendance had been rising steadily as the team's fortunes improved on the field.[15] Given the success of the Brewers in the late 1970s and early 1980s, it seemed clear that Major League Baseball had, in fact, succeeded in Milwaukee and that the Brewers would remain a viable franchise in the foreseeable future.

So why do young baseball fans in Milwaukee now share the insecurity long held by old Milwaukee Braves supporters, fearing that, if a new baseball stadium is not built, the Brewers will abandon the community?[16] Do these fears have a sound basis? If so, what, if anything, can (or should) community leaders and/or Major League Baseball do to ensure the survival of professional baseball in Milwaukee and other "small markets"?[17] These are some of the questions I will address in the remainder of this Article. In Part II, I analyze several arguments regarding the importance of small-market teams to the future success of Major League Baseball. I conclude that it is in the best interests of Major League Baseball to ensure that small market teams remain viable in order to discourage the formation of rival leagues, to preserve for the League the benefits of expansion opportunities, and to maintain the popularity of Major League Baseball throughout the country. In Part III, I analyze the viability of small-market teams given the current competitive structure of Major League Baseball and expected future trends. My conclusion is that the current governing structure of Major League Baseball inadequately addresses the needs of small-market franchises and seriously jeopardizes their future survival. In Part IV, I suggest the need for either increased revenue sharing or a salary cap as vehicles to ensure the survival of small-market clubs, with a preference for the former. I will also analyze relevant antitrust, labor, and contract issues. Finally, in Part V, I revisit the current status of the Milwaukee Brewers stadium proposal and offer some concluding thoughts.

II. Does Major League Baseball Need Small-Market Teams?

Why should it be important to Major League Baseball that franchises in Milwaukee and other small markets remain viable? After all, should not owners of individual franchises be free to relocate their teams at will whenever they believe that they can receive greater financial remuneration elsewhere?[18] Would not such a "free and open market" for professional baseball franchises ensure that teams are located where consumers will derive the most benefit (as measured by their ability to pay)? Clearly, it would be an inefficient allocation of resources to require baseball franchises to remain in existing locations when, due to changes in economic circumstances, other locales offer more profitable opportunities. Before addressing these issues, it is important to articulate how the interests of franchise owners may conflict with the interests of other owners under the current governing structure of Major League Baseball and with society at large.

A. Separating Conflicts Between the Interests of Baseball Owners and the Interests of Society From Conflicts Among the Interests of Individual Baseball Owners:

Clearly, the interests of franchise owners, as embodied by the Major League Agreement ("the Agreement"),[19] and the interests of society in encouraging market competition may conflict in the franchising of professional baseball teams. In general, society disfavors the concentration of economic power when it allows a small number of economic actors to control the forces of supply or demand in a given industry or geographic location. This sentiment, of course, is enforced through the nation's antitrust policy as embodied by the Sherman Act.[20] Antitrust principles dictate that, absent proof that a market restraint is *reasonable*,[21] any Major League Baseball policy that inhibits the "natural play" of market forces should be discouraged.[22] Presumably, this would include any restraints on the relocation of franchises imposed by the Agreement.[23] Major League Baseball owners, on the other hand, may desire some restrictions on franchise movement that ostensibly conflict with the policies of the Sherman Act.[24] Because owners may disagree as to the wisdom of a proposed move given its effects on the profitability of the relocating franchise and the League itself, they may find it in their best interests to agree ex-ante on certain restraints over each individual owner's power to unilaterally dictate where his or her team will be situated.

Apart from society's general interest in enforcing antitrust policy, the Agreement must also accommodate conflicting interests among individual owners. While franchise owners may covet the *power* to establish league policies that supersede the mandate of general anti-trust principles,[25] they may nevertheless wish to maintain a significant level of free-market activity in the relocation of franchises within the Agreement itself. Because owners generally have an interest in main-taining the freedom to move their teams in response to changing economic incentives, we would expect them to create a system that would generally favor unfettered franchise relocations. Again, how-ever, it is in each owner's interest to retain some degree of control over franchise movements by his or her brethren which adversely affect the financial position of his or her team or the League as a whole.[26] Presumably, the Agreement should accommodate these conflicting interests in a manner that best promotes the collective welfare of the franchise owners.

For several reasons, the above-referenced distinctions are significant when analyzing the importance of small-market teams to Major League Baseball. First of all, they have a direct effect on the decision over the types of measures (if any) that should be adopted to ensure the survival of small-market teams. Secondly, they help to answer the question of whether owners can be trusted to adopt the best measures, or if society, through antitrust policy and other laws, should also play a role. If society has a strong interest in promoting competition for Major League teams among cities, then antitrust policy should supersede self-regulation by owners,[27] and owners must justify as "reasonable" any restraints under the Agreement which were adopted to protect small-market franchises.[28] If, on the other hand, society has only a marginal interest in the policies of professional baseball, then the Agreement should supersede antitrust policy and the justifications for restraints adopted to protect small-market franchises need only be shown to be in the "best interests of baseball."[29] As discussed in Part III, Major League Baseball currently enjoys a special exemption from antitrust laws which gives owners more administrative discretion than owners in other professional leagues; however, we shall see that the exemption is by no means "ironclad."[30] In light of this, and because the best interests of the Major League Baseball owners may obviously conflict with those of society, one should consider whether purported justifications for adopting market restraints to preserve the integrity of small-market teams satisfies antitrust review under either regime.[31]

B. The Survival of Small-Market Teams Under the Free-Market Model of Franchise Relocation:

So what are some of the justifications that may be given to baseball owners or antitrust courts for adopting measures to ensure the viability of small-market teams? Before discussing purported justifications for market restraints to protect small-market teams, we should first imagine the state of affairs that would exist if there truly were open competition among cities for Major League Baseball franchises.[32] If other communities could freely bid with current Major League cities for franchises, the "proper" incentives would presumably be in place for owners and community leaders to determine whether moving a team would truly be economically efficient. The Brewers franchise, for example, would be encouraged to relocate under the free market model if Bud Selig could, in fact, find a more profitable location in which to operate. Under this model, the city of Milwaukee (as well as the state and other local municipalities) should subsidize the construction of a new stadium if the estimated six million dollars a year in increased revenue from luxury boxes and gate receipts adequately compares to the financial gain offered by a bidding locale *and* the cost of building the stadium is outweighed by the perceived benefits to the community.[33] If, on the other hand, the increased revenues from luxury box rentals and gate receipts are insufficient to keep the Brewers in Milwaukee, *or* the costs of building a new stadium outweigh the perceived benefits to the community, then the city should not subsidize its construction. In the latter scenario, the "invisible hand" of competition would channel the franchise to another city where it would be more highly valued by consumers as measured by their ability to pay.[34] While unfortunate for the baseball fans of Milwaukee, those in another city would be rewarded for presumably deriving more benefit from the "product" of Major League Baseball.

One should, however, also consider the creation of expansion franchises under the "free market model."[35] First of all, it is important to note that the free market model does not presuppose an optimal number of Major League Baseball teams. That is, a decision by an owner to move his or her team from a city does *not* prove that the city is unable to support a Major League franchise. Thus, a determination by Bud Selig that the Brewers franchise will be more profitable in another locale does *not* necessarily mean that the team is losing money in Milwaukee. The free market model only predicts that, absent the possibility of expansion and prohibitive transaction costs, Major League Baseball franchises will, over time, be located in the communities where owners expect to receive the greatest profits.[36] Major League Baseball is, in fact, a profitable venture in Milwaukee and other small markets, the removal of restrictions on expansion would result in the creation of new franchises to meet such demand.[37] Presumably, then, the optimal number of Major League Baseball franchises would be achieved under a free-market model if expansion were unrestricted. As a result, justifications for preserving existing small-market franchises must also address the arguments typically given for restrictions on League expansion.

C. Altering the Free-Market Model: Justifications for Owners to Adopt Measures to Ensure the Survival of Small Market Teams:

Why, then, is the free-market model of franchise relocation, coupled with unrestricted expansion, an insufficient response to the viability issue involving small-market teams? What are some of the arguments advanced for adopting measures to ensure that existing small-market teams are financially viable in the future? How do these justifications relate to the distinctions made in section A of Part II? The remainder of Part II discusses three common justifications for adopting measures to ensure the survival of small-market teams, as well as their compliance with antitrust policies and the interests of Major League Baseball owners.

1. The interest of baseball fans in keeping their local franchise:

One justification often given for protecting small-market clubs is that baseball fans in a team's current community have a significant interest in keeping their local franchise which should be factored into Major League Baseball's franchise relocation policy.[38] While not advocating that an owner be *forced* to continue operating in a non-profitable location, proponents of this view argue that an owner should not be permitted to move an existing franchise from one profitable location to another. They claim that, if an owner wishes to own a team in a different city, then he or she should sell his or her current team to someone willing to operate in its current city and then purchase or seek an expansion franchise in the desired locale. In discussing the relocation of the Dodgers franchise from Brooklyn to Los Angeles, one author argued this position as follows:

> Why should an individual like Walter O'Malley, who happened to be in the right place at the right time, be able to rob Brooklyn, as Bill Veeck put it, of a part of its heritage? There is a perfectly clear legal answer to this question. O'Malley had a property right in the team that enabled him to do this without legal reproach. But should not the borough of Brooklyn or New York City at least share in this right? After all, the city nurtured the team during its development, conferred upon the franchise part of its trademark, gave the team what amounted to daily, abundant, free advertising through sports coverage in its newspapers and media, and provided a variety of subsidies to the club over the years.[39]

This was likely Howard Cosell's view when, while testifying before the U.S. House of Representatives in 1981 regarding the lifting of Major League Baseball's antitrust exemption, he referred to Major League Baseball's policy regarding the movement of sports franchises as "the rape of the cities."[40]

Obviously, this justification directly conflicts with the free-market model previously discussed. If Major League Baseball enforced a non-relocation and non-expansion policy, then franchises would presumably be forced to remain in non-wealth maximizing locations.[41] That is, communities that value the presence of a Major League franchise more highly than existing Major League cities, based on their willingness to pay, would be denied the opportunity to attract an existing team or a new franchise.[42] Such a regime would also violate our common understanding of property rights and the notion that, to maximize efficient use, an owner must have freedom to do with his or her property as he or she desires. Under the free-market model, the rights commonly associated with the ownership of property must be enforced in order for resources to be properly allocated. Presumably, society is made better off when producers are able to respond quickly and accurately to changes in consumer preferences, and producers are best able to react to changes in market incentives through unfettered ownership of the forces of supply. It was this notion that likely prompted Ted Turner's response to Howard Cosell's above- referenced criticism when, while testifying at the same hearings, he noted that "it is a pretty rampant case of socialism to say that [baseball owners] cannot move."[43]

This justification also loses force when we consider the possibility of a Major League Baseball policy encouraging expansion.[44] In such an environment, a community losing an existing franchise could seek a replacement through expansion; and assuming that Major League Baseball is viewed as profitable in that community, we would expect investors to bid for new teams.[45] Under this regime, it is likely that owners of existing franchises would, in fact, be unable to find more profitable communities in which to move their teams. With free expansion, astute investors would seek out "up and coming" communities in which to establish expansion franchises well before those areas developed to a point where they would be able to attract an existing team; this is especially true if the transactions costs in relocating an existing franchise are high. Unrestricted expansion, then, may be viewed as a reasonable accommodation between the interests of owners wishing to relocate their franchises and baseball fans desiring to keep Major League Baseball in profitable communities. This accommodation, of course, rejects the notion that baseball fans in a particular community have "a special moral entitlement" under every circumstance to keep an existing team, as opposed to securing an expansion team.[46] As antitrust policy considers the aggregate interest of all consumers, including those of a new locale, the "moral entitlement" approach is not likely to win favor as a reasonable market restraint.[47] This is important given continued erosion of Major League Baseball's antitrust exemption.[48]

Apart from antitrust concerns, however, owners are not likely to find the "fan entitlement" justifications for adopting measures to protect small-market franchises persuasive. After all, no owner amassed his or her fortune by operating Major League Baseball franchises; they all accumulated wealth through other business ventures or inheritance. They are the "successes" of our capitalistic society; they have all mastered the nuances of the market and have learned how to react to market-created incentives in order to most efficiently allocate their resources to meet consumer demand. Given their success in these other markets, why should they be expected to adopt restrictions on their ability to react to consumer demand for Major League Baseball? Presumably, such restraints would lead to non-wealth maximizing behavior to the detriment of society. Furthermore, the skills most owners have developed in the market would be less useful in an environment characterized by restrictions on the use of productive resources. Finally, such restraints may also act as a disincentive for individuals wishing to enter the market in order to purchase Major League Baseball franchises. Potential owners would presumably be less inclined to purchase teams from existing owners if they were required to keep the team in its existing locale. Such a rule would increase the risks facing potential owners. As a result, some would exit the market and those remaining in the market would restrict the amount they would be willing to pay to purchase an existing or expansion franchise. Clearly, Major League Baseball owners would be reluctant to adopt such measures if they would decrease the value and liquidity of their holdings.

2. Preserving the benefits of expansion for the League:

A second justification for adopting measures to ensure the survival of small-market teams is to preserve for current owners the benefits of expanding into the most profitable markets. Major League Baseball can accommodate new geographic markets by either the relocation of an existing franchise from a different location or the creation of a new expansion team. When an existing team moves, the primary benefit of the relocation goes to that team's owner, who directly benefits from the increase in revenues of his or her team. Other owners may experience some residual effects in profits through changes in travel costs, gate receipts, and national television contracts. If the League feels that the abandoned locale is nevertheless profitable, it may approve an expansion team for that community and profit from the fee paid by the new owners, however, the expansion fee is likely to be less than the League could have charged for the right to secure a new team in the more desirable location.[49] On the other hand, if the League instead approved expansion into the desired location, the benefits from that location would be captured by the current owners. In theory, the League could charge a higher expansion fee than it could if it instead permitted an existing owner to move his or her team to the desired location and then approved expansion in that less profitable site.[50]

While again violative of the spirit of the above referenced free-market model, this justification may nevertheless carry some weight in a "reasonableness" analysis under antitrust law.[51] Baseball owners may claim, for example, that the addition of new cities has a tremendous impact on the viability and financial health of Major League Baseball (and, secondarily, on each individual owner), a "public good" to which they have been entrusted. Therefore, any decision to alter the mix of teams should be made by the League itself and not by an individual owner whose judgment may be "justifiably clouded" by his or her own shortterm financial interests or a court lacking expertise in this field. While this argument may explain why the League, and not individual owner, should decide whether or not to maintain the status quo, it does not explain why entry into a new market should be made through expansion rather than by encouraging an individual owner to relocate his or her existing franchise. The owners' response to this criticism may be that, as part of its analysis of the impact of new teams on the viability and financial health of Major League Baseball, the League should be allowed to consider the "reasonable expectations" of the general public. This is a "soft" version of the previously described "fan entitlement justification" for preserving small-market teams. While not claiming that the expectations of fans are determinative, owners would argue that, in circumstances where it is "reasonably clear" that a community will receive a Major League franchise in the near future, consideration should be given to the loyalty of baseball fans of existing Major League franchises. Such a preference, the owners may argue, would best enhance the image of Major League Baseball, minimize disappointment among existing fans, and promote fan development for the new franchise. As a result, League policy would reflect a preference for existing franchises to remain in their current communities, with expansion into new markets reserved for the League itself.[52] This outcome would, therefore, enhance the financial returns to current owners while appeasing those demanding removal of baseball's antitrust exemption.[53]

3. Discouraging the formation of rival baseball leagues:

A third justification for adopting measures to ensure the future viability of small-market teams is the owners' interest in discouraging the formation of rival leagues. The likelihood that this would occur, of course, depends significantly on the policy adopted by Major League Baseball regarding expansion. If the League adopted a restrictive expansion policy, then the relocation of an existing franchise may create an opportunity for the creation or expansion of a rival league. A rival league, for example, may gain a foothold in Milwaukee if the Brewers franchise is permitted to move to another community and Major League Baseball is dilatory in "filling the void." With a more permissive policy on expansion, Major League Baseball would be able to enter such markets in order to discourage the formation of a rival league. As stated by one source:

> Expansion into desirable cities targeted by a new league is a favorite tactic of established leagues, not only in hockey and in football, but also in baseball. Indeed, Major League Baseball, threatened in the late 1950's by Branch Rickey's proposed Continental Baseball League, hastily undertook its first expansion in this century, into New York and Houston in the National League and Washington and Kansas City in the American League.[54]

It therefore may be in the best interests of Major League Baseball owners to have both a permissive expansion policy and to ensure the survival of existing (and proposed) small-market franchises in order to protect their "monopoly" position.

Note that, under this view, it may, in fact, be in the best interests of Major League Baseball owners to adopt measures facilitating the existence of otherwise unprofitable franchises. We would fully expect the Major Leagues to expand into profitable communities in order to discourage the formation of rival leagues. However, the same logic dictates that it also maintain franchises in "non-profitable" communities, for the profitability of operating a team in a given location will be perceived very differently by an established league and a new league. For example, given the minimal amount of revenue sharing that currently exists in Major League Baseball pursuant to the Agreement,[55] small-market clubs with much lower revenues must compete with teams in more prosperous areas for talent and resources. Not surprisingly, many observers question whether such clubs can, in fact, field competitive teams over time without incurring tremendous losses. If Major League Baseball had significant revenue sharing (for example, as is the case in the National Football League), new franchises in small-markets would lower the revenues of existing clubs if, as is likely, the income they "bring to the common pool" is less than the League average.

A start-up league, on the other hand, would view the profitability of operations in such a community very differently. Since the primary concern of a new league is establishing a foothold in significant metropolitan areas across the United States, its owners would likely agree to subsidize sites which were initially unprofitable. In addition, even if such a league institutionalized revenue sharing among teams, it would not share the existing league's reservations about accepting a city whose team would earn revenues below the league average as many of its franchises would develop in small markets neglected by the existing league. As a result, and especially in light of the precarious position of its antitrust exemption,[56] it appears that Major League Baseball owners would be wise to consider steps to ensure the viability of teams in small markets.

Questions remain as to the optimal number of Major League Baseball franchises and the best way to protect small-market clubs. Part IV of this Article addresses the latter issue. The question of "how many teams is enough," however, is more difficult to assess. In theory, Major League Baseball owners should encourage the operation of as many teams as necessary to satisfy consumer demand, thereby discouraging the entry of competitors into the market. Presumably, this would include the presence of franchises in small markets that, absent contributions from more prosperous teams, would not be profitable in the long run. But how many such teams would Major League Baseball need to subsidize in order to satisfy the desires of baseball fans? If the Brewers left Milwaukee, for example, would baseball fans in Wisconsin be content to follow clubs in Chicago and Minneapolis?[57] Or would Milwaukee then become a viable target for entry by a rival league? One method to determine the number of new markets that Major League Baseball would need to accommodate would be to review the number of cities vying for teams in Major League Baseball's latest round of expansion in the National League. According to one source, at least fifteen cities were originally interested in landing an expansion team; ultimately, Denver and Miami were chosen.[58] Out of the remaining thirteen regions, eight are generally considered to be financially credible. These regions would include: Buffalo, Indianapolis, Nashville, New Orleans, Phoenix, Tampa-St. Petersburg, Washington D.C., and Vancouver.[59] Of these cities, five have populations less than that of the smallest current Major League city (Buffalo, Indianapolis, Nashville, New Orleans, and Vancouver); two are similar in size to existing small-market teams (Phoenix and Tampa-St. Petersburg); and one, Washington D.C., has already lost two franchises (in 1960 to Minnesota and in 1971 to Texas) and is close in proximity to Baltimore, the home city of the Orioles franchise.[60]

Clearly, Major League Baseball would not need to expand into each of the above-listed markets in order to deter the formation of a rival league. However, when faced with uncertainty over the number of communities they can "neglect" before aggrieved investors launch a rival league, it seems that Major League owners should, at a *minimum*, protect existing Major League franchises that are located in small markets. Some owners, of course, may question the likelihood that a rival league would ever arise to challenge the supremacy of Major League Baseball. These owners, however, may be placing too much confidence in the exemption from antitrust laws that Major League Baseball currently enjoys.[61] Most consider baseball's antitrust exemption to be a historical anomaly,[62] and many have recommended that it be lifted by Congress.[63] Recently, legislators from Florida, in light of the owners' disapproval of the sale of the San Francisco Giants to a Florida group intending to move the team to Tampa-St. Petersburg, have considered proposing legislation in Congress to have baseball's antitrust exemption removed.[64] Should this occur, under the previously discussed free market model, the creation of rival leagues should be encouraged to compete with the established league for consumer dollars. Competition may ensue from start-up leagues (both American and foreign), the entry of foreign leagues (for example, Japanese or Mexican) into the American market, or an upgrading in the level of play by existing minor league teams. It appears, then, that the competitive position of Major League Baseball vis-a-vis rival leagues is enhanced by the existence of franchises in small markets.

As indicated, this justification generally does not comport with antitrust policy and the interest of society in promoting competition among producers in a given industry. However, instead of focusing on its purported goal of preventing competition from rival leagues, owners could argue that they are, in fact, enhancing consumer welfare by increasing competition among teams within the league. Owners may further emphasize that their superior position in competing with potential rival leagues in small markets is the result of an inherent advantage due to the long history of Major League Baseball and its corresponding enhancement of fan loyalty and interest. Whether these justifications pass antitrust scrutiny, however, likely depends on whether or not a court believes that professional baseball is a "natural monopoly."[65] Also, with the essence of sports being competition designed to culminate in the crowning of a single champion, the owners may argue that, as history has shown, any rival league would ultimately be consumed by Major League Baseball.[66]

III. The Viability of Small-Market Teams Under Major League Baseball's Existing Regime

Once we conclude that small-market franchises are important to the future of Major League Baseball, we must determine whether or not such teams can survive under existing conditions. What are some of the special obstacles facing small-market franchises? How do the current rules governing Major League Baseball, as embodied by the Agreement,[67] address these challenges? What changes have occurred in the environment in which Major League Baseball franchises operate which threaten the viability of small-market teams, and what changes are likely to occur in the future? These are some of the questions addressed in Part III. We must first establish that the future viability of small-market franchises is, in fact, threatened within the current governing structure of Major League Baseball before considering measures that owners (or legislators) should adopt to ensure the viability of such teams.[68]

A. Antitrust Treatment of Major League Baseball:

Perhaps the best way to analyze the financial condition of small-market franchises is to first discuss the broader context in which Major League Baseball operates. This, in turn, will allow us to distinguish between those rules affecting small-market teams which are imposed by agreement among the owners, and those imposed by society, either directly or indirectly, on Major League Baseball. Baseball owners, of course, only have discretion to change the former.[69] If it is determined that the viability of small-market franchises is compromised under the existing regime, distinguishing between rules in this manner will allow us to identify those with the power to change relevant rules and enact measures to protect the integrity of such teams.[70]

1. The Historical Development of Major League Baseball's Antitrust Exemption:

The general power of owners to act is limited primarily by principles of contract, tort, criminal, labor, and antitrust law.[71] Of particular importance for this discussion is the influence of antitrust law on the policies implemented by Major League Baseball.[72] The applicability of § 2 of the Sherman Act to Major League Baseball was first raised in a case brought against Hal Chase involving the legality of baseball's "reserve clause."[73] Although not vital to its holding, the *Chase* court noted that:

[It] cannot agree to the proposition that the business of baseball for profit is interstate trade or commerce, and therefore subject to the provisions of the Sherman Act. . . Baseball is an amusement, a sport, a game that comes clearly within the civil and criminal law of the state, and it is not a commodity or an article of merchandise subject to the regulation of Congress on the theory that it is interstate commerce.[74]

That sentiment was echoed by Justice Oliver Wendell Holmes, a former amateur baseball player,[75] in a celebrated case brought in 1922 by the Federal Baseball Club of Baltimore, a member of a new rival league, against Major League Baseball for denying access to the players' market through the reserve system.[76] Holmes observed that:

[t]he business is giving exhibitions of baseball, which are purely state affairs . . . But the fact that in order to give the exhibitions the Leagues must induce free persons to cross state lines and must arrange and pay for their doing so is not enough to change the character of the business . . . [T]he transport is a mere incident, not the essential thing. That to which it is incident, the exhibition, although made for money, would not be called trade or commerce in the commonly accepted use of those words. As it is put by the defendant, personal effort, not related to production, is not a subject of commerce. That which in its consummation is not commerce does not become commerce among the States because the transportation that we have mentioned takes place. To repeat the illustrations given by the Court below, a firm of lawyers sending out a member to argue a case, or the Chautauqua lecture bureau sending out a member to argue a case, does not engage in such commerce because the lawyer or lecturer goes to another State . . . . If we are right the plaintiff's business is to be described in the same way and [this case does not involve] an interference with commerce among the States.[77]

Thus, Major League Baseball was held to be exempt from coverage under the Sherman Act.

With subsequent changes in the Supreme Court's interpretation of Congressional power under the Commerce Clause,[78] it was clear to many observers that baseball's antitrust exemption would soon be overruled.[79] Baseball's owners (and lawyers), anticipating a judicial response to Congress' failure to grant a statutory antitrust exemption, prepared themselves for the worst.[80] The Supreme Court, however, threw owners another curve when, in 1953, it held that it was up to

Congress, and not the courts, to remove baseball's antitrust exemption.[81] Specifically, the Court noted that:

> Congress has had the [*Federal Baseball*] ruling under consideration but has not seen fit to bring such business under [antitrust] laws by legislation having prospective effect. The business has thus been left for thirty years to develop, on the understanding that it was not subject to existing antitrust legislation . . . We think that if there are evils in this field which now warrant application to it of the antitrust laws it should be by legislation. Without re-examination of the underlying issues, the judgments below are affirmed on the authority of [*Federal Baseball*] so far as that decision determines that Congress had no intention of including the business of baseball within the scope of the federal antitrust laws.[82]

Congress and the Supreme Court, then, were both inclined to pass the buck. "Congress did not enact legislation because it believed the [*Gardella*] decision removing baseball's antitrust exemption was good law, not the [*Federal Baseball*] decision. . . [while] the Supreme Court putatively did not reverse the precedent of the Holmes decision because it interpreted congressional inaction in [the 1951 Cellar Hearings] as an endorsement of [*Federal Baseball*]."[83]

In 1972, the Supreme Court revisited the issue and again upheld the validity of baseball's antitrust exemption.[84] In *Flood*, the Court noted that:

> the slate with respect to baseball is not clean. Indeed, it has not been clean for half a century. . . We continue to loath, 50 years after *Federal Baseball* and almost two decades after *Toolson*, to overturn those cases judicially when Congress, by its positive inaction, has allowed those decisions to stand for so long and, far beyond mere inference and implication, has clearly evinced a desire not to disapprove them legislatively. . . If there is any inconsistency or illogic in all this, it is an inconsistency and illogic of long standing that is to be remedied by the Congress and not by this Court. . . Under these circumstances, there is merit in consistency even though some might claim that beneath that consistency is a layer of inconsistency.[85]

As a result, Major League Baseball continues to enjoy a unique exemption from antitrust legislation, based on an erroneous assumption made by the Supreme Court in 1922, not applicable to any other professional sports league.[86] As previously indicated, however, this exemption has come under increasing attack, and its continued viability is very much at issue.[87]

2. The Antitrust Exemption and Labor Law in Major League Baseball:

Not surprisingly, Major League Baseball's antitrust exemption has had a significant impact on the development of its policies towards players and among teams. Because of *Federal Baseball* and its progeny, baseball's player reserve system, including the rookie draft and veteran free agency, are exempt from the antitrust laws applicable to other professional sports leagues.[88]

Presumably, this protection would shelter Major League Baseball from antitrust scrutiny should it adopt a salary cap,[89] revenue sharing, or any other measure typically thought of as "non-competitive" in nature. At this point, however, it is again important to distinguish between owner-adopted measures affecting the teams' relations with one another, and those affecting the relationship between players and the League.[90] Though many owner-adopted rules may be properly categorized under either category, owners are, of course, constrained in adopting the latter types of measures by agreement with the Major League Baseball Players' Association.[91] The Supreme Court has held that collective agreements whose terms are principally felt by the immediate parties, and not outside competitors, are immune from antitrust scrutiny.[92] This "labor exemption" from antitrust scrutiny applies to any professional sports league where owner/player relations are governed by a collective bargaining agreement.[93] Since every major professional sports league in the United States is currently governed by such an agreement, and therefore exempt from antitrust law, the Major League Baseball's historical exemption may seem devalued. However, given this "special exemption," Major League Baseball players, unlike athletes in other professional leagues, are unable to seek antitrust protection by decertifying their union should they become dissatisfied with their gains in collective bargaining.[94] Major League Baseball's historical antitrust exemption, then, continues to define the contours of negotiations between the owners and the players' union by limiting an otherwise important option available to the players. As a result, it has great value to baseball owners, who currently have significantly more leeway than their brethren in other sports leagues in their power to adopt market restrictions affecting team relations, such as franchise relocations, and their bargaining position in labor negotiations.[95]

B. The Current State of Small-Market Teams in Major League Baseball:

So what effect (if any) has the antitrust exemption for Major League Baseball had on the profitability of small-market franchises? How have the rules adopted by Major League Baseball owners (after negotiating with the players' union) affected the competitive position and viability of small-market teams? Can small-market franchises survive in the future under Major League Baseball's current governing structure? In answering these questions, we must begin by comparing the current financial position of small-market teams with that of franchises with greater resources. Should we uncover significant disparities in financial health, we can then investigate whether they result from the policies enforced by Major League Baseball. Furthermore, should we conclude that the future viability of small-market franchises is at risk, we can propose measures that may be taken by owners to ensure the economic survival of such teams in the future.[96]

1. Franchise Values in Major League Baseball:

Major League Baseball owners profit from their franchises through appreciation in market value and the generation of income. Clearly, estimating the value of any business is an inexact science; this is especially true in Major League Baseball, where the profitability of a given franchise is often difficult to ascertain.[97] In general, the value of a franchise should "approximate the discounted value of future estimated profits, where profits are conceived broadly to include all forms of return."[98] Average franchise values in the 1980s were nearly seventy times greater than they were in the 1910s, and one small-market team, the Seattle Mariners, which was purchased for $13 million in 1981, was sold for $77 million in 1988.[99] Franchise values in all sports, in fact, grew at an annual rate of 20% per year during the latter portion of the 1980s.[100] With such a tremendous appreciation in value of baseball franchises over the last decade, it seems that owners have found it profitable to operate teams in small markets even if they experienced annual losses on their financial statements.[101]

These trends, however, are not likely to continue in the future. According to one source, the average franchise value in the Major Leagues *decreased* by 4.2% from 1990 to 1991, and the average value of five of the seven "small-market franchises"[102] declined over the same period.[103] In 1992, the average franchise value in the Major Leagues further decreased by 16.24%. The average value of six of the seven "small-market franchises," however, increased slightly due to "baseball's determination to redistribute local TV revenues."[104] Nevertheless, the overall decline in franchise values may be attributed to two sources: player costs continue to rise faster than revenues (causing operating income to decline), and owners are faced with a potential cut in national television broadcasting revenues of 20%.[105] As we shall later see, both factors will likely continue to negatively affect franchise values in the future, and also have a significant effect on the operating profits of Major League franchises. At this point, it is sufficient to note that any decline in the rate of increase of franchise values makes owners more reliant on operating income for profits, just as a decline in the rate of appreciation of a stock would make an investor more reliant on dividend payments in order to recognize investment profits. This effect is compounded when the value of Major League franchises decreases, as it did from 1990 through 1992.

2. Operating Profits in Major League Baseball:

As noted above, the second part of the owners' "profit equation" involves profits recognized from operations; this is what most people have in mind when referring to the profitability of baseball franchises. Again, one should keep in mind that it is extremely difficult to accurately measure the actual profits from operations of a franchise, especially given the malleability of accounting principles, specialized tax treatment, and specialized rules regarding the depreciation of player salaries.[106] By carefully considering each of the elements affecting the team's income statement and profitability, we can gain some insight into the status of small-market clubs, vis-a-vis franchises operating in larger communities. Operating profits equal revenues less operating expenses; from this figure, owners subtract depreciation from players' salaries, taxes, and interest to arrive at net income.[107] It is within this framework that we can ascertain relevant distinctions between small-market and large-market teams in order to better determine whether small- market clubs will remain profitable in the future.

In general, reported operating profits in Major League Baseball increased throughout the 1980s, from a $66.6 million loss in 1983, to a gain of $214.5 million in 1989. This figure, however, subsequently declined to approximately $142.9 million in 1990, $138.6 million in 1991, and $87.8 million in 1992.[108] Thus, according to industry figures, baseball first became profitable during the tenure of former Commissioner Peter Ueberroth, due in large part to the collusive practices of owners in the salary offers made to veteran free agents.[109] The decline in reported profits during the 1990s resulted from the end of collusive practices among the owners, which precipitated higher player salaries and compensatory payments which the owners were required to make to the players under the settlement agreement.[110]

For our purposes it is significant to note how Major League Baseball's operating profits are distributed among franchises to analyze the *disparity* between small-market and large-market teams. In 1990, for example, five Major League teams recognized operating losses, including three small- market franchises: the Kansas City Royals ($9.8 million), Cleveland Indians ($6.8 million), and Seattle Mariners ($3.1 million).[111] Of the remaining twenty-one teams, the most profitable were the New York Yankees ($24.5 million), New York Mets ($15.8 million), Toronto Blue Jays ($13.9 million), Oakland Athletics ($12.4 million), Boston Red Sox ($12.3 million), Philadelphia Phillies ($11.1 million), and Cincinnati Reds ($11.0 million).[112] In 1991, on the other hand, twelve clubs reported operating losses, including five small-market teams: the Milwaukee Brewers ($11.4 million), Kansas City Royals ($7.2 million), Cleveland Indians ($4.8 million), San Francisco Giants ($4.4 million), and Oakland Athletics ($1.7 million).[113] The most profitable teams in 1991 were the New York Yankees ($30.4 million), Toronto Blue Jays ($26.3 million), New York Mets ($20.7 million), Chicago White Sox ($18.0 million), Houston Astros ($14.5 million), Texas Rangers ($13.9 million), St. Louis Cardinals ($12.7 million), Baltimore Orioles ($11.1 million), and Boston Red Sox ($10.7 million).[114] Finally, in 1992, thirteen clubs reported operating losses, including six small-market clubs: the Milwaukee Brewers ($12.8 million), Oakland A's ($12.8 million), Cincinnati Reds ($11.8 million), San Francisco Giants ($11.1 million), Kansas City Royals ($5.1 million), and Seattle Mariners ($2.4 million).[115] The most profitable clubs that year were the Baltimore Orioles ($34.2 million), New York Yankees ($25.0 million), Chicago White Sox ($16.7 million), Texas Rangers ($14.8 million), and Los Angeles Dodgers ($14.7 million).[116] While not necessarily an accurate measure of the actual profits accruing to baseball owners,[117] these figures do suggest both a wide discrepancy between the profitability of small-market and largemarket teams and a growing trend where small-market teams are finding it more and more difficult to recognize operating profits at all within the current economic environment of Major League Baseball.[118]

Before investigating possible sources of this discrepancy, one important factor affecting the actual profits recognized by the owners needs to be discussed: the unique tax treatment given to the depreciation of player salaries.[119] In purchasing a team, an owner acquires three sets of assets: player contracts (constituting a club's major asset), a franchise right, and a set of contracts necessary for operations (for example, leases, concession agreements, and broadcast agreements).[120] Under the Internal Revenue Code, owners may treat player contracts as depreciable intangible assets.[121] As a result, player contracts are depreciated over the average length of a player's career.[122] This, in effect, forces the government to subsidize the purchase of the franchise by an amount equal to the present value of the amount allocated to players' contracts multiplied by the corporate tax rate.[123] However, as observed by one author:

> [f]rom an economic point of view, the loophole makes little sense. First, it is obvious that the overwhelming share of the value of a franchise belongs to the monopoly rent that is generated by belonging to Major League Baseball and the exclusive territorial rights membership confers, not to the players' contracts. The value of these rights does not depreciate over time. Second, baseball players do not depreciate as does a machine. In fact, most players reach their peak performances well after the midpoint of their careers. That is, for five years or more players appreciate in value from their on-the-job training before they begin to depreciate. Third, baseball players do not produce a net income stream unless the additional revenue they generate for a team (their marginal revenue product) is greater than their salary. In this sense, a ballplayer should be considered a depreciable asset no more than a factory production worker. Fourth, players can be replaced simply by promoting a player from the minors. If anything, the depreciable investment in players should be the amount spent on player development in the minor leagues, but this sum is expensed (the related expenses are fully deducted in each year) so it cannot also be amortized.[124]

The practice of amortizing player contracts, then, seems nothing more than "a taxpayer subsidy to franchise owners and consumers of sports."[125] Not surprisingly, the depreciation of players' contracts, first utilized in 1959 by owner Bill Veeck, has been called "his most important contribution to the baseball business."[126]

How should the depreciation of players' contracts factor into our analysis of the special problems facing owners of small-market clubs? First of all, just as they have considered removing baseball's antitrust exemption in response to increasing dissatisfaction with the way Major League Baseball is run, Congress may also consider eliminating this unique tax treatment given to the owners of professional sports franchises.[127] Secondly, the size of the tax shelter owners receive due to the depreciation of players' contracts, because it depends on the purchase price of a franchise, will be greater for large-market teams than for small-market teams. Thirdly, we should also remember that, because owners may only depreciate the value allocated to players' contracts *upon purchasing the franchise*, its value to owners "diminishe[s] to zero after the players' [contracts are] fully depreciated [typically, over five years]."[128] Thus, the tax savings realized by owners due to the depreciation of players' contracts is, in fact, short-lived.[129] Finally, this sheltering effect underlines the importance of basing financial analysis of franchises on book profits rather than operating profits as a team can clearly "suffer book losses but have positive cash flows."[130]

3. Elements Contributing to the Decline in Profitability of Small-Market Franchises:

So what has caused the recent decline in the profitability of small-market franchises? Should we expect this downward trend to continue in the future? Perhaps the best way to answer such questions is to look at the elements underlying "operating profits" to uncover sources of divergence between small-market and large-market teams. As noted earlier, operating profits equals the difference between operating revenues and operating expenses. Revenues in Major League Baseball are primarily derived from three sources: broadcasting revenues, gate and stadium revenues, and licensing revenues.[131] Costs, in turn, are mainly attributable to team costs (primarily player salaries), player development costs, game costs (primarily stadium operations), promotional expenses, and general and administrative expenses.[132] Each will be discussed in turn.

a. Broadcasting Revenues:

Broadcasting revenues currently account for approximately 50% of the total revenues in Major League Baseball.[133] Each team receives such revenues from both local and national sources.[134] Small-market franchises, however, derive a much greater percentage of broadcasting revenues from national sources.[135] This is because national broadcasting revenues are divided equally among the franchises, while local broadcasting revenues are not.[136] As a result, not only do small-market franchises receive significantly less in broadcasting revenues than large-market teams, but they are also much more dependent on national sources. In 1992, for example, the teams receiving the most total media revenues were the New York Yankees ($61 million), New York Mets ($50 million), Boston Red Sox ($40.1 million), Los Angeles Dodgers ($33 million), Detroit Tigers ($28.8 million), California Angels ($28.2 million), Toronto Blue Jays ($28 million), and Chicago Cubs ($28 million).[137] The teams receiving the least in total media revenues, on the other hand, were the Atlanta Braves ($17.3 million), Milwaukee Brewers ($19.8 million), Minnesota Twins ($20 million), Kansas City Royals ($21 million), Seattle Mariners ($22 million), and Cleveland Indians ($23 million).[138] The disparity in broadcasting revenues becomes even greater when we exclude the approximately $15 million each club received under the national television contract in 1992.[139] The New York Yankees, for example, realized over $40 million more in local broadcasting revenue than the Milwaukee Brewers in 1992 ($46.0 million to $4.8 million), a ratio of almost 10 to 1.

This does not give the complete picture. The above figures include an agreement between the clubs with superstation broadcasting agreements (Atlanta Braves, Chicago Cubs, New York Mets, and New York Yankees) and Major League Baseball to make compensatory payments to a central fund to be distributed among the remaining teams.[140] Furthermore, they also include a "modest revenue sharing [agreement among teams to share] 'net receipts' from pay television."[141] As a result, the actual disparity in local (and total) broadcasting revenues generated by small-market and large-market teams is even greater than indicated by the above figures. Finally, national television broadcasting revenues will decrease significantly in the future. CBS agreed to pay Major League Baseball $1.06 billion, which was divided equally among teams, for the right to broadcast nationally sixteen weekend games during the regular season, the All-Star game, the playoffs, and the World Series each year from 1990 to 1993. ESPN made a similar agreement to broadcast 175 regular-season games for $100 million a year during those years.[142] Both networks, however, lost a significant amount of money,[143] and Major League Baseball is bracing for a 20-30% drop in its new national television contract which will have to be divided among twenty-eight, rather than twenty-six, teams.[144] For reasons previously discussed, this will have a much greater impact on small-market clubs than large-market clubs. Coupled with the prospect of continued growth in local broadcasting revenues,[145] we can expect the disparity in total broadcasting revenues between the "haves" and the "have nots" to increase dramatically in the next several years.

b. Gate and Stadium Revenues:

As expected, small-market teams are also disadvantaged as compared to the large-market teams regarding gate and stadium revenues. In general, the percentage of total operating revenues in Major League Baseball attributable to gate and stadium receipts has fallen from 74.3% in 1975 to approximately 33% in 1992, due in most part to increases in broadcasting revenues over that same period.[146] The absolute amount of gate and stadium revenues has also grown dramatically over that same period due to rising attendance, higher ticket prices, higher parking and concessions prices, and luxury box revenues.[147] Gate receipts, of course, are a function of attendance and ticket prices, which are both affected by team quality. Not surprisingly, small-market teams fare worse, on average, than large-market teams on both counts.[148] Stadium receipts, on the other hand, depend on many factors; including whether the team owns or leases, the terms of the lease agreement, and the existence of luxury box revenues. Typically, the small- market teams fare worse than those in large-markets. In 1990, for example, the teams with the highest revenues from gate and stadium receipts were the Toronto Blue Jays ($47.3 million), New York Mets ($40.6 million), Oakland Athletics ($34.5 million), Los Angeles Dodgers ($32.5 million), Boston Red Sox ($32.2 million), and Kansas City Royals ($32 million).[149] That same year, the teams with the lowest revenues from gate and stadium receipts were the Atlanta Braves ($11.2 million), Cleveland Indians ($12.5 million), Montreal Expos ($13.1 million), Detroit Tigers ($13.5 million), Houston Astros ($13.6 million), and Seattle Mariners ($14.8 million).[150] In 1991 the teams with the highest gate and stadium revenues were the Toronto Blue Jays ($56.5 million), Chicago White Sox ($46.8 million), Los Angeles Dodgers ($44.6 million), New York Mets ($38.9 million), and Boston Red Sox ($38.8 million); the teams with the lowest amounts were the Montreal Expos ($13.7 million), Cleveland Indians ($16.1 million), Milwaukee Brewers ($17.2 million), Houston Astros ($18.6 million), Atlanta Braves ($19.2 million), Seattle Mariners ($20.5 million), and San Francisco Giants ($20.5 million).[151] Finally, the most profitable teams in this area in 1992 were the Toronto Blue Jays ($54.3 million), Baltimore Orioles ($52.1 million),[152] Chicago White Sox ($46.3 million), Boston Red Sox ($45.6 million), and Los Angeles Dodgers ($44.8 million); those with the lowest receipts were the Cleveland Indians ($13.0 million), Houston Astros ($15.3 million), Detroit Tigers ($17.8 million), San Francisco Giants ($18.6 million), Montreal Expos ($18.9 million), and Seattle Mariners ($19.5 million).[153] Thus, assuming that owners set ticket prices at a profit-maximizing level,[154] we should expect that the approximately $30 million disparity in gate and stadium revenues between small and large-market clubs will continue in the future. Furthermore, because the above figures include the gate sharing policy in effect in both the National and American Leagues, the absolute disparity between the gate revenues of small and large-market teams is actually much higher.[155]

c. Licensing Revenues:

The third primary source of operating revenues for teams, licensing revenues, brought approximately $77 million to Major League Baseball in 1990 and approximately $102 million in 1991.[156] Divided equally among teams, these funds do not contribute to the existing income disparity among teams, and added roughly $2.7 million to each team in 1990 and $3.7 million in 1991.[157]

d. Total Operating Revenues:

So what is the total disparity in operating revenues between small-market and large-market franchises? In 1990, the teams with the highest revenues were the New York Yankees ($98 million), New York Mets ($81.1 million), Toronto Blue Jays ($77.5 million), Boston Red Sox ($68.5 million), and the Los Angeles Dodgers ($64.4 million). The lowest-revenue producing teams were the Seattle Mariners ($34 million), Cleveland Indians ($34.8 million), Montreal Expos ($35.3 million), Atlanta Braves ($35.4 million), Detroit Tigers

($38 million), and the Milwaukee Brewers ($38.4 million).[158] In 1991, the top revenue producing teams were the New York Mets ($91.1 million), New York Yankees ($90 million), Toronto Blue Jays ($88.7 million), Boston Red Sox ($81.5 million), Los Angeles Dodgers ($79.3 million), and Chicago White Sox ($78 million). The teams with the lowest operating revenues were the Milwaukee Brewers ($38.8 million), Montreal Expos ($39.4 million), Atlanta Braves ($40.3 million), Cleveland Indians ($42 million), Minnesota Twins ($44.1 million), and the Seattle Mariners ($44.7 million).[159] Finally, the teams with the highest operating revenues in 1992 were the New York Yankees ($94.6 million), Boston Red Sox ($90.6 million), Toronto Blue Jays ($87.7 million), New York Mets ($86.9 million), and Los Angeles Dodgers ($84.2 million). Those with the lowest figures included the Cleveland Indians ($39.9 million), Houston Astros ($43.3 million), Milwaukee Brewers ($45.3 million), Seattle Mariners ($45.4 million), Montreal Expos ($46.7 million), and the San Francisco Giants ($47 million).[160] Large-market franchises bring in approximately twice the operating revenues of their small-market competitors, and as previously noted, this gap will likely increase as Major League Baseball's new national television contract becomes effective during the 1994 season.

e. Player Salaries and Other Operating Expenses:

Despite vast disparities in operating revenues, every Major League franchise faces similar operating costs since each club is in the same market for players.[161] While operating expenses[162] for baseball franchises also include costs for player development and training, stadium operations, sales and promotion, and general administrative expenses, the primary source of operating expenses in baseball is player salaries.[163] In 1992 player costs constituted 58 percent of Major League Baseball's gross intake, and averaged just over $35 million per team.[164]

There is a significant disparity in player salaries between small-market and large-market teams. In 1990, for example, the highest paying franchises were the Kansas City Royals ($23.6 million), Boston Red Sox ($22.7 million), San Francisco Giants ($22.5 million), Oakland Athletics ($22.3 million), New York Mets ($22.2 million), and the California Angels ($21.9 million); the lowest-paying teams were the Baltimore Orioles ($8.1 million), Seattle Mariners ($12.6 million), Texas Rangers ($12.7 million), Minnesota Twins ($14.2 million), Atlanta Braves ($14.2 million), and the Philadelphia Phillies ($14.2

million).[165] In 1991, the teams with the highest player salaries were the Oakland Athletics ($39.2 million), Los Angeles Dodgers ($36 million), Boston Red Sox ($35.4 million), New York Mets ($35.2 million), and the California Angels ($34.2 million); those with the lowest figures were the Houston Astros ($12.1 million), Seattle Mariners ($17.4 million), Atlanta Braves ($20.4 million), Philadelphia Phillies ($21.7 million), Cleveland Indians ($21.8 million), and the Montreal Expos ($21.8 million).[166] In 1993, the top paying teams were the Toronto Blue Jays ($59.3 million), Oakland Athletics ($53.2 million), New York Mets ($50.8 million), Boston Red Sox ($49.3 million), Los Angeles Dodgers ($46.3 million), and the New York Yankees ($43.5 million); the "stingiest" were the Cleveland Indians ($10.1 million), Houston Astros ($11.4 million), Montreal Expos ($18.4 million), Baltimore Orioles ($27.4 million), Philadelphia Phillies ($27.9 million), St. Louis Cardinals ($28.9 million), and the Seattle Mariners ($29.0 million).[167] Not surprisingly, a handful of large-market teams, with higher operating revenues, are able to appropriate more money toward player salaries than their small-market brethren; strangely, however, the lowest paying teams seem to include an equal number of small-market and large-market clubs. Nevertheless, the *ability* of large-market clubs to, on average, designate for players' salaries nearly twice the amount of small-market clubs is important in considering the viability of the latter, given that, while operating revenues in Major League Baseball increased by nearly 18% between 1990 and 1992, player salaries increased over 103% during that same period.[168]

What impact does the ability of large-market franchises to pay more in player salaries than small-market teams have on the viability of small-market teams? Does this mean that small-market teams are at a competitive disadvantage on the field? Because each Major League team is in the same market for player talent, it stands to reason that small-market teams lack the financial resources to attract the same number of proven quality players as large-market clubs. With fewer funds to work with, small-market clubs are generally less active in the market for veteran free agents, have a harder time resigning their own veteran free agents, and must rely more heavily on their minor league systems to supply Major-League caliber players.[169] Thus, it would seem that the rosters of small-market teams should be dominated by younger, less experienced, and lower-salaried players with, perhaps, a handful of highly-paid stars. Moreover, we should expect this state of affairs to worsen as the rate in growth of players' salaries continues to dwarf that of operating revenues. Thus, if veteran players are generally

more productive than their inexperienced cohorts, large-market franchises should, on average, field more competitive teams than those in
small markets.[170] Yet, naturally, poor performance on the field results
in still lower attendance, gate, and stadium revenues.[171]

There are several criticisms to this market analysis linking the level
of player salaries to success on the field. One is that either quality
management or an owner's willingness to lose money can compensate
for the financial disadvantages faced by small-market teams.[172] However, as small-market teams clearly do not have a monopoly over
quality management or philanthropic ownership, such factors cannot
be relied upon to preserve the viability of such teams once we
determine that their survival is important to Major League Baseball.
Another critique observes that, because veteran free-agency has proven
to be an inefficient manner of securing a player's services, large-
market teams do not have a competitive advantage over small-market
clubs despite their wealth. Using a model devised by economist
Gerald Scully for determining the value of a player's contribution to
a team's winning percentage and team revenues ("marginal revenue
product"), Andrew Zimbalist concluded that franchise owners typically pay veteran players, especially free agents, more than their
marginal revenue product.[173] However, whether an owner does this
because he or she misjudges the player's actual value to the team,
wishes to prevent the player from being signed by another club, wants
to use a popular player to "lure" baseball fans to the ballpark, or simply
prefers winning over profits,[174] the result is the same: a player is added
who contributes, in some small degree, to the team's winning percentage.

In an environment where large-market teams have the financial
resources to attract the greatest number of quality free agents,
small-market clubs must again operate at a competitive disadvantage.
Thus, assuming that each franchise is equally skilled at developing its
own players, wealthier teams may seek incremental gains in winning
percentage through the veteran free agent market; over time, this
should hurt the profitability of small-market teams. But why then,
some critics argue, has competitive balance increased, rather than
decreased, since the institution of free agency in 1976?[175] One answer,
of course, is that competitive bidding in free agency has made it harder
for any successful team to keep its nucleus of players. Again, however,
players are generally lost to large-market clubs. Other potential
explanations include the effect of long-term contracts on player
performance, the compression of baseball talent, and (of course) poor
judgment by owners in signing free agents.[176]

While it is not possible to quantify into a specific number of wins per season the advantage enjoyed by large-market teams over their small-market brethren in offering larger salaries, it is important to note that its effects are likely to increase in the future. As previously noted, a decline in national television broadcasting revenue will increase the discrepancy between revenues of small-market and large-market teams. This, coupled with the explosion in players' salaries realized through the end of owners' collusion in the veteran free agency market, will increase the discrepancy between small-market and large-market teams in the ability to pay competitive salaries to attract and keep quality players. Because they will, on average, be less competitive on the field than large-market clubs, small-market teams will experience further declines in gate and stadium revenues. Whether this cycle has already begun or will manifest itself in the future is not clear, however, now is the time for Major League Baseball leadership to take steps to prevent the demise, and utter collapse of, small-market franchises. As noted by Andy MacPhail, vice president and general manager of the Minnesota Twins who has long predicted that playing field inequality will emerge from the extreme disparity in revenues among teams: "Up to this point, I can't back that [prediction of imbalance] up, but do you have to have a nuclear bomb dropped on you to want some sort of disarmament?"[177]

IV. Measures That Major League Baseball Owners May Adopt To Ensure The Viability Of Small-Market Teams

What are the alternatives available to Major League Baseball owners once they have determined that the viability of small-market franchises is important and they have analyzed the precarious position of small-market teams under the existing framework? Which alternative will be most effective, and who will bear the costs? Finally, what are the legal impediments facing owners in adopting each measure? These are the questions addressed in the remainder of this Article. As reflected in Part III, Major League owners may take one of three approaches in dealing with the "small-market problem"; they may maintain the status quo, reduce the revenue disparity among teams, or reduce the cost disparity among teams. Each option will be discussed in turn.

A. Maintaining the Status Quo and Community Responses:

While acknowledging their common interest in ensuring the viability of small-market franchises, Major League Baseball owners may conclude that, despite the above-referenced revenue and cost disparities, such teams can survive in the existing governing structure. As a result, owners may decide that the current rules governing Major League Baseball are adequate to ensure on-the-field and financial competition among teams and that, therefore, the existing scheme requires no revision. If owners take this approach, what is likely to happen to small-market teams in the future?

1. Likely Future Trends:

As previously noted, small-market teams will suffer an inordinate decline in operating revenues under the new national television broadcasting contract, increasing the disparity in total revenues between small-market and large-market teams. This will permit large-market teams to further exploit their advantage over small market clubs in signing players with proven talent through veteran free agency, further increasing the disparity in players' salaries. Over time, small-market teams will find it harder to compete on-the-field, which will decrease gate and stadium revenues and further contribute to the variance in wealth between small-market and large-market franchises.

Some may argue that small-market clubs can remain competitive if they learn to operate more "resourcefully" than other teams. Clearly, any team with quality management or a free-spending owner should, on average, outperform other teams lacking on either front. As previously noted, however, there is no reason to expect that small-market teams will necessarily usurp such advantages. Also recall that, while we determined that small-market teams will be more reliant on their farm systems to develop talented players than will large-market teams due to their limited ability to enter the free agency market for proven talent, they will similarly have fewer financial resources to devote to this important player resource. One should expect that the small-market teams will compensate for their financial disadvantages by making better decisions than large-market clubs in player acquisition and development. Moreover, because small-market franchises lack the financial resources to enter the market for free agents to "shore-up" weak spots resulting from previous personnel decisions, any mistakes they make in player development or player selection will be magnified.[178]

2. Luxury Box Revenues:

Small-market franchises will be forced to find some way to increase operating revenues in order to remain competitive with large-market clubs in the search for quality players. Because gate and stadium revenues are linked to ticket prices and attendance, which are dependent on team performance, they are an unlikely source of increased revenue. Similarly, small-market teams will not be able to look to national or local broadcasting revenues as an increasing source of funds. As a result, many owners perceive that the revenues generated by luxury boxes is the best way to reduce the revenue disparity among clubs. In general, luxury boxes may add as much as $6 million a year to a team's revenues. For some teams, this constitutes over forty percent of total gate receipts.[179] In addition, luxury box revenues need not be shared with other teams.[180] With luxury boxes contributing so significantly to the revenues of many teams, it is not surprising that many communities, including Milwaukee, are faced with the choice of either using taxpayers' money to build a new stadium with luxury boxes or losing their teams to other cities willing to do so.[181]

Revenues from luxury boxes, however, are not a panacea. First of all, as of 1991, all but two baseball stadiums already contained luxury boxes.[182] For most teams, therefore, the incremental gain in revenues from building a new stadium with luxury boxes are much smaller than that of the Milwaukee Brewers. Secondly, there is often weak corporate demand for luxury boxes in small-market communities. Plans for constructing a new stadium in Milwaukee, for example, were stalled when the team had trouble pre-selling skyboxes to finance construction,[183] while weak demand for luxury boxes at the Kingdome contributed to the financial troubles of the Seattle Mariners.[184] Thirdly, most teams are unwilling, or, in the case of small- market clubs, unable, to construct a new stadium without a subsidy from taxpayers, many of whom "have grown weary of being held hostage by teams that threaten to move."[185] This has not proven to be the case in Milwaukee, where state and local government have already agreed to provide $67 million and a $35 million loan for the Brewers' proposed new stadium.[186] Finally, proposals to increase revenues from luxury boxes are probably best viewed as temporary solutions to long-term problems. We saw earlier that the disparity in operating revenues between small-market and large-market teams is likely to continue growing in the future, giving the latter an increasing advantage in attracting quality players. While temporarily closing the gap, luxury box revenues do not address the long-term trend of "richer teams getting richer faster than the poorer teams," with its resulting disparity in financial and on-the-field competitiveness.

B. Increased Revenue Sharing in Major League Baseball:

1 f reliance on luxury-box revenues to save small-market teams is misguided, then what alternatives are available to ensure their future viability? A second approach that Major League Baseball owners may take is to reduce the income disparity through increased revenue sharing. As previously noted, Major League Baseball currently divides licensing and national broadcasting revenues equally, and divides gate revenues between home and visiting teams by a ratio of 80 to 20 in the American League and 90 to 10 in the National League.[187] However, each team keeps 100% of its local media revenues. We saw that the continued increase in local broadcasting revenues is a primary source of income disparity between small-market and large-market teams. Clearly then, the existing level of revenue sharing is inadequate in dealing with the problems confronting small-market clubs.

Major League Baseball could implement several measures to further revenue sharing in decreasing the income disparity between small-market and large-market teams. Owners could agree to divide gate receipts more equally among teams, include luxury box revenues in the distribution of gate receipts, and/or share local broadcasting revenues.[188] The first two proposals, while reducing the current size of the income disparity among teams, does not address the increasing income gap between small-market and large-market teams given the growing disparity in local broadcasting revenues. As a result, the third option would appear to be the optimal long-term solution to the problem of revenue disparity in Major League Baseball. Owners must also determine the level at which revenue disparity between small-market and large-market teams no longer acts as an impediment to the on-the-field and financial competitiveness of small-market teams. In theory, the equal division of all sources of League revenues (with "cost-of-living adjustments" between large and small markets) would provide the optimal level of financial and on-the-field competitiveness within professional baseball. But achieving this standard of "perfect competition" is clearly not necessary. Even holding factors such as quality of management and ownership benevolence constant, lower-revenue franchises can surely survive as long as their competitive position reasonably approximates that of large-market teams. Deciding how much of an operating revenue disparity is too much, however, is a question best left to knowledgeable Major League Baseball insiders. Nevertheless, "it seems inevitable that some additional revenue sharing will be necessary" in the future.[189]

1. Labor Law Issues in Revenue Sharing:

Revenue sharing in Major League Baseball presents several important labor and antitrust law issues. Obviously, changes in the amount of revenue shared among teams will affect the ability of each team to pay players and therefore affect the dispersion of veteran and young players throughout the league. Presumably, these are changes in the "wages, hours and other terms and conditions of employment" which must be negotiated with the players' union through collective bargaining.[190] However, because revenue sharing would increase competition among teams in bidding for the services of players, salaries should rise; as a result, it should not be difficult for owners to negotiate desired changes in existing revenue sharing provisions. Revenue sharing is best viewed, then, as a method of redistributing profits among teams, rather than as a measure to limit player salaries.

2. Antitrust Law Issues in Revenue Sharing:

Finally, one should consider the treatment of revenue sharing arrangements under antitrust policy. We saw that, while Major League Baseball currently has a special exemption from antitrust not given to other professional sports leagues, this exemption is by no means "ironclad."[191] Without this exemption, the players, if dissatisfied with their gains under collective bargaining, could seek antitrust protection by decertifying the players' union, thereby eradicating the labor exemption from antitrust.[192] As a result, it is important to consider the implications of antitrust law on any agreement among owners to share revenues.

The Sherman Act makes unlawful "every contract, combination . . . or conspiracy in restraint of trade" in interstate commerce, and also prohibits monopolizing, attempts to monopolize, and combinations or conspiracies to monopolize any part of interstate commerce.[193] An initial issue, is whether Major League Baseball "consist[s] of a group of inherently economically competitive clubs who have come together to cooperate in some aspects of otherwise autonomous businesses, [thereby invoking § 1 of the Sherman Act], [or] a single integrated entity . . . which is thus incapable of *conspiracy* in restraint of trade when it establishes its internal operating rules and structure, [thereby invoking § 2 of the Sherman Act]."[194] Because antitrust challenges to revenue sharing in Major League Baseball would likely originate from players (rather than rival leagues), § 1, rather than § 2, of the Sherman Act seems applicable.[195] As a result, because revenue sharing does not involve *per se* price fixing or other unlawful activity,[196] it would have to pass a "reasonableness" test administered by a reviewing court to survive antitrust scrutiny.[197]

What are some factors that Major League Baseball owners could use to convince a court that its revenue sharing arrangement is "reasonable" for purposes of antitrust review? In general, courts focus on the impact that the challenged restraint would have on competitive conditions, considering the structure of the industry, facts peculiar to a firm's operation within an industry (including power and position), the history and duration of the restraint, and the reasons why it was adopted.[198] With increased revenue sharing, baseball owners would emphasize its effects on the financial and on the field competitiveness of small-market teams. Such measures, they would argue, are necessary to the success of their "joint venture," and benefit consumers to the extent that they increase on-the-field competition, limit franchise instability and relocation, and bring financial stability (and, perhaps, lower ticket prices) to the League. This especially holds true if baseball is regarded as a "natural monopoly" resulting from fans' desire to crown one champion.[199] Deflecting attention from the effects that revenue sharing may have in discouraging the creation of rival leagues, this view emphasizes its perceived pro-competitive effects on team performance and consumer welfare.[200]

C. Adopting a Salary Cap in Major League Baseball:

A third approach that owners could take in ensuring the viability of small-market teams is to reduce the widening discrepancy in player salaries by adopting a salary cap. While revenue sharing "distributes the total income pie" equally among owners, a salary cap is designed to "redivide the portions of the pie" received by owners and players. Thus, "the term 'cap' is actually something of a misnomer for this arrangement. . . [which] really . . . is an agreement between clubs and players associations about what 'share' of league revenues is to be spent on player salaries and other kinds of compensation."[201] A salary cap, of course, may be instituted in several ways; owners may set a maximum amount that each team may pay in total player salaries, a maximum amount that any team may pay a particular player, or some combination (or derivation) of both measures. Again, it may not be necessary for baseball owners to establish the same salary maximum for every franchise in order to achieve competitive balance within the Major Leagues.[202] However, if we hold management quality and owner benevolence constant among teams, then on-the-field competition should increase as player costs are brought into uniformity.[203] Nevertheless, as in the case of revenue sharing, the optimal method of implementing a salary cap, and whether or not it should be uniform among teams, is best left to the expertise of baseball insiders.

1. Labor Law Issues and the Salary Cap:

A salary cap and revenue sharing involve similar labor law issues. A salary cap would obviously affect the "wages, hours, and conditions of employment," thus qualifying as a mandatory subject of collective bargaining between owners and the players' union.[204] Intuitively, players typically resist the notion of a salary cap given its restrictions in the market for player talent and explicit goal of limiting the total share of revenues meted out to players. However, a salary cap may also inflate player salaries for teams below the cap, especially if the owners also incorporated a "salary floor."[205] Thus, the coupling of a salary minimum with a salary maximum may increase the overall share of team revenues allocated for player salaries.[206] Because the salary maximum must be set no higher than the amount that the least-wealthy teams can afford to pay, the players' union is not likely to accept a salary cap without increased revenue sharing among baseball owners.[207] Baseball owners recently agreed on such a proposal, which they will present to the players' union in their next round of collective bargaining.[208] Its palatability to the players, ultimately hinges on the percentage of revenues shared among teams.

As previously indicated, full revenue sharing would presumably adjust player salaries to a market-clearing rate. A salary cap, while offering little in terms of restoring fiscal equality to baseball, may nevertheless be acceptable to the players if set at or near the market rate. As the level of revenues shared diverges from this equilibrium point, however, the players are likely to become increasingly resistant to a salary cap which, is set based on the least-wealthy teams' ability to pay. Under such circumstances, the players receive a lower share of total revenues, with the difference accruing to the wealthiest teams (who can no longer use such funds to price other teams out of the free agent market). Moreover, even with partial revenue sharing, a salary cap offers little in terms of restoring fiscal and competitive equality, for teams, assuming that the amount of revenue shared by the owners allows small-market teams to reasonably bid with their brethren in the players' market. Under such circumstances, the players would receive a "cut" of the above-referenced excess revenues accruing to the wealthiest teams. If the amount of revenues shared is inadequate to allow small-market teams to competitively bid for players' services with their large-market brethren, a salary cap becomes vital to restoring fiscal equality among teams. Under such circumstances, the players receive a yet lower share of total revenues, with the difference again accruing to the wealthiest teams. Baseball owners, then, can likely solve the "small-market problem" through significant revenue sharing without the imposition of a salary cap on players. Their current proposal, linking both measures, may result from, (1) an inadequate degree of revenue sharing (thus necessitating a salary cap for fiscal competitiveness), (2) pressure by large-market owners reluctant to further share revenues *with players* through free agency, (3) pressure by small-market owners desiring equal competition in the bidding of players, and/or, (4) the owners' awareness of the pressure on the players' union to pass such proposal for fear that they will be viewed by the public as greedy, pampered athletes who killed the return of fiscal sanity to the game. Ultimately, the union is likely to condition acceptance of the owners' proposal on increased revenue sharing among teams.

2. Antitrust Law Issues and the Salary Cap:

Finally, just as in the case of revenue sharing, owners should consider whether justifications of a salary cap are "reasonable" under the laws of antitrust.[209] But while a salary cap, like revenue sharing, may increase competition on-the-field and preserve the financial integrity of small-market teams, some courts may determine that alternative measures are available to owners that are less restrictive on market forces.[210] A court may decide, for example, that owners, through redistribution of revenues generated from their "joint venture," rather than players, through salary limitations, should bear the burden of ensuring the survival of small-market teams. Owners, on the other hand, may argue that restrictions of player costs, as pro-consumer measures, actually demand less scrutiny under antitrust analysis because they bring lower ticket prices to baseball fans.[211] Ultimately, of course, any decision by the players' union to decertify for purposes of seeking antitrust protection would depend on the likelihood that a reviewing court would find a salary cap to be a proconsumer measure, rather than a naked price-fix by owners, as well as their negotiating position in collective bargaining.[212] Nevertheless, it seems clear that a court would more closely scrutinize an owner-adopted measure directly impacting a labor market than such a measure involving a mere redistribution of League revenues.

V. Conclusion

In 1951, William Wrigley observed that baseball was a "very peculiar business."[213] That observation, made over forty years ago, seems equally applicable today. As we have seen, Major League Baseball has experienced tremendous changes in its competitive environment in recent years regarding the rate of increase of player salaries and various sources of operating revenues. These trends have magnified the competitive disadvantages of small-market franchises both on-the-field and on the balance sheet. Many experts believe that recent growth in the rate of increase of the revenue disparity between small-market and large-market teams will accelerate in the future. Absent significant changes, the owners of small-market franchises can expect to operate in a still harsher environment in the years to come. I have suggested two measures, increased revenue sharing and a salary cap, that Major League Baseball owners may take to preserve the integrity of small-market teams. The former would be more palatable to the players' union and more likely to withstand antitrust scrutiny by a reviewing court.

Whatever measures baseball owners ultimately adopt to protect small-market teams, it is important that they act now. As the existing policies of Major League Baseball become less and less responsive to the problems confronting the game, an increasing number of people will become disenchanted with baseball's current governing structure and seek external review.[214] We also saw that, not only could removal of Major League Baseball's antitrust exemption subject owner-adopted market restrictions to court review, but it may also adversely affect their ability to negotiate desired changes with the players' union in collective bargaining. Finally, we saw that absent action by the League to preserve small-market franchises, community-based measures designed to help increase team revenues, such as financing the construction of a new stadium and luxury boxes, are inadequate to ensure the long-term survival of such teams.

It may offer little solace to baseball fans in Milwaukee (and other small markets) that their fears of losing their franchise are wellgrounded if the community cannot generate substantial public funding for the construction of a new stadium with a convertible roof and luxury boxes.[215] Under Bud Selig's latest stadium proposal, this entails a $35 million loan, $67 million for infrastructure costs, and over $250 million in tax exemptions and other costs over the stadium's thirty year mortgage. The franchise, in turn, would recognize an estimated $9.6 million in annual revenue.[216] These same fans, however, would probably be quite surprised to find out that this substantial community subsidy is not enough to guarantee the survival of the Brewers franchise in Milwaukee. Clubs competing in small and large markets will also take steps to maximize operating revenues through stadium construction and luxury box rentals. This will minimize the ability of small-market teams to use luxury box revenues as a method of decreasing the disparity in total operating revenues. With the increasing disparity in operating revenues between small-market and large-market teams, the initial boost in operating revenues created by a new stadium and luxury boxes represents a short-term solution to a long-term problem. At best, the Milwaukee community, by subsidizing the construction of a new stadium, is simply taking a calculated risk to "buy time" until Major League Baseball owners implement measures to ensure the financial integrity of small-market teams. Owners have recently taken the first step by unanimously approving a revenue sharing agreement contingent on the players' union acceptance of a salary cap.[217] Approval is not guaranteed, however, and the clock is still ticking; only time will tell if baseball owners have done enough.

Notes

1. "After intimating relocation, Selig convinced the city, county, and state governments to contribute $67 million (plus a $35 million loan) toward the construction of a new stadium that he and other private investors will own. Selig plans to finance his share of the construction costs by selling luxury boxes in advance." Andrew Zimbalist, Baseball and Billions 139 (1992). *See also* Bruce Murphy, *$pring Fever*, Milwaukee Mag., Apr.

1993, at 82. More recently, Selig revealed plans to build a stadium with a "convertible roof" at a cost of approximately $190 million; public funding may be sought through a statewide sports lottery. *See, e.g.,* Jeff Browne, *Stadium Lottery has Wide Appeal,* MILWAUKEE J., Mar. 21, 1994, at B6. One author estimates that the total government subsidy promised over the thirty-year mortgage of such facility may exceed $350 million dollars. *See* Bruce Murphy, *Trade Secrets,* MILWAUKEE MAG., Apr. 1994, at 21.

2. It has been estimated that luxury box rentals may add up to six million dollars to a team's operating revenues each year. *See* Kathleen Morris, *The Gimmicks,* FINANCIAL WORLD, July 7, 1992, at 48.

3. For a brief recounting of the circumstances preceding the Braves' departure for Atlanta, *see* ZIMBALIST, *supra* note 1, at 128-29.

4. *See* Id. at 129.

5. *Id.*

6. From 1962 to 1965, the Braves finished no higher than in fifth place. *Id.*

7. *Id.*

8. After moving to Atlanta, the Braves' local television revenues tripled from 1965 to 1966. *Id.* at 225.

9. *See Id.*; The Wisconsin Supreme Court stated that it would enforce baseball's exemption from antitrust statutes as articulated by the Supreme Court. State of Wisconsin v. Milwaukee Braves, Inc., 31 Wis. 2d 699, 144 N.W.2d 1 (1966). *See* JAMES EDWARD MILLER, THE BASEBALL BUSINESS: PURSUING PENNANTS AND PROFITS IN BALTIMORE 21-35 (1990) (detailing the attempts of St. Louis Browns owner Bill Veeck to move the team from St. Louis.) *See infra* Part III.

10. For a brief recounting of the events leading to the return of Major League Baseball to Milwaukee, *see* Selig v. United States, 565 F. Supp. 524, 530-33 (E.D.Wis. 1983), *aff'd* 740 F.2d 572 (7th Cir. 1984).

11. One author, in fact, has concluded that "baseball fans are more loyal than in any other sport — or have clouded minds. Maybe the inherent beauty of the game has blinded them to reality." Dave Nightingale, *Give Us Back the Game: Start With a New Commissioner and Quick, and Then* . . . , SPORTING NEWS, Feb. 22, 1993, at 11.

12. For a telling description of the abandonment felt by baseball fans when a Major League franchise relocates, *see* ZIMBALIST, *supra* note 1, at 125-29 (describing the circumstances surrounding relocations by the Brooklyn Dodgers to Los Angeles in 1957, the New York Giants to San Francisco in 1957, and the Milwaukee Braves to Atlanta in 1965). It is interesting to note that the Dodgers' move in 1957, like many proposed relocations today, was precipitated by the owner's (Walter O'Malley) dissatisfaction with the Brooklyn Dodgers' home field (Ebbetts Field). In response to the fans' claim that O'Malley was motivated by greed, Buzzie Bavasi, O'Malley's right-hand man, noted that "If [O'Malley] . . . saw the California gold [and] went prospecting . . . so be it. He was entitled." *Id.* at 128 (*citing* BUZZIE BAVASI, OFF THE RECORD 82 (1987)). Regarding the

Braves' move, Bill Veeck observed that it was "baseball's latest testimonial to the power of pure greed." *Id.* at 129 (*citing* BILL VEECK, VEECK—AS IN WRECK 301 (1962)). Finally, for an in-depth analysis of the move of the St. Louis Browns franchise to Baltimore in 1954, *see* Miller, *supra* note 9, at 21-35.

13. *See* ZIMBALIST, *supra* note 1, at 125-29.

14. *See* Selig, 565 F. Supp. at 531-33.

15. The average seasonal paid attendance for the Brewers from 1969-74 was 832,000. That figure rose to 1,372,000 for the years of 1975-79, and further rose to 1,744,000 from 1980-84. GERALD W. SCULLY, THE BUSINESS OF MAJOR LEAGUE BASEBALL 104 (1989).

16. While no Major League team has relocated since 1972, at least seven teams threatened to do so in 1990 and 1991; at least four of those teams may be properly classified as "small-market clubs" (Milwaukee Brewers, Montreal Expos, Seattle Mariners, and Cleveland Indians). *See* ZIMBALIST, *supra* note 1, at 129. Nor is the Brewers franchise alone in requesting government assistance to build a new facility. In the past six years, citizens of San Francisco, San Jose, Chicago, Detroit, Cleveland, Denver, Baltimore, Milwaukee, and Dallas-Fort Worth, "have been asked to go to the polls to approve issuance of a municipal bond and/or new taxes for the construction of new baseball stadiums. In each case there was the threat that if the bond and/or taxes were rejected, the city's baseball team would flee to greener pastures." *Id.* at xvi. Should a community fail to cave into an owner's demands, "'there are club-hungry cities out there that realize the value of a major league franchise and are prepared to make deals— often at the taxpayers' expense.'" Alexandria Biesada, *Gimme A Break*, FINANCIAL WORLD, July 9, 1991, at 40 (1991). The citizens of Tampa-St. Petersburg, for example, voted to finance the construction of a new ballpark in an attempt to attract an expansion or existing team; so far, their effort has not borne fruit. *See* ZIMBALIST, *supra* note 1, at xvi.

17. For the purposes of this Article, I define "small-markets" to include cities with municipal populations of two million people or less. Under this definition, there are currently eight Major League Baseball franchises residing in small markets; the Cleveland Indians, Kansas City Royals, Milwaukee Brewers, Oakland Athletics, and Seattle Mariners of the American League, and the Cincinnati Reds, Colorado Rockies, and San Francisco Giants of the National League. The average population in these cities is approximately 1.6 million people, while the average population of the other twenty major league cities is approximately 3.3 million people. *See* SCULLY, *supra* note 15, at 144.

18. *See* ZIMBALIST, *supra* note 1 (*citing* BAVASI, *supra* note 12).

19. The Major League Agreement acts as Major League Baseball's "constitution"; it is adhered to by all of the franchises in the major leagues. *See* PAUL C. WEILER & GARY R. ROBERTS, CASES, MATERIALS, AND PROBLEMS ON SPORTS AND THE LAW 2 (2d ed. 1993).

20. For a more complete discussion of antitrust policy as embodied by the Sherman Act and its implications for the policies of Major League Baseball, *see infra* Part III. For purposes of the discussion in Part II, however, it is sufficient to note that Section 1 of the Sherman Act proscribes "every contract, combination, . . . or conspiracy, in restraint of trade or commerce among the several States, or with foreign nations . . . ," while Section 2 of the Sherman Act prohibits any person from "monopoliz[ing], or attempt[ing] to monopolize, or combin[ing] or conspir[ing] with any other person or persons, to monopolize any part of the trade or commerce among the several States, or with foreign nations . . . " 15 U.S.C. §§ 1-2 (1988 & Supp. 1993).

21. *See, e.g.,* Standard Oil Co. v. United States, 221 U.S. 1, 60-62 (1911).

22. *See infra* Part III, which discusses the exemption from antitrust that Major League Baseball, but no other professional sports league enjoys. *See, e.g.,* Flood v. Kuhn, 407 U.S. 258, 270 (1972). For the purposes of Part II, however, it is sufficient to note the policies underlying antitrust legislation and defer consideration of the antitrust exemption itself.

23. Currently, three-fourths of the owners in the same league as a relocating team must approve the move; the Commissioner may block such a move under his or her "best interests" power. *See* ZIMBALIST, *supra* note 1, at 125, 131.

24. *Id.; See supra* note 20.

25. ZIMBALIST, *supra* note 1, at 131.

26. Such a system may take one of two forms. The owners could grant teams the absolute power to relocate unless doing so would violate important League policies as expressly articulated in the Agreement (for example, a requirement that teams cannot move to a new locale within one hundred miles of an existing team). Or, the owners could create a system that, while potentially subjecting all franchise relocations to significant restraints, would nevertheless encourage the non-enforceability of such restraints under most circumstances (for example, a rule that all relocations are permitted without restrictions unless a specified number of teams object). The current Agreement, by requiring Commissioner and super-majority owner approval for franchise relocations, appears to fall under the latter regime. It is important to recognize that, under such a system, current owners have an incentive to approve most proposed moves in order to "create goodwill" in the event that they desire to relocate their teams in the future. For example, between 1952 and 1972, only two owner-proposed moves were rejected; in both cases, however, the persons involved were considered "outcasts among owners" and the moves were later approved when new parties assumed ownership. *See* Zimbalist, *supra* note 1, at 125. Similarly, in 1992, the sale of the San Francisco Giants to a group that intended to move the team to Tampa/St. Petersburg was disapproved by vote of the owners, who wished for the franchise to remain in San Francisco.

27. *See supra* note 20.
28. *See supra* note 21.
29. *See supra* note 23. Absent antitrust concerns, Major League Baseball owners would presumably be willing to adopt rules to protect small-market franchises if such restrictions contributed to the financial well-being of the majority of individual teams and, by implication, the League itself. As shown in Part III, however, the mere threat of intrusion of antitrust policy may be sufficient to compel compliance with such laws even though such action may not be in the owners' collective (or, for that matter, individual) financial interest.
30. *Id.*; *See infra* Part III.
31. *See supra* note 23.
32. *See supra* note 23 for a discussion of the current rules for Major League Baseball franchise relocation. Because franchise relocations require a three-quarters majority vote among owners and Commissioner approval, the Agreement clearly does not ensure a free market for teams.
33. *See* Zimbalist, *supra* note 1, at 135-140.
34. *See generally* ADAM SMITH, AN INQUIRY INTO THE NATURE AND CAUSES OF THE WEALTH OF NATIONS (Glasgow ed. 1801) (discussing the invisible hand theory of competition).
35. *See* ZIMBALIST, *supra* note 1, at 140-46.
36. In addition, Major League Baseball owners have an incentive to restrict the creation of expansion teams; for as long as the "demand for teams from viable cities [is] greater than supply, then existing teams have greater leverage in bargaining for new stadium construction, new luxury boxes, lower rent, or a greater share of concession and parking revenues. They can threaten to leave." *Id.* at 124.
37. "Expansion to thirty-five or forty teams by the end of the century would mean that more cities would have their demand for a team satisfied, a more equitable relationship would develop between existing teams and host cities, and there would be a greater number of MLB players. This outcome sounds like something economists call a welfare maximizing solution. But economists never claimed that welfare maximization was a property of unregulated monopolies. A public policy is called for. . . . " *Id.* at 146.
38. *See generally* WEILER & ROBERTS, *supra* note 19, at 411-12.
39. ZIMBALIST, *supra* note 1, at 128.
40. *Id.* at 123.
41. *Id.*; *see* ZIMBALIST, *supra* note 1, at 146.
42. ZIMBALIST, *supra* note 1, at 123.
43. ZIMBALIST, *supra* note 1, at 123. Not surprisingly, however, Cosell got the last word. In response to Mr. Turner, Cosell stated emphatically: "I find that argument really could not appeal to anybody over the age of six . . . they [baseball owners] talk out of both sides of their mouths. They have

developed an everspinning spiral of hypocrisy and deceit that ascends up to the heavens." ZIMBALIST, *supra* note 1, at 129.

44. One antitrust issue involving expansion is whether a potential investor or city should have the right to insist that Major League Baseball offer a new franchise. *See* WEILER & ROBERTS, *supra* note 19, at 392-93. A federal court rejected such a claim in professional football. *See* Mid-South Grizzlies v. National Football League, 720 F.2d 772 (3rd Cir. 1983).

45. WEILER & ROBERTS, *supra* note 19, at 392-393.

46. *Id.*

47. *See supra* notes 20-21.

48. *See infra* Part III.

49. The factors underlying the calculation of expansion fees are often unclear. In theory, an expansion fee should be the present value of the annual profit loss (if any) to each of the existing clubs (primarily comprised of lost revenues from the national television contract and league profit sharing arrangements) plus the initial costs of organization and administration (for example, compensation to clubs for lost players). But while one source estimated such losses in Major League Baseball at between $8 to $9 million per year, the most recent National League expansion franchises (Colorado Rockies and Florida Marlins) paid $95 million each to join the League, which appears well above the present value of the former income stream. *See* Scully, *supra* note 15, at 147. Any payments above the theoretical amount would represent monopoly rents. Also note that expansion fees are often a poor measure of the actual value of the franchise created; if the theoretical value of a franchise is the value of its assets plus the present value of its expected profits, any expansion fee above that amount would also be evidence of monopoly profits in expansion fees. The $50 million expansion fee charged by the National Hockey League for the right to operate teams in Ottawa and San Jose, for example, was more than the estimated value of over half of the established National Hockey League franchises. *See* Michael K. Ozanian & Stephen Taub, *Financial World's Valuation Scoreboard*, FINANCIAL WORLD, July 7, 1992, at 50-51. The ability to extract monopoly profits in expansion fees may allow the owners to collect the same amount irrespective of the "degree of attractiveness" of the location of the expansion team.

50. *See* SCULLY, *supra* note 15, at 147; Ozanian & Taub, *supra* note 49, at 50-51.

51. *See supra* notes 20-21. Again, remember that this analysis does not take into consideration baseball's current exemption from antitrust laws. *See infra* Part III.

52. *See supra* note 49.

53. *See infra* Part III.

54. WEILER & ROBERTS, *supra* note 19, at 472. Weiler and Roberts also note that, despite the effectiveness of such "preemptive measures" in destroying rival leagues, judges are reluctant to prescribe them as "such a rule

would forever deny fans in 'virgin' cities the opportunity to secure a team in the established major league." *Id.* (discussing whether a rival team could demand access to the stadium owned or leased by an established team). *See also* ZIMBALIST, *supra* note 1, at 128.

55. *See infra* Part III.
56. *Id.*
57. Speaking from experience, I know that Brewers fans in Milwaukee would never adopt their American League rivals, the Chicago White Sox, as their team of choice. It is also interesting to note that baseball fans in western Wisconsin, who are geographically closer to Minneapolis than Milwaukee, generally support the Brewers franchise over the Twins. In fact, a significant number of these fans travel to Minneapolis to root for the Brewers against the home team.
58. *See* ZIMBALIST, *supra* note 1, at 124.
59. *See* SCULLY, *supra* note 15, at 145-46.
60. *Id.* Scully noted that the winning percentage of expansion clubs averages about .440 for the first decade of their existence. According to Scully, only half of the proposed expansion sites would produce revenues comparable to the clubs located in the seven smallest existing Major League cities given such a winning percentage. Scully predicted that expansion clubs in Denver, Miami, Phoenix, Tampa-St. Petersburg, and Washington D.C. would be as financially viable as existing small-market teams at such a winning percentage; expansion clubs in Buffalo, Indianapolis, New Orleans, and Vancouver would have to play .500 baseball to produce comparable revenues. Scully then concluded that, under the current regime, expansion into these sites would create financial instability to the detriment of Major League Baseball. *See Id.* at 146-47.
61. *See infra* Part III.
62. *See* ZIMBALIST, *supra* note 1, at xiv. *See generally* WEILER & ROBERTS, *supra* note 19, at 100-122.
63. More than fifty bills have been introduced in Congress seeking to remove or weaken Major League Baseball's exemption from antitrust laws. *See* SCULLY, *supra* note 15, at 13. Most recently, Bud Selig, Major League Baseball's acting commissioner and owner of the Milwaukee Brewers, testified at a March 21, 1994, congressional hearing before, among others, Senator Howard Metzenbaum (D. Ohio), a strong opponent of baseball's antitrust exemption. *Selig Spars with Senator at Hearing,* MILWAUKEE J., Mar. 22, 1994, at C2.
64. *See supra* Part III. In a suit brought by the aggrieved purchasers of the Giants, the district court concluded that antitrust law was applicable to franchise relocation because Major League Baseball's antitrust exemption "is limited to baseball's reserve system." Piazza v. Major League Baseball, 831 F. Supp. 420, 438 (E.D.Pa. 1993).
65. *See* WEILER & ROBERTS, *supra* note 19, at 493 ("... the essence of sports is competition, the high point of athletic competition is the crowning of

a champion, and the league whose champion is generally recognized by fans as supreme inevitably receives the lion's share of gate attendance and television revenues. . . . ").

66. *See* SCULLY, *supra* note 15, at 13-43 (noting the failed attempts of the Federal Baseball League and Continental Baseball League to compete with Major League Baseball).

67. *See supra* note 19.

68. *See infra* Part IV.

69. These "owner-controlled" restrictions govern teams' relationships with one another and with the players. *See* SCULLY, *supra* note 15, at 13. For the most part, I will be focusing on the former restrictions, although we will also see how the latter restraints affect relationships among teams.

70. *See supra* Part IV.

71. *See generally* WEILER & ROBERTS, *supra* note 19, chs. 2-7, 11.

72. For a summary of initial attempts to apply antitrust laws to the policies of Major League Baseball, *see* ZIMBALIST, *supra* note 1, at 8-10; SCULLY, *supra* note 15, at 5-7.

73. American League Baseball Club of Chicago v. Chase, 149 N.Y.S. 6 (1914). For a detailed discussion of Major League Baseball's reserve system and its treatment under antitrust policy, *see* WEILER & ROBERTS, *supra* note 19, at 100-109.

74. Chase, 149 N.Y.S. at 16-17.

75. *See* ZIMBALIST, *supra* note 1, at 10.

76. Federal Baseball Club of Baltimore v. National League, 259 U.S. 200 (1922).

77. *Id.* at 208-09.

78. *See e.g.*, Labor Relations Board v. Jones & Laughlin Steel Corp., 301 U.S. 1 (1937) (holding that Congress may regulate activity which has a "substantial economic effect" upon interstate commerce); Hodel v. Virginia Surface Min. & Recl. Ass'n, 452 U.S. 264 (1981) (explaining that Congress may regulate activity when there is a "rational basis" for its finding that the activity affects interstate commerce).

79. In one case, a former Major League player who had jumped to the Mexican League in 1946 found himself blacklisted by a policy adopted by Commissioner Chandler, and sued for damages and reinstatement. In overruling the district court, the Second Circuit ruled that baseball's involvement in radio and television had clearly involved baseball in interstate commerce and, as a result, subjected it to Sherman Act coverage. Gardella v. Chandler, 172 F.2d 402 (2d Cir. 1949). *See* ZIMBALIST, *supra* note 1, at 13. In 1951, the House of Representatives conducted hearings to determine whether baseball's antitrust exemption should be legislatively enacted. When the "Cellar Hearings" concluded without adopting any legislation, it was clear to observers that the Committee had, in fact, determined that *Gardella* had superseded *Federal*

Baseball and, by not adopting contrary legislation, had intended that baseball be subject to the Sherman Act. *See id.* at 13-14.

80. *Id.* at 15.

81. Toolson v. New York Yankees, 346 U.S. 356 (1953).

82. *Id.* at 357.

83. ZIMBALIST, *supra* note 1, at 15.

84. *Flood,* 407 U.S. 258.

85. *Id.* at 283-84.

86. "Baseball's exemption from antitrust statutes, based on the notion that it was not involved in interstate commerce, erroneous back in 1922 and more so in the 1950s, became even more anomalous in 1957, when the Supreme Court declared football to be subject to antitrust statutes and stated that baseball's antitrust exemption was 'unreasonable, illogical and inconsistent.'" ZIMBALIST, *supra* note 1, at 15 (*citing*, in part, LEE LOWENFISH & TONY LUPIEN, THE IMPERFECT DIAMOND: THE STORY OF BASEBALL'S RESERVE SYSTEM AND THE MEN WHO FOUGHT TO CHANGE IT 187 (1980)).

87. *See supra* notes 63, 64.

88. *See, e.g.,* Smith v. Pro Football, Inc., 593 F.2d 1173 (D.C. Cir. 1979) (finding that the National Football League's draft as it existed in 1968 constituted an unreasonable restraint of trade and therefore violated § 1 of the Sherman Act); Mackey v. Nat'l Football League, 543 F.2d 606 (8th Cir. 1976) (finding that the National Football League's "Rozelle Rule" requiring a team that signed a veteran free agent to provide "fair and equitable" compensation to the player's former team violated § 1 of the Sherman Act). Veteran free agency did, however, arrive to Major League Baseball in 1975 through collective bargaining with the Andy Messersmith and Dave McNally grievances. *See* Nat'l & Am. League Professional Baseball Clubs and Major League Baseball Players Ass'n, 66 Labor Arbitration 101 (1975). For a detailed discussion of these cases and the issues they pose regarding the application of antitrust policy to professional sports, *see* WEILER & ROBERTS, *supra* note 19, at 127-164.

89. *See, e.g.,* Brown v. Pro Football, Inc., 1992 U.S. Dist. LEXIS 2903 (D.D.C. Mar. 10, 1992) (holding that the National Football League's salary cap for players on each team's developmental squad violated § 1 of the Sherman Act). *See also* WEILER & ROBERTS, *supra* note 19, at 201-05.

90. *See supra* note 69.

91. In general, proper union activity, such as strikes, also enjoy an exemption from antitrust laws. *See* United States v. Hutcheson, 312 U.S. 219 (1941) (finding that Clayton Act protects labor disputes from substantive antitrust liability). Similarly, collective agreements whose terms are principally felt by the immediate parties (and not outside competitors) are immune from antitrust scrutiny. Amalgamated Meat Cutters v. Jewel Tea Co., 381 U.S. 676 (1965). As a result, collective agreements in the sports context also receive the labor exemption from antitrust. *See e.g. Mackey,* 543 F.2d 606 (finding that although labor exemption from antitrust is

available to terms of collective agreement, "Rozelle Rule" was found not to be exempt from the coverage of antitrust laws since it was not the "product of bona-fide arm's-length negotiations"). For an illuminating discussion of the labor exemption and its role in professional sports, *see* WEILER & ROBERTS, *supra* note 19, at 164-205.

92. *Amalgamated Meat Cutters*, 381 U.S. 676.

93. *See* note 91 (referencing Mackey).

94. The National Football League Players' Association, for example, "declared itself no longer a union representing players in collective bargaining and instigated another antitrust suit against the NFL's player restraints" after a court ruled that the labor exemption prohibited judicial review of a provision of the collective agreement where the parties had not yet bargained to an impasse. Powell v. Nat'l Football League, 888 F.2d 559 (8th Cir. 1989); *but see* Brown v. Pro Football, Inc., 1991 Trade Cases (CCH) 69, 454 (D.D.C. 1991) (holding that the labor exemption ends at the expiration of the collective bargaining agreement, not "at some indeterminable point beyond expiration which is labelled 'impasse'"). This move by the NFLPA prompted an antitrust suit brought by a player, Freeman McNeil, against the NFL regarding the League's free agency policy, precipitating the arrival of free agency to the League. *See* McNeil v. Nat'l Football League, 790 F. Supp. 871 (D.Minn. 1992). *See generally* WEILER & ROBERTS, *supra* note 19, at 188-205.

95. *See supra* notes 63, 64.

96. *See infra* Part IV.

97. *See generally* ZIMBALIST, *supra* note 1, at 61-73.

98. *Id.* at 62.

99. *Id.* at 67-68.

100. Ozanian & Taub, *supra* note 49, at 50-51.

101. A major reason that franchise values increased rapidly during the 1980s was the ability of the League to control player salaries in the market for free agents through collusive practices under former Commissioner Peter Ueberroth. For a summary of what happened, *see* WEILER & ROBERTS, *supra* note 19, at 277- 288.

102. *See supra* note 17.

103. Ozanian & Taub, *supra* note 49, at 50-51. Among small-market franchises, only Cleveland and Seattle experienced a gain in franchise value over the preceding year; however, Cleveland's gain was only $2 million and Seattle's gain of $8 million can, for the most part, be attributed to the sale of the franchise to a group of investors in 1991.

104. *See* Michael K. Ozanian & Stephen Taub, *Foul Ball*, FINANCIAL WORLD, May 25, 1993, at 20.

105. Michael K. Ozanian & Stephen Taub, *Big Leagues, Bad Business*, FINANCIAL WORLD, July 7, 1992, at 35-38. After the 1994 season, each club should expect a drop in national broadcasting fees from over $15

million a year to around $9 million. *See* Ozanian & Taub, *supra* note 104, at 20.

106. Paul Beeston, former vice president of business operations for the Toronto Blue Jays, noted that "[a]nyone who quotes profits of a baseball club is missing the point. Under generally accepted accounting principles, I can turn a $4 million profit into a $2 million loss, and I can get every national accounting firm to agree with me." The "Beeston principle" was in full swing from the years 1975-79, when, despite reported book losses in every year, Major League Baseball had "substantial and growing operating profits." ZIMBALIST, *supra* note 1, at 62-63. Much of the discrepancy is due to the depreciation of player salaries by owners, discussed later in Part III. Owners have also been known to participate in "accounting chicanery" in order to affect the bottom line. For example, the Turner Broadcasting System, which is owned by Ted Turner and owns the Atlanta Braves, paid the club $1 million in 1984 for television broadcasting rights, well below the league average of $2.7 million that year. Given the Braves' large geographic following, national exposure, and the number of games broadcast, the Braves made a bad deal. However, while the Braves lost money, Ted Turner received tax benefits from the transaction. For a detailed analysis of the Turner deal and other examples of the accounting games that baseball owners play, *see* ZIMBALIST, *supra* note 1, at 64-67.

107. *See* Ozanian & Taub, *supra* note 105, at 44.

108. *See* ZIMBALIST, *supra* note 1, at 64; Ozanian & Taub, *supra* notes 104, at 20; Ozanian & Taub, *supra* note 105, at 34-35.

109. *See* ZIMBALIST, *supra* note 1, at 64; *supra* note 101.

110. *Id. See* ZIMBALIST, *supra* note 1, at 64; *supra* note 101.

111. *See* Michael K. Ozanian & Stephen Taub, *Secrets of the Front Office*, FINANCIAL WORLD, July 9, 1991, at 42-43. Commissioner Fay Vincent, on the other hand, claimed that ten teams actually lost money in 1990. *See* ZIMBALIST, *supra* note 1, at 69.

112. *Id.* Note that in 1990, the small-market teams listed, the Oakland Athletics and Cincinnati Reds, each won their division and advanced to the World Series where the Reds defeated the A's, four games to none.

113. *See* Ozanian & Taub, *supra* note 49, at 50-51. The other teams reporting operating losses included the California Angels ($7.6 million), Montreal Expos ($4.2 million), Minnesota Twins ($4.1 million), Pittsburgh Pirates ($4.0 million), Detroit Tigers ($2.8 million), Atlanta Braves ($0.5 million), and the San Diego Padres ($0.4 million); of the small-market teams recognizing operating profits, the Seattle Mariners netted $2.9 million, while the Cincinnati Reds netted $0.2 million. *Id.*

114. *Id.*

115. *See* Ozanian & Taub, *supra* note 104, at 28.

116. *Id.*; The only small-market franchise in this category, the Cleveland Indians, realized $13.6 million in operating profits due to its inordinately

low player costs, which approached one-fourth that of most other teams. The Cleveland management has professed its commitment to fielding young players whom they sign to low-cost, long-term contracts.

117. *See supra* note 106.

118. Zimbalist claims that the losses recently suffered by at least three small-market franchises (the Pittsburgh Pirates, Seattle Mariners, and Kansas City Royals) may be due more to "accounting gimmickry" and owner-based preferences than true cost overruns. Nevertheless, while some teams that experience real operating losses may be able to turn profits the following year through shrewd management, "ominous signs are on the horizon. . . Most troubling . . . is the projected drop in national media revenues." ZIMBALIST, *supra* note 1, at 69-73.

119. *See generally* ZIMBALIST, *supra* note 1, at 34-36; SCULLY, *supra* note 15, at 130-32 (indicating that no other industry is permitted to depreciate employee contracts).

120. *See* SCULLY, *supra* note 15, at 130.

121. *Id.; see* 26 U.S.C. § 167(a) (1992).

122. *See* SCULLY, *supra* note 15, at 130. Note that "[t]he percentage of the purchase price of a franchise that may be allocated to player contracts and the estimated useful life of the players are subject to negotiation with the IRS. Until the mid-1970s, generally 90% of the franchise purchase price was allocated to player contracts in baseball and the useful life was set at seven years." *Id.; see, e.g.,* Selig v. United States, 740 F.2d 572, 580 (7th Cir. 1984)(approving district court ruling that it was proper for Bud Selig, when purchasing the Seattle Pilot franchise in order to move it to Milwaukee in 1970, to allocate $10.2 million of the $10.8 million purchase price to player contracts). Under Section 212 of the Tax Reform Act of 1976, however, a rebuttable presumption exists that no more than 50% of the purchase price of a sports franchise should be allocated to player contracts. 26 U.S.C. § 1056(d) (1992); *see also Selig,* 740 F.2d at 579, n. 17 (finding that Section 212 did not apply retroactively to the Selig purchase).

123. To recognize this tax shelter, an owner must have operating profits from the franchise or other holdings equal to or greater than the amount of depreciation taken for players' salaries. *See* Jennifer Reingold, *When Less is More,* FINANCIAL WORLD, May 23, 1993, at 38. The shelter was greater, of course, when the top corporate tax rate was higher (for example, 46% until 1987) and before the IRS capped the maximum amount allocable to players' salaries at 50%. *See* ZIMBALIST, *supra* note 1, at 34-35; WILLIAM D. ANDREWS, BASIC FEDERAL INCOME TAXATION 4 (1991); 26 U.S.C. § 11(b) (1992). For an example of how this tax shelter worked for Bud Selig and initial investors of the Milwaukee Brewers, *see* Murphy, *Trade Secrets, supra* note 1, at 21.

124. ZIMBALIST, *supra* note 1, at 35-36.

125. SCULLY, *supra* note 15, at 132.

126. ZIMBALIST, *supra* note 1, at 34. Commenting on the fairness of this special tax shelter for owners, Veeck smugly replied: "Look, we play the 'Star- Spangled Banner' before every game. You want us to pay income taxes too?" *Id.* at 35; *See also* SCULLY, *supra* note 15, at 130.

127. *See supra* notes 63, 64.

128. ZIMBALIST, *supra* note 1, at 35.

129. Note, however, that the tax shelter also has a long-term benefit for owners because in theory, it increases the value of each franchise by the present value of the expected tax savings. In addition, while the tax shelter should induce rapid turnover of club ownership as its short-term benefits to owners are fully realized, restrictions on franchise sale imposed under the Major League Agreement deter prospective investors from purchasing a team solely to recognize these gains. *See Id.*

130. SCULLY *supra* note 15, at 132.

131. *See* ZIMBALIST, *supra* note 1, at 48; SCULLY, *supra* note 15, at 117.

132. *See* SCULLY, *supra* note 15, at 123; ZIMBALIST, *supra* note 1, at 59-60.

133. *See* Ozanian & Taub, *supra* note 49, at 50-51; *see also* ZIMBALIST, *supra* note 1, at 48.

134. ZIMBALIST, *supra* note 1, at 48.

135. *Id.*

136. *Id.*

137. *See* Ozanian & Taub, *supra* note 104, at 28; *see supra* note 106 (teams such as the Atlanta Braves and Chicago Cubs, which share ownership with the local television network covering their games, receive less in local media revenues than otherwise expected).

138. Ozanian & Taub, *supra* note 104, at 28. Note that, excluding the Atlanta Braves (*see supra* note 106), four of the six teams listed qualify as "small-market teams;" the Oakland A's derived $25 million in media revenues in 1992, while the San Francisco Giants saw $24.5 in such revenues.

139. *Id.*

140. *See* ZIMBALIST, *supra* note 1, at 50.

141. *Id.*

142. *Id.* at 148, 158.

143. CBS claimed after-tax losses of $55 million in 1990 and estimated losses of $170 million over the term of the contract. Its profits were, no doubt, hurt by the fact that the World Series over those years generally involved small-market teams and few games. ESPN estimated that it lost at least $36 million in 1990 and $24 million after taxes in 1991. *Id.* at 159-60.

144. *See Id.* at 160.; *see* Ozanian & Taub, *supra* note 104, at 20.

145. *See* ZIMBALIST, *supra* note 1, at 161-65 (also noting that pay-per view will likely be a primary source of increased local broadcasting revenues in the future).

146. *See* Ozanian & Taub, *supra* note 104, at 28; ZIMBALIST, *supra* note 1, at 50-51.

147. *See* Ozanian & Taub, *supra* note 49, at 50-51; ZIMBALIST, *supra* note 1, at 50-51.

148. One author noted that, "holding ticket price and team quality constant, an extra one million in population size is worth 180,000 fans or $1,135,800 in ticket revenues to a club." SCULLY, *supra* note 15, at 114.

149. *See* Ozanian & Taub, *supra* note 111, at 42-43. Note that, in 1990, the Oakland Athletics advanced to the World Series before losing to the Cincinnati Reds, four games to none. The Kansas City Royals, on the other hand, have a free-spending owner. *See* ZIMBALIST, *supra* note 1, at 72.

150. Ozanian & Taub, *supra* note 111, at 42-43; *see supra* note 106.

151. *See* Ozanian & Taub, *supra* note 49, at 50-51; *see supra* note 106.

152. 1992 marked the opening of Oriole Park at Camden Yards.

153. *See* Ozanian & Taub, *supra* note 104, at 28. The figures for other small market teams were as follows: Milwaukee Brewers ($21.6 million), Kansas City Royals ($26.6 million), and Oakland A's ($33.0 million).

154. *See* SCULLY, *supra* note 15, at 113.

155. The National League splits gate revenues between the home and visiting teams at approximately a 90 to 10 ratio (specifically, the home team must share 71 cents per admission; 22 cents to the league office and 49 cents to the visiting team); the American League uses an 80 to 20 split. Significantly, luxury box revenues and concession revenues are not included. *See* ZIMBALIST, *supra* note 1, at 57.

156. ZIMBALIST, *supra* note 1, at 57-58.

157. *Id.*

158. *See* Ozanian & Taub, *supra* note 111, at 42-43.

159. *See* Ozanian & Taub, *supra* note 49, at 50-51.

160. *See* Ozanian & Taub, *supra* note 104, at 28.

161. *See generally* Ozanian & Taub, *supra* note 111, at 42.

162. As previously indicated, operating expenses does not include costs for depreciation, amortization, taxes, and interest.

163. *See generally* SCULLY, *supra* note 15, at 123-26; ZIMBALIST, *supra* note 1, at 59-61.

164. *See* Ozanian & Taub, *supra* note 104, at 28.

165. *See* Ozanian & Taub, *supra* note 111, at 42-43. The Oakland and San Francisco franchises were, no doubt, paying for their success in 1989, where both teams advanced to the World Series, while the owner of the Kansas City Royals, Ewing Kauffman, was "perceived by some to be baseball's last big- spending sportsman owner . . . in baseball to massage his passions, not his profits." ZIMBALIST, *supra* note 1, at 72.

166. *See* Ozanian & Taub, *supra* note 49, at 50-51. The significant jump in player salaries from 1990 to 1991 is attributable to the big increase in national television broadcasting and the end of collusive practices by baseball owners in veteran free agency. *See supra* note 101.

167. *See* Ozanian & Taub, *supra* note 104, at 28.

168.*Id.*; Ozanian & Taub, *supra* note 105 at 34. A major factor affecting the increase in players' salaries over this time was the demise of collusive practices by the owners. *See supra* note 101.

169. Apart from ability to pay, we would still expect large-market franchises to attract the best players because such players would bring more additional people to the ballpark, enlarge the local media contract by a greater amount, and attract more promotional income than they would in a small market. *See* ZIMBALIST, *supra* note 1, at 101.

170. *See* SCULLY, *supra* note 15, at 125 (concluding that, based on salary figures and team performance from 1978-87, "clearly, average player pay and average club record are linked"). *But see* ZIMBALIST, *supra* note 1, at 96 (concluding that, from 1984-89, average team salary has been related only tenuously to team performance, as it explained less than 10% of the variance in team win percentage and less than 12% of the variance in team standing). Note, however, that the salary figures used by Zimbalist occurred during the height of owner collusion in the veteran free agency market, which significantly decreased the disparity in player salaries among teams, thereby undermining his conclusion.

171. *See* SCULLY, *supra* note 15, at 113 (noting that, based on the 1984 season, each additional game won by a team brought in an additional 21,511 fans or $135,730 in ticket revenues based on average ticket price).

172. *See, e.g.,* ZIMBALIST, *supra* note 1, at 69-72 (noting that Ewing Kauffman, the owner of the Kansas City Royals, is "perceived by some to be baseball's last big-spending sportsman owner," who "is in baseball to massage his passions, not his profits").

173. *Id.* at 90-94 (also noting that the marginal revenue product of a star player will be higher in a large market than a small market); *see* SCULLY, *supra* note 15, at 154-58.

174. *See* ZIMBALIST, *supra* note 1, at 93-94. *See also* Andrew Zimbalist, *Salaries and Performance: Beyond the Scully Model,* DIAMONDS ARE FOR-EVER 107, 130-132 (Paul M. Sommers ed. 1992).

175. *See* ZIMBALIST, *supra* note 1, at 95-101 (noting that, since 1976, twelve different teams have won the World Series, and sixteen different teams have qualified for the World Series [those figures have since increased to thirteen and seventeen, respectively]; only three teams have failed to win division titles; and team winning percentages have narrowed over time).

176. *See id.* at 96-97. Zimbalist also suggests that, what may initially appear to be "ownership stupidity" in the signing of free agents, may actually be a conscious attempt to maintain competitive balance with small-market teams to escape pressure to share revenues. *Id.*

177. *Id.* at 99.

178. Milwaukee Brewers management, for example, claimed that costly free-agent acquisitions and long-term signings of ineffective and injured players precluded them from resigning their best player, veteran Paul

Molitor, in 1993; Molitor joined the World Series champion Toronto Blue Jays through free agency. *See, e.g.*, Murphy, *supra* note 123, at 25.

179.*See supra* note 2; Ozanian & Taub, *supra* note 104, at 28. The amount of money generated from luxury boxes, of course, depends a great deal on the obsolescence of the stadium involved and the affluence of the surrounding community.

180.*See* ZIMBALIST, *supra* note 1, at 57.

181.*See supra* note 16; *see* Murphy, *Trade Secrets, supra* note 1, at 21.

182.*See* ZIMBALIST, *supra* note 1, at 55.

183.*See* Morris, *supra* note 2, at 48; Murphy, *Trade Secrets, supra* note 1, at 22.

184.*See* Anthony Baldo, *Edifice Complex*, FINANCIAL WORLD, Nov. 26, 1991, at 36.

185.*Id.* at 34 (noting that stadium referenda in San Francisco, Oakland and Miami have failed in recent years, while civic groups have opposed new projects in Detroit and Chicago). To get around taxpayer disapproval, some areas have created "sports authorities," which "provide public financial support to stadiums—without public consent" (for example, the Georgia Dome in Atlanta and Oriole Park at Camden Yards in Baltimore). *Id.* at 35. *See supra* notes 1, 16.

186.*See* Murphy, *Spring Fever supra* note 1, at 82; Murphy, *Trade Secrets supra* note 1, at 21.

187.*See supra* note 155.

188.In particular, "because the clubs can no longer rely on the reserve system to insulate equality of team playing talent from inequality in team earnings, there is considerable interest in league-wide revenue sharing in major league baseball—particulary sharing of local broadcast revenue." WEILER & ROBERTS, *supra* note 19, at 438-39.

189.*See* ZIMBALIST, *supra* note 1, at 173. Recognizing this, the owners, after much debate, unanimously agreed on a plan to share local broadcasting revenue on January 18, 1994; that plan, conditioned on approval of a salary cap by the players' union, promises small-market clubs between $5 and $9 million a year in additional revenue. *See* Bob Berghaus, *Revenue Plan a Victory for Selig to Savor*, MILWAUKEE J., Jan. 19, 1994, at A1.

190.*See* 29 U.S.C. § 158(d) (1993).

191.*See supra* Part III, notes 63, 64.

192.*Id.*

193.15 U.S.C. §§ 1,2 (1993).

194.WEILER & ROBERTS, *supra* note 19, at 353. At least one court held that the National Football League was not a "single entity" for purposes of § 1 of the Sherman Act and, in fact, constituted "separate economic entities engaged in a joint venture." North American Soccer League v. National Football League, 670 F.2d 1249, 1254 (2d Cir. 1982).

195.*See generally* Gary R. Roberts, *Professional Sports and the Antitrust Laws*, THE BUSINESS OF PROFESSIONAL SPORTS 135, 136-48 (Paul D. Staudohar

& James A. Mangan eds. 1991) (historically, interleague disputes have involved § 2 of the Sherman Act, while intraleague disputes have involved § 1 of the Sherman Act); WEILER & ROBERTS, *supra* note 19, at 445-456.

196.*See, e.g.,* United States v. Socony-Vacuum Oil Co., Inc., 310 U.S. 150, 212-18 (1939).

197.*See generally* Board of Trade v. United States, 246 U.S. 231 (1918); National Society of Professional Engineers v. United States, 435 U.S. 679 (1978).

198.*Id.*

199.*See supra* note 65.

200.*See supra* Part II.

201.WEILER & ROBERTS, *supra* note 19, at 303.

202.Salaries may be adjusted, for example, based on the cost of living and promotional income in different locales.

203.*See id.* As previously noted, players are also attracted to teams by the number of endorsement opportunities available in a given location. As a result, if an unadjusted uniform salary cap was applied to every team, the best players would generally migrate to large-market teams. *See* ZIMBALIST, *supra* note 169.

204.*See supra* note 190.

205.The National Basketball Association, for example, has, in principle, both a team salary maximum and team salary minimum. Its principles are outlined in WEILER & ROBERTS, *supra* note 19, at 300-304.

206.*See id.*

207.According to one observer, "[t]he union has always been ready to listen to proposals on revenue sharing and a salary cap—one based on equal sacrifice, not just as a means of saving owners money." Larry Whiteside, *Baseball Owners in a Sharing Mood,* BOSTON GLOBE, Feb. 18, 1993, at 39, 41.

208.*See supra* note 189.

209.*See supra* Part III; notes 63, 64, and 197.

210.*See, e.g., Board of Trade,* 246 U.S. at 239.

211.*See, e.g.,* Kartell v. Blue Shield of Massachusetts Inc., 749 F.2d 922 (1st Cir. 1984) (finding no antitrust violation where the health insurer's practice of requiring all doctors who performed patient services to accept its fee schedule because it held medical and insurance costs down for consumers). *See also* WEILER & ROBERTS, *supra* note 19, at 127-131.

212.*See supra* Part III, notes 63, 64.

213.*See* MILLER, *supra* note 9, at 1.

214.*See supra* notes 63, 64.

215.*See supra* note 1.

216.*Id.*; Daniel P. Handley Jr., *Selig Intent on Another Big Victory,* MILWAU-KEE J., Feb. 27, 1994, at A1.

217.*See supra* note 189.

Planning for Effective Risk Management: A Guide for Stadium and Arena Management*

Bernard P. Maloy

Bernard Maloy's essay focuses, not on the questions of where franchises will locate, but upon the equally important question of the liability of stadium and arena operators for personal injuries suffered by spectators. This is one of the oldest sports law questions, but also one that has long defied easy resolution. In Maloy's view, excessive liability costs incurred by facility operators are the product of poor management practices which is often the consequence of the inadequacies of the traditional hierarchical management strategies. Maloy advocates an approach to risk management which relies upon a non-traditional, integrated organizational structure.

I. Introduction

Astadium or an arena's legal liability for a personal injury claim is generally predicated upon the facility's failure to meet minimum standards of "safety, suitability, or sanitation."[1] Significant concerns regarding facility safety started to manifest themselves with the abolition or limitation of immunity, and the enactment of Tort Claim statutes. Consequently, management interest in risk management programs grew as the specter of legal liability loomed over public facilities.[2] Many facility risk management programs were implemented with the specific purpose of preventing or reducing personal injury risks.[3]

*From Volume 2, Number 1, Fall 1991, pp. 89-101.

It is not uncommon for personal injury attorneys to trace the failure to provide minimum facility standards to the seemingly enduring incompetencies of the facility management. Often, management incompetency is the result of a lackadaisical management attitude toward risk management. In addition, sometimes it is caused by the inherent constraints of the facility's organizational structure. In other words:

1. Facility management incompetency is usually evident from management's misconduct regarding its own safety policies or procedures. That is, management has failed to communicate safety responsibility to its staff, has disregarded or neglected proper safety procedures, or has imprudently delegated safety obligations; or,

2. Facility management has adopted the traditional organizational structure of American business which tends to be hierarchal in form and militaristic in style. Therefore, it works within an organizational structure which has been known to stunt the flow of information, doubt the virtue of employee motivation, and inhibit staff participation in the work place.[4] In many cases, risk management incompetency is not the result of malicious intent. As noted, it may be the unfortunate consequence of managerial attitudes which are bred in a hierarchal organizational structure. That structure subscribes to vertical levels of communication, and the separation of tasks and duties.[5]

The thrust of this article is to encourage American stadium and arena managers to utilize non-traditional organizational structure and management methods when implementing their risk management programs. This article suggests that "effective" risk management is the result of a number of steps. First, effective risk management requires an awareness that risk identification is only one process of a comprehensive risk management program, not its entire purpose. Second, effective risk management means that legal concepts which focus on the risk management process should be simplified to three simple concepts: legal knowledge, instruction, and warning. Third, the management component of a facility risk management program requires open organizational communication focusing on participatory risk management. Finally, all steps need to be integrated in order to provide the most comprehensive program of facility safety and protection.

II. The Risk Identification Process

The identification of facility risks is often initiated by assessing facility functions.[6] There are a number of methods by which stadium or arena functions can be appraised. First, there are the risks created by the interaction of the spectator with the facility which include:

1. *Areas of Heavy Use*, such as entrances and exits, concourses, portals, rest rooms, and concession areas, present safety problems simply because they are places where fans congregate. There is always a safety concern when large groups of people congregate or cluster around a heavy traffic area.[7]

2. *Areas of Specialized Use*, such as toilets, sinks, concession tables, and doors create risk management problems due to the unorthodox means in which they may be used. Many sports fans open doors by pushing on the glass rather than the handle, are heavy-handed with toilet attachments, or lean on rest room sinks and tables while waiting their turns.

3. *Areas of Expectation* means that fans expect that their seats are in proper working condition, that facility floors will be reasonably clean, and that concession products are safe and edible. These spectator expectations are justified since there is little that fans can do to protect themselves from the related risks.[8]

Another way of evaluating facility use is to examine known or anticipated defects in the facility itself which may include:

1. *Roofing Systems* are a major concern since they can stimulate or accelerate the deterioration of the facility.[9] The effects of leakage always poses a facility risk.

2. *Steps*, though generally installed according to city, county, or state building code, are always affected by the type and location of lighting, varied height and width of risers, length of handrails, and the type of step covering.[10]

3. *Floor surface* is a critical area because most stadiums and arenas host various types of events and convocations which require a variety of surfaces and coverings. These can present multiple risks and hazards for spectators and participants.[11]

A third approach to facility use is to review the services provided by the facility, including:

1. *Trash or garbage created from concession and souvenir sales* is a primary area of concern to facility operators because it literally covers a large area of spectator use: parking lots, entrances and exits, concourses and hallways, toilets, portals, rows, and seats.[12]

2. *Alcohol* is a always a facility problem. Obviously, if the stadium or arena serves alcohol, then strict liability may attach under applicable dram shop laws.[13] In most instances, it is alcohol-induced conduct which is the major hazard to spectators and participants.[14]

3. *Security and Supervision* are always risk concerns for facilities because spectators generally believe that most personal injuries could have been prevented if the facility had taken greater care to provide adequate security or supervision.[15]

Nevertheless, the process of generating lists of facility risks is only one step or process of a risk management program. Unfortunately, it often is accepted as the entire plan. It is impractical, if not impossible, to list or categorize the potential hazards and risks that may be found in a stadium or arena. In order to list every potential facility risk, one would have to consider all the potential sources of injury from the design, construction, maintenance, operation, or administration of the facility itself. Add to that all the potential risks which have not yet revealed themselves in the facility. There are other problems associated with risk identification. For example, the size of the facility, the ages and maturity of its users, and the types of events hosted in the facility. In short, there are so many variables involved that all the possible risks of injury in a facility cannot be adequately and prudently listed. For that very reason, any administrative or management belief that risk management can be reduced to a simple check list is naive.

Airline pilots and crews use checklists in order to assure that proper procedures are followed so that the aircraft safely takes off, flies, and lands. The safe operation of the aircraft, however, does not begin by putting an untrained pilot in the cockpit with a check list. Safe operation begins with a purpose, communication, and training. The same is true with the safe operation of a stadium or arena. A risk identification list merely facilitates the risk management program. It does not replace the mission, communication, or training required for a competent risk management plan.

Sooner or later, a risk list will have to be produced for the facility risk management program. However, the list should result from research in the construction, maintenance, and use of the facility as well as analysis of the facility management program. The results of facility risk management appraisals usually focus on the legal obligations or duties of the stadium or arena. Ultimately, those liability concerns should be reduced to three simple legal obligations: legal knowledge, instruction, and warning. This process of consolidating a facility's legal duties to the three legal obligations will clarify the procedure for risk identification.

III. Communicating Legal Concepts

Stadiums and arenas have to sell themselves to survive in business. They cannot merely be concerned with the operation, maintenance, and administration of the facility but, equally, they are dependent on their marketing, promotion, and public relations. For that reason, the law distinguishes them from facilities which are merely open to business visitors or customers, such as office buildings or stores. Stadiums and arenas are legally termed places of amusement. That distinction is made for facilities which invite the public to use their premises *and* charge a fee for entry.[16] The legal obligations owed by places of amusement are more strictly applied than those of a facility which merely invites public use. It is not uncommon, therefore, for facility risk management manuals to preface their risk identification process with a brief explanation of tort liability, especially the law of negligence.[17]

Many lawyers have difficulty explaining legal concepts in anything other than the language of the law. It is important that risk management manuals avoid explaining legal concepts in "legalese" or applying examples exclusively in legal settings. In a risk management program, the language of safety has to be expressed in terms understood by the facility management and staff. Spectators and participants of all ages have to be directed, instructed, and guided in safe facility use by common language. Therefore, a more simplified method of risk identification, utilizing legal concepts, could concentrate its attention to the legal obligations of knowledge, instruction, and warning. These are not the only legal obligations with which a facility needs to concern itself.[18] However, a review of the many areas of risk identification discussed in the previous section should reveal that the reasonable application of legal knowledge, instruction, or warning will alleviate a majority of the risks identified.

Legal knowledge is not a term distinguishable from the word "knowledge." Legal knowledge refers to the decision to apply knowledge. The word knowledge is defined as "[a]cquaintance with facts, truths, or principles, as from study or investigation."[19] In more relevant risk management parlance, knowledge might be defined as experience and expertise in facility risk appraisal. Legal knowledge is its judicial expectation. It is the expectation that a stadium or arena manager will use his or her knowledge to maintain a reasonably safe facility. The facility whose manager has failed to use his or her knowledge to keep the facility safe will be liable for personal injuries. Legal knowledge is also the expectation that a facility manager will expand his or her knowledge of risks through continuing education, industry journals, and trade publications. Additionally, legal knowledge is the expectation that the facility manager will regularly inspect the facility in order to be prepared for any unexpected or undiscovered problems that may threaten the facility's patrons. Finally, legal knowledge is the expectation that a facility manager will prudently react to spectator risks once they are discovered.[20]

Facility managers can react to their knowledge of facility risks by instructing or warning spectators about the safe use of the stadium or arena. Safe facility use depends upon instruction. From the time a spectator arrives at the facility, he or she relies on instructions regarding traffic flow, where to park, which entrance to use, where to sit, where the concession and rest rooms are located, and where to smoke. Obviously, instructions play a major part of effective facility risk management. The risks associated with instruction are generally created from the manner in which the instructions are communicated, not their content. Facility communication has to be sensitive to senior citizens who may have hearing difficulties, to children whose attention may be directed elsewhere, and to fans whose interests are directed to the field of play, not to their own personal protection.[21]

The legal obligation to warn of risks is related to the instruction concept. In regard to facility risks, the functions of warnings are to instruct, to inform, and to warn.[22] To be effective, the warning message must be reasonably conveyed. For example, a "do not run" sign merely posted over a portal may not be reasonable warning for an 11-year-old spectator anxious to get to his or her seat. Warnings should always be posted for any facility conditions or problems which cannot be immediately remedied. For example, if the source of flooding of a rest room floor cannot be located or stopped, a warning of the danger together with an alternative plan for rest room relief should be communicated to spectators needing those services.

The importance of legal knowledge, instruction, and warning cannot be overemphasized. For example, the law recognizes that spectators assume some risks of injury or may contribute to their own injury by their inattention. Further, the law is clear that spectators assume most of the risks inherent to the type of event they are attending.[23] Nevertheless, before the court weighs the contributory actions of an injured spectator, it will generally look to see if the facility knew of the risk and failed to instruct the spectator or did not effectively warn the spectator.[24]

Legal knowledge, instruction, and warning can serve as a sufficient basis for a facility risk management program. If the management and staff embrace and apply the three concepts, then the facility will have a foundation for its risk identification process. However, the three legal concepts share a common trait which first has to be competently managed before the legal concepts can be utilized effectively. That element is communication. "The effectiveness of any risk management program is in direct proportion to the effectiveness of communications, for when communication is non-existent, incomplete, or inadequate in any way, the program becomes inoperable and the risks, then, are not reduced as they might be."[25] Communication is the common element of legal knowledge, instruction, and warning. The communication between management and staff, as well as communication between staff and facility patrons is vitally important to a facility's competent performance of the three legal tasks. It should be apparent that the "risk" component of facility risk management is rooted in the legal concepts which direct the process of risk identification. It should be equally evident that the "management" part of facility risk management relies on effective communication. Communication is not a legal concept. It is a social concept and a business concept. As a business concept, the effectiveness of communication can be thwarted by managerial attitudes, or limited by the confines of organizational structure.[26]

IV. MANAGING COMMUNICATION

Recently, American business has been the target of some critics for its multi-tiered organizational structure.[27] Other criticism places the blame for the apparent deterioration of American business on the incompetence, even fraudulent intent, of management.[28] Certainly the savings and loan crisis, American auto manufacturing woes, or the impending insurance crisis serve as strong testaments for those opinions. It is unclear, however, whether organizational structure and management incompetence are separable, or whether they are inter-related. It is exasperating to discover whether organizational structure or inferior management is the cause of poor management. The argument begins to take on shades of the chicken or the egg dispute. Nevertheless, managerial attitude and organizational structure are vital elements which greatly affect the communication within any organization. Since communication has been identified as the key element of a facility risk management plan, it is essential to discover how it is best adapted to the organizational work place.

It has been posed that today's predominant office structure is really nothing more than the organized assembly line adopted for the early 20th Century mass production.[29] Many modern business persons accept that business organization should be a tiered structure. Its levels and processes are comparable and similar to the military organizational structure.[30] A feature of the hierarchal structure is command from the top down. An important criticism of that command structure is the reservation of information by the higher management levels of the organization. Peters and Waterman asserted that a dominant feature of their "excellent" companies was the loose flow of shared information. "Another of the more striking characteristics of the excellent companies is the *apparent absence of a rigidly followed chain of command.* Of course, the chain of command does exist for big decisions, but it is not used much for day-to-day communication."[31] It is maintained that management's reluctance to share information stunts employee participation in the organizational mission or process, and permits little employee autonomy over the job process. This is usually reflected by management's desire that employee duties and responsibilities be standardized into simple, repetitive tasks. Unfortunately, those corollaries seem to result in minimal employee performance.[32]

It could be assumed that the hierarchal organizational structure inhibits communication from the top to the bottom simply because of the difficulty in transmitting information through the levels of management. In other words, not all communication problems may be the result of close-mouthed or patronizing managers. The problems may result merely from the inherent problems of organizational structure. If the organization designs communication to flow from top to bottom, the hierarchal structure becomes an impediment. In addition, if information is supposed to flow from the bottom to the top as well, its dissemination faces similar hierarchal obstacles.

A stadium or arena whose administration is organized along traditional organization lines with multi-layered, hierarchal management should be aware of these communication impediments. This is not to suggest that the free flow of information cannot exist in a hierarchal organization. Nor does it mean that a stadium or arena management process is guilty by association merely because it has adopted a layered structure. It does mean, however, that facility management framed in the multi-tiered organization must be managed by uniquely open people. The hierarchal organization places greater emphasis on the quality of the management personnel to facilitate a good communication process. The evidence suggests that hierarchal organizations usually do not breed such managers.

Management incompetence is not easily defined. Actually, it probably belongs in the eyes of the beholder. Management which fails to maximize profits and dividends may be viewed as incompetent by the shareholders.[33] Further, management which fails to effectively plan, organize, staff, control, and lead employees in the performance of their tasks may be measured as incompetent by experts and consultants.[34] Management which has little respect for the individual is probably considered incompetent by employees.[35] In any event, management has many antagonists when it attempts to define its purpose and goals. In regard to service industry management, however, Peter Drucker defends the quality of management, and blames perceived incompetencies on the structure of the organization:

> If service institutions cannot be run and managed by men of normal and fairly low endowment; if, in other words, we cannot organize the task so that it will be done adequately by men who only try hard, it cannot be done at all ... there is no reason to believe that business managers, put in control of service institutions, would do better than the 'bureaucrats.' Indeed, we know that they immediately become bureaucrats themselves.[36]

The bottom line, unfortunately, is that many facility risk management programs implemented in a layered organizational structure, with its inherent bureaucratic management, will be ineffective. Stadium and arena risk management cannot succeed because communication, so important to the risk management concept, is curtailed.

It is equally apparent, however, that change in the organizational structure, or in the method of management, starts with management. It is not a task for which employees or staff are held accountable. If communication is going to be the main ingredient in organizational structure, or management philosophy, then it is a charge which management alone has to bear.

> In performing these essential functions [leadership, direction, objectives, and organization], management everywhere faces the same problems. It has to organize work for productivity, it has to lead the worker toward productivity *and* achievement. It is responsible for the social impact of its enterprise. Above all, it is responsible for producing the results — whether economic performance, student learning, or patient care - for the sake of which the institution exists.[37]

In the late 1970s, many changes were made by Preston Trucking.[38] The focus of that change was to make the company more competitive in an increasingly difficult transportation market. Most of the difficulty centered on communication. At the time of the change, employee performance and morale was at an all-time low. Levering noted that open communication became a natural by-product of the company's decision to change. More importantly, the change came strictly from management. Employees were not called upon to make any change, were not asked to forego any established union privileges, and were not given "lip service" regarding their efforts for company growth.[39] Management alone was required to change. For example, Levering discussed the positive reinforcement method wherein a manager had to find four good things to say regarding an employee's performance for every one criticism.[40] In establishing vital communication, and recapturing employee performance, the program was a success. However, management did not readily buy into the precept that it had to change, nor did the program guarantee future company success.

The idea that Preston management alone had to change its employee communication and interaction was not easily accepted. One-quarter of the management structure quit because of the change in management philosophy.[41] When management training is directed to managerial functions within a multitiered organizational structure, it would be difficult for a manager to accept less than the absolute authority he or she held. However, if communication is to be a shared process, management has to learn the processes of employee participation. At Preston, it was also realized that the new management emphasis was not a guaranteed success. The Preston story had to be repeated everyday. The communication of goals, purpose, and procedures became an everyday effort. It required the constant commitment of management.

V. INTEGRATING THE RISK MANAGEMENT PLAN

One of the methods adopted by management, as a means of integrating risk management programs, has been the appointment of a risk manager. The role of a risk manager can be a positive one for the stadium or arena. However, such an appointment does pose some problems. First, if the position is merely a delegated duty which management does wish to deal with, then it will fail due to management's own incompetency. Second, the position may be just another layer or tier in the organizational structure which means that the flow of information will have another obstacle. Therefore, the success of a risk management program should not be left solely with the appointment of a risk manager. A successful program depends on its integration of risk management communication within the organization.

There are a number of steps required for an integrated risk management program. They utilize each of the lessons reviewed concerning risk identification, the applicable legal concepts and, more importantly, an open or participatory management approach to facility safety.

1. The traditional concept and perception of the management role has to be re-defined. It is doubtful, for instance, that middle management engages in a daily process of decision-making, planning, and organizing. It is suggested that management's real function, literally and figuratively, is to facilitate. In other words, making it easier for employees to perform their jobs is the real function of management. Such a role is almost totally dependent on loose, unstructured communication.[42] A management model based on facilitating, rather than ruling, should be adopted for the management which establishes the facility risk management program and for the risk manager it wishes to appoint.

2. There can be no qualifications to the communication process at any level of the stadium or arena organization. The major factors to be considered in reducing risks are conditions of the facility environment, its participants and spectators, emergency procedures, and related information. The ability to deal with these risks is dependent on open and honest communication.[43]

3. The hindrances posed by organizational structure or delegated responsibilities have to be overcome. Usually, this means effort, renewed effort, and then more effort to make risk management work.

If a risk management program becomes the victim of organizational indifference due to the framework of the facility or is forgotten by management under the guise of a delegated duty to a risk manager or staff, it usually fails.

"Risk management is an on-going process. Not only must it be integrated into the very fiber of an organization, but also its effectiveness must be systematically evaluated and adjustments made as appropriate. Neither the implementation of the plan nor its effectiveness assessment just happen ..."[44]

NOTES

1. Francis Gregory & Arthur H. Goldsmith, *The Sports Spectator as Plaintiff,* 16 TRIAL 26, 28 (March, 1980). For purposes of this article, which is primarily addressed to the stadium and arena industry, the term "facility" may be substituted for "stadium or arena" for purposes of brevity.
2. BETTY VAN DER SMISSEN, LEGAL LIABILITY AND RISK MANAGEMENT FOR PUBLIC AND PRIVATE ENTITIES vol. 2, ch. 23, at 1-2.
3. *Id.* at 3.
4. PETER F. DRUCKER, MANAGEMENT: TASKS, RESPONSIBILITIES, AND PRACTICES 137- 147 (1974). Drucker alleges that the government, higher education, the armed services, and the health industry are growing faster than American business He distinguishes American business as that industry which produces products. The goal of the service industry is to be efficient and control costs. By its nature, it is bureaucratic; and, it is not "effective" which is the distinctive aspect of American business. *Id.*
5. ROSABETH MOSS KANTER, THE CHANGEMASTERS: INNOVATION AND ENTREPRENEURSHIP IN THE AMERICAN CORPORATION 28-29 (1983). The author terms "segmentalization" as the foundation upon which hierarchal organizational structure is built. Its effects are the isolation of actions, events, and problems in the organization. Segmentalization "means that each [organizational] segment works independently, with minimum need for communication." *Id.*
6. *See* RICHARD B. FLYNN, PLANNING FACILITIES FOR ATHLETICS, PHYSICAL EDUCATION, AND RECREATION 131 (1985). Flynn's risk identification process begins with concepts rather than specifics. For example, stadiums and arenas should "provide adequate storage space." Adequate storage has many meanings. From the legal perspective, what is adequate depends upon the circumstances. From a management viewpoint, adequacy is measured by one's experience and knowledge regarding needs. Therefore, to be safely understood and implemented, "providing adequate storage space" would require communication between facility management and staff.

7. Ross v. City of Minneapolis, 408 N.W.2d 910 (Minn.Ct.App.1987) (A spectator is assaulted by unidentified persons while exiting a Minneapolis arena after a wrestling match); Greenville Memorial Auditorium v. Martin, 301 S.C. 242, 391 S.E.2d 546 (1990) (A glass bottle is thrown into a crowd at a rock concert); *see also*, Annotation, *Injury to Customer by Crowd*, 20 A.L.R.2d 12 (1951).

8. *See* Lindgren v. Voge, 260 Minn. 262, 109 N.W.2d 754 (1961) (a flooded rest room floor and a broken flushbox cause a spectator injury); *see also* League of Minnesota Cities Ins. Trust v. City of Coon Rapids, 446 N.W.2d 419 (Minn.Ct.App.1989) (spectators at an ice arena are injured from pollutants discharged from the Zamboni); *see also* Annen v. McNab, 192 Ill.App.3d 711, 548 N.E.2d 1383 (1990) (child is injured when a rest room sink falls on her).

9. RICHARD B. FLYNN, *supra* note 6, at 114-119; See also Monex, Inc. v. Anthony A. Nunes, Inc., 576 A.2d 1206 (R.I.1990) (Products liability claim regarding a 2-ply built-up roofing system).

10. Jacobs v. Commonwealth Highland Theatres, Inc., 738 P.2d 6 (Colo.Ct.App.1986).

11. RICHARD B. FLYNN, *supra* note 6 at 119, 130.

12. Maryland Maintenance Service, Inc. v. Palmieri, 559 So.2d 74 (Fla.Dist.Ct.App. 1990) (Spectator slipped on a wet substance on the grandstand floor of a race track).

13. Allen v. Rutgers, The State University of New Jersey, 216 N.J.Super. 189, 523 A.2d 262, *cert. denied*, 527 A.2d 472 (1987) (Rutgers University is immune from the claim of a student who became intoxicated at a football game. Although university personnel at Rutgers Stadium failed to follow the procedures for administering to intoxicated fans, the university did not sell or provide the intoxicants. Therefore, strict liability under New Jersey's Dram Shop law did not apply).

14. Bearman v. University of Notre Dame, 453 N.E.2d 1196 (Ind.App.1983) (A football fan exiting Notre Dame Stadium is injured by two intoxicated fans). *See also* Francis X. Dealy, *Win at Any Cost* 125-143 (1990).

15. Vanchieri v. New Jersey Sports and Exposition Authority, 104 N.J. 80, 514 A.2d 1323 (1986) (a fan exiting Giants Stadium at the Meadowlands is knocked down by some young men who are engaged in a game of roughhouse). *See also* Betty van der Smissen, *supra* note 2, 163 ("Lack of inadequate supervision is the most common allegation of negligence").

16. Lindgren v. Voge, 260 Minn. 262, 272, 109 N.W.2d 754, 761 (1961); *see also*, Annotation, *Liability of Owner or Operator of Theater or Other Amusement to Patron Assaulted by Another Patron*, 75 A.L.R.3d 441 (1977).

17. *See* Ian McGregor & Joseph MacDonald, RISK MANAGEMENT MANUAL FOR SPORT AND RECREATION ORGANIZATIONS 2-21 (1990).

18. There is a legal obligation to supervise facilities. That obligation may be implicit, however, in the legal duties to instruct and warn. *See* BETTY VAN DER SMISSEN, *supra* note 2, at 221-233.

19. THE LIVING WEBSTER ENCYCLOPEDIC DICTIONARY OF THE ENGLISH LANGUAGE 531 (1974).

20. Maryland Maintenance Service, Inc. v. Palmieri, 559 So.2d 74, 76 (Fla.Dist.Ct.App. 1990).

21. VAN DER SMISSEN, *supra* note 2, at 22-26 (conducting activities or managing services is based on giving instructions).

22. *Id.* at 37-44.

23. Friedman v. Houston Sports Association, 731 S.W.2d 572 (Tex.Ct.App.1987) (An 11-year-old child assumed the risk of injury from a foul ball at a baseball game); Accold Chareas v. Township High School District No. 214, 195 Ill.App.3d 540, 553 N.E.2d 23 (1990) (A youngster assumes the risk of injury when he stands inside the fence at a tennis match instead of sitting in the bleachers provided).

24. VAN DER SMISSEN, *supra* note 2, at 11 ("In regard to assumption of risk, concern is with knowingly encountering danger, which is to be contrasted with negligently encountering risk").

25. *Id.* at 20.

26. THOMAS J. PETERS & ROBERT H. WATERMAN, IN SEARCH OF EXCELLENCE 121-125 (1982). (Corporate projects often become mired in corporate bureaucracy. The authors suggest that getting things done in an organization requires informal, open communication between management and staff; and, positive reinforcement from management to staff).

27. MARK H. MCCORMACK, WHAT THEY DON'T TEACH YOU AT HARVARD BUSINESS SCHOOL 175 (1984). (McCormack cites a former Ford executive who termed that company's organizational structure as a "wall of molasses - nothing gets in, nothing gets out, nothing goes up, or goes sideways, and is too slow to go down.")

28. *See* ROBERT LEVERING, A GREAT PLACE TO WORK 239-253 (1988).

29. *Id.* at 48-49 and 79-89.

30. PETERS & WATERMAN, *supra* note 26, at 7.

31. *Id.* at 262; (Peters and Waterman also cite a FORTUNE magazine article which notes that sharing information at the "shop floor" level is the single most important act in bridging the gap between management and staff).

32. See LEVERING, *supra* note 28, at 72-76; *see also* PETERS & WATERMAN, *supra* note 26, at 39 (Authors present Japanese organizational beliefs which recognize job performance as an organizational natural resource and, which, view organization and employees as synonymous).

33. LEVERING, *supra* note 28, at 239.

34. *See* HAROLD KOONTZ & HIENZ WEIHRICH, ESSENTIALS OF MANAGEMENT, 22-24 (5th ed. 1990); *see also* MURRAY SPERBER, COLLEGE SPORTS, INC. 20-21 (1990) (Sperber questions the management expertise of many college athletic directors whose main qualification appears to be their participation as a player or coach in football).

35. LEVERING, *supra* note 28, at 225-226 (Author poses that bad workplaces have management which lives by arbitrary rules, permits abusive supervision, and generally has little regard for employee well-being).

36. *See* DRUCKER, *supra* note 4, at 139.

37. *Id.* at 17.

38. LEVERING, *supra* note 28, at 151.

39. PETERS & WATERMAN, *supra* note 26, at 238-241 (Lip service is a management gimmick. It is used by management, usually in times of crisis, to inspire employees to renew their efforts, expresses management's concern for the employees well-being, and directs that positive change will result if each side makes a concerted effort. Implicitly, it is management's placing some blame for its own failure on the employees).

40. ROBERT LEVERING, *supra* note 28, at 139-161.

41. *Id.* at 154.

42. HENRY MINTZBERG, THE MANAGER'S JOB: FOLKLORE AND FACT 163-176 (1990).

43. VAN DER SMISSEN, *supra* note 2, at 45-58.

44. *Id.* at 15.

PART II

LABOR
AND
DISCIPLINARY
ISSUES

PLAYER DISCIPLINE IN TEAM SPORTS*

Jan Stiglitz

The right of a professional sports team to discipline its players has been the source of much controversy in recent years. Traditionally, the right of teams to exercise such authority generally went unchallenged; however, with the rise of militant players associations, the nature and format of discipline have become subjects for the collective bargaining agreement between the league and its players. Illegal drug usage by athletes has led to a large number of public controversies over questions of discipline.

In this essay, Jan Stiglitz examines the way in which disciplinary issues are addressed in the four major team sports—baseball, football, basketball, and hockey.

I. INTRODUCTION

The purpose of this paper is to briefly outline the issues involved in disciplining athletes in this country's four major team sports: baseball, football, hockey and basketball. As anyone familiar with the industry knows, we live in changing times; only football has a long term labor agreement. This makes it particularly difficult to definitively explicate the disciplinary process. Similarly, one can hardly speak with any authority about the power of the Commissioner of baseball when there isn't one, and the owners have just recently rewritten the rules which define the Commissioner's powers. But there are enough similarities in the historical disciplinary structures of the four leagues to create a framework for analysis and highlight the major problem areas.

*From Volume 5, Number 2, Spring 1995, pp. 167-188.

This article will first present an overview of the structure of the industry, its disciplinary mechanisms, and the legal issues that are implicated. The article will then outline the specific disciplinary framework which exists (or has recently existed) in each of the four major team sports.

II. Industry Structure

A. "The Players"

In order to understand the issues involved in athlete discipline in team sports, it is necessary to understand the particular structure of the typical sports league. In this structure, there are a number of individuals and entities who have significant rights and power. Unlike the traditional employment setting, where the "company" is the only source of discipline, in professional team sports, there is an additional source of discipline: the league.

In team sports, the "company" is the player's club. But athletes in the four major team sports are also subject to discipline by the league, which acts through its president or commissioner. Moreover, in the case of baseball, there is an additional level of disciplinary authority because Major League Baseball is comprised of two, somewhat autonomous leagues. Each league has a President, who exercises a certain amount of disciplinary authority.[1]

Another significant "player," in terms of disciplinary authority, is the on the field official. Misconduct on the playing field is a very common basis for discipline. The actions of the umpire or referee, and that official's report of the incident, may ultimately determine whether an athlete is disciplined and what the level of discipline will be. For example, in football, ejection from a game can be the basis of a fine.[2] Similarly, in hockey, the on-ice officials have the power to suspend a player for up to twenty games.[3]

B. The "Rules"

The relationships between these actors are governed by a set of interrelated documents which need to be reviewed in order to determine who can impose discipline, under what circumstances, subject to what limits, and with what scope of review. Typically there are three basic documents to be considered.

1. The Collective Bargaining Agreement

When all goes well, there is the collective bargaining agreement, entered into between the union and the league, which governs the terms and conditions of employment. The typical collective bargaining agreement will have one or more sections devoted to discipline.[4] This part of the collective bargaining agreement will be a primary source for the rules determining who can impose discipline and under what circumstances. The collective bargaining agreement will also have a grievance procedure.[5] In the event of a dispute over the imposition of discipline, the collective bargaining agreement will establish who ultimately decides whether the discipline was appropriate. Finally, the collective bargaining agreement will contain important procedural rules, regarding such issues as notice, time limits, discovery, and representational rights.

For example, the article on discipline in the current collective bargaining agreement in baseball provides that a player can be subjected to discipline for "just cause" by "his Club, League or the Commissioner."[6] The agreement also provides for notice[7] and discovery rights.[8] Finally, the agreement sets out a grievance procedure, which gives the player the right to have most disputes resolved by a neutral arbitrator.[9]

2. The Uniform Player Contract

In the traditional industrial setting, the collective bargaining agreement governs salaries for all covered employees. By tradition, in team sports, the collective bargaining agreement contains the general terms and conditions of employment but only sets forth the minimum salary. Athletes have been allowed to individually negotiate salaries and certain other perks and benefits with their teams, so long as these agreements do not diminish the minimum rights and benefits awarded under the collective bargaining agreement.[10] The vehicle for memorializing and governing this individual player-club agreement is the "Uniform" or "Standard" player contract. This contract may contain provisions which directly affect discipline.

For example, the ultimate discipline is discharge. The Uniform Player's Contract in baseball contains the provisions under which the club can terminate the contract and thus the player's employment.[11] Paragraph 7(b)(1) of the Uniform Player's Contract states that the club may terminate the contract if the player shall: "fail, refuse or neglect to conform his personal conduct to the standards of good citizenship and good sportsmanship or to keep himself in first-class physical condition or to obey the Club's training rules."

The Uniform Player's Contract in baseball also has "Regulations" which govern a player's conduct and give the clubs the right to discipline the player. Paragraph 5 of the Regulations provides that the club may impose a "reasonable fine" or suspend a player for up to thirty days for a violation of a regulation or provision of the contract.

Additionally, a player's contract may contain special covenants, like a weight clause, or an agreement not to participate in certain other sports. The breach of one of these special covenants might also give rise to discipline by the club.

A special covenant may also be included to more precisely define conduct that could give rise to discipline or termination. For example, one recommended addendum to the Uniform Player Contract in basketball contains a provision under which a player acknowledges that a criminal conviction for a felony would constitute a basis for discharge under the "personal conduct" standards of the contract.[12]

Conversely, special covenants may limit the effect of discipline. In basketball, a player and team may enter into a covenant which guarantees that the player's salary will be paid even if the player's contract is terminated by reason of his personal conduct.[13]

3. The League Constitution and By-Laws

Each league is an entity unto itself, which has been created by certain governing documents. These documents generally call for a chief executive and give that chief executive some plenary power to act in the best interests of the sport. That power can be exercised to discipline league participants including owners, coaches and players.

For example, until the recent debacle involving the firing of Fay Vincent, Major League Baseball gave its commissioner the power to reprimand, fine, suspend or remove any player who engages in conduct "which is deemed by the Commissioner not to be in the best interests of Baseball."[14] Similar disciplinary power is given to the Commissioner of the NFL,[15] the Commissioner of the NBA,[16] and the President of the NHL.[17]

4. Other Relevant Documents

While the uniform contract, the collective bargaining agreement, and the constitutions are implicated in most discipline cases, there are often other agreements or rules which come into play. For example, one of the most important disciplinary rules in baseball is Rule 21 of the "Major League Rules." Rule 21 proscribes a variety of misconduct, including fixing games or failing to report an attempt to induce a player to fix a game,[18] accepting gifts for defeating a competing club,[19] giving gifts to umpires,[20] betting on baseball games,[21] and attacking another player or an umpire during a game.[22] Rule 21 also has a catchall "best interests of Baseball" provision.[23]

Similarly, the individual clubs, as employers, may have their own rules which modify or govern the relationship between the player and the club. In basketball, for example, the collective bargaining agreement provides for a set of Standard Club Rules which govern a player's conduct.[24]

Finally, since discipline frequently arises as a result of on the field conduct, the playing rules of a sport may be relevant.

5. The Interplay of the Rules

Careful attention must always be given to how the various documents relate to each other. While the constitution of a league may purport to give its commissioner unlimited authority to impose discipline, that authority may be curtailed or subject to outside review as a result of the collective bargaining process and provisions incorporated into the collective bargaining agreement.

One illustration of the interplay of these documents is what happened in the early baseball drug cases. Pursuant to the catchall "best interests of baseball" provision of Rule 21, the Commissioner had adopted a rule that "[a] nyone involved in the illegal possession or use of drugs or illegal trafficking with drugs . . . will be subject to discipline." In 1983, four members of the Kansas City Royals were convicted of possessing cocaine and sentenced to jail. As a result of these drug convictions, and under the authority of Rule 21, Commissioner Bowie Kuhn suspended each player for one year.

The players challenged the Commissioner's action. In deciding these cases, the arbitrator ruled that the Commissioner did have a legitimate interest in the problem of drug use and had the right to impose discipline. But the players were successful in arguing that the action of the Commissioner was subject to the grievance procedure and reviewable through binding neutral arbitration.[25] Since that time, the Major League Baseball Players Association has successfully challenged the imposition of discipline by the Commissioner in a number of cases and had that discipline reduced.[26]

C. The Law

It is important to remember that the industry doesn't exist in a vacuum or get to create it's own legal world. With one notable exception,[27] sports are subject to external law. In the context of understanding the disciplinary process, two bodies of substantive law have particular application: labor law and private association law.

1. Labor Law

As indicated, the disciplinary structures in the major team sports have been incorporated into collective agreements, negotiated by the various players associations. These associations are labor unions, which derive their authority from virtue of Section 7 of the National Labor Relations Act.[28]

One critical feature of labor law is that the union is the exclusive representative of the employees in the bargaining unit.[29] As a result, attorneys and player agents can only participate in a collectively bargained grievance procedure if the union consents to such representation. In some cases, the unions have welcomed participation by representatives chosen by the players.[30] In other cases, the union is designated as the official representative and the appearance and participation of an agent or attorney is a matter of discretion.[31]

The flip side of the principle of exclusive representation in the union's "duty of fair representation." A union must represent all of its members "fairly, impartially, and in good faith."[32] So even if the employee is not allowed to select his own representative, the union is obligated to provide fair representation to all.

Another critical feature of the labor law is that it makes the collective bargaining agreement the supreme governing authority regarding the terms and conditions of employment. It also precludes an employer from changing those terms and conditions without engaging in collective bargaining.[33] This has served to dramatically limit the authority of the commissioners.

For example, in one case, Pete Rozelle was precluded from promulgating a rule regarding players leaving the bench and imposing fines on players under that rule, because his action was held to be the action of the employer, and constituted a unilateral change in the rights negotiated under the collective bargaining agreement.[34] In another case, an arbitrator ruled that Pete Rozelle could not unilaterally impose a new drug program, which included the unscheduled drug testing of players' because that too constituted a unilateral change in the terms and conditions of employment which could only be effectuated through collective bargaining.[35]

Another important consequence of the fact that the grievance procedure is a creature of and governed by labor law, is the way in which arbitration awards are treated. Under a group of cases known as the Steelworkers Trilogy,[36] the courts give great deference to arbitration awards and will almost never overturn them.[37] Thus, as a practical matter, once an arbitrator has made a ruling on the propriety of discipline, that ruling is final.

2. Private Association Law

Equally important is an area of law known as private association law. One general principle in private association law is that courts will hesitate to interfere with internal disputes involving members of a private association.[38] This principle will have application in any case where a player has been disciplined by a commissioner and seeks to have that decision reviewed by a court.

One famous illustration of this was the case of *Finley v. Kuhn*.[39] In 1976, Charles Finley sold the rights to Joe Rudi and Rollie Fingers to the Boston Red Sox and the rights to Vida Blue to the New York Yankees. Commissioner Bowie Kuhn disapproved the assignments as "inconsistent with the best interests of baseball." Finley then sued, challenging Kuhn's authority. The court looked to see whether the Commissioner had acted in good faith. Once the court determined that Kuhn had acted in good faith, it refused to look at whether Kuhn was "right or wrong." That issue was "beyond the competence" of the court. Similarly, most courts would not want to second guess David Stern as to what fine is appropriate when two players get into a fight during a basketball.

But there are other principles of private association law which may give a player a basis for challenging disciplinary action by a commissioner.[40] First, one can challenge any action that exceeds the legitimate authority granted to the commissioner. In *Atlanta National League Baseball Club & Ted Turner v. Bowie Kuhn*,[41] the Commissioner suspended Ted Turner for one year for tampering with another club's player. Kuhn also took away Atlanta's first round draft pick. Turner sued and the court held that it must not look closely at the reasons advanced for the discipline: "What conduct is 'not in the best interests of baseball' is of course, a question which addresses itself to the Commissioner, not this court." But the court reversed Kuhn as to the forfeiture of the draft pick, finding that such a penalty was not authorized by the Major League Agreement, which was the source of the Kuhn's power. This principle of *ultra vires* was also the basis upon which the Chicago Cubs was able to successfully challenge Fay Vincent's unilateral realignment of the divisions in the National League.[42]

Finally, a commissioner's actions may be challenged for procedural correctness. While private actors are not subject to the due process clause of the U.S. Constitution, certain principles of procedural fairness are required when discipline is imposed by a private association upon a member or employee. This was the basis of Pete Rose's challenge to the discipline by Bart Giamatti.

Under the Major League Agreement, the Commissioner had the power to both investigate and impose appropriate discipline for gambling.[43] The Commissioner was also given the power to promulgate rules of procedure, which rules were to recognize the right of any party to appear and be heard.[44] When Bart Giamatti heard rumors about gambling by Pete Rose, he hired John Dowd, a Washington D.C. lawyer, to investigate. Dowd's investigation resulted in a lengthy report, which based its conclusions on the accusations and testimony of two key informants: Ron Peters and Paul Janszen.

After receiving the report, but prior to holding any hearing on the Rose matter, Giamatti wrote a letter to a U.S. District Court judge who was about to sentence Peters for drug and income tax related crimes. In that letter, Giamatti stated that Peters had been "candid, forthright and truthful" in providing testimony against Rose.

The judge sent a copy of that letter to Rose's attorney. Rose's attorney then filed an action to enjoin the Commissioner from taking any further disciplinary action against Rose. He argued that the letter showed that Giamatti had literally "pre" judged the matter and that Rose was being denied his right to a proceeding conducted with "due regard for all the principles of natural justice and fair play." Based on this argument, Rose was successful in winning a 10-day restraining order.

The Rose case was ultimately settled, with Rose acceding to discipline by the Commissioner. But the notion that some kind of fundamental fairness and due process is required was, nonetheless, established.[45]

III. Categories of Discipline

The way discipline in imposed, contested and resolved, i.e., the structural mechanism is usually a function of the nature of the discipline and the kind of conduct that is involved. In this regard, it might be helpful to think of discipline as falling into three thematic groups: on the field misconduct, contract related discipline, and integrity related misconduct.

A. On the Field Misconduct

On the field discipline would include actions taken against a player for excessive violence, attacking another player, or misconduct involving an umpire or referee. As a general rule, discipline for on the field misconduct is initiated by a representative of the league (either a game official or someone appointed by the commissioner) and is ultimately resolved by a representative of the league (usually, the commissioner). While it is a frequent source of discipline, the issues are relatively simple. In addition, because the discipline stems from the game itself, the appropriateness of discipline, and the legitimacy of league self-rule, are generally accepted.

Examples of this kind of discipline are legion. In 1991, Ed Balfour of the Chicago Blackhawks was fined $600 for entering a referees dressing room after a game to dispute a call. Vince Coleman was suspended for seven days and fined an undisclosed amount for arguing with and bumping an umpire. Roger Clemens was suspended for five games and fined $10,000 for the dispute which led to his ejection in a 1990 American League Play-Off game. Mark Bavaro was fined $7,500 by Commissioner Tagliabue for a 1990 incident where he made accidentally knocked down an umpire who tried to break up a argument Bavaro was having with another player.[46]

B. Contract Related Discipline

Contract related discipline would involve violations of club rules, or the regulatory provisions of the contract between the player and the club. Contractual discipline is usually initiated by the club, and in most cases, the ultimate authority is a neutral arbitrator. The issues here, e.g., discipline for lateness, violating a weight clause, are ones that are analogous to non- sports settings and the typical labor relations grievance process seems most appropriate.

C. Integrity Related Misconduct

Integrity related discipline would include issues like gambling, drugs, and other off the field conduct which might effect the public's view of the player or the sport. Integrity related discipline is the most difficult area. On the one hand, the leagues have a legitimate interest in ensuring public respect for the product. And historically, giving broad disciplinary power to a commissioner has helped to keep the public's respect.[47] But from the players' perspective, there are core privacy issues involved in the regulation of off the field behavior. Moreover, the level of discipline implicated in cases of serious off the field misconduct is such that having a neutral decision maker can be of critical importance.

Some examples of the kinds of discipline which fall under the umbrella of integrity related misconduct are well known. Gambling is one important category. Pete Rose was banned for life as a result of gambling.[48] So too was Jack Molinas, of NBA infamy.[49] In football, Paul Hornung and Alex Karras were each suspended for one year for gambling on a football game.

Perhaps the largest group of cases under this category relate to drugs. As a result, they will be treated separately. But there is a wide variety of behavior that can come under this heading. For example, Zeke Mowatt and other members of the New England Patriots were fined for sexually harassing Lisa Olson, a female reporter, in the locker room. Vince Coleman's throwing a firecracker towards some fans and the almost daily assortment of police blotter items that involve athletes are also in this category.[50]

D. Drug Related Discipline

An unfortunate number of professional athletes have used drugs and this has created host of special problems. Drug use can tarnish the public's view of a sport, can impair an athlete's ability to perform (and thus destroy a club's investment), and can pose serious health problems for the athlete. From the athlete's perspective, there are some serious privacy issues, especially with regard to the question of testing.[51]

Because this is a particularly sensitive area, each league has struggled to come up with a comprehensive program that is acceptable to the players. In some cases agreement has been reached. For example, the NBA has a comprehensive anti-drug program which is incorporated in its collective bargaining agreement with the players. The league offers treatment for players who seek help but permanently disqualifies a player who does not come forward and gets caught.[52] But in baseball, the parties have not agreed to a comprehensive drug program. Instead, the Commissioner has promulgated and acted under his own guidelines. In response, the Players Association has accepted some of his decisions and challenged others.[53]

IV. An Analysis of League Disciplinary Systems

This section will examine the specific disciplinary system that is or was recently in place in each of the four major team sports. Although it is organized structurally; discipline by the club, discipline by the commissioner or president, and the applicable grievance procedures, some attempt is made to highlight the "thematic" issues articulated in section III.

A. Major League Baseball

In baseball, discipline may be imposed at three levels: by the club, by the President of the League, and by the Commissioner. But common to all is the rule that discipline may only be imposed for "just cause."[54] In almost every case, the entity imposing discipline is required to give written notice of such discipline to the player and the Players Association.[55] Players have the right to discover all documents and evidence "adduced during any investigation."[56] In addition, when possible, the Players Association must be notified in advance of any disciplinary interview of the player.[57]

1. Discipline by the Club

The club's right to impose discipline is explicitly recognized in the Collective Bargaining Agreement.[58] The specific power to discipline is contained in the regulations incorporated in the Uniform Player's Contract, which authorizes the club to impose a reasonable fine and/ or a suspension not to exceed thirty days, for a violation of any regulation or provision of the Uniform Player's Contract.[59] The club also has the right to terminate the contract if the player fails to conform to standards of good conduct or good citizenship, fails to keep himself in good condition, or fails to obey the club's training rules.[60]

2. Discipline by the Commissioner and League Presidents

As indicated previously, the Major League Agreement gave the Commissioner in baseball broad authority to discipline any player for any conduct deemed not to be in the "best interests of baseball."[61] Similar authority to discipline is contained in Rule 21 of the Major League Rules. In each Uniform Player's Contract, the player expressly agrees to abide by the Major League Agreement, the Major League Rules, in addition to League Rules and Professional Baseball Rules, so long as those rules do not conflict with specific provisions of the collective bargaining agreement and the Uniform Player's Contract.[62]

The collective bargaining agreement generally calls for binding resolution through neutral arbitration for any grievance. But discipline for on the field misconduct and some integrity related misconduct are handled in a different manner.

a. On the Field Misconduct

Where a dispute involves a fine or suspension which has been imposed by the League President or the Commissioner, for conduct on the playing field, the player has no recourse to neutral arbitration.[63] Binding "appellate" authority is retained in most cases by the very person who has imposed the discipline.[64]

b. Integrity Issues

Although the Commissioner is given binding authority with respect to action taken which involves "the preservation of the integrity of, or the maintenance of public confidence in, the game of baseball,"[65] this provision is narrowly construed. It was intended to cover disciplinary action for gambling and not for other related discipline such as that for drugs.[66] In baseball, discipline for misconduct like drug use is initiated by the Commissioner, but can be reviewed and modified by a neutral arbitrator.[67]

3. Grievance Procedure

Grievances with regard to discipline may be initiated by the player. Generally, the player is initially required to resolve any dispute with his club. If the matter is not resolved in that manner, step two calls for appeal by the player or the Players Association to the Player Relations Committee (an arm of Major League Baseball) and then to binding arbitration.[68] But in the case of discipline, the Players Association may only appeal if the player agrees.[69]

B. Football

The new Collective Bargaining Agreement between the National Football League Players Association and the National Football League in May of 1993 has two articles on discipline: one governs discipline by the club[70], the other governs discipline by the Commissioner[71]. While a player can be disciplined by either, he may not be disciplined by both the club and the Commissioner for the same act. When the Commissioner imposes discipline it will supersede or preclude discipline by the club.[72]

1. Discipline by the Club

With regard to discipline by the club, the collective bargaining agreement itemizes maximum fines for various violations. For example, the maximum fine for reporting overweight is $50 per lb., per day.[73] Each club is required to publish a list of the fines that it will impose for each of the designated violations.[74] The club is also admonished to impose discipline on a uniform basis but may treat players differently if there are "events which create an escalation of the discipline."[75]

The items covered include conduct which does not take place on the field, such as reporting late, losing equipment, failing to follow a rehabilitation program, and losing a playbook.[76] It also includes some misconduct on the playing field. For example, it subjects a player to a maximum fine of $200 for throwing a football into the stands and a maximum fine of $2,000 if a player is ejected from the game.[77]

The most serious discipline which can be imposed is for "conduct detrimental to the club." For such conduct, the player can be fined up to one week's salary or suspended without pay for up to four weeks.[78]

Finally, the collective bargaining agreement provides that a player may bring a "non-injury" grievance if he disagrees with the discipline.[79]

2. Discipline by the Commissioner

The NFL's Commissioner is given disciplinary authority of two types of matters: conduct on the playing field and conduct which is detrimental to the integrity and public confidence in the game.[80]

a. On the Field Conduct.

With regard to on the field conduct, discipline for "unnecessary roughness or unsportsmanlike conduct" is initially imposed by a person designated by the Commissioner after consultation with a representative of the NFLPA.[81] An appeal from that person's decision may be taken to the Commissioner. Discipline for other on the field conduct is imposed by the Commissioner in the first instance and the player, upon notice of the Commissioner's action, may appeal to the Commissioner.

b. Conduct Detrimental to the Integrity of the Game

The NFL Player Contract created by the collective bargaining agreement has a provision entitled "Integrity of Game" under which the player "recognizes the detriment to the League and professional football that would be result from impairment of public confidence in the honest and orderly conduct of NFL games or the integrity and good character of NFL players."[82] Under that provision, the player gives the Commissioner the right to fine, suspend or terminate the contract of a player, if he accepts a bribe, agrees to fix a game, fails to report an offer of a bribe, associates with gamblers, uses or provides any players with performance enhancing drugs, or "is guilty of any other form of conduct reasonably judged by the League Commissioner to be detrimental to the League or professional football."[83]

c. Rights on Appeal

Where a player or the NFLPA disagrees with the decision of the Commissioner or, in the case of on the field conduct, his representative, they may appeal back to the Commissioner. Upon such appeal, a hearing will be held where the player has a right to be represented by counsel of his choice.[84] But the Commissioner's decision is final and binding.[85]

3. Grievance Procedure

The collective bargaining agreement specifically allows a player to file a grievance, and he need not wait for the union to do so.[86] The collective bargaining agreement also authorizes a player to be represented by an attorney of his own choosing or the NFLPA at any hearing held.[87]

The collective bargaining agreement provides two different methods resolving grievances. First, it provides for binding arbitration by a neutral arbitrator jointly selected by the NFL and the NFLPA.[88] It also provides for resolution by a "Grievance Settlement Committee." This committee consists of the Executive Director of the NFLPA and the Executive Vice President for Labor Relations of the NFL. If these two agree on a resolution, that decision will be binding so long as no arbitration hearing on the grievance has been convened.[89]

C. Basketball

As in the other sports, players in basketball can be disciplined at two levels: by their clubs and by the league. Although there is a right to neutral binding arbitration for most grievances, the Commissioner is given certain disciplinary rights with regard to on the field conduct and integrity issues which are not subject to review.

1. Discipline by the Club

The club's right to discipline a player is expressly recognized by both the Uniform Player Contract[90] and the collective bargaining agreement.[91] Exhibit G to the NBA-CBA contains a set of Standard Club Rules which govern player conduct. Each club may draft its own supplemental rules, but those rules must be reviewed by the Players Association. If the Players Association objects and files a grievance, the rules do not become effective unless they are found to be reasonable by either a Grievance Panel or an Impartial Arbitrator.[92]

The Standard Rules start out by telling the player that he is expected to conduct himself both on and off the court according to the "highest standards of honesty, morality, fair play and sportsmanship," to conform his personal conduct to "standards of good citizenship," and to refrain from any conduct that might be "detrimental to the best interests of the club or the NBA." If a player does not meet the standards or engages in conduct detrimental to the club or the league, he is subject to fine, suspension or may be held to be in material breach of his contract.[93]

More specific rules relating to good conduct are also included. These include rules covering discipline for criminal conduct,[94] gambling,[95] violence,[96] and alcohol use.[97] These rules also deal with less serious conduct and provide for fines for a variety of infractions including the failure to have a proper uniform,[98] being late to a flight,[99] missing a practice,[100] and missing a promotional appearance.[101]

2. Discipline by the Commissioner and the Board of Governors

Under the collective bargaining agreement and the Uniform Player Contract, basketball players have agreed to subject themselves to discipline by the Commissioner and the Board of Governors in accordance with Rule 35 of the N.B.A. Constitution and By-Laws.[102] Rule 35 calls for dismissal and a lifetime ban for anyone caught fixing a basketball game and gives the Commissioner the power to impose discipline, at his discretion, for gambling on any basketball game.[103] It also allows the Commissioner to fine a player for any statement he makes or endorses which is prejudicial or detrimental to the best interests of basketball, and to suspend or fine the player for conduct that is detrimental to the NBA.[104] Finally, Rule 35 allows the Commissioner to discipline a player for contract tampering[105] and for conduct during a basketball game.[106]

Except where the Commissioner has disciplined a player for gambling, the Commissioner's actions under Rule 35 are subject to review by the Board of Governors.[107]

3. Grievance Procedure

Grievances for disciplinary action can be initiated by a player or, with the player's permission, by the Players Association.[108] In all grievances regarding discipline, the issue to be determined is whether there has been "just cause" for the penalty imposed.[109]

Grievances that are not resolved by the parties to the grievance can be appealed to a Grievance Panel, consisting of two persons appointed by the NBA and two persons appointed by the Players Association.[110] If a majority of the Grievance Panel agrees on a resolution, that resolution is binding.[111] If the matter is not resolved, it may be heard by the Impartial Arbitrator.[112]

The Impartial Arbitrator is given broad power to interpret and determine compliance with the collective bargaining agreement and player contracts, but there are some special limits and procedures with regard to discipline.[113] Any discipline imposed by the Commissioner (or his designee) for conduct on the playing court or "concerning the preservation of the integrity of, or the maintenance of public confidence in, the game of basketball," is not heard by the Impartial Arbitrator and may only be appealed to the Commissioner.[114] There is also a kind of minimum "amount in controversy requirement." A player cannot appeal to the Impartial Arbitrator from any suspension which is less than five days and cannot appeal a fine unless it exceeds $ 500 (if imposed by the club) or $ 5,000 (if imposed by the Commissioner).[115]

D. Hockey

The discipline system in hockey is somewhat different then the system in other sports in that a neutral arbitrator may be given jurisdiction over part of a dispute, i.e., determining the underlying facts, but at the same time limited in his or her ability to interpret the operative rules. As a result, careful attention must be paid not just to whether discipline is subject to review by a neutral arbitrator, but also to the scope of power given to the arbitrator.

1. Discipline by the Club

Hockey players may be disciplined by their club for violations of club rules, so long as these rules are reasonable and the players receive proper notice of the rules.[116] The only articulated limit on these rules is that a player may not be fined for " 'indifferent' play."[117] Conversely, the collective bargaining agreement specifically authorizes clubs to impose reasonable fines for players who report to work in an "over-weight condition."[118] Under the Standard Player's Contract, a player is also subject to discipline by the club for "any conduct impairing the thorough and faithful discharge of the duties incumbent upon the Player."[119] The normal discipline imposed may be a "reasonable fine" or suspension.[120] But if the player's conduct amounts to a material breach, the contract may be terminated.[121]

2. Discipline by the President

A player can be disciplined by the league in a variety of circumstances. Section 17 of the N.H.L. Constitution and By-Laws contains comprehensive guidelines on the circumstances and conduct which may give rise to discipline, the nature of the discipline, and certain procedures with regard to its implementation. For example, the rules provide for immediate expulsion, at the discretion of the President, for throwing a game or failing to report a solicitation to throw a game.[122] The President is also given broad power to fine, suspend or expel any player for any act which is "dishonorable, prejudicial to or against the welfare of the League or the game of hockey," whether this act takes place "during or outside the playing season."[123] Players may also be disciplined for public statements which are critical of the League, or the League "Officiating Staff."[124]

3. Grievance Procedure

The NHL has an somewhat intricate grievance mechanism which divides disciplinary grievances into two categories. Unresolved disputes as to the facts giving rise to discipline, and disputes concerning an interpretation of club rules or the collective bargaining agreement go to binding arbitration before an independent arbitrator.[125] While a player may request arbitration when there is a factual dispute, only the club or the NHLPA may seek arbitration where the dispute involves the interpretation of a club rule or the collective bargaining agreement. Disputes regarding the "severity" of discipline or the interpretation of the standard player contract, the NHL Constitution, or By-Laws or league rules, go to the binding arbitration by the league President.[126] In the case of discipline ordered by the President, there is a right of appeal to the Board of Governors.[127]

The power of the arbitrator is somewhat circumscribed even where the arbitrator does have jurisdiction. For example, an arbitrator is bound by a club's interpretation of its own rules so long as such an interpretation is not "arbitrary and capricious." Moreover, the arbitrator may not find a club's interpretation of a rule to be arbitrary or capricious if there is a "rational basis" for the club's interpretation.[128]

Disputes which involve more than one issue may be the subject of two arbitration proceedings. For example, if there is a factual dispute and a dispute as to the severity of the punishment, the factual issues may be resolved initially by the arbitrator. His or her written decision will be binding as to those facts, but the President will then get to decide on the severity of the penalty.[129]

V. CONCLUSION

This article has focused, primarily, on an analysis of the systems under which discipline may be imposed and challenged. Although there are some complexities, for each sport there should be one or more persons who work for the league or the players association who are familiar with the rules and with relevant precedent. Since the league and the players associations are ultimately responsible for making the collective bargaining relationship work, you should be able to get immediate assistance in the event that you or a client has a question.

In addition, you should recognize that whether an athlete gets disciplined, and the extent of discipline might depend as much on the skills of an advocate, as on the rules. As in most areas of the law, settlement is preferable to litigation. Even if a settlement cannot be reached, the decision of an arbitrator or commissioner will be a product of the case that is presented. The combination of thorough investigation and persuasive presentation is the *sine qua non* of effective advocacy in this field of law.

NOTES

1. *See* BASIC AGREEMENT BETWEEN THE AMERICAN LEAGUE OF BASEBALL CLUBS AND THE NATIONAL LEAGUE OF BASEBALL CLUBS AND MAJOR LEAGUE BASEBALL PLAYERS ASSOCIATION of January 1, 1990, Art. XII (A). [Hereinafter "MLB-CBA"].

2. NFL COLLECTIVE BARGAINING AGREEMENT 1993-2000, Art. VIII, Sec. 1 (a). [Hereinafter "NFL-CBA"].

3. *See* NHL CONSTITUTION , Art's. 2.1 (c) & 11.1 (1989).

4. *See* MLB-CBA Art. XII; NFL-CBA Art. VII & XI; COLLECTIVE BARGAINING AGREEMENT BETWEEN THE NATIONAL BASKETBALL ASSOCIATION AND THE NATIONAL BASKETBALL PLAYERS ASSOCIATION of November 1, 1988, Art. XXVII, § 3 (d), [hereinafter "NBA-CBA"]; MEMORANDUM OF UNDERSTANDING BETWEEN THE NATIONAL HOCKEY LEAGUE AND NATIONAL HOCKEY LEAGUE PLAYERS' ASSOCIATION — September 16, 1991, to September 15, 1993, Art. IV, § 4.02, [hereinafter "NHL-CBA"].

5. MLB-CBA Art. XI; NFL-CBA Art. IX; NBA-CBA Art. XXVIII; NHL-CBA Art. IV.

6. MLB-CBA Art. XII (A).

7. *Id.* at Art. XII (B).

8. *Id.* at Art. XII (C).

9. *Id.* at Art. XI (A)(1). Technically, the arbitration is held before a tripartite panel. But in reality, there is one arbitrator and two party advocates.

10. The collective bargaining agreement will usually have some language which amounts to a "supremacy clause." *See, e.g., id.* at Art. III — UNIFORM PLAYERS' CONTRACT. *See also, id.* at Art. II — Recognition, which allows a player to individually negotiate salary "over and above the minimum requirements" and special covenants which "actually or potentially provide additional benefits to the Player."

11. *See id.* at UNIFORM PLAYER'S CONTRACT, Art. 7.

12. *See* MARTIN J. GREENBERG, SPORTS LAW PRACTICE 247 (Vol. 2) |(1993).

13. NBA-CBA Art. 1, §§ 3 (d)(ii) and 4 (b).

14. MAJOR LEAGUE AGREEMENT, Art. I, § 3 (1988).

15. *See* NATIONAL FOOTBALL LEAGUE CONSTITUTION AND BY-LAWS, Art. VIII, §§ 8.13 and 8.14 (1988).

16. *See* NATIONAL BASKETBALL ASSOCIATION CONSTITUTION AND BY-LAWS, par. 24 & 35 (1989).

17. *See* NATIONAL HOCKEY LEAGUE CONSTITUTION AND BY-LAWS, §§ 17 and 18 (1991).

18. MAJOR LEAGUE RULES, Rule 21 (a).

19. *Id.* at Rule 21 (b).

20. *Id.* at Rule 21 (d).

21. *Id.* As the followers of the Pete Rose saga may already know, this rule calls for a one year suspension for any player (or umpire or club or league

official) who bets on any game, and a lifetime ban for any player (or umpire or club or league official) who bets on a game in which "he has a duty to perform."

22. *Id.* at Rule 21 (e).

23. *Id.* at Rule 21 (f).

24. NBA-CBA Art. XXIII.

25. *See* In the Matter of Arbitration Between Major League Players Ass'n (Ferguson Jenkins) and Major League Player Relations Comm. (Commissioner Bowie Kuhn), Decision No. 41, Gr. No. 80-25 (1980); In the Matter of Arbitration Between Bowie K. Kuhn, Commissioner of Baseball and Major League Players Ass'n (Willie Wilson, Jerry Martin) Panel Decision No. 54, Gr. Nos. 84-1 and 84-2 (April 3, 1984); In the Matter of Arbitration Between Major League Players Ass'n (Pascual Perez) and Bowie K. Kuhn, Commissioner of Baseball, Gr. No. 84-0 (April 27, 1984).

26. The most recent illustration of this was the reinstatement of pitcher Steve Howe after his suspension by Commissioner Vincent. *See* In the Matter of the Arbitration Between Major League Baseball Players Ass'n. and The Commissioner of Baseball, Gr. No. 92-7, 1992 (George Nicolou, Ch.).

27. *See* the infamous decision in *Flood v. Kuhn*, 407 U.S. 258 (1972), which reaffirmed the proposition that baseball was not subject to antitrust law.

28. 29 U.S.C. § 167.

29. *See* § 9(a) of the National Labor Relations Act, 29 U.S.C. § 159(a).

30. Art. IX, § 9 of the NFL-CBA allows a player to be represented by an attorney of his own choosing at any disciplinary hearing.

31. Under the Rules of Procedure for grievance arbitration in baseball, (which also govern hearings before the Commissioner and the League Presidents), a player has the right to be represented by the Players Association. Unless an attorney or agent has a "direct interest in the arbitration," his or her attendance appears to be discretionary with whoever is presiding. (*See* MAJOR LEAGUE RULES, Rules 2 [Attendance at Hearings] and 3 [Conduct of Hearings]). As a matter of practice, however, agents and attorneys have been allowed to be present and participate.

32. Steele v. Louisville & N.R.R., 323 U.S. 192 (1944).

33. The author recognizes that this is a gross oversimplification and apologizes to any labor law aficionado who is offended by this cursory treatment of a subject fraught with exception and nuance.

34. *See* National Football League Players Association v. National Labor Relations Board, 503 F.2d 12 (1974). For a history of football's struggle with the issue of drug testing *see* David Sisson & Brian Trexell, *The National Football League's Substance Abuse Policy: Is Further Conflict Between Player and Management Inevitable:*, 2 MARQ. SPORTS L.J. 1 (1991).

35. *See* National Football League Players Ass'n and National Football League Management Council and the National Football League (Kasher, Arb.) (October 25, 1986). For a history of baseball's struggle over the Commissioner's power to institute drug testing, *see*, Glenn Wong & Richard Ensor, *Major League Baseball and Drugs: Fight the Problem or the Player?*, 11 Nova L. Rev. 779 (1987).

36. Steelworkers v. American Manufacturing Co., 363 U.S. 564 (1960); Steelworkers v. Warrior & Gulf Navigation Co., 363 U.S. 574 (1960); Steelworkers v. Enterprise Wheel & Car Corp., 363 U.S. 593 (1960).

37. The most dramatic illustration of this in the sports context relates to free agency in baseball. Free agency was originally the product of an arbitration award in the so-called Messersmith-McNally case. (In re The Twelve Clubs Comprising National League of Professional Baseball Clubs and Twelve Clubs Comprising American League of Professional Baseball Clubs, Los Angeles and Montreal Clubs and Major League Baseball Players Association, Gr. Nos. 75 -27 and 75 -23, 66 Lab. Arb. 101 (Seitz, Chairman) (December 23, 1975.) Although the decision dramatically changed the entire structure of the industry, the courts refused to interfere and overturn it. *See* Kansas City Royals Baseball Corp. v. Major League Baseball Players Association, 532 F.2d 615 (8th Cir. 1976).

38. A most dramatic illustration of this principal occurred in *Carr v. St.John's University*, 17 A.D.2d 632, 231 N.Y.S.2d 410 (1962), where the court refused to interfere with a university's decision to expel Catholic students who had participated in a civil marriage ceremony.

39. 569 F.2d 527 (1978).

40. *See generally* Matthew Conway, *Sports Commissioners or Judges: Who Should Make the Call When the Game Is Over?*, XXIV Sulfolk U. L. Rev. 1043 (1990).

41. 432 F. Supp. 1213 (1977).

42. Chicago National League Ball Club Inc. v. Francis Vincent, Jr., No. 92 C 4398 (U.S.D.C., N.D.Ill. 1992) (unreported). *See also* Professional Sports, Ltd. v. Virginia Squires Basketball Club Limited Partnership, 373 F. Supp. 946 (W.D. Tex. 1974) (the court disagreed with a commissioner's broad interpretation of his powers); Riko Enterprises v. Seattle Supersonics, Inc., 357 F. Supp. 521 (S.D.N.Y. 1993).

43. Major League Agreement, Art. I, § 2 (a) & (b).

44. Major League Rules, Art. I, § 2 (d).

45. For a more comprehensive treatment of the Pete Rose saga and the power of commissioners, *see*, Matthew Pachman, *Limits on the Discretionary Powers of professional Sports Commissioners: A Historical and Legal Analysis of Issues Raised by the Pete Rose Controversy*, 76 Va. L. Rev. 1409 (1990).

46. Martin J. Greenberg , Sports Law Practice 1177 (Vol 1.) (1993).

47. For example, the general sports public was supportive of Fay Vincent's suspension of Steve Howe and outraged when it was overturned through arbitration.
48. Although Pete Rose was a manager at the time, the lifetime ban is the same for players and managers and in both cases, the Commissioner has the right to impose discipline.
49. *See* Molinas v. National Basketball Ass'n, 190 F. Supp. 241 (S.D.N.Y. 1961).
50. Just imagine the difficult issue that would face Commissioner Tagliabue if O.J. Simpson were an active player.
51. *See* Charles Palmer, *Drugs v. Privacy: The New Game In Sports*, 2 MARQ. SPORTS L. J. 175 (1992).
52. NBA-CBA Art. XXXIII.
53. For a review of the status of the Commissioner's Drug Policy in baseball *see* Edward Rippey, *Contractual Freedom Over Substance-Related Issues In Major League Baseball*, 1 SPORTS LAW. J. 143 (1994).
54. MLB-CBA Art. XII (A).
55. *Id.* at Art. XII (B).
56. *Id.* at Art. XII (C).
57. *Id.* at Art. XII (E).
58. *Id.* at Art. XII (A).
59. *Id.* at 96, Regulation 5.
60. *Id.* at UNIFORM PLAYERS CONTRACT, ¶ 7.
61. MAJOR LEAGUE AGREEMENT, Art. I, § 3.
62. MLB-CBA, UNIFORM PLAYERS CONTRACT, ¶ 9 (a).
63. *Id.* at Art. XI (C).
64. If a League President initially imposes a fine in excess of $500 or a suspension which exceeds ten days, it may be appealed to the Commissioner. *Id.* at Art. XI (C)(2).
65. *Id.* at Art. XI (A) (1) (b).
66. This has been a sensitive issue for baseball. The original language was negotiated while Bowie Kuhn was Commissioner. *See* MARVIN MILLER, A WHOLE DIFFERENT BALL GAME: THE INSIDE STORY OF BASEBALL'S NEW DEAL 214-215 (1991). Successive Commissioners have agreed to the original understanding behind and interpretation of that provision. *See, e.g.*, letter from Francis Vincent to Donald M. Fehr, Attachment 4 to the MLB-CBA. In addition, the players have reserved the right to reopen collective bargaining in the event that a Commissioner attempts to exercise authority in a way that is inconsistent with that understanding. (MLB-CBA Art. XI (A)(1)).
67. *See* Major League Players Ass'n (Ferguson Jenkins), Dec. No. 41, Gr. No. 80-25; Bowie K. Kuhn, Panel Dec. No. 54, Gr. No.s 84-1 and 84-2; Major League Players Ass'n (Pascual Perez), Gr. No. 84-0, *supra* note 26.
68. MLB-CBA Art. XII (B).
69. *Id.* at Art. XII (E).

70. NFL-CBA Art. VIII.
71. *Id.* at Art. XI.
72. *Id.* at Art. VIII, § 3.
73. *Id.* at Art. VIII, § 1 (a).
74. *Id.* at Art. VIII, § 2.
75. *Id.* at Art. VIII, § 3.
76. *Id.*
77. *Id.* at Art. VIII, § 1 (a).
78. *Id.*
79. *Id.* at Art. VIII, § 4.
80. *Id.* at Art. XI, § 1.
81. *Id.* at Art. XI, § 1 (b).
82. *Id.* at Appendix C: NFL PLAYER CONTRACT, § 15.
83. *Id.*
84. *Id.* at Art. XI, § 3.
85. *Id.* at Art. XI, § 1 (c).
86. *Id.* at Art. IX, § 2.
87. *Id.* at Art. IX, § 10.
88. *Id.* at Art. IX, §§ 6 & 8.
89. *Id.* at Art. IX, § 13.
90. NBA-CBA, UNIFORM PLAYER CONTRACT, para. 4.
91. *Id.* at Art. XXVIII, § 3 (f).
92. *Id.* at Art. XXIII. *See also* Art. I, § 5 (f).
93. *Id.* at Exhibit G "Introduction."
94. *Id.* at Exhibit G "Professional Conduct."
95. *Id.* at Exhibit G "Gambling."
96. *Id.* at Exhibit G "Violence."
97. *Id.* at Exhibit G "Alcoholic Beverages."
98. *Id.* at Exhibit G "Equipment."
99. *Id.* at Exhibit G "Travel Arrangements."
100. *Id.* at Exhibit G "Attendance and Punctuality at and for Practices, Meetings and Games."
101. *Id.* at Exhibit G "Promotional Appearances."
102. *See id.* at Art. I, § 5 (l) and UNIFORM PLAYER CONTRACT, para. 15.
103. NBA CONSTITUTION AND BY-LAWS, Rule 35 (a) & (g). A similar rule found the basis of the discharge in *Molinas*, 190 F.Supp. at 241.
104. NBA CONSTITUTION AND BY-LAWS, Rule 35 (c) & (e).
105. *Id.* at Rule 35 (f).
106. *Id.* at Rule 35 (d).
107. *Id.* at Rule 35 (h).
108. NBA-CBA Art. XXVIII, § 2 (a) (1).
109. *Id.* at Art. XXVIII, § 3 (d).
110. *Id.* at Art. XXVIII, § 2 (c). The parties can agree to skip this step and go directly to the Impartial Arbitrator.
111. *Id.* at Art. XXVIII, § 2 (c) (4).

112.*Id.* at Art. XXVIII, § 2 (c) (5).

113.*Id.* at Art. XXVIII, § 2 (d) (3).

114.*Id.* at Art. XXVIII, § 2 (f) (2).

115.*Id.* at Art. XXVIII, § 3 (g).

116.NHL-CBA Art. VII, § 7.02. *See also* par. 4 of the STANDARD PLAYER'S CONTRACT (1986 Form; Revised 1988) [hereinafter "NHL-SPC"].

117.NHL-CBA Art. VII, § 7.03

118.*Id.*

119.NHL-SPC para. 4.

120.*Id.*

121.*Id.* at para. 14 (a).

122.NHL CONSTITUTION AND BY-LAWS , Rule 17.2.

123.*Id.* at Rule 17.3 (a). The President may delegate disciplinary authority that comes under this rule for "incidents arising under the playing rules," i.e., game related misconduct. This appears to supplement the power of on-ice officials to suspend players for up to twenty games for on-ice misconduct.

124.*Id.* at Rule 17.4 (a). With regard to criticism of the officials or of the officiating, the player may be fined up to $1,000.

125.NHL-CBA Art. 4.01, 4.02, and 4.03. Rule 17.8 of the NHL Constitution and By-Laws also gives the player the right to a suspension reviewed by the President.

126.NHL-CBA Art. 4.05.

127.NHL CONSTITUTION AND BY-LAWS, Rule 17.11. This right of appeal does not include action taken by the President for betting on a championship game.

128.NHL-CBA Art. 4.07.

129.*Id.* at Art. 4.06.

Sudden Death: League Labor Disputes, Sports Licensing, and Force Majeure Neglect[*]

Gary D. Way

Since the 1970s, lockouts and strikes have become an almost annual feature of American professional team sports. Gary Way's essay explores an important, though not always anticipated, consequence of work stoppages in the sport on sports marketing arrangements. Licensing agreements are invariably created with the expectation that play will proceed as normal. When that expectation is not met, the situation for sports licensees can quickly become critical.

Way explores this phenomenon from the perspective of the force majeure clause—a provision in a contract that addresses the occurrence of an unforeseeable natural or human event beyond the control of the parties to the contract. Although force majeure (literally, "superior force") clauses have not been unknown in the world of sports licensing, Way argues that in practice sports licensees have usually failed to obtain effective protection against such events in spite of the recurrence of work stoppages.

Way's essay is both an analysis of a particular problem and a prescription for avoiding that problem.

I. Introduction

In most rights agreements entered into with a major professional sports league, team or player association, *force majeure*[1] protection is badly neglected—to the extent it is addressed at all. Until relatively recently, where such protection existed, frequently the provision had been "thrown-in" at the 12th-hour request of the licensee or sponsor ("licensee") with minimal care given to the exact formulation of the clause. Often, the resulting language was simply recycled *force majeure* "boilerplate" long ago

*From Volume 7, Number 2, Sprint 1997, pp. 427-463.

borrowed from some other party's agreement. The relative importance of such provisions within an agreement is perhaps best signaled by their typical insertion at the end of the contract, just before the provision that states that "paragraph captions are for convenience only." However, the unprecedented extent of labor strife in Major League Baseball ("MLB"), the National Hockey League (the "NHL") and the National Basketball Association (the "NBA") experienced during the 1994-95 and 1995-96 playing seasons[2] sent many licensees and licensors alike flipping furiously to the last pages of their agreements to determine what contractual protection was afforded them in the event of a League work stoppage. Too often, the answer was none, or the answer was unclear. Prior to the opening of MLB's spring training in 1995, that precise state of uncertainty metastasized into a suit being filed against the New York Yankees by their radio broadcast partner over the Yankees' use of replacement players[3] —a suit that could have been easily avoided with the mere addition of a single sentence to their agreement.

While the average contract lawyer is undoubtedly familiar with *force majeure* provisions, and views the drafting or negotiation of such provisions as a routine matter, relatively few have much experience with them in a sports licensing context. Unfortunately, this inexperience was often painfully brought to light amid the multi-sport labor discord that reached its zenith in Autumn 1994.[4] In the wake of the then-current MLB player strike, and threatened disruptions of the upcoming NHL and NBA seasons, *force majeure* provisions contained in pre-existing agreements came under close scrutiny. Moreover, such provisions came to be viewed as essential components of every contemplated pro sports rights agreement and were often elevated to "deal breaker" points in many negotiations.

This article is intended to help the attorney casually involved with sports licensing to negotiate these critical provisions, as well as provide some useful suggestions for the well-versed. Part I of this article provides a comparative view of the negotiating posture of parties towards *force majeure*. Part II catalogs the *force majuere* provisions currently in use in professional sports licensing. Part III subsequently analyzes the protection afforded by these provisions under various labor dispute scenarios. Part IV then examines and explains the serious defects commonly found in such provisions and, lastly, Part V provides practical drafting advice coupled with recommended approaches to various *force majeure* issues.

II. THE FACE-OFF

Providing licensees with *force majeure* protection is outside the licensing modality of the Leagues. The agreements generated by Major League Baseball Properties ("MLBP"), NBA Properties ("NBAP"), National Football League Properties ("NFLP") and NHL Enterprises ("NHLE")—the licensing arms of the respective Leagues (collectively, "Properties")—do not, as a matter of routine, include *force majeure* provisions.[5] A survey of the form merchandise licenses issued by the various Properties (the most numerous forms of agreement in effect[6]), and the three professional player associations ("PAs") engaged in licensing,[7] will reveal that *force majeure* is not included as a standard term or condition. An understanding of the rationale behind this conspicuous absence is critical to developing intelligent and coherent strategies for negotiating these sensitive provisions.

Underlying all licensor aversion to *force majeure* relief is a single universal imperative—the desperate need to meet its earning goals. Over the past decade, licensing has evolved from essentially a public relations function, and negligible source of income, to a major profit center. Fueled by a long string of successive team merchandise sales records, team owners (the exclusive shareholders in each League's Properties) have come to expect ever-increasing royalty and rights fee payments. For each season, benchmarks are established based upon licensing payments made by Properties to their owners the preceding season and revenue projections made based upon guaranteed royalties and scheduled rights fee payments. The high owner expectations created by the extraordinary marketing success of the past ten years, coupled with soaring team operation costs, places enormous pressure on each League's Properties (or team marketing department in the case of direct licensing arrangements such as local market sponsorships, as opposed to league- wide, sponsorship arrangements) to exceed the past year's performance and to meet their forecasted revenue level.

That pressure has, in recent years, been greatly exacerbated by the new economics wrought by collective bargaining among the Leagues and their respective PAs. Two of the last four collective bargaining agreements ("CBA") negotiated—the NFL and NBA CBAs—0provide for profit sharing that guarantees their players near-equal (and even majority) share of broadly defined League revenues,[8] while the recently ratified MLB labor agreement provides for "an unprecedented level of revenue sharing between rich and poor clubs."[9]

Furthermore, the NFL/NBA kinds of CBAs provide players with participation in league revenue streams that historically have not been shared with players, such as luxury suite revenues and international television rights fees.[10] As a consequence of the new advent of owner sharing of previously sheltered revenue, leagues and teams are extremely reluctant to assume any financial risk in the licensing area—unlike in their core business (i.e., competitive team sports) where risk is commonplace (e.g., long-term guaranteed player contracts, or the private financing of stadium/arena construction).

Hand-in-hand with the organization imperative is a deeply held fundamental belief about the nature of the merchandise licensing business. Licensors view licensed product agreements as unique investment vehicles. A League license provides a manufacturer entree into the $11.5 billion sports licensing market (pre-baseball strike)[11]—a market that has enjoyed sustained, often double-digit, growth for over a decade. In light of that, licensors feel justified in insisting upon a guaranteed fee in return for providing a licensee with such an extraordinary investment opportunity. Moreover, a valid argument can be made that every team sport and/or event property carries with it certain inherent risks that are properly borne by the licensee. Team popularity, measured by either merchandise sales or television ratings, has always been a function of on-field success which, by its very nature, is speculative. Event-based licensing is similarly speculative. Typically, licensees are often required to commit to large royalty guarantees well in advance of the event and are, thus, forced to "roll the dice." No protection against under performance is given to them. For example, as a condition to participation in the 1994 World Cup soccer licensing program, manufacturers were required to make significant royalty guarantees without any assurance as to how the event would be received in the United States—a first-time host country. In view of the inherent speculative nature of sports merchandise licensing, licensors of a proven property such as the Leagues do not believe that they should have to share with the manufacturer the risk that their property may be temporarily rendered unpopular, such as by a labor dispute—particularly when diminished popularity has always been a licensee risk. Moreover, licensors are particularly unsympathetic to sharing business loss consequent of a work stoppage in view of the fact that the licensor's loss of revenue and damage to its business will invariably far exceed that of any particular licensee.

There are also technical reasons for the absence of *force majeure* provisions in most sports licenses. The purposes of a *force majeure* provision are "to limit damages in a case where the reasonable expectations of the parties and the performance of the contract have been frustrated by circumstances beyond the control of the parties."[12] The essence of a trademark license (or agreement granting rights of publicity) is the conveyance of intellectual property rights. Because of the nature of such rights, the occurrence of a *force majeure* provision arguably should neither impair the ability of the licensor to convey its property rights nor arguably the licensee's ability to exercise them. Accordingly, since a *force majeure* provision should not frustrate a party's performance, protection against such occurrences is not required.

From the licensor's perspective, there are also two significant practical reasons for its distaste for *force majeure* provisions. First, it is simply sound business and legal practice for a licensor to not gratuitously include any provision that primarily, if not exclusively, operates to the benefit of the licensee. This is particularly true in merchandise licensing. Under a merchandise license, the grantor has few affirmative obligations: to convey incontestable rights; to provide guidance on proper usage of the licensed properties; to exercise reasonable quality control, and to maintain and enforce its rights in and to the licensed properties. All of these obligations can be performed notwithstanding any manner of *force majeure*. On the other hand, a merchandise license imposes numerous non-waivable requirements upon the licensee such as: meeting a product launch date; the manufacture of specific numbers of product lines or styles; the maintenance of prescribed inventory levels; merchandise support obligations; the active advertisement and promotion of the licensed products; and minimum royalty payments to name a few. These types of obligations may be difficult, if not impossible, to meet in the face of the more "common" *force majeure* conditions such as fire, natural disasters and other "acts of God." Until the acute labor strife of the past three years, it was usually with these more common events in mind—occurrences affecting product manufacture or distribution--that licensees were motivated to request *force majeure* protection.[13]

The second, and in some circumstances the most compelling, reason for licensor resistance to labor-based *force majeure* is that in the event of a work stoppage, royalties and rights fee payments may be the licensor's principal or only source of revenue. This is particularly true of player associations. For PAs, licensing revenues are even more critical than they are for Leagues or teams; they constitute their single-largest source of income and fund such union work stoppage related activities as litigation and hardship benefits for players.[14] As Donald Fehr, Executive Director of the Baseball PA, has stated with respect to licensing revenues, "[t]he ability to generate income on behalf of the players provides [the Players Association] with resources that otherwise would be difficult to secure".[15]

It is against the above backdrop that a licensee must negotiate for relief against League labor disputes.[16] While licensors are reluctant to grant such concessions, chiefly because of their risk aversion, relief is often available to a licensee making a substantial financial commitment to the League and willing to support a League's brand building activities through significant electronic media and event sponsorship support.

III. Reading the Coverage

A. Checking The Formation

To the extent *force majeure* protection can be found in sports marketing agreements, three types are the most common: (i) the generic *force majeure* provision ("Generic Provision"); (ii) the so-called "Strike Clause;" and (iii) the sports-specific *force majeure* provision ("Sports FM").

Generic Provisions tend to be formulated in one of two ways. One is the truly generic form. This form simply provides that relief is available "[i]f either party hereto shall have been prevented, in whole or in part, from performing its obligations hereunder by virtue of any cause beyond such party's control . . ." The other common form of Generic Provision contains an enumeration of specific *force majeure* conditions limited to casualties, "acts of God" and governmental prohibitions. Typical of this latter form is the following clause which relieves performance in the event of "fire, flood, war, governmental law or restrictions, natural disaster, Acts of God, or other similar causes beyond the reasonable control of such party."

A Strike Clause is essentially a generic provision containing a reference to labor disputes in the form of a strike. *Force majeure* provisions containing strike language generally follow the same construction as the Generic Provision but include a non-specific reference to strike. The following enumeration is typical: "fire, flood, war, riot, strike, natural disaster, compliance with law or governmental regulation, or any other event beyond the control of the party."

The third variation, the Sports FM, is tailored to relationships involving sports property licensors and specifically contemplates

League labor disputes. The following examples are common forms of this type of provision:

> Neither party shall hold the other responsible for any delay or failure of performance occasioned or caused by acts beyond the reasonable control of the party including, but not limited to, acts of war, fire, natural disaster or other acts of God, *interruption of the . . . Season . . .* (emphasis added)

or

> Neither party shall hold the other responsible for any delay or failure of performance occasioned or caused by acts beyond the reasonable control of the party including, but not limited to, labor disputes [*between the League and its players*], acts of war, fire, natural disaster . . . (emphasis added)

B. Zone Coverage

As the Generic Provision illustrates, it is not uncommon to find a *force majeure* provision that does not list labor disputes in its enumeration. To a party seeking to take advantage of such a provision in the event of a League labor dispute, the availability of relief will depend on the form of the particular provision. If the provision does not contain an enumeration, then a labor dispute is likely to be deemed covered consistent with the principle of *contra proferentem* which provides that an ambiguous provision is construed against the party that selected the language[17]—which in most cases, will have been the licensor/drafter. Conversely, if the provision contains an enumeration, the omitted reference to strike will be fatal to the charging party. With respect to enumerations, it is a well-settled principle of contract interpretation that "only if the *force majeure* clause specifically includes the event that actually prevents a party's performance will that party be excused."[18]

In the absence of specific reference to labor events, a party could nonetheless assert that a League work stoppage is covered under the commonly included catch-all clause "and other acts beyond the control of a party." However, a party is unlikely to prevail on this theory either. Applying the principle of *ejusdem generis* that governs the interpretation of such clauses, general words following a detailed enumeration are not to be given expansive meaning; they are confined to things of the same nature as the particular matter aforementioned.[19] Since the recited conditions all pertain to occurrences affecting the ability to manufacture or distribute merchandise, a League work stoppage is different in kind and nature from the enumerated *force majeure* events and, therefore, falls outside the events contemplated by the provision.

A licensee fortunate enough to have a Strike Clause in its agreement may well consider itself protected in the event of a League labor dispute. However, even when strike is included in the *force majeure* enumeration, whether such language will provide the licensee with protection in the event of various forms of labor dispute is far from clear.

If the reference to strike is non-specific, and therefore may refer to those of a manufacturer's workers, material supplier, shippers, *et cetera*, and a licensee seeks to take advantage of a Strike Clause in the event of a player strike, a licensor may be able to successfully rebut the presumption that a Strike Clause contemplates player strikes. The mere reference to strike in this kind of generic *force majeure* provision is not so free from ambiguity as to preclude extrinsic evidence. The proper interpretation of words in an agreement frequently depends on the circumstances that existed when the contract was concluded and then within the contemplation of the parties.[20] As discussed above, it has usually been with production or distribution thwarting events in mind that manufacturers have sought *force majeure* protection. Upon a trial or in arbitration, a licensor may be able to show that such occurrences were the expressed and exclusive concern of the licensee and, thus, establish the understanding of the parties as of the inception of the agreement.[21] As any such case will necessarily turn on its particular facts, it is impossible to predict the likelihood of a licensor's success under such a scenario.

The likely result is much clearer in a case where a licensee seeks to invoke a Strike Clause in response to an owner lock-out; the licensee is unlikely to prevail. Many Strike Clauses are silent on the effect of a lock-out. Typically, licensees are narrow in their request for *force majeure* protection. In negotiating such a provision, licensees regularly make a specific request for the inclusion of the word "strike." The experienced drafter, in keeping with the time-honored principle of providing for only as much as was expressly requested and agreed upon, will only provide for strikes. Unfortunately, such an oversight on the part of the licensee can have devastating consequences.

While it is not uncommon for lay people and licensing lawyers unfamiliar with labor law—as is sometimes the case with those responsible for negotiating licensing agreements—to think of strike and lock-out as being interchangeable, the two terms clearly are not. The term strike is statutorily defined[22] and distinguished from lock-out throughout the National Labor Relations Act ("NLRA").[23] Consequently, the term strike is unlikely to be interpreted by any court as being inclusive of lock-out. Accordingly, absent specific reference to lock-out, the doctrine that only the occurrence of a specifically enumerated event will excuse a party's non-performance should obtain to bar reliance upon a Strike Clause in the event of a lock-out.[24] While a licensee can argue that a lock-out is an event of the same kind and nature as a strike and, therefore, should be covered under the principle of *ejusdem generis*, such argument should be unpersuasive since a lock-out is a clearly foreseeable event that could have been easily guarded against in the agreement.[25] Indeed, in view of an express reference to strike in an enumeration, a court should conclude that the omission of lock-out from such a provision was intentional.

C. The Curve Ball: Use of Replacements

Assuming the existence of a *force majeure* provision that covers a "work stoppage" or "interruption of the season," what is the effect of conducting games using replacement players? For instance, the NFL played three regular season games using replacement players during the 1987 strike-shortened season.[26] More recently, MLB opened Spring Training and the 1995 exhibition season with replacement players. The use of replacement players raises a unique paradox—the existence of a covered force majeure occurrence (i.e., a strike or lock-out), but a continuation of play. If this contingency is not specifically addressed in an agreement, it may be left to the courts to determine the obligations of the parties. Such was the case in *WABC-AM Radio v. New York Yankees*.

WABC-AM Radio holds the radio broadcast rights to New York Yankee games and earns revenues in connection therewith through its sale of advertising time in these broadcasts.[27] In its complaint, WABC asserted that it "would not have agreed to pay millions of dollars to [the Yankees] for such rights unless it was understood that professional Major League baseball games by the real Yankees would be scheduled and made available for broadcast."[28] Following the Yankees' announced plan to provide for broadcast games to be played by replacement players, and WABC's determination that such games were "valueless" to [the station] because virtually no advertiser will pay to advertise on broadcasts of such games" and that the provision of such games was "a breach by [the Yankees] of its contractual obligations,"[29] WABC filed an action seeking a court declaration of each

party's contractual obligations and seeking $10 million in damages—
a suit necessitated only because of the failure of the parties to address
this foreseeable occurrence in their contract.[30]

Presumably, it is only because the agreement between the parties
does not contain a *force majeure* provision dealing with labor disputes
that the station was compelled to resort to litigation for a determination of its rights.[31] As a result of this same omission, Plaintiff's claim
was fashioned to rely upon classic principles of contract law. The
gravamen of WABC's claim was that the Yankees' decision to provide
the station with "replacement games" to broadcast because of the
player strike "deprive[d] WABC of its reasonably expected benefits
under the Agreement"[32] and "breach[ed] the implied covenant of
good faith and fair dealing in the Agreement."[33] While the players'
return to work effectively mooted this action and resulted in the suit
being dropped,[34] the fact remains that without a *force majeure* frame
of reference in which to interpret the rights of the parties, it would
have been difficult to predict the outcome of this suit. However, it is
clear that with the inclusion of a Sports FM, the Court's decision
would have at least been based on an interpretation of specific
agreement terms rather than basic contract principles.[35]

IV. Technical Fouls

As a result of the cursory consideration often involved in last-minute
agreement to include a *force majeure* provision in a particular license,
it is not surprising that a close reading of such provisions often reveals
a variety of drafting flaws. The most serious of these flaws are found
in their scope of coverage, the triggering language used, tolling clauses
and in the lack of a damage requirement.

A. Scope of Coverage

For the reasons discussed in Section III above, the failure to fully
address the scope of coverage can have disastrous consequences.
Often, in order to ensure the fullest extent of coverage, parties will use
terms such as "labor dispute," "work stoppage" or "season interruption," rather than specific reference to strike and lock-out. While the
use of such terms will avoid the interpretation problems discussed
above, nonetheless, underlying each of these word choices is a

potential dispute. Typical of the above-described provisions is the following:

> Neither party shall hold the other responsible for any delay or failure of performance occasioned or caused by acts beyond the reasonable control of the party including, but not limited to, *labor disputes*, acts of war, fire, natural disaster . . . (emphasis added).

While the term "labor disputes" provides maximum breadth of coverage, its use can lead to issues as to what kind of occurrence can trigger the operation of the provision.[36] The cited language begs the question of what constitutes a "dispute." Does the expiration of a collective bargaining agreement without reaching a new accord qualify?[37] What about the initiation of antitrust litigation? The pronouncement by a principal that the parties are "far apart," or declaration of an impasse? These are all fairly typical occurrences during a labor negotiation and invariably precede a strike or a lock out. These types of occurrences create an atmosphere of uncertainty in the marketplace and, more often, it is this uncertainty that is the proximate cause of the injury to a licensee's business. Typically, it is the fear of a work stoppage that prompts retailers to curtail their up-front commitment for merchandise or to adopt a "wait and see" approach to ordering.[38] Given certain kinds of saber rattling, orders for merchandise for the particular sport often decline substantially long before a work stoppage materializes.[39] Consequently, if the reason for inclusion of the provision is to protect a licensee against the adverse affect of a labor dispute, then logically the affected party should be entitled to avail itself of such protection at the earliest point at which its business is demonstrably injured.

Other terms popular with many drafters are the phrases "work stoppage," "interruption of season," or similar language. As with the use of labor dispute, utilizing work stoppage language is an effective means of "covering the bases." While there can be no serious debate that such language encompasses both strike and lock-out scenarios, this language can give rise to issues of coverage as well. Specifically, it is possible for there to be a strike or lock-out, yet for an affected party to not be able to avail itself of protection afforded by these types of provisions precisely because of that language choice. Since these types of provisions are triggered by a halt in play, absent a specific contract carve-out, the use of replacement players would deprive a licensee of a *force majeure* claim based on work stoppage/interruption for any period of play using replacements. Moreover, should an agreement be entered into during a League's off-season, if a League engages replacement players and opens its season as scheduled (pre-season or regular) using replacements then there will have been no "work stoppage" or "interruption" at all. Finally, if the work action commences during the off-season, such as the NBA's 1995 summer long lock-out, an injured licensee will not be able to seek relief if its entitlement is based on season pre-emption or lost games language.[40]

One of the most common drafting mistakes in the area of coverage is to over describe the labor event. In an effort to be precise, some drafters will gratuitously include modifiers, the unintended effect of which is to convert language that is inclusive into language of exclusion. For example, consider the above-quoted provision but modified as follows:

> Neither party shall hold the other responsible for any delay or failure of performance occasioned or caused by acts beyond the reasonable control of the party including, but not limited to, labor disputes [*between the League and its players*], acts of war, fire, natural disaster . . . (emphasis added).

By the addition of the emphasized language, the extent of coverage is actually lessened. Whereas the clause without the qualifying language was not limited simply to those involving players, with the addition of the adverbial phrase, the type of disputes now covered is specifically limited to those between the League and its players. Nevertheless, given that player-owner labor disputes have been of late the paramount *force majeure* concern of a licensee, and that the addition of qualifying language makes the coverage of any such disputes unequivocal, it may appear that whatever other coverage that is lost by this additional language is of little consequence. However, when one views the other labor dispute potentialities, it is obvious that the risks that have been assumed by virtue of over specification can have equally devastating consequences. For instance, by solely specifying labor disputes involving players, in the event of a strike by game officials (e.g., referees, umpires, etc.) that forces the cancellation or relocation of games a licensee would not be entitled to any relief. Such an occurrence is no phantom risk. Prior to the start of the 1995 MLB Season, league umpires—who had been locked out since the first of that year—successfully petitioned the Ontario Labour Relations Board to bar MLB's use of replacement umpires in the province.[41] Obviously, in the face of that decision, had the parties not reached a settlement, the removal of Blue Jay games out of the province would have had a significant adverse economic impact upon the team's broadcast partners,[42] sponsors and Canadian licensees. More recently, the NBA played its entire exhibition season schedule, and the first month of the 1995- 96 regular season, using replacement officials.

Another common pitfall, and similar to the above, resulting from the ill-considered use of modifiers can be found in clauses that are based upon the interruption of a "Season." As with the over-specification of labor disputes, the addition of qualifying language to the term "Season" can create more problems than it solves. Consider the following clause:

> Neither party shall hold the other responsible for any delay or failure of performance occasioned or caused by acts beyond the reasonable control of the party including, but not limited to, acts of war, fire, natural disaster or other acts of God, *interruption of the [name of League]* Season . . . (emphasis added).

As drafted, the emphasized language provides the broadest coverage possible with respect to the interruption of a League's season. Now, consider the effect of this provision as commonly modified. Insert the word "Regular" before season, and by definition you exclude the interruption of League playoffs. To cover that possibility, some will sandwich Season between the words "Regular" and "Playoffs" so as to read ". . . interruption of the League's Regular Season or Playoffs." The result of such variation is to leave a licensee remediless against an interruption of pre-season play. Add "Pre- Season" to the list, and the clause remains ambiguous as to a cancellation of a League's All-Star event. For example, the NFL's Pro-Bowl is neither part of the Pre-Season, Regular Season or Playoffs.[43] All of the issues presented by this paragraph can be avoided simply by using "Season" on a stand-alone basis. As to the distinctions between the Pre, Regular and Playoff Seasons, all are clearly covered by the term "Season." As to events such as All-Star games, inasmuch as each is typically a "scheduled" event on a League's season calendar—absent specification that renders them not susceptible to categorization—it would be extremely difficult to argue that they are not part of the "Season."[44] As the foregoing illustrates, in this area, general language is superior to specific language.

Finally, a licensee should insist upon *force majeure* protection throughout the term of its agreement. Too often, when a licensee is negotiating an agreement during a period of labor instability, its focus will be locked on the immediately threatened season. As a result, some licensees will readily settle for a provision that provides protection for the upcoming season. Unfortunately for such licensees, as the labor negotiating history of MLB, the NBA, NFL and NHL each demonstrate, once a CBA expires, it often takes far in excess of a single season to conclude a new pact.[45] Consequently, for the MLB or NBA licensees that accepted a provision that specifically provided relief in the event of an interruption of the 1994 Season of each respective League, it found its hard-won right extinguished by its terms when the MLB strike carried over into the following season and the NBA's lock-out did not commence until after the conclusion of its 1994-95 Season.

B. Triggering Devices

In addition to the coverage problems discussed above, there are a number of other common drafting flaws that can render the applicability of a *force majeure* provision ambiguous. Chief among them is the language that triggers the protection of the provision.

Invariably, the right to invoke the labor-related clause of a *force majeure* provision is based upon the occurrence of some specified event. Unfortunately, some drafters will use as the triggering occurrence an event or scenario that is expressed in vague or ambiguous terms. For example:

> If as a result of a labor dispute . . . there is an interruption of any commercial announcements to be telecast hereunder, which continues for a *prolonged period of time* . . . (emphasis added)

or

> If a *material number* of games cannot be broadcast because of . . . strike . . . (emphasis added).

The injection of subjective terms provides fertile ground for good faith disagreement. A pre-requisite condition, such as the loss of "material number of games," in addition to being subjective, is necessarily a relative term. What constitutes a "material number" depends on, among other factors, the number of games in the particular season and number of games covered by the particular agreement. For instance, if a regular season is 162 games, a loss of several games may be *de minimus*. On the other hand, if a broadcaster only has the right to broadcast a small fraction of the total number of games in a season, the loss of even a few games can be material.

In addition to the potential interpretation problems, use of subjective terms and relative standards can force a licensor into having to take a position with respect to one licensee that may operate to the licensor's detriment *vis-a-vis* another licensee or, worse, inconsistent positions with licensees. For example, in the area of game broadcasts Leagues and teams invariably have multiple media outlets: an over-the-air TV carrier; a cable TV station; and a radio broadcaster. Assuming the inclusion in each broadcast agreement of an identical provision that conditions relief upon the loss of a "material number" of games, even though the claim of each licensee would arise from the same *force majeure* occurrence, the materiality threshold could vary widely depending on the number of broadcasts each carrier is authorized.[46]

Finally, in the event of a dispute over the availability of the remedy at a particular point in time, a party believing itself to have the right to withhold certain performances based upon the *force majeure* can be faced with the dilemma of either having to forego the opportunity to mitigate the injury to its business at the earliest opportunity, or withholding performance at its peril. If a licensee fully performs during a period when it may have properly withheld performance, it will likely compound its losses.[47] Conversely, if a licensee withholds performance over the objection of the licensor, and to the licensor's injury,[48] the licensor may terminate the agreement (which is an option incorporated into many *force majeure* provisions) or even bring a claim based upon breach of contract.

C. Tolling Clauses

Many *force majeure* provisions contain a clause that tolls the running of the contract term and a concomitant clause that extends the agreement for a period corresponding to the length of the work stoppage. The following is representative of such clauses: "in the event of such delay, interruption or diminution [as a result a *force majeure*], the Term of this Agreement shall be extended for a period equal to the period of such delay, interruption or diminution."

This type of relief can be attractive to both licensees and licensors. Licensees receive the full benefit of the term of agreement for which they bargained, and licensors enjoy guaranteed payments over an extended period and in compensation for a period in which it may have received reduced or no revenues. At first blush, this would seem an equitable solution that would make whole the party seeking relief. However, such an *ad hoc* approach can have many unintended adverse consequences for the licensor while providing no real benefit for the licensee.

In the event of a lengthy work stoppage, an automatic extension for a comparable period can severely hamstring a licensor's normal business practices and disrupt its business operations. Since the contract year for the purposes of League and team agreements generally coincides with the licensor's fiscal year (which usually coincides with it season),[49] in a case involving a prolonged interruption such as the MLB players' strike, an agreement extension on the foregoing basis would add 232 days to the term of the contract. As a consequence, the so-fixed expiration date will, instead of ending proximate to the conclusion of their season, fall some two months into a new season. Such an abrupt and unscheduled ending can have significant adverse consequences to the licensor.

1. Leverage Considerations

The in-season expiration of any agreement is certain to severely reduce the negotiating leverage of the licensor in a number of ways. For instance, in virtually every significant business or licensing category, because of the considerable lead time necessary to effectively enter a market—whether it be a licensing category, corporate sponsorship of a newly acquired property or producing broadcasts—the licensor will be faced with the inescapable reality that if it does not renew the incumbent, there will be some period of transition when it will have to conduct business without the benefit of the services and revenue provided by the non-renewed party. The inability to reach renewal of certain types of agreements can have disastrous consequences for the League or team. For example, in the case of a broadcast agreement that expires in-season, if a renewal cannot be reached with the incumbent broadcast partner, the League or team may find itself without a carrier for its games.[50] This would be doubly disastrous because, in addition to the loss of the broadcast outlet, the licensor might then be unable to perform the media placement obligations owed to various corporate sponsors. Because the risk of loss in such key areas as broadcasting and sponsorship of certain promotions (e.g., All-Star balloting) or licensor-controlled television programming may be unacceptable, the licensor may be forced to accept considerably less fees than it could command for the same rights, if up for negotiation at the end of a season or during the off-season.

As in the broadcast agreement context, the advent of an in-season expiration can drastically alter the negotiating leverage in the merchandise licensing arena. Given the new end-of-term months covered by an 8-month extension, coupled with the standard 90-day sell-off period at a minimum, a licensee up for renewal goes into negotiations knowing that, in the event terms of renewal cannot be reached, it will have the benefit of selling through the critically important selling windows of: (i) start of season; (ii) the All-Star period; and (iii) the all important "back-to-school" period.[51] Perhaps even through the equally important Christmas selling season.[52] This gives the licensee a significant negotiating advantage. The incumbent licensee, the licensor and any potential competitor for the license will all recognize that because of the foregoing sales rights, the rights of any licensee other than the incumbent will be seriously devalued for its first contract year. Indeed, given that, manufacturers that might otherwise vie for a particular license may opt not to enter into contention because the licensor cannot deliver a "clean" category. If an incumbent licensee is in effect "running unopposed," its leverage is clearly enhanced.

2. Benefits?

For the reasons detailed above, a lengthy extension of an agreement can be of greater detriment than benefit to a licensor. In a similar vain, the extension of the term of a contract may be of minimal value to a licensee under various circumstances. Depending on the part of the season lost to a work stoppage, the extension of a license for a corresponding period may leave a licensee far from whole and without any effective relief.

As a result of the August 12th walkout by the Major League Baseball Players, the 1994 playoffs and World Series were ultimately canceled. As a consequence, baseball experienced massive fan disillusionment that left MLB licensees and sponsors unable to maximize their rights during the peak period of fan interest—the pennant races and the World Series. Deprived of that heightened period of interest, and with the strike's ill effects carrying through the holiday season, many rights holders suffered irreparable harm to their business. League (and many team) broadcast partners and advertisers lost the opportunity to reach the largest viewer audiences of the season, corporate sponsors lost their most important promotional platform, and licensees watched their business free-fall. Licensees, in particular, were perhaps the hardest hit. For most licensees, particularly in the apparel categories, the majority of their sales are made during the final months of the season (a period which overlaps the back-to-school buying season) together with the Christmas shopping season.[53]

Sponsors and licensees of the NHL found themselves in a position similar to that of their MLB counterparts. With the owners' October 1st lock-out of its players, and the warnings and threats that preceded it, hockey's business partners, like baseball's, were unable to capitalize on several periods of heightened attention: the Season's opening and the unique circumstances surrounding it;[54] and the All-Star lead-in. Moreover, as was the case with the baseball strike, the consequences of the lock-out were felt by licensees for a period extending from back-to-school through the holiday shopping season.

Given the timing of both the MLB and NHL work stoppages, the addition of 232 or 75 days (as the case may be) to an agreement is hardly salve for some wounds. To a corporate sponsor or merchandise licensee, the addition to their contract term of days that will run in the off-season is of little or no value. For the sponsor, there are no games to advertise in and no available platform upon which to build any promotion. As for merchandise licensees, there is no adequate substitute for a lost Christmas season or special event opportunity such as the All-Star game. For a marketing partner that has been severely injured, an extension under the foregoing circumstances is a hollow remedy—if it is one's sole remedy. Indeed, for licensees in some product category segments, an extension may prove to be no remedy at all. Given the extent of lost sales during a work stoppage coupled with the residual fan disaffection,[55] loss of popularity compared to other sports, and failing League promotional support,[56] a licensee may be unable to meet its minimum royalty payment obligation to the League even with an extension. For example, in the trading card category where baseball accounts for about half of all cards sales, in the immediate aftermath of the strike, the Topps Company—the market leader with a $1.2 billion card business—experienced a third-quarter earnings dive of 68%,[57] saw its fourth-quarter net income down by 77%[58] and its first quarter sales decline by close to $30 million.[59] In that case, the licensee's damages will have been compounded, as it will have lost sales, and will be required to pay "out of pocket" to meet its minimum payment guaranty.

3. Operation Concerns

As discussed in the first subsection, long-term contract extensions resulting from a work stoppage can materially affect the business decision-making process. They can also severely disturb normal business operational matters. As noted above, it is generally broadcast partners, sponsors and "key" licensees that have *force majeure* protection in their agreements. This class of marketing partners typically accounts for a disproportionate percentage of a League or team's non-gate revenues. If these partners, as a class, receive extensions, it can create a myriad of operational complications. For instance, with large advertising and promotion contributions being held in abeyance, budgeting becomes difficult. Similarly, continuing royalty reporting and payments makes revenue forecasting difficult. And, lastly, in view of the foregoing, closing the books on the fiscal year becomes a problem which in turn raises share holder issues because Leagues are normally required to make their annual distribution to their shareholders (i.e., the teams) within a time-certain following the close of the fiscal year.

As illustrated above, while the equitable extension of an agreement may be a mutually satisfactory form of relief and, equally important, be a compromise that is easily reached, such relief should not be settled upon without full consideration and appreciation of all of its repercussions.

D. Damages

Unless a licensee's damages are apparent, such as with a broadcaster that is unable to air games, or an in-game TV advertiser whose commercials cannot be run, because of a work stoppage, the licensor should incorporate into its *force majeure* provision a damage requirement. While a strike or lock-out will undoubtedly have an adverse affect on anyone involved with the particular sport, every work stoppage does not necessarily have such a severe economic impact upon a licensee as to justify any extraordinary relief. For instance, the work stoppage may have been *de minimus* like the recent July 1996 lock-out of players by the NBA which lasted a mere few hours,[60] or the 2-day walkout by the Major League Baseball Players at the start of the 1985 season. Alternatively, it may have occurred late in the season at a point when a licensee has already met its minimum payment obligation or during the off-season when its direct affects are muted.

Because the "purpose of a *force majeure* clause is to limit damages,"[61] and a work stoppage does not necessarily result in a licensee sustaining any significant damages, a licensee should not be permitted to invoke such a provision without meeting some damage standard. Further, the standard should include the notion of materiality, particularly under a merchandise license, because a licensee cannot truly be said to have been damaged, at least not in the "frustration" of expectation sense,[62] if it has been able to meet its minimum payment guarantee which, after all, is based on the sales projections provided by the licensee. Without such a standard, a license may use the event of a work stoppage as a pretext to renegotiate more favorable terms or gain some other concession, notwithstanding the fact that it may have already met (or be able to meet) its minimum. Therefore, it is recommended that a licensor include in its *force majeure* provision a clause that provides that relief is only available if the work stoppage "has had a material adverse affect on the sale of the Licensed Products." A final rebuttal argument in support of a materiality standard is philosophical. A licensor should not be a guarantor of a manufacturer's level of profitability with respect to product it licenses. If a licensee has met, or can meet, its minimum guarantee, then *a fortiori* it has profited on its license.

Concededly, the term "material" is subjective and subjective terms should be avoided in the drafting process. However, unlike the problems discussed above with respect to subjective language, in this one context, materiality is easily determined. Since a merchandise licensee is typically required by contract to submit regular periodic sales statements, its sales can simply be compared to its sales figures for a comparable period of the past season (or several seasons) or to even the last pre-work stoppage accounting period. As an alternative to the inclusion of an explicit materiality standard, the parties may elect to include a durational requirement upon the elapse of which material damage is presumed. The following type of clause has such an affect: "if any such [*force majeure*] event prevents performance for a period of time in excess of sixty (60) days, either party may terminate this agreement upon written notice."

V. Draft Choices

While many licensors and licensees tend to view a *force majeure* provision as simply part of the boilerplate, if included at all, this is the first provision the parties will review at the hint of any potential work stoppage. In the event of a work stoppage, the obligations of each party will be dictated by the terms of such provision. Accordingly, each party should be as attentive to the language of this clause as they are to the so-called "business terms" of their agreement. The well-drafted sports *force majeure* provision should be based upon thorough consideration of the following elements: (i) scope of coverage; (ii) triggering event; and (iii) type of relief. This section discusses the critical considerations relative to these clauses and recommends drafting solutions that avoid the common pitfalls.

A. Scope of Coverage & Triggers

Obviously, the scope of coverage is the most critical element of any *force majeure* provision because it is dispositive on the issue of a party's rights in the event of a labor disputes. Licensees should request a broadly worded provision covering all of the traditional *force majeures* (e.g., acts of God, war, fire, governmental restriction, carrier failure, etc.) as well as specific protection against all forms of League labor disputes. A licensor may, however, justifiably resist such broad coverage. Such expansive coverage can be fairly viewed as an attempt to shift certain business risks that are customarily borne by a licensee. For example, with respect to apparel manufacturers, for many major licensees a significant percentage of their business is attributable to their sale of branded merchandise[63]—and in some cases, even a majority of their overall business[64]—and for which they should assume all *force majeure* risk. Thus, for such manufacturers, a request for broad coverage can be seen as a "grab;" an effort to shift certain inherent business risks, that in all other contexts the licensee assumes sole responsibility for, to a party that may be willing to share them for no compelling reason.

A frequent compromise is to limit *force majeure* protection to strikes. Content with having extracted any concession on protection against strikes, some licensees will rest. However, as discussed in Section III(B) above, to do so is a grave mistake. If the grantor is a League or team and has consented to include a Strike Clause, then the licensee will have gained the high ground in negotiating this particular provision. A licensee should then insist upon specific protection against lock-out. Having acknowledged the appropriateness of work stoppage relief by virtue of the agreement to include a Strike Clause, the licensor is left with no principled reason for not further extending coverage to lock-out if the licensee requests such protection. The cogent argument that follows is that if the licensor consents to protection against a player strike, it can hardly object to extending similar protection to a lock-out; a situation of the League's own making and a matter exclusively within its control.

To avoid any potential ambiguity, the well-drafted Sports FM enumeration should explicitly refer to strikes or lock-outs in which the League is involved. Consistent with the particular form of provision and style employed by the drafter, the following language is suggested to provide for excuse (or suspension) of a party's performance as a result of "strike or lock-out to which the League is party." This sample language will avert the myriad interpretation/construction problems discussed above. The language by its terms expressly applies to both player strike and lock-out as well as covering any disputes involving League officiating personnel. Moreover, it removes any uncertainty as to the affect of the use of replacements. Since a strike or lock-out is a prerequisite to the use of replacements, relief will be available to a party under a so-drafted provision notwithstanding the fact that no work stoppage or interruption of the season may exist, or may have been *de minimus*. If the League wishes to reserve the right to utilize replacements and receive full performance from its licensee (or otherwise provide for some form of modified performance), the drafter should expressly carve out the terms and conditions. If on the other hand, the licensee wishes to be protected against labor disputes involving non-League personnel as well, then the sample language should be modified as follows: "strike or lock-out (including those to which the League is party) . . ."[65]

Finally, in addition to the foregoing benefits of using the recommended language, use of the words strike and lock-out provide ideal triggering events. They are objectively determinable events that are not susceptible to dispute over the point at which a party may properly invoke the *force majeure* provision. Moreover, these events often provide early warning in that the effective date of these occurrences is typically preceded by an announcement of a deadline.

B. Type of Relief

A *force majeure* provision, like any athletic protective equipment, can only provide the user with maximum protection if it fits. These provisions come in a number of different configurations; one-size does not fit all. To ensure adequate protection, it is essential that the form of relief provided is fitted to the nature of a licensee's obligations, to its business and to practical realities.

Force majeure provisions commonly provide for one or more of the following forms of relief: (i) excuse of performance; (ii) suspension of performance; (iii) right of termination; (iii) credit, or rebate; or (iv) equitable adjustment.

1. Excuse vs. Suspension

A typical form of *force majeure* clause that excuses performance provides in pertinent part as follows:

> If either party hereto shall have been prevented in whole, or in part, from performing its obligations hereunder by virtue of acts beyond the reasonable control of the party including, but not limited to, acts of war, fire, natural disaster or other acts of God, then the obligation of such party shall be excused . . . (emphasis added).

Suspension-type *force majeure* provisions are similarly constructed. The following is typical:

> Neither party shall be deemed in default of any obligation under this Agreement to the extent that such default results from acts of God, strike, fire, flood, acts of the public enemy or other *Force majeure* causes; provided that all performances affected by said *Force majeure* shall be *suspended* during the currency of such cause; and provided that the obligor shall resume the performance of its obligations in good faith as soon as possible . . . (emphasis added).

While excusal and suspension effect the same immediate result— the discharge of a party from the performance of a present obligation—these two forms of relief are not equivalents.

In drafting a *force majeure* provision, the words "excuse" and "suspend" should not be used loosely, and only with full consideration of the import of the term used. Whereas suspension merely postpones performance for a period of time, excuse permanently discharges a party from the affected specific obligation. The failure to take into account this hyper-technical distinction can have significant repercussions. It can mean the difference between receiving an expected benefit late, and not receiving the benefit at all.

2. Right of Termination

As an alternative to the foregoing forms of relief, a licensor can elect to provide a right of termination in the event a *force majeure* condition prevents a party's performance for a specified period. A typical form of this type of provision provides in pertinent part that "if any such [*force majeure*] event prevents performance for a period of time in excess of sixty (60) days, either party may terminate this agreement upon written notice." Some licensees may view such a termination right as an adequate remedy inasmuch as it allows a party a means of complete discharge. Because of the "out" this provides, and given that a licensee can rightly consider it a major achievement to have extracted a concession on *force majeure* at all, many licensees will accept such relief if proffered without further negotiation. While a licensee should be pleased at prevailing on the macro issue of work stoppage relief, a licensee should not be so quick to acquiesce as to this particular form of relief. As discussed below, this form of relief may not be suitable for a particular company.

If the decision to provide a licensee with a right to terminate as its sole form of relief reflects a strategic choice on the part of the licensor, it is a shrewd gambit. This approach preserves for the licensor the full performance by the licensee through the currency of a strike or lock-out (at least until a specified length of time, which can be quite significant)—a fact that a licensee should consider—while providing relief that is, as discussed below, somewhat specious.

At first blush, it may seem that providing a right of termination puts a licensor at considerable risk. In reality, the risk of actual termination is relatively remote for several reasons. First, by the terms of the provision, relief may not be available even in the event of a work stoppage. The option to terminate is contingent upon the continuation of a strike or lock-out for more than the specified period. That period can be as long as mutually agreed: 60 days, 90 days, or even longer. It is worth noting, that only twice in the approximately 40-year history of PAs has a work stoppage continued for more than a 60-day period.[66]

Second, a licensee is unlikely to take advantage of the right to terminate (if the durational requirement has been met) because business reality militates against taking such a drastic measure. Typically, the only licensees able to secure protection against a player strike or owner lock-out are sponsors and a League's most substantial (in terms of royalties generated) merchandise licensees. Invariably, these types of licensees fall into three categories. In one category are those companies whose brands are synonymous with a particular sport such as NIKE with basketball, the ubiquitous CCM and Bauer brands in hockey, or Topps with baseball. In a second category are companies whose overall sales are disproportionately dependent upon the sale of the licensed product of a particular sport — again, such as Topps with baseball cards. Falling within the third category are so-called "authentics" licensees, whose overall sales are driven by a particular League's endorsement or use of their signature product such as an "official" game jersey manufacturer like Champion, or a game ball supplier like Wilson (NFL footballs) or Spalding (NBA basketballs). For these types of companies, to give-up their license is not a real alternative. For Topps to exit the baseball card business would be suicidal; if a company like Spalding gave up its designation as the supplier of the "Official Game Ball of the NBA," its market share in the basketball category would likely plummet. In view of these often symbiotic relationships, it is highly improbable that any so-situated licensee would opt to terminate its League license.

Finally, even if a licensee is inclined to terminate its agreement, a licensor would still have an unarticulated fall-back position that makes termination unlikely. Upon notice of termination, a licensor can simply offer other forms of relief such as excusing or suspending the party's performance, extending the term of the license, or reducing minimum payment guarantees or rights fees. Given such concessions, the probability of a licensee resigning its license is virtually zero.

Not every licensee has the same amount of negotiating leverage. A licensee with minimal royalty guarantees, or whose royalties can easily be replaced by another (or new) licensee, that requests protection against a work stoppage may well be offered the above form of relief on a "take it or leave it" basis. The most common mistake made by a licensee confronted with this set of circumstances is to assume that there is nothing negotiable. While a licensor may be steadfast as to the basic form of relief it has chosen, there may still be areas within the provision that are negotiable. A licensee should request interim relief such as excuse or the suspension of performance during the waiting period. Moreover, the licensor may be willing to reduce the "waiting period" from 60 days to 30 days. For the licensee, it should be noted that four out of the last five League work stoppages have lasted more than 30 days.[67] If the licensor has already agreed that work stoppage relief is warranted, then it will likely exhibit some flexibility on these micro points.[68] However, such concessions will not be volunteered. A licensee must specifically request such further modifications.

If, in the end, the licensor opts for the right of termination as the form of relief, the termination option should not be left open-ended, as is in the above-cited provision. The option should be made exercisable within a time-certain following the elapse of the specified period of disability. The following type of clause is recommended: "if any such [*force majeure*] event prevents performance for a period of time in excess of sixty (60) days, either party may terminate this agreement upon *thirty (30) days' written notice served upon the other party not later than ten (10) days after the elapse of the 60- day period*" (emphasis added). This additional language will prevent a licensee from using the *force majeure* as a pretext for terminating an agreement that it comes to view as unfavorable, or from using the threat of termination as a "re-opener" device. Moreover, a fixed deadline will force the licensee to make a timely determination and permit the licensor to proceed forward, either one way or another, with a needed degree of certainty.

3. Credit or Rebate

As mentioned, a particular form of relief may not be suited for a particular licensee or types of business. For example, the mere right to terminate is not a meaningful choice for a licensee whose business is dependent upon a specific license. An incremental extension of an agreement's term can be meaningless for some licensees. For a licensee that is thinly capitalized or has a heavy debt burden, a requirement to fully perform during the pendency of a work stoppage can be crippling. On the other hand, to permit certain types of licensees to suspend their performance could be disastrous for the licensor. Into this last category falls "key" sponsors and broadcast partners in particular.

Unlike merchandise licenses where the rights granted are bundled and indivisible (e.g., right to manufacture, distribute, sell and promote Licensed Product), the elements of a sponsorship agreement (e.g., use of trademarks and "Official Sponsor" designation in advertising, specific promotion rights, purchase of League-controlled media, etc.) or broadcast agreement are severable. Moreover, unlike royalty payments which are based on actual sales and generally payable on a monthly basis, sponsorship rights fees are typically allocated to specific elements and payable in relatively large installments that are fewer and farther between than royalty payments. If such substantial fees were withheld or diminished, it would severely impact a licensor's ability to meet its operational expenses as well as other financial commitments. Accordingly, as to "cash cow" licensees, excuse or suspension of certain performances should be avoided. Thus, in the first instance, the licensor should offer relief in the form of a rights fee credit or other forms of credit.

From a licensor's perspective, agreement by a licensee to accept a credit or rebate in lieu of other relief is an extremely licensor-favorable resolution of the relief issue: full payment is ensured through the work stoppage; the relief afforded is all post-stoppage; and the relief does not require any out-of-pocket payment. While such a resolution can be equitable, a licensee may balk nonetheless. The discerning sponsor or broadcast partner is likely to find such a proposal unsatisfactory for a number of reasons.

First, depending on the point in the term of the agreement that the work stoppage occurs, there may not be a guaranteed subsequent season in which to apply the credit; for instance, if a strike occurs in the final year of an agreement. Secondly, for a myriad of reasons, comparable advertising inventory or promotional opportunities may not be available in a subsequent season. For instance, some sponsored events are not available on an annual basis such as the NBA's McDonald's Championship—a pre-season tournament played abroad and featuring the reigning NBA champions team in tournament play against championship teams representing various foreign basketball leagues—which is staged every other year. Other events, such as League all-star games, are hosted by different cities each year and therefore can have differing promotional value for a particular sponsor. Other opportunities are truly unique, such as a League anniversary season like the NFL's recent diamond anniversary or the NBA's current 50th anniversary season. Finally, opportunities may not be available simply because of prior commitments made by the licensor to other sponsors or advertisers. Moreover, in the case of corporate sponsors, companies routinely review marketing plans weighing costs against effectiveness and decide alternative promotional activities will be more efficient and therefore change their marketing focus.

In addition to the foregoing reasons why a licensee may find make-goods unattractive, make-goods may be of little value to certain licensees, given the potential for severe diminished interest in the sport following a prolonged work stoppage. This was evident by the lagging attendance[69] and reduced TV viewership experienced by MLB last season.[70] For a broadcast partner that has been left with unsold advertising inventory as a result of a work stoppage, or has been forced to deeply discount its ad rates, the last thing it will want is additional units to sell or games to broadcast.[71]

Faced with a cool response to the offer of credit, the licensor's fall-back is to combine the offer of credit with one or more additional forms of relief. The usual alternative is to combine credit with the option to terminate and/or receive a rebate. The following form of construction is typical:

> If the performance of either party shall be delayed, interrupted or diminished by any cause beyond its reasonable control, such as war, national emergency, fire, restrictions imposed by law, natural disaster or other acts of God, Grantor may in its sole discretion (i) terminate this Agreement, pro rate the fees due to the time of termination, and neither party shall be under any further obligation to the other; or (ii) apply a pro rata credit or make-good.

A good strategy in some cases is to first offer the licensee the right of termination as the alternative form of relief. The reasons are twofold. First, the return of funds is to be avoided if at all possible. Secondly, neither a broadcaster nor a sponsor in a highly competitive product category (and whose target consumers are efficiently delivered by a league's programming such as the case in the soft drink, malt beverage and athletic footwear categories) is likely to exercise the right to terminate for many of the same types of reasons discussed in the above subsection with respect to authentics licensees.

If a rebate is to be provided, to avoid any potential dispute regarding the amount of the rebate, the provision should provide for a means of calculating the refund. This can be achieved by incorporating a formula such as: (a) number of opportunities lost (e.g., games, weeks of play), (b) divided by a base number that is equal to the total number of opportunities, (c) multiplied by the annual rights fee due, (d) the sum of which equals the amount of the rebate. The following examples are illustrative of this approach:

$$\frac{\text{\# Games Lost (8)}}{\text{Total \# Games in Season (16)}} \times \text{Annual Rights Fee (\$1,000,000)} =$$

$$\text{Amount of the Rebate (\$500,000)}$$

or

Weeks Lost (6)
_____   x Annual Rights Fee ($1,000,000) =

Total Weeks in Season (24)

Amount of the Rebate ($250,000)

To minimize the revenue placed at risk, a licensor should include some type of "cap" device. Such a mechanism might include providing that a refund will only be available if a designated percentage of games are canceled and, further limiting the amount to a pro rata portion of the rights fee payments and capped at a designated percentage of the fee.[72]

Formulas can be structured in any number of different ways. However, whatever formula is adopted should be tailored to the mutual agreement of the parties and take into account the particular rights granted, the nature of the performance obligations, and the fee structure and payment schedule involved.

4. Equitable Adjustment

In contrast to the credit/rebate form of relief that is particularly suited for sponsors and broadcasters, and wholly unsuitable for many types of licensing arrangements, equitable adjustment is a form of relief that is universally applicable and particularly fitting for merchandise licensees. The following is typical of a *force majeure* provision that provides for such relief:

> [i]n the event of a strike or lock-out ("Work Stoppage") involving the League and its players that causes the pre-emption, in whole or in part, of the Season, all obligations of LICENSEE hereunder shall continue, including all payment obligations, and when such Work Stoppage has ceased, if such Work Stoppage has had a material adverse affect on LICENSEE's Licensed Product sales, LICEN-SOR and LICENSEE shall in good faith confer with each other to negotiate with respect to an equitable adjustment to LICENSEE's obligations hereunder.

From a licensor's perspective, this is the optimal form of *force majeure* relief. It requires full performance through the duration of the work stoppage; relief, if warranted, is post-stoppage; and it provides the licensor with the maximum amount of flexibility to fashion appropriate relief.

The flexibility such provision provides is perhaps its most attractive feature. By not locking into particular relief, it affords the parties the latitude to customize the relief to their specific circumstances. This can actually be more advantageous to a licensee than prescribed relief because it provides the licensee with a contractual basis to press for what may be more useful relief under the prevailing circumstances. As discussed above, a licensee can come to find that a right of termination is useless or that an extension will still not enable it to meet its minimum royalty payment guarantee. With the flexibility provided by this type of provision, a full menu of relief is available that can include more desirable relief options such as product additions, reduction of minimum guarantees or advertising support, or cross collateralization of royalty payments.

Notwithstanding some of the advantages that the above form of relief can provide a licensee, a licensee may oppose this type of provision for precisely the same reasons licensors find it desirable: the relief is post-stoppage and is not assured. However, because the most valued marketing relationships are typically long-term, and often long-standing, there is a built-in element of self-policing that militates against any grossly inequitable adjustment. Moreover, a prophylactic can be added by tying the equitable adjustment provision to an arbitration clause. In this way, the parties can avail themselves of an expedient, and cost-efficient, dispute resolution mechanism in the event the parties cannot reach agreement on the extent of the adjustment.

VI. The Point After

The MLB and NHL work stoppages in particular have had a profound impact on sports marketing relationships. The enduring aspect of their strife has been to shock Leagues, players and their marketing partners into the realization that true licensing disaster is possible. This realization should forever after make parties to a pro sports licensing arrangement routinely take such possibilities into consideration in their negotiations. As a result of licensee consolidation through corporate acquisition,[73] the steady movement of the Leagues towards the "less is more" philosophy and "marketing partner" model,[74] and ever-increasing League creation of controlled media and special events, allows major licensees now to enjoy the greatest negotiating leverage since the dawn of sports licensing. Given this, the Leagues must be prepared to share some financial risk, and should be more willing to bargain on the issue of *force majeure* protection. In dealing with such matters, counsel must recognize that each licensing situation is unique and must be approached as such. A multi-League and entertainment property license holder can divert resources (e.g., production capacity, raw material, etc.) to the production of other merchandise in ways a single license holder cannot. A domestic manufacturer can react more quickly to changing conditions than a licensee that sources offshore. An unaligned apparel company has different risks than a vertical mill. A conglomerate (e.g., Sara Lee) is better able to lay-off business loss than a privately owned sportswear company. A corporate sponsor can switch gears faster and reallocate funds to another sport more easily than a merchandise licensee. A television network is better able to tolerate significant financial pain than is any merchandise licensee.

Because of the widely divergent sizes and resources of licensees and licensors alike, in addressing *force majeure* concerns, counsel should strive for the adoption of a provision that is fully understood and that suits his or her client's goals and the requirements of the client's particular business. As the drafter, once an election is made on the type of provision to be provided, the licensor should steadfastly insist upon acceptance of its standard terms unless circumstances of a particular negotiation dictate an exception, in which case, based on the thorough understanding of the purpose of each clause of the *force majeure* provision, adapt the provision so that as much of that purpose can nevertheless be achieved. The attorney that approaches this now highly-charged area of contract in the foregoing manner will, no doubt, find himself or herself having a distinct advantage over the adversary that approaches this area with nonchalance. More importantly, counsel will ensure that its client is not "blind-sided" by unforeseen, but foreseeable, risk.

NOTES

1. "Force majeure," a French term, literally meaning "superior force." An unforeseeable natural or human event beyond the control of the parties to a contract, rendering performance of a contract impossible. RANDOM HOUSE LEGAL DICTIONARY 101 (1st ed. 1996).
2. A 232-day MLB player strike that forced the cancellation of the final third of the 1994 season, all post-season play, and a 3-week postponement of the 1995 "Opening Day;" an NHL lock-out that delayed the start of their

1994 season from October 1st to January 20, 1995, reducing the season to a 48-game schedule, and resulting in the cancellation of the 1995 All-Star Game; and the 11 week NBA lock-out of its players during the summer of 1995, followed by a 9 week lock-out of its referees. While the major sports leagues are finally enjoying a period of relative labor peace, war drums can be heard in the distance. The National Football League (the "NFL") has recently expressed its dissatisfaction with their current labor contract with Commissioner Paul Tagliabue publicly stating that "[a] number of clubs are really struggling with this agreement" and indicating that the league may seek an early out. Don Cronin, *Sportline*, USA TODAY, Apr. 4, 1997, at 1C. Just a few weeks earlier, Major League Soccer ("MLS"), in only its second season of existence, was sued by its players association alleging, among other anti-competitive practices, that the league illegally secured from its players group licensing rights for merchandising. Paul Gardner, *Players Association Sues MLS*, SOCCER AMERICA, Mar. 3, 1997, at 12. For purposes of this article, MLB, MLS, the NBA, the NFL and the NHL are collectively referred to as the "Leagues."

3. WABC-AM Radio, Inc. v. New York Yankees Partnership, No. 95-106671 (N.Y. Sup. Ct. filed March 17, 1995). *See infra* part III(c).

4. October 1994 saw the cancellation of the World Series for the first time in 90 years and the indefinite postponement of the start of the 1994 NHL Season. In addition, only a 12th hour "no strike, no lock-out" agreement reached between the NBA and its players averted a MLB-NHL-NBA work stoppage trifecta.

5. However, *force majeure* provisions are not uncommon in broadcast agreements, and in sponsorship agreements to a lesser extent, for many of the reasons discussed at note 16 *infra*.

6. While each league (and member team) typically has fewer than 20-30 sponsors, and perhaps 2 or 3 broadcast partners, each league has 150 or more licensees (not including local licensees and premium item manufacturers) and both MLB and the NFL have in excess of 300. Because merchandise licenses are by far the most widely circulated forms of agreements, they are, accordingly, the primary focus of this article.

7. The Major League Baseball Players Association ("Baseball PA"), National Football Players Association ("Football PA") and NHL Players Association ("Hockey PA") maintain and administer a so-called "Group" licensing program on behalf of their players (i.e., licensing covering the collective use of a designated minimum number of players). The National Basketball Players Association has by license agreement granted to NBAP the exclusive right to license to third parties the use of current NBA players on a Group basis. MLS, through its form of uniform player contract, has secured such rights directly through their individual players. *See generally* Gardner, *supra* note 2, at 13.

8. The NFL CBA currently guarantees the players 63% of "Designated Gross Revenues" (i.e., ticket and broadcast revenues). *See* Larry Weisman, *Judge Tells NFL to Raise Salary Cap $2 Million,* USA TODAY, Feb. 16, 1996, at 1C. At the same time, the NBA CBA guarantees its players up to 50.8% of "Basketball Related Revenues" (i.e., broadcast and licensing revenues, and miscellaneous arena-generated revenues). Clifton Brown, *Labor Agreement Ratified by N.B.A. Players,* N.Y. TIMES, Sept. 14, 1995, at B17, B22.

9. Murray Chass, *Reluctantly, Baseball Owners Approve a Pact With Players,* N.Y. TIMES, Nov. 27, 1996, at A1.

10. For purposes of the NFL CBA, "Designated Gross Revenues" includes ticket revenue, "luxury boxes" revenue, and all broadcast revenues "without limitation." NFL COLLECTIVE BARGAINING AGREEMENT 1993-2000, Art. XXIV, § 1(a)(i). The NBA's Basketball Related Revenues definition, for the first time, includes revenue from luxury suites, parking, concessions sales, international television and arena signage. NBA NEWS, vol. 50, Sept. 25, 1995, at 3.

11. *Sport-Anon: A 12-Step Program Developed to Get the Sporting Goods Business Back On Its Feet,* SPORTSTYLE, July 1995, at 23.

12. United Equities Co. v. First Nat. City Bank, 383 N.Y.S.2d 6, 9 (1st Dept. 1976), *aff'd mem,* 41 N.Y.2d 1032 (1977); *See generally* 407 East 61st Garage v. Savoy Corp., 23 N.Y.2d 275, 282 (1968).

13. In many of the most profitable licensing categories for the Leagues, the outerwear, headwear and technology categories (e.g., video games, CD-ROM products, etc.), the licensees typically subcontract the manufacture of all or part of their products to third-party operations located in countries in the Asian Pacific and Latin America. Because of the long lead times required for the manufacture of these products, the frequency of natural disasters (monsoons, floods, etc.) in many of these areas, the political and/or economic instability that exist in many countries within these regions, coupled with the vagaries of ocean transit, much is beyond the reasonable control of the licensee. Consequently, this "key" group of licensees has powerful incentives to insulate themselves from the types of risks characterized above as "common" *force majeures*.

14. Mike Freeman, *Sports Unions Flex Muscles With Financial Clout,* N.Y. TIMES, Mar. 21, 1995, at B11, B15.

15. *Id.* In addition to the foregoing practical reasons, in some cases, *force majeure* protection is simply superfluous. If a League has a signed CBA that extends through the term of a license agreement to be entered into, the licensor will not be vulnerable to the one type of *force majeure* occurrence that can arguably disable it, namely a work stoppage. Under such circumstances, sometimes a licensor will unwisely include work stoppage protection at the behest of a licensee. Typically, this concession is made as a display of a licensor's flexibility and justified as a "no-harm, no-foul" accommodation. This cavalier approach can seriously under-

mine a licensor's position on the issue in a subsequent negotiation. If a licensor is going to "throw-in" a *force majeure* provision, it should only do so mindful of the reality that non-standard terms generally have a life-span that is coterminous with the length of the particular licensing relationship. Invariably, the point of departure in any contract renewal discussions are the terms of the current agreement. Given that, and the fact that there is frequently a different League lawyer involved in each successive contract negotiation, it is likely that any specifically requested provision will be grandfathered into successor agreements without any further discussion or renewed deliberation, and even though there has been a "sea change" in circumstances. Put simply, having once agreed to a provision, it may be impossible to object to its inclusion in subsequent agreements with the same party. This is particularly true in the case of work stoppage protection. If such a provision is included under circumstances where the risk is remote (i.e., where a CBA is in place), there cannot be any principled justification for not including such protection where the risk is significant.

16. While the reasons discussed above in this section with respect to merchandise licensing are equally applicable within the sponsorship context, *force majeure* provisions are not uncommon in broadcast and sponsorship agreements. Unlike in the merchandise licensing setting, under a broadcast or sponsor agreement, the League or team frequently has numerous affirmative   performance obligations that it may not be able meet in the event of a work stoppage. The most obvious example is in the case of broadcast agreements where the licensor is responsible for the delivery of the product to the broadcaster. Less apparent examples include TV ratings and audience delivery guarantees promised to advertisers, media placement obligations and League commitment to execute specific promotional programs (e.g., All-Star balloting) or stage specific events (e.g., League championships or All-Star Game).

17.   United States v. Seckinger, 397 U.S. 203, 216, 25 L.Ed.2d 224, 235 (1970), *reh'g denied*, 397 U.S. 1031 (1970).

18.   Kel Kim Corp. v. Central Markets, Inc., 70 N.Y.2d 900, 902-03, 519 N.E.2d 295, 296 (1987). This article assumes the application of New York substantive law pursuant to either the choice of law designation contained in MLBP, NBAP, NFLP, NHLE and Baseball PA agreements (each of these licensors, as well as the recently relocated offices of MLS, are headquartered in New York City; the Football PA is headquartered in Washington D.C. and the Hockey PA in Toronto), or conflicts principles. *See generally* Gould Entertainment Corporation v. Bodo, 107 F.R.D. 308, 312 n.3 (S.D.N.Y. 1985) (Finding New York law applicable in an action for a breach of a licensing agreement, brought by a New York corporation, even though defendants were Italian residents and the territory for the license was Italy. In reaching this conclusion, the Court placed great weight upon, among other considerations, the fact

that the license was negotiated in New York, the contract was signed in New York, and the payments under the license were made to plaintiff in New York.).

19. *Kel Kim,* 70 N.Y.2d at 903, 519 N.E.2d at 297; WILLISTON, CONTRACTS § 1968 209 (3d. ed. 1979).

20. Osborn v. Wilson & Co., 193 N.Y.S. 241 (1922), *aff'd,* 206 A.D. 787 (1923); WILLISTON, *supra* note 19, at 209.

21. There is another inchoate issue raised by the ambiguity in the use of the term strike. Under the principle of *contra proferentem,* ambiguous contract language is resolved against the drafter. WILLISTON, *supra* note 19, §621, at 760-62. However, such language could be just as easily construed against the licensee, the party that frequently provides the exact language.

22. 29 U.S.C. §142(2) (1988).

23. 29 U.S.C. §151 *et seq., passim.* While the NLRA contains no specific definition of "lock-out," the term is given statutory recognition in four separate sections: §8(d)(4) prohibits lock-outs (and strikes) for the purposes of terminating or modifying a collective bargaining contract until the 60-day notice period has run, 29 U.S.C. §158(d)(4); §203(c) requires the Director of Federal Mediation and Conciliation Service to seek settlements of disputes "without resort to strike, lock-out, or other coercion" by the parties, 29 U.S.C. §173(c); and §206 and §208(a) both grant powers to the President to deal with "threatened or actual strike or lock-out" which constitute national emergencies, 29 U.S.C. §176; §178(a).

24. See text accompanying note 18 *supra.*

25. *See Kel Kim,* 70 N.Y.2d at 902, 519 N.E.2d at 296.

26. THE OFFICIAL NATIONAL FOOTBALL LEAGUE 1996 RECORD & FACT BOOK 274, col. 2 (1996).

27. The Complaint at P1.

28. *Id.*

29. *Id.*

30. While the parties entered into the subject agreement as of September 24, 1986, it must be noted that WABC had been the Yankees' radio station through two previous League work stoppages: the 50-day player strike during the 1981 Season and the 2-day strike during the 1985 Season. In view of these experiences, WABC should have, at the very least, foreseen the possibility of a strike or lock-out (and, arguably, even the potential use of replacement players given the NFL's conduct of replacement games in 1987) and explicitly addressed such an occurrence. The Complaint at ¶4.

31. As plaintiff states: "WABC faces the prospect of having to perform its obligations under the Agreement, including payment of substantial sums of money and broadcast of Replacement Baseball games, to its considerable loss and damage, for an indefinite period of time. [The New York Yankees] den[y] that its scheduling and making available of Replacement Baseball games is in breach of its obligations pursuant to the Agreement.

A real and live legal controversy between the parties therefore exists as to their respective obligations under the Agreement." The Complaint at ¶¶24-26.

32. *Id.* at ¶16.

33. *Id.* at ¶20.

34. *Airwaves*, N.Y. TIMES, Apr. 7, 1995, at B10. The players' return likely averted a spate of similar litigation. Less than two weeks earlier, an industry survey cited television outlets of 12 MLB teams as having decided, or considering, dramatically changing their broadcast plans because of the use of replacement players. The extent of their stated contractual rights to do so was unclear from the survey, however, based upon individual team responses, few parties appeared to have provisions in their contracts covering labor-related issues. *Baseball On TV: Who Will Carry Replacement Games?*, SPORTS BUS. DAILY, Mar. 23, 1995, at 6.

35. In the absence of a *force majeure* provision, under the alleged facts it appears that Plaintiff may have had a meritorious defense to nonperformance based upon the principle of commercial frustration, a defense that may be similarly viable under certain types of merchandise and sponsor agreements. However, an examination of this defense is beyond the scope of this article.

36. The NLRA provides that "[t]he term 'labor dispute' includes any controversy concerning terms, tenure or conditions of employment ..." 29 U.S.C. §152(9) (1988).

37. If that is the case, then virtually every negotiation will trigger such a provision. In the past 15 years, only once have Leagues and PAs renewed a collective bargaining agreement without any lapse.

38. Jeff Jensen, *NBA Lockout Slows Licensing Juggernaut*, ADVERTISING AGE, July 17, 1995, at 6.

39. *Id. See generally Topps Co.*, THE WALL ST. J., Mar. 27, 1995, at A2; Bruce Horovitz, *Opening Day, and Nothing to Pitch*, USA TODAY, Mar. 31, 1995, at 1B, 2B.

40. The corollary to this loophole is whether a licensee is entitled to relief during the off-season period in a situation where a work stoppage results in the loss of games, and then carries into the off-season–a period when there is no loss of games. Does this occurrence suspend relief?

41. AP News Wire Service, Apr. 28, 1995.

42. This was, in part, borne out by the decision by the Blue Jays' cable TV partner TSN who advised that the team's usual 25 scheduled game broadcasts would not be carried by the network because of the costs of producing Blue Jays' replacement games from Florida, a circumstance that itself was necessitated by Provincial labor law.

43. Arguably, the same can be said of the mid-season All-Star games staged by MLB, the NBA and the NHL. These events, along with certain other regularly televised and sponsored events such as the draft, do not fit neatly into the specified categories of "Pre-Season, Regular Season or Playoffs."

44. However, depending on the League in question, the status of the respective League's drafts can present different analytical challenges. Whereas the NBA's draft takes place within a few days of the conclusion of the NBA Finals, and is expressly deemed the final event of its season for a number of purposes, the NHL and NFL drafts are scheduled several months after the conclusion of their respective seasons. Accordingly, it would be an extreme stretch to maintain that these events are part of their season.

45. For example, the NFL operated from 1987 to June 29, 1993 without a signed CBA. NFL FACT BOOK, *supra* note 26, at 275, col. 4. The MLB took three years to reach a new labor agreement, and the NBA conducted its last two seasons without a signed CBA.

46. The following baseball-based hypothetical illustrates this potentiality. For the strike-shortened 1994 MLB regular season, a team grants the following rights: (a) to a radio station, the right to broadcast all of its regular season games; (b) to a cable station, the right to televise up to 100 games; and (c) to a "free TV" station, the right to televise 20 specific games. At the point the Baseball Players' commenced their strike each team had played roughly 110 of its scheduled 162 games. In total, approximately 50 games were lost resulting in each of the team's three broadcasters losing the same number of scheduled game broadcasts — ten. Based on such a scenario, it is easy to see how results may differ even though the *force majeure* condition vis-a-vis each licensee is identical. As to the radio station, the loss of ten games (less than 10% of its inventory) may not be a material number of games. As to the cable station, the loss of ten dates is arguably a material number of games. As to the over-the-air rights holder, the loss of ten games, 50% of its available inventory, is clearly a material loss of games. If after three weeks of the work stoppage, the over-the-air broadcast partner sought relief under the subject *force majeure* provision and the team agreed that the loss of games had been material, then if either, or both, of the television broadcast partners shortly thereafter sought that same relief, the team would find itself in the difficult position of having already deemed the loss of games to have been material.

47. While *force majeure* was not at issue in *WABC Radio*, plaintiff faced just such a predicament. The station maintained, in essence, that it could only perform its broadcast obligations (i.e., airing replacement games) at a financial loss.

48. For example, the typical retail product license agreement requires that the licensee contribute to a League-administered promotional fund that is used by the League to execute advertising and promotion of League "Official Licensed Product." These funds are budgeted well in advance of each season. The campaigns funded by these dollars have numerous "hard" costs that the League would have to absorb in the event licensees wrongfully withheld their contributions.

49. For example, an NBA "Contract Year" is a 12-month accounting period that commences August 1st and concludes July 31st, the same as its fiscal year, encompassing a full exhibition, regular and playoff season (a period that runs from October through June).

50. It should be noted that, because it is quite common for broadcast partners and corporate sponsors to have exclusive negotiation windows contained in their agreements, a licensor may be contractually prohibited from even discussing the sale of rights to another party until the 11th-hour of the agreement in effect. Moreover, if a licensee has a right of first refusal, the licensor may be unable to find a party willing to negotiate for the available rights under the circumstances.

51. "Back-to-school" is the second-biggest shopping season of the year, second only to the Christmas holiday-shopping period. Alice Z. Cuneo, *Back-to-School 'Season' Gets Extended Spending*, ADVERTISING AGE, Sept. 23, 1996, at 16. Indeed, for apparel manufacturers, the back-to-school season is even bigger than the Christmas shopping season. Donna Rosato, *Shopping Season Off to Slow Start*, USA TODAY, Aug. 14, 1995, at 1B.

52. It is fairly common for licensees with significant minimum payment guarantees to successfully negotiate extended sell-off periods.

53. *See supra* note 51.

54. The return of the Stanley Cup to New York (the media and advertising center of North America) for the first time in over 50 years and the lack of competition with the baseball playoffs and World Series as a result of their own work stoppage.

55. By baseball's own account, 38% of its fans are angry and 58% are "disgusted." SPORTS BUS. DAILY, Dec. 9, 1996, at #11 (quoting the MLB Enterprises CEO, Greg Murphy, state of MLB marketing address at the 1996 MLB winter meetings). This disaffection is also readily evident in post-strike attendance and television viewership figures. For example, attendance for the strike-shortened 1995 MLB Season was down approximately 19% league-wide. *See generally, Ballpark Figures Slide*, USA TODAY, Aug. 11, 1995, at 3 C; Tom Verducci, *Baseball: The Bad News*, SPORTS ILLUSTRATED, July 10, 1995, at 32. Television viewership was also down sharply. *See generally* Rudy Martzke, *All-Star Ratings Take Nosedive*, USA TODAY, July 13, 1995, at 2C (reporting that the national TV ratings for the 1995 All-Star Game was an all-time low since the telecast was moved to prime-time in 1967). Indeed, two full seasons after the strike, the 1996 All-Star Game posted a second consecutive record low TV rating. *Baseball All-Star Game Plummets to Lowest Rating*, USA TODAY, July 11, 1996, at 2C. The 1996 World Series ratings were down 9% from the low-rated 1995 Series, making the '96 Series the third least-watched Series in history. Rudy Martzke, *Sports on TV*, USA TODAY, Oct. 29, 1996, at 2C; Erik Brady, *Series Ratings 14% Behind Last Season's*, USA TODAY, Oct. 25, 1996, at 4C (projecting final Series ratings based on then to-date ratings for games 1 through 4). The 1996 ratings are even more

disappointing in view of the two large television markets involved and a "dream" match-up between the defending world champion Atlanta Braves against the most storied franchise in American sports, the New York Yankees.

56. *See* David Leonhardt, *Baseball's Slump is Far From Over*, BUS. WEEK, Nov. 4, 1996, at 82; *see also* Andy Bernstein, *Can Baseball Be Cool Again?*, SPORTING GOODS BUS., June, 1996, at 52.

57. Nancy J. Kim, *Checked Swings*, WASH. POST, Dec. 31, 1994, at Section C.

58. Richard Sandomir, *The Players Are Back, But Are Card Collectors?*, N.Y. TIMES, Apr. 13, 1995, at B14.

59. Topps net sales for its first quarter ending May 27, 1995 were $67,432,000, down from $94,498,000 in 1994. *Topps First Quarter Sales Down Close to $30M From Last Year*, SPORTS BUS. DAILY, June 16, 1995, at 1 (citing Topps press release). Almost two years after the baseball players walkout, the trading card industry is still suffering from the ill effects of the strike. According to one industry executive, even though the baseball card business was, by some estimates, down by as much as 50% in 1995, THE SPORTS BUS. DAILY, July 1, 1996, at 3 (quoting television interview of Brian Burr, the president of the Upper Deck Company, on ESPN's SportsCenter, June 28, 1996), sales of a number of the leading cards brands "have not increased at all" and have "probably decreased." *Id.* (quoting collectibles executive Norm Klemonski).

60. David DuPree, *On, Off-Again NBA Lockout Stalls Signings*, USA TODAY, July 10, 1996, at 1C.

61. United Equities Co. v. First Nat. City Bank, 383 N.Y.S.2d 6, 9 (1st Dept. 1976), *aff'd mem*, 41 N.Y.2d 1032, 363 N.E.2d 1385 (1977).

62. *Id.*

63. For example, NIKE, Champion, Russell and Starter to name a few. Indeed, branded product is one of the "hottest" areas in apparel sales. Kim-Van Dang, *Brand News*, SPORTSTYLE, Feb., 1996, at 82.

64. For example, several large publicly traded companies are involved in team sport licensing: textile giant, VF Corporation, through its subsidiaries Nutmeg Mills and Cutler Sports, holds a number of League merchandise licenses as well as being the maker of the famous "Lee" brand of jeans; the same is true of Fruit of the Loom, best-known for its underwear business but also owns Pro Players among other sports licensing companies; and uniform and apparel maker Champion Products is owned by frozen food giant Sara Lee Corporation.

65. If a party's performance obligations are heavily dependent upon services provided by an organized labor force, such as broadcasters who are necessarily dependent upon cameramen, engineers, electricians and the like, then such general protection should be desirable. Indeed, last year, only a 12th hour agreement reached between the Canadian Broadcast Company and its major unions averted "the largest strike in the history

of the CBC." Adrienne Tanner, *Deals Met, CBC Strike Averted,* THE GAZETTE (Montreal), May 24, 1996, at A7. A strike that would have crippled all CBC operations. Christopher Harris, *Focus at CBC Shifts to Cutbacks: Deal With Unions Lifts Strike Threat,* TORONTO GLOBE & MAIL, May 25, 1996, at A1, A11. Such a strike would have affected NHL playoff coverage in Canada.

66. The 1994 baseball strike and hockey lock-out.

67. The most recent baseball strike, the hockey lock-out, the 1982 Football Players strike and the 1981 baseball strike.

68. Indeed, if the licensor is willing to accommodate the licensee on these further modifications, it may well elect to reverse itself and simply provide the licensee with a suspension-type relief since the net effect will be the same, and the licensor would not have to expose itself to the risk of licensee termination.

69. *See supra* note 55. While it must be noted that the average attendance for the 1996 season, 26,804 fans per game, was the fourth-highest in MLB history and represented a 6.1% increase over the 1995 season average, it was still more than 4000 less fans per game than the 1994 pre-strike average. *Attendance Is Up,* USA TODAY, Sept. 27, 1996, at 7C.

70. *See supra* note 55. The majority of MLB's 30 teams saw an increase in local television viewership over 1995 levels. Michael Freeman, ... *A Long Way to Go,* MEDIAWEEK, Sept. 23, 1996, at 4. This increase in viewership was fueled largely by a record-setting season of home runs and a wild-card system that kept more than half of the teams in playoff contention well into September. *See* Mark Starr, *Diamond Jubilee,* NEWSWEEK, Sept. 16, 1996, at 78. Only 11 teams "managed to creep back up to the same or similar rating netted before the strike," meaning that 12 teams have lost ratings from last season and 19 have still not recovered to where they were in 1993. MEDIAWEEK, *supra* at 4. Nationally, television ratings are even dimmer. *Id.*

71. Indeed, two full seasons after the 1994 baseball strike, at the conclusion of the 1996 MLB regular season, Fox Sports had only sold 75% of its ad time for the upcoming World Series and felt it necessary to cut the price of a 30-second ad by $75,000. *World Series Just Got $75G Cheaper, Id.* at 3. With ad time still available as of the start of the series, remaining inventory was further discounted by another $25,000. *See* Rudy Martzke, *Sports on TV,* USA TODAY, Oct. 17, 1996, at 2C. The saleability of the World Series, the crown jewel of baseball's events, stands in sharp contrast to ad sales for the 1997 Super Bowl, also on Fox. Fox sold out all 58 available 30-second ad slots (at a rate of $1.2 million a spot, up from $1.1 million from the previous year) three weeks in advance of the game. Dottie Enrico, *Super Bowl Ad Roster Filled at $1.2 Million a Spot,* USA TODAY, Jan. 7, 1997, at 1B.

72. Capping devices can also be applied within the retail licensing context. Under a retail licensing arrangement, one possible approach to limit the

extent of any required reduction in the minimum guarantee, and provided the license calls for scheduled minimum installment payments throughout the contract year, is to (i) provide that the mechanism be only triggered by the loss of a minimum number of games, and (ii) cap the maximum amount of the reduction to a designated percentage of the minimum guarantee, and then require licensee to only pay earned royalties on sales in excess of the reduced minimum guarantee.

73. For example: VF Corporation owns Nutmeg Mills and Cutler Sports; Rusell owns The Game and Chalkline; Fruit of the Loom owns Salem Sportswear, Pro Player and Artex; NIKE owns Sports Specialties and Bauer; and Tultex owns Logo Athletics and Discus Athletics.

74. That is, having fewer overall merchandise licensees and sponsors but in turn requiring those selected companies to make substantially greater commitments and investments in the licensor's sport. McGee, *supra* note 11; Nichols et al., *The 1994 Annual Industry Report*, TEAM LICENSING BUS., May 1994, at 18, 26. In many instances, the financial commitment of some merchandise licensees now rivals that of corporate sponsors—the long favored participants in a League's licensing program (because of their in-game advertising in national broadcasts and national consumer promotions).

Why Is the PGA Teed Off at Casey Martin? An Exemple of How the Americans with Disabilities Act (ADA) Has Changed Sports Law[*]

W. Kent Davis

Should a disabled golfer be permitted to ride in a golf cart when PGA rules prohibit such actions? Does allowing the golfer to ride in the cart significantly alter then nature of the sporting event? For several years now Americans have been debating such questions.

The Americans With Disabilities Act has clearly had an impact on American sports. However, the proper dimensions of that impact are still a matter of great controversy. In this essay, Kent Davis explores the history of the application of the ADA to sports and offers insights into what the ADA does, and doesn't, mean for the world of sports.

[*]From Volume 9, Number 1, Fall 1998, pp. 1-44.

I. INTRODUCTION

Golf is a good walk spoiled.

- Mark Twain

When Mark Twain made his humorous observation, he probably had no idea that the link between golf and walking would one day become a topic of national debate. In the early months of 1998, Americans found themselves divided over the issue of whether a disabled professional golfer should be allowed to use a motorized cart during Professional Golfers Association (PGA) tournaments. This time, however, the issue would not be a laughing matter, as the two sides of the debate rallied around such American icons as Arnold Palmer and Jack Nicklaus on the one hand and the sympathetic plaintiff, Casey Martin, on the other.

To Casey Martin, golf is not "a good walk spoiled." Stricken with a disability ominously labeled Klippel-Trenaunay-Weber Syndrome, he finds walking as daunting as the game of golf itself; just limping around eighteen holes is "a victory of sorts" for him. Given this limitation, it would be difficult not to see Martin as a hero in his simple request to use a golf cart to make his way around tournament courses. Americans have long put athletes on a pedestal and made them the topics of *causes cJlPbres*. Disabled athletes have been the object of special adoration by the public. For example, Kenny Walker has achieved fame and sympathy as a football player for the University of Nebraska and the Denver Broncos despite being deaf. Jimmy Connors became a popular championship tennis player while afflicted with asthma. Several famous athletes, such as basketball's Terry Cummings, have become sports heroes while suffering from serious heart conditions. And Gail Devers won a gold medal in the women's 100 meter dash at the Olympics even though she has Graves disease. A recent empirical study points to one of the reasons why disabled athletes are held in such high regard for their courage: these disabled sports stars "would rather play with physical pain than suffer the emotional pain of not playing." Americans, it has often been noted, love an underdog, especially one perceived as suffering special hardship.

The Casey Martin debate would not remain a discussion confined to the sports pages of newspapers. Unfortunately, like too many

American disagreements, the decision over whether to allow Martin to use a golf cart would ultimately be decided in a courtroom. However, the judicial decision-making would present some unique questions. Despite the long history of public support for disabled athletes, the law had been silent on the rights of these figures until relatively recently, and judicial wrangling over the rights of the disabled had largely been confined to amateur athletics. The passage of the Americans with Disabilities Act (ADA) in 1990, however, gave Martin the legal means of pursuing his desire to use a golf cart. In fact, his case would prove to be the first to apply this antidiscrimination law—requiring reasonable accommodation for people with disabilities—to professional sports.

Using the *Martin* case as a backdrop, this paper will discuss how the passage of the ADA has affected the rights of disabled athletes. Part II will outline a history of disability discrimination laws in the United States, particularly as they affect athletics. Part III will discuss how these statutes had been applied to disabled athletes by courts in the years preceding the *Martin* case. Part IV will discuss the *Martin* case in detail, including a history of the PGA, a biography of Casey Martin himself, and a discussion of the public debate that preceded and followed the trial. After examining all of these issues, the paper will conclude by asserting that the *Martin* case, though not legally earth shattering in its holding, may ultimately prove to be a watershed event by injecting the ADA into professional sports.

II. A History Of Disability Discrimination Statutes In The United States

A. The Pre-ADA Statutes

Before the ADA was passed, several statutes protected the rights of the disabled in the United States. Congress took tentative steps toward eliminating discrimination against the disabled when it passed the Rehabilitation Act in 1973. Section 504 of that Act provides that "[n]o otherwise qualified [disabled] individual with a disability in the United States . . . shall, solely by reason of her or his disability, be excluded from the participation in, be denied the benefits of, or be subjected to discrimination under any program or activity receiving federal financial assistance." As part of its legal bite, "the Rehabilitation Act requires federally funded programs to make reasonable accommodations [for] disabled persons." In order for a plaintiff to successfully bring suit against a defendant, he must prove four elements: "1) he is 'disabled' under the Rehabilitation Act; 2) he is 'otherwise qualified' to participate in the activity or program in question; 3) he was excluded from the activity or program solely on the basis of his disability; and 4) the activity or program receives federal funding." The Rehabilitation Act remains an important piece of legislation to this day for several reasons. First, many sports programs are recipients of federal aid, particularly high school and college activities. Second, the ADA works in conjunction with the Rehabilitation Act in many ways, even though it subsumes the earlier statute in some respects and extends beyond any previous statutory provisions to provide clearer regulations. Most important, however, is the analogy that courts often draw between the Rehabilitation Act and the ADA; courts have repeatedly used decisions on the Rehabilitation Act as precedent to formulate holdings on the ADA. This is a valuable link for ADA plaintiffs, for the mere fact that the Rehabilitation Act is seventeen years older than the ADA means that there is much more case law on point involving the older statute.

In the years between passage of the Rehabilitation Act and the ADA, Congress took further steps to eliminate discrimination against the disabled. Perhaps the strongest legislation existed in the area of education. For example, the Individuals with Disabilities Education Act (IDEA) is a civil rights statute that requires schools to provide disabled students an "individualized education plan" so that they can receive an "appropriate" education. Part of an appropriate education is athletics, so the IDEA presumably applies to school sports activities. Other statutes that Congress passed in the years leading up to the ADA included the Developmental Disabilities Bill of Rights Act of 1975, the Air Carrier Access Act of 1986, the Voting Accessibility for the Elderly and Handicapped Act of 1984, and the Fair Housing Act Amendments of 1988.

B. The Americans with Disabilities Act (ADA)

In 1990, Congress sought to ensure that the federal government would play an even bigger role in ensuring the rights of the disabled when it passed the ADA. Finding a "continuing existence of unfair and unnecessary discrimination and prejudice" against the disabled, Congress sweepingly sought "the elimination of discrimination against individuals with disabilities." Drafted by Senator Tom Harkin, and backed by Senator Bob Dole, "[t]he ADA prohibits discrimination on the basis of disability in employment, programs and services provided by state and local governments, goods and services provided by private companies, and in commercial facilities." When "President [Bush] signed the ADA into law on July 26, 1990," he described it as "the world's first comprehensive declaration of equality for people with disabilities." The ADA was subsequently codified under five Titles. In the parts most relevant to sports law, "Title I covers private employment discrimination; Title II covers the provision of programs and services by state and local governments; and Title III covers the provision of services by public accommodations and commercial facilities such as restaurants, hotels, and . . ."—most applicable here— golf courses. The arrival of these Titles "has resulted in a booming area of law" for the disabled.

The ADA requires the Equal Employment Opportunity Commission (EEOC) to issue regulations and guidelines implementing Title I; a similar provision requires the Department of Justice (DOJ) to issue federal regulations governing Titles II and III. These regulations are very important, for the Supreme Court has stated that they "are of significant assistance" in fleshing out the basic provisions of federal disability discrimination statutes. When Casey Martin brought his ADA claim against the PGA, he based his claims on Titles I and III. Thus, a closer examination of these two titles is helpful to understanding the rest of this article.

1. Title I of the ADA

Title I states rather bluntly that "[n]o covered entity shall discriminate against a qualified individual with a disability because of the disability of such individual in regard to job application procedures, the hiring, advancement, or discharge of employees, employee compensation, job training, and other terms, conditions, and privileges of employment." Looking at the plain language of this passage, it is clear that one must first prove himself to be "disabled." There are several ways that a person can be qualified as disabled: 1) having "a physical or mental impairment that substantially limits one or more of the 'major life activities of such individual'; 2) having a record of such impairment; or 3) being regarded as having such an impairment."

According to Congress, qualifying as disabled should be rather common under these three prongs, for the findings which introduce the ADA state that "some 43,000,000 Americans have one or more physical or mental disabilities, and this number is increasing . . . ." At times, however, proving that one is disabled can be a tough burden, or at least a confusing one. For example, rejection for one job application due to physical impairments, by itself, has been repeatedly held to lack the impact necessary to prove the ADA's prerequisite that a person is substantially limited in the life activity of work under the first prong of the ADA's disability definition, assuming of course that the person is able to work elsewhere. On the other hand, under the third prong of the definition ("being regarded as having such an impairment"), if a prospective employer treats an impairment (either actual or perceived) as substantially limiting one or more of life's major activities, and discriminates based on this treatment, then a person is deemed "disabled" and a violation of the ADA has occurred. This is especially true when the prospective employer treats a perceived disability as a blanket disqualifier for employment. Under this reasoning, even a single refusal to hire based on this perception may adequately make out a case of an employee "being regarded as having such an impairment"; in other words, a pattern of such perceptions may not be necessary. These are subtle distinctions, but ones that could make or break a plaintiff's case.

Returning to the plain language of the ADA's prohibition of discrimination, having proven that he is disabled, a plaintiff must next prove that he is nonetheless "qualified" for the job in question. To be "qualified," the person must be able to "perform the essential functions of the employment position that such individual holds or desires." It is the definition of "essential functions" that often proves a sticky point for litigants under the ADA.

Finally, to succeed under Title I's plain language, a plaintiff must prove that he has been discriminated against in an employment situation. Employment discrimination includes not only excluding one from employment based on a disability, but also "not making reasonable accommodations to the known physical or mental limitations of an otherwise qualified individual with a disability."

Courts looking at the plain language of the ADA have begun to encapsulate these elements and the associated burdens of proof. To establish a prima facie disparate employment treatment case under the ADA, the employee has the initial burden of proving that he is a disabled person, "that he or she is qualified to perform the essential functions of the job (either with or without reasonable accommodation), and that he or she has suffered an adverse employment action under circumstances from which an inference of unlawful discrimination arises." In meeting this initial burden, the employee need only show that the discrimination based on disability was "a" cause of the action taken, not necessarily the "sole" cause. If the employee is successful in this initial step, the employer would then have the burden of proving that the employee was not an otherwise qualified person or that the alleged discrimination was for reasons other than the disability. Finally, if the employer is successful with its argument, the burden shifts back to the employee to prove that the employer's reasons for the alleged actions are based on misconceptions or unfounded conclusions, and that the reasons articulated for the alleged action entail unjustified consideration of the disability.

Another factor that affects Title I is the traditional law of disparate impact. Under the ADA, an employer may not use selection criteria or tests that "tend to screen out" qualified disabled employees unless the criteria "is shown to be job-related for the position in question." To make out a prima facie case in such disparate impact situations, the plaintiff need only prove that the challenged standard disparately impacts the group of disabled people of which he is a member, and that the plaintiff is otherwise qualified for the position. The burden then shifts back to the employer to prove that the challenged tests are job-related or are required by business necessity.

Before ending the discussion of Title I, it should be noted that defendants have several general defenses against employment discrimination claims. First, an employer does not have to hire a disabled person if that person would constitute a "direct threat to the health or safety of other individuals in the workplace." The EEOC has extended this defense by regulation to cover situations where the individual may be a direct threat to himself instead of others. However, the direct threat defense is a high hurdle for defendants, for the EEOC has deemed that the threat to personal safety may not involve "slightly increased risk. The risk can only be considered when it poses a significant risk, i.e., high probability, of substantial harm."

Another defense available to employers is proof that a reasonable accommodation would constitute an "undue hardship" due to "significant difficulty or expense" in achieving it. "In determining whether an accommodation would cause undue hardship on a covered entity," courts consider the following factors, among others: "the nature and [net] cost of the accommodation . . ., the overall financial resources" of the employer, and the impact of the accommodation upon the operation of the employer's facility.

2. Title III of the ADA

Title III broadly states that "[n]o individual shall be discriminated against on the basis of disability in the full and equal enjoyment of the goods, services, facilities, privileges, advantages, or accommodations of any place of public accommodation by any person who owns, leases (or leases to), or operates a place of public accommodation." Turning once more to the plain language of the statute, a defendant must first be shown to be a place of public accommodation under Title III. In fleshing out the entities covered by this first element, section 12181(7) of the statute gives a very detailed list of facilities that qualify as a public accommodation, including among many others a "golf course, or other place of exercise or recreation." One commentator has noted that "[a] type of entity that is not explicitly covered [by section 12181(7)] but would seem to fit many of the criteria of other covered entities is 'professional or business organizations'," which could easily include such sports organizations as the NCAA or PGA. It should additionally be noted that a separate provision of Title III, section 12189, is equally determinative in deciding whether an entity is covered as a public accommodation, for it states that "[a]ny person that offers examinations or courses related to applications, licensing, certifications, or credentialing for secondary or post-secondary education, professional, or trade purposes shall offer such examinations or courses in a place and manner accessible to persons with disabilities or offer alternative accessible arrangements for such individuals." Any sports organization that falls within this definition would thus qualify as a public accommodation.

Once a defendant is proven to be a public accommodation, the next step is to show that it has discriminated against a disabled person in some manner under the text of Title III. There are several ways that a public accommodation can discriminate under Title III, and each specific offense carries its own particular defense. For example:

> - Section 12182(b)(2)(i) deems the imposition of eligibility criteria that tends to screen out disabled individuals discriminatory "unless [the screening] can be shown to be necessary for the provision of the service."
> - Section 12182(b)(2)(A)(ii) deems "a failure to make a 'reasonable modification' in policies" affecting public accommodations discriminatory unless it can be shown that the "modification would fundamentally alter" the services or facilities.

- Section 12182(b)(2)(A)(iii) states that a public accommodation discriminates when it fails to take steps to ensure that the disabled are not treated differently because of the absence of auxiliary aids and services, unless the provision of these would fundamentally alter the nature of the service/facility or would result in an undue burden.

- Section 12182(b)(2)(A)(iv) states that "a failure to remove architectural barriers [or] communication barriers" in places of public accommodation is discriminatory if it affects access for the disabled, but only where such removal is "readily achievable."

In further explaining all of these potential violations, the DOJ regulations require a public accommodation to afford facilities "in the most integrated setting appropriate to the needs of the individual."

In addition to the specific defenses available under the individual categories of discrimination, there are some general defenses available under Title III. Perhaps the most important for the Casey Martin case is the simple exception that Title III does "not apply to private clubs or establishments." Another example is the "direct threat" defense, which is described in terms similar to what we saw under Title I. Once again, the direct threat defense is a high hurdle for defendants, for Title III itself and the DOJ regulations define this defense as "a significant risk to the health or safety of others" by the disabled individuals, require an individualized assessment of such risk, and demand that defendants consider modifications and auxiliary aids/services to eliminate such risks if they are found to exist.

C. The Critics of the ADA

Despite its lofty goals, the ADA has been a source of controversy since its passage, with many arguing that it reaches too far into every aspect of American society. One of the most vocal critics has been attorney Philip K. Howard, who wrote the 1994 best-selling book THE DEATH OF COMMON SENSE. Though largely sympathetic toward the plight of the disabled, Mr. Howard spends several pages of his book pointing out some unfortunate paradoxes of the Rehabilitation Act and the ADA. For example:

- Largely because of the dictates of federal disability laws, "[g]ifted students, in contrast with disabled children, receive virtually no support or attention from America's school systems . . . . The ratio of funding of special education programs to gifted programs is about eleven dollars to one cent."

- The ADA fails to acknowledge that "what benefits a person with one disability may harm someone with another disability. Low drinking fountains and telephones are harder to use for the elderly or those with bad backs . . . . Curb cuts are more dangerous for the blind, who have more difficulty knowing when they have reached the end of the block."

- Though the ADA purports to protect upwards of 43 million Americans,

the overwhelming preponderance of the ADA regulations, . . . and virtually all cost and conflict, relate to wheelchair users . . . . It turns out, in a number that seems to have been actively suppressed [in the Congressional findings], that not 2[sic] percent of the disabled are in wheelchairs, and many of those are confined to nursing homes. Billions are being spent to make every nook and cranny of every facility in America wheelchair accessible . . ., when children die of malnutrition and finish almost dead last in math.

- "Under ADA regulations, doorknobs are now illegal in the workplace (they are hard to turn for someone without full use of his hands). So is carpet that is more than one quarter-inch thick (it causes too much friction for wheelchairs.)"

In summing up his criticisms of the ADA, Mr. Howard notes that "[t]he ADA gave the disabled the right to sue virtually every establishment, public or private, for discrimination," but argues that the fight for rights under the ADA has become "obsessive" and that handing out these rights "does not resolve conflict. It aggravates it."

Mr. Howard has found a kindred spirit in the most unlikely of places, for a few African-American leaders have noted that the ADA potentially dilutes the advances of the black civil rights movement. One such leader well-known to Georgians, Julian Bond, has caustically made some observations about the growth of rights symbolized by the ADA:

Today, the protected classes extend to a majority of all Americans, including white men over forty, short people, the chemically addicted, the left-handed, the obese, members of all religions. Surely there is a scholar somewhere who can tell us how we came to this state of affairs and how the road to civil rights became so crowded. . . . In our society, there were only so many fruits to go

around. When short, fat, old white men step to the front of the line
. . . then our civil rights are as endangered as they were by Bull
Connor . . . .

Critics of the ADA have not confined themselves to general
discussions of the law, for tough comments have accompanied the
statute's foray into sports law. For example, Professor Matthew
Mitten has commented on the dilemma faced by Loyola Marymount
University over the disability of star basketball player Hank Gathers.
Gathers suffered from a known irregular heartbeat. When he col-
lapsed and died during a basketball game, the university was sued
heavily in two suits. Yet Mitten notes that, "[i]ronically, Loyola
Marymount's refusal to permit Gathers to continue playing basketball with his heart condition also could have resulted in litigation"
under the ADA. This obviously presents tough choices for some sports
programs. Equally biting criticisms have accompanied the Casey
Martin case. Syndicated columnist Tony Snow, though largely sympathetic toward Martin himself, takes a dim view of the ADA, arguing
that "the feds ought to butt out. The government already has an
annoying knack for making everybody's business its business—with
the result that federal 'help' costs more and does less good than ever."
Finally, *Sports Illustrated* magazine, in commenting on the Martin
case, has quipped that the ADA "has pushed sports enterprises like
[the PGA] to the mouth of a very dark cave" and "has invited a rash
of litigation that is testing the best minds in sports and law." This
alleged rash of litigation is our next topic of discussion.

III. Prior Court Cases Involving Disability Discrimination In Sports Law

Bringing lawsuits to support the rights of the disabled is largely a
twentieth century phenomenon. One commentator has observed that
the use of lawsuits to support the rights of the disabled—particularly
disabled athletes—is inherently unfortunate. Instead, he argues that
"[t]he decision to participate in . . . sports should be the product of
mutual agreement between the handicapped or physically impaired
athlete and family, school officials, and physicians." One should not
forget that the ADA itself urges "the use of alternative means of
dispute resolution . . . to resolve disputes." Despite these earnest
appeals, like too many facets of American life, these decisions have
often spilled into the courtroom. The complaints by plaintiffs have

generally involved two areas: constitutional claims and statutory claims (under the Rehabilitation Act and/or ADA).

A. Constitutional Claims

The use of constitutional claims on behalf of the disabled has seen a rather brief and now largely settled history. One of the earliest suits specifically involving a disabled athlete was *Neeld v. American Hockey League*, in which a hockey player claimed that the league's policy banning one-eyed players violated the Equal Protection Clause. This case is interesting because the court rejected the Equal Protection Clause claim when it found that the action resulted from private conduct, not state action subject to constitutional scrutiny; however, the court also included in dicta the statement that a disabled athlete has an enforceable constitutional right to participate in college sports if such program constitutes state action. Despite this promising language for disabled athletes, no other court has recognized a fundamental right to play college or high school sports.

Other attempts to lay constitutional claims for the disabled (and disabled athletes in particular) have met similar doom, mainly because of a watershed disability case heard by the Supreme Court in 1985, *City of Cleburne v. Cleburne Living Center. Cleburne* involved mentally retarded citizens who sued under the Equal Protection Clause of the Fourteenth Amendment, claiming they were members of a protected class (i.e. the disabled) much like members of racial minorities. If this argument had been successful, the actions of the defendant in requiring building permits for group homes for the retarded would have been subject to "heightened scrutiny," a very tough hurdle for defendants. However, the Court disagreed with the plaintiffs and found that they were not part of a protected class; thus, the Equal Protection Clause only required a much easier rationality test. In the wake of *Cleburne*, a "school can justify the exclusion of [certain] handicapped athletes from its athletics program if its decision is rationally related to a legitimate objective."

Suits have also attempted to invoke the Due Process Clause as a method of securing rights. These attempts have largely been unsuccessful, and one commentator has noted that there is little chance that one could successfully prove there is a liberty or property interest in playing interscholastic or intercollegiate athletics; thus, there is little way to argue a violation of due process in these settings. Even if the disabled athlete *could* prove a property or liberty interest, however, a team "could rationally justify such exclusion based on concern for the athlete's health [or other justifications]." This reasoning may doom due process claims in the professional sports world as well.

Given this history, the bottom line on constitutional claims appears to be that they are largely ineffective in the context of disabled athletes. The futility of constitutional claims has been offset, however, by the enactment of statutes prohibiting discrimination against the disabled.

B. Statutory Claims

The use of statutory law as a basis for lawsuits has a richer history than constitutional claims. Perhaps the first attempt to seek a judicial remedy for discrimination against the disabled occurred in 1934, when a father unsuccessfully sued a school system under an Ohio statute to have his mentally retarded son admitted to public school. The enactments of the Rehabilitation Act and the ADA have resulted in more and more private litigants asserting discrimination claims in the courts. Unlike the federal constitution, these statutes require a "substantial justification" rather than a mere rational basis for discriminating against a disabled athlete. Before the Casey Martin case, these statutes had never been applied to professional sports. However, a wide variety of claims had been brought at the high school and collegiate levels, disabled coaches had sued over discriminatory job requirements under the ADA, and some disabled professional athletes had brought state claims based on laws similar to the ADA. These prior cases, especially the high school and college athletics cases, provide some persuasive precedent for the new link between the ADA and professional sports, as the court in the *Martin* case noted:

> Although the PGA Tour is a professional sports organization and professional sports enjoys certainly, a much higher profile and display of skills than collegiate or other lower levels of competitive sports, the analysis of the issues does not change from one level to the next. High school athletic associations have just as much interest in the equal application of their rules and the integrity of their games as do professionals.

1. The High School Cases

State high school athletic associations generally ban students who turn nineteen prior to the start of the school year from participating in sports. The reasons for this widespread ban are threefold: 1) "to prevent a competitive advantage for teams that use older players"; 2) "to protect younger [presumably smaller] players from injury;" and 3) "to discourage 'red-shirting,' the practice of delaying education to gain athletic maturity." At times, these policies have inadvertently affected the eligibility of students who were held back in school purely because of a learning disability. Courts have differed as to whether waiver of these age requirements is a reasonable modification under the federal disability discrimination statutes.

The early trend among courts seemed to be that the federal laws required a waiver of the age requirement when it came to disabled athletes. For example, the Court of Appeals of Texas, in the 1993 case of *University Interscholastic League v. Buchanan*, examined the ban imposed by the defendant League (which regulated high school athletics in Texas), finding that "the underlying purpose of the over-19 rule is to ensure the safety of the participating student athletes and the equality of competitors." Buchanan, who had been held back in school because of a learning disability, requested a waiver of the League rule so that he could play football, a move the League resisted. Because Buchanan had not participated in red-shirting and was average in size for the team, the court found that the concerns that made the rule necessary were not present if he were allowed to play. Thus, as the court reasoned, "[a] waiver mechanism for the over-19 rule would permit the [League] to consider the facts of particular situations in order to make individualized determinations as to the enforcement of the rule. Such determinations are *reasonable accommodations*."

The reasoning of the *Buchanan* case found support shortly thereafter in a federal court. In *Johnson v. Florida High School Activities Association, Inc.*, the U.S. District Court for the Middle District of Florida in 1995 addressed a situation very similar to the *Buchanan* case. Johnson had been held back in school because of a hearing disability, preventing his participation in high school sports under the Florida over-19 rule. Much like the *Buchanan* court, the district court here held that; "[r]esolution of this issue requires an examination of the purposes of age requirement as applied to the instant case." It quickly reasoned that:

> [T]he relationship between the age requirement and its purposes must be such that waiving the age requirement in the instant case would necessarily undermine the purposes of the requirement . . .
> . [W]aiving the age requirement in the instant case does not

fundamentally alter the nature of the program. . . . Therefore, waiving the age requirement constitutes a 'reasonable accommodation' and must be undertaken.

Despite these victories for plaintiffs, the tide in the over-19 cases seems to be turning toward the defendants. The first wave of this tide came in 1994 with the Eighth Circuit decision in *Pottgen v. Missouri State High School Activities Association*. Pottgen, much like the other litigants discussed above, was held back in school because of a learning disability, which made him ineligible to play high school baseball. The court here rather bluntly stated that "the age limit is an essential eligibility requirement of the interscholastic baseball program," however. It then explained that "[w]aiving an essential eligibility standard would constitute a fundamental alteration in the nature of the baseball program. Other than waiving the age limit, no manner, method, or means is available which would permit Pottgen to satisfy the age limit. Consequently, no reasonable accommodation exists." In stark contrast to the *Buchanan* and *Johnson* cases, the court took specific issue with the argument that these situations required an individualized "essential eligibility requirement" inquiry, reasoning that if this were required "[a] public entity would never know the outer boundaries of its 'services, programs, or activities.' . . . Clearly the ADA imposes no such duty." Given this reasoning, the court held that waiving the rule is not a reasonable modification.

Pottgen was quickly followed in 1995 by the Sixth Circuit's decision in *Sandison v. Michigan High School Athletic Association, Inc.* Under a similar fact pattern, the *Sandison* court quickly sided with the *Pottgen* decision:

> [W]e agree with the court in *Pottgen* that waiver of the age restriction fundamentally alters the sports program . . . . Removing the age restriction injects into competition students older than the vast majority of other students, and the record shows that the older students are generally more physically mature than younger students. Expanding the sports program to include older students works a fundamental alteration . . . .

> . . . .

> [T]he plaintiffs are not subjected to "discrimination on the basis of disability," and waiver is not in this case a "reasonable modification."

The *Pottgen* and *Sandison* decisions seem to be holding water, as they have already been cited with favor in at least one lower court in another Circuit. However, they have sparked some fierce commentary in law reviews. One author, for instance, chastises the *Sandison* court for failing "to assess whether an individualized waiver [of the over-19 rule] is a reasonable accommodation" and argues that courts need to be more willing to accommodate the needs of disabled athletes in general, in order "to further the goals of the ADA and Rehabilitation Act to eliminate the neglect and discrimination of disabled individuals." A fellow commentator has been more specific, urging the adoption (by the Fifth Circuit) of the "case-by-case" analysis used in *Johnson, Buchanan,* and *Dennin* which weighs the individual interest of the disabled student and the purposes of the over-19 rule. This author also urges high school athletic associations to adopt their own waiver procedures that apply to the disabled, dismissing the additional work required as "not an undue burden," but conversely mandated by the Rehabilitation Act and the ADA.

Despite the voices of these critics, the trend represented by *Pottgen* and *Sandison* seems to comport with the views of one eminent sports law scholar. Professor Mitten argues that a sports organization does not have to substantially modify its standards by changing its rules of play or reducing the quality of team play to enable a disabled athlete to participate, given Supreme Court precedent. Furthermore, he states that a disabled "athlete is not 'otherwise qualified' if physically unable to perform or function effectively in a particular sport," and organizations may validly exclude disabled athletes for safety reasons. These arguments, along with the *Pottgen* and *Sandison* decisions themselves, seem to raise the bar on the definition of "reasonable accommodations" and "reasonable modifications" for plaintiffs. Thus, it is not clear from the high school cases alone that Casey Martin would have an easy time in his simple request to waive the "no cart" rule of the PGA.

2. The College Cases

Resort to the federal disability discrimination laws has also begun to appear in college sports. Several federal district courts have found themselves deciding what is a reasonable accommodation or modification in this setting. Unfortunately for the sake of clarity, the results are diverse. A landmark case in this area is the 1995 district court decision in *Pahulu v. University of Kansas.* Pahulu had a scholarship to play football at Kansas. During a scrimmage, he suffered a hit to the head. Afterward, the team doctors determined that he had a congenitally narrow cervical canal and disqualified him from the team. Pahulu went to several other doctors on his own, all of whom said it was safe for him to play, but the team still barred him. He sued under the Rehabilitation Act, asking that he be allowed to play. The court's ruling on his claim is revealing:

> [T]his court finds that for Pahulu, intercollegiate football may be a major life activity, i.e., learning. The defendants' action, however, is not a substantial limitation upon the plaintiff's opportunity to learn . . . . [T]here are a myriad of other educational opportunities available to Pahulu at KU. Consequently, Pahulu is not disabled . . . .
>
>   . . . .
>
> Even if the plaintiff is disabled, he is not otherwise qualified . . . . Whether a person is "otherwise qualified" . . . primarily is a factual inquiry . . . . The defendants argue that Pahulu must satisfy the program's requirements, e.g., medical clearance for participation, in order to be otherwise qualified . . . .
>
>   . . . .
>
> [T]he conclusion of the KU physicians, although conservative, is reasonable and rational. Thus, the defendants' decision regarding disqualification has a rational and reasonable basis and is supported by substantial competent evidence for which the court is unwilling to substitute its own judgment.

Another federal district court took a similarly dim view of a plaintiff's claim in the 1997 case of *Bowers v. National Collegiate Athletic Association*. Bowers, a learning disabled student, wished to play football at Temple University. However, the NCAA required students to finish "core course" requirements while in high school before eligibility for college football could be granted. When he applied, the NCAA's Clearinghouse (set up to review academic qualifications of players) ruled that he had only met three of the requisite thirteen core course requirements, which made him ineligible for college football. Bowers, claiming that the failure to meet the core course requirements stemmed from his disability, sued the NCAA under the ADA, seeking a waiver of the core course requirements. The court was not sympathetic:

> Eligibility requirements are "essential" or "necessary" when they are reasonably necessary to accomplish the purposes of a program. The basic purpose of the NCAA is to maintain intercollegiate athletics as an integral part of the educational program and to assure that those individuals representing an institution in intercollegiate athletics competition maintain satisfactory progress in their education . . . .
>
> . . . .
>
> [T]he NCAA initial eligibility criteria are essentially minimum requirements which assure that freshmen student-athletes are sufficiently able to handle college academic work, along with the demand of participating in intercollegiate athletics during their first year of college . . . .
>
> . . . .
>
> [T]he NCAA "core course" definition [is] essential to the NCAA's provision of the privilege of participation in the NCAA's intercollegiate athletic program . . . . [A] complete abandonment of the "core course" requirement would fundamentally alter the nature of the privilege of participation in the NCAA's intercollegiate athletic program.

These cases may have been the beginning of a consistent trend were it not for the 1996 case of *Knapp v. Northwestern University*, in which a U.S. district court took the opposite stance of the *Pahulu* and *Bowers* courts. Knapp was a basketball player at Northwestern on a scholarship. When the team discovered that he suffered from a heart condition—ventricular fibrillation—it barred him from practicing or competing with the team. Knapp sued the university, claiming that allowing him to play with an internal defibrillator (with bi-weekly interrogation of the device) would be a reasonable modification of team policy. The court here took direct issue with the stance of the other federal courts. For example, it disputed the *Pahulu* court's logic (though without naming *Pahulu* directly) that a rationality test applied to cases involving discrimination against disabled college athletes. Moreover, the judge issuing the opinion took direct issue against other courts by name (including *Pahulu*) when he said that:

> The district courts, and these are the only courts that have addressed the issue, are split over whether participation in sports is a 'major life activity . . . .
>
>   . . . .
>
> While the issue is not free from doubt, I find that intercollegiate sports competition may constitute a major life activity. I find, without doubt, that it is for Nicholas Knapp.

Finally, the court noted that "[i]t also undermines the purpose of the Rehabilitation Act not to allow a disabled individual to pursue his chosen field," and "the Rehabilitation Act requires that remote or minimal risks not be used to legitimize discrimination." With all of these considerations in mind, the court decided that the only reasonable accommodation was to allow Knapp to play with an internal defibrillator interrogated bi-weekly. The bar had been lowered much closer to the ground for plaintiffs like Casey Martin with this case.

3. Tentative Steps into Professional Sports

Though Casey Martin was the first to apply federal disability laws to professional sports, several cases had danced on the perimeter of this area in the past. In combination with the amateur sports case discussed above, these cases may shed a little light on how successful a leap into the professional arena might prove to be. To begin, professional athletes had successfully challenged professional sports league rules prohibiting athletes with certain disabilities from competing on the field of play under state employment discrimination laws. A prime example is the case of *Neeld v. American Hockey League*, in which a U.S. district court forced waiver of a league's rule that prohibited one-eyed players from competing; the court reasoned that the rule violated New York's Human Right Law, which prohibited discrimination on the basis of disability unless the disability is a bona fide occupational hazard. Though obviously not binding precedent, this case might at least be persuasive in the Martin situation.

A perhaps more tenuous—but nonetheless helpful—comparison could be made to the 1992 U.S. district court case of *Anderson v. Little League Baseball, Inc.* Anderson, who was confined to a wheelchair, had been acting as a Little League coach for several years. The national company controlling Little League adopted a new policy forbidding people in wheelchairs from coaching on the field for the safety of children (i.e. concerns that children would collide with the wheelchairs). Anderson filed suit under Title III of the ADA, seeking an injunction against the new policy. In deciding against Little League Baseball, the court chastised it for enacting a blanket policy without engaging in an individual assessment over whether Anderson was a safety threat or whether reasonable modifications could be made that would allow him to coach. As the court put it, "[r]egrettably, such a policy—implemented without public discourse—falls markedly short of the requirements enunciated in the Americans with Disabilities Act and its implementing regulations." The link to Casey Martin might not seem obvious, but here was a case where an employee in a sports setting was granted relief by the court, all because a sports league had implemented a blanket policy which banned him from participating. The bar had apparently been lowered again for Martin.

IV. THE CASEY MARTIN CASE

Given this sometimes confusing and diverse case history, it would be easy to see why the Casey Martin case was not a slam dunk for either party. For one thing, Martin could not bring a constitutional claim against the PGA with any hope of success. In addition, the courts' definitions of "reasonable modification" and "fundamental alteration" under Title III and similar statutory provisions had been murky at best, for no consensus had been reached across the nation. Furthermore, no court had directly applied Title III to the world of professional sports, and it remained to be seen whether this setting would make a difference in defining the relevant terms. Finally, and perhaps most importantly, no case had directly applied Title I to sports leagues. It remained to be seen whether these organizations would indeed be seen by a court as employers subject to the ADA's prohibition of employment discrimination.

On top of the indecisive history of caselaw governing disabled athletes, the Martin case presented two unusual litigants: Martin himself and the PGA. The unique characteristics of these two parties, as with many court cases, would help guide the court's decision. Thus, a greater understanding of the two litigants is helpful.

A. The Litigants

1. The Professional Golf Association

Evidence of golf in America dates back to 1659, when some historical accounts relate the game being played in upstate New York. Similar accounts discuss the game being played around Savannah, Georgia, and Charleston, South Carolina, by early settlers. After 1811, these accounts disappeared in newspaper stories, and the curiosity seems to have died out. The history of golf in America really begins on February 22, 1888, when six men assembled in a cow pasture in Yonkers, New York with a set of golf clubs and balls brought back from Scotland by Robert Lockhart. By November of 1888 the men had come to enjoy this new pastime so much that they decided to form a club that would provide funds for maintenance of the pastureland course and "cement the comradeship that had evolved among the handful of golf lovers." Accordingly, they adopted a set of simple resolutions—a sort of "Magna Carta" of American golf according to historians. This simple act would prove to spark an amazing growth of the sport. By the dawn of the twentieth century, the number of organized golf clubs would reach one thousand.

In the first two or three decades after its birth in Yonkers, golf had no pro tour. In 1916, however, the PGA was founded. Though it was not even close to being a labor union that would protect the players, the PGA gave the pros an organizational entity, with a constitution, bylaws, and its own seal. The early tour was not very successful, and the professionals who played on it were not very good compared to their counterparts in Europe. To add to the problem, the PGA almost immediately split into two camps—touring pros and teaching pros. The war between these two camps raged for thirty years, and gave the game a poor public image. By the late 1940's, however, players began to understand the value of a good image, and good behavior began to prevail among all members of the PGA. The arrival of television coverage in 1954, however, was the real unifying force in the PGA, and the game has grown tremendously in power and money since that time. By 1967, the PGA had grown so powerful that the players owned the television rights to all tournaments in which they participated, were able to control many aspects of production (such as choice of networks, announcers, and advertisers), and oversaw the budget priorities of the PGA itself.

Despite its sometimes rancorous past, pro golf remains a sport ruled by tradition. At the heart of this tradition are the rigid rules by which pro golf governs itself. The PGA "has a powerful interest in the clear [enforcement] of its rules" and has seldom been swayed to bend its rules in matters of personal safety or comfort. Many of the PGA's rule decisions have involved questions of equipment (such as golf carts) and these questions have also supplied the biggest headaches for the PGA over its history. Despite the rigidity of many of the rules governing PGA play, the general game of golf is also inherently subject to notions of equity, both in deciding on rules questions themselves and in attempting to equalize competition between players. As one author has put it, "[t]he underlying philosophy of all this is to create equity among players of contrasting abilities, thus, in theory at least, increasing the pleasure for everyone." This is an interesting notion when one considers the situation that Casey Martin found himself, a dilemma that could go either way under this philosophy.

When looking at the history of the PGA, it is helpful to examine two areas that have often touched it—charges of discrimination and its dealings with the disabled—sometimes with results that are germane here. On the discrimination front, when the PGA was born in 1916, its constitution required members to be of the Caucasian race. It took until 1961 to get that clause removed from the constitution. Remnants of that policy lingered, however. As late as 1973, eighteen U.S. congressmen sent a letter to the PGA complaining that a "form of subtle discrimination taints the image of the tournament and brings no credit to the world of professional golf." Amazingly, "no black man was invited to [one of the premier pro tournaments,] The Masters, until 1975." These incidents may have contributed to a negative public image for the PGA, one that advertises a willingness to discriminate, whether the subject is race or disability, and may explain some of the public debate that accompanied the Casey Martin case.

Despite the seemingly unique nature of the Martin case, the PGA has often had to deal with the plight of disabled golfers, or at least those suffering from temporary infirmities. For example, Ben Hogan limped around the course and won the U.S. Open in 1950, sixteen months after suffering a near-fatal auto accident. In 1954, in the first televised PGA tournament, Ed Furgol won the U.S. Open despite having a withered left arm from a childhood accident. In the 1964 U.S. Open, Ken Venturi literally staggered his way through the last nine holes of play after finishing eighteen holes in sweltering heat, nearly collapsing at the end but pulling off an unlikely victory. The drama of incidents such as these had largely endeared the PGA to the public, but the tide may have begun to change by the 1980's. By then, the cart issue had become a reality for disabled players. In 1987, Charlie Owens, who had been injured in a parachuting incident while in the Army, petitioned for use of a cart during a professional tournament. When permission was denied, Owens walked the first nine holes on crutches before withdrawing. Similarly, in 1987 Lee Elder asked for permission to use a cart after he suffered a mild heart attack. His request was similarly denied. Of course, both of these requests came before the ADA was passed, which put Casey Martin in a whole new ball park (or golf course, perhaps). Conversely, in the 1990's the PGA has seen players such as Paul Asinger, battling cancer and weakened by the effects of chemotherapy but still walking with the rest of the players, apparently without complaint. Thus, the PGA apparently had some public image factors in its favor as well going into the Martin court case.

Today, the PGA remains a non-profit association of pro golfers. It sponsors three tours for professionals: the PGA Tour, the Senior PGA Tour, and the Nike Tour. The Nike Tour operates as sort of a "minor league" tour for players who are less talented or are developing their skills. There are several ways for a young golfer to enter either the PGA Tour or the Nike Tour. The most important way is the PGA's "three-stage qualifying school tournament." To enter this tournament, the young player must pay a $3,000 entry fee and submit two letters of reference. The first stage of the tournament is 72 holes of golf. Those who do well enough to make the cut in this round move on to a second stage consisting of another 72 holes of golf. The top finishers after this stage, approximately 168 players, move on to stage three, which consists of 108 holes. The 35 players with the lowest scores after stage three are given invitations to play on the PGA Tour, while the next 70 are given invitations to play on the Nike Tour. Of critical importance to this discussion, participants are allowed to use a golf cart in the first two stages of the tournament, but must walk during the stage three rounds. A player on the Nike Tour can later move up to the PGA Tour by winning three Nike Tour tournaments during a single season or by finishing in the top fifteen money-winners for the year. Another route for Nike Tour players to enter the PGA Tour is to obtain a sponsor's exemption for individual tournaments. This entire process is overseen by the current PGA Commissioner, Tim Finchem, a former Democratic activist.

2. Casey Martin

If ADA advocates had wanted a poster child, they could not have asked for one better than Casey Martin, for his life is clearly one of over-achievement and accomplishment despite adversity. Martin "was born with Klippel-Trenaunay-Weber syndrome, a rare . . . disorder that causes blood to pool in his lower right leg." Lacking the rich circulatory system in this leg that most people have, his bones below the knee have "become increasingly brittle." Despite this disability, he played sports all throughout secondary school and became an accomplished shooter for his school basketball team in the sixth and seventh grade. As his condition worsened as a child, however, he "had to constantly ice his knee, where blood [settled and eroded] the cartilage."

After high school, Martin attended Stanford University on an athletic scholarship, where he played golf from 1990 to 1995 and became a two-time Academic All-American. While at Stanford, he captained the team to a national championship and roomed with no less than Tiger Woods himself. To add to the mystique, while at Stanford he studied economics, played piano at fraternity parties (he has long been an accomplished pianist), studied the Bible, and mentored a Hispanic youth. Midway through his college career, however, his leg began to worsen, with x-rays showing erosion of both bones and muscles in his afflicted leg. As a result, he developed shinsplints and asked the NCAA for permission to use a cart in the 1994 NCAA Championship in Texas. The NCAA not only consented for the tournament, but also let him use a cart for the remainder of his junior year and his entire senior year as well.

After leaving Stanford, Martin walked during his two years on the Hooters mini-tour, though he also sometimes played on the Tommy Armour mini-tour because it allowed carts. After this two year period, Martin entered the PGA's qualifying school tournament hoping to make the PGA or Nike Tours. He made it through the first two stages, utilizing a cart as allowed by the PGA rules. PGA rules, however, did not allow him to use a cart for stage three, and he filed for an injunction under the ADA in federal district court seeking a waiver of the no-cart rule. The district court granted a preliminary injunction directing the PGA to allow him to use a cart during the third stage of the qualifying school tournament, and the PGA promptly lifted the no cart rule for all players taking part in the third stage rounds. Unfortunately, Martin missed qualifying for the PGA Tour by two strokes, though he did qualify for the Nike Tour. The federal district court quickly extended the preliminary injunction to include Martin's first two tournaments on the Nike Tour. In his first Nike tournament, in January 1998, Martin won and was soon starring in his own Nike ad. PGA lawyers soon stipulated that he could ride in all Nike Tour tournaments until his court case was heard in full. As the full trial on Martin's ADA case neared, his doctors warned that his leg was getting worse, describing his right knee as "that of a 70- or 80-year-old," and telling him that he may face amputation. Meanwhile, Martin himself, when asked why he was so insistent on participating in the pro golf tour despite his disability, cheerfully replied, "[t]his is what I've wanted to do since I was a kid." The stage was now set for a unique, if somewhat melodramatic, showdown that would test the limits of the ADA.

B. The Pretrial Phase

In the months between the federal district court's granting of a preliminary injunction and the full trial, the Martin case received an incredible airing with the American public, in the press, and among fellow pro golfers. In many respects, like too many cases these days, the trial seemed to occur even before the court heard the legal merits of the case, so vocal was the public debate. For its part, the PGA, in the guise of Commissioner Tim Finchem, while expressing sympathy for Martin, basically advanced two arguments in public leading up to the trial: 1) that walking is essential to the game of pro golf; and 2) the PGA Tour has the legal right to make its own rules for competition. (One writer quickly noted that this second argument was precisely the same justification that golf used to exclude blacks for so many years.)

Some of the first people to pick sides in the debate were fellow pro gofers. Lining up behind the PGA were such legends as Arnold Palmer, who gave a deposition arguing that "walking is a traditional and intrinsic part" of pro golf and that Martin would gain an unfair advantage if allowed to walk, and Jack Nicklaus, who offered to do the same. Ken Venturi, who had staggered through the U.S. Open in 1964, argued that "[t]his is not a case of personality. This is a case of an athletic event, which you have to do." Tour veteran Brad Faxon was even more pointed in his comments, referring to fellow pro Jose Maria Olazabal, a former Masters champion who has suffered a series of foot injuries in recent years: "I don't see guys in the NFL who have knee injuries getting mopeds. I didn't see Jose Maria Olazabal getting a cart

when he was hurt. Where do you draw the line?" Another pro, David
Frost, quipped, "I don't think it's right. . . . If he's riding and we're
walking, it's not the way the game was meant to be played." Even
Lonnie Nielsen, who had to abandon the PGA Tour prematurely
several years ago due to an arthritic knee, "joined the chorus of pros
who sided with the longtime PGA practice of walking: 'I feel bad for
Casey Martin and the condition that he has. It's a tragedy . . . but I
really feel like walking is an integral part of the game.'"

Lining up behind Casey Martin were some equally impressive pros.
Greg Norman personally called Martin in the pretrial days, telling
him the following: "The [PGA] is putting pressure on me to testify on
its behalf . . . . But I won't make a very good witness for them because
I'm on your side. I hope you get your cart, and I look forward to
playing with you someday." The Nike Tour's leading money winner,
Eric Johnson, even provided some legal evidence for the Martin legal
team when he stated that walking actually helped with his rhythm and
that it was a part of the game "only as a purpose to get to the next shot."
Fellow pros Brian Henninger and Peter Jacobsen were also publicly
supportive of Martin.

In the middle of the road were several golfers who apparently could
not pick a definite side in the debate. Some could see merits in both
sides' arguments. Phil Mickelson was typical, saying, "[I]f we could
make an exception in this one case, I might be for it, . . . but you have
to ask yourself, . . . where does it end?" Martin's old buddy Tiger
Woods noted at first that if he had to ride in a cart he would be "off
rhythm" and argued that walking allowed a player to work off nervous
energy. Later, however, when asked if riding in a cart would be an
advantage, he said that "it could be." Even golfers that you would
expect to stand solidly behind Martin expressed empathy for both
sides. Specifically, Greg Jones, founder and president of the advocacy
group Association of Disabled American Golfers, noted that "Casey
deserves to have the opportunity to try to make a living. At the same
time, if he has a cart and it's 100 degrees and 90 percent humidity,
there certainly is the potential to change the competitive nature of the
game." Some of those with sympathies in both camps eventually came
up with novel solutions to the impasse. For example, professional
Steve Lamontagne proposed that doctor's put a percentage figure on
Martin's disability (say 66 percent) and require him to walk a
commensurate number of golf holes to reflect this percentage (six of
the nine holes using the 66 percent example).

With all of this open discussion among pro golfers, the press seemed
to have a field day with the Martin case in the days leading up to trial,

sometimes in tasteless fashion as we have regrettably come to expect from the American media. *Hard Copy* even offered a videographer several thousand dollars if he could come up with a clear image of Martin's withered leg. Most comments by the media seemed to favor Martin in his quest. For example, *Sports Illustrated* magazine poked fun at the PGA by noting that "no one has succeeded at tournament golf by virtue of his walking ability." Columnist Tony Snow remarked, "[A]s far as I'm concerned, Martin stands on the side of the angels in his battle against the Lords of the Country Clubs." A newspaper sports writer in Florida accused the PGA of using the same philosophy as first-grade teachers: "If I do it for you, then I'll have to do it for everyone." Even *Time Magazine* jumped on the bandwagon when it poked fun at the PGA's argument that walking is integral to golf by derisively asking "how many golfers really look like they've done a lot of distance training?"

The media was not the only outside body to support Martin, as politicians soon jumped on his bandwagon. The California legislature passed a resolution supporting his request to use a cart, and the San Francisco Board of Supervisors praised his "courage and honor in tackling an issue of great interest to all Americans." The original sponsor of the ADA, Senator Tom Harkin, held a press conference with Martin to support his case, and Bob Dole publicly wondered if the letters PGA stood for "Please Go Away."

With all of the comments by public figures, it was inevitable that the public would quickly choose sides. Most people aligned with Martin, but the choice was not unanimous, as the public found itself split much like the pro golfers themselves. Newspapers and other outlets eagerly conducted polls of the public to get a pulse on the nation's sentiments. One polling site on the Internet even went so far as to delineate the best opposing arguments of the PGA and Martin. Against this entire backdrop, Casey Martin began to find hope that he would be the victor no matter what happened, saying, "[I]f this goes to trial and they win, I don't know if they really win." With the public relations battle having been waged for several months now, the entire matter was ready to move to trial.

C. The District Court Decision

When Martin filed his request for an injunction in the U.S. District Court for the District of Oregon, Magistrate Judge Thomas Coffin was assigned to the case. Judge Coffin's holdings are spread over two reported decisions: his rulings on the PGA's motion for summary judgment issued January 30, 1998, and his final finding of fact and conclusions of law issued February 19, 1998. Judge Coffin's reasoning on Martin's claims are spread throughout both opinions, so a combined discussion of the two reported decisions is necessary.

Martin based his claims against the PGA on Titles I and III of the ADA. In his Title I claim, he asserted that the PGA was an employer as described in Section 12111(5) of the ADA and had discriminated against him "because of his disability in regard to job application procedures, the hiring, advancement, or discharge of employees, employee compensation, job training, and other terms, conditions, and privileges of employment." In ruling on this Title I claim, the court did not have to decide whether Martin was indeed "disabled," for the PGA chose not to contest this issue. Thus, the only real issue to decide under the Title I claim was whether the PGA is an employer at all, which would determine if it was even capable of employment discrimination. Surprisingly, the judge made very short work of this issue by issuing just one sentence: "As I reject (without detailed elaboration) plaintiff's claim that he is a PGA Tour employee..., I will discuss only his remaining claim . . . under Title III."

Judge Coffin's cursory treatment of the Title I claim is surprising because he could have easily cited past cases dealing with the issue of whether a non-profit sports association is an employer or not. A prime example is the case of *Graves v. Women's Professional Rodeo Association, Inc.*, a Title VII case. (Though falling under a different statute, courts have long analogized ADA claims to Title VII cases when defining "employer.). *Graves* put the issue as follows:

> [E]xistence of . . . coverage requires a two-part analysis. The claimant must first demonstrate that the defendant is a covered employer within the meaning of [the statute], thus conferring subject matter jurisdiction on the court. After that is determined, and only if it is determined affirmatively, the claimant must demonstrate the existence of an employment-type relationship which he alleges is being unlawfully interfered with by the defendant.

> . . . .

> In the case at hand, the defendant is a voluntary association whose members pay dues. The WPRA does not pay wages, withhold taxes, or provide insurance. The WPRA has a comprehensive set of

rules and regulations that are to be followed by members who wish to compete in a particular contest. The WPRA cannot tell its members when and where to participate. Rather the members elect when to compete. *This association differs little from numerous other associations, i.e. golfing associations,* bowling association, etc. The members of the association who compete agree to abide by the association's rules. In other words, the competing members agree to "play by the rules."

. . . .

[P]laintiff could not have met the second prong of the test. The existence of an employment-type relationship is of crucial significance for those seeking to redress alleged discriminatory actions . . . . Here the only interference alleged is plaintiff's inability to participate in a competition for prize money. As such, plaintiff has not shown the existence of an employment-type relationship.

Inclusion of this explanation would have done much to explain Judge Coffin's decision on Martin's Title I claims.

Martin's Title III claims consisted of two parts. First, he claimed that the PGA was subject to Section 12189 of the ADA, which requires that "any person [offering] examinations or courses related to applications, licensing, certification, or credentialing for . . . professional or trade purposes shall [do so] in a place and manner accessible to persons with disabilities." Again, Judge Coffin made incredibly short work of this claim, rejecting it in one brief sentence without any elaboration. Thus, the overwhelming majority of his decision encompassed Martin's final Title III claim, that the PGA was subject to ADA Section 12182's prohibition of discrimination in the full and equal enjoyment of the goods, services, facilities, privileges, advantages, or accommodations of any place of public accommodation by any person who owns, leases (or leases to) or operates a place of public accommodation.

The PGA raised three defenses to Martin's remaining Title III claim. First, it asserted that it was exempt from Title III as a private club under Section 12187. In making this assertion, PGA lawyer William Maledon argued that the PGA was analogous to the Boy Scouts and should be similarly exempt from Title III. The court looked at seven factors used to determine whether an entity qualifies as a private club: 1) genuine selectivity; 2) membership control; 3) history of the organization; 4) use of facilities by non-members; 5) the club's purpose; 6) whether the club advertises for members; and 7) whether the club is non-profit. Finding marked differences between the PGA and the Boy Scouts when looking at these factors, the court rejected the PGA's defense, finding it much more akin to a "commercial enterprise" than a private club.

In its second defense to Martin's remaining Title III claim, the PGA argued that it was not a place of public accommodation at all because the courses it operates are not open to the general public between the boundaries of play during tournaments. The court rejected this argument as "flawed" for several reasons. First, it noted that Section 12181(7) of the ADA specifically included golf courses on its list of public accommodations. Secondly, the court noted that the PGA's argument would render the private club exemption virtually irrelevant in many cases. Finally, the court noted that the ADA and its associated regulations "do not support the concept that places of public accommodation have zones of ADA application," while chastising the PGA for overlooking the fact that "people other than its own Tour members [such as caddies] are allowed within the boundary lines of play during its tournaments."

The PGA's final defense to Martin's Title III public accommodation claim—that allowing Martin to use a cart would not be reasonable because it would mark a fundamental alteration of the game—occupied the greatest portion of the court's attention. On this issue, the court cited such cases as *Sandison* and *Pottgen*, noting that—despite the holdings for the defendant in these cases—"the courts examined the purpose of each of the rules in question to determine if the requested modification was reasonable." In attempting to find the purpose of the PGA's asserted no-cart rule in Martin's case, the court seemed perplexed, for it could not find any justification for it; as Judge Coffin put it rather succinctly, "[n]othing in the Rules of Golf requires or defines walking as part of the game." Nonetheless, the court accepted the PGA's proposition that the purpose of the walking rule was to inject the element of fatigue into the skill of shot-making. Despite this acceptance, the court stated that an individual assessment of Casey Martin's situation was necessary to see if the rule could be reasonably modified, citing past circuit court decisions for support of this proposition. In making this individualized assessment, the court relied on the testimony of several doctors (including Martin's) and the statements of fellow pros (such as Eric Johnson) in determining that "the fatigue factor injected into the game of golf by walking the course cannot be deemed significant under normal circumstances." On the other hand, the court, again relying on the testimony of doctors, determined that "[w]alking for Casey Martin is a different story," concluding from an individual assessment of his disability that "it does not fundamentally alter the nature of the PGA Tour's game to accommodate him with a cart." In other words, the court found the requested accommodation of a golf cart "eminently reasonable" under Title III. Casey Martin had won.

D. The Immediate Aftermath of the District Court Decision

The *Martin* decision seemed immediately to spawn as much commentary as the pre-trial hoopla had. This time, however, many seemed more conciliatory and able to sympathize with both parties. Even Judge Coffin joined in this trend, for when he delivered his verdict he praised both sides for their arguments and singled out PGA Commissioner Finchem's testimony for its professionalism. "I don't see how anyone can fault the PGA Tour for its stand," said Judge Coffin. Even the Martin family was complimentary of Finchem, with Casey's father commenting, "[T]he thing that's awkward for me . . . is that I totally understand the other point of view." *Sports Illustrated* and other publications suddenly found themselves congratulating Finchem for showing courage and backbone in the whole debate. The public, though still apparently divided on the issue, appeared largely sympathetic to Casey Martin while more understanding toward the PGA. This was quite a change from the pre-trial stage, when newspaper columnists portrayed Finchem as a callous Chief Executive Officer and politicians denounced the PGA as a club for greedy, self-centered athletes.

Despite the amiable comments in these quarters, there were some who were clearly upset by the ruling. Pro golfers were some of the most vocal. Fred Couples called Judge Coffin's ruling " a farce." Arnold Palmer worried that when the gates of change open like this, "we may not have a Tour at all. It may disappear." Tom Watson said, "[A]s much compassion as I have for Casey, I have contempt for the decision." And Paul Azinger, who had walked tournament courses while suffering through cancer treatments, "insinuat[ed] that Martin [was] trying to get an advantage when he [really did not] need one." The governing bodies of other professional sports seemed equally alarmed at the prospects of the *Martin* decision. Even a noted legal scholar chimed in with some concerns, noting that 1) golf has always been a game of overcoming the odds, regardless of one's individual abilities, and 2) changes in procedures often look minor to outsiders, but can nonetheless be very big to those involved.

In the wake of the decision, PGA sponsors seemed eager to have Martin compete in their events, with one sponsor predicting that having Casey in the field "might be bigger mediawise than having Tiger [Woods]." For his part, Casey Martin immediately turned down several sponsors' exemptions to play in PGA Tour events, believing that his game had slacked a bit after taking three weeks off for the legal battle and worrying that other players might be offended "if he took advantage of his situation too early." Martin returned to the Nike Tour, hoping to debut on the PGA Tour in 1999 (provided he can win two more Nike tournaments), according to his agent. No matter what his level of participation, commentators galore predicted that Martin would now be a boon to the game of golf, and would attract a healthy following on tour. Advertisers seemed to salivate over the prospects of endorsements by Martin, with one writer predicting that his golf cart would soon be festooned with corporate decals much like NASCAR automobiles.

Meanwhile, the PGA quietly planned to appeal Judge Coffin's ruling to the 9th U.S. Circuit Court of Appeals, though it seemed reluctant to pursue the appeal aggressively. As Commissioner Finchem put it, "[I]t's going to take years for the appellate process to resolve this issue. In the meantime, let's see how well Casey can play." In other words, we may not see a final resolution to the Casey Martin saga for quite awhile.

V. CONCLUSION

Golf is the most human of games. In it a man can become the hero of an unbelievable melodrama, the clown in a side-splitting comedy, the dogged victim of inexorable fate, all without having to bury a corpse or repair a tangled personality.

- Bobby Jones

There are several lessons to be learned from the preceding discussion. First, the ADA, despite its brief history, has already caused significant changes for the lives of disabled people in America. It can be perhaps argued that not all of these changes have been positive for the nation as a whole, as some critics have pointed out. The Casey Martin case points out some of the dilemmas presented by the ADA, and the deep divisions that this statute can foster.

Despite its seemingly unique character, the *Martin* decision is really just one in a line of cases dealing with public accommodations having to make reasonable modifications for disabled athletes. Courts for years have been wrangling over the level of modification that sports organizations are required to make under Title III. It appears, given the *Martin* decision, that the amateur or professional status of these organizations matters little in deciding Title III claims. Thus, the *Martin* case, as a district court decision, ultimately seems to be but a small voice in the chorus of Title III claims on behalf of disabled athletes.

The biggest unanswered question after *Martin* is the scope of Title I claims in the world of professional sports. Because the judge in *Martin* gave such short attention to this claim, it remains to be fully seen how employment discrimination will be viewed in the world of disabled pro athletes. Perhaps the only thing one can take from the *Martin* decision in this regard is that sports associations do not meet the Title I definition of "employer." Only time and new litigants will tell how Title I applies to more direct employment relationships such as sports teams.

Despite these shortcomings, the *Martin* case does stand as a watershed case in one aspect: The ADA has finally made a foray into the world of professional sports. This event is significant, for it may encourage others to wield the ADA as a means of seeking redress in this field and prepare the legal mind set for this eventuality. Thus, the tepid steps taken by the *Martin* case may just be the beginning of a new area of sports law.

NOTES

1 GEORGE EBERL, GOLF IS A GOOD WALK SPOILED xiii (1992).

2 *See* Rick Maloney, *Nielsen Sides with PGA in Debate About Use of Carts*, BUS. FIRST - BUFF., Feb. 9, 1998, at 22 (describing the Casey Martin dilemma as "the topic of discussion in the sports world these days" (emphasis added)).

3 *See, e.g., Backtalk: Can Casey Get a Lift?*, FLORIDA TODAY, Jan. 25, 1998, at 2C.

4 *See* John Garrity, Golf Plus, *Out on a Limb: His Parents Hoped Casey Martin Would Lead a Normal Life. Instead He's Living an Extraordinary One*, SPORTS ILLUSTRATED, Feb. 9, 1998, at G10.

5 Maloney, *supra* note 2, at 22.

6 *Id.*

7 *See* Matthew J. Mitten, *Amateur Athletes with Handicaps or Physical Abnormalities: Who Makes the Participation Decision*, 71 NEB. L. REV. 987, 993 (1992)[hereinafter *"Abnormalities"*] ("Athletes are one of the most revered groups in American society and are among its highest paid members.")

8 *See id.* at 989.

9 *See id.*

10 *See id.*

11 *See id.*

12 Mitten, *Abnormalities, supra* note 7, at 989.

13 *Id.* at 994. Mitten also notes that "[e]conomic pressure such as the loss of a potential scholarship or professional career or the fear of losing a starting position provides strong incentive to any star athlete to play with a handicap or impairment." *Id.*

14 *See Dateline NBC* (NBC television broadcast, Mar. 22, 1998) (transcript available at 1998 WL 6615281).

15 *See* Martin v. PGA Tour, Inc., 994 F. Supp. 1242 (D. Or. 1998); Martin v. PGA Tour, Inc., 984 F. Supp. 1320 (D. Or. 1998).

16 *See* Mitten, *Abnormalities, supra* note 7, at 1003-04.

17 42 U.S.C. §§ 12101-12213 (1994).

18 *See Dateline NBC, supra* note 14.

19 *See* Jason L. Thomas, Comment, *Through the ADA and the Rehabilitation Act, High School Athletes are Saying "Put Me In Coach":* Sandison v. Michigan High School Athletic Ass'n, 65 CIN. L. REV. 727, 730 (1997).

20 29 U.S.C. § 794(a) (1994); Thomas, *supra* note 19, at 730; Julia V. Kasperski, *Disabled High School Athletes and the Right to Participate: Are Age Waivers Reasonable Modifications Under the Rehabilitation Act and the Americans with Disabilities Act?*, 49 BAYLOR L. REV. 175, 178 (1997).

21 Thomas, *supra* note 19, at 736.

22 Pahulu v. Univ. of Kan., 897 F. Supp. 1387, 1389 (D. Kan. 1995); *see also* Mitten, *Abnormalities, supra* note 7, at 1008.

23 *See* Thomas, *supra* note 19, at 738.

24 *See* Sandison v. Mich. High Sch. Athletic Ass'n, Inc., 64 F.3d 1026, 1035 (6th Cir. 1995)("Our analysis of the plaintiffs' ADA claim closely tracks our [Rehabilitation Act] section 504 analysis."); Bolton v. Scrivner, 36 F.3d 939, 943 (10th Cir. 1994)("Congress intended that the relevant caselaw developed under the Rehabilitation Act be generally applicable to the term 'disability' as used in the ADA."); Reaves v. Mills, 904 F. Supp. 120, 123 (W.D.N.Y. 1995)(taking to heart the ADA's language that "[t]he remedies, procedures, and rights set forth in . . . [section 504a of the Rehabilitation Act] shall be the remedies, procedures, and rights this subchapter provides to any person alleging discrimination on the basis of disability in violation of [the ADA]"); Eckles v. Consolidated Rail Corp., 890 F. Supp. 1391, 1403 (S.D. Ind. 1995) ("[T]he ADA is to be interpreted consistently with the Rehabilitation Act.").

25 This is probably why attorneys often bring suits under both statutes to this day. Though the many Rehabilitation Act decisions would apply to the ADA, lawyers often appear to be more comfortable when precedent directly addresses a statute by name. In addition, it never hurts to bring suit under two statutes when possible rather than under the ADA alone. Of course, this is impossible if the defendant is not a recipient of federal funds, as the Casey Martin case illustrates. The extension of the ADA into activities not funded by the federal government is probably its most dramatic development. See *infra* Parts II and III for further discussion of the interplay between the Rehabilitation Act and the ADA in case law.

26 *See* RUTH COLKER, THE LAW OF DISABILITY DISCRIMINATION 19 (1995 & Supp. 1996-97).

27 20 U.S.C. §§ 1401-1491 (1994).

28 COLKER, *supra* note 26, at 19. "In order for a school district to be covered by the IDEA, it must accept federal funding and agree to abide by an extensive set of funding criteria." *Id.*

29 Despite this fact, it is doubtful that IDEA goes very far in the area of reasonable accommodations for the disabled. For example, in *Board of Education v. Rowley*, 458 U.S. 176, 178 (1982), the Supreme Court held that a school did not have to employ an interpreter for a deaf student in order to meet IDEA's requirements. Given this decision, one can only imagine the hesitancy to require accommodations for athletic programs under IDEA. *See* COLKER, *supra* note 26, at 19. The ADA has helped fill this gap by mandating more exacting accommodations for the disabled in all areas of education, including athletics. *See id.*

30 *See* COLKER, *supra* note 26, at 19.

31 42 U.S.C. § 12101(b)(3)-(4) (1994).

32 *Id.* § 12101(a)(9).

33 *Id.* § 12101(b)(1).

34 *See* Garrity, *supra* note 4.

35 Americans with Disabilities (ADA) Homepage of the U.S. Department of Justice (visited March 6, 1998) <http://www.usdoj.gov/crt/ada/adahom1.htm>. Readers should note that this coverage marks a big difference over the Rehabilitation Act, for the federal government now had the power to go after institutions that were not recipients of federal funding.

36 See ADA HANDBOOK, DISABILITY DISCRIMINATION: STATUTES, REGULATIONS AND RELATED MATERIALS 92 (1995).

37 Robert L. Burgdorf, Jr., *The Americans with Disabilities Act: Analysis and Implications of a Second-Generation Civil Rights Statute*, 26 HARV. C.R.-C.L. L. REV. 413, 413-14 (1991) (quoting remarks made by President Bush during the ADA signing ceremony).

38 *See* ADA HANDBOOK, *supra* note 36, at i.

39 *Id.* For the record, Title IV covers telecommunications relay services for hearing and speech impaired individuals (including closed-captioning of

public service announcements), and Title V contains miscellaneous provisions such as special rules for insurance providers. *See id.* Though possibly of indirect importance to matters of sports law, these last two Titles will not be discussed in this paper, with the following brief exception: Section 12212 (in Title V) encourages alternative dispute resolution as a means of resolving disputes under the ADA. *See* 42 U.S.C. _ 12212. However, one federal court has ruled that this section does not require an athlete to arbitrate his discrimination claims against an athletic association because this provision was meant to supplement, not supplant, judicial remedies. *See Case Law Development: Mobility/Access,* 20 MENTAL & PHYSICAL DISABILITY L. REP. 382, 386 (citing Devlin v. Arizona Youth Soccer Ass'n, No. Civ. 95-745 TUC ACM (D. Ariz. Feb. 8, 1996)).

40 COLKER, *supra* note 26, at xvii.

41 *See id.* There is one exception to this provision: the Department of Transportation is charged with issuing regulations to enforce the transportation aspects of Title III. *See id.* As another important side note, the ADA requires DOJ to issue regulations governing Title II which are consistent with the existing regulations under section 504 of the Rehabilitation Act, yet another link between the two statutes. *See id.*

42 School Bd. of Nassau County v. Arline, 480 U.S. 273, 279 (1987) (discussing Department of Health and Human Services regulations issued pursuant to the Rehabilitation Act).

43 *See* Martin v. PGA Tour, Inc., 984 F. Supp. 1320, 1323 (D. Or. 1998).

44 42 U.S.C. § 12112(a).

45 "Major life activities" include functions such as "caring for oneself, performing manual tasks, walking, seeing, hearing, speaking, breathing, learning, and working." 29 C.F.R. § 1630.2(I). Sports may qualify by themselves as a "major life activity" under the ADA. As one federal court has put it, "some courts and commentators . . . have concluded athletics comes within the purview of 'learning,' [an] enumerated major life activity, and others have implied athletics in and of itself is a major life activity for certain individuals." *Pahulu,* 897 F. Supp. at 1391. Interestingly, the EEOC has stated that "[t]he determination of whether an individual is substantially limited in a major life activity must be made on a case by case basis, without regard to mitigating measures such as medicines, or assistive or prosthetic devices." Americans with Disabilities Act Title I Equal Employment Opportunity Commission Interpretive Guidance, 29 C.F.R. § 1630.2(j). The EEOC's guidance seems to conflict with the language of the ADA itself, which requires that a disability "substantially limits one or more of the major life activities" before it is covered. *Compare id., with* 42 U.S.C. § 12102(2)(A).

46 42 U.S.C. § 12102(2)

47 42 U.S.C. § 12101(a)(1).

48 *See* 29 C.F.R. § 1630.2(j)((3)(I) ("The inability to perform a single, particular job does not constitute a substantial limitation in the major life activity of working."); *see also* Taylor v. U. S. Postal Serv., 946 F.2d 1214 (6th Cir. 1991); Bolton v. Scrivner, Inc., 36 F.3d 939 (10th Cir. 1994); Byrne v. Bd. of Educ., 979 F.2d 560 (7th Cir. 1992).

49 *See* Cook v. R.I., 10 F.3d 17, 17 (1st Cir. 1993).

50 *Id.*

51 *See* 42 U.S.C. § 12112(a).

52 42 U.S.C. § 12111(8).

53 *See, e.g.,* Treadwell v. Alexander, 707 F.2d 473, 477 (11th Cir. 1983) (finding that even rarely-performed duties can be essential functions of a job); Davis v. Frank, 711 F. Supp. 447, 454 (N.D. Ill. 1989) (addressing whether answering the phone was an essential function of a postal clerk's position); Ackerman v. Western Elec., 643 F. Supp. 836, 844 (N.D. Cal. 1986) (finding that an employee's actual prior tasks—versus her job description—determine what are the essential functions of a job).

54 *See* 42 U.S.C. § 12112(a).

55 42 U.S.C. § 12112(5)(A). "Reasonable accommodation" requires "making existing facilities used by employees readily accessible to and usable by individuals with disabilities," *Id.* at § 12111(9)(A), and making "[m]odifications or adjustments to the work environment, or to the manner or circumstances under which the position held or desired is customarily performed, that enable a qualified individual with a disability to perform the essential functions of that position." 29 C.F.R. § 1630.2(o)(ii).

56 Price v. S-B Power Tool, 75 F.3d 362 (8th Cir. 1996), *cert. denied* 117 S. Ct. 274 (1996)

57 *See* Newman v. GHS Osteopathic, Inc., 4 A.D. Cases 1051, 1055 (3d Cir. 1995).

58 *See* Pushkin v. Regents of the Univ. of Colo., 658 F.2d 1372, 1384 (10th Cir. 1981).

59 *See id.* at 1385.

60 42 U.S.C. § 12112(b)(6); *see also* Davis v. Frank, 711 F. Supp. 447 (N.D. Ill. 1989). In contrast, one federal court has stated that "it remains . . . an open question whether [the Rehabilitation Act] forbids recipients of federal financial assistance from engaging in 'conduct that has an unjustifiable disparate impact' on the disabled." *Sandison,* 64 F.3d at 1032.

61 *See* Prewitt v. U.S. Postal Serv., 662 F.2d 292, 306 (5th Cir. 1980).

62 *See id.*

63 42 U.S.C. § 12113(b).

64 *See* Chiari v. City of League City, 920 F.2d 311, 317 (5th Cir. 1991)(*citing* 29 C.F.R. § 1613.702(f) (1990)).

65 Americans with Disabilities Act Title I Equal Employment Opportunity Commission Interpretive Guidance, 29 C.F.R. § 1630.2(r). The EEOC further explains that, in weighing the direct threat, the employer must

make an individual assessment using factual data, considering potential reasonable accommodations, and taking into account four factors: the duration of the risk, the nature and severity of the potential harm, the likelihood that the harm will occur, and the imminence of the potential harm. *See id.*; 29 C.F.R. § 1630.3(r).

66 42 U.S.C. §§ 12111(10), 12112(b)(5)(A).

67 42 U.S.C. § 12111(10)(B); 29 C.F.R. § 1630.2(p)(2). For a list of other Title I defenses available to an employer, see 42 U.S.C. § 12113, 29 C.F.R. § 1630.15, and Americans with Disabilities Act Title I Equal Employment Opportunity Commission Interpretive Guidance, 29 C.F.R. § 1630.15.

68 42 U.S.C. § 12182(a).

69 Title III uses the same definition of "disabled" as Title I. *See* 42 U.S.C. § 12102.

70 42 U.S.C. § 12181(7)(L). Moreover, the DOJ regulations implementing this provision state that a "facility means all or any portion of . . . sites." 28 C.F.R. § 36.104.

71 COLKER, *supra* note 26, at 345. Colker uses the American Bar Association as a specific example, *see id.*, but this definition could presumably apply to such organizations as the NCAA or PGA as well. *See* Martin v. PGA Tour, Inc., 994 F. Supp. 1242, 1246 (D. Or. 1998) ("It is also worth noting that the ADA does not distinguish between sports organizations and other entities when it comes to applying the ADA to a specific situation. Businesses and schools have rules governing their operations which are of equal importance (in their sphere) as the rules of sporting events. Conversely, the disabled have just as much interest in being free from discrimination in the athletic world as they do in other aspects of everyday life. The key questions are the same: does the ADA apply, and may a reasonable modification be made to accommodate a disabled individual?")

72 42 U.S.C. § 12189. This provision figured into the Casey Martin case, as the PGA conducts a qualifying school tournament for golfers who wish to join the pro tour. *See* Martin v. PGA Tour, Inc., 984 F. Supp. 1320, 1321-22 (D. Or. 1998).

73 COLKER, *supra* note 26, at 344.

74 Readers should note that the "reasonable accommodation" language that is used in Title I has a counterpart in the "reasonable modification" language of Title III. *Id.*

75 Though the DOJ has largely been silent on what constitutes a "fundamental alteration," the applicable regulations define undue burden as "significant difficulty or expense." 28 C.F.R. § 36.303(a).

76 Title III defines "readily achievable" as "easily accomplishable and able to be carried out without much difficulty or expense," an apparently easier

standard for defendants than the undue burden definition. 42 U.S.C. §
12181(9). This is not the end of the inquiry under this provision,
however, for Title III goes on to explain that when the removal of a barrier
is not readily achievable, a public accommodation is still guilty of
discrimination if it fails to implement alternative methods of providing
access to its facilities. *See id.* at § 12182(b)(A)(v). This additional
provision is also subject to the "readily achievable" defense, however. *See
id.*

77 28 C.F.R. § 36.203(a).

78 42 U.S.C. § 12187.

79 42 U.S.C. § 12182(b)(3); 28 C.F.R. § 36.208; *see also* Anderson v. Little
League Baseball, Inc., 794 F. Supp. 342 (D. Ariz. 1992).

80 *See generally* John J. Coleman, III & Marcel L. Debruge, *A Practitioner's
Introduction to ADA Title II*, 45 ALA. L. REV. 55 (1993).

81 PHILIP K. HOWARD, THE DEATH OF COMMON SENSE: HOW LAW IS
SUFFOCATING AMERICA (1994).

82 *See id.* at 129 (noting that, prior to passage of the Rehabilitation Act,
"[d]isabled citizens had been largely ignored by law, probably because of
society's tendency to want to forget about the misfortunes of those
suffering from serious handicaps. Indignities were their daily routine: To
someone in a wheelchair, every six-inch curb, every step, is like a high
wall.")

83 *Id.* at 151.

84 *Id.*

85 *Id.* at 153.

86 HOWARD, *supra* note 80, at 130-31.

87 *Id.* at 130.

88 *Id.* at 150.

89 *See id.* at 132.

90 *Id.* at 132-33.

91 *See* Matthew J. Mitten, *Sports Participation by "Handicapped" Athletes*, 10
ENT. & SPORTS L. 15, 15 (1992)[hereinafter "*Handicapped*"].

92 *See id.*

93 *See id.*

94 *Id.*

95 Tony Snow, *Editorial: PGA Needs to Do Right Thing for Casey Martin*,
FLORIDA TODAY, Jan. 19, 1998, at 9A.

96 John Garrity, *Taking One for the Team Battered by the Martin Case, Tim
Finchem Nonetheless Deserves Respect*, SPORTS ILLUSTRATED, Feb. 23, 1998,
at 63.

97 *See* COLKER, *supra* note 26, at 3.

98 Mitten, *Handicapped*, *supra* note 89, at 15; *see also* Mitten, *Abnormalities*,
supra note 7, at 990.

99 42 U.S.C. § 12212.

100 439 F. Supp. 459 (W.D.N.Y. 1977).

101 *See* Mitten, *Abnormalities, supra* note 7, at 1004. The plaintiff was successful on claims brought under state employment discrimination laws, however. *See infra* section II.B.3.

102 *See* Mitten, *Abnormalities, supra* note 7, at 1004.

103 *Id.* at 1005.

104 473 U.S. 432 (1985).

105 *See id.* at 437.

106 *See id.* at 440-42.

107 *See id.* at 446. A couple of caveats should be noted, however. First, despite the Court's rule, it found that the actions of the defendant did not pass the rationality test. *See id.* at 448-50. Thus, it could be said that the disabled community won the battle but lost the war in this case. Secondly, Justice Marshall argued in dissent that the mentally retarded should be a quasi-suspect class because of the interest in establishing a home and the tragic history of discrimination against the retarded. *See id.* at 460-78 (Marshall, J., dissenting).

108 Mitten, *Abnormalities, supra* note 7, at 1005.

109 *See* Mitten, *Handicapped, supra* note 89, at 17.

110 *See id.*

111 *Id.*

112 *See* Board of Educ. v. State ex rel. Goldman, 191 N.E. 914 (1934) ("Apparently this is a case of first impression in Ohio, and counsel have been unable to find a case anywhere in the United States which gives the right to exclude from all educational facilities any child within the prescribed ages upon the basis of an intelligence test. It is, therefore, necessary to look to the provisions of the statutes of Ohio with reference to the right to refuse this child admission to the schools."); *see also* COLKER, *supra* note 26, at 3.

113 *See* Thomas, *supra* note 19, at 741.

114 Mitten, *Handicapped, supra* note 89, at 19.

115 *See Dateline NBC, supra* note 14.

116 Martin v. PGA Tour, Inc., 994 F. Supp. 1242, 1246 (D. Or. 1998).

117 *See* Kasperski, *supra* note 20, at 186.

118 *Id.*

119 *Id.*

120 *Id.*

121 *See* Kasperski, at 176, 186, 193.

122 848 S.W.2d 298 (Tex. Ct. App. 1993) (addressing the IDEA and Rehabilitation Act).

123 *Id.* at 300.

124 *See id.* at 300.

125 *See id.* at 301-02.

126 *Id.* at 302.

127 899 F. Supp. 579 (M.D. Fla. 1995), *vacated*, 102 F.3d 1172 (11th Cir. 1997).

128 *See id.* at 581-82.

129 *Id.* at 584.

130 *Id.* at 585-86 & n.8. For comments on other federal district court cases sympathetic to plaintiffs in the over-19 rule setting, see Kasperski, *supra* note 20, at 188 & n.82 (citing Dennin v. Conn. Interscholastic Athletic Conference, Inc., 913 F. Supp. 663 (D. Conn.), *rev'd in part, appeal dismissed in part*, 94 F.3d 96 (2d Cir. 1996)), and Thomas, *supra* note 19, at 744-45 (citing Booth v. Univ. Interscholastic League, No. Civ. A-90-CA-764, 1990 WL 484414 (W.D. Tex. 1990).

131 40 F.3d 926 (8th Cir. 1994).

132 *See id.* at 927-28.

133 *Id.* at 931.

134 *Id.* at 930.

135 *Id.* at 931.

136 *See Pottgen*, 40 F.3d at 931. It should be noted that the case was accompanied by a strong dissent. The dissent argued that the court was obligated to look at the reasons behind the over-19 rule and make an individual assessment of the plaintiff to see if "the age requirement could be modified for this individual player without doing violence to the admittedly salutary purposes underlying the age rule." *Id.* at 932 (Arnold, C.J., dissenting). If so, the dissent reasoned, then it cannot be " 'essential' to the nature of the program or activity to refuse to modify the rule." *Id.* at 932-33 (Arnold, C.J., dissenting). The dissenting opinion was cited with favor in *Johnson. See* 899 F. Supp. at 585.

137 *Sandison*, 64 F.3d 1026.

138 *Id.* at 1035-37.

139 Reaves v. Mills, 904 F. Supp. 120, 123 (W.D.N.Y. 1995).

140 Thomas, *supra* note 19, at 757, 762.

141 *See* Kasperski, *supra* note 20, at 193-94.

142 *Id.* at 194-96. Kasperski notes with favor that the Colorado High School Activities Association has already "demonstrated such foresight in developing such a process." *Id.* at 194.

143 *See* Mitten, *Handicapped*, *supra* note 89, at 18 (citing Southeastern Community College v. Davis, 442 U.S. 397 (1979) *and* Alexander v. Choate, 469 U.S. 287 (1985)). For example, Mitten states that "it is not necessary to require able-bodied athletes to use wheelchairs to enable paraplegics to play college basketball." *Id.*

144 *Id.* at 18.

145 897 F. Supp. 1387 (D. Kan. 1995).

146 *See id.* at 1388.

147 *See id.*

148 *See id.*

149 *See id.* at 1388-89.

150 *See Pahula*, 897 F.Supp at 1389

151 *Id.* at 1393-94.

152 974 F. Supp. 459 (D.N.J. 1997)

153 *See id.* at 462.

154 *See id.* at 461.

155 *See id.* at 463.

156 *See id.*

157 *Bowers*, 974 F.Supp. at 466-67.

158 942 F. Supp. 1191 (N.D. Ill 1996).

159 *See id.* at 1194.

160 *See id.*

161 *See id.*

162 *See id.* ("In deciding a case under the Rehabilitation Act the rational basis test is not applicable.")

163 *Knapp*, 942 F.Supp at 1195.

164 *Id.*

165 *Id.* at 1195, 1197.

166 *See* Mitten, *Abnormalities, supra* note 7, at 1003.

167 439 F. Supp. 459 (W.D.N.Y. 1977).

168 *See id.*; *see also* Mitten, *Abnormalities, supra* note 7, at 1003 & n.96.

169 794 F. Supp. 342 (D. Ariz. 1992).

170 *See id.* at 343.

171 *See id.*

172 *See id.* at 344.

173 *See id.* at 345.

174 *Anderson*, 794 F.Supp at 345.

175 The judge in the Casey Martin court case actually alluded to this scenario when he asked rhetorically in support of Martin's claims the following: "What about a disabled manager of a team? May the St. Louis Cardinals refuse to construct a wheelchair ramp to the visitor's dugout to accommodate a disabled manager of the Chicago Cubs simply because spectators cannot go into the dugout?" Martin v. PGA Tour, Inc., 984 F. Supp. 1320, 1327 (D. Or. 1998).

176 *See* Al Barkow, Golf's Golden Grind: The History of the Tour 28 (1974).

177 *See id.*

178 *See* George Peper, Golf in America: The First One Hundred Years 8 (1988).

179 *See id.* at 8-9.

180 *Id.* at 11-12.

181 *See id.* at 12.

182 *See id.*

183 *See* Peper, *supra* note 174, at 57.

184 See Barkow, *supra* note 172, at 56.

185 *See id.* at 57.

186 *See* PEPER, *supra* note 174, at 57.

187 *See id.* at 69.

188 *See* BARKOW, *supra* note 172, at 98.

189 *See id.* at 104. For example, by this time players had agreed to a code of conduct which prohibited, among other things, criticizing golf courses in public; however, the players refused to support a prohibition of profanity! *See id.*

190 *See id.* at 248, 250-51.

191 *See* BARKOW, *supra* note 172, at 254-55.

192 *See* Maloney, *supra* note 2 (quoting pro golfer Lonnie Nielsen: "It's such a game of tradition. Walking and having a caddie is the way the game has been played for years. I don't know how important tradition is in a decision like [the Casey Martin case], but when people think of golf on the uppermost levels, that's how we envision the game being played."); *see generally* EBERL, *supra* note 1.

193 *See* EBERL, *supra* note 1, at 3.

194 *Id.* at 8.

195 *See id.* at 23. Eberl offers this as an (amusing but true) example:

[T]wo players on the final nine holes arrived at a teeing area where they discovered some water buffalo placidly grazing. The beasts glanced at the players with bleak and suspicious eyes. The players, properly apprehensive, decided to forego that tee area and headed for the forward tees, from where they played, far removed from the buffalo. Upon their return to the clubhouse when their rounds were completed, the two men turned in their scorecards to the committee and amiably reported the incident with the animals.

To their astonishment, they were disqualified from the tournament for playing from outside the teeing ground.

Id.

196 *See id.* at 112. It is interesting to note that the rigidness of the PGA's rules, especially on the use of golf carts in its tournaments, comes at a time when the use of caddies is dying out on most golf courses and golf carts are becoming the norm. *See id.* at 55.

197 *See id.* at 39. The handicapping system, though not used in the PGA, is one example of this philosophy. *See id.* at 127-28.

198 EBERL, *supra* note 1, at 128.

199 *See* BARKOW, *supra* note 172, at 206. Economics, rather than overt racism, appears to be the driving force behind this clause; the PGA's founders feared that a contrary policy might cause them to "lose control over a lot of cheap caddie and club-cleaning labor." *Id.* at 207.

200 *See id.* at 206; PEPER, *supra* note 174, at 69.

201 BARKOW, *supra* note 172, at 216.

202 PEPER, *supra* note 174, at 69.
203 *See* Nick Charles & Don Sider, *Fairway or Now Way? Fellow Pros Say Using a Cart Would Give Disabled Golfer Casey Martin an Unfair Advantage, But Would They Care to Walk a Mile in His Spikes?*, PEOPLE, Feb. 9, 1998, at 48.
204 *See* BARKOW, *supra* note 172, at 228-29.
205 *See* Charles & Sider, *supra* note 199, at 48.
206 In commenting on these earlier incidents, Casey Martin's father stated: "I love the stories about Venturi and Hogan, but those stories miss the point. Neither Venturi nor Hogan was disabled. They had hope, and they had the opportunity to recover. Casey doesn't." Garrity, *supra* note 4.
207 *See* Cameron Morfit, Golf Plus, *Winning A La Cart While Preparing to Fight the Tour for the Right to Ride, Casey Martin Won the Nike Opener*, SPORTS ILLUSTRATED, Jan. 19, 1998, at G6.
208 *See id.*
209 *See id.*
210 *See id.*
211 *See Dateline NBC*, *supra* note 14.
212 *See* Martin v. PGA Tour, Inc., 984 F. Supp. 1320, 1321 (D. Or. 1998).
213 *See id.*
214 *See* Snow, *supra* note 93, at 9A.
215 *See Martin*, 984 F. Supp. at 1321.
216 *Id.*
217 *See id.* at 1322.
218 *See id.* at 1321.
219 *See id.*
220 *See Martin*, 984 F. Supp. at 1321.
221 *See id.*
222 *See id.* at 1322. Carts are also used on the entire Senior Tour. *See* Charles & Sider, *supra* note 199, at 48.
223 *See Martin*, 984 F. Supp. at 1321-22.
224 *See* Kevin Cook, *Golf Plus/News & Notes*, SPORTS ILLUSTRATED, Feb. 23, 1998, at G4. This entire process has changed a bit over the years. Most notably, until the late 1950's, the PGA required new professionals to put in a six-month apprenticeship, during which they could not collect any prize money. *See* BARKOW, *supra* note 172, at 234.
225 *See* Snow, *supra* note 93, at 9A.
226 Garrity, *supra* note 4, at G10.
227 *Id.*
228 *See* Morfit, *supra* note 203, at G6.
229 *Id.*
230 *See id.*; Snow, *supra* note 93, at 9A.
231 *See Dateline NBC*, *supra* note 14; Peter Kerasotis, *PGA's Rule Takes Martin for a Ride*, FLORIDA TODAY, Jan. 18, 1998, at 1C.
232 *See* Snow, *supra* note 93, at 9A.

233 *See* Garrity, *supra* note 4, G10; Charles & Sider, *supra* note 199.
234 *See Dateline NBC, supra* note 14. To counter the pooling of blood in his legs, Martin was forced to wear two sets of support stockings. *See* Martin v. PGA Tour, Inc., 994 F. Supp. 1242, 1244 (D. Or. 1998).
235 *See* Morfit, *supra* note 203, at G6.
236 *See id.*
237 *See id.*; Garrity, *supra* note 4, at G10.
238 Morfit, *supra* note 203, at G4.
239 *See Martin*, 984 F. Supp. at 1322.
240 *See id.*
241 *See id.*
242 *See id.* About twenty players (of the 168 competing) took advantage of the opportunity to use a cart. *Spring Second in Q-School*, FLORIDA TODAY, Dec. 4, 1997, at 2C.
243 *See* Kerasotis, *supra* note 227, at 1C.
244 *See* 984 F. Supp. at 1322.
245 *See Dateline NBC, supra* note 14; *see also* Kerasotis, *supra* note 227, at 1C.
246 *See* Garrity, *supra* note 4.
247 *Id.*; *see also* Morfit, *supra* note 203, at G6.
248 Morfit, *supra* note 203, at G6.
249 *See* Maloney, *supra* note 2 (quoting Tim Finchem: "This is a very unfortunate system we find ourselves in, having to litigate whether a fellow we think a great deal of can play the game.").
250 *See Judge Rules Martin Lawsuit to Go to Trial*, ATLANTA J.-CONST., Jan. 28, 1998, at C3.
251 *See* Snow, *supra* note 93.
252 *See* Garrity, *supra* note 4, at G10; Charles & Sider, *supra* note 199.
253 Glenn Sheeley, *Martin Case Not Simple*, ATLANTA J.-CONST., Jan. 21, 1998, at D5; Kerasotis, *supra* note 227.

254 Sheeley, *supra* note 249, at D5.
255 *Id.*
256 Maloney, *supra* note 2, at 22.
257 Garrity, *supra* note 4, at G10.
258 *Golf Pro Supports Martin's Case, Says Walking Keeps Scores Low*, FLORIDA TODAY, Feb. 4, 1998, at 2C. Johnson's sentiments were shared by Stanford golf coach Wally Goodwin, who coached Martin to the 1994 NCAA championship and stated that carts hinder more than help a player's game. *See id.*
259 *See* Morfit, *supra* note 203, at G6.
260 *Id.*
261 Kerasotis, *supra* note 227, at 1C.

262 Charles & Sider, *supra* note 199, at 48. Columnist Tony Snow reported Woods' comment more emphatically as "It *probably is.*" Snow, *supra* note 93 (emphasis added).

263 Morfit, *supra* note 203, at G6.

264 *See* Peter Kerasotis, *O'Neals Ignore Loss, Manners,* FLORIDA TODAY, Feb. 24, 1998, at 1C.

265 *See* Garrity, *supra* note 4, at G10.

266 *Id.* This statement appears a bit hypercritical on *Sports Illustrated's* part, for it had earlier argued that "in a five-hour round, roughly five minutes are spent hitting the ball. The rest of the time you're chasing it. Stamina counts." Morfit, *supra* note 203, at G6.

267 Snow, *supra* note 93, at 9A.

268 Kerasotis, *supra* note 227, at 1C.

269 Kathleen Adams et. al, *Notebook: Winners & Losers Spanning the World,* TIME, Feb. 16, 1998, at 25.

270 Garrity, *supra* note 4, at G10.

271 *Id.*

272 *See* Sheeley, *supra* note 249, at D5.

273 *Backtalk: Can Casey Get a Lift?, supra* note 3 (reporting that readers were split over Martin's case and listing some of the public's revealing comments on both sides).

274 *See, e.g., Backtalk: Should the PGA Bend?,* FLORIDA TODAY, Jan. 18, 1998, at 1C.

275 *See* Golf Viewpoint (visited March 6, 1998) <http://www.igolf.com/viewpoint/survey/martin/kangaroo.htm>. The site did a remarkable job in summarizing the valid legal and public relations arguments that this paper has highlighted. To be specific, the site listed the PGA's arguments as 1) Riding a golf cart is a decided advantage to a player; 2) Walking is integral to the spirit and conduct of the game of golf; 3) The PGA Tour should be able to decide on its own destiny without the interference of the court; 4) Professional sports are not the place for accommodations to be made for disabled people; 5) Allowing Casey Martin to ride diminishes the achievement of players like Ben Hogan and Ken Venturi; and 6) Carts were never a part of the game before the 1960's and should not be now. Conversely, the site listed Martin's arguments as 1) The PGA Tour already uses carts on the Senior Tour and as shuttles between certain holes to speed play; 2) The ADA requires that accommodations for disabled players be made; the PGA is a public place and employer and must adhere; 3) Riding a cart is not an advantage; in many ways it is a disadvantage; 4) Modern courses are designed with golf carts in mind; 5) Walking is no longer part of the game; and 6) Most players would not use a cart even if they could. *See id.*

276 Morfit, *supra* note 203, at G6.

277 *See* Martin v. PGA Tour, Inc., 984 F. Supp. 1320 (D. Or. 1998).

278 *See* Martin v. PGA Tour, Inc., 994 F. Supp. 1242 (D. Or. 1998).

279 *See* 984 F. Supp. at 1323.
280 *Id.*
281 *See* 994 F. Supp. at 1244.
282 *See* 984 F. Supp. at 1323.
283 994 F. Supp. at 1247 & n.7.
284 708 F. Supp. 233 (W.D. Ark. 1989).
285 *See* COLKER, *supra* note 26, at 229-42 (citing Spirides v. Reinhardt, 613 F.2d 826 (D.C. Cir. 1979) and Doe v. Shapiro, 852 F. Supp. 1246 (E.D. Pa. 1994)).
286 708 F. Supp. at 236-38 (emphasis added). On appeal, the Eighth Circuit stated the following: "We find no flaw in the District Court's analysis and may affirm because we, too, find that the relationship between WPRA and its members categorically resists classification as 'employment' according to the ordinary usage of that term." Graves v. Women's Prof'l Rodeo Ass'n, Inc., 907 F.2d 71, 72-73 (8th Cir. 1990).
287 984 F. Supp. at 1323.
288 *See* 994 F. Supp. at 1247 & n.7.
289 *See* 984 F. Supp. at 1323.
290 *See id.*; 994 F. Supp. at 1244. One defense the PGA did not use was the "direct threat" argument (i.e. that Martin's participation in the PGA tournaments under any circumstances would pose a significant risk to his own health). See *infra* sections I.B.1 and I.B.2 for a general discussion of this defense. For a discussion of the "direct threat" problem in Casey Martin's specific situation, see Eldon L. Ham, *When Athletes Want to Play But Doctors Say No, It's Off to Court,* CHI. DAILY L. BULL., Feb. 20, 1998, at 6.
291 *See* 984 F. Supp. at 1323.
292 *See PGA, Martin Head to Court,* FLORIDA TODAY, Jan. 27, 1998, at 1C.
293 *See* 984 F. Supp. at 1324-26.
294 *See id.* at 1323.
295 *See id.* at 1326.
296 *Id.* at 1326-27.
297 *See id.* at 1326.
298 *See* 984 F. Supp. at 1326.
299 *Id.*

300 *Id.* at 1326-27. In comparison, one federal appeals court has found that the National Football League is not a place of public accommodation. Ted Curtis, *"Cart" Blanche? A Decision Requiring Accommodation for a Disabled Golfer Has Sports Lawyers Wondering What's Next,* A.B.A.J., Apr. 1998, at 34 (citing Stoutenborough v. NFL, 59 F.3d 580 (6th Cir. 1995)).
301 *See* 994 F. Supp. at 1249 ("[T]he ultimate question in this case is whether allowing plaintiff, given his individual circumstances, the re-

quested modification would fundamentally alter PGA and Nike Tour golf competitions.")

302 *Id.* at 1246.

303 *Id.* at 1249.

304 *See id.* at 1250.

305 *See id.* The court specifically rejected, without explanation, *Pottgen's* reasoning on this question. *See id.* at 1249 & n.10, 1250.

306 *Martin*, 994 F.Supp at 1250.

307 *Id.* at 1251-52.

308 *Id.* at 1253.

309 *See* Garrity, *supra* note 94, at 63.

310 *Id.*

311 *Id.*

312 *See id.*; *see also* Rance Crain, *PGA Tour Stand on Disabled Golfer Shields the Sport from PR Bonanza*, ADVERT. AGE, Feb. 23, 1998, at 22.

313 *See Sportsview Backtalk: Debate Continues After Martin Ruling*, FLORIDA TODAY, Feb. 15, 1998, at 3C.

314 *See id.*

315 Cook, *supra* note 220, at G4.

316 Garrity, *supra* note 94, at 63.

317 *Dateline NBC, supra* note 14.

318 Kerasotis, *supra* note 259.

319 *See* Garrity, *supra* note 94, at 63.

320 *See* Interview with Richard A. Epstein, James Parker Hall Distinguished Service Professor of Law, University of Chicago, in Atlanta, Ga. (March 12, 1998). *See also* Curtis, *supra* note 294.

321 Cook, *supra* note 220, at G4.

322 *See Martin Not Ready to Use Exemptions*, FLORIDA TODAY, Feb. 15, 1998, at 3C.

323 Cook, *supra* note 220, at G4.

324 *See Martin Returns to Course Next Week*, FLORIDA TODAY, Feb. 25, 1998, at 2C.

325 *See* Kerasotis, *supra* note 227, at 1C.

326 *See* Crain, *supra* note 306, at 22.

327 *See Dateline NBC, supra* note 14; *Martin Returns to Course Next Week*, *supra* note 318, at 2C. For an assessment of the PGA's appeal by selected sports lawyers, see Curtis, *supra* note 294.

328 Cook, *supra* note 220, at G4.

329 EBERL, *supra* note

PART III

SPORTS CONTRACTS

COLLEGE COACHING CONTRACTS: A PRACTICAL PERSPECTIVE*

Martin J. Greenberg

Negotiating contracts for athletes is the activity most often associated with the label "sports lawyers." While representing athletes may be glamorous, the representation of coaches actually gives rise to a larger and more complex set of issues. In this essay, Martin Greenberg discusses the considerations involved in the representation of coaches and offers extensive recommendations for those involved in the process.

I. COLLEGE COACHES CONTRACTS

A. Introduction -"The Environment"

When is a contract not a contract? Where is job security as fleeting as the last seconds of a basketball victory? In what field is an employment contract broken as easily as made? None other than in the world of college coaching. At the commencement of the 1988-89 college basketball season, a total of 39 schools or approximately 13.4% of the 294 Division I institutions had new coaches at the helm.[1] This compares with an all-time high of 66 new coaches or approximately 22.8% of Division I schools during the previous season.[2] During the 1980s, approximately 384 coaching changes have taken place in Division I schools.[3] Approximately 53 basketball coaches have changed jobs since the end of the 1989-90 season.[4] The American Football

*From Volume 1, Number 2, Spring 1991, pp. 207-282.

Coaches Association indicates that head football coaches remain in
NCAA Division I-A football programs for an average of only 2.8
years.[5] The number of coaches employed at the 279 schools that have
played in Division I Men's Basketball for all of the past 15 seasons include:

> 10 schools employed 6 coaches (average tenure, 2.5 years)
> 30 schools employed 5 coaches (3.0 years)
> 68 schools employed 4 coaches (3.75 years)
> 102 schools employed 3 coaches (5.0 years)
> 45 schools employed 2 coaches (7.5 years)
> 24 schools employed 1 coach (15.0 years)[6]

Why is job movement, contract jumping, retirement and firing so
characteristic of college coaching? The Job Related Almanac indicates
that an NCAA basketball coach has the 15th most stressful job out of
the 260 jobs listed.[7] A coach is defined as "one who trains intensively
by instruction, demonstration, and practice."[8] This definition certainly does not recognize the current job environment and employment conditions of the modern day coach.

The coach of the 1990s is not only required to be an instructor, but
also a fundraiser, recruiter, academic coordinator, public figure,
budget director, television and radio personality, alumni glad hander,
and whatever else the university's athletic director or president may
direct the coach to do in the best interest of the university's athletic
program.

Indeed, today's college coach has become a prominent public
figure. In many instances, the coach's name recognition is greater than
that of the university president. In some cases, a coach who exhibits
interest in employment elsewhere other than old "U" may cause a
statewide crisis. For instance, when Bobby Knight, head basketball
coach of Indiana University, entertained an offer of employment from
the University of New Mexico, Knight's actions, and the resultant
public furor became a featured story on network news and even drew
the attention of the Indiana legislators.

Stress and the changing nature of the job may be the primary cause
for job movement. Some coaches indicate that "they spend less than
20% of their working time actually coaching on the court or the
field."[9] Jack Hartman, former men's basketball mentor at Kansas
State University who had coached for 35 years stated, "[t]he fun was
actual on-court coaching, and working with a kid on and off the court
and seeing him grow as a person. That's what attracted us originally
and has become obscured by all the other time demands."[10]

In addition to the pressures of college athletics, the coach now faces the added pressures of the public concern involving student eligibility, academic progress and, most recently, the posting and disclosure of grades and graduation rates of student athletes.

The NCAA has passed legislation requiring member institutions to publish graduation rates for student-athletes making them available to the public.[11] The legislation calls for disclosure of graduation rates for the entire student body and for student-athletes to the NCAA. The athlete's data must be broken down by sports and in football and basketball broken down by race. Thus, the information on graduation rates that have been disclosed to the NCAA for many years will now be available to the public. The first reporting date is October, 1991, at which time the graduation rates for the last four years will be disclosed.[12]

The Chronicle of Higher Education recently published a survey which included responses from 262 of 295 Division I schools. It took freshmen going into school in fall of 1984 and counted how many had graduated by August 1989. The survey indicates:

Some good: The five-year graduation rate for all Division I athletes entering school in 1984 was 56.1%, far ahead of the 47.9% graduation rate for all students in general.

Some bad: The graduation rate for football players at Division I-A schools was only 42.5%, including 32.2% by the Southeastern Conference, 32.5% by the Southwest and 39.4% by the Big Eight.

Some ugly: The graduation rate for basketball players in Division I was only 39%, and only 31.9% at schools that are Division I in basketball and Division I-A in football. This includes 14% by the Southeastern Converence, 18.9% by the Big West Conference, whose rate for football players was 23.8%.[13]

The article concludes that, "The overall signal is undeniable; schools are much more lax in graduating football and basketball players than other athletes. There is a crisis of non-graduated students in the sports of big names and big money."[14]

Because of public disclosure, coaches can no longer just be satisfied with winning. Coaches cannot afford to ignore when their star athlete misses his chemistry class or threatens to drop out of school.

College sports has become a big business with high financial stakes. If the coach is not bringing in enough revenue, or is not perceived positively by the alumni or public, a university may be forced to terminate his employment for fear of losing large amounts of money.

Coach Rich Haddad was fired as the basketball coach of Jacksonville, concluding a 6-21 season. "Winning is the bottom line."[15] Added Haddad, "Schools are looking for coaches who run clean programs, graduate their players and win big. If you stumble in any area, you're in trouble. But winning big is the big factor. And that translates into money."[16] But, even winning doesn't guarantee job security. J.D. Barnett had a winning record including two NCAA tournament appearances, a clean slate with the NCAA and a rollover five year contract at Tulsa when he joined the roll call of fired basketball coaches in March of 1991. "Where did Barnett go wrong? Tulsa Athletic Director Rick Dickson said Barnett was fired for not making enough money for the school. He cited dwindling attendance, contributions and season ticket sales. He also cited the turnover in the assistant coaches and the student-athletes not completing his program."[17] Twenty-four College Football Association teams that played in 1989-90 bowl games earned a total of $33 million.[18] The 1990 NCAA Men's Basketball Final Four participants, Arkansas, Duke, Georgia Tech, and UNLV, earned an estimated 1.23 million each for their participation in the Tournament.[19] Further, the advent of major television and cable network contracts for the right to broadcast these events has created even more revenue for the NCAA and its constituent universities. CBS has agreed to pay the NCAA $143 million for television rights to the NCAA College Basketball Tournament from 1991 to 1997.[20] Before Notre Dame left the CFA (College Football Association), ABC agreed to pay $210 million for five years for the right to telecast CFA games.[21] In 1989, ABC paid $11.8 million for the rights fees to telecast the Rose Bowl with each team receiving approximately $6.3 million.[22] Today's coaches are faced with a win at any cost dilemma. The pressure to generate revenues from television, gate receipts, alumni donations and tournament participation has put the bottom line or balance sheet psychology on an equal basis with "wins and losses."

    The student athlete of today may be a different athlete than of years ago. The reverence paid to the coach as a father-figure or surrogate parent may no longer be. Recent revolts by players have forced coaches out of their jobs. For instance, San Jose University in January of 1989, experienced a rebellion among its basketball players. The players announced they would not play for the team unless coach Bill Berry was fired.[23] They accused the coach of verbal abuse and mental cruelty.[24] A players rebellion also occurred in February of 1990 at Drake University when Coach Tom Abatemarco was reassigned to other athletic department duties 24-hours after the players stated that they would no longer practice or play for Abatemarco because of alleged verbal and mental abuse. Drake University officials denied that they let the basketball players take control over the program by giving in to player demands.[25]

With the rise of college sports as a big business, college coaching has become a game of high stakes where money talks. The position of head coach may offer not only a salary with institutional fringe benefits, but additional compensation opportunities which are generally referred to as the "package." The package might include shoe, apparel and equipment endorsements, television and radio shows, speaking engagements, personal or public appearances, and summer instructional camps. In addition, the job may also mean such related perquisites as housing, insurance premiums, membership in health and country clubs, financial gifts from alumni and boosters, business opportunities, and the use or the gift of automobiles.

For instance, the income of Vince Dooley, Georgia's athletic director and football coach, and the income of Hugh Durham, Georgia's basketball coach illustrate the types of compensation packages in college athletics:

1. Vince Dooley, Athletic Director and Head Football Coach income from sources outside of University of Georgia Athletic Association (UGA).

$103,000	TV and radio shows
15,000	Endorsement contract with shoe company
12,000	Speaking engagements
5,250	Summer camps
2,406.12	Endorsement contracts with various athletic equipment and clothing companies
$137,656.12	SUBTOTAL

Income provided by UGA Athletic Association

$ Value (unknown)	Home (provided by Athletic Association)
$ Value (unknown)	Luxury automobile
$ 95,000	Salary
$ 4,500	Allowance for incidental expenses
$ 26,000	Premium on deferred-income annuity
$ 125,500	Subtotal
$ 263,156.12	Total Sports-Related Income (without value of house and car)

2. Hugh Durham, Men's Basketball Coach

Income from sources outside of UGA Athletic Association

    $ 73,000   TV and radio shows
    $ 40,000   Speaking engagements
    $ 35,000   Endorsement contract with shoe manufacturer
    $ 3,000   Endorsement contract with basketball manufacturer
    $ 1,500   Endorsement contract with uniform manufacturer
    $ 3,600   Housing subsidy
    $ Value   Basketball camps (unreported)
    $ 156,100 SUBTOTAL (plus any unreported income)
Income provided by Durham by UGA Athletic Association

    $ 75,000   Salary
    $ Value   Luxury automobile
    $ 75,000   SUBTOTAL
    $ 231,000 TOTAL SPORTS-RELATED INCOME (without value of
               car)[26]

Because of the lack of job security in coaching, and the amount of money paid to the coaches for their services, meticulously drafted employment contracts have become a necessity for both the coach and the university. According to Judson Graves,

> College athletics is big business. Whatever else they may be-master strategists, charismatic inspirers of young athletes, or national celebrities-today's college athletic coaches are big businessmen. In the high-stakes, win at all costs atmosphere of major college athletics, job security for coaches can be as fleeting as last Saturday's victory, and complex, tightly drawn employment contracts have become a necessity for those coaches with enough negotiating leverage to obtain them. These relatively new entrants to the business world operate in a volatile atmosphere in which hirings and firings often occur in rapid sequence, and hard legal questions are being raised about the proper methods of enforcing their employment contracts when breaches occur.[27]

This article is organized as a practical guide for those representing the coach or university when drafting an employment contract. The commentary will focus on Division I coaches' contracts, but the contents herein also apply to Divisions II and III coaches' contracts. Two essential areas will be discussed in order that a tightly drawn employment contract can be created. First, the practitioner must understand the effect of the law on the employment contract in a sports industry context. General contract principles regarding coaching contracts, the implications of *Rodgers v. Georgia Tech. Athletic Ass'n.*,[28] NCAA rules, and the effect of state open record laws on the coaching contract will be discussed. Second, this chapter will discuss and provide examples of clauses that may be contained in the coach's contract. Employment contracts will vary depending upon the factual circumstance because of the divergent goals and strategies of the university and coach. However, a discussion of the important clauses that are generally found in coaches contracts is the starting point for the practitioner when drafting the coaching contract. The clauses used in this chapter originated from actual coaches' contracts, "'The Model University Coaching Contract' (MCC): A Better Starting Point For Your Next Negotiation,"[29] and "Coaching Contracts: Some Suggestions on Your Next Coaching Contract Negotiation And Report From Our Survey."[30] When reviewing MCC clauses, one should note that the MCC is university oriented and drafted for purposes of protecting the university and not the coach. Coaches' contracts can take many forms, unlike the standard player contracts utilized in the NBA, NFL, NHL and Major League Baseball, varying from a simple letter of appointment, to a letter agreement, to a standard university contract or to a fully negotiated contract covering many of the legal nuances of this unique position.

B. Knowing the Law

As a general principle of law, a promise to tender personal services will not be specifically enforced by an affirmative decree. This is so primarily because courts will not force a person to engage in activity against his will, regardless of a contractual obligation to perform. When this rule is applied in the area of coaches contracts, the result is that neither the university nor the court can require a coach to work, even if the coach is contractually bound to do so. Similarly, a coach cannot force a university to allow him to work if the university decides to terminate his position or to replace him with another coach. The university, therefore, may remove the coach from his position at any time, with or without a valid reason. However, the university may have to compensate the coach with monetary damages if the coach challenges the premature contract termination.

In *Coaches in the Courtroom*, Judson Graves states that in the context of coaching contracts, the relationship between the university and the coach becomes somewhat unbalanced, in that while the coach has clear contractual remedies against the university for breach of contract, the same may not be true if the coach decides to terminate performance.[31] Graves believes that the advantage here lies with the coach "who can breach the contract and leave the relationship with virtual impunity...."[32] Graves states that the problem is even more acute when the university, in attempting to enforce its contract, tries to prove precisely how, in monetary terms, it has been damaged by the coach's termination of the contract.[33] According to Graves:

> In theory, at least, an employer is clearly entitled to bring an action for damages against any employee in breach, and coaches are no exception. In such cases the recoverable damages are normally measured by the cost to the employer of obtaining equivalent services elsewhere, plus consequential damages. Some cases indicated that in assessing such damages, the market value of the lost services must be measured against that of the substitute services procured by the employer to remedy the breach.[34]

Although these criteria may seem simple and reasonable, a judge or jury may find it impossible to determine the market value of coaches' contracts. In addition, most premature terminations are met with animosity on at least one side, and litigation could serve merely to prolong those negative public relations and cast a shadow over the institution's athletic program for years. It may provide difficult to estimate—or compensate for—the vast array of payments and fringe benefits a coach may have been receiving prior to the breach. For these reasons, many institutions avoid litigation, even if the coach is the breaching party.[35] Graves concludes that: "As a result, most employees, and certainly most coaches, have historically been able to leave their employment virtually at will despite their prior contractual commitments."[36]

On the other hand, a university may attempt to obtain equitable relief by acquiring an injunction to prohibit a contract "jumping" coach from working for another entity. For example, in 1973, Charles "Chuck" Fairbanks contracted with the New England Patriots, to act as its general manager and head coach. A later agreement specified that employment should continue until January, 1983, and also read:

> 10 (b) Fairbanks shall not render services directly connected with football during the period of his employment other than for the Patriots except with the express written permission of the Patriots, which permission shall not be unreasonably withheld.

(d) Fairbanks shall not render services to another entity not connected with football during the period of employment except with the express written permission of the Patriots, which permission shall not be unreasonably withheld.[37]

In 1978, Fairbanks was approached by persons affiliated with the University of Colorado who tried to convince Fairbanks to leave the Patriots and become the Colorado head football coach. The Patriots sought a court injunction enjoining Colorado from contracting with Fairbanks while he was still under contract with the Patriots.[38] The District Court in Colorado entered a preliminary injunction enjoining the University of Colorado, its regents, president, athletic director, and certain fans from contacting Fairbanks for the purpose of hiring him for the University.[39] On Appeal, the first district upheld the preliminary injunction forbidding Colorado from soliciting Fairbanks' services reasoning that Fairbanks' services where unique and the loss of his services would cause irreparable harm to the Patriots, and money damages would be difficult to determine.[40] The court also held that the contractual provisions that required Fairbanks, while under contract with the Patriots, to refrain from contracting for "services directly connected with football ... [or with] another entity not connected with football," covered entities not in direct competition with the Patriots.[41] Therefore, the clause also prohibited Fairbanks from entering into an employment agreement with the University of Colorado.

A similar situation arose regarding Michigan State University's attempt to hire George Perles, then under contract with the Philadelphia Stars of the former United States Football League. In response to the university's action, the Stars sued the university for $1 million.[42] The case ultimately ended in a settlement, with the university paying $175,000 in order to obtain Perles' services and protect itself from legal liability.[43]

In many instances, a coach's contract will contain a unique services clause, to protect the university from a breaching coach. By agreeing to this clause, the coach acknowledges that he has a special, unique and exceptional skill, and that the university's need for continuity in its coaching—as well as any further acquisition of coaching experience—will reflect that uniqueness. The contract will also require the coach to agree that the loss of his services, prior to the expiration of the contractual term, and without the university approval, will cause an inestimable loss to the university which cannot be fairly or adequately compensated for by money damages. Finally, the coach will be required to promise not to accept employment under any circumstances as a coach at any other institution, or with any professional league, or with any other competing entity without first obtaining permission from the university.

These clauses are necessary because a university may be unable to obtain a negative injunction due to the "difficulty of proving a coach exceptional, difficulty in proving irreplaceability or irreparable harm, difficulty in proving money damages and difficulty in proving that the coach would not be unreasonably burdened."[44]

Because of the university's inability to force the coach to work, and because of the possibility of protracted litigation, adverse publicity, a cloud over the athletic department, and presumably a relationship that has deteriorated, most universities will let their restless or ambitious coach go without further ado. Unless, of course, the contract contains some type of financial "buy out" or "release" clause.[45]

However, when the coach's contract is terminated by a university prior to its expiration, the courts have generally allowed the coach to recover money damages, measured by the "full-rate of contract compensation." The coach's right to receive this compensation may be reduced if a mitigation of damages clause in the contract states that the coach's relief will be offset if he obtains other employment or has earnings from a new job.

Judsen Graves concludes that the victimized coach has a remedy in the form of full monetary compensation:

> Most institutions recognize their continuing liability under the contract and either continue to pay the coach through the contract term (even though there are no employment duties) or "buy out" the contract for a lump sum. It has been suggested that a lump sum buyout at the time of the termination, based on the present value of future payments to come due, is the proper measure of damages in such a situation rather than the installment method ... and this method has been used with many coaches. The theory is that since the breach is complete upon contract termination, complete damages are then due as well. The principle is the same, however, and the adequacy of the remedy clears under either measure.[46]

The coach's contract today is no longer monetarily a simple matter of salary and fringe benefits provided by the university. The total compensation received by the coach commonly referred to as the "package," may include those financial opportunities normally attendant to the position of head coach such as "anticipated earnings" from television, radio shows, athletic summer camps, product endorsements or similar personal appearance opportunities, as well as certain incidental benefits and perquisites sometimes bestowed by alumni and boosters such as a free car, free housing, life insurance, lodging, complimentary club memberships, trust funds, annuities, complimentary athletic tickets, and attractive investment and business opportunities.[47]

The component parts of the package may flow from a variety of sources, "... some of which may provide their component part pursuant to an obligation (such as the employer's obligation to pay salary), while others may provide elements of the package under no legal obligation, but simply out of a desire to aid the athletic program or curry favor with the celebrity coach."[48]

The legal question becomes to what extent may a terminated coach recover consequential loss of his collateral opportunities even when the university did not agree to be contractually liable for them, or their aggregate value is substantially in excess of the coach's basic salary and university provided fringe benefits.[49]

C. Rodger v. Georgia Tech. Athletic Association[50]

Rodgers v. Georgia Tech Athletic Association,[51] is the leading case as to whether a coach may recover monetary damages for breach of contract including consequential loss of collateral opportunities. Franklin C. "Pepper" Rodgers was removed by Georgia Tech from his head football coaching position on December 18, 1979, two years before the expiration of his contract. Rodgers' initial contract was in the form of a letter dated April 20, 1977 with the defendant, a non-profit corporate entity separate from the university, but responsible for the university's varsity's athletic program.

Rodgers' contract provided that in addition to regular compensation, as an employee of the Association, you would be entitled "to various insurance and pension benefits and perquisites" as you become eligible therefor.[52] After termination, the Association had continued to pay Rodgers his normal monthly salary plus pension-insurance benefits.[53] Rodgers suit which was for damages in excess of $496,000.00 was for "perquisites" over and above the normal compensation covered under his coaching contract.[54]

Rodgers argued he was entitled to twenty-nine perquisites for which he grouped into two categories.[55] The first category included items provided directly to him by the Association but discontinued when he was fired.[56] The second category included items provided through sources other than the Association by virtue of his position as head football coach.[57] What follows is a list of those perquisites as included in the appendix to the case:

A. Benefits and Perquisites Received by Rodgers *Directly* from Georgia Tech Athletic Association.

(1) gas, oil, maintenance, repairs, other automobile expenses;

(2) automobile liability and collision insurance;

(3) general expense money;

(4) meals available at the Georgia Tech training table;

(5) eight season tickets to Georgia Tech home football games during fall of 1980 and 1981;

(6) two reserved booths, consisting of approximately 40 seats at Georgia Tech home football games during fall of 1980 and 1981;

(7) six season tickets to Georgia Tech home basketball games for 1980 and 1981;

(8) four season tickets to Atlanta Falcon home football games for 1980 and 1981;

(9) four game tickets to each out-of-town Georgia Tech football game during fall of 1980 and 1981;

(10) pocket money at each home football game during fall of 1980 and 1981;

(11) pocket money at each out-of-town Georgia Tech football game during fall of 1980 and 1981;

(12) parking privileges at all Georgia Tech home sporting events;

(13) the services of a secretary;

(14) the services of an administrative assistant;

(15) the cost of admission to Georgia Tech home baseball games during spring of 1980 and 1981;

(16) the cost of trips to football coaches' conventions, clinics, and meetings and to observe football practice sessions of professional and college football terms;

(17) initiation fee, dues, monthly bills, and cost of membership at the Capital City Club;

(18) initiation fee, dues, monthly bills, and cost of membership at the Cherokee County Club;

(19) initiation fee and dues at the East Lake Country Club.

B. Benefits and Perquisites Received by Rodgers from Sources *Other Than* the Georgia Tech Athletic Association by Virtue of Being Head Coach of Football.

(1) profits from Rodgers' television football show, "The Pepper Rodgers Show," on Station WSB-TV in Atlanta for the fall of 1980 and 1981;

(2) profits from Rodgers' radio football show on Station WGST in Atlanta for the fall of 1980 and 1981;

(3) use of a new Cadillac automobile during 1980 and 1981;

(4) profits from Rodgers' summer football camp, known as the "Pepper Rodgers Football School," for June 1980 and June 1981;

(5) financial gifts from alumni and supporters of Georgia Tech for 1980 and 1981;

(6) lodging at any of the Holiday Inns owned by Topeka Inn Management, Inc. of Topeka, Kansas, for the time period from December 18, 1979 through December 31, 1981;

(7) the cost of membership to Terminus International Tennis Club in Atlanta for 1980 and 1981;

(8) individual game tickets to Hawks basketball and Braves baseball games during 1980 and 1981 seasons;

(9) housing for Rodgers and his family in Atlanta for the period from December 18, 1979 through December 31, 1981;

(10) the cost of premiums of a $400,000.00 policy on the life of Rodgers for the time period from December 18, 1979 through December 31, 1981.[58]

These perquisites were not defined in Pepper Rodgers' contract. The Association moved for summary judgment arguing that (1) it had met its contractual obligation by continuing to pay Rodgers as required under the contract, (2) it could not be held responsible for Rodgers' collateral opportunities with third party providers, or (3) it could not be held liable for actions of individuals not related to the contract who decided to cease providing Rodgers gratuitous items as a result of his position as head coach.[59]

The trial court granted the Association's motion for summary judgment dismissing Rodgers' suit in its entirety. According to Judson Graves:

> Had this decision gone unchallenged, it would have essentially preserved the traditional view described previously, by which the breaching employer's liability is limited to the amount of direct compensation and related compensatory benefits (such as pension contributions, for example) which the employee would have

received for the balance of the term of employment had the contract not been terminated early.[60]

Rodgers' appeal, and the appellate decision "broke new ground in Georgia and that may help litigants elsewhere do the same, in expanding the elements of damages potentially recoverable in these coaches' contract cases."[61]

The Court of Appeals held that some perquisites may be recoverable even though received by Rodgers from third parties not controlled or related to the defendant, if the defendant knew that their loss may be occasioned by relieving Rodgers of his position.[62] In essence, the Court of Appeals found that perquisites could be recovered if all of the following elements were met:

1. The damages must be traced solely to the breach;
2. The damages must be capable of exact computation;
3. The damages must have arisen naturally and according to the usual course of things from such breach; and
4. The damages must be such as the parties contemplated them as a probable result of the breach.[63]

As result, the Court of Appeals' decision excluded certain damages as a matter of law, while other categories of damages were remanded for a jury trial on the merits.[64]

Of the twenty-nine perquisites that Rodgers tried to collect, eight were thrown out by the court and the other twenty-one were sent to the jury to decide if they were perquisites that were recoverable under the contract and under the elements as previously stated.[65] Graves states that the importance of the case is that the *Rodgers* decision:

> ... acknowledged that some collateral losses may be recovered if they can be proven with specificity and that in a special class of cases, extraordinary damages may be probably recoverable by an employee if the employment position is such that it provides a unique status and presents the employee with special opportunities to further one's name and reputation, as well as to earn money substantially over and above salary and fringe benefits.[66]

The case of *McLaughlin v. Union-Leader Corp.*,[67] also provides guidance for the construction of personal service contracts. *McLaughlin* involved a five year personal service contract of an advertising manager who worked for a New Hampshire newspaper. After the execution of the agreement, the newspaper installed a new advertising manager and placed McLaughlin on an "indefinite leave of absence" with pay. When McLaughlin sued for breach of contract, the newspaper stopped paying his salary, asserting that McLaughlin had breached the contract by rendering inadequate performance. The jury rejected the newspaper's argument and awarded McLaughlin a substantial verdict which was upheld on appeal.[68]

The turning point of the case was when the court recognized a breach on the part of the newspaper, both in its refusal to pay McLaughlin's salary and its denial of the position he had contracted to receive.[69] To support its holding, the court cited Section 433 of the Restatement of Agency:

> If the [agent] ... is to receive a fixed salary, a promise by the principal to furnish him with work is inferred from a promise to the employee only if it is found that the anticipated benefit to the agent from doing the work is a material part of the advantage to be received by him from the employment. This anticipated benefit may be the acquisition of skill or reputation by the employee or the acquisition of subsidiary pecuniary advantages, as in the case of the employment of public performers whose reputation will be enhanced by their appearance or diminished by their failure to appear beginners in a trade or profession, and those whose compensation is likely to be enhanced by receiving gratuities from outside sources....[70]

In holding that the removal of McLaughlin from the position promised to him constituted a separate and distinct breach of his contract, the New Hampshire court took a significant step toward recognizing certain employment positions as including far more than merely the opportunity to work for an employer and earn the agreed upon compensation.

Under this reasoning, preventing an employee ascending to a sufficiently unique employment position (such as that of a coach) could constitute a separate breach of contract, and render the employer liable in damages, even if that employer continued to pay the full contract compensation. Damages in such a situation could flow from the loss of the kinds of "subsidiary pecuniary advantages" and the "gratuities from outside sources" described in the Restatement.[71] In sum, relieving an employee from a position could constitute a compensable loss in addition to the paid compensation to which the employee is clearly entitled under the contract. Moreover, in the area of major college coaching, the value of the lost "subsidiary pecuniary advantages" and "gratuities," such as alumni gifts, television revenues, endorsements, etc., could easily (and often does) exceed the combination of a base salary and related compensation paid by an employer.[72] Based on decisions such as *Rodgers*[73] and *McLaughlin*,[74] a coach relieved of a position prior to the expiration of the contract can assert that unless the contract specifically precluded such recovery, the coach may be entitled to damages for the monetary losses the employer knew or should have known would be occasioned by a breach. To prevent the occurrence of such damages, the contract should specifically state how collateral business opportunities are to be addressed. The contract should not leave any doubt as to what is within the contemplation of both parties with respect to liability for such items, in the event the relationship is prematurely dissolved.

D. National Collegiate Athletic Association (NCAA) Regulations

The drafters of any coach's contract should consider external rules and policies which will have an impact upon the contractual terms. Such external rules and policies will come from the NCAA, the conference to which the university belongs, and the university itself. Current NCAA rules affecting coach's contracts are as follows:

a. Article 11, Section 2.1, Stipulation That NCAA Enforcement Provisions Apply:

Contractual agreements or appointments between a coach and a institution shall include the stipulation that a coach who is found in violation of NCAA regulations shall be subject to disciplinary or corrective action as set forth in the provisions of the NCAA enforcement procedures.[75]

b. Section 11.2.1.1, Termination of Employment:

Contractual agreements or appointments between a coach and an institution shall include the stipulation that a coach may be terminated if the coach is found to be involved in deliberate and serious violations of NCAA regulations.[76]

c. Section 11.2.2, Report of Athletically Related Income:

Contract agreements, including letters of appoint, between a full-time or part-time coach and an institution shall include the stipulation that the coach is required to report annually (in writing or orally) all athletically related income and benefits from sources outside of the institution through the athletics director to the institution's chief executive officer. Sources of such income shall include, but are not limited to, the following: (a) Income from annuities; (b) sports camps; (c) housing benefits (including preferential housing arrangements); (c) country-club memberships (e) complimentary ticket sales; (f) television and radio programs, and (g) endorsement or consultation contracts with athletic shoe, apparel or equipment manufacturers.[77]

d. Section 11.3.2.1, Bona Fide Outside Employment:

A staff member may earn income in addition to the institutional salary by performing services for outside groups, provided the compensation is for additional work actually performed and at a rate commensurate with the going rate in that locality for services of like character, further, such outside work must be in conformity with institutional policy and with the approval of the institution.[78]

e. Section 11.3.2.2, Supplemental Pay:

An outside source is prohibited from paying or regularly supplementing an athletics department staff member's annual salary and from arranging to supplement that salary for an unspecified achievement. This includes the donation of cash from outside sources to the institution earmarked for the staff member's salary or supplemental income. It would be permissible for an outside source to donate funds to the institution to be used as determined by the institution, and it would be permissible for the institution, at its sole discretion, to use such funds to pay or supplement a staff member's salary.[79]

f. Section 11.3.2.3, Bonuses for Specific and Extraordinary Achievement:

An institution may permit an outside individual, group or agency to supplement an athletics department staff member's salary with a direct cash payment in recognition of a specific and extraordinary achievement (e.g., contribution during career to the athletics department of the institution, winning a conference or national championship, number of games or meets won during career), provided such a cash supplement is in recognition of a specific achievement and is in conformance with institutional policy.[80]

g. Section 11.3.2.4, Extra Compensation Restriction for Division II and Division III Coaches:

A member institution shall not give extra compensation or renumeration of any sort to any coach conditioned upon or because of the number of games the coach's team wins, or because the team goes to a bowl game or tournament or participates in championships. These limitations on extra compensation to coaches do not apply where enforceable contracts or formal security-of-employment commitments in effect on August 15, 1976, make it impossible to comply with the limitations. These exceptions are continued until existing contracts or formal security-of-employment commitments expire.[81]

h. Section 11.3.2.5, Endorsement of Commercial Products:

Athletic department staff members shall not use, directly or by implication, the institution's name or logo in the endorsement of commercial products or services for personal gain without prior approval from the institution.[82]

i. Section 11.3.2.6, Promotional Activities:

A staff member of a member institution's athletics department may not be compensated by an individual or commercial business outside of the institution for employment or assistance in the production, distribution or sale of items (e.g., calendars, pictures, posters, advertisements, cards) bearing the names or pictures of student athletes. The use of the names or pictures of student-athletes on promotional items is limited to institutionally controlled activities involving the sale of official institutional publications and team or individual pictures by the institution. This restriction shall apply even if the promotional item is provided without charge to the public by an outside individual or commercial business that produces or purchases the item through the assistance of institution's staff member.[83]

j. Section 11.3.2.7, Compensation in Exchange for Use of Merchandise:

Staff members of a member institution's athletics department shall not accept, prior to receiving approval from the institution's chief executive officer, compensation or gratuities (excluding institutionally administered funds) from an athletics shoe, apparel or equipment manufacturer in exchange for the use of such merchandise during practice or competition by the institution's student-athletes.[84]

k. Section 11.3.2.8, Compensation for Scheduling Contests/ Individual Participation:

Staff members of a member institution's athletics department shall not accept compensation or gratuities for scheduling athletics contests or individual meet participation with another institution or a sponsor of athletics competition. This specifically precludes the acceptance of compensation or gratuities from other institutions, schedule brokers or agents, and television networks or syndicators.[85]

At the 1991 NCAA Convention, legislation was passed that would require Division I coaches to be certified on an annual basis in order to contact or evaluate prospects off-campus.[86] The certification procedures would be established by the NCAA national office and be administered by the respective conference offices.[87] The certification process would include a standardized national test.[88] The legislation would go into effect on August 1, 1992.[89]

Finally, the drafter should review the NCAA's "Recommended Policy 6" sections.[90] Although these are not found in the NCAA Constitution or By-Laws, these recommendations provide some guidance in what should be included in a coaches employment agreement. The NCAA recommendations are as follows:

Section 1. An individual as well as an institution should recognize the moral responsibilities inherent in respecting and fulfilling contractual agreements.

Section 2. An institution should enter into a contractual agreement with a coach similar to those entered into with the other members of the faculty; and such a contract should include the assignment of faculty rank, benefits of tenure and retirement, and such other rights and privileges as are enjoyed by other members of the contracting institution's faculty.

Section 3. When a contracting institution makes special concessions to a coach, they should be set forth in detail in the contract and accepted as legal and binding in the same manner as the other provisions of the contractual agreement.

Section 4. All salary agreements between a coach and an institution should be stated in the contract, and such salary should come from sources under the administrative control of the institution.

Section 5. An educational institution seeking a coach who is under contract to another educational institution is morally obligated first to contact the institution that holds the agreement with the coach and secure permission to negotiate with the individual.

Section 6. A coach should not enter into negotiations with a second institution during the term of the contract without first notifying the institution that is a party to this contractual agreement, and the coach should then keep the first institution's administration informed concerning the negotiations.

Section 7. No institution should engage the services of a coach prior to the coach's release from any contractual obligation to another institution.[91]

An interpretation of Section 11.3.1 of the NCAA Manual "Control of Employment and Salaries"[92] has had a recent affect on coaches. The rule has now been interpreted to forbid a head coach from supplementing assistant coaches' salaries. The rule states that, "The institution, as opposed to any outside source, shall remain in control in determining who is to be its employee and the amount of salary the employee is to receive within the restrictions specified by NCAA legislation."[93] The head coach for purposes of this rule is considered an outside source.

Galen Hall, who resigned October 8, 1989, as head football coach at the University of Florida, amid allegations of rule violations including paying his assistant coaches extra money, may not have been the only college football coach to pay his assistants.[94] Hall, admitted at the time of his resignation that he paid $22,000.00 to two assistants.[95] Former University of Notre Dame coach Ara Parseghian and University of Oklahoma coach Barry Switzer, admitted that they also supplemented their assistants' salaries. "I will tell you right now, when I was at Notre Dame, I co-shared income that I received," said Parseghian. "But that was after the fact. It was commercial and television money I had received as a reward for our success. I shared it at Christmas, as bonuses, with my assistant coaches."[96] Switzer said he gave Christmas bonuses to secretaries and graduate assistants when he was head coach at Oklahoma.[97] He also stated that he gave former assistant Mack Brown, now head coach at North Carolina, a $30,000 supplement when Brown was hired as the Sooners' offensive coordinator in 1984.[98] Florida State head football coach, Bobby Bowden, said 90% of coaches do not or did not know that rules existed forbidding the coach from supplementing assistants' salaries.[99] Don Morton, former University of Wisconsin head football coach, was found by the NCAA to have violated its rules when he took out a loan in August of 1989 in the amount of $14,100.00 to pay nine assistant coaches their compensation for salary cuts ordered by the Wisconsin Athletic Board as part of a budget balancing measure.[100] Morton received approval to incur the loan to pay the coaches salaries from former Athletic Director Ade Sponberg, who assumed that "outside sources" referred to non-university sources such as boosters.[101]

E. The Knight Foundation Commission Report on Intercollegiate Athletics

On March 19, 1991, The Knight Foundation Commission on Intercollegiate Athletics presented its forty-seven page report entitled "Keeping Faith With the Student Athlete: A New Model for Intercollegiate Athletics." The report issued by the twenty-two member Commission after more than eighteen months of study and five hearings does deal with the issue of coaches' athletic-related income. The Commission recommended as follows:

> The Commission believes that in considering non-coaching income for its coaches, universities should follow a well-established practice with all faculty members: If the outside income involves the university's functions, facilities or name, contracts for particular services should be negotiated with the university. As part of the effort to bring athletics-related income into the university, we recommend that the NCAA ban shoe and equipment contracts with individual coaches. If a company is eager to have an institution's athletes using its product, it should approach the institution not the coach.[102]

In addition, the Commission addressed the insecurity of the position of coach and long-term contracts. The Commission recommended:

Academic tenure is not appropriate for most coaches, unless they are bona fide members of the faculty. But greater security in an insecure field is clearly reasonable. The Commission suggests that within the first five years of contractual employment, head and assistant coaches who meet the university's expectations, including its academic expectations, should be offered renewable, long-term contracts. These contracts should specifically address the university's obligations in the event of termination, as well as the coach's obligations in the event he or she breaks the contract by leaving the institution.[103]

The Commission recognized the great import and impact that the coach has in their day-to-day contact with student-athletes:

> You and your colleagues are the adults with the greatest day-to-day contact with our student-athletes. You must make them understand that fewer than one in a hundred will ever make a living from their athletic ability. Emphasize to them the value of a college degree. Insist that the privilege of being a member of your squad carries with it the obligation of being a student in good standing. Search out every opportunity to drive home the point that your athletes' behavior, on and off the field, is important not merely because it reflects on your institution or on you, but most significantly because of what it says about them. Your satisfaction will be a lifetime associated with adults who have, with your assistance, achieved their full potential.[104]

Rev. Theodore Hesburgh, President-Emeritus of the University of Notre Dame and co-chair of the Knight Foundation Commission on Intercollegiate Athletics indicated that:

> "Power coaches, the CEOs of multimillion-dollar athletic enterprises, can become laws unto themselves."
> "The surest path to reform lies in reaffirming the integrity of athletics as part of the educational enterprise."
> "All funds spent and raised on sports will be under the control of the university ..."
> "Shoe contract income will be negotiated through the university, not with individual coaches."[105]

Rev. Theodore Hesburgh concludes that, "But only by restoring the balance between athletics and academics can we keep faith with the student-athlete, with our institutions and with the American public that wants the best for both of them."[106]

F. State Open-Records Law

The representative of a coach or university should know the applicable Open-Records law or Freedom of Information statute of the state where the contract is situated. These laws are significant in that the coach may have to allow access by the public to the financial details of his contract. The confidentiality clause inserted in the contract by the lawyer for the university or coach may be rendered ineffective by virtue of such laws. The underlying public policy behind state open-records laws is to "insure accountability of public officers and to enhance public confidence in the political system through disclosure and increased awareness."[107]

Three questions must be considered in order to decide whether the public will be able to gain access to the coach's income reports or the coach's contract itself. First, who may use a state's open-records law? Most state laws provide that any person may request a disclosure of documents by an agency; however, a minority of states require that the requester be a citizen of that state.[108]

Second, what definition does the state's statute afford the term "public records"? Implicit in any definition of "public records" is that the custodial agency is a governmental agency or body.[109] Normally, state-funded colleges or universities are considered governmental bodies within the meaning of state open-records laws.[110] Some private entities may be subject to such laws as a result of receipt of public funds and, as such, would qualify therefor as governmental agencies.[111]

Finally, what exemptions are allowed under the particular state open-records law? The exemption most often found in state open records laws that could pertain to a coaching employment contract would be the invasion of privacy exemption.[112] Typically, statutes exempt personnel files, medical files, and similar type files the disclosure of which would constitute an unwarranted invasion of privacy.[113] If, however, the privacy exemption does not specifically include the solicited document or information requested, the courts often will balance the public's need to know against the harm which might result in the invasion of privacy of the person to whom the records relate. While a majority of laws allow the disclosure of elected official's financial information and the financial information of public employees, it is not clear whether states may compel disclosure of a non-elected public employee outside income, even if job related.[114]

In June of 1988, Peter Gavitt resigned his position as head coach of the University of Maine's women's basketball team. Gavitt's resignation lead Gannett Publishing Company to make a series of requests for information under the Maine Freedom of Access Act. The university denied all requests and Gannett filed an action to compel the university to turn over documents and records concerning Gavitt's resignation.[115] The university contended that the Maine Freedom of Access Act contained two exceptions to disclosure. There is a exception to disclosure for public employee's personnel records and "[m]edical information of any kind, including information pertaining to diagnosis or treatment of mental or emotional disorders...."[116] There is also an exception for records containing complaints, charges or accusations of misconduct that may result in disciplinary action.[117] The university argued that these two exceptions mandated that the settlement agreement between it and Gavitt should remain confidential.[118] The court found, however, that there were several sentences in the settlement agreement concerning medical information which should indeed remain confidential, but the remainder of the agreement should be disclosed.[119]

There is before the Georgia Supreme Court, a suit testing whether Georgia's Open-Records Act requires coaches to make public documentation regarding their outside sources of income.[120] The Atlantic Journal-Constitution newspaper petitioned the University of Georgia for release of all documents detailing the athletically-related income of University of Georgia, Football Coach and Athletic Director, Vince Dooley, Men's Basketball Coach, Hugh Durham and Women's Basketball Coach, Andy Landers. The newspaper claims access to the memoranda under which the coaches reported their income to University of Georgia's (UGA) President Charles Knapp under the Georgia-Records Act. The coaches in order to block release of documents detailing their income, filed suit against the newspaper. The coaches contended that the documents are not "public records" within the meaning of the Georgia Records Act as interpreted by the case of *Macon Telegraph v. Board of Regents*.[121] In *Macon*, the Georgia Supreme Court held that documents relating to the income and expenses of the University of Georgia Athletic Association are "public records", because the Athletic Association is the management tool by which the University operates its intercollegiate athletic program.[122] However, the court limited its decision by holding that records of the UGA are subject to disclosure only if "the maintenance of documents relating to ... the intercollegiate sports program is an integral part" of the University President's control of the school's intercollegiate sports program.[123] Ironically, the coaches released figures detailing their athletically-related outside income to the newspaper in January of

1988. However, the coaches refused to allow inspection of the documentation with respect to such athletically-related outside income. As a result, the primary issue in the lawsuit is the newspaper's right to inspect and copy certain of the coaches' documents, including federal tax returns, communication with certified public accountants, personal checking accounts, endorsement contracts, letters between the coaches and manufacturers and the forms the coaches used to report verbally to their reporting superior.[124]

II. Coach's Employment Contract - Contract Clauses And Issues

A. Introduction

As previously stated, there is no standard form coach's employment contract, like standard players' contracts in the NBA, NFL, NHL or MLB. A coach's contract can take the form of a simple letter agreement, standard university appointment form or a negotiated contract. This section will discuss contract clauses and issues that are important to the coach's contract from both the university and coach's perspective.

The environment in which some coaches' contracts are negotiated should be understood. Newly appointed head coaches are often so elated to get the "job" that, as long as the package number is respectable, they will execute the proffered contract without the advice of counsel. Universities "often negotiate coaching contracts in a frenzy, making impossible a careful 'invent-the-wheel' legal drafting job within the time constraints."[125] Further, "the 'general' terms of university coaching contracts often are negotiated by persons who lack knowledge of university's interests and how to protect them."[126] Consequently, lawyers become the beneficiaries of contracts that have already been negotiated and drafted resulting in a contract which fails to protect the parties' interests.[127] Because of the complexity of the issues in today's coach's contract, those skilled in legal training and knowledgable about the contractual provisions of coaching contracts should be both involved in the negotiation and drafting process.

Edward N. Stoner II, in his speech at the 1987 National Association of College and University Attorneys (NACUA), Section of Athletics', 27th Annual Conference in Albuquerque, New Mexico,[128] proposed model coaches contract in order to protect the university's interest. In an accompanying article prepared by Edward N. Stoner II and Arlie

R. Nogay, details were laid out as to how university and college attorneys should negotiate and draft college coaching contracts.[129]

As the unions in the professional sports have negotiated the contract language for their players, so too should the associations representing college football and basketball coaches. They should take a more active role and interest in not only the format of their coaches contracts, but also the economics of a coaches contract and what the coach and the representative should be negotiating. A central and open source, such as a college coaches contract data bank, should be made available to the attorneys representing coaches so that a format of negotiation agenda and statistical information is available to each representative.

What follows is a discussion of the various clauses and provisions that are normally found in a college coach's contract, along with some specific examples.

B. Duties and Responsibilities of the Coach.

Before a contract can be entered into listing the specific duties of the coach, the coach must agree to devote his best efforts and full-time to the performance of all duties and responsibilities attendant to the position of head coach of that university's particular athletic team. Moreover, the coach must agree to abide by and to comply with the constitution, bylaws and interpretations of the NCAA and all NCAA, Conference and university rules and regulations relating to the conduct and administration of that particular athletic program. Beyond the general responsibilities and best efforts clause, the employment contract will normally list specific responsibilities. For example, a former Midwestern Collegiate Conference (MCC) head basketball coach's contract lists the following specific responsibilities:

> A) Assume all of the support services that are necessary for coaching the sport (For instance, recommend competitive schedule, budget, necessary equipment, etc.);
> B) Conduct the program with integrity and in a financially responsible manner which reflects favorably upon the university as a whole;
> C) Maintain a level of performance in the program which is consistent with the goals established by the University;
> D) Provide for and encourage academic counseling for the students-athletes coached by him within the program as their individual circumstances may warrant;

E) Provide individual and group training and instruction to team members at all practices;
F) Prepare for and accompany teams to both home and away competitions;
G) Possess a thorough and up-to-date knowledge of the sport;
H) Assess talent of prospective students-athletes and recruit high caliber prospects who are capable of performing effectively against the University's scheduled opponents at the highest Division One Level;
I) Answer all correspondence relative to the sport;
J) Be available for various community and alumni speaking engagements;
K) Promote and stimulate interest in the program among students and season ticket holders;
L) Hire and fire, but only after consultation with the University's Director of Athletics, the Assistant Coaches for the Men's Varsity Basketball Program;
M) Work effectively with the media;
N) Perform related duties as assigned.[130]

Specific responsibilities listed in the MCC contract include:

A) Supervise assistant coaches, including compliance with such coaches with _____ Conference and NCAA rules and regulations;
B) Participate in the instruction and coaching of student-athletes;
C) Determine scouting schedules for high school and college games;
D) Interview prospective players, their parents and coaches;
E) Contact media, alumni and civic groups;
F) Work to integrate sports into the whole spectrum of academic life to complement the University and its mission in the community;
G) Work within the confines of rules, regulations, guidelines and policies of the University athletic department;
H) Keep public statements complimentary to the athletic program and to the University;
I) Make every effort, working in cooperation with and support of the University's faculty and administrative officials, to ensure that all student-athletes' academic requirements are met;
J) Have complete knowledge of the rules and regulations governing intercollegiate athletic competition and maintain strict compliance therewith by the program;
K) Apply effectively experience in recruiting, training and coaching of student-athletes;

L) Be a disciplinarian but be fair, sympathetic and protective of student- athletes while motivating them to excellence;

M) Maintain a mature and rational attitude, keep emotions in control and downplay defeats;

N) Prepare players for each game and each season with dedication; and

O) Establish and maintain a frequent and systematic program of personal communication with the University's student body.[131]

The university will want, in addition to a list of specific duties, a clause indicating that the coach will perform such other duties as are incident and consistent with his position and as may be prescribed from time-to-time by mutual agreement between the parties. From the university's perspective, a listing of specific duties is advantageous especially in attempting to enforce the termination provisions for just cause, i.e., failure to perform the duties and responsibilities specifically assigned.

On the other hand, the coach will probably desire a broad form responsibility statement, such as "performance of such duties as are incidental to the position and as may be prescribed from time-to-time by mutual agreement between the parties" to give the coach an arguable position with respect to the university's charge that the coach has failed to perform the duties of the position.

C. Term of Employment

This clause normally creates a term that is for a stated number of years. Coaching contracts are normally 3 to 5 years in length. Earle Bruce's, former head football coach at Ohio State University, employment contract with respect to term provided: "Subject to the terms of this Agreement, Earle Bruce is appointed by The Ohio State University ("University") to the position of Head Football Coach ("Head Coach") for a term of three (3) years commencing July 1, 1986, and terminating June 30, 1989."[132]

With respect to the term of employment, the MCC contract provides:

> The Coach's employment hereunder shall commence _____, and shall continue until this Agreement terminates on _____; provided that this provision is subject to the terms and conditions of Article VI hereof concerning termination and Article VII hereof concerning restrictions on competition and neither party shall

have any right to terminate this Agreement prior to ___ except as provided therein.[133]

The case of *Roberts v. Wake Forest University*[134] was an instructive case with respect to the term of the employment contract. The plaintiff, Roberts, was hired pursuant to an oral agreement to become the golf coach and associate athletic director of Wake Forest University. There was an oral agreement on salary, but there was no specific request as to a definite term of employment.[135] Golf coaches traditionally have a very long tenure.[136] The plaintiff understood from circumstances surrounding his initial visit to the university that he would be given a reasonable amount of time to demonstrate that he could coach the golf team.[137]

Although the duration of his contract was not fixed, the plaintiff alleged the parties intended employment to be for a substantial period, at least six years.[138] After less than a year with the program, the President of the University on December 2, 1977 requested plaintiff to relinquish his duties and accept other duties in the athletic program.[139]

The North Carolina court indicated, "[e]mployment for an indefinite term is regarded as an employment at will which may be terminated at any time by either party."[140] In this case, the court indicated that the record falls far short of showing the intention of the parties for a fixed term of employment.[141] In addition, the plaintiff relied on the Wake Forest University Personnel Policies and Regulation Manual to support his argument that he was a permanent employee and could not be dismissed without cause.[142]

Although the court admitted that the coach was a permanent employee, at least pursuant to the manual, it did, however, indicate that a permanent employee in a general sense means a position of some permanence as contrasted with a temporary employment and ordinarily, where there is no additional expression as to duration, a contract for permanent employment implies an indefinite hiring terminable at will.[143] The *Roberts* case is a clear expression of the coaches' need to define in writing the term of his intended employment contract, rather than let custom, usage, or the intentions of the parties bind the pathway of the future term of employment.

Another interesting case with respect to the issue of term of employment is *Lindsey v. University of Arizona*.[144] In the spring of 1982, the University of Arizona attempted to locate a new coach for the Men's Basketball Program. Ben Lindsey, who had successfully coached men's basketball at Grand Canyon College for several years, was ultimately chosen. Lindsey said that at a meeting with the Search Committee, the members therein stated that no one would be hired for the coaching position for less than three to four years.[145] Lindsey also testified that during discussions with the University of Arizona Athletic Director, Dave Strack, Lindsey was told that it was the university's policy to give coaches a minimum of four years before being evaluated.[146] On July 6, 1982, Lindsey accepted a formal appointment as Adjunct Professor of Physical Education from 1982 to 1983.[147] A coaching contract, in the form of a letter to Lindsey from the then University of Arizona President, John P. Schaefer, stated:

Dear Mr. Lindsey:
You are requested to serve as Head Coach of Men's Basketball at the University of Arizona, effective July 1, 1982 and ending no later than June 30, 1983.
It is the policy of the Arizona Board of Regents that an academic-administrative assignment is not a contract and that it can be terminated by the President of the University at any time. It is also policy that the assignment is renewable at my option and that renewal must be confirmed by a letter from my office. I would appreciate it if you would sign the enclosed copy of the letter to indicate your willingness to serve in this assignment. Please return it to Faculty Records (Administration 507) within ten days.
Sincerely
/a/ John P. Schaefer
JOHN P. SCHAEFFER[148]

Lindsey signed the bottom of a copy of the Schaefer letter on July 7, 1982.[149] Above his signature and date he noted, "I hereby accept the foregoing assignment."[150]

Lindsey was to receive approximately $90,000 per year as compensation.[151] "This consisted of a $49,115 annual salary, approximately $30,000 per year arising from a contract with a shoe company which Lindsey promoted, and an additional $10,000 anticipated from conducting a basketball camp and other benefits associated with the position."[152]

After Lindsey was hired, the University men's basketball team experienced its worst record in history (4 wins and 24 losses). Sometime around March 15, 1983, the new athletic director, Cedric Dempsey, notified Lindsey that his appointment would not be renewed after June 30, 1983.[153] The University provided Lindsey two checks totalling $49,115 as severance pay.[154] Lindsey brought suit, alleging breach of contract, fraud, intentional interference with contractual realations, and intentional infliction of emotional distress.[155]

The jury awarded Lindsey $215,000 for deprivation of three years of employment.[156] The appellate court indicated that:

> Despite the specific language contained in the letter from President Schaefer, Lindsey presented evidence from which the jury could have concluded that he would have the security of coaching for four years at the University of Arizona. An employer's oral representation may modify the terms of a contract and create a question of fact for the jury as to the terms of the contract.[157]

The court found that the evidence at trial was sufficient to sustain a verdict that the University breached an express contract with Lindsey by terminating his employment before four years of employment elapsed.[158]

Implicit in this finding is the holding that Lindsey accepted a one year renewable contract which the University promised to renew for three additional years.[159] Thus, the appellate court, held that the University violated an oral promise to renew Lindsey's contract for three additional years; therefore, they affirmed the $215,000 trial court judgment.[160]

Obviously, oral promises inducing performance which may be in opposition to the stated letter of appointment were significant in the Lindsey case. Discussions, promises, intentions, customs and usages, need to become part of the written document so that there is no mistake with respect to the term and conditions of employment.

D. "Rollover" Provisions

If the university is satisfied with the coach's performance after the completion of each season, the contract may be extended for an additional year so that at all times the remaining term of the contract at the commencement of each succeeding season is the same as the original term of the contract. This is commonly referred to as a rollover clause. To illustrate, Coach Jones has a five year contract with a rollover provision. At the end of each season, the university, with Coach Jones' consent, has a right to extend the contract an additional year, provided the university is pleased with the performance of the coach. Thus, if the university continues to exercise its rollover provision, Coach Jones will have at all times a five year contract. Coach Jones may want the rollover provision to state that if the university does not extend the contract for two consecutive years, the coach has a right to terminate the contract without needing to comply with the release or buy-out provision.

An example of a rollover contract provision suiting Coach Jones' needs is as follows:

> The term of this Agreement shall be for a period of five (5) years commencing on April 1, 1989 and ending on March 31, 1994. In addition thereto, the University shall have the right to extend the term of this Agreement with the prior written approval of the Coach for one (1) additional year following the completion of each Men's Varsity Basketball season (but in no event later than May 1st of each year) during the term of this Agreement. Upon the completion of each season, the Coach will meet with the Athletic Director of the University to review the season. Following such review, a decision shall then be made by the Athletic Director whether or not to exercise this one-year extension option for that year. In the event of a decision to exercise such extension option, then the University shall extend the term of this Agreement for an additional one (1) year in accordance with such decision. If this extension option is not exercised in a given year, however, but is exercised in a subsequent year in the above-described manner, the University may in the event, with the Coach's consent, increase the term of such subsequent extension to a full five (5) year period from the effective date of said extension. In the event the term of the employment is not extended by the University in any two (2) successive years, then the Coach shall have the right to terminate his employment under and pursuant to this Agreement without the necessity of complying with the release provisions as more specifically described in paragraph 9.3 hereinafter.[161]

Such, a rollover clause has at least four drawbacks to the university.[162] First, a university's notice of a decision not to extend the contract for the extra year could be considered by some to be a current breach of the contract which allegedly and immediately entitles the coach to x-1 year's of severance pay, or some other remedy.[163] Second, "[r]ollover clauses are typically poorly drafted because drafters write them in the euphoria of the moment ..."[164] Third, "[t]he rollover clauses require the university to give years of notice of its intention to let the contract expire."[165] Finally, "[r]ollover clauses are typically one-sided.[166] While they bar the university from removing the coach without paying for the balance of the term, contracts with such clauses tend not to guarantee the university that the coach will not terminate the agreement and coach elsewhere."[167]

Some state institutions are prohibited from entering into contracts that bind the institution for more than a period of one (1) year. Often times, even though those contracts are only binding for one (1) year, there will be an expression between the parties of an intent to continue the employment relationship providing the terms of the original contract are met. An example of such a clause is as follows:

> The term of this Employment Agreement shall be for one (1) year, commencing____,____, and terminating____. The parties hereby acknowledge that the University is an agency of the State of____ and that the law of the State of____ prohibit the University from entering into legally binding agreements for periods longer than one year. The parties also agree, however, that absent the occurrence of an event or events that would allow for termination of this Agreement in accordance with the provisions set forth in Article VI hereof or events beyond their control prohibiting such action, it is their intent to enter into successive one-year Agreements on substantially the same terms and conditions as this Agreement for the next ____ ( ) year(s).[168]

In *The University of Arizona v. County of Pima*,[169] the University of Arizona attempted to utilize a "fiscal out statute" to nullify contentions of former University of Arizona head basketball coach, Ben Lindsey, that he had an employment contract with the state for longer than one year duration. Arizona Revised Statute Section 35-154 provides as follows:

Unauthorized obligations, effect; liability

A. No person shall incur, order or vote for the incurrence of any obligation against the state or for any expenditure not authorized by an appropriation and an allocation. Any obligation incurred in contravention of this chapter shall not be binding upon the state and shall be null and void and incapable of ratification by any executive authority to give effect thereto against the state.

B. Every person incurring, or ordering or voting for the incurrence of such obligations, and his bondsmen, shall be jointly and severally liable therefor. Every payment made in violation of the provisions of this chapter shall be deemed illegal, and every official authorizing or approving such payment, or taking part therein, and every person receiving such payment, or any part thereof, shall be jointly and severally liable to the state for the full amount so paid, or received.[170]

This public statute is referred to as the "fiscal out statute". The court in this case, however, interpreted the statute as to operate as a condition subsequent, allowing the University of Arizona to avoid its obligations if prerequisite funding is not forthcoming.[171] "Subject to this implicit condition, contracts for more than one year are valid and do not violate the statutory provision against financial obligation for which there is no appropriation."[172] While neither Arizona nor Lindsey had so pleaded, the court indicated that it could take judicial notice of the fact that the University of Arizona had maintained a men's basketball program after Lindsey's termination.[173] Legislative funding for Lindsey's position must necessarily have been approved.[174] Thus, the court held that the University of Arizona was not prevented from promising a basketball coach a four year period in which to rebuild the basketball program by statutory provision even though the legislature of the State of Arizona could avoid obligations of more than one year if requisite funding was not forthcoming.

E. Reassignment Clause

A reassignment clause allows the university to remove a person as head coach without terminating the employment contract by assigning the coach to a new title and different duties. Often such a clause will contain a statement that the coach is not to be assigned to any job which is not consistent with his education and experience.

An example of a reassignment clause is found in Don Morton's (former University of Wisconsin head football coach) contract. The clause is found under the heading of "Title and Duties During Appointment Term". This clause states that "During the Appointment Term, you shall hold the appointment title and duties of Head Coach in the University's football program, except that at any time during the Appointment Term with 30 days notice, the appointment title and duties as Head Coach may be terminated and another title and duties assigned."[175]

If the coach refuses to accept such reassignment, the university may attempt to terminate the contract pursuant to the termination provisions. In essence then, the university wishes to avoid an accusation by the coach that he was constructively discharged by such reassignment. The university will want to shift the burden of refusing to accept reassignment to the coach and such refusal to accept reassignment may be a just cause for the university to terminate the employment contract and, thus, limit the university's liability for liquidated damages. Careful drafting of reassignment clauses must be undertaken to protect the university. Any language as contained in the contract which gives the coach the apparent right to be the "Head Coach" during the term of the contract should be avoided. Such language could result in the coach bringing a suit for injunctive relief for the right to continue as head coach for the balance of the term of the contract. The coach could also contend that reassignment is, in legal fact, a constructive discharge, thus, entitling the coach to perform no duties at all and get paid pursuant to the terms of the contract.[176] There is case law in an employment context[177] that would conclude that when a coach contracts to fill a particular position, any material change in duties or significant reduction in rank could constitute a constructive discharge which, if found unjustified, is a breach of the contract. The fact that the coach receives the same salary is immaterial because the status associated with the original position may well have been the primary inducement for making the contract.[178]

To ensure maximum protection, the attorney for the head coach will seek a prohibition against reassignment in the employment contract. An example of a clause prohibiting reassignment is as follows:

> It is hereby acknowledged by the university that the position in which the coach is hired is unique and requires special talents. The position as herein specified in this agreement is the only position for which the coach is hereby being employed. The university shall have no right pursuant to this agreement to reassign the coach to any other position of employment for the university during the term of this employment or any renewal therefor.[179]

Another issue which needs to be defined in any reassignment clause is the compensation that the coach will receive in the newly assigned position, if accepted. For instance, does the coach receive only the guaranteed base salary plus university fringe benefits, or does the coach also receive those other compensation perquisites that are normally associated with the position of head coach?

More recently, the presence of a reassignment clause in a coach's contract has been used by the university as leverage with respect to a buy out of the remaining term of the contract. Essentially, the university will reassign the coach. There will be some confusion or conflict with respect to the salary, fringe benefits and other compensation perquisites available to the coach by virtue of the reassignment. This will eventually lead to a negotiated settlement between the coach and the university with the university using the reassignment clause as leverage in such negotiations. For example, Don Morton, former head football coach of the University of Wisconsin, did not bring football fortunes to the University. Morton was reassigned, pursuant to his contract, from the position of head coach to the position of assistant athletic director in the third year of his five year contract.[180]

The issue in the Morton case was not the reassignment clause, but the compensation that Morton would receive for the remaining two years of his contract. The University agreed that Morton had a right to his salary, University fringe benefits, plus a car and country club membership.[181] Morton, however, demanded the additional outside income, i.e., his radio and television shows and summer camps that were directly a result of his position of head coach.[182] Although the parties battled their differences in the newspapers, and a lawsuit was Morton's game play, the parties eventually settled their differences with the University buying out the contract and Morton terminating his employment.[183]

F. Compensation Clauses

Compensation clauses address the monetary aspects of a coaching contract. Unfortunately, parties often believe that what one side gains, the other side loses, causing each side to maintain rigid negotiating postures in order to ensure that their interests are protected. However, benefits can be realized by both sides since the success of one party can often benefit the other. For instance, a clause granting a coach autonomy in running his own television and radio show may produce a more aggressive and quality program since the coach is directly interested. This in turn may produce higher viewership, greater fan interest and ultimately higher ticket sales. Therefore, it is important to focus on the beneficial aspects of compensation clauses of both sides to objectively realize their true impact upon the contract.

1. Guaranteed Base Salary

The first clause normally considered in every coaching contract is the guaranteed base salary (GBS). Simply put, this clause states the amount of money the institution employing the coach's services is willing to pay. An example follows:

> The guaranteed base salary paid by the University to the coach for services and satisfactory performance under the terms and conditions of this Employment Agreement shall be at the rate of $_____ per year, payable in ___ installments by the University to the Coach on the ___ day of each calendar month during the term of this Agreement.[184]

The university may be faced with various limitations as to the extent of such salary in the sense that the coach is no more or less an employee of the university than any other university professor. Therefore, the salary granted a coach is scrutinized and must be justified in light of other coaches' salaries and in the interest of preserving the university's emphasis upon its academic purpose. Even so, many coaches nonetheless retain healthy base salaries despite concerns over the school's academic prestige. Many universities believe a top-rated coach should be compensated as well as a top-rated university professor.

What follows are some sample *estimated* base salaries for head or former head footbal and basketball coaches from various Division I schools as reported by the news media (the figures as herein expressed have not been verified or corroborated as being true or correct):

SCHOOL	COACH	BASE SALARY
Georgia Tech	Bobby Cremins	$ 95,000[185]
Georgia	Hugh Durham	75,000[186]
Arizona	Lute Olsen	130,000[187]
Florida	Norm Sloan	99,000[188]
Kentucky	Rick Pitino	105,000[189]
Wisconsin	Barry Alvarez	135,000[190]
Ohio State	Earle Bruce	87,120[191]
UNLV	Jim Strong	100,000[192]
Florida	Lon Kruger	110,000[193]
NC State	Les Robinson	95,000[194]

The employment contract should also direct its attention, presuming that the coach's contract is long-term in nature, to periodic increases in the GBS during the contract term. In essence, the coach will be entitled to merit increases based upon periodic evaluations. Normally, merit increases based on periodic evaluations will occur on the same basis as evaluations and increases available to other university coaches within the coach's employment classification. In some instances, the coach, depending upon his leverage, will want to negotiate a guaranteed minimum base increase. The following example illustrates this point:

> The coach should be eligible to be paid a merit increase or raise, which raise shall be determined by using the same procedures for evaluating and rewarding meritorious performance as used for other coaches of the coach's classification within the university system. Provided, however, that in no event shall the merit increase during each year during the term of this employment agreement be less than 5% of the previous year's GBS.[195]

Some coaches' contracts will contain conditional compensation clauses subject to approval of the university's budget and appropriations. This clause will normally indicate that payment of the compensation as set forth in the contract is subject to approval of annual operating budgets by the university's governing body and appropriations of sufficient funds to pay the coach's compensation. An example of such a clause is as follows:

> The payment of all forms of compensation set forth in this agreement is subject to the approval of the annual operating budget by the university's governing body, and the sufficiency of appropriations or the availability of sufficient funds within the athletic department's budget to pay such compensation.[196]

2. Fringe Benefits

The employment contract will also contain a provision for fringe benefits. Normally, the coach will be entitled to the standard university fringe benefits appropriate to the coach's university employment classification including but not limited to group life insurance, health insurance, vacation with pay, TIAA/CREF, etc. In addition, there will be a provision covering reimbursement for expenses including all travel and out-of-pocket expenses reasonably incurred for the purposes of and in connection with the performance of the coach's duties. Reimbursement of expenses are normally made pursuant to and in accordance with standard procedures of the university upon presentation of vouchers or other statements itemizing such expenses in reasonable detail. The university, as additional compensation, may provide the coach with the use of an automobile during the term of the employment contract. If the university provides a coach with an automobile, there should be a periodic auto replacement provision and a provision for the use of a university provided gasoline credit card. Finally, the university should provide comprehensive liability insurance and be responsible for all costs of maintenance and repair with respect to the subject automobile.

Other forms of fringe benefits may be offered to the coach depending upon his contractual leverage including tuition waivers for his immediate family members, season and complimentary tickets to each of the university's team games including post-season games and tournaments, club memberships to either golf, country club or health club facilities and living accommodations to name a few. For example, Jerry Tarkanian, Head Men's Basketball Coach of the University of Nevada at Las Vegas is alleged to receive as a fringe benefit 234 season basketball tickets (with a face value of over $40,000) for the coach to dispose of at his will.[197] Joe B. Hall, former Head Men's Basketball Coach of the University of Kentucky was alleged to have received more than 322 complimentary tickets and at one point faced criminal charges for selling those tickets for more than face value, i.e., scalping.[198]

Clemson provided former head football coach Danny Ford with a home and made payment on his $280,000 home mortgage for him.[199] Auburn head football coach, Pat Dye, lives rent-free in a $500,000 house.[200] Both head football and men's basketball coaches at the University of Arkansas have $10,000 housing allowances.[201] When Jackie Sherrill signed his Texas A & M contract he was promised as much as $75,000 toward the purchase of a new home.[202] When John Thompson considered leaving Georgetown for a coaching position at the University of Oklahoma, a group of Georgetown alumni purchased a $300,000 house in the District of Columbia donating the same to the University with the proviso that Thompson be allowed to live in it for as long as he remains at Georgetown.[203] He pays rent, although no one will reveal how much.[204]

It is extremely important for both the coach and the university to specifically list every fringe benefit provided as part of the employment relationship to avoid any future assertion by the coach of any assumed fringe benefit not listed in the contractual arrangement.

3. Moving – Relocation Expense Allowance

The coach is bound to incur expenses in his move from his old employment to his new coaching position. The coaches' representative may want to negotiate for a moving - relocation expense allowance. The allowance should cover some, if not all, of the following moving related expenses: house hunting expenses, travel expenses, expenses for moving household goods and personal affects, including packing, storage and insurance, temporary lodging, extraordinary costs incurred to dispose of former residence, such as a mortgage prepayment penalty, costs incurred in the buy out of an existing leasehold obligation, and costs such as attorney fees, commissions or other expenses incurred in the purchase of the new residence, etc. The contractual clause should either cap out the total amount of dollars that the university is willing to expend on such allowance or specifically list without limit those expenses for which the moving - relocation expense allowance applies.

4. Bonuses

Bonus clauses in employment contracts are in the nature of supplemental compensation as an incentive based upon a coach's performance. These incentives may come in the form of a predetermined set amount or in the form of percentages of either the coach's base salary or of the net revenues received by the university as a result of post-season play. What follows is a listing of some bonus types:

1. Signing bonus. (Execution of original employment contract or renewal contract)
2. Participation in post-season tournaments or Bowl games
3. Regular season win/loss record
4. Regular season or conference championship
5. End of year conference championship tournament
6. Home game attendance
7. Graduation rates or grade attainment levels
8. Length of service based on years of employment (annuity)

Lon Kruger, head basketball coach at the University of Florida, will earn a $1,000.00 bonus if 40% of his scholarship players graduate and $2,000.00 bonus if 50% of his scholarship players graduate.[205] He will gain an extra month's salary in any year that 60% of his scholarship players earn their degree.[206]

Bill Frieder, head basketball coach of Arizona State University can earn up to $14,000.00 for winning the NCAA Tournament, $10,000.00 for improving the academic performance of his players and $30,000.00 if season home attendance exceeds 11,000.[207]

Lute Olsen, head basketball coach of the University of Arizona, has performance bonus clauses in his contract which could earn him an additional $33,000.00 per year.[208] These clauses are triggered if the team goes to the Final Four and if players achieve a specified academic performance.[209]

Jerry Tarkanian, by virtue of taking his team into the 1990 Final Four, earned 10% of the team's net revenue for its appearance.[210] Since each team in the Final Four earned approximately $1,432,500.00, Tarkanian can expect to receive $143,250.00 in addition to his regular salary.[211]

The popular coach will be in demand for personal appearances and speaking engagements by local and national alumni and booster groups. The coach and university will normally negotiate a specific number of appearances to be made by the coach as part of his salary compensation package. Appearnaces over and above the base minimum should result in the coach being compensated in the form of additional compensation or bonus. A sample clause is as follows:

> As part of the compensation as hereinstated, coach shall be required to participate in at least ___ alumni-booster personal appearances or speaking engagements. The university shall be responsible for incurring all expenses with respect to the making of such speeches or appearances. In the event that in any contract year the coach is required to make in excess of the minimum amount of personal appearances or speaking engagements as required herein, coach shall receive as additional compensation, $_____ per speaking engagement or public appearance. This paragraph shall not in any way prohibit the coach from separately entering into agreements or making public appearances on his own behalf and not for the university wherein the coach is compensated from a third party other than the university, all as provided by the outside employment provisions of this contract.[212]

5. Additional Retirement Benefits

Retirement benefits separate from the university's fringe benefits in the form of an annuity seems to be popular today in college coaching. Such benefits are used as additional incentives for the coach, not only in recognition of his accomplishments, but in hope of retaining the coach for the full term of his contract. There are two methods for providing additional retirement benefits.[213] Under the first method, the university can purchase an annuity which the coach owns. As the university pays premiums, the coach includes those premiums in income.[214] The advantage for the coach is that, the earnings are tax deferred until they are withdrawn.[215] The advantage of annuities are that if the interest or earnings are allowed to compound on a tax deferred basis, there can be a substantial increase in the net worth of the annuity in a very short period of time.[216] Annuities are normally purchased through insurance companies and take on such form as straight or life annuity, joint and survivorship annuity, refund annuity, deferred annuity and variable annuity to name a few. It is suggested that the coach seek assistance of not only a financial advisor, but a life insurance agent when attempting to structure an annuity that most perfectly fits his economic and retirement situation.

Under the second method, the university agrees to pay a retirement benefit as deferred compensation.[217] The university can use a commercial annuity to accumulate funds to pay the deferred compensation benefits, but the annuity must be owned by the university and the retirement benefits are paid by the university.[218] There are special income tax considerations that must be kept in mind when negotiating deferred compensation for university coaches.[219] Section 457 of the Internal Revenue Code imposes limitations on the amount that an employee of a tax-exempt organization can defer under a nonqualified deferred compensation plan.[220] As a general rule, an employee of a tax-exempt organization, such as a university, will be taxed on any amount he defers if the "amount of compensation deferred" exceeds $7500.[221] While the rule is defined in terms of the amount that the employee actually defers, the Internal Revenue Service has taken the position that the limitations of section 457 also apply to nonqualified retirement plans that do not involve elective deferrals by the employee.[222] Consequently, additional retirement benefits provided as an incentive would be includible in the coach's income currently if the section 457 limit is exceeded.[223] Presumably, in cases where the coach does not actually defer current compensation but rather the university agrees to pay an additional retirement benefit, the "amount of compensation deferred" would be determined by calculating the present value today of the benefit that is promised in the future.[224] In those situations where the university agrees to set aside a specified amount for the benefit of the coach, the amount set aside would be the "amount of compensation deferred".[225] The limits imposed by section 457 can be exceeded without targeting current taxation on the deferred amount if there is a substantial risk of forfeiture on the right to receive the benefits.[226] Section 457 defines substantial risk of forfeiture as a condition requiring the future performance of substantial services by an individual.[227] In a case where the university wants to provide a substantial nonqualified retirement benefit, taxation of the promised benefit can be postponed until retirement if the right of the coach to receive the benefit is conditioned on his continuing to perform services for the university until the time when benefits are due.[228] Since it is not likely that the coach will provide substantial services after retirement, the risk of forfeiture will lapse and the coach will be taxed on the present value of the future benefits or the value of the account set aside for his benefit at the time he retires.[229] Because of the acceleration of the income tax, it is necessary to structure the payments so that there is a balloon payment at retirement so that the coach can pay the tax and still receive the retirement income desired.[230] As subsequent payments are made, a portion of the payment will be tax-free to the coach as representing the amount on which he already paid tax.[231]

Pat Dye's, head football coach of Auburn University, financial package will be augmented by a retirement plan including an annuity with $1 million at age 65.[232] Nolan Richardson, whose Arkansas basketball team made the 1990 Final Four, has obtained a $1 million annuity to make certain of his stay at Arkansas.[233] Xavier University is alleged to have given basketball coach Pete Gillen an annuity or insurance policy worth $1 million after he rejected overtures to fill the coaching vacancy at Virginia.[234] Denny Crum, the Head Men's Basketball Coach at the University of Louisville will obtain a lump sum payment of $1 million in 1993, if he fulfills the obligations of his long-term contract with the school.[235] An example of an annuity or endowment fund clause is as follows:

> In recognition of the contribution by coach to the university's athletic program in general and to the basketball program in particular, the university shall establish a special endowment fund and on August 31st of each year during the term of this Agreement,

the university shall deposit the sum of $100,000 to the fund from gifts and/or grants received for athletic purposes. The payments, as to principal made to this fund as well interest as all capital appreciation realized within the fund shall be fully vested in coach. The total value of the fund shall be determined as of August 31, 1995 and subsequently paid to coach within 120 days thereafter pursuant to a withdrawal program mutually agreeable to the coach and the university. In the event of coach's death prior to August 31, 1995, the university shall be obligated to continue to make such principal payments to said fund and the total value of such fund as of August 31, 1995 shall then be paid within 120 days thereof to coach's surviving spouse or designee pursuant to withdrawal program mutually agreeable to said surviving spouse or designee pursuant to a withdrawal program mutually agreeable to said surviving spouse or designee and the university.[236]

G. Provisions Concerning Outside or Supplemental Income Sources

Contrary to popular belief, a successful coach's life-style is not conducive to long vacations, lazy afternoons during the off-season and three hours of fun and excitement on game day during the season. The majority of the successful coaches are either on the road recruiting or in the film room strategizing and/or performing the multitude of duties of what could be a 24-hour a day job. Equally misconceived is the notion that all college coaches earn top salaries. Again, the majority earn only modest incomes.

For this reason, there exist clauses within the framework of the contract which provide coaches with the opportunity to supplement their income through outside sources. Outside income significantly affects the economics of high visibility college sports. Coaches of successful football and basketball programs often make more money from outside income than they do from their base salaries which may be restricted either by law or budgetary limitations.

Generally, the university will require that certain requisite conditions be followed by the coach prior to engaging in any outside business or entrepreneurial endeavor. First, and foremost, the university will require that its interest and the obligations owed to it by the coach remain primary. This is based on the fiduciary relationship between the university and the coach and the duty of loyalty owed by each to the other. This covenant is an attempt to avoid inferior performance in the coach's duties resulting from conflicts of interest and compromises.

Secondly, the coach is subject to all NCAA rules regulating the coach's sources of income. In this way, the coach's independent judgment cannot be persuaded by outside interest groups.

Thirdly, the university will normally retain the right of final approval before the coach is allowed to enter into such agreements. However, the university's right of approval may not be used to unreasonably deny the coach's justifiable request or income expectancies.

The coach may or may not retain all of the proceeds which result from outside sources. Whether the income is the university's or the coach's should be specifically designated in the contract. Presumably, if the coach acts independent of the university, he will retain the proceeds from such outside sources. If, on the other hand, the university supplies the means or personnel to assist the coach, it may require a certain percentage of the proceeds or a predetermined fee.

The university will also want a statement that such outside employment is independent of the university's employment and the university will have no responsibility or liability for any claims arising from the performance therefrom. An example of an outside employment clause is as follows:

> Coach shall devote such time, attention and efforts as necessary to fulfill the duties under and pursuant to this Agreement and shall not become associated directly or indirectly in any "other business or employment" without first obtaining the prior written consent of the University, which consent shall not be unreasonably withheld. For purposes of this provision, Coach's participation in speaking engagements and personal appearances, coaches clinics, basketball camps, radio and T.V. appearances other than those to be compensated pursuant to this Agreement, and athletic shoe, apparel and equipment endorsement contracts shall not be deemed, for purposes of this Agreement, to be "other business or employment" requiring the consent of the University. Coach shall schedule such activities so as not to interfere with his responsibilities hereunder. It is hereby further understood and acknowledged by the University that any compensation received by Coach with respect to permitted "other business or employment" shall be the sole compensation of the Coach hereunder.[237]

1. Radio and Television

Common to any sporting organization is the media attention it attracts. Radio and television talk show programs featuring the coach offering direct contact between the coach and the fans are a lucrative source of income for coaches.

There are various alternatives as to how these radio and television show contracts are structured and negotiated. First, the coach may negotiate independent of the university with a radio or television station. The coach would receive the compensation from such show with the university not being responsible for any amounts due and owing under such agreement. A second alternative is where the university has an agreement with a particular radio or television broadcaster for the production of a show in conjunction with its athletic program. The coach is paid directly by the media representative. The coach in these instances should require a minimum dollar guarantee with respect to such shows each year.

Another alternative is where the university itself owns all rights to the program and controls the production and marketing. The coach may be required under, such university controlled and produced shows to assist in procuring sponsors and to make commercial endorsements on behalf of program sponsors. The coach will normally participate in the financial success of such university program on a negotiated basis. If the university controls production and marketing of its television and radio programming, it may require the coach not to appear in any competing radio or television program during the season except routine news media interviews.

While the structuring of radio and television deals make take different formats, some coaches are alleged to enjoy enormous profits from their enterprises. When Bill Dooley was football coach at Virginia Tech, he was paid a talent fee by the school for appearing on television and radio shows for an estimated $85,000.[238] When Jackie Sherrill was at Texas A & M it was alleged that he received at least $135,000 a year from the sponsors of his television and radio shows.[239] In Sherrill's case and in similar deals, many of the sponsors are athletic department boosters who see the payments as a way of helping their favorite athletic programs. However, sponsors-boosters can write-off the money spent as a deductible business expense (part of their company's advertising).[240]

2. Endorsements

As a result of their high public profile and stature, coaches may often times attract product or organizational endorsement offers, especially if the coach is enjoying enormous popularity among boosters and the public. Basically, three important ingredients can combine to create a marketable coach: (1) Television or media exposure; (2) a creative personality; and, (3) a big win.[241] Typically, the university will require that the coach not utilize his university association with any product endorsement. However, the coach will require that he be permitted to identify himself as the coach of the particular athletic team.

Former North Carolina State head basketball coach, Jim Valvano, is a prime example of how endorsements can be utilized to create a lucrative supplemental income. After his team won the NCAA national basketball championship in 1983, Valvano was hailed as one of the top-rated coaches and strategists in the game. His reputation as a colorful speaker and unique personality soared, and his comfort in front of a camera all combined to make him an endorsement gold mine. As a result, Valvano came out with his own line of clothes called Coach "V's", authored an Italian cookbook and served as spokesman for Ronzoni Pasta.[242] This was in addition to the numerous other product endorsements, (car companies, Washington Speakers Bureau, corporate art, etc.) which allegedly earned him as much as $750,000.00 a year.[243]

3. Shoe, Apparel and Equipment Contracts

Shoe contracts are generally negotiated between the coach and the shoe company. In most cases, the company will pay the coach a certain sum of money as a consultant and provide a supply of shoes, warm-up togs and gym bags in exchange for the coach's team players wearing the shoes. The benefits are readily apparent to the shoe company in that high profile teams advertise their product during every game. At almost every major collegiate program, a shoe company contracts to have its shoes worn by the coach and team members. When considering the hundreds of thousands of dollars television broadcasters are demanding for 30 second commercial slots, $100,000 for 25 games at 40 minutes a game is a bargain. In a typical shoe contract provision, the coach will want the university's agreement that the coach may require the athletic team to wear the shoes during competition. In addition, the coach will also want the university to consent that he may be permitted to wear, promote, endorse or consult with the shoe, apparel or equipment manufacturer concerning the design or marketing of such shoe, apparel or equipment without such activities being in violation of the employment agreement.

Mark Thomasshaw, corporate counsel for the Nike Shoe Company, states that the four or five top college basketball coaches in the country can earn as much as $200,000 apiece to sign endorsement contracts with shoe companies. Others in the top ten can expect between $100,000 and $200,000.[244] The Nike Shoe Company has about 60 major college coaches under contract.[245] Converse has 41 coaches under contract and Reebok's roster includes 26 coaches.[246] For example, it has been reported that John Thompson (Georgetown) received $200,000.00 annually, Eddie Sutton (formerly of the University of Kentucky) received $160,000.00 annually, Jim Valvano (formerly of North Carolina State) received $160,000.00 annually, Jerry Tarkanian (University of Nevada Las Vegas) received $120,000.00 annually, and Jim Boeheim (Syracuse University) received $120,000.00 annually.[247] It has also been reported that Bobby Cremins, head basketball coach of Georgia Tech, first shoe contract with Converse paid him $5,000.00 in 1981.[248] After winning the 1984-85 Atlantic Coast Championship, Converse signed Cremins to a four year contract at $70,000.00 per year.[249] In 1989, he signed a multi-year contract with Nike for $160,000 per year.[250]

Below the six figure echelon, at least 75 NCAA Division I Men's Basketball head coaches have contracts in the $40,000 or higher range and the leading women's head coaches average $10,000 a year.[251]

Sporting News in its February 4, 1991 issue reported the top shoe deals for college basketball head coaches for the 1991 season from information obtained from the Newport News Daily Press:

Shoe Companies

Top Shoe Deals For College And Basketball Coaches:

No.	Coach	Team	Company	Per Year
1	Dale Brown	LSU	L.A. Gear	$300,000
2	Mike Krzzewski	Duke	Adidas	$260,000
3	Bob Knight	Indiana	Adidas	$200,000
4	John Thompson	Georgetown	Nike	$200,000
5	Dean Smith	N.Carolina	Converse	$200,000
6	Jim Boeheim	Syracuse	Nike	$150,000
7	Lute Olson	Arizona	Nike	$150,000
8	Jerry Tarkanian	UNLV	Nike	$150,000[252]

Not all universities permit the coach to contract directly with the shoe company. For instance, University of Virginia coaches instead of having contracts directly with shoe companies have the athletic department handle the Cavaliers endorsement contracts by seeking bids.[253] The Virginia's Attorney General's office issued an opinion that any coach at a state university who accepted promotional money from athletic shoe companies was violating the state conflict of interest laws.[254]

One of the legacies of Lefty Driesel's departure from Maryland after the death of Len Bias was a rule that Terrapin coaches could no longer negotiate private endorsement contracts.[255] The new Maryland policy requires the university to negotiate all endorsement contracts and the coach shares in the revenues on a negotiated basis.[256]

4. Income from Speeches and Written Material

The contract should permit the coach to deliver speeches, make public appearances, grant media interviews, write and release books and magazine articles and receive the compensation therefor. The coach will also want permission to utilize publicly his reference to the university as coach. The university, however, will want some type of limiting clause that the coach represents the university in a professional manner and does not bring any discredit or disrespect upon the university in such spoken and written materials.

Success breeds success on the rubber chicken circuit. Southern Cal head coach Larry Smith, who makes only $97,000 in base salary is guaranteed $150,000 annually from the USC Speakers Bureau.[257] He earns $6,000 for each speaking engagement.[258] Terry Donahue of UCLA also earns $6,000 for every speaking engagement while former Pitt head coach, Mike Gottfried, earned $5,000.00.[259] Lou Holtz of Notre Dame, however, is the king of college football coaches when it comes to speaking engagements. He commands $18,000 per speech and accepts as many as 30 speaking dates during the off-season.[260] Companies interested in retaining Holtz must book him six months in advance.[261]

5. Summer Camps

Another source of income for the coach is summer athletic camps and clinics. The first issue to be considered is whether the university or the coach is the sponsor of such camps. Normally, the coach will want the opportunity to use the university's facilities in connection with such summer camp without cost or at a minimum cost. Another vital question will be which party is to provide and pay for the camp's liability insurance. An example of a summer camp provision is as follows:

> As additional consideration for the services to be rendered by the Coach hereunder, the University shall make available to Coach for summer basketball camps the use of the University gyms and facilities at a rate not to exceed $3.00 per camper per week and will charge Coach lodging and food costs for the campers at normal University rates. The $3.00 per camper per week shall include the use of the University's gym and related facilities, including locker room, swimming pool and the like and shall further include any and all insurance required for the purposes of operating such summer basketball camps.[262]

Murray Sperber in his book, College Sports, Inc., provides the following commentary on the profits many coaches earn from their summer camps:

> Unlike intercollegiate athletics, with its tremendous start-up costs and huge ongoing expenses, camps can be established and run on a small amount of capital. Because costs tend to be low __ thanks to the university __ summer camp profits for many coaches are outstanding, in many cases double their annual salaries.
>
> Coaches run their camps in one-week sessions, for as many as ten weeks during a summer; campers who board pay an average of $200 to $300 a week; day campers, $150 to $250. Bill Frieder, when at Michigan, is reported to have grossed over $350,000 for his 1986 basketball summer camps. Charles "Lefty" Driesell, the former coach at Maryland, resigned from his coaching job after his star player, Len Bias, died from a cocaine-induced seizure; Driesell, however, insisted on keeping his camps at the university and, in 1986, had 875 kids pay $264 each for a $231,000 gross. Moreover, in his settlement agreement with Maryland, the school continued its $20,000 subsidy to defray Driesell's dorm and facility bill. Even when Driesell moved to James Madison University, he got to keep his Maryland camps and subsidies.[263]

H. Disclosure of Outside Income

Article 3, Section 2g of the NCAA Constitution requires annual disclosure by the coach to the president of the university through the athletic director of all athletically-related income and benefits earned or received from outside sources.[264] The purpose of this requirement is to monitor the sources of a coach's outside income and to increase and maintain university control over intercollegiate athletic programs. The rule also was intended to have university presidents informed of possible conflicts of interest and commercial influences on coaches. Hofmann and Greenberg in *Sport$ Biz* provide an interesting interpretation of the disclosure issue:

> There was a move in 1988 to get some kind of handle on coaches' outside income. A proposal was drafted that would require institution approval before a coach could take the money directly. To no one's great surprise, 77% of the university presidents surveyed were all for the idea, and 94% of the basketball coaches were against it. The coaches fought off outright limits on outside income with a compromise measure requiring them to report what they made to school administrators. But they weren't really crazy about that either, because they figured the administrators would disclose what the coaches told them, thereby creating pressure for income limits.[265]

Former University of Kansas head basketball coach, Larry Brown, was not pleased with NCAA efforts involving controlling sources of outside income. Brown stated, "[d]o universities oversee the money professors make from royalties and from being on corporate boards ... I'll accept them limiting what I earn if they will grant me tenure."[266]

Some coaches are not only against limits on their outside income, but are also reluctant to release income information to the public. For instance, the Charleston Gazette completed a story about West Virginia head football coach, Don Nehlen's and head basketball coach, Gale Catlett's income sources only after the newspaper filed a Freedom of Information request.[267] This request revealed that outside income, including an endowment, shoe contract and sports camps more than tripled the base salary of Nehlen and Catlett.[268] The Gazette reported that Nehlen earned $224,909 to coach football and Catlett earned $198,484 a year.[269] Nehlen's base salary from the State of West Virginia was $71,208.[270] This amount was increased by $3,800 from his football camp, $49,000 from the athletic department endowment fund and $25,000 from the Mountaineer Athletic Club (MAC), the newspaper reported.[271]

The football coach also earned $40,000 from the Mountaineer Sports Network and $11,900 from West Virginia Radio for his radio and television shows; $12,000 for advertising Chrysler automobiles; $10,000 from a shoe contract and $2,000 for personal appearances, the Gazette added.[272] Catlett, who earned a state base pay of $60,684, earned an additional $21,000 from his summer basketball camps and $36,000 from the endowment fund.[273] He also earned $31,000 from a shoe contract; $30,000 from the Mountaineer Sports Network and $19,600 from West Virginia Radio, the newspaper reported.[274]

Both Catlett and Nehlen had received large income increases during the last several years. During the 1984-85 fiscal year, Nehlen earned $154,824 while Catlett earned $143,842.[275]

By contrast, the average West Virginia University professor earns $35,500.[276]

I. Guaranteed Contracts

College coaches, should attempt to negotiate a "guaranteed contract" with the university. This may be a quid pro quo for a long-term contract. The university agrees to guarantee a portion or all of the coach's salary regardless if the coach should die or become disabled during the term of the contract. An example of a "guaranteed contract" provision is as follows:

> Notwithstanding anything to the contrary, the compensation as stated in Paragraph 4 shall be deemed to be a Guaranteed Base Salary. "Guaranteed Base Salary" as used herein shall mean that Coach shall be paid said Base Salary as hereinbefore stated through the term of this Agreement regardless of and in the event that the Coach shall die or become partially and/or totally disabled so that the services as hereinbefore referenced cannot be performed pursuant to the terms hereof. The intention as hereinstated is that the Base Salary as from time-to-time increased and determined during each year of the term of this Agreement shall be deemed to be guaranteed and paid as a contractual obligation of the University for the entire term of this Agreement as extended. It shall be the University's sole financial responsibility to fund the guarantee as herein contemplated either with its own financial resources and/or the purchase of such insurance policies as to guarantee the payment as herein required.[277]

J. Termination Clauses

The volatility of the coaching profession and the number of firings, removals and job movements make termination clauses one of the most significant provisions in the coaching contract. Often times, a coach's career is launched upon a contract which has been poorly drafted since it is not prepared to handle the many situations which may arise during the course of the contract term including premature termination. The end result is that one side is forced to abandon ship and often amid rocky waters.

1. Death – Disability

The university will want the employment contract to automatically terminate if the coach dies or becomes totally disabled with the coach's salary and all other benefits terminating as of the calendar month in which death occurs, except that the coach's personal representative shall be entitled to such other death benefits, if any, and such disability/salary continuation benefits to which he is entitled under the university's disability program.

The coach's representative will attempt to negotiate a guarantee provision in the contract at least with respect to the base salary so that in the event the coach should die or become partially or totally disabled, the base salary would be guaranteed and paid by the university for the entire term of the contract either through the university's funds or through the purchase of such insurance policies as are necessary to guarantee the required payments.

2. Termination by the University for Just Cause

Termination clauses whether or not they require "just cause," are generally the most difficult to negotiate in the employment contract. Termination controversies between coaches and universities have drawn and will continue to draw great attention from the media. A coach's contract will almost always contain "termination for just cause" provisions empowering the university to terminate the contract at any time at its sole discretion if there is a determination by the university that the coach has committed a violation, intentionally or not, of any law, rule, regulation, constitutional provisions or by-law of the university, United States, the state of jurisdiction, the participating conference or the NCAA and such violation reflects adversely upon or may impugn the image of the coach, university or its athletic program, including any deliberate or serious violation which may result in the university being placed on probation. The NCAA requires that contractual agreements between a coach and a university include a stipulation that the coach may be suspended for a period of time, without pay, or that the coach's employment may be terminated if the coach is found to be involved in deliberate and serious violations of NCAA regulations.[278]

The Knight Commission reports that approximately one-half of all Division I-A institutions (the 106 colleges and universities with the most competitive and expensive football programs) were the object of sanctions of varying severity from the NCAA during the 1980s.[279] Rules, rules, rules, it seems that college sports has become a panoply of rules and interpretations. The Knight Commission Report indicates that, "[s]ome rules have been developed to manage potential abuse in particular sports, in particular schools, or in response to particular circumstances of individual athletes. Whatever the origin of these regulations, the administration of intercollegiate athletics is now so over burdened with legalism and detail that the NCAA Manual more clearly resembles the IRS Code than it does a guide to action."[280] Even the simplest of rules may taint the coach and trigger sanctions in his contract. The Knight Commission further requests that the NCAA applies itself to the task of simplifying and codifying complex NCAA rules and procedures.[281]

> Any man or woman on the street should be able to understand what the NCAA does, how it works, how it makes its decisions and, in particular, how it determines its sanctions. As it stands, not only can the average person not answer those questions, but very few presidents, athletic directors, coaches or student-athletes can predict what it is likely to do in any given circumstance.[282]

Therefore, the coach will need to protect himself with respect to this required "termination for cause" provision. The coach may want to require that in order for a termination for cause to exist, (1) that such rules violation be determined or adjudicated by the university, the NCAA or any other equivalent body and/or a court of law and (2) that the coach has committed a *MAJOR* violation, and did so knowingly or intentionally in violation of those rules.

There is a second category of just cause provisions calling for termination of the head coach if a member of the coaching staff commits a serious violation of NCAA rules providing that such acts were either under the control or direction of the head coach. In essence, the head coach becomes responsible for the acts of his coaching staff. While a principal/agent - respondeat superior relationship may exist, once again, the head coach needs to protect himself by specifying that the acts of assistants would have an effect on his employment only if the coach had actual knowledge of such violations or directed that such violations occur. The same should hold true with respect to student-athletes who also can violate the rules of the NCAA.

Finally, there are provisions for immediate termination in the event the head coach refuses to perform any of the duties which are reasonably related to his position and/or where such duties cannot be performed because of such disability or illness which would make the head coach unavailable to perform such duties. Termination clauses are normally accompanied by a clause exonerating the university from any further liability for salary benefits or other compensation after termination.

By their very nature, termination provisions should be negotiated between the parties. A statement of what constitutes grounds for termination is necessary. The coach will also want to establish some independent dispute resolution process such as a due process hearing, arbitration hearing or third party mediator for determining whether grounds for termination exist. If the university retains the right to make such determinations unilaterally, the coach's interests may be compromised.

The MCC Agreement defines just cause as:

(1) deliberate and serious violations of the duties outlined in Section 3.02 of this Agreement or refusal or unwillingness to perform such duties in good faith and to the best of the Coaches abilities;
(2) violations by the Coach of any of the other terms and conditions of this Agreement not remedied after _____ (___) days' written notice thereof to the employee;
(3) situations in which the University determines that the best interests of the University and of its intercollegiate _____ program require that the Coach no longer retain the position of Coach of the University's _____ team initially assigned to him under this Agreement and the employee does not accept reassignment of responsibilities in accordance with the provisions of Section 3.01 above;
(4) any conduct of the employee in violation of any criminal statute of moral turpitude;

(5) a serious or intentional violation of any law, rule, regulation, constitutional provision, bylaw or interpretation of the University, the _____ Conference or the NCAA, which violation may, in the sole judgment of the University, reflect adversely upon the University or its athletic program, including any serious violation which may result in the University being placed on probation by the _____ Conference or the NCAA and including any violation which may have occurred during prior employment of the employee at another NCAA member institution;

(6) a serious or intentional violation of any law, rule, regulation, constitutional provision, bylaw or interpretation of the University, the _____ Conference or the NCAA by a member of the _____ coaching staff or any other person under the employee's supervision and direction, including student-athletes in the _____ program, which violation may, in the sole judgment of the University, reflect adversely upon the University or its athletic program, including any serious violation which may result in the University being placed on probation by the _____ Conference or the NCAA;

(7) conduct of the employee seriously prejudicial to the best interests of the University or its athletic program or which violates the University's mission;

(8) prolonged absence from duty without the consent of the employee's reporting superior; or

(9) any cause adequate to sustain the termination of any other University coach of the Coach's classification.[283]

Another definition of "just cause" for termination purposes is as follows:

> COACH'S employment being terminated by the Board of Directors of the University "for cause." Termination "for cause" shall be limited solely to termination by the action of the Board of Directors because of (a) gross negligence of Coach in the performance of his obligations under this Agreement; (b) the habitual intoxication or inexcusable repeated or prolonged absence from work of COACH; (c) the perpetration by Coach of a willful fraud against the University or its programs; (d) the failure of COACH to perform faithfully the duties of his office or the duties which are otherwise assigned to him by the Board of Directors of the University or its President, so long as such duties are consistent with the skills and experiences of COACH; (e) COACH's complicity in an immoral act which is inconsistent with the University's stated objectives and philosophies; or (f) the indictment of COACH for a felony as same is defined by the laws of the State of _____.

Termination "for cause" shall occur upon delivery to COACH of a notice of such action by the Board of Directors of the University, which notice shall specify the grounds for such termination. If COACH's employment is terminated "for cause," the University's only obligation to COACH shall be payment of the salary through the end of the month in which such termination occurs....[284]

From a coach's perspective, specific acts constituting just cause for termination need to be strictly defined rather than couched in broad based statements. Such clauses as wilful fraud, moral turpitude or habitual intoxication may have a different meaning to different parties. Therefore, these terms should be specifically defined in terms of specific prohibited acts.

In negotiating termination for just cause provisions, the definition of "just cause" is factual in nature (such as moral turpitude, prejudicial conduct, prolonged absences, willful fraud, complicity in an immoral act, habitual intoxication, etc.) and, therefore, need to be determined by an impartial hearing examiner. A due process procedure should be established for purposes of an objective and impartial hearing to determine whether termination for just cause exists. Such procedure should include a statement of the charges against the coach, the right to a hearing, the opportunity for a coach to be present and to present a defense, the right to have an attorney present to advise the coach and to counsel and state his case and/or such other procedures as shall be governed by normal university grievance procedures.

Affording a coach some opportunity to a hearing and the right to challenge the university's charges for termination for cause is especially significant if a state institution is involved since the termination itself may be considered "state action" subject to due process provisions. In virtually all litigation in which an individual argues that his constitutional rights have been violated, the court can grant relief only if it finds that there has been state action, i.e., some sort of participation by a government entity sufficient to make the particular constitutional provision applicable.

When Earle Bruce was fired by Ohio State and filed a $7.45 million lawsuit against the institution,[285] one of his contentions was that his unlawful termination involved state action and, therefore, his constitutional rights were violated including denial of due process and equal protection of the law and deprivation of property without just compensation.[286]

An example of a due process procedure is as follows:

(a)   Employment may be suspended for a period of time, without pay, or terminated, with immediate cessation of salary payments and fringe benefits, for cause. Cause for suspension or termination shall be a violation by a Coach, or a violation by a coach under that Coach's supervision of which that Coach was aware or was of a character or extent that the Coach should have been aware, of any of the rules, regulations or policies of the Big Ten Conference or the National Collegiate Athletic Association, as modified from time to time.

(b)   Prior to suspension or termination, an Employe (i) shall be provided with written notice of contemplated suspension or termination, a statement of the reasons and facts in support thereof and (ii) shall have five calendar days from receipt of such notice to deliver a written request for a hearing on the contemplated action. Written requests shall be delivered to the Office of the Chancellor. If no written request is received by the Chancellor as provided herein, a contemplated suspension or termination shall become final five calendar days following the coach's receipt of such notice.

(c)   Upon receipt of a written request for hearing, the Chancellor will appoint a three person hearing board, composed of two individuals from the Athletic board and one other University coach, to consider the matter and hear reasons for and against the contemplated action. The Coach has the right to appear before the hearing board, with a representative if he desires, to comment on the reasons given for the contemplated action and to present reasons against it. The hearing board shall not be bound by formal or technical rules of evidence. It will send written findings of fact and recommendations on the matter to the Chancellor or, if the Chancellor designates someone else, his designee. The Chancellor or his designee may seek counsel from the Athletic Board, shall consider the matter and notify, in writing, the Coach, the Director of Intercollegiate Athletics and the hearing board of the decision, which shall be final.[287]

Finally, if the coach is dismissed for cause, the contract should state the effect therefor including cessation of compensation and fringe benefits as of the end of the month in which such termination occurs. The university will also want to indicate that it has no liability for loss of any collateral business opportunities or any other benefits, perquisites, or income resulting from the job as a result of said termination.

Murray Sperber in his book, *College Sports, Inc.*, indicates that Universities, even though they may have cause to dismiss a coach, and even though that coach may cause a NCAA investigation and ensuing penalties, prefer to settle their differences with a breaching coach rather than fire them outright.[288] This is so, even though the university is absolved from its obligations if the coach violates NCAA rules:

> When Mike White, after years of incurring NCAA sanctions and negative publicity for the University of Illinois, finally quit, the school rewarded him with $300,000 settlement. Barry Switzer settled with the University of Oklahoma for $225,000 during its recent troubles. After the NCAA put Texas A & M on probation for over twenty-five violations during Jackie Sherrill's regime, the school waved goodbye to this football coach and AD with a $684,000 cash settlement and a house. And when Danny Ford resigned in 1990 at Clemson, with the NCAA cops at the gates, he was rewarded with a settlement that could top $1.1 million.[289]

Because of the potential for litigation that may ensue after a coach is terminated for "just cause" and the coach's probable contesting of the facts therefor, the representatives of the coach and the university may want to simply ease the burden of a continued dispute. If there is a proceeding for just cause the university and the coach may mutually agree to a resignation format with the payment of some termination fee or liquidated damages.

3. Termination Without Cause or for Any Other Reason

The coach's contract will also reserve to the university the right to terminate the coach's employment for reasons other than those set forth in the termination for "just cause" provision or for no reason at all. This termination provision is more concerned with defining the university's financial liability than the reasons for termination. Thus, when the coach is terminated without cause, the issue centers on the determination of the amount of damages that the coach will receive, the nature of the damages and the method of payment. A number of options are available, including:

1. A negotiated stated amount.
2. The coach's base salary or other compensation items for the remainder of the contract term.
3. The percentage of the base salary and other compensation packages for the remainder of the agreement.
4. De-escalating amount depending upon the year of the agreement and the termination therefor.
5. A lump sum settlement.

What benefits the coach will receive should be strictly defined in the contract upon a premature termination. If liquidated damages are agreed to, the university will want a provision indicating it will not be liable for the loss of any collateral benefits, perquisites or income resulting from activities such as but not limited to camps, clinics, media appearances, apparel, shoe contracts, consulting relationship or from any other sources that may ensue as a result of the university's termination of this agreement without cause or because of the coach's position as such. The liquidated damage provision will also indicate that said damages are bargained for damages and constitute a reasonable and adequate consideration to the coach and shall not be construed to be in the nature of a penalty.

Another issue is the coach's obligation to mitigate damages, i.e., obtaining reasonably comparable employment or other employment for purposes of offsetting the damages agreed to be paid by the university. If other employment is obtained, a question will arise as to whether or not the liquidated damages agreed to be paid by the university ceases or the university's obligation is modified to be the difference between the amount the university agreed to pay and the amount received from the new employer, if any.

Most universities recognize their continuing liability under the contract and continue to pay the coach throughout the contract term or buy-out the contract for a lump sum. It has been suggested that a lump sum buy-out at the time of the termination, based on the present value of the future payments to become due, is the proper measure of damages in such a situation rather than the installment method. The theory is that since the breach is complete upon contract termination, complete damages are then due as well. When negotiating the buy-out or the liquidated damages provisions of a termination without just cause, consideration should also be given to continuation of some collateral benefits such as continued health insurance for a time certain and the payment of moving expenses. An example of termination without cause provision favorable to the coach is as follows:

> *Termination Without Cause.* In the event of the Employee's termination by the University for reasons other than as previously set forth in this Agreement during the term of this Agreement, including any extensions therefore, the Employee shall be entitled to the remainder of any Annual Salary plus the University's contribution to TIAA-CREF (retirement plan) owed under and pursuant to the terms of this Agreement plus 50% of the then scheduled radio and T.V. income as hereinbefore referenced to be

paid on the same date as if Employee was still employed under and pursuant to this Agreement for the term under which said amount shall be paid. In addition, the University shall continue to provide Employee after such termination with such medical and health insurance benefits for the balance of the term of this Agreement, including any extensions therefor or until Employee obtains other full-time employment with replacement policies whichever is the lesser period. It is the intention of this paragraph that in the event Employee should be terminated without cause that Employee would continue to receive the compensation and benefits as herein specified for the full remaining term of this Agreement without any obligation to mitigate damages and, in addition to compensation he may be receiving from other employment, even if the employment is similar to the employment as hereinstated. In the event Employee is terminated without cause, Employee shall be entitled to conduct the summer camp and receive all benefits therefrom pursuant to paragraph 8 of this Agreement during the summer subsequent to said termination. In no case shall the University be liable for loss of any collateral business opportunity or other benefits, perquisites or income from any sources that may ensue as a result of the University's termination of this Agreement.[290]

There are a number of celebrated termination cases that need to be reviewed.

On November 20, 1987, Earl Bruce was fired by Ohio State University. He filed a $7.45 million lawsuit against the institution and its president.[291] Bruce charged breach of contract, wrongful dismissal and slander.[292] Because the termination involved state action, constitutional law violations were also alleged, including denial of due process and equal protection and the deprivation of property without just compensation.[293] In the ad damnum clause to Bruce's complaint, the following damages were requested:

A. $448,800 for breach of contract (salary and package).
B. $2 million for violation of Bruce's constitutional rights.
C. $5 million in compensation and punitive damages.[294]

It should be noted that Bruce's contract specifically stated that the university was not liable for consequential damages of any kind in the event of early termination.[295] The university only contractual obligation was to pay salary and employee benefits, subject to the usual offset.[296] The case was ultimately settled for $471,000.[297]

In *Yukica v. Leland*,[298] in December of 1986, Joe Yukica, prevented Dartmouth College's attempt to fire him when he obtained a temporary court order restraining the athletic director from hiring a replacement coach.[299] The coach argued that he was not given 12-months' notice of termination as required by his contract. Yukica's contract had been renewed in the summer of 1986 and extended to June of 1987. In November, after his second straight losing season, Dartmouth athletic director, Ted Leland, told Yukica that he was being relieved of his coaching duties and would be reassigned elsewhere in the college.[300] In December of 1986, the coach filed suit. In January 1987, a settlement was reached allowing Yukica to remain as coach through the 1987 season.[301] The settlement called for Yukica to get roughly a $1,700.00 pay increase, $57,511 in 1986, retention of the use of a car and house while serving as coach, and $70,000 in settlement of his claims.[302]

Another celebrated case is that of Ben Lindsey, former head basketball coach at the University of Arizona.[303] Lindsey brought various actions against the University of Arizona for breach of contract and breach of the implied covenant of good faith and fair dealing and for loss of future earning capacity.[304] In addition, he sued Cedric Dempsey, former athletic director and Henry Koffler, President of the University for breach of contract, fraud, intentional interference with contractual relations and intentional infliction of emotional distress.[305] In *Lindsey*, the court affirmed a judgment in favor of Lindsey for $215,000 for loss of employment[306] for three years, and an additional $91,312 for attorney's fees. However, the court also vacated a judgment insofar as an award of $480,000 for loss of future earning capacity.[307] With respect to this aspect of the case, Lindsey maintained that he should receive damages because of the difficulty that he would have and would, in the future, encounter in obtaining employment as a coach in view of his premature termination as coach of the University of Arizona.[308] The court indicated that damages for diminution of future earning power capacity are not recoverable in action for breach of an employment contract.[309] The jury, the court held, could do nothing more than engage in speculation and conjecture as to the effect Lindsey's termination would have on his future earning capacity.[310]

Probably the most celebrated case is the demise of former North Carolina State head basketball coach Jim Valvano. With the release of *Personal Fouls* by Peter Golenbock,[311] the announcement by the NCAA that North Carolina State was to be placed on probation for two years because of players selling shoes and complimentary tickets and the announcement by former Valvano player, Charles Shackleford, currently of the New Jersey Nets, that he accepted loans while playing at State, the fate of Valvano had already been determined.[312] Evidently, Valvano's contract contained both a buy out clause and a termination provision. Valvano was required to pay $500,000 if he left the university and the university was required to pay $500,000 if Valvano was prematurely terminated.[313] Valvano even offered to coach the basketball team for $1 (presumably to preserve his lucrative outside income sources and the name position of head coach) for the ensuing season.[314] An out-of-court settlement was reached between Valvano and the university. He agreed to leave the university voluntarily and not to sue the school in exchange for $238,000 ($26,509.24 for salary payments through May 15, 1990 and $212,000 buy out for the remaining term of his contract).[315] In addition, Valvano expected to receive $375,000 from the university's booster club, The Wolf-Pack Club, in the form of a $250,000 annuity and $125,000 under a "loss revenue provision".[316]

K. Buy Out - Release Provisions

Generally, an employer cannot obtain specific performance of a personal service contract. That is, neither the employer nor the courts can require a coach to work even if the contract specifically provides for such services. Courts are reluctant to issue injunctions compelling employment because of the inherent logistical problems in effectively supervising and enforcing such decrees. Courts have historically viewed this form of affirmative relief as violating public policy and the Thirteenth Amendment of the United States Constitution, as it subjects individuals to a form of involuntary servitude.

With respect to a contract jumping coach, it would appear, at least in theory, that the university could bring an action for monetary damages against the coach in breach of contract. In such cases the recoverable damages are normally measured by the cost of the employer in obtaining equivalent services elsewhere, plus consequential damages. Some cases indicate that in assessing such damages, the "market value" of the lost services must be measured against that of the substitute services procured by the employer to remedy the breach.

These rules sound reasonable but they may be quite difficult to apply, particularly for an institution contemplating suit against a departed coach. First, measuring the 'value' of one coach's services

compared to another's is an inherently difficult problem unlikely
to provide an easy answer. Second, due to the intense publicity
involved, to engage in litigation with the departing coach can
prolong the parties' bad feelings and put a cloud over the institution's
entire athletic program. This adverse publicity can easily continue
for years while a complex case is pending in court. Third, while
some damages, such as the expenses of searching out a new coach,
are easily ascertainable, the complex compensation arrangements
under which most coaches operate, where base salary is but one
element in the compensation "package," could make it extremely
difficult for a jury to calculate exactly what it has cost the institution
to obtain the services of the new coach."[317]

As a result, most institutions allow their restless or ambitious
coaches to leave gracefully without further legal recourse.

Recently, however, universities are imposing buy out provisions on
coaches who wish to depart early. Normally, the buy out provision
will be for a predetermined lump sum or an amount predicated on a
de-escalating scale, depending upon when the coach terminates.
Washington State University seems to be an anomaly in the field of
enforcement of coach's contracts. It is alleged that the university is the
first institution of higher education to sue a jumping coach and to
generate a settlement therefor.[318] With two years remaining on his
contract, Warren Powers, the then head football coach, left for better
pastures for the same job at the University of Missouri.[319] Washington
State University sued and ultimately ended up with a $55,000
settlement.[320] In 1989, Washington State University was, once again,
faced with a jumping coach.[321] Dennis Erickson decided to depart for
Miami, as a result therefor, ended up paying the university $150,000
to settle his contract.

Gene Keady, Purdue head basketball coach, was recently offered the
job at Arizona State University for a greater compensation package
than he had at Purdue.[322] However, his Purdue contract had a buy out
provision of $200,000.[323] Keady chose to stay at Purdue rather than
expending the required buy out figure, or asking his new employer to
incur the obligation to release him of his prior contractual obligations.[324]

Some examples of a buy out-release provision are as follows:

If at any time during the term of this agreement, coach shall submit
his resignation as head basketball coach for any reason other than
disability due to illness or accident, then he shall pay to the

university the sum of $_____ to compensate the university for injury suffered by reason of a breach of this contract resulting from such resignation, it being very difficult to ascertain or estimate the entire exact cost, damage or injury which the university as employer may sustain by reason of such breach. The parties agree that such sum is reasonable and appropriate compensation for the injuries suffered by the university under the same circumstances and that it is not a penalty.[325]

Another example of a buy out release provision is as follows:

Voluntary Termination by Coach. In the event Coach voluntarily terminates his employment with the University during the term of this Agreement, the University shall be discharged of any and all further obligations of this Agreement with respect to the obligation to pay and/or provide the benefits as herein specified to Coach. In the event the Coach desires to voluntarily terminate this Employment Agreement and take another position as a Division One Coach, Coach will be required to buy-out the terms of this Agreement and pay the University according and pursuant to the following schedule:

a. Without regards to the rollover provisions as herein contained, if Coach desires to terminate the terms of this Agreement after the first year of employment hereunder, Coach shall pay to the University 80% of the Annual Salary for the remaining term of this Agreement.

b. Without regards to the rollover provisions as herein contained, if Coach desires to terminate the terms of this Agreement after the second year of employment hereunder, Coach shall pay to the University 60% of the Annual Salary for the remaining term of the Agreement.

c. Without regards to the rollover provisions as herein contained, if Coach desires to terminate the terms of this Agreement after the third year of employment hereunder, Coach shall pay to the University 40% of the Annual Salary for the remaining term of the Agreement.

d. Without regards to the rollover provisions as herein contained, if Coach desires to terminate the terms of this Agreement after the fourth year of employment hereunder, Coach shall pay to the University 20% of the Annual Salary for the remaining term of the Agreement.

e. Without regards to the rollover provisions as herein contained, if Coach desires to terminate the terms of this Agreement after the fifth year of employment hereunder, Coach no buy-out shall be required.

At the sole option and discretion of the Coach, said buy out payments may be made in lump-sum within ten (10) days after notification of voluntary termination and/or on May 1st of each year of the term of this Agreement with respect to the amount owed by Coach. It is understood that this buy-out provision shall only apply to the original term of this Agreement and shall not be included and/or apply to any extensions of the original term hereof.[326]

Some coaches will take a job with specific language in their contract that they have the right to terminate their position with the university in the event a specific named school offers a position of head coach.[327] For instance, it was rumored that when Lou Holtz signed a contract with the Minnesota Gopher football team, he had a contract clause that would permit him to terminate that contract in the event he was offered the head football coaching job at Notre Dame University. In essence then, the contract advisor is negotiating an opt out clause wherein the coach is permitted to terminate his employment and obligations pursuant to the employment contract without any further obligation to the university on a condition subsequent basis if a specific job was offered to the coach during the term of the employment contract with the university.

L. Support of Program

The coach will want a covenant and commitment requiring the university to provide academic, economic and other forms of support to the athletic program at least equal to the level of support given to other athletic programs by other universities in the athletic conference to which the university is a member. Included in academic support would be: (1) academic counselors, (2) tutoring, and (3) other educational services. Included in economic support would be: (1) maintenance and improvement of physical facilities, (i.e., office facilities, locker room facility, dining and dormitory facilities as well as training and exercise facilities), (2) budgets sufficient to hire and retain the maximum number of assistant coaches, (3) budgets necessary to cover expenses associated with first class recruiting, (4) awarding the maximum number of scholarships to athletes permissible under NCAA rules. A coach will also want to be involved in the scheduling of games subject to final authority being reposed in the university's athletic director.

M. Tenure

Normally, only ordinary faculty members can be given tenure. Tenure is only granted in a specific academic capacity and a faculty member could not achieve tenure in connection with his administration or athletic department duties. At the January, 1990, NCAA Convention, Executive Director Dick Schultz suggested that schools give tenure to coaches. In any discussion of tenure for coaches, the issue of job security versus job flexibility must be weighed.[328] Therefore, under present circumstances, the university will want a clause indicating and confirming that the position of head coach of an athletic team is not a tenured track position, and will not ultimately lead to tenure.

N. Scheduling and Assistant Coaches

There will be some negotiation between the university and the coach with respect to the coach's authority relative to the hiring and firing of assistant coaches and the scheduling and rescheduling of games with respect to the university's program. While the coach will request control over the hiring and firing of his own assistants and the scheduling of the games, the athletic director will probably want the right of approval or the right to participate in the scheduling or hiring process itself.

O. Confidentiality

To the extent permitted by law and not prohibited by state open-record laws or freedom of information acts, the university and coach will want the terms and conditions of the employment arrangements to be kept confidential. Each party will agree to refrain from disclosing the terms and conditions of the employment agreement without the prior written consent of the other. Unless, of course, disclosure is required by applicable state law. In addition, the parties will probably want a confidentiality agreement concerning disagreement and non-disclosure to third parties and the submission of any disagreements to some form of arbitration procedure.

Any public announcement with regards to the employment contract shall be jointly agreed to concerning the agreement itself and/or any extensions or modifications thereof.

The university will also want the coach, upon termination, to immediately cause certain information developed as a result of the position of head coach to be delivered to the university as the sole and confidential property of the university upon such termination. Such materials, without limitation, may include personnel records, recruiting records, team information, films, statistics, any other memoranda or data furnished to the coach by the university or developed by the coach on behalf of the university as a result of the position of coach.

P. Arbitration

During the course of the contract period there may be disputes between the university and coach arising out of or concerning the scope, interpretation or provisions of the employment contract. Obviously, if there is a dispute with respect to the contract either party has their legal remedies, including injunctions against further continued breach, specific performance, if any, or damages arising out of such breaches. Another alternative, other than utilization of the courts, is arbitration or some other form of dispute resolution procedure where such disputes are submitted to an impartial third party. Obviously, any such clause would need to define the disputes to be so submitted, the party to act as the objective third party arbitrator, the rules under which the arbitration would be conducted and the agreement that the decision of the arbitrator shall be binding without further ability to appeal. Although the utilization of the courts may be a leverage factor, a dispute resolution device may be more efficient, cost saving, time saving and ultimately equitable for both parties.

III. Conclusion

The Knight Commission characterizes the power coach as often enjoying greater recognition throughout the state than most elected officials, and as the chief operating officer of a multimillion dollar business.[329] Indeed, college sports is a business, but so is the relationship between a university and its coach a business and contractual package. As such, that relationship should be treated in the strictest contractual and legal sense. Kevin O'Neill, Marquette University Basketball Coach, in a speech at Marquette University Law School, on March 26, 1991 gave some important perspectives to the real world of college coaching and contracts. O'Neill suggested:

1. Get a lawyer.
2. Get all compensation terms in writing, nothing oral. Hand shake deals are a custom of the past.
3. The day of the long-term contract is gone. Three to five year stays will become normal.
4. Don't trust anyone. Contract negotiations is a business deal and ultimately adversarial.
5. Because violation of NCAA Rules can mean an end to your contract and maybe your career, document all activities on a daily basis by the use of a diary.
6. Limit your liability with respect to the acts of other, especially student-athletes and assistant coaches.
7. College athletics is big business and universities should not be limiting the outside sources of income of coaches.
8. Plan for termination.[330]

Yes, job volatility and movement in the coaching industry is the main concern and topic of most coaches today. On April 3, 1989, Jud Heathcote, head basketball coach at Michigan State University and outgoing President of the National Association of Basketball Coaches, announced that a fund would be created for the rehabilitation and counselling of those coaches who were dismissed. He stated that $2,000.00 will be made available to any coach or member of his family for use, for counselling, self-rehabilitation or career guidance.[331] It appears that lawyers will have a more heavy-handed role in the contractual relationships between universities and coaches. Not only in the contractual stage, but in the legal adversity in negotiated settlements that seem to highlight those events that terminate the relationship between universities and their coaches.

NOTES

1. BASKETBALL WEEKLY, May 2, 1989, at 4, col. 1.
2. *Id.*
3. *Id.*
4. *The Coaching Game: Turnovers Tell The Story How Long They Stay*, USA TODAY, Mar. 26, 1990, at 10C, col. 1. Indicated is the number of Division I Basketball coaches hired in the past 10 years according to BASKETBALL WEEKLY, May 1, 1990, at 15, col. 2.
1989-90 .. 53
1988-89 .. 42
1987-88 .. 39

1986-87 .. 66
1985-86 .. 56
1984-85 .. 26
1983-84 .. 38
1982-83 .. 37
1981-82 .. 37
1980-81 .. 42
5. MURRAY SPERBER, COLLEGE SPORTS, INC. 158 (1990). According to
   Sperber,

> Even when other divisions are factored in, the average stay is only
> 6.5 years. Similar statistics used to prevail for men's basketball
> coaches, but now in Division I, like molecules being heated by
> NCAA tourney and TV fever, coaches are moving increasingly fast
> and have surpassed the football rate. Almost 50 percent of all head
> basketball coaches changed jobs between 1986 and 1989.

6. USA TODAY, Mar. 28, 1990, at 10C, col. 1
7. BASKETBALL WEEKLY, May 2, 1989 at 4, col. 4.
8. WEBSTER'S NEW WORLD DICTIONARY 118 (2d ed. 1983).
9. CHRON. OF HIGHER EDUC., Mar. 19, 1986, at 39, 40, col. 2.
10. Id.
11. 1990-1991 NCAA DIVISION I BYLAWS. The 84th NCAA Convention
    adopted this provision effective 1/10/90 for data collection, 10/1/91 for
    Division I and 7/1/93 for Division II.
12. Id.
13. CHRON. OF HIGHER EDUC., Mar. 27, 1991, at A1 & A38.
14. Id.
15. USA TODAY, Mar. 27, 1991, at 4C, col. 4.
16. Id.
17. Id.
18. PALM BEACH POST, Apr. 30, 1989, at 8C, col. 6.
19. Symonds, *March Madness is Getting Even Crazier*, BUS. WK., Apr. 2,
    1990, at 102.

> This year, the NCAA expects to clear about $65 million on
> tournament receipts of $72.3 million. Next year, the tournament
> could easily gross $1230 million, thus exacerbating the problem.
> The NCAA gets 40% of this year's $65 million, while the other
> 60% goes to the 64 colleges in the tourney. The 32 teams
> eliminated in the first round go home with $286,500 apiece; teams
> that go to the Final Four each get $1.4 million.

BASKETBALL WEEKLY, May 2, 1989, at 4; T.V. revenue from the Final Four
in 1970: $500,000; 1973: $1.1 million; 1979: $5.2 million; 1980: $8.9

million; 1981: $10.3 million; 1982: $14.6 million; 1987: $36.6 million; 1988: $57.8 million;

An NCAA committee is working on a plan that would change the way basketball tournament money is distributed. The new plan would, in part, reward schools for the number of sports sponsored, participation in NCAA championships the last three years and the number of grants-in-aid provided, rather than simply on progression through the tournament. Hearings will be held in San Francisco, Chicago and Arlington, Va., June 14, to explain the plan. If implemented, it would represent a drastic change from the current payoff system. A look at how round-by-round rewards have grown:

Year	Teams	Round 1	Round 2	Regional Semifinal	Regional	Final 4
1970	25	8,263	8,263	24,788	24,788	49,576
1975	32	22,230	22,230	66,691	66,691	133,381
1980	48	81,594	81,594	203,986	203,986	326,378
1985	64	150,380	300,760	451,139	601,510	751,899
1990*	64	286,500	573,000	859,500	1,146,000	1,432,500

* Estimated, final figures should be available by June 27.

Source: NCAA & *NCAA Basketball Tournament Pay Outs Grow*, USA TODAY, May 31, 1990, at 10C, col. 5.

20. USA TODAY, December 14, 1989, at 12C; SPORTS INDUSTRY NEWS, March 2, 1990, at 67, col. 1; CBS will televise the Division I Men's College Basketball Tournament and fifteen other championships, including the Men's College Basketball Tournament for a seven year period from 1991 to 1997. The $1 billion dollar deal represents approximately $143 million a year. This package is worth two and one half times the networks' previous television deal which garnered $55.3 million per year. The annual rights fee in 1980 was $9.3 million (NBA network), in 1982, $13.3 million (CBS network), and in 1985 $55.3 (CBS network).

21. E. Comte, *College Football Focus: Going Regional With ABC*, SPORTING NEWS, Feb. 5, 1990, at 47. Details of the Notre Dame NBC television agreement: All home football games, six a year from 1991-95 to be telecast nationally on NBC. The package will begin with a Sept. 7, 1991 visit by Indiana. The Irish will play at home against 16 opponents: Three games each: Southern California, Boston College, Navy; Two: Michigan, Michigan State, Pittsburgh, Penn State, Purdue, Stanford, Brigham Young, Northwestern; One: Indiana, Tennessee, Air Force, Vanderbilt, Texas. Revenue is $30 million-split evenly between Notre Dame and visiting schools. ABC or ESPN retain rights, under their 1991-95 deal with the College Football Association, to broadcast games when Notre Dame is playing on the road. ABC aired two Notre Dame games in 1989 under its Big Ten-Pacific 10 contracts; CBS three, under its current CFA deal;

ESPN two, under the CFA cable package; SportsChannel America aired two games on cable. The South Bend, Ind., NBC affiliate, WNDU, owned by Notre Dame, will continue to telecast all sold-out home games, and some road games. SportsChannel America retains tape-delay TV rights.

22. USA TODAY, Nov. 5, 1990, at 2C.

A Look at the Postseason Bowls

Bowl	Date	Time	TV	Payout	Location
California Raisin Poulan/Weed Eater	Dec. 8	4 p.m.	SportChannel	$275,000	Fresno
Independence	Dec. 15	8 p.m.	Mizlou	600,000	Shreveport
Eagle/Aloha	Dec. 25	3:30 p.m.	ABC	600,000	Honolulu
Liberty	Dec. 27	8 p.m.	ESPN	1 million	Memphis
Blockbuster	Dec. 28	8 p.m.	Raycom	1.25 mill +	Miami
All American	Dec. 28	7:30 p.m.	ESPN	600,000	Birmingham
Peach	Dec. 29	12:30 p.m.	ABC	900,000	Atlanta
Anaheim Freedom	Dec. 29	8 p.m.	Raycom	600,000	Anaheim
Sea World Holiday	Dec. 29	7:30 p.m.	ESPN	1.2 mill.	San Diego
John Hancock	Dec. 31	2:30 p.m.	CBS	750,000 +	El Paso
Domino's Pizza Copper	Dec. 31	5 p.m.	TBS	600,000	Tucson
Mazda Gator	Jan. 1	11:30 p.m.	ESPN	1.2 mill.	Jacksonville
Hall of Fame	Jan. 1	1 p.m.	NBC	1 mill.	Tampa
Florida Citrus	Jan. 1	1:30 p.m.	ABC	1.3 mill.	Orlando
Mobil Cotton	Jan. 1	1:30 p.m.	CBS	3 mill.	Dallas
Sunkist Fiesta	Jan. 1	4:30 p.m.	NBC	2.5 mill. +	Tempe
Rose	Jan. 1	5 p.m.	ABC	? mill.	Pasadena
Federal Express Orange	Jan. 1	8 p.m.	NBC	4.2 mill.	Miami
USF & G Sugar	Jan. 1	8:30 p.m.	ABC	3.25 mill.	New Orleans

See also, The Sports Industry News, Aug. 5, 1988, at 247, which provides:

Bowl	Network	Payment	Payment Per Team-1988	Payment Per Team
Rose	ABC	$11.8 million	$5.8 million	$6.3 million
Orange	ABC	5.0 million	2.5 million	3.5 million
Sugar	ABC	2.5 million	2.6 million	2.7 million
Cotton	CBS	3.4 million	2.4 million	2.5 million
Fiesta	NBC	2.5 million	2.0 million	2.5 million
Citrus	ABC	500,000/barter	1.0 million	1.1 million
Hall of Fame	ABC	barter	$800,000	1.0 million

23. CHRON. OF HIGHER EDUC., Feb. 1, 1989, at A31, col. 5.
24. *Id.*
25. B. Loop, *Administrators Deny Basketball Players' Staged Coup*, UPI, Feb. 8, 1990.

26. Note, *State Open Records Acts and the NCAA Bylaw Requiring Coaches to Disclose Their "Athletically-Related" Outside Income: Emptying the Coaches' Pocket For Public Inspection*, 16 J. OF C.& U.L. 497, 513 n. 104 (1990).

27. Graves, *Coaches in the Courtroom*, 12 J. OF C. & U.L. 545, 545 (1986).

28. Rodgers v. Georgia Tech Athletic Association, 166 Ga.App. 156, 303 S.E.2d 467 (1983).

29. Stoner & Nogay, *The Model University Coaching Contract (MCC): A Better Starting Point For Your Next Negotiation*, 16 J. OF C. & U.L. 43 (1989).

30. Stoner, *Coaching Contracts: Some Suggestions on Your Next Coaching Contract Negotiation and Report from our Survey*, 27th Annual NACUA Conference (June 23-26, 1987).

31. Graves, *supra* note 27, at 548.

32. *Id.*

33. *Id.*

34. *Id.*

35. *Id.* at 549.

36. Graves, *supra* note 27, at 549.

37. New England Patriots Football Club, Inc. v. University of Colorado, 592 F.2d 1196, 1998 n. 1 (1st Cir.1979).

38. *Id.* at 1200.

39. *Id.* at 1198.

40. *Id.* at 1198, 1199.

41. *Id.*

42. SPERBER, *supra* note 5, at 164, 165.

43. *Id.* at 165.

44. Stoner, *supra* note 30, at 6.

45. A "release" clause is defined as a provision "discharg[ing] a claim one has against another." BLACK'S LAW DICTIONARY 1159 (5th ed. 1979).

46. Graves, *supra* note 27, at 550.

47. *Id.* at 551.

48. *Id.* at 551.

49. *Id.* at 551.

50. *Rodgers*, 303 S.E.2d 457 (1983).

51. *Id.*

52. *Id.* at 469.

53. *Id.* at 470.

54. *Id.*

55. *Id.*

56. *Id.*

57. *Id.*

58. *Id.* at 474 (1983).

59. *Id.* at 474 (1983).

60. Graves, *supra* note 27, at 553.

61. *Id.*
62. *Rodgers*, 303 S.E.2d at 467, 471.
63. *Id.* at 472, 473.
64. *Id.* at 474.
65. *Id.* at 474, 475.
66. Graves, *supra* note 27, at 554.
67. 99 N.H. 492, 116 A.2d 489 (1955).
68. *Id.* at 491.
69. *Id.* at 492.
70. *Id.* at 492, 493.
71. *Id.*
72. Graves, *supra* note 27, at 555, 556.
73. 166 Ga.App. 156, 303 S.E.2d 467 (1983).
74. 99 N.H. 492, 115 A.2d 489 (1955).
75. 1991-92 NCAA DIVISION I BYLAWS, Art. 11.2.1.
76. *Id.* at 11.2.1.1.
77. *Id.* at 11.2.2.
78. *Id.* at 11.3.2.1.
79. *Id.* at 11.3.2.2.
80. *Id.* at 11.3.2.3.
81. 1991-92 NCAA DIVISION II & III BYLAWS, Art. 11.3.2.4.
82. 1991-92 NCAA DIVISION I BYLAWS, Art. 11.3.2.6.
83. *Id.* at 11.3.2.6.
84. *Id.* at 11.3.2.7.
85. *Id.* at 11.3.2.8.
86. *Id.* at 11.5.1.1.
87. *Id.* at 11.5.1.1.1.
88. *Id.*
89. *Id.* at 11.5.1.1.2.
90. JEFFREY ORLEANS & EDWARD STONER, LEGAL ISSUES IN ATHLETICS 155 (2nd ed. 1989) (quoting NCAA's "Recommended Policy 6").
91. *Id.*
92. 1991-1992 NCAA MANUAL DIVISION I BYLAWS, Art. 11.3.1.
93. *Id.*
94. SPORTING NEWS, Oct. 23, 1989, at 56.
95. *Id.*
96. CHICAGO TRIB., Oct. 11, 1989, at 2C; Milw.J., Oct. 11, 1989.
97. *Id.*
98. THE SPORTING NEWS, Oct. 23, 1989, at 34.
99. L.A. TIMES, Oct. 12, 1989, at 9C, col. 1.
100. *Wisconsin Not Likely to Pay for Mistake*, UPI, Feb. 15, 1990; USA TODAY, ct. 25, 1989, at 11C.
101. *Id.*
102. THE KNIGHT FOUNDATION COMMISSION REPORT ON INTERCOLLEGIATE ATHLETICS, Mar. 8, 1991, at 20.

103.*Id.* at 21.
104.*Id.* at 27.
105.SPORTING NEWS, Mar. 25, 1991, at 6, col. 2.
106.*Id.* at 6, col. 4.
107.Note, *supra* note 26, at 503-05.
108.*Id.* at 505.
109.*Id.* at 506.
110.*Id.* at 507.
111.*Id.*
112.*Id.* at 507-08.
113.*Id.* at 508; *see, e.g.*, 5 U.S.C. § 552(b)(6) (1979).
114.*Id.*
115.Gannett Publishing v. University of Maine, 555 A.2d 470 (Me.Ct.App.1989).
116.*Id.* at 471.
117.*Id.* at 472.
118.*Id.*
119.*Id.* at 473.
120.Note, *supra* note 26, at 511 (*citing* Durham and Landers v. Davidson & Cox Enterprise, Inc. (Super.Ct.Fulton, Ga.) (filed January 1, 1989) (No. 55-1187))
121.Note, *supra* note 26, at 511 (*citing* Macon Telegraph v. Board of Regents, 256 Ga. 443, 350 S.E.2d 23 (1986)).
122.*Id.*
123.*Id.* (*citing Macon Telegraph*, 350 S.E.2d at 25).
124.*Id.*
125.Stoner & Nogay, *supra* note 29, at 44.
126.*Id.*
127.*Id.*
128.*Id.*
129.Stoner & Nogay, *supra* note 29, at 44.
130.Provisions disclosed under condition name of Coach and University remain confidential.
131.Stoner & Nogay, *supra* note 29, at 59-60.
132.Coach Earl Bruce, Ohio State University, Football Contract.
133.Stoner & Nogay, *supra* note 29, at 59-60.
134.55 N.C.App. 430 (1982).
135.*Id.* at 433.
136.*Id.*
137.*Id.*
138.*Id.* at 435.
139.*Id.*
140.*Id.*
141.*Id.*
142.*Id.* at 435-36.

143.*Id.*
144.754 P.2d 1152 (Ariz.Ct.App.1987).
145.*Id.* at 50.
146.*Id.*
147.*Id.*
148.*Id.*
149.*Id.* at 51.
150.*Id.*
151.*Id.*
152.*Id.*
153.*Id.*
154.*Id.*
155.*Id.* at 52.
156.*Id.*
157.*Id.* at 53.
158.*Id.*
159.*Id.*
160.*Id.*
161.Stoner & Nogay, *supra* note 29, at 47.
162.*Id.* at 48.
163.*Id.*
164.*Id.*
165.*Id.*
166.*Id.*
167.*Id.*
168.*Id.* at 63.
169.150 Ariz. 184, 722 P.2d 352 (Ariz.Ct.App.1986).
170.Ariz. Rev. Stat. Ann. § 35-154 (1986).
171.The University of Arizona v. County of Pima, 187 722 P.2d 352, 355 (Ariz.Ct.App.1986).
172.*Id.* at 35.
173.*Id.*
174.*Id.*
175.Former coach Don Morton, University of Wisconsin, Football Contract.
176.Stoner, *supra* note 30, at 4.
177.*Id.*
178.*Id.* (quoting Brock v. Mutual Reports, Inc., 397 A.2d 149 (D.C.App.1979).
179.Clause utilized in undisclosed and confidential coaching conrtacts drafted by M. Greenberg.
180.Milw.J., Nov. 29, 1989, at 1A, col. 1; Milw. Sentinel, Dec. 12, 1989, at 1, col. 1.
181.*Id.*
182.*Id.*

183. *Id.* Morton's Ultimate settlement was for $300,000; *see also* THE BOSTON GLOBE, Dec. 22, 1989, at 34C.
184. Stoner & Nogay, *supra* note 29, at 63-64.
185. PALM BEACH POST, Apr. 30, 1989, at 8C.
186. *Id.*
187. USA TODAY, Apr. 13, 1989 at 1C, col. 3.
188. *Id.*
189. *The Blue Grass Isn't So Blue*, SPORTS ILL., Dec. 11, 1989, at 54.
190. SPORTS INDUSTRY NEWS, January 5, 1991, at 9.
191. *The Mystery of Earle Bruce*, L.A. TIMES, Jan. 17, 1988, Part 3, at 3, col. 2.
192. *UNLV Picks Notre Dame Assistant*, L.A. TIMES, Dec. 23, 1989, at 2C, col. 1.
193. N.Y. TIMES, May 2, 1990, at B4, col. 4.
194. SPORTING NEWS, May 7, 1990, at 37.
195. *See supra* note 179.
196. Stoner & Nogay, *supra* note 29, at 89.
197. SPERBER, *supra* note 5, at 177.
198. *Id.* at 178.
199. *Id.* at 196.
200. *Id.*
201. *Id.*
202. *Id.* at 196, 197.
203. Gellitt, *The Gospel According to John*, SPORTS ILL., Dec., 1980 at 90, 102.
204. *Id.*
205. SPORTS INDUSTRY NEWS, June 1, 1990, at 165.
206. *Id.*
207. SPORTS INDUSTRY NEWS, Mar. 24, 1989, at Data Page.
208. USA TODAY, Apr. 13, 1989, at C1, col. 3.
209. *Id.*
210. N.Y. TIMES, Apr. 1, 1990 at 6, col. 2.
211. *Id.* With an annual base salary of $203,976, Tarkanian is Nevada's Highest Paid State Employee, MILW.J., June 5, 1991 at C5.
212. *See supra* note 179.
213. Interview with John K. O'Meara, Assistant Director Advanced Marketing, Northwestern Mutual, May 20, 1991.
214. *Id.*
215. *Id.*
216. *Id.*
217. *Id.*
218. *Id.*
219. *Id.*
220. *Id.*
221. *Id.*

222.*Id.* (*citing* Internal Revenue Notice 87.13, 1987-1 C.B. 432, QSA 26 (1991)).
223.*Id.*
224.*Id.*
225.*Id.*
226.*Id.* (*citing* I.R.C. § 457(f) (1991)).
227.*Id.* (*citing* I.R.C. § 457(f)(3)(b) (1991)).
228.*Id.*
229.*Id.*
230.*Id.*
231.*Id.* (*citing* I.R.C. § 457(f)(1)(B) (1991)).
232.SPERBER, *supra* note 5, at 194.
233.WASH. POST, Apr. 3, 1990, at B5, col. 2.
234.SPORTING NEWS, Apr. 16, 1990, at 29.
235.SPERBER, *supra* note 5, at 194. Sperber stated that an

> Increasing number of schools are using future bonuses and annu-
> ities as an attempt to insure that a coach will not jump contract for
> another job. In Crum's case, the promised $1 million appears to
> have kept him from accepting various attractive coaching offers,
> including one from UCLA, his alma mater. This use of future
> annuities as a defensive strategy against the Coach in Motion Play
> also contradicts the standard coaches' complaint that schools are
> ready to fire them after the first losing season.

236.*See supra* note 179.
237.*Id.*
238.*Id.* at 186.
239.*Id.* at 187.
240.*Id.*
241.Comte, *Coaches for Sale*, SPORTS INC., Apr. 18, 1988, at 40. Comte states: "Athletes aren't the only sports figures who can make big endorse-ment dollars. Madison Avenue has its eye on college coaches, especially those with personality, TV exposure and most importantly, a big win."
242.B. Jacobs, *Endorsements: Coaching For Dollars*, SPORTS INC., Feb. 8, 1988, at 42.
243.*Id*; "One Man's Enterprise": North Carolina State head coach, Jim Valvano's outside income:

> -Four-year shoe endorsement contract with Nike at more than
> $100,000 a year.
> -Three-year contract to serve as spokesman for a Durham, N.C.,
> Nissan Dealership.
> -Contract with the Washington Speakers Bureau for a guaranteed
> 25 appearances at $8,500 per appearance ($212,500).

-Endorsement contract with a national insurance company (pending).

-Host of Jim Valvano's Road to the Final Four, airing on New York's MSG Network and Sports Channel.

-Pilot episode of another national sports show.

-Host of the Jim Valvano Show, which airs on six network affiliates in North Carolina, ESPN, Home Team Sports, Dimension Cable in Arizona and Sportsvision in Chicago.

-Jim Valvano Basketball Camps on the North Carolina State campus.

-Four-year contract with Capitol Broadcasting in Raleigh, N.C., for personal services and appearances on radio and television shows.

-Half-owner of Center-Vitale, a subsidiary of JTV enterprises, which creates corporate art. Among the life-size statutes already commissioned are one of Aristides, the first winner of the Kentucky Derby, for Churchill Downs; one of Julius Erving for the Spectrum in Philadelphia; and one of Walter Payton that will be given to the city of Philadelphia; and one of Walter Payton that will be given to the city of Chicago. Miniatures of the originals are made and sold for up to $2,000 each. Source: JTV Enterprises. *Id.*

244. DALE HOFMANN & MARTIN GREENBERG, SPORT$ BIZ 101, 102 (1989).
245. *Id.* at 102.
246. Kirkpatrick, *The Old Soft Shoe*, SPORTS ILL., Nov. 16, 1988, at 98.
247. SPERBER, *supra* note 5, at 184.
248. Kirkpatrick, *supra* note 246, at 98.
249. *Socking Away 160,000 in Shoe Deal*, SPORTING NEWS, Feb. 1, 1988.
250. *Id.*
251. SPERBER, *supra* note 5, at 184.
252. SPORTING NEWS, February 4, 1991, at 42. "In 1985, Americans paid $1.4 billion for athletic footwear. This year we will spend an estimated $5.5 billion. Long range predictions put sales over $20 billion by the end of the century." Milw. J., June 24, 1990, at C3, col 1; "In 1990, Nike became the largest sports and fitness footwear and apparel company in the world. Profit for Nike's entire 1990 fiscal year rose 45% to $242.96 million or $6.24 a share form $166.05 million or $4.45 a share in 1989. Annual revenue rose 31% to $2.24 billion from 1989's $1.71 billion. In the United States alone, Nike estimates that it holds about 28% of the market. Its closest competitors, Reebok International Inc., and L.A. Gear Inc., hold 22% and 12% of the US market respectively." MILW. SENTINEL, July 10, 1990 Part 2, at 2, col. 4.
253. SPORTING NEWS, Nov. 24, 1986, at 38, col. 1.
254. *Id.*
255. *Id.*

256.*Id.*

257.SPORTING NEWS, Oct. 23, 1989, at 56, col. 2.

258.*Id.*

259.*Id.*

260.*Id.*

261.*Id.* at col. 3, 4.

262.*See supra* note 179.

263.SPERBER, *supra* note 5, at 180.

264.1991-1992 NCAA DIVISION I BYLAWS, Art. 11.2.2.

265.HOFMANN & GREENBERG, *supra* note 244, at 101-02.

266.Douglas Lederman, *Will Proposal to Oversee Coaches' Pay Trip the Great Sneakers Sweepstakes,* CHRON. OF HIGHER EDUC., October 29, 1986, at 38, col. 1.

267.Catlett, *Nehlen Earns $200,000 Annually,* UPI, May 5, 1989.

268.*Id.*

269.*Id.*

270.*Id.*

271.*Id.*

272.*Id.*

273.*Id.*

274.*Id.*

275.*Id.*

276.*Id.*

277.*See supra* note 179.

278.1991-92 NCAA DIVISION I BYLAWS, Art. 11.2.1.1.

279.THE KNIGHT FOUNDATION COMMISSION REPORT ON INTERCOLLEGIATE ATHLETICS, *supra* note 102, at 6.

280.*Id.* at 8.

281.*Id.* at 29.

282.*Id.* at 30.

283.Stoner & Nogay, *supra* note 29, at 75, 76.

284.Stoner, *supra* note 30, at 28.

285.Earl Bruce v. The Ohio State University, Case No. 87 CV-11-7430.; "Fired Cleveland State men's basketball coach Kevin Mackey plans to challenge his dismissal, claiming he was discriminated against because he is an alcoholic, the News-Herald of Willoughby, Ohio reported Thursday. Mackey's attorney, David Roth, filed a complaint with the Ohio Civil Rights Commission charging the school failed to provide him with reasonable accommodation for his chemical dependency. Mackey pleaded no contest last fall to charges of cocaine abuse and driving under the influence. Cleveland State fired Mackey six days after his July 13 arrest. 'We think we can defend our position,' said university spokesman Ed Mayer." USA TODAY, Mar. 29, 1991, at 1C, col. 1.

286.*Id.* From the pleadings of Bruce, paragraph 11, "The actions taken by the defendant, Edward H. Jennings and defendant, The Ohio University, acting under the color of state law and authority, deprived plaintiff of his contracted for and non-contracted for property rights and have further denied the plaintiff due process and equal protection, in violation of the laws of the State of Ohio and the United States of America, including the first Amendment, the Fifth Amendment and the Fourteenth Amendment."

287. University of Illinois Due Process Procedures as Part of Employment contract, Title, Supervision & Termination; CHRON. OF HIGHER EDUC., February 1, 1989, at 29, 31; CHRON. OF HIGHER EDUC., February 15, 1989, at 36; Gary Moss, the former men's basketball coach at Sam Houston State University has sued the university, the NCAA and several of their officials claiming that his rights under the Texas lawyer claimed that he has been fired without receiving a hearing as required for all state employees in Texas. The lawyer indicated the Sam Houston State University used the findings of the NCAA investigation, which he said does not meet due process standards under Texas law, to support the dismissal. Moss's attorney said that Moss should have been able to examine the evidence and confront his accusers. The law suit was ultimately settled when the university assigned Moss to a non-athletic post. CHRON. OF HIGHER EDUC., February 1, 1989, at 29, 31; CHRON. OF HIGHER EDUC., February 15, 1989, at 6.

288. SPERBER, *supra* note 5, at 165.

289. *Id.* at 155-66; Gone But Not Forgotten; Clemson football coach Danny Ford resigned Thursday, but will continue to be compensated by the university. Under the terms of his resignation he will receive:

--$190,000 a year for three years.
--Additional payments: For six months if he is hired elsewhere before Nov. 15, 1991; and two years if he is not hired before Nov. 15, 1992. there will be no payments beyond five years. As long as he is receiving payments, he will receive six football season tickets.
--He may stay in his home through May, 1990 and keep the automobile (van) he is using.
--The university will pay $13,000 in mortgage interest on his farm in 1990, pay the balance of the mortgage, $100,000, and maintain health insurance for Ford and his family through Dec. 31, 1990.
Gone But Not Forgotten, USA TODAY, Jan. 19, 1990, at 8C.

290. *See supra* note 179.

291. Earl Bruce v. The Ohio State University and Edward H. Jennings, President and Edward H. Jennings Individually; Franklin county Ohio, Case N. 87-CV11-7430; N.Y. TIMES, Nov. 17, 1987, at D31, col. 4; Nov. 28, 1987, at 43, col. 1; CHRON. OF HIGHER EDUC., Dec. 2, 1987, at A37, col. 2.

292. CHRON. OF HIGHER EDUC., Dec. 2, 1987, at 37, col. 2.

293. Earl Bruce, Case No. 87 CV-11-7430, complaint at 6.
294. *Id.* at 89.
295. Earl Bruce, Case No. 87 CV-11-7430, Exhibit A at 3.
296. *Id.*
297. *Id.*
298. Yukica v. Leland, Farrel, Dartmouth; CHRON. OF HIGHER EDUC., Nov. 19, 1986, at 39, col. 1; N.Y. Times, Dec. 3, 1985, at B20, col. 1.
299. *Id.*
300. *Id.*
301. *Id.*
302. *Id.* An out of court settlement was reached by former University of Wisconsin-Stevens Point coach, D.J. LeRoy, who was fired following a scandal involving ineligible players. LeRoy was fired a year ago when the school was forced to forfeit its 12 victories in 1987, the Wisconsin State University Conference title and a share of the NAIA Division II championship because two players were ineligible. The settlement absolves LeRoy of any responsibility regarding the athletic eligibility of the two players. It also call for the State to pay him $40,000. Said LeRoy, "My primary objectives since last May have been to obtain a respect to the loss of the 1987 football season and the national co-championship. I consider this settlement as a total vindication." LeRoy is now a coach at Coe College in Cedar Rapids, Iowa; SPORTING NEWS, May 15, 1989, at 49, col. 1. Bob Wade, former University of Maryland basketball coach, was the subject of an NCAA investigation involving allegations that Wade gave improper rides to class to a player. Wade misstated this role to investigators thereafter. Wade helped players accumulate frequent flyer bonus points from airline tickets purchased by the Athletic Department and received small sums of cash on occasions. For his resignation, Wade received $120,000 cash settlement which amounted to about 60% of Wade's salary for the remaining two years of his five year contract and the settlement further calls for the University foundation to buy his house near campus and to pay $5,000 towards moving expenses. WASH. POST, May 13, 1989, at A1, A6, col. 1, col. 2.
303. Lindsey v. University of Arizona, 157 Ariz. 48, 754 P.2d 1152 (Ariz.App.1987).
304. *Id.* at 1152.
305. *Id.*
306. *Id.* at 1157, 1159.
307. *Id.* at 1158.
308. *Id.* at 1157, 1158.
309. *Id.* at 1158.
310. *Id.*
311. P. GOLENBOCK, PERSONAL FOULS (1989).
312. L.A. TIMES, July 26, 1990, at 16C, col. 6.
313. *Id.*

314. *Id.*
315. *Buyout Accord Reached By Valvano, N.C. State*, SPORTS INDUSTRY NEWS, Apr. 13, 1990, at 111; *see also*, WASH. POST, Apr. 8, 1990, at C1.
316. *Id.*
317. Graves, *supra* note 27, at 548.
318. SPERBER, *supra* note 5, at 165.
319. *Id.*
320. *Id.*
321. SPORTING NEWS, Mar. 20, 1989, at 26.
322. SPORTS INDUSTRY NEWS, Mar. 24, 1989, at Data Page.
323. *Id.*
324. *Id.*
325. Stoner, *supra* note 30, at 34.
326. *Id.*
327. SPERBER, *supra* note 5, at 167.
328. *Coaches Not United on Tenure*, SAN FRANCISCO CHRONICLE, Jan. 10, 1990, at D8, col. __. The following are cases related to the tenure issue for college coaches: *see generally* Hanlon v. Providence College, 615 F.2d 535 (1st Cir.1980); Hennessey v. NCAA, 564 F.2d 1136 (5th Cir.1977).
329. THE KNIGHT FOUNDATION COMMISSION REPORT ON INTERCOLLEGIATE ATHLETICS, *supra* note 102, at 5.
330. Remarks by Kevin O'Neil, Marquette University Men's Head Basketball Coach, (Mar. 26, 1991).
331. *Coaches Organize Fund For the Fired*, USA TODAY, Apr. 5, 1989, at 2C.

THE ART OF CONTRACT NEGOTIATION*

David B. Falk

David Falk is perhaps the best known sports agent in the United States, having represented Michael Jordan and a host of other high profile professional athletes. In this essay, he recounts his own experiences as a sports lawyer/agent and offers recommendations as to the effective representation of professional athletes.

I. INTRODUCTION

Twenty years ago, I was a young student aspiring to a career in sports law. Following law school, I have had the good fortune to achieve my personal ambition and become a sports attorney while representing some of the best athletes in the country. In the process, I have visited many of the top universities and met many athletes throughout the country.

For me, it all began when I attended law school at George Washington University and made the decision to combine my love for sports with my desire for law. Through some networking, I met two of the giants in the business, Bob Woolf and the late Larry Fleisher. They gave me two pieces of advice: First, take a lot of tax courses in law school, which was some of the worst advice I got in my life, because my professor in income tax failed one-third of my class in 1975; and second, since I was in Washington, D.C., look into a very small law firm there that represented tennis players called Dell, Craighill, Fentress & Benton. When Bob Woolf and I meet the same player, I

*From Volume 3, Number 1, Fall 1992, pp. 1-27.

often tweak him: "Don't forget your recommendation to me that this is a great firm. I hope you tell that to the players."

One of the most difficult and challenging deals I made with the firm was to get Donald Dell on the telephone, which took six to seven weeks. I met his assistants, his secretaries, and one day I decided I was going to get a personal reply from Donald Dell, even if it was X-rated. So on that fateful day, I called him about eighteen times until he finally took my call. We met and negotiated my first position, which was working evenings during the summer following my second year of law school, after completing my fulltime job each day at Sidley & Austin in Washington, D.C. My starting salary was zero. I celebrated my position by getting married, going on my honeymoon, and enrolling in a summer course in negotiations.

By the close of the summer, I had learned enough in my class to negotiate a job at the law firm beginning in September. I did not realize part-time meant about sixty hours a week, but for me it might as well have been sixty hours a day. About one day before graduating law school and shortly before my classmates would have burned the building down, Dell broke down and offered me a full-time job.

We went to lunch to negotiate my salary. I vividly remember: We had lunch at about 4:30 in the afternoon. One of the associates in the firm had advised me to have a good breakfast. I thought it was to prepare me for the negotiations, but it really was to prepare me for the hour of day. I sat down and Dell asked: "What do you think a fair salary would be?" In 1979, starting salaries for government attorneys were $15,500 annually. Dell replied, "Starting attorneys here make $13,000." We then reached a compromise: $13,000. Eighteen years later I am the chairman of my own company called Falk Associates Management Enterprises, Inc., representing about thirty players in two sports.

Over the eighteen years I have been in business, there has been an explosion of players' salaries. One of my first clients was a point guard from the University of Maryland named John Lucas. Lucas was the first player drafted in the National Basketball Association in 1976, and the last player to sign before the NBA-ABA player merger. Lucas received a salary of about $300,000 a year for his five-year contract. Ten years later, I had the opportunity to represent Patrick Ewing from Georgetown University, who was also the number one pick in the draft. I negotiated a contract for Ewing that averaged about $3 million a year — which represented an increase of about 900 percent since Lucas signed. This year, Shaquille O'Neal signed a contract with the Orlando Magic for seven years, averaging $5.7 million a year. To say that the salaries in basketball have exploded is probably an understatement. The number of people who want to be in the representation business is also increasing. There are 324 players on NBA active rosters, and there are over 400 registered agents to represent them. I would guess that just ten individuals or groups represent about two-thirds of the players in the League. So, there are another 400 people competing for less than 100 players.

The explosion in salaries reminds me of the Texas millionaire who is walking down the street in New York and encounters a bum. The bum says: "Excuse me, can you spare a quarter?" The Texas millionaire looks down at him and says, "Son, look at me; this hat is a custom-made Stetson that cost a thousand dollars. These boots are hand-tooled Tony Lamas that cost two thousand dollars. Do you think I got where I am by thinking small? The next time someone walks up to you, don't ask him for a quarter. Ask him for a $5 bill." The bum looks up at the millionaire and says: "Just what I need, some loud-mouthed Texan telling me how to run MY business."

This raises an interesting question, which just happens to be the topic of this conference: How do I run my business negotiating professional sports contracts, and how do I approach negotiating professional sports contracts?

II. FACTORS IN NEGOTIATING

A. Knowing the Agreements, Terms, and Talk

Despite my longevity in the sports representation business, I always prepare thoroughly. I spend a considerable amount of time before every negotiation preparing, taking copious steps to understand the task I am about to approach. The first step is understanding the collective bargaining agreement, for which it is very helpful to have a legal background. In football there has not been an agreement for a number of years.[1] On the other hand, the basketball collective bargaining agreement is a very complex document that includes the salary cap. There are probably not even ten people in America who really understand the salary cap. There are so many gaps in the cap that Gary Bettman, senior vice president and general counsel of the NBA, creates new rules every time he interprets the cap.[2] So, it is difficult to really stay on top of the salary cap.

There are a variety of rules. For example, there is the "30 percent rule" that provides that the increases in salary in the NBA from the first year of the contract cannot exceed thirty percent of the first year salary. There are rules on how many options a player can have, termination rules, etc. So to properly negotiate a contract in today's NBA, I think you do have to be a lawyer, you have to be an expert on the salary cap, and you have to be creative and try to invent ways — not to circumvent the cap because that is not permitted — but to negotiate around the cap to get your client fair market value. Unfortunately, I think that very few people on either side of the table — very few general managers and very few player representatives — truly understand the salary cap.

The second thing I like to do is try to understand trends in the business. I believe every industry has trends, and the sports industry is no different. There are trends in the length of the contract. For example, because many teams in basketball are close to the salary cap, and because the contract can only be increased by thirty percent of the first-year salary, there has been a tendency in the last few years to negotiate very long contracts. Frankly, this concerns me. Whatever amount seems high today does not seem so high a few years down the road. In 1992, when I was negotiating with the Charlotte Hornets for Alonzo Mourning, I reminded the owner, George Shinn, that I represented the very first player Charlotte ever drafted, Rex Chapman, in 1988. As the eighth pick, Chapman signed a four-year contract averaging $675,000 per year. We had just turned down an offer for Mourning averaging $3 million more than that. I asked George Shinn if he ever thought four years ago that he would sit with a player who could turn down $3.6 million a year? When he said, "No," I replied, "Well, that's exactly why I don't want a long-term contract, because if salaries continue to change as fast as they have over the last four years, Mourning's contract will never stay in line with the salary explosion."

About fifteen months ago, I negotiated the biggest contract in the history of professional basketball for a player named Danny Ferry. He signed a ten-year contract for $3.75 million a year. Since Ferry's record-breaking signing, Patrick Ewing, Magic Johnson, Shaquille O'Neal, David Robinson and Brad Daugherty have all exploded past $3.75 million, $4 million, $5 million, and a few even past $6 million per year. Ewing passed $10 million. Therefore, in that kind of environment, the length of the contract is a very important issue. Without criticizing some of my colleagues, I believe that there is a real pressure when negotiating for young players, particularly rookies, to be able to point to a deal you have negotiated whose average compensation is higher than the player picked before or after you. As a result, sometimes individuals negotiate deals that are too long for their own client because they are trying to make the deal look good. I believe the substance of the deal is more important than how it looks.

B. Knowing the Structure of Contracts

A representative needs to understand the structure of contracts in conjunction with the increase in the lengths of contracts in professional basketball. A lot of us have come to question what happens if you have a player like Patrick Ewing, and you are about to sign him for one and a half times what the highest player has ever received in the history of the sport as a rookie. However, you really believe the salary structure is going to dramatically change. How do you protect yourself? The answer is that you put in a right to terminate the contract. In Ewing's first contract, we negotiated a clause that provided that after the first six years, if four players in the NBA earned more salary than Ewing, he could terminate. Subsequently, Larry Bird signed a one-year contract whose entire $7.1 million compensation was denominated a signing bonus. We then went to arbitration to determine whether salary in a one-year contract was the same as a signing bonus in a one-year contract, and unfortunately we lost. That did not really affect the final outcome of the negotiations, though. Since then, there has been an increase in the number of clauses providing early rights to terminate the contract. Gary Bettman is a very good friend of mine. I call him "the Pope." When I was in Rome several years ago, Gary's wife, Shelly, came up to me and asked: "Are you the famous David Falk who calls my husband 'the Pope'? Don't you know he is Jewish?" I said I knew he was Jewish, as I am. She asked, "Then why do you call him the Pope?" "Because," I replied, "he makes the rules as he makes them up." After you have concluded a negotiation, the contract is submitted for approval to Bettman. Recently, we concluded a four-year deal for Xavier McDaniel with the Boston Celtics that included a right to terminate in favor of the player after the first year. Bettman informed us that we were not allowed to do that. I asked, "What rule are we violating?" He said, "No rules, we just interpret a termination after one year as circumventing the cap, so you can't do it." You have two choices, either accept it or arbitrate it. Unfortunately, the teams are so afraid of Bettman being difficult to deal with in the future that they do not even want to go to arbitration with him to enforce the deals they have negotiated.

C. Being Aware of Salary Growth

I believe the third step is understanding the growth of salaries in relation to the growth of the cap. The cap has gone up dramatically since its inception in 1983 from $3.6 million to $14 million in 1992-93, and next year it will be $15 million. That is about four times its initial amount. When you are representing a player, you have to question how large the increase in his contract will be over the previous year's pick, relative to the increase in the cap from year to year. Such analysis is a new trend. From my standpoint, the pre-negotiation analysis has gotten a lot more scientific, like doing a baseball contract. When you go to arbitration in baseball, you want to develop as much economic evidence as you can in order to justify your position.

D. Fair Market Value Rather Than Ability

Most people would be foolish to walk into a room with Red Auerbach or Jerry West and try to negotiate a contract based on their perception of how good their player is. If you walked in and said, "I'm representing Jimmy Jackson; I think he has a great spin move on the base-line, nice rotation on his jump shot, and he is a good rebounder in traffic," most general managers would laugh you out of the room. They do not think you are qualified to make those determinations. However, when they draft Jackson number four, a whole host of economic considerations immediately come into play, relative to what the number three player gets, what the number five player gets, what the number four player received the year before and perhaps the year before that. These are the kinds of considerations that professional representatives need to concern themselves with. These considerations are quite different from the fans' perspective, which focuses on how good the player is.

Every year there are definitive break points in the compensation paid to rookies. If you took the list of rookie players and examined it from top to bottom, you would find that there are gaps in the compensation packages players receive. It is not a symmetrical progression where each player is slotted, as is done in football. For example, in 1990 we represented the fourth player taken in the draft, Dennis Scott, who was picked by the Orlando Magic. Scott received $600,000 a year more in guaranteed compensation than the player selected one pick behind him. That $600,000 represented the biggest gap in the entire first round; it was an even bigger gap than the differential between Scott and the player drafted number one. The gap indicates that there is a consensus by general managers that the talent pool reached a plateau at the fourth pick, and that the players selected below four were at a different level.

The identical situation occurred the following year. Dikembe Mutombo was selected fourth and received $500,000 a year more in guaranteed compensation than Steve Smith, who was selected number five. This represented the biggest gap between any two picks in the draft. This year there will probably be several gaps. Shaquille O'Neal will likely set his own market, and there will probably be a very big gap between the third pick, Christian Laettner, and the fourth pick, Jimmy Jackson. You must understand that when you try to compare your client with the players picked ahead of him in the draft, you may be creating more of an anomaly than the rule.

There are other unwritten rules, such as centers always receive a premium, much like quarterback in the NFL. If you represent a NFL quarterback as a rookie, he has traditionally been worth roughly a half-a-round in the draft. It is important to understand these little nuances because they have a big impact on a player's value. In a general sense, professional representatives must be experts in value, not necessarily experts in the sport.

The experts in the sport are the scouts and general managers. They determine that your client is drafted, for example, number six. You must then understand what impact your client will make as the number six pick based on the year, the composition of the team, and the players around him. You must translate his position into economic value. There are easy ways of making this economic translation for the rookies. But if a player is a veteran free agent, you can obviously negotiate with all the other teams, and in this open market environment, another team may determine what is fair.

E. The Negotiation Position

Once you understand the collective bargaining agreement and the trends, the second step is to try to understand the client's negotiation position. Aside from preparation, this is perhaps the most important step because it is not simply a function of what the name of your client is or what number he is picked. Rather, it is really a question of how much leverage you have. Leverage is the bottom line in my business. The obvious question is: Where does leverage come from? The first place is competition from other bidders. I previously mentioned the rule that quarterbacks are worth half-a-round. The first quarterback I represented was Boomer Esiason of the Cincinnati Bengals. Esiason was drafted number thirty-eight in 1984 during the "glory years" when there was another league (USFL). Despite his draft position, Esiason received the seventh highest rookie contract in professional football in 1984. Afterwards, everyone asked me how I got such a good deal? I explained that it was such a good deal because we had three teams in the USFL, whose owners do business with us on a regular basis, bidding to sign Esiason. The competition made the negotiations much easier. When you have another league, like we used to have in basketball (ABA) — or in football (USFL), it provides tremendous leverage. In the global scope of basketball in the 1990s, the other league might actually be another country, such as the Italian or Spanish league. A few years ago, my client, Danny Ferry, signed a five-year contract with an Italian team, Il Messaggero, that was owned by a giant agro-chemical company called the Ferruzzi group. (Those of you who are fans of sailing know that the owner of the company, Raul Gardini, was in the America's Cup last year. Most of the participants spent $30 million for their boats and Gardini reportedly spent $60 million. He ran his basketball team the same way.) Ferry had a five-year contract in Italy that had an "out clause" at the end of each year. He had been selected by the Los Angeles Clippers as the number two pick in the draft. At Ferry's request, I indicated to the Clippers that Ferry would prefer to play for a team other than the Clippers, but management was a little stubborn. After Ferry spent his first year in Rome with Il Messaggero, the Clippers began to realize that we were sincere. They made a major trade with the Cleveland Cavaliers, who gave up two first-round picks and Ron Harper, one of their best players, for Danny Ferry and Reggie Williams, who is also a client of mine. By the time Ferry returned from Italy and we were ready to commence negotiations for him, Williams had been cut. In essence, Cleveland had traded two first-round picks and probably its best, most exciting player for Ferry, who had a fifteen-day window to either make a deal with Cleveland or go back to Rome.

Needless to say, Ferry's negotiating position was very advantageous, and his rookie contract made him the highest paid player in the league for fifteen months. This happened because we had tremendous leverage—probably all the leverage. To reiterate an old theme, because the team had given up a lot of value in the form of Ron Harper and the two first-round picks, they simply had to sign Ferry.

F. Two Sport Players as a Factor

There has been a recent, albeit limited, trend of players talented enough to play two professional sports at the same time. Bo Jackson started the trend. More recently, Deion Sanders and Brian Jordan have played two sports simultaneously. Obviously, the ability to tell a team that it is not offering enough money and that you can play for another professional team, sometimes in the same city, gives you a tremendous edge in negotiations.

III. KNOWING THE TEAM(S) YOU ARE DEALING WITH

The second source of leverage comes from the team's position in its market. As an example, in 1986, Bo Jackson was the first pick in the NFL draft by the Tampa Bay Buccaneers. He had the highest rating at the scouting combines of any football player between 1968 and 1986. Jackson decided that Hugh Culverhouse's offer simply was not sufficient for him to sign with Tampa Bay, so he signed instead with the Kansas City Royals baseball team. He earned a substantial signing bonus from his baseball contract and sat the year out in football. One year later, Tampa Bay again had the number one pick in the NFL draft and selected the Heisman trophy winner from the University of Miami, Vinny Testaverde. Imagine that you are Testaverde's attorney. You have a star quarterback from one of the premier college football programs in the country. When you sit down to negotiate and tell Hugh Culverhouse that if your client does not get paid enough money, he is going to sit the year out, Culverhouse is going to listen to you a little more attentively in 1987, after losing Bo Jackson, than he would otherwise, when he really did not believe the first pick in the draft would sit out an entire year. So, Testaverde did quite well. His negotiating position was obviously a fluke. You are not going to be in that position often. But when you are, you must take advantage of it.

A. Impact of Player on a Team

Another situation where the team's position in the market will give you great leverage is when your player can make an impact at the gate. In 1985, Patrick Ewing was the first player in the history of the NBA to be selected in the draft lottery. The lottery changed the old draft system in which the two worst teams in the league flipped a coin for the first pick to a blind draw by the seven worst teams in the League. Some cynical fans thought the draft was not so blind, and that it was influenced by Commissioner David Stern picking envelopes treated with dry ice, or using infra-red glasses or alpha waves, or other ways to make sure the New York Knicks got the number one pick to revive the team in the biggest media market. Regardless of how it happened, we were glad the Knicks won the lottery. Between the lottery and the draft, which was exactly five weeks, the Knicks were not permitted to commence negotiations. During this period, they asked us a very interesting question: "Would we object to their use of Patrick's picture on the cover of the Knicks' season ticket brochure?"

I thought it was a joke. However, it was anything but a joke. In that five-week window, the Knicks sold $5 million worth of new season tickets. With $5 million in incremental revenues, we commenced negotiations. The players drafted number one the previous two years were two very special centers, Ralph Sampson and Akeem Olajuwon, who were picked back to back by the Houston Rockets in 1983 and 1984. They both signed for approximately $1 million a year for four to six years. The Knicks' opening offer was in that neighborhood, but it was very difficult to accept the notion that Ewing should get paid the same as Sampson or Olajuwon because he had already made a $5 million economic impact on the Knicks in terms of new season ticket revenues. I presented an opening offer of $30 million for ten years. Three months later, we signed a ten-year contract for $32.1 million. Ewing had all the leverage because the New York did not want to be forced to contact season ticket holders and explain, "Refunds will be available next week because Ewing's decided not to play." So his position in the market, independent of his talent, made a huge impact.

B. Realize When the Team Has Already Committed

Sometimes a team has a huge investment in a player. This is more common for a veteran than a rookie, but in the case of Danny Ferry, Cleveland had invested two number one picks and Ron Harper to obtain Ferry's rights. If he decided not to play for Cleveland and returned to Italy, the team would have lost its premier player, two important draft picks, and Ferry's services. The investment that they made translated into a lot more dollars for him. Similarly, this year the Orlando Magic won the lottery and obtained the right to draft Shaquille O'Neal. All the other teams figured it was easy pickings to get Stanley Roberts, Orlando's starting center who was a restricted free agent. NBA rules provide that when a restricted free agent receives an offer from a "new team," his prior team has fifteen days to match the offer or allow the player to sign with the "new team." Most NBA teams felt that if they gave Roberts an offer for significant dollars, Orlando would only have fifteen days to sign Shaquille O'Neal. If Orlando was not able to sign O'Neal before the fifteen day deadline for matching Stanley Roberts' offer, they would have been so far over the salary cap they would not be able to sign O'Neal at all. But everyone was wrong. Pat Williams, Orlando's general manager, did a masterful job of restructuring four or five players' contracts and signed O'Neal for the princely sum of $5.7 million a year within the fifteen day window. He then matched Roberts' $3 million offer and subsequently traded him. But, the leverage represented by Orlando's investment in the number one pick in the draft gave O'Neal tremendous negotiating clout.

There are several areas that I like to look at in trying to understand how much leverage I have. Specifically, how badly does the team need to sign my player? Let's look at Alonzo Mourning from Georgetown, who was drafted number two by the Charlotte Hornets in 1992.

I believe the Hornets absolutely had to sign him. He is a franchise center and has a precedent setting contract with Nike, which has been written about extensively. Charlotte finished number two in the lottery, although its record would have dictated they pick ninth. The "luck of the draw" provided their last real opportunity to obtain a great center. As a result, I think Mourning did not have some of the leverage or even most of the leverage; he had ALL of the leverage. It is a situation where ultimately the team must come to you and meet your terms. It is simply a matter of timing.

C. Know Your Negotiating Opponent

Once you have analyzed your own position, there is a person on the other side of the table who is going to be really tough, and you have to analyze their position as well. You have to evaluate the same criteria, particularly how much leverage they have. However, there are other criteria I would like to look to at this point.

1. What is Their Authority?

First, what authority does the person you are negotiating with have to make the deal? In professional sports, you are frequently dealing with a person whose title is General Manager or President of the team, but they do not own the team. You find yourself in a situation where you are negotiating through a filter. The offers a general manager is throwing at you may just be an attempt to get you into a more comfortable range so the owner can come in and close the deal.

About twelve or fourteen years ago, we represented a very talented basketball player from the University of North Carolina named Phil Ford. Ford was the number two pick in the draft by the Kansas City Kings. Joe Axelson was the King's general manager. We negotiated all summer with Axelson. Finally, one night at about two o'clock in the morning, we made a deal which we both agreed to recommend to our respective principals. However, Axelson called me at about four o'clock in the morning and said he realized on the way home that he had added up the numbers wrong and he could not sell the deal to his owner. Based on our protocol, I said, "Well, I guess you are going to have to resign now as general manager and have the owner finish the deal." It was our agreement, that if we could not sell the deal to Ford, we would resign and if Axelson could not sell it, he would resign. Of course, Axelson, as he always did, had a great one-liner, even at 4:30 in the morning. "You know, there's a difference," he explained, "You have a lot of clients, and I only have one job, so I'm not going to resign." Fortunately, we finally made the deal.

2. Your Opponent's Objective

Often the person you are negotiating with has a different objective than you do. His job is not to close the deal, but simply to get you to a lower level or to change your expectations. I think it is very important, particularly if you are experienced enough, to ask the person you are negotiating with, "Can you close the deal?" If the person cannot, I think it has to affect your strategy as to how far to compromise, knowing that you could end up compromising on a compromise to make a deal.

You have to analyze how important it is for the person you are negotiating with to sign the deal. You may think that is obvious; of course, it is important. Sometimes it may be unexpectedly important for the person you are dealing with to close the deal, rather than having to go back to his or her boss to get help or approval to close the deal. I deal with a general manager, whom I would prefer not to name, who has never made me an offer that has been within fifty percent of what I have finally signed my client for on that particular team. Over the past six or seven years, this individual always low- balls us regardless of who the player is, a superstar or a reserve. One day, I called him up and said, "You know, ultimately we are going to make this deal. I think it would be a good idea for you to show your owner that you can make the deal, instead of always aggravating him into asking, "Do I have to cancel another meeting and sit down with Falk again?" Apparently, closing the deal is not important to him. Perhaps the strategy on this team is to have the general manager always low-ball the offer. At some point, we are simply not going to deal with him anymore, or I will send one of my junior associates to deal with him. When they finally get into a range they both can deal with, then the first team will come in and close the deal.

Sometimes, you want to find out how important it is to the team to sign your player because if the player is not very important and you delay the deal, the market may pass him by. But if you have a great player of the stature of a Mourning or a Ewing, the team will always come back to you. It is critical that you analyze your opponent's position and try to understand how you can attack his strengths.

3. Trade-offs

The next step is to identify the trade-offs in the deal. Every deal has trade-offs; they are the essence of the bargaining process. You can call it bargaining, negotiating, or horse-trading. There are some basic trade-offs I use when I am negotiating a deal. The first is the length of the contract. You must understand the needs and goals of your client. Does he want security? Does he want to maximize the amount of dollars protected in case he fails to reach an expected level of performance? Or does he want flexibility, so if the market changes substantially in the first two or three years of his contract, he has the ability to renegotiate as a free agent? I mentioned Patrick Ewing, who actually signed the highest contract in NBA history in 1985. Subsequently, the market changed so dramatically that by 1991, it no longer reflected his market value. This occurred because he set such a high standard that everybody else strived to reach. As more players approached his level, the market changed and Ewing's contract no longer reflected his market value. We attempt to obtain both security and flexibility. But the first issue is length, or what I call aggregate dollars and flexibility, so you can come back and renegotiate. I mentioned the case of Stanley Roberts, which is a very interesting one because he was the twenty-third pick in the 1991 draft, and because of the salary cap. He signed a one-year contract. Most general managers thought that he was overweight, was not a very hard worker, and therefore was a risky pick. Roberts averaged ten points and six rebounds a game as a rookie. But he was a center, and centers are extremely hard to obtain in the NBA. As a result, at the conclusion of his one-year contract, four or five teams bid for him. He signed a contract averaging in excess of $3 million a year. Had he come out of school and signed a great contract for the twenty-third pick, let's say $1 million a year, but locked himself up for five years, he would have cost himself a tremendous amount of money. Because he was in a position to get only a one-year deal, it ended up working to his benefit. The decision whether to sign long-term or short-term is a critical one that demands full discussion with your client. You cannot make judgments *for* your client. You have to make judgments *with* your client. You have to point out the benefits of security and the detriments of locking him in for a long period of time and having to renegotiate a contract when you do not have a lot of leverage.

The second trade-off is guarantees. In basketball, eighty-three percent of all contracts are guaranteed for either skill or injury. This means that if the club terminates the contract, it remains obligated to pay the player. In football, a very small percentage of contracts are guaranteed. Since guarantees provide security, teams will often pay a player more dollars if he will take fewer guarantees. Conversely, teams may propose that the player sacrifice dollars in order to get the entire contract guaranteed.

The third trade-off is current cash dollars versus deferred money. I believe deferred money is one of the most abused areas in professional sports contracts. That is why I like to call it "funny money." Years ago, before the salary cap, I used to say that I could get a million dollars a year for any player I represent if you gave me enough playing years and deferred the money long enough, because it becomes almost worthless. There is a simple rule, called the rule of 72's, which states that if you take the number 72 and divide it by a given interest rate, it will tell you how long it takes a dollar to double. At the current prime interest rate of six percent, every twelve years a dollar is worth half of what it is today. Many players negotiate deals with money deferred as many as twenty to thirty years out. As interest rates climb, the deferred monies are worth as little as one-fourth of what they are worth today.

Sometimes there are pressures on player representatives to try to obtain a certain amount of money for a client. This pressure may force the representative to make a bad deal by signing an unduly long contract, or deferring large amounts of money, or both. I believe this type of response to the pressures of signing players represents a troubling development in our industry. Rookie players often do not understand how little deferred money is worth. When they agree to defer large amounts of money in their contracts and they receive it many years later, it is literally like monopoly money. Obviously, a team would much prefer to pay a player in deferred dollars than in cash today. In the NBA, this trade-off is affected by the salary cap. For purposes of the cap, a dollar deferred is not discounted and is treated the same as a cash dollar. Thus, suppose two players make a $1 million a year, one all current, and the other $800,000 current and $200,000 deferred. For purposes of the salary cap, they would both be treated as making $1 million. Therefore, there is a disincentive for a team to defer money from a salary cap standpoint, but a strong incentive for the team to do so from a financial standpoint.

Another area of trade-offs is incentive bonuses. As with deferred compensation, incentive bonuses represent an area of abuse. Obviously, if a player could choose between earning a dollar guaranteed or a dollar in incentive bonuses, always insist on getting the dollar guaranteed. However, when you are negotiating a contract and you are apart in your positions, one area available to you to close the deal is incentive bonuses. I am not against bonuses, but I always recommend to a client that we try to maximize the amount of guaranteed current dollars. When you have "maxed out" guaranteed cash, but you have not closed the deal, bonuses are a creative trade-off in closing the gap.

I am amused sometimes by the type of bonuses that people put into contracts. Several years ago, one of our clients was drafted in the lottery. The player was deciding between another agent and me. The player told me how impressed he was by the other agent's claim that he negotiates many bonuses. I indicated that the other agent either did not understand the NBA salary cap or he was simply misleading him. I explained that when the league reviews a new contract, there has to be sufficient salary cap room for every single bonus that can potentially be earned in order for the contract to receive NBA approval. Accordingly, if you negotiate a bonus of $1 million if the player wins the Most Valuable Player award in his rookie year, the League will require the team to have $1 million of salary cap room to approve the contract. I would recommend that my client accept $500,000 in guaranteed salary rather than to try to be the third player in the history of the League to win the MVP as a rookie and receive $1 million.

Unfortunately, players sometimes do not understand the nuances of the cap any more than some of the people in our business. While incentive bonuses are a creative way to bridge the gap and close a deal, they should not be abused. You must tailor the bonuses to your particular client as you are negotiating.

D. Prepare a Negotiation Strategy

The next step and one of the most interesting, perhaps even humorous, areas in contract negotiation is developing a negotiation strategy. This strategy has nothing to do with your client or his position. It really has everything to do with you and your personality. You need to adopt a strategy that fits comfortably with your personality and that can be maintained on a consistent basis throughout the negotiation. We could easily spend a day on different negotiating styles, but let me point out a few by way of example.

1. High-ball/Low-ball

The first one is what I call "high-ball, low-ball." This style is reflected in many football negotiations. Typically, you propose an offer significantly higher than fair market value and the team proposes an offer significantly lower than fair market value. You then inch down like a snail from the top, and the team inches up from the bottom, and each side emphasizes how far it has moved from its initial offer, which was totally unrealistic. You end up somewhere in the middle of two distorted offers. I do not subscribe to this approach because I find it the most amateurish. However, it is the safest approach, because you start so far away from what you expect to get and put a lot of "fat" in the offer. It is not an approach that I like, but it is a legitimate approach.

2. Hard-ball

The second one is hard-ball. There is an individual who used to negotiate a lot of football contracts who is a very bright attorney, Howard Slusher. Slusher probably was the hardest hard-ball player in professional sports. He would put an offer on the table and he would not budge. He would hold a player out if the team did not capitulate. He would really go to the mat for his client. He is a very intelligent man and a good negotiator, and everyone in sports knew if you drafted a Slusher client, you were in for a long, tough, bruising battle because he was going to play hard-ball. Teams often play hard-ball, particularly in football, because they have all the leverage. Football teams know you really have nowhere to go — no other leagues, no Europe, and as a result, the deals are negotiated in hard-ball fashion.

3. The "Phantom" Negotiation

The third style is what I call the "phantom" negotiation. In this situation, you are dealing with an individual who cannot "sell" the deal to his or her superior. For example, your opponent will tell you, "It sounds like a really fair deal, but I don't think I can sell it to my owner." You are negotiating with one individual, but there is a phantom in the background that you never meet and who is never present. There is a phantom in the background that you simply cannot break through to. It is like negotiating with a ghost and it is very frustrating.

Sometimes, you are able to break through to the ghost. About ten years ago, I was negotiating a deal with the New Jersey Nets for their best player. I had a very friendly relationship with the owners. The general manager expressed repeatedly, "We are really close, but we just do not really feel comfortable with the deal." I responded, "Our client is your best player and he is one of the top rebounders in the League. What's the problem?" One day, we finally closed the deal and the general manager explained: "We have a deal, but we want a clause that if your client misses team functions, we can deduct $100,000 from his salary. He's been late for a couple of team sponsored community functions." This shocked me because our client is a very conscientious individual. Nevertheless, we responded, "No problem; if he misses three team functions in a year, you can fine him $100,000." I flew up to the Meadowlands to sign the deal, and as we were about to sign the contract, the general manager said, "Okay, everything's fine, but what happens if he fails to get 1,000 rebounds in a season?" And I responded, "Well, I guess it's tough luck. You pay him a salary and hope he has the best season possible and gets 1,000 rebounds." He said, "No, no, we can't do that. We are paying him all this money and we want a clause providing that if he does not get 1,000 rebounds for the season, we can deduct $100,000." I said, "Wait a minute, I thought you were worried about him missing team functions." He said, "No, we are really not worried about team functions. Joe Taub, our owner, is really worried that if he does not get 1,000 rebounds, we are over-paying him." I became very angry and said, "This is ridiculous. Where is Joe?" To my surprise, the general manager walked out of the room to call Taub and upon returning said, "I'm sorry, Joe can not be here until 6:30 tonight." New Jersey had a pre-season game against the Knicks, and at 6:45 that evening, Taub arrived. He did not want to negotiate. He wanted to go his sky-box and watch the game. He said to us, "What on earth are we doing at 6:45 on the night of a game, negotiating a deal; why couldn't we have worked it out this afternoon?"

So I looked at the general manager of the team, who was sporting rings around his arm-pits that made his dress shirt appear like a L.A. Rams uniform, and I said, "Well, Joe, when your general manager called you four hours ago, you said you could not be here until 6:30." He replied, "What are you talking about? He never even called me." Needless to say, the general manager was very embarassed. He got caught playing this phantom game, inventing various versions of deals that the owner wanted. On the other hand, it was a very effective strategy because we kept shifting gears. We wanted to close the deal so much that we kept giving into him on these different protective clauses.

4. Bluffing, Puffing, and Other Styles

There are many other kinds of negotiating styles. Sometimes you project false deadlines. You say to the team, "If this deal is not done by next Friday, I cannot be responsible for what is going to happen." Now, you may be telling the truth or you may be bluffing. I do not like to bluff, because if you are in this business long enough and you bluff, you may lose your credibility. But timing is a very important issue in almost any kind of negotiation, and especially in sports where you have training camp and regular season games scheduled. Often, when I make an offer, I will limit its acceptance to a certain period of time. If you have sufficient information and you really know what is going on in your business, and you know what other deals are being transacted around you, you can develop an instinct for how the timing affects the deal. In 1981, we represented the third and fourth picks in the NBA draft. The third pick signed a deal that was worth about $100,000 a year higher than the picks that went one and two, Mark Aguirre and Isiah Thomas. In our negotiating for the fourth player, we kept reminding the general manager, "We need to finalize this deal because there are developments on the horizon that will affect our negotiations." He did not believe us. One day, we made an offer and explained, "It is good until 5:00 p.m. on Friday, but after that we cannot commit to honor it." The general manager thought it was a bluff, but on Thursday we signed the number three pick to a contract that was significantly higher than the first and second picks, and on Friday we withdrew our offer and submitted a higher one. The general manager went absolutely crazy in Atlanta because he thought it was very unfair to withdraw the offer, even though we had given him notice. The fourth pick ended up getting a very strong contract, piggy-backing the third pick.

The timing of the offers and acceptances was very important. The next time you deal with the same individual and tell him that it is really important to close the deal at a certain time, you hope that the credibility you established in the first negotiation will assist you through the second one.

Many people adopt the philosophy of "splitting the difference" in negotiations. To me, this is an offshoot of high-ball, low-ball. You are at X dollars and they are at Y dollars, and you suggest, "Well, why don't we just split the difference?" I do not like to split the difference. I am not a split the difference negotiator. I like to try to open very close to the final number I want and not put a lot of fat in the offers. Again, splitting the difference is a very legitimate style.

Another style is to negotiate with teams and play "good cop, bad cop." One individual is a really nice guy; he is trying hard to work with you, while the other individual is really tough: whatever you say, the answer is no. You could propose reducing your offer — the answer is no. Whatever you propose, it is no. Naturally, you have a tendency to try to work with the good guy and do whatever they propose. You feel the good guy is the only person who is responsive to what you are doing. Often, this approach is a well-orchestrated scenario by the other side to try to soften your position, because you feel that one of the two people you are dealing with is absolutely impossible.

Whatever strategy you adopt, it has to be you. I am not a very low-key person. I often get very intense when I negotiate. If I attempted to adopt a Californian, laid-back kind of attitude, it would not last very long. The first time my opponent would say something that got me angry, I would change my demeanor like a chameleon. Therefore, I never try to be low-key in a negotiation because it does not fit my personality or my reputation.

You have to do something that works for you. Every person has a different style. Whatever style you have, I believe it is very important that you establish yourself as a negotiator in that kind of mold and stick with it. The bottom line is credibility. When you are down to the moment of truth, trying to close the deal, and you say, "This is it, I'm not going to go a dime less than this number," the person on the other side has got to know that you really mean it. Whether you said that nineteen times in the past ten years and you have never gotten your number, or you have said it nineteen times in the past ten years and you have always gotten your number makes all the difference in the world. Your credibility is on the line.

E. The Importance of Atmosphere

1. Home Court Advantage

Once you have established your style and approach, the next thing I like to try to do, which will sound a little strange to some of you who have not done it before, is create an atmosphere that is suitable for your approach. I can give you a couple of variables on atmosphere. First, and most important to me, is what I call "home court advantage." I like to negotiate in my own office, behind my own desk, with my own notes, my own calculator, etc. These are the same reasons that teams like to play at home. I am more comfortable in my own office than anywhere else. If someone comes from San Diego to negotiate with me, and I am getting nowhere, I can say, "Thanks a million for coming why don't we hook up again in two weeks." If the guy has flown five hours to see me, perhaps taking the red-eye, he is going to have a lot more incentive to be reasonable. If I have to fly to San Diego to see him and I have to take the red-eye home, I am probably going to try to get more accomplished. Therefore, working on your home court is a big advantage.

2. Having the Client Present

Another critical issue is whether you have the client present in the negotiation. I have undergone a change in my own philosophy on this issue. Early in my career, I never had my clients directly participate in the negotiations, and I still do not have rookies present because they are not experienced in business and they tend to get more emotional over the ebb and flow of discussions. Today, I believe that a veteran player, particularly if he is bright, can dramatically change the range of options the team has and affect what the team can say about your player. I have brought most of my veteran clients into their negotiations over the past three years. Some of them are terrific. Buck Williams of the Portland Trail Blazers was absolutely fantastic. He was tough and he was firm, but he was very personal with the management of the team, and it was a really good partnership. Patrick Ewing was fantastic. He was in every single meeting we had with the New York Knicks last summer. After we lost his arbitration, I am certain there were many times that David Checketts had to bite his lip with things he would have liked to have said to me, but could not say because Ewing was sitting in the room. Whether you have the client present or not is certainly a strategic decision you have to make. In my opinion, I would counsel against having a young client present in the room. However, if you have a veteran who knows what is going on, and he has a good relationship with the owner, I think it could add a lot to the atmosphere.

3. Number of People Present

How many people do you put in the room? Do you bring in seven or eight accountants to the meeting so they can plug in their calculators? They may have a lot of "horsepower," but it is definitely going to affect the tenor of the meeting. It is also going to affect the very atmosphere you are negotiating in. If the team responds in kind and they bring in four or five of their accountants, you may have a United Nations conference. You then have to decide what shape table you want, whether to meet in a hotel room or in an arena, or at the United Nations. How many people are in the room affects how personal you get with the ultimate decision-maker.

I like to keep the number of people very small. However, I do like to negotiate in teams. I usually bring in a younger person from my office who can learn from the experience. The best way to learn to negotiate is to be involved. But the number of people clearly affects the dynamics of the negotiation. If you are not going one-on-one with the decision-maker, you will oftentimes get into a "good cop, bad cop" routine with the second person in command who will intercept every signal you are throwing out to the decision-maker. You will ask, "Gary, what do you think of this?" and the assistant will respond, "Let me answer that." Consequently, you never really develop the kind of personal rapport with the decision-maker that you want to have in order to make a break-through.

4. Oral or Written Offer?

Whether you make your offers orally or in writing has a big impact. When you put things in writing, they have tendency to become carved in stone. Once a person has a letter sitting in front him, it is very difficult to say, "I never said that" or "I did not mean that." He is reading your writing, and it has a tendency to really harden positions versus something you communicate orally, where you can say, "Yes, I said that, but I changed my mind."

5 Appearance

How do you dress? Depending on who you are meeting with, how you dress can have an impact. I took an individual with a beard who worked for me into negotiations about five years ago, and the first comment the owner made was, "I normally do not like guys with beards, but if he works for you, I guess he is okay." It never occurred to me before that having a beard or a moustache would impact what you are doing, but this particular owner reacted to my assistant's personal grooming habits. If you are a woman, how you dress can clearly have an impact in a male-dominated sports industry like football, basketball, or baseball.

6. Gridlock

A classic issue is: Do you walk out of a negotiation? I have been negotiating for eighteen years and I have only threatened to walk out of one meeting. This occurred when a general manager told me that his offer was absolutely non-negotiable. The general manager of my client's team told me that we were $500,000 a year apart, but we had to accept his offer. I asked, "Why is that? Isn't my input important enough, or how my client feels important?" He responded, "No, it really isn't important." I was a little stunned, and he continued, "We are the ones paying the money, so we are going to determine what's fair." I very calmly packed up my briefcase and started to leave. He asked, "Where are you going?" and I explained, "Obviously, neither my client nor I are very important to this process. You are going to determine what is fair and since we can not accept your offer, I guess it's time to leave." An hour later we made the deal at our numbers. I guess the whole thing was just for show, but I am not a big believer in histrionics in negotiations. I attempt to be very up front with the person I am dealing with because I expect to have more dealings with them. Many people find it effective to storm out of a meeting to show they are truly upset. That move certainly affects the atmosphere.

7. Scheduling the Meeting

How you schedule a meeting is a very important part of the negotiating process. The former president of the Minnesota Vikings, Mike Lynn, had a well known reputation for being very difficult to deal with. I represented one of his best players, All-Pro defensive end Chris Doleman. Lynn and I actually had a very good relationship. However, he told me that I was absolutely out of my mind when it came to salary numbers — that I was mistakenly giving him basketball numbers for football contracts. When I would travel to Minnesota to negotiate Doleman's contract, I would always have a flight planned to Los Angeles or San Francisco or somewhere else about two hours after my meeting was scheduled to start. I would walk in the room, and the first thing Lynn would say would be, "What did I offer you last time — $410,000? I can't believe I offered you that much. It's so high. And you did not accept it? I really should be at about $210,000." I would reply, "Mike, don't worry about it. We are never going to get the deal done today. Let's just go out and have breakfast. I've got a plane to Los Angeles in an hour and a half." Then, he would get serious when he realized that the meeting was finite and I was not going to be there for nine hours — which is what he actually did to me when Doleman was a rookie. Lynn put me up at Lake Minnetonka, gave me a lot of wine, a nice dinner, and we negotiated for about thirteen hours overnight. Fortunately, I have a lot of staying power. The point is that how you schedule and where you schedule are important. Do you schedule a meeting at the airport, so you can hop on a plane right away if the meeting is not working out? Or do you sit in a general manager's office with six or seven hours to kill? You have to know that some people like to string you out.

8. Managing the Media

Last, but certainly not least, is management of the media. The media is one of the most important tools and one of the most important booby-traps in negotiations. Generally, I do not like to use the media in negotiations. First, the public is not very sympathetic to your client when he complains, "Gee, $3.5 million is really unfair." With unemployment rising and a lot of people out of work, you are not going to get a lot of public sympathy by whining in the newspaper that the few million dollars your client is being offered is unfair. Second, in most team sports, the team controls the media's access to the players. If you get a writer who is too sympathetic to your position, the team will subtly tell him that his press pass is being restricted or the number of interviews he is scheduled to do is being limited, or they might not want to talk with him as much as they have in the past. You are not likely to win the media battle with the team and, therefore, it is a battle you should not engage in. I have always said that the press is like a derringer. You have one shot and you have to know when to shoot it. In 1992, in Charlotte, the Hornets held a daily press briefing on the Alonzo Mourning negotiation, even though the team promised me they would not discuss what was going on with the press. Every day I woke up, an article was faxed to me that I felt was inaccurate and distorted. We are all human, and we all have a tendency to want to respond and straighten it out. I tried to do this for about three weeks. However, a media black-out resulted, and we did not talk to the press. All it did was hype the negotiations, raise everybody's emotions and ultimately made the atmosphere more difficult to make a deal that both sides could live with. Getting drawn into this media battle with the team is really counter-productive and I regret doing it.

The use of the media is critical. A lot of people who have never seen their name in the newspaper love to wake up in the morning over coffee and say, "There I am on page three." There may be one line that says, "Joe Smith's a jerk; he's asking for six million dollars," but you are in there anyway and it is really fun to show to your girlfriend, your wife, or your kids. However, doing the play-by-play in the press is something you should try to avoid.

IV. First Offers: Getting Off the Ground

You have developed a strategy, created the atmosphere, you have your opponent coming to see you, and you have twenty five minutes to make the deal or you are going to leave the room. Who makes the first offer? It depends. Is that a good answer? It depends. I like to make the first offer because I believe you set the market most of the time if you make the first offer.

When we sat down with the New York Knicks in 1985, we knew they were going to offer us $1 million a year for Ewing, because that is what the number one picks had made in 1983 and 1984. I did not think that number remotely reflected the market for Ewing, so I made the first offer. In fact, I made it in writing. A lot of people will tell players they do not need an agent, and that they can get the deal by themselves. Players are told they simply need to get the offer and then hire someone to negotiate the deal on the excess. I think that is a disastrous suggestion because if the team makes the offer directly to the player and then you come in and dramatically change it, it is going to appear to the player that the team was really being unfair to him. Nobody wants to go to work for somebody who has been unfair. If you know what you are doing, if you have done your homework, if you are confident, it is important for you to set the market, as opposed to having the team come in first. They are not as likely to move on their own offer if they come in first as they are if you come in first. Sometimes, you can come in at the same time. You say to the team, "We're going to exchange offers. I don't want you to go to school on my offer, and I'm not going to go to school on your offer. Get to the fax machine; we'll both exchange offers at 3:00." In team sports, particularly football, there is a system you may have heard of called "slotting." Who makes the first offer in a sport like football sometimes is not that important, because all of the teams are going to wait and see what the player ahead of you got and what the player behind you got, in order to determine what is fair. I like to set the market in my negotiations. I think it has a psychological impact. If historically you have finalized contracts close to your opening offer, it sets a tone in your negotiations. Conversely, if your opening offer bears no relationship whatsoever to the final deal, I do not think it is that important who makes the first offer.

V. NARROWING THE ISSUES

A. Get Down to Business

Now, you have made the offer, you have the right atmosphere and you negotiate back and forth. As you try to close the deal, you need to narrow the issues. If you have seven or eight different issues on the table (I do not know too many people who can simultaneously "horse-trade" so many different issues), you have to narrow the negotiation down to two or three really key issues and trade-off dollars for length, guarantees for bonuses, cash for deferred, or whatever the issues are. You have to narrow the negotiation. Many of the issues really are not important; a number of them are red herrings. There are issues people will concede readily — they may have been thrown in to make you think that your opponent is making compromises. You need to ascertain the two or three most critical issues and deal points and go to them. Depending on how well you know the person you are dealing with, you might suggest to them, "We've been at this for three months. What is it going to take to close this deal? You've been asking X and I'm offering Y."

If your opponent respects you and you have dealt with him before, he is going to tell you, "You want to close the deal? I can't go five years, I can't go over three years. My owner won't let me do it. The Chancellor won't let me do it. My wife won't let me do it." If you have a good relationship, at some point you have to stop playing games; training camp is around the corner and you must get the player into camp. You have to get beyond the verbiage.

B. Identifying "Deal-Breakers"

You must identify what I call the deal-breakers. Certain points in the deal are probably non-negotiable. If I represent the number one pick in the country, I am not going to accept an option from the team. I do not care how much money they pay us; I do not want any options. That is a deal-breaker. I am not going to give any non-guaranteed years. That is a deal-breaker. We can talk for six months or six years; we are not going to give them a non-guaranteed year for this player. I think you need to identify that. Ultimately, you need to identify the paramount issue to each side. What is the single, most important issue that each side needs to get? If you boil the negotiating process down, each side needs to get certain basic points, one or two or three basic points to make the deal. And you have to figure out a way to get the opponent most of what he needs, while you get most of what you need. For example, I am in negotiation now and I do not want to lock up my client on a long-term deal. The team keeps reminding me, "I'm giving you all the security." I reply, "I don't want security. I'm very confident that my client is going to be a terrific player. I want to go short and you want to go long. You're not doing me a favor by putting all these additional dollars on the table, because I'm not interested in a long-term contract. You're not giving me what I need, so quit pushing it. If I wanted the security, I'd say, 'Thanks a million for the extra ten million dollars; I'll give you something.' But, that's not important to me here. The reason we haven't made the deal is because you haven't understood that what you're offering me isn't what I need to make the deal."

C. Be Flexible

You need to identify the single most important issue. Sometimes, it is what I call a magic number. If you want to get $1 million, $999,000 just does not have the same appeal. If your client is absolutely fixated on a number, whether you go above or below the magic level will have a huge impact on him. At times, the team is really hung up on how much total dollars they pay out. They may not be concerned about paying you $4 million a year for two years, but they simply are not going to pay you $4 million a year for eight years. You must figure out what the break-point is in each deal, and then you have to horse-trade.

Figure out how to give up some things that you want, but maybe you cannot get, for the things that you absolutely have to have to make the deal and go home. When you have done all these things, you must narrow the gap. That is the art of being creative.

D. Closing

Last, but not least, you have to take the most important step; you have to close the deal. You can talk and talk; you can have the greatest strategy; you can do all your research — know every salary in the League by heart for the last twenty years; but you have not closed the deal yet. There are no style points in negotiations. You have to close the deal. To do that, you have to set a tone for the close. You have been negotiating back and forth, plenty of offers and counter-offers. You have to somehow communicate to the other party that you are ready to make the deal now. Make your closing offer and clearly and unambiguously identify this offer as a closing offer. Suppose you are at $1 million, and your opponent is at $800,000 and you respond, "I'm going to break the million dollar barrier." You can close the deal for $950,000. The other party says, "Great, now if you just come down to $900,000, you have a deal." You wanted to close the deal at $950,000. However, you did not signal that $950,000 was your closing offer. When you are making the close, your opponent needs to know that you are not going to have anymore room to compromise the deal. Maybe you walk out, maybe you terminate the session, but you have to let your opponent know that you are at the close.

The cardinal rule of negotiations is that you must be prepared to say no. If you do not get what you want, whether it is one dollar less or a million dollars less, if you really believe you are below market and you have the leverage, you have to be prepared to say no. If you are lucky, and your opponent says, "Okay, I can accept the last compromise," then you say some magic words to signify that you have a deal, so that there is no confusion later. When I deal with someone I know well, whether I am on the phone or in person, I say, "Do we have a deal?" If the reply is, "Yes, we have a deal," I shake hands if I am in person, or I say on the telephone, "We have a deal," and I immediately send something in writing.

If you are in person, you could take a yellow pad of paper and jot some principal deal points down and sign it. You want to have something tangible that states you have a deal, so that a week later the other party does not say, "I thought it was a seven-year deal, not a five-year deal." Once you get away from the discussion, everyone is going to have a different recollection of the final deal. Therefore, if you are negotiating in person, find a way to reduce it to writing, even if you have to write on a napkin or a paper plate. Always have the person you are negotiating with signify you have a deal. At that point, I like to review the deal points and go through all the principal terms to make certain you are both on the same page. If you have a misunderstanding at the moment you are making the deal, you are certain to have a misunderstanding a week later. It is important to reduce the terms to writing, even if it is informal, and schedule an exchange of a more formal writing or final contract.

V. Conclusion

In summary, five points must be emphasized:

1) Do your homework. I have negotiated contracts for eighteen years. I have an almost photographic memory. However, when I get on an airplane to meet someone, I pull out the League salary numbers, review them, and write down my arguments. I do not think I *need* to do that, but it gives me a sense of confidence that I am really prepared. Know your opponent. Find out as much as you can about the person with whom you are negotiating. What is his style? What is his authority? How long has he been doing it? Is he easy or difficult to deal with?

2) Prepare your principal arguments in writing. What is the worth of your client? Write it down. Do not just wing it. I write down my offers. Sometimes, I write down counter-offers and even potential counter-offers, which are called "fall-backs." Can you go shorter? Can you take deferred money? Can you get bonuses? I try to have as much information as possible at my fingertips so that when I am in the room, I am really prepared. I am not thinking about the issues and how to approach the deal for the first time.

3) Be creative. In today's environment of big dollars, people will respect you for coming up with creative ways to make a deal. Ultimately, the process of making a deal — negotiating — is simply an exercise in creative problem- solving. You have certain things you have to get, your opponent has certain things he has to get and you are trying to creatively find a way to match up as many points on both sides of the table as you can.

4) Maintain your flexibility. Sometimes you put yourself in a corner by giving ultimatums or by being unnecessarily difficult. Never forget that never is a long, long time. People who say, "I'm never going to do this" or "I'm never going to do that," lose a lot of credibility the next time around if you persuade them to "just do it." My good friend, Angelo Drosses, often got to the point where he would say, "I will swear on my dead mother's grave that I'll never accept your offer." I would respond, "Angelo, please don't swear on your dead mother's grave. I get the message. You don't have to carve it in cement." Never say never.

Likewise, I think you need to allow your opponent to maintain his flexibility. As you get more rigid, threatening and difficult, the chances are that your opponent is either going to cave-in because he is weak, or he is also going to get rigid and difficult and make it a lot harder to close the deal. Allow your opponent to maintain his integrity. Perhaps this is the most difficult lesson to learn — something that only comes with maturity as a deal-maker. Sometimes, you know you can get a little more money, but the last concession, the last $10,000 a year, will so impair the relationship between the team and you and even your client that it is just not worth it. I recall Xavier McDaniel's negotiation with the Seattle SuperSonics. I was determined to get him $800,000 a year as a rookie. Toward the end of the negotiation, we got a big break and the team offered $750,000. I felt strongly we could get to our $800,000 goal, but in my judgment it would have been so embarrassing to the team that when they offered $762,000, we closed the deal. I knew we could have obtained the last $38,000, but McDaniel had to live in Seattle and if the coach thought that the team had been gouged, it really was not worth it. When I negotiated Danny Ferry's contract, I really wanted to get him $4 million. Ferry thought $4 million was simply too much. When we finally signed the deal, the owner was very complimentary to me at dinner about how reasonable we had been, even though we had all the leverage. Ferry replied, "If you think David was reasonable, you should have seen what he really wanted to ask for." I had to kick Ferry under the table.

5) Last, but not least, as they say at Holiday Inn, "The best surprise is no surprise." Do not try to wing it. Know what the market is and understand the collective bargaining agreement, the salary trends, the salary cap, or whatever the restrictions are. Do not be surprised. Do not make a deal and find out later that someone who really impacts your client has made a deal you did not know about it. *Semper paratis.* You must always be prepared. The stakes are far too large in today's economy, with players breaking the $2 million, $3 million, $5 million, $6 million, and $10 million a year barriers. The stakes are simply too high to be surprised. You are a professional and this is not a hobby. This is a big business. You have to be prepared.

* This article is primarily based upon the transcript of Mr. Falk's presentation at the Sports Dollars & Sense Conference, which was held on October 22, 23, and 24, 1992 in Milwaukee, Wisconsin. The staff of the *Marquette Sports Law Journal* is especially grateful to Mr. Don Watz, Editor, *For The Record Extra*, for transcribing Mr. Falk's presentation.

Notes

1. The NFL and its players reached a settlement agreement on January 6, 1993. The settlement agreement will be replaced by a collective bargaining agreement when the NFLPA resumes as a union. Bob Oates, *Analysis; Players' Victory Not Easy*, L.A. TIMES, Jan. 8, 1993, at C1.
2. Gary Bettman was appointed National Hockey League Commissioner on December 11, 1992.

PART IV

AMATEUR
AND
COLLEGIATE
SPORTS

A Comprehensive Blueprint for the Reform of Intercollegiate Athletics*

Raymond L. Yasser

For all its successes, the National Collegiate Athletic Association is always subject to a variety of criticisms. Given the contradictory nature of its mission—to preserve amateurism in athletics and to make as much money as possible for its member schools—this is probably not surprising. While the NCAA has many critics, the critics are infrequently on the same page and much of the criticism levelled against big-time college sports is reactive and piecemeal.

This essay by Ray Yasser is one of the most thoughtful and measured critiques ever advanced. Yasser begins with an overview of the NCAA and its operations and then makes the case that the existing intercollegiate sports structure is very seriously flawed.

I. Introduction

Recent world events, like the tearing down of the Berlin Wall and the rapid disintegration of the "Evil Empire," provide solace and hope to architects of social change. While the problems connected with what was previously regarded as the Communist bloc are no doubt on a wholly different plane than those connected to "big-time" intercollegiate athletics in this country, the similarity resides with the solution. A point is reached when an existing system is so seriously flawed that a consensus begins to emerge among thoughtful people that something like "perestroika" is necessary. It is

*From Volume 3, Number 2, Sprint 1993, pp. 123-159.

my contention that "big-time" intercollegiate athletics in this country is at that point. What I will attempt to do in the pages that follow is to offer a working draft of a blueprint for this restructuring.

Any blueprint for reform of an extant system must of course take full account of the existing structure. This is a blueprint for restructuring, not a call for demolition. The format for discussion, then, is to look at the structure, piece by piece, and to describe it "fairly." The next step is to suggest how each piece of the structure can be changed into something stronger and more beautiful. I begin with a descriptive overview of the National Collegiate Athletic Association (hereinafter, the NCAA). In order to understand intercollegiate sports in this country, it is essential to appreciate how the NCAA is structured and how it works. While it is true that other organizations also govern intercollegiate sports, the NCAA is the dominant governing body as far as "big time" intercollegiate sports is concerned. This descriptive overview is followed by somewhat more critical and normative observations about the various components of the intercollegiate sports scene. In this more critical vein, I start at the portal by discussing the recruitment and admission of "student-athletes" who receive "athletic scholarships." The campus life of athletes once they are enrolled is examined — from where they live to how they spend their day to what happens when they leave the university. The role of coaches, faculty, boosters, and university presidents is of course a big part of the picture. Each group is looked at in turn. In the course of the discussion, I will attempt to articulate what the reality is and what the problems are and to offer what I consider to be radical but sensible solutions. I say "radical" because oftentimes the solutions I will propose are not within the established contours of the current debate — a debate which has come to be dominated by specially interested, well-entrenched and powerful proponents. However, I do believe that many of the solutions I propose reflect the views of a growing body of sports-intellectuals (no, the term is not oxymoronic) who care deeply about sports and wish for it to occupy a more appropriate role in the life of the university. The solutions offered are, I believe, "sensible."

The world's political restructuring has made it clear to all that it is no longer simply naive, pie-in-the-sky utopianism to suggest that existing systems can be rapidly transformed into something starkly different and hopefully better. So, I do believe that a workable blueprint can be developed for an intercollegiate sports system in this country which mirrors our best values, not our worst traits. This paper, however, is designed as a starting point. The blueprint itself will no doubt be revised over and over again before the building is completed. I consider this a "working draft"; I welcome input from all those putative sports architects out there.

A few final observations are in order before the blueprint is presented. The "fair" description of the reality of the current sports structure referred to earlier is, of course, my own. Undoubtedly, the reader will find some aspect of it "unfair." I invite and welcome scrutiny of my descriptions. For what it's worth, my own descriptions are based on the observations of a 42 year old white male law professor who lives in what is reputed to be the most typical American city (Tulsa) and who has spent a lifetime deeply immersed in sports— playing, watching, reading about, writing about and just pondering. I regard it as a "fairly" healthy obsession. (Others who know me well would quarrel with the categorization "healthy.") In any event, I acknowledge that my own view of the existing reality is skewed by my experience, and so my recommendations for restructuring are also subjective.

I should also note that I have struggled to make this piece readable for lawyers and non-lawyers alike. I say "struggled" because "readability" appears not to have a high value in traditional legal writing. I have, for example, written a footnote-free manuscript. I have always believed that footnotes separate from the text are an evil to be avoided. I must admit I have never understood why lawyers are so committed to their use. An extensive "additional notes and sources" section appears in the Appendix, in lieu of footnotes. When helpful, citations, quotes, and references to other works are included in the text. Afterthoughts which are often the grist of extended footnotes are either woven into the text, included in the additional notes and sources section, or omitted entirely because of their inherent unworthiness in the final analysis.

II. THE NCAA—AN OVERVIEW

CONSTITUTION OF THE
NATIONAL COLLEGIATE ATHLETIC ASSOCIATION
ARTICLE TWO, SECTION 2.

Fundamental Policy (a) The competitive athletic programs of the colleges are designed to be a critical part of the educational system. A basic purpose of this Association is to maintain intercollegiate athletics as an integral part of the educational program and the athlete as an integral part of the student body, and, by so doing, retain a clear line of demarcation between college athletics and professional sports.

The NCAA is an unincorporated, voluntary association, made up of some one thousand member schools, both public and private. Public universities constitute approximately 55 percent of the membership. All member schools and member conferences are required to pay dues, the amounts varying depending upon the division in which membership is held. The association is divided essentially into three divisions: Division I, Division II, and Division III. Within one sport, football, Division I is itself divided into Division I-A and Division I-AA. The organization has a permanent professional staff, with individual departments for administration, business, championships, communications, compliance services, enforcement, legislative services, and publishing. The Association is headquartered in Overland Park, Kansas, a suburb of Kansas City.

The membership governs the organization and holds annual conventions to accomplish this. In the interim periods, the NCAA operates through the Council, the Executive Committee, and the President's Commission. The authority and make-up of these bodies is noted below, along with a discussion of selected aspects of the NCAA Constitutions and By-laws. The NCAA regulates athletic competition among its member schools, sets rules for eligibility to participate, establishes restrictions and guidelines for recruitment of prospective student athletes, conducts several dozen championship events in the various sports sanctioned by the Association, and enters into television and promotional contracts relating to these championship events.

The NCAA openly states that one of its primary purposes is to promote the concept of amateurism. Related to this is the idea that athletics are an integral part of the educational experience at the intercollegiate level. The NCAA, of course, is big business. It administers a multi-million dollar budget, which includes among other things a huge television contract for collegiate basketball and smaller contracts for other sports. In short, the Association is the governing body and, to a great extent, the business agent for intercollegiate sports.

In order to understand the more difficult issues faced by the NCAA and its individual member schools it is necessary to have an understanding of the critical portions of the NCAA Constitution and Bylaws. The following is a summary of these sections.

A basic purpose of the Association is to ensure that intercollegiate athletics are maintained as "an integral part of the educational program and that the athlete [is] an integral part of the student body." (NCAA Constitution, Section 1.3.1.) Theoretically, this would promote a clear delineation between amateur sports and professional sports. Another linchpin of the Association is the concept of institutional control of intercollegiate athletics. (NCAA Constitution, Section 2.1.) The chief executive officer of the institution is ultimately responsible for the program at a given member school. The athletes who make up the program at a school are to be amateurs. Amateur is defined as one whose participation is "motivated primarily by education and by the physical, mental and social benefits to be derived." (NCAA Constitution, Section 2.6.)

As noted above, three separate bodies are actively involved in operating the Association. The Council consists of 46 members, including 22 from Division I schools and 11 each from Division II and III schools. The president and secretary-treasurer are ex officio members. At least 12 of the members must be women and at least 6 must be chief executive officers of institutions. (NCAA Constitution, Section 4.1.) The Council has the authority to:

(a) Establish and direct the general policy of the Association in the interim between Conventions;

(b) Appoint such committees as may be necessary for executing the provisions of this constitution or the bylaws;

(c) Report its proceedings to the general business session of the annual Convention;

(d) Make interpretations of the constitution and bylaws in the interim between Conventions;

(e) Review and approve policies and procedures governing the administration of the enforcement program in the interim between Conventions;

(f) Adopt administrative regulations for the efficient implementation of the Association's general legislative policies; and

(g) Fill vacancies that occur among the officers of the Association or on the Council, the Executive Committee or other committees of the Association. The Council shall fill such vacancies by majority vote and only for the unexpired term, except that a person so elected to the Council shall serve until the next annual Convention. (NCAA Constitution, Section 4.1.3.)

The Executive Committee consists of 14 members, including at least three women and the president and secretary-treasurer. The Executive Committee has the authority to:

(a)   Transact the business and administer the affairs of the Association in accordance with the policies of the Association and the Council;

(b)   Employ an executive director, with the approval of the Council and the President's Commission, who shall be administratively responsible to the Executive Committee and who shall be authorized to employ such other persons as may be necessary to conduct efficiently the business of the Association;

(c)   Require all income from membership dues, from activities of the Association and from other sources (except as may be provided in the constitution and bylaws) to be deposited in the general fund;

(d)   Adopt a budget for the ensuing fiscal year prior to the end of any current fiscal year;

(e)   Adopt regulations providing for the expenditure of Association funds, administration of NCAA championships and distribution of the income of the Association;

(f)   Arrange for the bonding of the officers and employees of the Association charged with the handling of funds;

(g)   Provide for the various accounts and arrange for the auditing of them;

(h)   Report its proceedings to the Council and to the business session of the annual Convention;

(i)   Prescribe, through the executive regulations and general policies, requirements, standards and conditions governing the conduct of all NCAA championships; and

(j)   Adopt executive regulations not inconsistent with the provisions of the constitution or other bylaws. Criteria for the establishment and continuation of NCAA championships may be revised only at an annual Convention according to procedures specified in Bylaw 18.

The President's Commission consists of 44 members, 22 from Division I schools and 11 each from Division II and III schools. At least three women are to be members of the President's Commission. The group is empowered to:

(a)   Review any activity of the Association;

(b)   Place any matter of concern on the agenda for any meeting of the Council or for any NCAA Convention;

(c) Commission studies of intercollegiate athletics issues and urge certain courses of action;

(d) Propose legislation directly to any Convention;

(e) Establish the final sequence of legislative proposals in any Convention agenda, within the provisions of 5.1.4.3.1;

(f) Call for a special meeting of the Association under the provisions of 5.1.1.2;

(g) Designate, prior to the printing of the notice of any Convention, specific proposals for which a roll-call vote of the eligible voters will be mandatory; and

(h) Approve the appointment of an executive director of the Association. (NCAA Constitution, Section 4.5.3.)

The NCAA also has an extensive enforcement arm. The Association has a full time enforcement staff which handles investigations. Matters which proceed to a hearing come before the Committee on Infractions. Any cases which are appealed by an institution under scrutiny go to the NCAA Council for this final stage of the enforcement process.

An investigation may begin either as a result of information being given to the enforcement staff by some outside source or on the initiation of the enforcement staff itself. All investigations are treated as confidential until announcements are made according to prescribed procedures. (NCAA Administrative Bylaw, Section 32.1, 32.2.) The first step in the process is the forwarding of a preliminary inquiry letter to the institution. If, following further investigation, the enforcement staff finds a violation and it appears to be a major infraction, an official inquiry is sent to the chief executive officer of the institution. (NCAA Administrative Bylaw, Section 32.5.) This letter fully informs the school of the allegations against it and requests full cooperation from the school. The institution will then conduct its own investigation in order to provide a written response to the charges and to prepare for any hearing which might be held before the Committee on Infractions. If a hearing is conducted, the institution will be allowed to present its case and the enforcement staff will represent the Association. In addition to the institution itself, anyone who could be penalized will also be allowed to appear. The Committee then reaches a decision, makes findings, and proposes penalties. The potential penalties range from limitations on recruiting visits to bans on television appearances to suspension of an entire program. (NCAA Bylaw, Section 19.4.) If the institution is not content with the decision of the Committee on Infractions it may appeal to the NCAA Council. (NCAA Administrative Bylaw, Section 32.8.)

The NCAA governs athletics at its member institutions through regulations affecting the coaches, athletes, and representatives (boosters) of the schools. For example, all contracts between a coach and a school must include a stipulation that a coach found in violation of NCAA rules will be subject to disciplinary action, including termination of the contract. (NCAA Bylaw, Section 11.2.2.) Coaches are also required to report income or benefits from sources outside the institution, including that from annuities, camps, housing arrangements, club memberships, complimentary tickets, television and radio programs, and endorsement or consultation contracts with shoe, apparel, or equipment manufacturers. (NCAA Bylaw, Section 11.2.2.)

The primary focal points of the regulations regarding athletes are aspects of amateurism, education status and progress. As noted, only an amateur student-athlete is eligible for participation in a particular sport. (NCAA Bylaw, Section 12.01.1.) An athlete may be a professional in one sport and still retain eligibility in other sports, however. An athlete will be deemed a professional, and thus lose his or her eligibility if the individual:

(a) Uses his or her athletics skill (directly or indirectly) for pay in any form in that sport;
(b) Accepts a promise of pay even if such pay is to be received following completion of intercollegiate athletics participation;
(c) Signs a contract or commitment of any kind to play professional athletics, regardless of its legal enforceability or any consideration received;
(d) Receives, directly or indirectly, a salary, reimbursement of expenses or any other form of financial assistance from a professional sports organization based upon athletic skill or participation, except as permitted by NCAA rules and regulations;
(e) Competes on any professional athletic team and knows (or has reason to know) that the team is a professional athletic team, even if no pay or remuneration for expenses was received; or
(f) Enters into a professional draft or an agreement with an agent or other entity to negotiate a professional contract. (NCAA Bylaw, Section 12.1.1.)

The NCAA defines "pay" to include the following:

(a) Educational expenses not permitted by the governing legislation of this Association;

(b) Any direct or indirect salary, gratuity or comparable compensation;

(c) Any division or split of surplus (bonuses, game receipts, etc.);

(d) Excessive or improper expenses, awards and benefits;

(e) Expenses received from an outside amateur sports team or organization in excess of actual and necessary travel, room and board expenses for practice and game competition;

(f) Actual and necessary expenses or any other form of compensation to participate in athletic competition (while not representing an educational institution) from a sponsor other than an individual upon whom the athlete is naturally or legally dependent or the nonprofessional organization that is sponsoring the competition;

(g) Payment to individual team members or individual competitors for unspecified or unitemized expenses beyond actual and necessary travel, room and board expenses for practice and competition;

(h) Expenses incurred or awards received by an individual that are prohibited by the rules governing an amateur, noncollegiate event in which the individual participates;

(i) Any payment, including actual and necessary expenses, conditioned on the individual's or team's place, finish or performance or given on an incentive basis, or receipt of expenses in excess of the same reasonable amount for permissible expenses given to all individuals or team members involved in the competition;

(j) Education expenses provided to an individual by an outside sports team or organization that are based in any degree upon the recipient's athletic ability, even if the funds are given to the institution to administer to the recipient;

(k) Cash, or the equivalent thereof (e.g., trust fund), as an award for participation in competition at any time, even if such an award is permitted under the rules governing an amateur, noncollegiate event in which the individual is participating. An award or a cash prize that an individual could not receive under NCAA legislation may not be forwarded in the individual's name to a different individual or agency.

(l) Preferential treatment, benefits or services (e.g., loans with deferred pay-back) because of the individual's athletic reputation or skill or pay-back potential as a professional athlete, unless such treatment, benefits or services are specifically permitted under NCAA legislation;

(m) Receipt of a prize for participation (involving the utilization of athletic ability) in a member institution's promotional activity that is inconsistent with the provisions of 12.5 or official interpretations approved by the NCAA Council. (NCAA Bylaw, Section 12.1.2.)

An individual becomes a professional in a sport if he or she signs a professional contract, regardless of its enforceability. Participation on a professional sports team makes an athlete a professional. (NCAA Bylaw, Section 12.1.3.) As noted, an athlete may be a professional in one sport and retain eligibility in other NCAA sports. That individual, however, may not accept institutional financial aid while involved in professional sports or receiving remuneration from a professional sports organization. (NCAA Bylaw, Section 12.1.4.) An athlete becomes ineligible if he asks to have his name placed on a draft list for a professional sport prior to the actual draft, regardless of whether the athlete is drafted, or ultimately reaches a contractual agreement. (NCAA Bylaw, Section 12.2.4.1.) This rule would have no relevance to baseball since baseball conducts its draft in a manner which does not require affirmative actions in order for underclass athletes to be included in the draft. The athlete will also lose eligibility if the athlete reaches any kind of an agreement with an agent for representation, either written or verbal, regardless of whether that agreement is for present or future services. (NCAA Bylaw, Section 12.3.1.) An athlete may, however, secure advice from an attorney concerning a proposed contract, so long as the attorney does not become involved in negotiating the contract.

The NCAA has also been concerned about athletes becoming involved in promotional activities which benefit them solely because of their athletic abilities. Perhaps the most absurd example of previously stringent policies occurred when University of Indiana basketball player Steve Alford was suspended for one game because he appeared on a sorority calendar, the proceeds from which went to charity. This rule has been relaxed somewhat. Athletes may now appear or have their picture used for charitable or educational purposes if written permission is secured, no class time is missed, and there is not co-sponsorship by a commercial entity. (NCAA Bylaw, Section 12.5.)

The Association regulations also govern the educational status and progress of student-athletes. This area has recently been extremely controversial as related to eligibility for entering freshmen athletes. An athlete at an NCAA member institution generally has four years of eligibility for competition. The four years must be completed within five years of the time the athlete first registers for a minimum full time program of studies in a collegiate institution. (NCAA Bylaw, Section 14.2.) "To be eligible to represent an institution in intercollegiate athletics competition, a student-athlete shall be enrolled in at least a minimum full-time program of studies, be in good academic standing and maintain satisfactory progress toward a baccalaureate degree." (NCAA Bylaw, section 14.01.1.)

The most controversial aspect of the NCAA academic eligibility rules is that dealing with freshman eligibility. In 1983, the NCAA enacted legislation which became effective in 1986 and was intended to regulate eligibility of incoming freshmen athletes. As modified, an entering freshman, in order to be eligible for competition, must be a high school graduate and have a minimum cumulative grade point average of 2.000 based on a maximum of 4.000 in a core curriculum specified by the rule. (NCAA Bylaw, Section 14.3.1.1.) The athlete must also have scored either a minimum score of 700 on the SAT or a minimum score of 15 on the ACT. Any freshman not meeting these criteria is ineligible for financial aid, practice, and competition during the first academic year in residence. This rule has been controversial due to its alleged adverse racial impact. Statistics show that most of the athletes affected by the rule are black.

III. Athletes at the Portal of the University

A. Recruiting and Compensation of Athletes

> I think it would be a wonderful thing if a coach would just forget all about the high school and prep school wonders of the world and develop a team from among the students of his institution who came to his school because they liked it best and not because of any attractive offers made for athletic ability.
>
> Knute Rockne, Notre Dame Football Coach,
> bemoaning recruiting in 1929.

> If you're going to the Final Four, you have to recruit athletes, not Christians.
>
> Luke Kelley, former Oral Roberts University
> Basketball Coach, on contemporary recruiting.

In the current recruiting milieu, colleges and universities participating in "big-time" intercollegiate athletics spend considerable resources ferreting out athletic talent and luring the talented to their respective campuses. Well-paid head coaches designate full-time assistants to have special responsibilities for recruitment. This search-and-bring-back mission takes place in the context of "amateurism." While the recruiters are paid professionals, the recruited are expected to maintain the facade of amateurism. A complex web of NCAA rules makes it illegal for the recruits to receive any "illegal" benefits — low, or no-interest loans for cars, money for travel, cash for game tickets, and favors from boosters are all forbidden by NCAA rules. The receipt by a recruit of any excessive or improper expenses, benefits, or awards jeopardizes both the athletic eligibility of the recruit, and the status of the athletic program in the eyes of the NCAA.

From the perspective of most coaches, academic and athletic administrators, and boosters and fans, the recruiting arrangement is viewed as a competition among schools for the best talent. Occasionally, a coach decries the recruiting violations of competitors. Digger Phelps, former basketball coach at Notre Dame, once had the temerity to suggest that many universities maintained slush funds to channel illegal money to athletes. The news media regularly reports about suspected abuses. The NCAA tries to enforce the rules by investigating reports of illegal recruiting and punishing transgressors. One of the more common reasons for an institution to be sanctioned in some way is for providing improper benefits to players. Every once in a while, an outspoken coach (one usually noted for being a "players' coach") points out that it would make sense to allow athletes to receive some additional benefits, like a small allowance — something along the lines of the "laundry money" that at one time was allowed. Even some NCAA cognoscenti have indicated that they are not entirely averse to this idea. But the overriding sentiment among coaches, academic and athletic administrators, and boosters and fans, is that the overall scheme of benefit limitations is basically fair. It needs to be enforced more evenhandedly, perhaps, and maybe athletes ought to get a little more. However, very few people from these groups seriously question the efficacy of limiting the benefits of athletes to the athletic scholarship — tuition, fees, books, room and board — and maybe, sometime down the road, a little allowance, a modicum of travel and expense money.

The perspective of those upon whom the restraints operate, however, is startlingly different. Professor Allen Sack (a Professor of Sociology at the University of New Haven and a former defensive end on Notre Dame's 1966 National Championship team) has extensively surveyed college basketball players concerning their attitudes towards "illegal benefits." Sack has found that many athletes believe it is unfair to so severely limit their benefits. In short, many athletes do not accept the legitimacy of the NCAA rules. In particular, athletes from lower socio-economic backgrounds are more likely to see nothing wrong with accepting money "under the table." Unsurprisingly, black athletes — who are disproportionately poor — are the most likely to view "amateurism" as exploitative. A substantial majority of the black basketball players playing at the most competitive level (NCAA Division I) see nothing wrong with accepting money and other benefits under the table, and believe that they deserve a share of the television revenue generated by the sport. Additionally, many college athletes (and it appears that most black college athletes) believe that they should receive other benefits like workers' compensation and disability insurance. The dominant self-perception is that they are university employees — compensated to play their sport. In short, the athletes' point of view contrasts sharply with the perspective of most coaches, administrators, and fans. Many athletes simply find it difficult to accept that so many others are making so much money watching them perform and they are not able to afford bus fare home. The prevailing view among athletes is that the myth of amateurism is an ideology which functions to suppress their ability to support themselves.

One way of dealing with the so-called corruption in intercollegiate sports is to recognize that what the NCAA has defined as corruption (excessive benefits to athletes) is really not corruption at all. Efforts to prevent athletes from receiving additional benefits are doomed to fail because such artificial constraints are viewed by those upon whom they are imposed as inherently unfair. Moreover, the restraints are imposed by an organization (the NCAA) in which the athlete has no representative voice. The disempowered athlete therefore feels little compunction about violating rules imposed by an organization which does not represent the athlete's real interests. As a result, these kinds of rule violations are as American as apple pie. (Remember, Jim Thorpe was stripped of his Olympic medal for having received benefits inconsistent with his amateur status). It would make sense to redefine corruption so as to simply legalize additional benefits in fairness to athletes.

The starting point is to provide expense money for athletes above, rather than under, the table. A percentage of the television revenue generated by big-time intercollegiate sports ought to be earmarked as a special fund for the benefit of athletes. This fund could be used to provide this additional stipend. Moreover, this fund should be used to provide additional scholarship assistance to athletes who have completed their athletic eligibility but who have not completed their education. In fact, the NCAA already administers such a fund for athletes who return to school. This fund should be vastly expanded to guarantee additional support for athletes. (NCAA member schools might also consider joining an already existing consortium administered by the Center for the Study of Sport in Society at Northeastern University which allows athletes without degrees to further their education at member schools).

More fundamentally, serious consideration should be given to allowing and even encouraging supporters and boosters to provide assistance to athletes. Why is it that in the context of intercollegiate sports, willing donors are precluded from providing financial and other assistance to needy recipients? The tradition of both free market forces and patronage, which exist to support budding artists, musicians and writers, is a noble one. Why is it that in the sports setting that free market forces and patronage are viewed as corrupt? There is, I think, no adequate justification for making it illegal for athletes to receive assistance benefits well beyond those currently permitted by the NCAA. If we truly believe in free and open markets, athletes should not be forbidden from participating in them. Patrons of athletes should be encouraged to provide additional benefits to athletes in much the same way as patrons of the arts are encouraged to support and nurture artists. There is nothing inherently wrong or corrupt about a sports booster providing an athlete with a summer job or with cash for tickets. In fact, I believe that no other group in our society, engaged in otherwise legal and socially desirable activities, is singled-out to be excluded from participation in what is supposed to be a free and open economy. (Imagine Princeton declaring Brooke Shields ineligible to participate in the school play because of her earlier acceptance of improper benefits). Simply put, there is nothing "corrupt" about athletes sharing in the fruits of the marketplace.

B. Admissions

> I never graduated from Iowa. I was only there for two terms—
> Truman's and Eisenhower's.
>> Alex Karras, Detroit Lions defensive linesman.

Under the prevailing system, recruited "student-athletes" ordinarily do not gain admission to the university through anything remotely resembling the regular admission process. Although details may vary from one institution to the next and some schools may take extra care to make the decision to admit look like it has been accomplished through regular channels, the reality is that the highly sought-after athlete is usually admitted de facto by the university athletic interests. "Student-athletes" are admitted with credentials that would not get a non-athlete in the door. Occasionally, scuffles break out between the athletic powers-that-be and the regular admissions personnel of the university, but perhaps the most revealing thing about these scuffles is that both sides seem to agree that athletes may be "specially admitted." The argument, then, becomes a kind of admissions limbo dance about just how low the admissions people are willing to go. Even the most persnickety of the admissions officers has apparently caved-in on the most significant presumption that recruited student-athletes do not have to meet the same academic requirements of other regularly admitted students. And, in what must at best be regarded as a remarkable and perverse irony, the NCAA has regularly entered the picture, articulating eligibility floors in the guise of "academic standards."

The entry of the NCAA upon the college admission scene is not new. Over 20 years ago, the NCAA adopted a "1.6 predictor" rule which limited admission to student athletes who were regarded as statistically likely to achieve at least a 1.6 g.p.a. in their freshman year of college. More recently, the NCAA adopted Proposition 48, which in one of its formulations required incoming athletes to have maintained a 2.0 g.p.a. in 11 college preparatory classes and a minimum of 700 combined SAT or 18 ACT score to be eligible to play sports as a freshman. (The NCAA regularly fiddles with the requirements, more recently adopting a sliding scale approach.) The significance of these plans is not in the details. It is in the fact that individual schools have allowed the NCAA to meddle in the process. These "stringent academic standards" in reality represent the floor beneath which no school is to be permitted to sink. These standards do have the practical effect of cutting down on the admission of many students who are not prepared to do college level work. But the mere articulation of the standard bespeaks the problem. Individual schools are in essence saying, "stop me before I admit again." Indeed, it should be pointed out that some schools even admit "non-qualifiers," and attempt to make them eligible for sports by their second year by nursing them through a specially prepared year of course work.

One by-product of this "special admit" system is the creation of what might be called a "sub-college-level-curriculum." In order to accommodate the special needs of the specially admitted, special

offerings have flourished. Many student-athletes have found it possible to remain athletically eligible while making little or no real
progress towards a degree. Horror stories are legion. Athletes are able
to work the system to remain eligible while making no real progress
towards a degree by taking courses which do not lead to a degree. The
existence of this substandard curriculum functions to compromise the
academic integrity of the institution that offers it. Unsurprisingly,
though, there is little organized opposition to it. Real students make
an occasional foray into it to relieve the rigors and tedium connected
with real college courses, and many of the athletes enrolled in these
courses are focused more on eligibility than on graduation.

The answer to these problems is surprisingly simple. The
all-important admission decision should be turned over to the admissions office of the school, where it belongs. Being an athlete should
count about as much as being an outstanding pianist or an accomplished artist. It should be a factor to be considered in the admissions
calculus. It should not be outcome-determinative. Individual schools
have to muster the courage to dismantle substandard curriculum. No
student should be admitted who does not have a legitimate chance to
attain a meaningful education. And no student properly admitted
should be permitted to take anything less than a college-level curriculum. The answer to the problem of the academically unqualified
athlete is for individual institutions to take control of their admissions
process to ensure that only academically qualified college students are
admitted. This is not unrealistic reform. It only requires that colleges
and universities act with integrity in the process of admitting students.
The NCAA could pass a rule which, rather than mandating uniform
academic "standards," mandates institutional control of the admission process--no school shall admit any student who does not have a
reasonable chance of attaining a degree in a reasonable amount of
time.

C. Athletic Scholarships

> Shelby Metcalf, basketball coach at Texas A&M, giving advice to
> a player who received four F's and one D: "Son, looks to me like
> you're spending too much time on one subject."

In the world of big-time intercollegiate sports, the highly recruited
athlete receives an athletic scholarship. To be sure, in the vast majority
of cases the award has nothing whatsoever to do with "scholarship,"

and everything to do with athletic ability. (Indeed, the term "athletic scholarship" is an oxymoron.) Many recipients of athletic scholarships are marginal students at the university they attend. The receipt of free tuition, fees, room and board, and books, is an award for athletic prowess, given with the understanding that the recipient will make a good faith effort to "play ball." The modern scholarship is a one year deal, renewable at the discretion of the university. Athletes who are able to compete on the playing field and remain eligible by staying above the school's academic floor typically will have their scholarship renewed for an additional year. Real progress toward a degree is not ordinarily a condition precedent to the renewal of the award.

The NCAA dictates to individual member schools the maximum number of athletic scholarships which are permitted for each sport in the various divisions. Year to year the numbers vary as the partisan interests of particular divisions and sports jostle for position at the annual convention. For example, the 1992 NCAA convention revised the limit on the number of awards permitted in a variety of Division I sports. Baseball, which had been limited to 13 awards, was dropped to 11.7. Soccer dropped from 11 to 9.9, while tennis went from 5 to 4.5. This was a cost-cutting convention. For the most part, schools may carve up the awards to provide assistance to a greater number of people. For example, a school limited by the NCAA to 6 scholarships might be able to provide 12 half scholarships to what the NCAA calls "counters." In the lexicon of the NCAA, a "counter" is one who receives a full or partial athletic scholarship. Thus, the NCAA limits both the number of awards and the number of recipients. The number of "counters," like the number of awards, is a regular subject of controversy.

The most lively and recent source of controversy has to do with the limits on football scholarships. Alarmed by recent cost reduction moves, coaches are lobbying to have the overall grant limit set at 90 grants-in-aid. The current rule will reduce the overall total to 85 beginning in the Fall of 1994. The concern of coaches is apparently that they can not administer effective programs with only 85 scholarships. The lament of coaches in other sports is similar; coaches invariably lobby for more scholarships. And the NCAA steps in to resolve it all, setting the limits.

As with the academic standards, perhaps the most startling fact about this is that individual schools have even felt the need for the

NCAA to limit them in this way. It's as though the schools are saying, "stop me before I give still another athletic scholarship to a marginally qualified athlete." Again, the answer, I think, is institutional autonomy and control with a national mandate for what I call "athletic scholarship disarmament." I would start with a proposal for a national across-the-board cut of 50% in the number of athletic scholarships available for men. This disarmament mandate must be accompanied by a commitment from each university to allocate the 50% saved to academic scholarships for disadvantaged, academically motivated applicants. What this means is that we would have a cost-free reallocation of scholarship resources. The new recipients of the old "athletic scholarships" would simply be composed of students rather than athletes. The lament of the coaches notwithstanding, the scholarship limits (which in reality operate as the actual number awarded, particularly in football and basketball) are unconscionably high. Consider the salubrious effects of athletic scholarship disarmament.

1. The Message to the Community

This type of cut will send an important message to the national community about the proper role of athletics in the life of a university. It will also send an important message to people in disadvantaged communities. The prevalent message in disadvantaged communities today is that athletic prowess provides the most readily available ticket to the university. Athletic achievement is more highly valued than academic achievement. Universities must take responsibility for communicating this flawed message. They must also take responsible action to communicate a new and more sensible message. The most readily available ticket to the university must be provided to those people in the community who have shown a commitment to academic excellence. Clearly, scholarship reallocation in the form of athletic scholarship disarmament sends the most sensible message.

2. The Effect on Competition and Marketability

Powerful athletic interests will, of course, blanch at the mere mention of such a proposal. But athletic scholarship disarmament does not mean the destruction of highly competitive and marketable intercollegiate athletics. In fact, such a move will, I believe, reinvigorate intercollegiate competition, because more schools will be able to compete at the highest levels. Athletic talent will be spread about more broadly. Traditional collegiate powerhouses will not be able to "warehouse" athletic talent. New fans, many of whom are now turned off by the hypocrisy of intercollegiate athletics, will be drawn to the more pure intercollegiate system. Old fans are unlikely to turn away from intercollegiate sports just because more of the athletes are now really students, too.

The powerful and well-entrenched athletic interests will claim that this kind of "radical" step will destroy intercollegiate competition. But think about this claim. Why is it that Oklahoma, for example, cannot field a highly competitive football team with "just" 45 athletic scholarships? Or that Duke could not field a highly competitive basketball team with "just" 6 athletic scholarships? Remember too that the disarmament is across-the-board. It is possible that the overall performance level would drop, but isn't it clear that the drop, if there is one, would be imperceptible to the fan? Moreover, the fan would see fewer "entrenched" sports powers and more broad-based competition for national prominence. The better argument is that this "radical" step—what I have called athletic scholarship disarmament—will prevent big-time intercollegiate sports from destroying itself.

3. The Effect on Campus Diversity

a. Blacks

> People see me and immediately assume I'm on the track team,. . . [T]hey ask, 'What sport do you play?' My response is, 'I'm on the art team'.
>
> Ziddi Msangi, a black fine arts major
> at Boise State University.

It is extremely important that this disarmament not be viewed by the black community as an attempt to "whiten" intercollegiate sports. Rather, it must be both implemented and viewed as a profound national commitment to increase the number of black lawyers, doctors, engineers, and other professionals. This, after all, is what the disarmament program is all about. That is why the disarmament plan must be accompanied by detailed and verifiable plans to allocate those scholarship resources that are no longer going to be spent on athletic scholarships to academic scholarships for disadvantaged minority applicants. If this is done honestly, the number of black and minority students on each campus will be increased because scholarships previously given to white athletes will now go to academically promising disadvantaged students. In fact, the disarmament plan should serve to increase the number of black and minority students on the campus.

While the number of black students on campus will increase as a result of the disarmament plan, another very important change will be taking place. Where before disarmament a disproportionate number of black students were athletes, disarmament will significantly reduce this disproportion. It will also decrease the perceptions which lead to the damaging stereotypes which in turn contribute to our racial problems. And as a very practical matter, it simply makes more sense for a "university" to recruit and enroll academically talented black students than it does to recruit and enroll athletically talented but often academically marginal black athletes. As I once heard Dean Marilyn Yarbrough (Law Dean at the University of Tennessee and a black woman) put it, "in our current system, we just have the wrong black students on our campuses."

b. Women

In 1972, Congress enacted a law which prohibited educational programs from discrimination on the basis of sex. As a result of recent case law and amendments by Congress, there is now no doubt that this important law, commonly referred to as Title IX, applies to the administration of intercollegiate sports programs. In fact, current regulations designed to implement the mandate of Title IX spell out with specificity the responsibility of athletic departments to provide equal opportunity for women who participate in intercollegiate sports. One particular regulation has been interpreted to require that schools provide athletic scholarships on a "substantially proportional basis to the number of male and female participants in the institution's athletic program." Schools have been told that the government will measure compliance with Title IX by simply "dividing the amounts of aid available for the members of each sex by the numbers of male or female participants in the athletic program and comparing the results."

The reality is that the vast majority of schools in Division I are in violation of the scholarship-to-participant ratio rule. Another reality is that the Reagan and Bush administrations have done very little to

enforce this Title IX mandate. The result is that college and universities have placed themselves in the unenviable position of ignoring
the mandate of a beneficent civil rights law.

Most schools, in fact, agree that providing equal opportunity for
women in sports is a desirable social goal. The justifications for
flouting the federal mandate vary. Some schools appear to think that
very gradual progress is all that is required. Others cling to the idea that
revenue-producing sports are not to be included in the
scholarship-to-participant ratio formula. (This idea has been rejected
by the governmental agency empowered to enforce the Title IX
mandate.) The reality here is that the powerful athletic interests have,
for the most part, simply chosen not to comply and the federal
government has done very little about it.

The scholarship disarmament plan discussed earlier, if implemented, will have the very positive side-effect of bringing many
schools into compliance with Title IX. The scholarship disarmament
plan as it applies to men's sports should also be accompanied by a
genuine commitment to upgrade women's sport to bring schools into
meaningful compliance with Title IX. As required by the regulations
which implement the Title IX mandate, schools should commit to
providing additional support to women's sports in the areas of
equipment and supplies, travel, practice site availability, publicity,
and salaries for coaches. As a practical matter, this may result in a
certain de-emphasis of men's sports. Athletic administrators must be
willing to come to grips with the fact that the strictures of Title IX
reflect both existing law and sound policy.

IV. CAMPUS LIFE

If I make a set of rules, then a guy goes out and steals an airplane.
He comes back and says, 'It wasn't on the list of rules'.
                    Abe Lemons, former Texas basketball coach.

The life of the big-time college athlete is regulated to a far greater
degree than the life of the average college student. Athletes are
engulfed by a complex regulatory scheme from the moment they
arrive on campus. The athlete's life is managed and controlled in what
can perhaps best be described as a militaristic fashion. Regulations
which would be viewed as entirely inappropriate for "civilians" are
commonplace for athletes. The sections that follow deal critically with
the various regulations which effect the lives of the athletes.

A. Housing

A large majority of Division I schools still maintain athletic dormitories. Often, these "jock dorms" are located close to the athletic facilities, and separate from regular student residential communities. Additionally, student-athletes often eat their meals in a separate cafeteria.

The rationales for establishing and maintaining these separate facilities reflect the power of coaches to influence university housing policies. Coaches have succeeded in convincing university administrators that these dorms will help the school to compete at the highest level. First, coaches point out that they will use the jock dorms to recruit. The jock dorms are usually somehow nicer (bigger and/or better equipped) than the regular dorms. And the food service is enhanced (more "feed" for the jocks). So the coaches use these special features to lure their prospects to the university, and without them, the coaches say, they would be at a disadvantage. Once the recruit is landed, coaches argue that they need the dorm to control and regulate the lives of the athletes. Coaches can call important meetings on short notice without having to scurry all around looking for team members. Bed-checks are made more simple. Coaches can find out just who is doing what and when and this is important to avoid embarrassing situations. Jock dorms give coaches the ability to be on top of things — heading off problems before they occur. These spurious rationales don't work to support the continued maintenance of these housing projects. First of all, the ABSENCE of jock dorms is the proper recruiting tool if coaches really want to attract "student-athletes." And in a university setting, coaches simply should not exert the kind of control over the lives of young people that they currently exercise. For it is this type of separateness and control that gives athletes the message that they are not really "student-athletes"--rather, the view is reinforced that they are athletes first and foremost and only second-class students.

Even the NCAA has come to realize that separate facilities for athletes is really not defensible. At the 1991 Convention, the NCAA adopted a proposal which made it impermissible to devote floors, wings or residence halls exclusively to athletes. This proposal is to be implemented over a 5 year period. A companion proposal prohibited Division I schools from providing more than one training-table meal per day if other university dining facilities are open. As is usually the case with NCAA "reform" proposals, these proposals do not go far enough.

The maintenance of segregated housing facilities for athletes stigmatizes athletes as non-students, as athletic mercenaries. This kind of isolation and separation is segregation in its most pernicious form. The solution here is to integrate athletes into the university by allowing them to live and dine with students, as students.

B. Practices, Games, and Classes

It is common knowledge that inordinate time demands are placed on student-athletes, who must expertly juggle the myriad responsibilities associated with being both a student and a big-time intercollegiate athlete in order to succeed. It is not at all surprising to most observers that, under the circumstances, few are really able to pull it off. While the NCAA regularly holds up some latter-day Bill Bradley as the model of the student-athlete, the truth is that there aren't too many out there who even remotely resemble Bill Bradley. Even the NCAA has come to appreciate that it is extremely difficult to play big-time intercollegiate sports and to be a bona fide student at the same time. In an effort to deal with this problem, the NCAA has enacted an extensive body of regulations concerning practice times and game scheduling. The NCAA manual has taken on the prolixity of a collective bargaining agreement detailing permissible conditions of employment.

In regard to practice times, the NCAA regulatory scheme covers the waterfront. The NCAA says when seasons begin and end. With a few exceptions for physical fitness activities, supervised practice sessions are only permitted in-season. The NCAA now requires that institutions limit the number of hours during the day and week that can be spent on activities connected with sports participation — in other words, schools must establish limits on working hours. Athletes must be given one day off per week during the season. Institutions must now keep records and develop a methodology for computing hourly limitations. Schools must also prescribe the number of class hours that can be missed because of athletic activities. One specification here is that class time may not be missed for practices but permits the missing of a limited number of classes to participate in away games.

As far as games are concerned, the NCAA limits the number of games that can be played in each sport in each division. (The NCAA recently reduced the permissible number of Division I basketball contests from 28 to 27 in partial response to the problem of athletes missing class to participate in games.) An NCAA bylaw dealing with games requires that teams leave no earlier than 48 hours prior to game time and depart from the game site within 36 hours of completion of the game. (Limited exceptions apply to games played off the mainland.)

These kinds of proposals will do little to solve the very difficult problem of fairly accommodating the competing demands of school work and athletic development. The NCAA proposals are significant in that their very existence is evidence that even athletic administrators realize that this is a most delicate problem. If we are to maintain a system where our athletes are really students too, a system which regulates practices and games must be devised. But it must be a system which takes full account of the fact that many athletes are especially vulnerable to academic pressures. While there are no easy formulae here, rethinking some basic assumptions will provide some relief.

The limiting of practice times to an artificially defined season is counterproductive. First of all, athletes and coaches at the intercollegiate level really know no season. The limitation of practice to the season creates tremendous pressure to over-practice during the season, because practices are illegal out of season. In my view, it would make more sense to simply jettison the assumption that limiting practices to the season reduces the pressures on athletes. Allowing athletes to practice all year, and particularly in the summer, will alleviate the pressure to overpractice during the season, when the academic pressures are also present. If practices were permitted all year, coaches would be provided with the opportunity to sensibly train athletes without having to "pack it all in" to the season. Coaches would also be relieved of the hopelessly artificial constraint of the current system, where they have to be careful to not even be present when their players are practicing on their own. This expansion of the season, accompanied by reasonable practice time limits, would help to provide an environment where athletes have a legitimate chance to succeed as students.

The problem of game scheduling is an intractable one. If anything like the current system is to be maintained, athletes are going to miss class in order to participate in games. But there now exists a somewhat cavalier attitude toward missed classes that seriously undermines the academic mission. Steps must be taken to directly confront this problem. Of course, athletic administrators must take real care to schedule games in such a way as to minimize lost class time. Meaningful guidelines should be articulated to ensure that this is in fact done with a serious purpose. The NCAA rules in regard to departure to and from games, previously alluded to, make sense. But isn't it clear that a system needs to be devised which provides athletes with some facsimile of the class missed? Surely with available technology athletes could be provided with either an audio or video tape of missed class. After returning from a road trip, it is commonplace for athletes and coaches to go over the "game films." Doesn't it make even better sense to set aside a time to go over the tape of the class missed? And if some professors object to the taping (as no doubt some will be wont to do), shouldn't the athlete meet with a dependable student who was present to go over what was missed as a matter of course. Isn't this what good students do? Is it stretching things too far to ask that athletes should behave as good students do? Shouldn't the athletic department expend as much time and energy providing athletes with an opportunity to review missed classes as it currently does in regard to game films?

C. Drug Testing

Many intercollegiate athletes are required to submit to drug testing as a condition of participation. In many cases, the individual school administers the testing. In other instances, the NCAA itself requires that athletes be tested for drugs as a condition precedent to participation in certain championship events. Typically, the athlete is asked to sign a waiver or consent form which allows for the collection of a urine sample. Refusal to consent renders an athlete ineligible to participate. At some schools, all athletes are tested at one time or another. For example, the mandatory physical exam might include a drug test. At other schools, the athletes to be tested are supposedly randomly selected. Still others permit the testing of an individual athlete based on something akin to probable cause to believe the athlete is using illegal drugs. Myriad variations are in place as one moves from school to school. Following the collection of what is usually a urine sample, chemical tests are performed to detect the presence of illegal substances, including marijuana, cocaine, amphetamines, and steroids. Positive test results are verified with follow-up tests. Procedures and punishments at individual schools also vary. One common methodology would be to suspend a first time offender pending the completion of a drug education course. A second or third failed test might result in either lengthier suspensions or expulsion. But the one outstanding aspect of all the various drug testing schemes is that athletes are separated out from the rest of the student body for special treatment in regard to drugs.

In order to wage a meaningful war on drugs it is important that we begin to draw some distinctions. One distinction that is not drawn by most of the drug testing schemes is the distinction that should be drawn between performance enhancing drugs (like steroids and the human growth hormone) and recreational drugs (like alcohol, marijuana and cocaine). If the distinction is drawn and examined, it makes good sense to test athletes for performance enhancers. And it doesn't make sense to single out athletes to be tested for recreational drugs.

1. Performance Enhancers

The athlete who takes performance-enhancing drugs is a cheater. This kind of cheating cuts at the soul of competitive sport. It is sound policy to institute a fair and effective drug screening program to protect the integrity of sport and to protect athletes who are under pressure to cheat in order to compete. In a very real sense, the problem of performance-enhancing drugs is a sports problem. Somewhat ironically, sports organizations like the NCAA are typically ineffective when it comes to testing for performance-enhancers, but efficacious when it comes to detecting recreational drug use. But it is screening for performance-enhancers to detect cheating that is essential to the preservation of the competitive environment. In short, it makes sense to single out athletes to test them for performance-enhancing drugs.

2. Recreational Drugs

The athlete who takes recreational drugs is a different kind of cheater. It makes little sense, however, to single out athletes for special treatment when it comes to the use of recreational drugs. Think about it: Is there any justification for testing the football team for marijuana and not the debate team? When it comes to the use of recreational drugs, athletes simply are no differently situated than non-athletes. The problem is not particularly related to participation in athletics. If we deem it sound policy to test for recreational drug use, fairness dictates that we test the population more broadly - all students should be tested, not just athletes. The point is, an effective war against recreational drug use cannot be fought with only athletes on the front lines. We cheat ourselves and athletes when we force athletes to fight what is everyone's war.

3. Toward Sound Policy

It may well be that it is entirely appropriate to draw other distinctions as well. The distinction I offer here is merely a starting point. But it seems to me that the "war on drugs" can not be fought in a meaningful way until rational distinctions are drawn. The "war on drugs" cannot be won if athletes are the primary foot-soldiers. The athletes' contribution to the war is to get policy makers to think critically about how best to fight it fairly—without cheating.

D. Freedom Issues: The Right to Transfer and The Right to Test the Professional Sports Market

The NCAA has a set of regulations designed to serve a governing principle—athletes are to be discouraged from transferring from one school to another. One rule which helps to effectuate the basic principle declares that an athlete who does choose to transfer must sit out a year before regaining eligibility. (Since another rule requires that an athlete complete his eligibility in 5 years, the requirement that an athlete sit out one year is especially coercive.) A concomitant regulation is that such an athlete can not receive financial assistance at the school transferred to unless the school transferred from agrees to "release" the athlete. To make absolutely sure that transferring is effectively prevented, the NCAA has adopted a web of by-laws. For example, one recently passed bylaw requires an NCAA member to obtain a written release from another member school before any contact is made with a student-athlete regarding the possibility of the student-athlete transferring schools. In short, the regulatory framework serves to severely limit an athlete's ability to move to another school. Even if the coach leaves, these anti-transfer rules don't loosen.

A related set of regulations prevents many athletes from effectively testing the professional sports market. One rule renders a student-athlete ineligible to participate as soon as the athlete agrees to be represented by an agent. Another rule makes an athlete ineligible the moment the athlete requests to be included in the professional draft. (With the exception of baseball, professional leagues typically will draft only those players who have either exhausted their eligibility or renounced their remaining eligibility by petitioning for inclusion in the draft.) The effect of these rules, combined with the predominant practices of the professional sports industry, is to preclude an athlete from testing the professional sports market without sacrificing eligibility. In short, an athlete with eligibility remaining has no opportunity to determine whether market forces warrant relinquishing of remaining eligibility without first giving up the remaining eligibility.

Imagine a theater major being told that if she transferred to another school, the rules of the National Collegiate Theatrical Association mandated that she would be ineligible to participate in any theatrical productions at her new school for a full year. Imagine a music major being told that if he wanted to audition for a spot as a percussionist with a popular group that he would first have to agree to relinquish his right to play with the school's well-regarded ensemble. Imagine both being told that if they hired an agent or received advice from an attorney who subsequently represented them in connection with securing employment, they would be barred from participating in school-sponsored presentations. Imagine being told that you couldn't find out whether you would receive the job you sought, or even what the job would pay, unless you first unequivocally quit your old job. Eligibility rules in any other context but sports make little sense. I would contend that such rules make little more sense in the sports milieu.

The myriad limitations on an athlete's freedom to change schools or to test the professional sports market exist to serve the interests of the athletic powers-that-be. The NCAA and its member schools are primarily concerned with the maintenance of high quality, low-cost athletic programs. Transfers and attempts to test the professional sports market create administrative problems for coaches and athletic administrators. In fact, the vast array of NCAA regulations restricting the freedom of athletes to make decisions which other students make in the regular course of their lives are designed not with the athlete's interest in mind, but with an eye on protecting the economic interests of the NCAA and its member schools. These rules have the purpose and effect of forcing talented athletes to remain at the school where they first enrolled in order to minimize disruption and inconvenience for athletic administrators. The rationales proposed by the NCAA—that the rules are designed to promote amateurism and to further educational goals--are both chimerical and disingenuous.

An athlete ought to be able to make a decision to transfer in much the same way as any other student does. An athlete ought to be able to contract with a lawyer or agent to get information concerning his potential as a professional without jettisoning his college career. An athlete ought to be able to find out if he has market value by requesting inclusion in the draft without sacrificing eligibility. In short, what is required here is a move toward the drastic deregulation of the lives of athletes. At the very least, the rules that limit transfers, the so-called "no agent" rules, and the rules which require athletes to give up eligibility in order to be considered for the draft, ought to be repealed. In fairness to athletes, the NCAA has to get out of the way. But whether the NCAA has the political wherewithal to get out of the way is an entirely different matter. I think that if the NCAA doesn't start legislating with the interests of athletes in mind, it will be eventually pushed out of the way by lawsuits and legislation.

V. COACHES

I thought I had a lifetime contract. Then I found out the other day that if I have a losing season, they're going to declare me legally dead.

> Hayden Fry, Iowa Football coach.

What the hell's the matter with a society that offers a football coach a million dollars?

> Joe Paterno, Penn State Football Coach,
> after receiving an offer to coach the
> New England Patriots.

. . .I'll accept them limiting what I earn if they will grant me tenure.

Former University of Kansas head basketball coach Larry Brown.

Big-time college coaches work under incredible pressure to win. They also make an awful lot of money, much of which is often derived from sources outside the university. To bring perspective back to intercollegiate sports, the pressure to win must be reduced along with the money from outside sources. Coaches should be provided with an opportunity to attain the special kind of security enjoyed by those in the academic community. At the same time, it must be made clear that coaches work for the university and they are not independent, roving entrepreneurs.

A. Job Security for Coaches

Perhaps the one thing that marks the university as a distinctively different employer is that faculty can earn and enjoy tenure. We all know what this means. An employee with academic tenure has a lifetime contract, terminable only in the event of specific, well-proven financial exigency at the university, gross incompetence or neglect of duties, or egregious crimes of moral turpitude. In short, tenure provides a unique kind of job security in American life. Coaches should be brought more fully into the university community by being offered an opportunity to earn tenure. Once earned, tenure would not mean that a coach had to be retained as coach. It would simply mean that a coach with tenure, once relieved of coaching responsibilities, still had a job to do at the university.

Under this type of arrangement, a coach under consideration for tenure would be evaluated with reference to more than a win-loss record. This is not to suggest that success on the playing field is irrelevant—only that it is far less relevant than prevailing wisdom holds. A good coach is a good teacher and it follows that there is a connection between winning and effective teaching. (Most coaches know, however, that winning and losing is primarily a function of athletic talent. Some coaches who are very effective at teaching the game may not have the glittering records of the more effective recruiters. Universities must be willing to look beyond the win-loss record in evaluating the performance of coaches.) But a successful coach is one who teaches in areas that go well beyond the playing of the game. A coach should be evaluated for tenure with reference to the seriousness with which players are offered a truly meaningful opportunity to attain a college education. Graduate rates are relevant criteria. The extent to which players are truly integrated into the university community is a relevant consideration in the evaluation of the coach. Coaches should, in short, be evaluated as teachers in the university community, and the successful ones should be provided with something akin to academic tenure.

B. Shoe Contracts, Camps, Television and Radio Shows, and Other Perks

As a trade-off for increased job security, the rampant entrepreneurialism of coaches must be curtailed. University administrators have acquiesced in giving peculiar and unwarranted permission to coaches to exploit their connection with the university in ways that are not permissible for any other members of the academic community. Tenure carries with it special responsibility to the university. While tenured faculty enjoy the special freedom associated with a lifetime appointment, they also understand that they are tethered to the university in a distinct and special fiduciary relationship. Guidelines concerning outside work are taken seriously by most, who understand that their primary allegiance is to the university which has tenured them. Universities must be zealous in reclaiming university assets that have been ceded to coaches. The goodwill and the value of the university name belong not to the coach but to the university. Money from shoe contracts, camps, and television and radio shows more properly belongs to the university than the coach.

Coaches who sign lucrative shoe contracts have been permitted to exploit a university resource by overly-permissive athletic administrators. University presidents have looked the other way. If a contract is to be signed for athletes to wear a certain shoe, it should be signed by the university, not the coach. If shoe companies are willing to pay this money, it is money that belongs to the university, not the coach. (Imagine a professor being paid by a book publisher for requiring students to use a certain book.) Summer camps which operate as cash cows for coaches should be producing revenue for the university. (Imagine a professor being allowed to use university facilities at little or no cost to run a summer camp, and to keep the money generated from the camp.) Coaches can be employed at these camps in the same manner that faculty are employed to teach over the summer. Public relations is part of the job of the coach. A weekly television or radio show is an aspect of the public relations component of the job. A coaches' contract ought to contemplate that the money paid for this part of the job belongs to the university, not the coach.

The receipt of other "perks" by coaches (like cars, country club memberships, and the like) serve to further separate coaches from the university community. University presidents should discourage, if not prohibit, these perks, and should take pains to steer the donors in the direction of providing "perks" that benefit the wider university community.

This fairly radical restructuring of the relationship between coach and university is attainable. In fact, the current mood of the coaches, revealed most clearly in pronouncements from their national associations (for example, the National Association of Basketball Coaches), indicates that coaches are deeply concerned with lifestyle issues and very committed to the prospect of making academic style tenure available to its members. These kinds of changes can be made by university presidents as they hire new coaches. Moreover, the changes are cost effective because the university will be claiming significant assets that had previously been relinquished to coaches. These additional assets ought to more than offset the costs connected to providing job security to coaches.

VI. Faculty (and Students)— The Fans and the Disaffected

When it comes to big-time intercollegiate sports, faculty members tend to fall into one or the other of two distinct camps. The same is probably true of students. A significant number can simply be described as "fans." Relatively uncritical of the rampant hypocrisy endemic to their athletic programs, these faculty and students are willing to look the other way or explain away problems in the athletic program in exchange for the mostly psychic joys of being a part of a sports program. This observation is not intended as a pejorative put-down of fans. The fact of the matter is that being a fan does provide significant pleasures to many. (The size and scope of the sports industry in this country is proof of the phenomenon.) To cheer for the home team—to forcefully identify with a community beyond self and family—is uniquely fulfilling for many. Savvy administrators know who the fans are. When it comes time to designate students or faculty to the various university-wide committees that have some oversight over the program, or to name the faculty representative to the NCAA, one can be quite sure that the designees came from among the fans and not the disaffected. Occasional miscalculations result in the appointment of a disaffected faculty member or student, but these mistakes are usually short-lived. Those who serve on these various committees or as institutional representatives are then often further co-opted by little perks that mean a lot to a fan—better seats, an opportunity to travel with the team or to attend a convention, access to the players and coaches, and a general feeling of being part of the team.

A significant number of faculty and students, however, are alienated from and somewhat hostile to the sports program. This disaffected group falls into two categories. The "entirely disaffected" have little interest in or appreciation of sports and believe that intercollegiate athletic competition is almost entirely unconnected to the educational mission. They would favor elimination of the sports program. There is no way these people will ever become fans. But a significant number of the disaffected are only partially disaffected. Concerned by the hypocrisy in the program, particularly by the fact that many of the players are really not students, the partially disaffected meander in and out of the program. Their love of sports and the joy that comes with being a fan occasionally pull them into the fan camp. Their awareness of abuses in the program alienate them. While their ambivalence is apparent, potential exists to transform the partially disaffected into fans. An honest effort to reduce the hypocrisy would make fans of many of the partially disaffected. And it goes without saying that those who are already fans will remain fans should some of the hypocrisy be removed.

It would serve the interests of the university to undertake honest efforts to eliminate some of the abuses. The disaffected must be brought into the process of governing intercollegiate sport to act as agents for change. While at first glance this appears to be a counter-intuitive proposition, the truly savvy administrator would utilize the disaffected as catalysts for changes. The changes are not particularly controversial—there exists a shared consensus in the university community in favor of them. Admit only students who have a bona fide chance of attaining a degree. Require real progress towards a degree as a condition of continued attendance. Eliminate the sub-standard jock curriculum. With these changes, the disaffected become part of the athletic program and the athletic program becomes a real part of the university. Without them, the disaffection worsens, and the prospects for the university athletic program are, in the long run, bleak.

In the current milieu, can these changes be accomplished? The answer, I think, is that it depends largely on the presence of academic leadership from university presidents, who have the power but perhaps not the stomach to effectuate meaningful reform.

VII. University Presidents

[College Presidents] are far too politic a class of men to take any really effective steps against an enterprise that brings in such large sums of money. . . .

Journalist and social critic H. L. Mencken,
commenting about intercollegiate athletics.

I know this is going to sound facetious, but it really isn't: if any
person is interested in becoming president or chancellor of a
Division I-A institution and he or she doesn't like football, then
that person better look for a job somewhere else; because you've
just got to spend an awful lot of time at it. The intercollegiate
athletic program is not something you can leave for someone else
to take care of.

An anonymous university president.

If there is one group that bears major responsibility for allowing
intercollegiate sports to spin wildly out of control, it is university
presidents. Even the NCAA acknowledges, in its Constitution, that
the president "has ultimate responsibility and final authority for the
conduct of the intercollegiate sports program." For the most part,
university presidents have failed miserably in administering intercollegiate sports programs — allowing the athletic tail to wag the
university dog.

A. Failure to Insist on the Admission of Qualified Students

One of the most serious failures of university presidents is the failure
to ensure that only students who have some reasonable likelihood of
academic success are admitted. Leadership from the top in connection
with the all-important decision to admit is sorely lacking. This failing
is not a difficult one to cure. All that is really required is resolve and
commitment, along with a willingness to face the powerful athletic
lobby both within and without the university.

B. Failure to Control the Athletic Lobby

The "athletic lobby" at the university consists of university athletic
administrators, fans, the media, and boosters. In many instances,
members of the athletic lobby serve on the university's board of
trustees or governing board.

As big-time sports programs have grown, presidents have increasingly turned to professional sports administrators to run the university's
sports business. A typical big-time athletic program employs a highly
paid athletic director along with a professional staff ranging from
influential public relations staff to surprisingly powerful ticket dis-
pensers. Coaches are of course part of the athletic lobby. Some schools
even have autonomous legal corporations to assist in the administra-

tion of the athletic program. Other schools utilize advisory athletic boards which lobby on behalf of the already powerful and entrenched athletic interests. Often, a fawning local press contributes to an environment which lionizes the athletic program. To a certain extent, university presidents have contracted out the running of the athletic program. So long as the school does not run up deep red ink or run afoul of NCAA rules in such a way as to embarrass the school, the President looks the other way. This laissez-faire attitude gives carte blanche to athletic interests to consolidate their independent power base at the university. The dissidents and the disaffected in the university community are viewed with suspicion and hostility. The athletic lobbyists within the academic community—the athletic administrators, the faculty who teach jock courses or serve on athletic oversight committees, the hard-core supporters, and the wealthy boosters—are for the most part treated like the valued customers that they are. Although already committed to the program, key lobbyists are further co-opted by the perks that come along with being associated with the program (complimentary tickets, preferential seating, and subsidized travel, to name a few.) Presidents often are both kept at a distance and keep themselves at a distance in order to avoid being sullied by the muck.

The athletic lobby works to create the perception that big money pours in to support athletics and that much of this money would not be forthcoming were it not for athletics. In COLLEGE SPORTS INC., Professor Sperber very persuasively describes the false economies of big-time intercollegiate sport. In essence, Sperber convincingly demonstrates that the data supports the view that the great bulk of big-time sports programs in this country do not turn a profit. Sperber points out that a fair accounting system reveals that big-time sports is subsidized in a big-time way at most universities. While many chase the holy grail of big pay-offs, very few come into possession of it.

Many universities play accounting shell games to avoid disclosure of just how serious the budgetary deficits really are. For example, while an academic unit might budget academic scholarships, the athletic departments might be permitted to treat athletic scholarships as unbudgeted tuition waivers. Funds raised by the athletic lobby might be considered revenue by the athletic department even though the evidence exists that this money would be contributed to the university's general fund anyway. The range of all this economic abracadabra is wide. The common theme is that university presidents have both failed to control the costs associated with the running of the athletic program, and do not even have accurate financial data upon which to base decisions concerning the administration of the program.

C. The Failure to Resist Their Own "CEO-ification"

At the same time, the presidency itself has been "CEO-ified." The modern university president is no longer primarily an academic leader with a commitment to "the vision thing." Rather, presidents are more like corporate CEOs, enjoying salaries and benefits which clearly place them separate and apart from the rest of the academic community. Even though most are provided with the soft landing of a university professorship should the presidency be lost, few are willing to jeopardize their position by risking principled action with regard to athletics. Very few are willing to confront their Boards about the issue of putting sports in perspective. As one president put it,

> The ideal situation is to not have your board mucking around in athletics. The only way that you are going to stop that from happening is to be willing to put your job on the line.

The "CEO-ified" president is typically unwilling to put his or her job on the line over anything, let alone athletics. As one *former* president put it,

> Some chief executive officers are just going to have to lose their jobs. That's the bottom line of this whole enterprise. It's easy for me to say because I'm not going to be one of them at this point; but I've been recruited during this past year by two major Division I institutions and it was clear to me that athletic problems were going to be an issue right off the bat. . . .I believe that these things can't be handled diplomatically. In the end the chief officer has to say, "Look, friends, there's a way we're not going to run this place. I'm not looking for trouble, but I'm telling you I want to meet my responsibilities and I can't meet them in the way you guys are operating. Now you can either have me as your president or you can get somebody else." Now that's tough, but what other remedy is there to a basic structural question of who's in charge of the program? You say, "What happens to people like that?" Well, _____ lost his job at _____, came to _____. Where is he now? He's chancellor at _____. He took a punch in the course of all that, but no one in higher education thinks any less of him for it. . . . Why some presidents seem reluctant to lose their jobs over athletics, I don't know. It's a badge of honor these days.

A new generation of presidential leadership is essential to the reform of intercollegiate athletics. The President's Commission of the NCAA, which thus far has failed miserably in effectuating meaningful reform, at least provides an institutional structure within the NCAA to effectuate reform. But so far, the Commission has been unwilling to fully subscribe to basic reform principles to restore perspective to athletics. Presidents are, to a large degree, captivated by and held captive to the entrenched athletic interest. It is not entirely unforeseeable however, that as it becomes apparent that fewer and fewer schools are really sharing in the largesse produced by big-time intercollegiate sport, a new generation of leadership, spurred first by economic imperatives and empowered by an academic vision, will emerge to initiate real reform. The existing intercollegiate sports structure is very seriously flawed. With the leadership of just a few far-looking presidents, the structure can be renovated.

VIII. The NCAA Revisited

Any blueprint for the reform of intercollegiate athletics must at least address the possibility that the NCAA is not capable of governing intercollegiate athletics in a principled way. Much of what has been observed thus far indicates that the NCAA, the most visible and powerful of our amateur sports governing bodies, has perhaps lost the ability to govern intercollegiate sports in a principled way. This inability can be attributed to its inherently faulty structure, its fundamental hypocrisy, and its pattern of arbitrary and selective enforcement of its rules.

One damning fault in the structure of the organization is that athletes are not represented in the organization. Admittedly, the ideals of representative democracy are shared values in our culture. The NCAA is inherently undemocratic. Although the NCAA governs intercollegiate athletics, intercollegiate athletes—those people whose lives are most directly affected by what the NCAA does—have no direct representation. The result is a not-so-surprising amalgam of complex rules which protect the interests of member schools represented by member administrators with little regard for the real interests of athletes. Thus the NCAA clings to a myth of "amateurism," reigning over a big-time intercollegiate sports system in which all the actors except the athletes are permitted and encouraged to be profiteers, while the athletes are held to the out-dated myth of playing for fun.

While clinging to this out-dated myth of amateurism in so far as athletes are concerned, the NCAA operates as a business entity for most other purposes. It recently sold the television rights to the Division I intercollegiate basketball championship tournament for approximately 1 billion dollars. It maintains an elaborate formula for disbursing money to member schools which takes into full account the relative degree of athletic success of the school's athletic program, while minimizing the academic achievements of its members. The NCAA markets products through various licensing schemes, while vigorously "selling" the myth of the student-athlete to the consuming public. To the slightly sophisticated observer, the hypocrisy is appalling.

The NCAA's record of unfair and haphazard enforcement of the rules governing college athletic programs is equally appalling. In *Undue Process: The NCAA's Injustice for All*, Don Yeager offers a compelling and persuasive indictment of the NCAA's enforcement arm. Selective and arbitrary initiation of proceedings, secrecy, delay, and distortion of testimony (the NCAA doesn't usually tape record testimony; it allows its own investigators to write summaries of testimony) are but a few of the hallmarks of the existing regime. While it is true that the Supreme Court has said that the NCAA is not technically a "state actor", and therefore doesn't have to provide constitutional safeguards in the course of its proceedings, the current framework contributes to the malaise; member schools feel vulnerable and view the organization with suspicion and distrust. The process is so obviously flawed that many state legislatures have introduced bills that would require that the NCAA provide rudimentary due process protections to those caught up in the NCAA's byzantine enforcement mechanisms.

Whether the organization is capable of reforming itself is problematical. Its own record indicates it probably can not. The most obvious catalyst for reform is the President's Commission. But unless this Commission undertakes a serious commitment to change, internal reform of the NCAA is unlikely.

It might well be that meaningful reform will come about not as a result of internal reform of the NCAA, but as a consequence of secession of some powerful member schools from the NCAA. These renegade schools would then form their own organization to administer big-time intercollegiate sport in a more principled, less hypocritical way. This is not a wholly unlikely possibility.

Attempting to construct a blueprint for the fundamental reform of big time intercollegiate sports, it must be admitted, is an act of incredible hubris. I offer the preceding with humility, and the hope that it will contribute something towards the creation of a system which places sports in a better perspective for all of us.

APPENDIX

ADDITIONAL NOTES AND SOURCES

There is a vast and constantly growing body of what might aptly be called "sports reform" literature. The genre first flourished, I think, with the breakthrough book BALL FOUR, written by Jim Bouton in 1970. Bouton's book was one of the first to de-mystify athletes by detailing what life as a professional baseball player really was like. Football's analogue to Bouton's book appeared shortly thereafter. OUT OF THEIR LEAGUE, by Dave Meggyesy, is a scathing and brilliant expose of both college and professional football. These two books laid the groundwork for a more rigorous examination of sports in American society and the now existing body of realistic sports non-fiction is vast. I have been deeply influenced by this body of literature. Among the more recent important contributions to the field are BLACKBOARDS AND BACKBOARDS, by Patti and Pete Adler; PERSONAL FOULS, by Peter Golenbock; Murray Sperber's COLLEGE SPORTS INC.: THE ATHLETIC DEPARTMENT V. THE UNIVERSITY; RAW RECRUITS, by Alexander Wolff and Armen Keteyian; and Don Yeager's UNDUE PROCESS: THE NCAA'S INJUSTICE FOR ALL. While I am sure there are many other very worthwhile works, the ones listed above are the books that have most deeply influenced my thinking.

I have also read and been influenced by what might be regarded as a more moderate set of works. Among these very thoughtful and helpful works, I would include ATHLETES AND ACADEME, by Wilford S. Bailey and Taylor D. Littleton; THE CHARACTER OF AMERICAN HIGHER EDUCATION & INTERCOLLEGIATE SPORT, by Donald Chu; UNSPORTSMANLIKE CONDUCT, by Paul Lawrence; and THE RULES OF THE GAME, edited by Richard E. Lapchick and John Brooks Slaughter. Allen Sack's, "Are Improper Benefits Really Improper?" appears as one of the edited pieces in Slaughter and Lapchick and my own views are influenced by Professor Sack's work.

Intercollegiate sports reform issues have also found their way into the law reviews. In this regard, I found the CAPITAL UNIVERSITY LAW

REVIEW *1991 Symposium on the Reform of Big-Time Athletics* particularly helpful. Most noteworthy here were the very insightful articles of Robert N. Davis and Ethan Lock. The fledgling MARQUETTE SPORTS LAW JOURNAL promises to make some lasting contributions to the field. Martin Greenberg's, "College Coaching Contracts: A Practical Perspective" provided me with the background I needed to critically examine the relationship of the big-time coach to the university.

For what I would call "deep background" on the structure of sports in this country, and on the myriad legal issues that arise in connection with sport, one must make mention of THE LAW OF SPORTS, by John C. Weistart and Cym Lowell. This 1,000 page treatise introduced me to the world of sports law and I may well be the only person in America who has read it cover-to-cover twice (such was my youthful zeal). An outgrowth of the Weistart and Lowell hornbook is my own casebook, with coauthors Jim McCurdy and Pete Goplerud, SPORTS LAW: CASES AND MATERIALS, which is now the most widely used sports law casebook in the country. The NCAA overview is drawn largely from our casebook. I might also point out that the NCAA manual, revised annually, is must skimming.

To stay current on sports issues, I regularly read my local paper (THE TULSA WORLD), the NEW YORK TIMES, SPORTS ILLUSTRATED, and the weekly periodical, SPORTS INDUSTRY NEWS, which focuses on the business and financial aspects of the sports industry. THE CHRONICLE OF HIGHER EDUCATION offers interesting and provocative coverage of intercollegiate sports.

Unless otherwise noted below, the quotes used to set out the topics in my blueprint are from SPORTSWIT, by Lee Green, The quote from Ziddi Msangi, the black fine arts major at Boise State, was reported in THE CHRONICLE OF HIGHER EDUCATION on June 17, 1992. The quote from Larry Brown is reported in Greenberg's coaching contracts piece alluded to earlier at page 263. The Mencken quote appears at page 185 of Slaughter and Lapchick, and the quotes from the anonymous university presidents appear at page 66-72 of Bailey and Littleton.

Enhanced Risk of Harm to One's Self As a Justification for Exclusion from Athletics*

Matthew J. Mitten

The rights of athletes with disabilities to compete has always been a socially sensitive issue. The problem has taken on a legal dimension as well in recent years with the application of the federal Rehabilitation Act and the Americans With Disabilities Act to the world of amateur athletics. In this essay, Matthew Mitten examines the situation where an athlete possesses a physical abnormality that does not affect his or her ability to participate in the sport but which exposes the athlete to an enhanced risk of harm.

Mitten maintains that there is no simple solution to this problem under the relevant statutes and that varying views of the proper resolution is closely linked can be explained in terms of broader social values. He also suggests that the proper standard be different in amateur and professional sports.

This article discusses an athlete's legal right to participate in sponsored athletic competition[1] with a physical abnormality that exposes him or her to an enhanced risk of injury or death. For purposes of this discussion, I assume that the athlete has the necessary physical skills and abilities to successfully play the sport with a physical impairment (*e.g.,* a cardiovascular or spinal abnormality or a missing or non-functioning paired organ such as an eye or kidney) and that his or her participation does not create an increased risk of physical injury to others. However, the athlete may be exposed to a substantially enhanced risk of personal injury by

*From Volume 8, Number 2, Spring 1998, pp. 189-223.

participating in a sport. A lack of available scientific data and reliable clinical studies may cause sports medicine experts to disagree regarding whether this increased risk of harm, created by the athlete's physical abnormality, justifies medical disqualification from athletic competition.

Considering the uncertainties present in sports medicine and the impossibility of accurately predicting whether a physically impaired athlete will actually experience serious injury or death during sports participation as a result of his or her medical condition what is the appropriate judicial construction of federal laws prohibiting medically unjustified discrimination? Resolution of this issue requires proper delineation of the respective bounds of an impaired athlete's liberty interest in having an opportunity to participate in sports and a team's right (or that of a sports league or sponsoring organization) to establish reasonable minimum physical standards that must be satisfied by all participants. How we resolve this question implicates broader social values such as the limits of libertarianism and acceptable communitarian protection of others' health and safety, because sports is a microcosm of society in many respects.[2]

I begin by considering the legal nature of an amateur athlete's protected interest in participating in organized athletic competition and the legal rights and duties arising out of sponsorship of amateur sports by a team or other organization. Next I review and analyze the historical development of case law concerning the federal rights of physically impaired amateur athletes to participate in their chosen sports under the Rehabilitation Act of 1973[3] and propose a legal framework for resolving participation disputes involving amateur athletes. I then discuss the implications of this analysis for future claims under the Americans With Disabilities Act of 1990[4] (hereinafter "ADA") by impaired professional athletes who have been medically disqualified to play a sport because of a physical impairment.

I. Parties' Respective Legal Rights and Protected Interests

A. Athletes

Organized amateur athletic competition begins with youth sports during elementary school years such as Little League baseball and gymnastics, includes interscholastic competition during high school, extends to intercollegiate sports during college, and encompasses Olympic sports during the teens through mid-life. Youth and high school sports are extracurricular activities engaged in by athletes who generally are minors. Participants typically play these sports mainly for the social, educational, and physical benefits of athletic competition, but some particularly talented high school athletes seek a college athletic scholarship. Most participants in intercollegiate athletics are adults, and although they are primarily considered to be students, playing a sport at the college varsity level often is more than merely an extracurricular activity for the participating athletes. In some instances, a college athlete plays a sport to develop the skills necessary for future participation at the professional or Olympic levels of competition. Olympic athletes usually are adults (although some, such as most female gymnasts, are minors) with unique talents providing them with the opportunity to participate in international competition against other elite athletes.

Participation in amateur sports at any level of athletic competition generally is considered to be a privilege rather than a legally protected right. Although some courts hold that a high school student cannot be arbitrarily denied an opportunity to participate in interscholastic sports competition,[5] that sports are an integral part of one's scholastic and social development,[6] or that athletic competition is vital to obtaining a college education by means of an athletic scholarship,[7] courts generally refuse to recognize a constitutional right to play interscholastic sports.[8] Similarly, there is no constitutionally protected liberty or property interest in playing intercollegiate athletics.[9] Although a college athletic scholarship is a contract between the student-athlete and his or her university,[10] it does not guarantee either a position on the team or playing time.[11] The national governing body for each Olympic sport has a contractual relationship with its member athletes,[12] and the Amateur Sports Act of 1978 gives the organization the exclusive right to determine the membership of its national team for purposes of international competition, so there is no legal right to participate in Olympic sports.[13] Thus, the relationship between an amateur athlete and the sponsoring educational institution or athletics organization is legally considered to be consensual in nature.

B. Teams and Athletics-Event-Sponsoring Entities

An athlete may be medically disqualified by the team physician, or event sponsor's medical personnel, if a physical abnormality exposes him or her to a medically unreasonable risk of injury. A sponsoring educational institution or athletic organization may be reluctant to permit a talented, but physically impaired athlete, to participate in a competitive sport without medical clearance. The organization may also be concerned about potential legal liability from allowing an impaired athlete to participate. Apart from legal liability, the team or event sponsor also may have a paternalistic desire to protect a physically impaired athlete's health and safety by refusing to allow potential exposure to a risk of serious harm during athletic competition. In addition, there may be concern about potential psychological harm to others participating in the game or event or the detrimental effects of adverse publicity on the team or event sponsor's reputation if a physically impaired athlete suffers serious injury or death.

Courts have held that both public educational institutions[14] and private athletic governing bodies[15] have a legitimate interest in protecting an athlete from injury during athletic competition. Although these cases involved federal or state constitutional challenges to mandatory drug testing (rather than Rehabilitation Act or ADA claims), they recognize that a team or athletic event sponsor has at least some inherent right to protect an athlete's health and safety.[16] Moreover, outside the context of athletics, there are several judicially recognized social justifications for preventing people from engaging in potentially dangerous activities and harming themselves. For example, minimizing the public cost of injury treatment and disability;[17] avoiding the loss of productive members of society;[18] and preventing the loss of economic support and/or consortium to the injury victim's family[19] are valid objectives.

Even if a team or sponsor of an athletic event has a general *legal right* to protect the health and safety of participating athletes, the extent of its *legal duty* to protect an athlete from a voluntarily assumed enhanced risk of injury is uncertain. In *Orr v. Brigham Young University*,[20] a federal district court refused to impose a legal duty on a university to prevent an adult athlete from continuing to play intercollegiate football to avoid aggravating a pre-existing injury. The court rejected the player's contention that, by allowing him to participate, the university "assumed the responsibility for his safety and deprived him of the normal opportunity for self protection."[21] Another court has suggested that a high school's legal duty to protect a physically impaired athlete from voluntarily assumed risks is limited to ensuring that the athlete (and parents if he or she is a minor) is fully informed of an enhanced risk or severity of threatened injury, in order to enable him or her to make a rational participation decision.[22]

Although the doctrines of express assumption of risk[23] or sovereign immunity[24] may immunize a team or event sponsor from tort liability for allowing a physically impaired athlete to participate, uncertainty concerning legal liability is a legitimate interest to a team or sponsor of an athletic event.

Although a sponsor of an amateur athletic event has both a legitimate interest in protecting an impaired athlete's health and safety, and a justifiable fear of legal liability if it does not do so, its interest in safeguarding other participants from psychological injury and protecting its own reputation seem less compelling. Considered alone, possible harm to team morale is not entitled to as significant weight when balanced against the exercise of an athlete's federally protected civil liberties.[25] And, it may be difficult to establish that serious injury to, or even the death of, a physically impaired athlete who voluntarily chooses to participate in a sport, with full knowledge of an enhanced potential risk of harm, will significantly injure the reputation of the team or event sponsor.[26]

II. Rehabilitation Act Cases Defining Amateur Athletes' Participation Rights

To prevail on a claim that exclusion from a sport or athletic event violates the Rehabilitation Act, an athlete must prove: 1) he or she is "disabled"; 2) he or she is "otherwise qualified" for the position or opportunity sought; 3) he or she has been excluded from the position solely because of his or her disability; and 4) the position or opportunity exists as part of a program or activity receiving federal financial assistance.[27] It is not necessary that an entity's athletic program directly benefits from federal funds. A public or private elementary or secondary educational institution, as well as any other sponsor of an athletic event, is covered by the Rehabilitation Act if any aspect of it receives any form of federal funding.[28]

A physically impaired athlete also could assert that his or her exclusion from a sport violates the ADA, although cases challenging such exclusion, because of increased risk of injury to one's self, thus far have only been brought under the Rehabilitation Act. Such a claim requires proof of essentially the same elements as a Rehabilitation Act claim[29] except that, instead of showing that the defendant receives federal funds, the athlete must prove that the defendant is covered by the ADA's "public entity"[30] or "public accommodation"[31] provisions. A sponsor of an amateur athletic event that is not covered by the

Rehabilitation Act because it does not receive federal funds may nevertheless be covered under the ADA's public entity or public accommodation sections.[32] Unless otherwise noted, I will consider both laws together in addressing a physically impaired amateur athlete's legal right to participate in sports.[33]

A person with a physical impairment which substantially limits one or more of his or her major life activities, or has a record of such impairment, or is regarded as having such an impairment, is considered to be "disabled" and covered by the Act.[34] The first Rehabilitation Act suits were brought by high school or college athletes with either a missing or non-functioning eye or kidney who had been excluded from participating in a contact sport. Courts either assumed that these athletes satisfied the Act's definition of an individual with a "disability," or found this requirement satisfied without engaging in extensive analysis.[35]

In resolving these initial cases, courts focused on the requirement that an athlete be "otherwise qualified" to participate in a sport despite a physical abnormality. In a 1977 case, *Kampmeier v. Nyquist*,[36] the Second Circuit ruled that a high school's refusal to permit one-eyed athletes to play contact sports complied with the Act despite conflicting physician participation recommendations. Although the plaintiffs had the requisite ability and skill to play basketball, and their medical condition did not expose others to an enhanced risk of injury, they were not allowed to participate because of an enhanced risk of injury to themselves.

Neither the Act nor its implementing regulations regarding inter-scholastic or intercollegiate sports directly address whether an enhanced risk or severity of injury to an athlete is a legally valid justification for exclusion from school-sponsored athletics.[37] Without citing any judicial precedent, the *Kampmeier* court held that a "substantial justification" is required to exclude an impaired athlete from participation in a sport.[38]

The court found that the team physician's medical recommendation, against participation, which was consistent with then current American Medical Association guidelines, because plaintiffs would be subjected to a perceived "high risk" of injury during athletic competition, provided a "substantial justification" for the school's decision.[39] Other examining physicians medically cleared the plaintiffs to play interscholastic basketball, based on their belief that special goggles would adequately protect the plaintiffs' eyes from injury during competition. Observing that the team physician had nevertheless concluded that participation in contact sports with protective gear would still present an unreasonable risk of eye injury, the court found "little evidence – medical, statistical, or otherwise – which would cast doubt on the substantiality of this rationale."[40]

Finding that public high schools have "a parens patriae interest in protecting the well-being of their students,"[41] the court held that the plaintiffs are not "otherwise qualified" to play interscholastic basketball. Despite recognizing the important role of athletics in the life and growth of children, and that the plaintiffs were being deprived of an opportunity to play their chosen sports, the court observed that they still had the option of participating in noncontact sports.[42]

In a 1979 case not involving athletics, *Southeastern Community College v. Davis*,[43] the Supreme Court held that, under the Act, an educational institution may require a person to possess "reasonable physical qualifications" necessary to *protect others' safety* as a condition of participating in its programs and activities. Although "mere possession of a handicap is not a permissible ground for assuming an inability to function," the Court ruled that a school need "not lower or substantially modify its standards to accommodate a handicapped person."[44] The Court concluded that an individual is "otherwise qualified" if "able to meet all of a program's requirements *in spite of his handicap*,"[45] but did not determine whether risk of harm to one's self is a valid reason to exclude him or her from an activity.

In *Poole v. South Plainfield Board of Education*,[46] a federal district court held that a high school's refusal to permit a student to wrestle with only one kidney violated the Act because other "respectable medical authority" cleared him to participate. Without citing or discussing *Kampmeier*, the court rejected the school's argument that the student was not "otherwise qualified" because he was unable to obtain medical clearance from the team physician with only one kidney. Relying on *Davis*, the court found that the student was "otherwise qualified" because, with the exception of his failure to pass the team physician's examination, he satisfied all of the wrestling program's requirements and did not pose a risk of increased injury to others "in spite of the fact he was born with one kidney."[47]

The *Poole* court did not directly address whether requiring an athlete to pass the team physician's medical examination, *to protect his or her own safety*, is a permissible "reasonable physical qualification" under *Davis*. *Poole* also did not consider whether an athlete's failure to satisfy this school-established requirement was a legally valid "substantial justification" for exclusion under *Kampmeier*. Instead, *Poole* relied on a 1978 Department of Health, Education, and Welfare policy interpretation of the Act's regulations prohibiting schools from categorically excluding athletes who have a missing or non-functioning organ from playing contact sports.[48]

The *Poole* court found that the Act's purpose is "to permit handicapped individuals to live life as fully as they are able, without paternalistic authorities deciding that certain activities are too risky for them,"[49] thereby according great weight to an impaired athlete's interest in individual autonomy. The court held that the school's interest in protecting a student's physical health did not justify excluding him from contact sports and was not a proper exercise of its *in loco parentis* authority when his parents supported his decision to participate in wrestling.[50] The court also suggested that, because the school had alerted plaintiff and his parents of the potential health risks of playing with his physical abnormality, it would not be legally liable for any injuries he suffered as a result of wrestling in his condition.[51]

Similarly, in *Wright v. Columbia University*,[52] another federal district court held that the Act required a university to permit an outstanding athlete with sight in only one eye to play football. Distinguishing *Kampmeier* by accepting the testimony of the plaintiff's ophthalmologist that, "no substantial risk of serious eye injury related to football exists[,]" the court rejected the school's reliance on the team physician's contrary medical opinion.[53] The plaintiff testified that "he seriously considered and appreciates the risks incident to playing football with impaired vision and willingly accepts them."[54]

The court found that he was "otherwise qualified" to play, and the university was not forced to "lower or . . . effect substantial modifications of its standards,"[55] which would be a valid defense to his exclusion under *Davis*. Following *Poole*, the court found that the plaintiff "is indeed an intelligent, motivated young man who is capable of making this decision which affects his health and well-being."[56] Holding that the Act "prohibits 'paternalistic authorities' from deciding that certain activities are 'too risky' for a handicapped person,"[57] the court noted that excluding the plaintiff would deprive him of an opportunity to participate fully in an intercollegiate football program that also may preclude him from a future professional football career.[58]

In *Grube v. Bethlehem Area School District*,[59] a federal district court held that a high school's decision to exclude an excellent player with one kidney from its football team in accordance with its team physician's recommendation violated the Act. While adopting *Kampmeier's* "substantial justification" standard, the court found it was not satisfied based on the evidence of record. The court framed the key issue as whether the risk of injury to the plaintiff "is significant enough to make this concern any justification" for the school's action.[60] Because the plaintiff's personal physician concluded that "there is no medical reason why [he] cannot play football" with appropriate protective padding, and, most importantly, the opinion of other physicians recommending against his participation "lacks a medical basis," the court found no "substantial justification" for preventing the plaintiff from playing football.[61]

The school was concerned about potential legal liability if the plaintiff lost his one functioning kidney while playing football. According to the court, this also was not a "substantial justification" for excluding him from the sport, because he and his parents were willing to release the school from liability if he injured his kidney, while playing football.[62] Concluding that the "plaintiff is being deprived of an important right guaranteed by federal legislation," the court noted that he is a "collegiate caliber football player" who might earn a college athletic scholarship if allowed to continue playing high school football.[63]

After *Poole, Wright,* and *Grube* were decided, in *Alexander v. Choate,*[64] the United States Supreme Court clarified *Davis* by holding that an entity covered by the Rehabilitation Act "need not be required to make 'fundamental' or 'substantial' modifications to accommodate the handicapped, [but] it may be required to make 'reasonable' ones." This case did not involve the application of the Act to athletics, but suggests that physically impaired athletes are legally entitled to reasonable accommodations necessary to enable them to compete in a sport with their medical condition.

In 1987, the United States Supreme Court decided another important case under the Act by considering when it is legally permissible to exclude a physically impaired person from an activity or program to *prevent a risk of harm to others. In School Board of Nassau County, Fla. v Arline,*[65] the Court held that the Act does not prohibit disparate treatment of the handicapped necessary to avoid "exposing others to significant health and safety risks." The Court explained that "in determining whether an individual is 'otherwise qualified,' she or he is entitled to an opportunity to have [one's] condition evaluated in light of medical evidence."[66] The decision to exclude an individual from a particular program or activity must be based on "reasonable medical judgments given the state of medical knowledge."[67] The nature, duration, probability, and severity of harm likely to result from the handicapped individual's participation, and whether it can be effectively reduced by reasonable accommodation, are factors to be considered.[68]

After *Arline*, a minor athlete asserted an absolute right to play high school football under the Act, despite unanimous agreement by examining physicians that he should not play with a serious heart condition that could be fatal. In *Larkin v. Archdiocese of Cincinnati*,[69] in an unreported oral opinion issued from the bench, Judge Herman J. Weber held that, although the plaintiff was "handicapped," the school's acceptance of unanimous physician recommendations that he not continue playing football, did not violate the Act. The court ruled that the plaintiff's inability to satisfy an Ohio High School Athletics Association by-law requiring "a physician certification" of medical fitness as a condition of participation in interscholastic athletics was a "substantial justification" for the school's decision to exclude him.[70] The court also recognized that, under Ohio law, the plaintiff's parents could not validly waive their minor son's potential legal claims if he were injured while playing football.[71] Without citing *Arline* or *Kampmeier*, *Larkin* implicitly relies on their holdings in concluding that exclusion of an athlete from a sport, based on a reasonable medical judgment that athletic participation would expose him or her to an enhanced risk of serious injury or death, does not violate the Act.

Recent Rehabilitation Act cases brought by athletes challenging their medical disqualification from a sport, specifically consider whether an athlete is "disabled" under the statute, as well as whether he or she is "otherwise qualified" to participate. In *Pahulu v. University of Kansas*,[72] the court upheld a public university's decision not to allow Alani Pahulu to continue playing college football after being medically disqualified by the team physician. After experiencing transient quadriplegia while making a tackle during a scrimmage, he was found to have an abnormally narrow cervical canal. After consulting with a neurosurgeon, the team physician concluded that he was at extremely high risk for sustaining permanent, severe neurological injury, including permanent quadriplegia, if he resumed playing college football. The university agreed to honor his athletic scholarship, although he was not permitted to play football. Nevertheless, he wanted to continue playing because three other medical specialists concluded that his spinal abnormality did not expose him to a greater risk of permanent paralysis than any other player.

The court first considered the Act's requirement that the plaintiff have a physical impairment which substantially limits one or more of his major life activities. It found that his congenitally narrow cervical canal is a physical impairment, and applying a subjective standard, that intercollegiate football is a part of the student's major life activity of learning.[73] However, the court held that he is not "disabled" under the Act because his exclusion from football does not substantially limit his opportunity to learn since he retained his athletic scholarship, which provided him with continued access to all academic services, and he was allowed to participate in the university's football program in a role other than as a player.[74]

Without citing any of the foregoing cases, the court also held that the student is not "otherwise qualified" because he was not able to satisfy all of the football program's requirements in spite of his disability, namely, medical clearance from the university's team physician to play football. The court found that the team physician's "conservative" medical opinion is "reasonable and rational" and "supported by substantial competent evidence" for which it is "unwilling to substitute its judgment."[75]

In *Knapp v. Northwestern University*,[76] the Seventh Circuit reversed the lower court's holding that Northwestern University violated the Rehabilitation Act in following its team physician's medical recommendation that an athlete with a heart condition known as idiopathic ventricular fibrillation not play intercollegiate basketball. As a high school senior, Nicholas Knapp suffered sudden cardiac arrest while playing recreational basketball, which required cardiopulmonary resuscitation and defibrillation to restart his heart. Thereafter, he had an internal cardioverter-defibrillator implanted in his abdomen. He subsequently played competitive recreational basketball without any incidents of cardiac arrest for two years and received medical clearance to play college basketball from three cardiologists who examined him.

Northwestern agreed to honor its commitment to provide Knapp with an athletic scholarship, although it adhered to its team physician's medical disqualification from intercollegiate basketball. This recommendation was based on Knapp's medical records and history, the 26th Bethesda Conference guidelines for athletic participation with cardiovascular abnormalities,[77] and opinions from two consulting cardiologists who concluded that Knapp would expose himself to a significant risk of ventricular fibrillation or cardiac arrest during competitive athletics.

All medical experts agreed on the following facts: Knapp had suffered sudden cardiac death due to ventricular fibrillation; even with the internal defibrillator; playing college basketball placed Knapp at a higher risk for suffering another event of sudden cardiac death compared to other male college basketball players; the internal defibrillator has never been tested under the conditions of intercollegiate basketball; and no person currently plays or has ever played college or professional basketball after suffering sudden cardiac death and having a defibrillator implanted.[78]

The lower court held that Knapp is "disabled" under the Act. The parties did not dispute that Knapp is perceived as having a permanent cardiovascular impairment, which is a physical impairment under the statute. The court found that intercollegiate basketball is a major life activity for Knapp, because it "is an important and integral part of [his] education and learning experience."[79] Because practicing with the team and competing in games is necessary for learning discipline, teamwork, and perseverance, the trial court concluded that Northwestern's refusal to allow Knapp to play substantially limits his ability to play college basketball.

The Seventh Circuit disagreed with the lower court's conclusion and held that Knapp is not "disabled" under the Act. The appellate court held that "[p]laying intercollegiate basketball obviously is not in and of itself a major life activity."[80] Finding that learning is the affected major life activity, the court concluded that playing intercollegiate basketball is "only one part of the education available to Knapp at Northwestern."[81] Consistent with *Pahulu*, the court observed that Knapp's "inability to play intercollegiate basketball at Northwestern forecloses only a small portion of his collegiate [learning] opportunities"[82] and does not substantially limit his college education because his athletic scholarship continues, thereby allowing him full access to all of the university's other programs and activities.

The parties agreed that Knapp is not "otherwise qualified" under the Act if there is a "genuine substantial risk" that he could be seriously injured while playing basketball at Northwestern.[83] The lower court noted that all medical experts agreed on the underlying basic scientific and medical principles, but that, because no one had ever played college basketball with an implanted defibrillator, the risk that Knapp would suffer another incident of cardiac arrest while playing could not be objectively quantified.[84] Medical experts disagreed whether the risk of injury to Knapp was substantial enough to medically justify his exclusion from intercollegiate basketball.

The lower court conceded that excluding Knapp from an "'unessential' activity," such as intercollegiate basketball, that creates an increased uncertain risk of serious personal injury "is clearly rational in the medical profession," given the absence of proven safety.[85] However, the court concluded that the Act "require[s] a judicial decision on the substantiality of the risk" necessitating consideration of "the testimony of all the experts who testified and determin[ing] which are most persuasive."[86] After weighing the experts' testimony, the court found that the risk of injury to Knapp while playing college basketball is not medically substantial and that the implanted defibrillator most likely would restore his heart beat to normal if Knapp's heart rate became abnormal during strenuous physical exertion.[87]

The Seventh Circuit again disagreed with the lower court and concluded that Knapp is not "otherwise qualified" to play basketball at Northwestern under the Act. Citing *Davis*, the appellate court held that a university legally may establish legitimate physical qualifications that an individual must satisfy in order to participate in its athletic program.[88] Agreeing with the lower court and the parties that a "significant risk of personal physical injury" that cannot be eliminated justifies medical disqualification from an activity, the court framed the controlling issue as, "[W]ho should make such an assessment[?]"[89]

Holding that Knapp's exclusion from Northwestern's basketball team was legally justified, the Seventh Circuit explained:

> We disagree with the district court's legal determination that such decisions are to be made by the courts and believe instead that medical determinations of this sort are best left to team doctors and universities as long as they are made with reason and rationality and with full regard to possible and reasonable accommodations. In cases such as ours, where Northwestern has examined both Knapp and his medical records, and considered his medical history and the relation between his prior sudden cardiac death and the possibility of future occurrences, has considered the severity of the potential injury, and has rationally and reasonably reviewed consensus medical opinions or recommendations in the pertinent field – regardless whether conflicting medical opinions exist – the university has the right to determine that an individual is not otherwise medically qualified to play without violating the Rehabilitation Act. The place of the court in such cases is to make sure that the decision-maker has reasonably considered and relied upon suffi-cient evidence specific to the individual and the potential injury, not to determine on its own which evidence it believes is more persuasive.
>
> ...
>
> We do not believe that, in cases where medical experts disagree in their assessment of the extent of a real risk of serious harm or death, Congress intended that the courts – neutral arbiters but generally less skilled in medicine than the experts involved – should make the final medical decision. Instead, in the midst of conflicting expert testimony regarding the degree of serious risk of harm or death, the

court's place is to ensure that the exclusion or disqualification of an individual was individualized, reasonably made, and based upon competent medical evidence. So long as these factors exist, it will be the rare case regarding participation in athletics where a court may substitute its judgment for that of the school's team physicians.

...

In closing, we wish to make clear that we are *not* saying Northwestern's decision necessarily is the right decision. We say only that it is not an illegal one under the Rehabilitation Act. On the same facts, another team physician at another university, reviewing the same medical history, physical evaluation, and medical recommendations, might reasonably decide that Knapp met the physical qualifications for playing on an intercollegiate basketball team. Simply put, all universities need not evaluate risk the same way. What we say in this case is that if substantial evidence supports the decision-maker – here Northwestern – that decision must be respected.[90]

III. Synthesis and Critique of Rehabilitation Act Precedent

Federal trial and appellate courts, thus far, have resolved claims brought by physically impaired amateur athletes on a case-by-case basis, without clear direction from Congress or explicit guidance from the Supreme Court. Neither the Rehabilitation Act nor its accompanying regulations specifically address whether exclusion of a skilled athlete, with a physical abnormality from a desired sport substantially limits a "major life activity."[91] Moreover, the Act is silent regarding whether a risk of physical harm solely to one's self precludes an athlete from being "otherwise qualified," and the Supreme Court has not yet considered this issue.

In construing the Act's requirements that an athlete be both "disabled" and "otherwise qualified" to participate, it appears that courts are implicitly balancing the athlete's interest in playing a sport with the sponsoring institution's interest in protecting the health and safety of participants. The foregoing cases illustrate that courts recognize that athletic competition is a valued component of both high school and college education, but are divided regarding the importance of athletics in a student's learning experience. On the other hand, the judiciary considers the protection of an athlete's health to be a legitimate objective, regardless of whether an educational institution has an affirmative legal duty to prevent a student from harming one's self, but does not always consider this interest to be paramount. Courts usually struggle to weigh appropriately the parties' conflicting interests particularly when medical experts are divided in their participation recommendations.

A. Exclusion From Amateur Athletics as Substantially Limiting a Major Life Activity

In determining whether an individual athlete's exclusion from athletics substantially limits a major life activity, courts should accord greater weight to the importance of athletic competition in high school and college education. Although most students do not participate in intercollegiate or interscholastic sports, it is appropriate to apply a subjective test in resolving this issue because the Act references "such person's major life activities,"[92] thereby indicating the necessary individualized nature of this inquiry. Consistent with this language, some courts have held that athletics are sufficiently intertwined with education, such that they constitute a major life activity for particular individuals playing interscholastic or intercollegiate sports.[93]

At the high school level, interscholastic athletics play an integral role in enabling participants to earn better grades and develop social skills by teaching discipline, teamwork, commitment, motivation, and hard work.[94] The vast majority of people do not participate in structured competitive athletics beyond high school, and their last opportunity to take advantage of these important educational benefits occurs during this formative four-year period.

Intercollegiate athletics play a different role in the educational process for the relatively small number of college students participating in them, but they are an important part of a university's primary mission of helping an individual maximize one's learning and career potential – whether it be academic, physical, or artistic prowess or a combination of these talents. Moreover, in other contexts, courts have recognized that intercollegiate athletics are an integral component of American higher education and provide invaluable lessons that help further general life success and careers outside of professional sports.[95]

Whether exclusion from intercollegiate or interscholastic athletics substantially limits one's opportunity to learn must necessarily be considered on an individualized basis.[96] Even if there are other

educational benefits available to excluded physically impaired athletes, they are being denied an equal opportunity to participate fully
in all of an educational institution's programs and activities which are
generally available to all persons with the requisite skills and abilities.[97]
If physically impaired high school and college athletes are not covered
by the Act, such an athlete is deprived of his or her federal right to have
one's medical condition individually evaluated as well as the full
potential educational benefits of competitive athletics if he or she is
found to be "otherwise qualified" under the Act. Accordingly, it
would further the Act's objectives of prohibiting medically unjustified
discrimination against physically impaired persons by ensuring that
these athletes are protected by the Act.

B. "Otherwise Qualified" to Participate in Amateur Athletics

In *City of Cleburne v. Cleburne Living Center, Inc.*,[98] the United
States Supreme Court ruled that handicapped persons are not a
suspect or quasi-suspect class justifying heightened scrutiny of alleged
discrimination. Under *Cleburne*, to successfully defend a denial of
equal protection of the law claim, a public school can justify the
exclusion of a physically impaired athlete from a sport if its decision
is rationally related to a legitimate objective such as protecting his or
her health and safety. However, unlike the federal Constitution, the
Rehabilitation Act requires that a covered educational institution or
entity have more than merely a rational basis for discriminating
against a physically impaired athlete.[99] Courts have struggled to
formulate the appropriate legal standard justifying exclusion of a
physically impaired athlete from a sport for medial reasons.

The *Larkin* court properly rejected the contention that the Act
creates an absolute right for a physically impaired amateur athlete to
participate in a sport, even if there is universal agreement among
physicians that his or her medical condition creates a significant risk
of serious personal injury or death.[100] Absent clear legislative intent
supporting such a position, it is extremely unlikely that Congress
intended the Rehabilitation Act to be a means of forcing covered
entities to enable amateur athletes to take potentially life-threatening
risks in a sport that is merely an avocation. To the contrary, in *Davis*,
the Supreme Court held that the Act does not prohibit an educational
institution from requiring that its students possess "reasonable physical qualifications" in order to participate in its programs and activities.[101]

In construing the Act's "otherwise qualified" requirement, as applied to athletics, some courts hold that an athlete with a physical abnormality may be excluded from a sport only if there is a "substantial justification" for doing so.[102] Even if this specific terminology is not used, or the appropriate legal standard is phrased somewhat differently, courts generally agree that the Act permits an athlete to be medically disqualified, if necessary to prevent a significant risk of serious personal injury such as a permanently crippling injury or death.[103] Courts have adopted a similar judicial standard regarding the legally permissible exclusion of handicapped persons from covered employment opportunities under the Act.[104]

Judicial formulation and acceptance of the "significant risk of serious injury" standard as a legal justification for excluding a physically impaired athlete from a sport does not, however, resolve the key issue in determining whether an athlete is "otherwise qualified" to participate. As the *Knapp* appellate court recognized, this issue is, "Who should make such an assessment"[105] when there is no definitive scientific evidence and medical experts conflict in their athletic participation recommendations? There are three theoretical models of decision-making that have been adopted by courts in construing the Act as it governs athletes which I will term as: 1) the judicial/medical fact-finding model; 2) the athlete informed consent model; and 3) the team physician medical judgment model.

1. Overview of Three Decision-Making Models

Under the judicial/medical fact-finding model, which was used by the *Knapp* trial court, a court resolves conflicting medical testimony regarding whether a disabled athlete's condition creates a significant risk of substantial injury while playing a sport. The *Knapp* trial court judge concluded: "Congress has required a judicial decision on the substantiality of the risk" and "I must consider the testimony of all the experts who testified and determine which are most persuasive."[106] This model requires a court to determine whether there is a valid basis for medically disqualifying an athlete from participation as a matter of fact.

The athlete informed consent model permits the athlete (and his or her parents or guardian if he or she is a minor) to decide whether to participate if respectable medical authority provides clearance to play the sport. Under this model, the athlete is allowed to participate even if he or she has been medically disqualified by the team physician if

willing to waive any potential legal claims against the educational
institution or sports event sponsor for injury that occurs while playing
with his or her physical impairment.[107] As the *Poole* court explained:

> Life has risks. The purpose of [the Act], however, is to permit
> handicapped individuals to live life as fully as they are able, without
> paternalistic authorities deciding that certain activities are too risky
> for them. . . . The [school's] responsibility is to see that he does not
> pursue this course in a foolish manner. They therefore have a duty
> to alert Richard and his parents to the dangers involved and to
> require them to deal with the matter rationally.[108]

Poole suggests that an athlete must obtain medical clearance from
his or her chosen physician in order to have an autonomy right to
participate in sports under the Act.

Under the team physician model, a school has a valid legal justification, as a matter of law, for excluding an athlete who has been
medically disqualified by the team physician. The school is entitled to
rely on its team physician's reasonable opinion that the athlete's
disability exposes him or her to a significant risk of substantial injury
during athletic competition, even if other physicians have provided
medical clearance.[109] In *Knapp*, the Seventh Circuit held:

> [M]edical determinations of this sort are best left to team doctors
> and universities as long as they are made with reason and rationally
> and with full regard to possible and reasonable accommodations.
> . . The place of the court in such cases is to make sure that the
> decision-maker has reasonably considered and relied upon suffi-
> cient evidence specific to the individual and potential injury, not
> to determine on its own which evidence it believes is more
> persuasive.[110]

Each of these three models has its respective pluses and minuses.
The litmus test, however, is which model best furthers Congressional
intent in formulating the Rehabilitation Act, accords with Supreme
Court precedent construing the Act, and furthers public policy? For
the following reasons, I believe the team physician model accom-
plishes these objectives better than the other two models.

2 Judicial/Medical Fact-finding Model

The judicial/medical fact-finding model is consistent with some other cases construing the Act outside of the athletics context. These cases hold that the trial court must make a *de novo* assessment of the risk of personal injury to a disabled person.[111] This model enables the court to disregard a reasonably conservative medical opinion disqualifying a disabled athlete to protect his or her health in favor of a more liberal medical opinion that would permit participation, contrary to the school's legitimate safety interests. In determining whether there is a significant risk of substantial harm to a disabled athlete as a matter of fact, a court would not be bound by the team physician's medical opinion.

This model, however, conflicts with Supreme Court precedent under the Act. *Davis* holds that an educational institution legally may require that its students possess "reasonable physical qualifications" in order to participate in its programs and activities.[112] It also contravenes the *Arline* holding that physically impaired persons may be legally excluded from activities "based on reasoned and medically sound judgments."[113] According to the Court, the purpose of the Act is to protect a physically impaired person "from deprivations based on prejudice, stereotypes, or unfounded fear" and to provide an opportunity to have one's condition individually evaluated in light of medical evidence."[114] The Act should not be construed to require courts to exhaust scarce judicial resources attempting to resolve an issue of medical uncertainty on which there is no consensus among medical experts.[115]

If Congress had actually intended to limit a school's legal ability to exclude an athlete from a sport, consistent with its team physician's medical judgment, it could have established an explicit statutory framework for this purpose. For example, a New York education law statute expressly provides a judicial procedure for enabling a physically impaired athlete to participate in interscholastic athletics despite an inability to obtain medical clearance from the school physician.[116] A petition seeking court-ordered participation must be accompanied by affidavits from two physicians testifying that the athlete's participation would be "reasonably safe."[117] The court will order the school to permit participation if it finds that participation in a sport would be in the athlete's best interests and reasonably safe.[118] The statute immunizes a school district from liability for injury sustained by a physically impaired student while participating in athletics pursuant to a court order.[119]

The New York statute effectively requires a court to resolve conflicting medical opinions, as a matter of fact, in determining whether athletic participation would be reasonably safe. This is consistent with the state legislature's intent as reflected in the express language of the statute. In accordance with this explicit statutory authorization, a New York appellate court affirmed the lower court's order allowing an athlete to participate in a sport contrary to the team physician's medical judgment.[120] However, the Second Circuit, refusing to resolve conflicting testimony by medical experts, held that the same athlete did not have a federal right to participate under the Rehabilitation Act without medical clearance from the team physician.[121]

The judicial/medical fact-finding model allows a court to substitute its judgment on medical issues for that of the team physician, which may thereby adversely affect the quality of sports medicine care rendered to athletes. The law should not create an incentive for a team physician to place greater weight on legal rather than medical considerations when evaluating athletes' physical fitness.[122] This model encourages athletes, motivated by economic or psychological reasons, to shop for favorable opinions in order to obtain medical clearance to play a sport and facilitates second-guessing of the team physician's medical judgment. The team physician/athlete relationship is based on a trust relationship that will be seriously compromised if a court interferes with the exercise of medical judgment exercised to protect an amateur athlete's health and safety.[123]

3. Athlete Informed Consent Model

The athlete informed consent model is based on a strong libertarian philosophy that would enable a physically impaired athlete to voluntarily assume the risk of a potentially serious injury, which is not medically certain, or even likely, to occur.[124] This philosophy promotes individual autonomy over communality and is espoused in John Stuart Mill's seminal work ON LIBERTY.[125] In relevant part, Mill states:

> That the only purpose for which power can be rightfully exercised over any member of a civilized community, against his will, is to prevent harm to others. His own good, either physical or moral, is not a sufficient warrant.

· · ·

[The] principle requires liberty of tastes and pursuits; of framing the plan of our life to suit our own character; of doing as we like, subject to such consequences as may follow; without impediment from our fellow-creatures, so long as what we do does not harm them even though they should think our conduct foolish, perverse, or wrong.

· · ·

Each is the proper guardian of his own health, whether bodily, or mental or spiritual.[126]

When I initially considered this issue, I adopted a libertarian position and argued that there is no legal justification under the Act for excluding a physically impaired athlete from intercollegiate or interscholastic athletics if competent physicians have conflicting participation recommendations based on an individualized examination of the athlete and a differing evaluation of the medical risks.[127] I asserted that, when there is no definite scientific answer or consensus among medical experts, and there are different credible conclusions regarding the medical risks of participating, a physically impaired athlete (and parents or guardian if he or she is a minor) has a legal right to choose to participate in school-sponsored athletics. Arguably, the Act's "reasonable accommodation" requirement mandates that the team or athletic event sponsor allow the athlete to choose the physician(s) whose assessment of the medical risks controls. Court-ordered athletic participation under the Act should create an implied immunity absolving a school from tort liability if an athlete suffers injury relating to or caused by one's physical abnormality.[128]

This model embodies the philosophy that the Act prohibits a school or sponsor of an athletic event from substituting its decision for that of a fully informed athlete who chooses to participate in athletics based on credible medical clearance. The physically impaired athlete has a right to exercise his or her individual autonomy and choose to accept an enhanced, but medically uncertain risk of injury, free of a school's paternalistic concerns.

The primary weakness of the athlete informed consent model is its de-emphasis of a school's legitimate interest in protecting a physically impaired athlete's health and safety.[129] Courts have recognized that the relationship between an educational institution and its athletes is consensual in nature.[130] Also, *Davis* holds that a school may legally establish reasonable physical qualifications to ensure the safety standards that must be satisfied in order to participate in its programs and activities.[131] Nevertheless, this model provides a physically impaired athlete who has been medically disqualified by the team physician with a federal right to participate in a sport if he or she is able to obtain medical clearance from another physician.

Even if one accepts Mill's libertarian view that an individual should not be prevented from engaging in activities that may endanger one's health, this philosophy does not support a construction of the Act requiring a school to involuntarily permit a medically disqualified athlete to participate in its athletic program. Properly interpreted, Mill's philosophy supports a physically impaired athlete's right to refuse medical treatment and to individually engage in athletic activities that threaten his or her health, but it does not justify requiring the sponsor of an athletics event to involuntarily provide a playing field for endangering one's personal health. For example, a long distance runner with a potentially life-threatening cardiovascular abnormality that may be aggravated by strenuous exercise cannot be forced to undergo a recommended medical procedure or prevented from running on one's own. However, he or she should not have a legal right to participate on the university's cross country team even if physically able to do so, after being medically disqualified by the team physician. Properly considered, Mill's libertarian philosophy does not affirmatively support requiring the school to allow him to participate even if other physicians provide medical clearance. A team or sponsor of an amateur athletic event should not be legally required to provide the arena for an uncontrolled medical experiment that may have tragic consequences.[132]

4. Team Physician Medical Judgment Model

All things considered, the team physician medical judgment model strikes the appropriate balance between an amateur athlete's interest in athletic participation and the team or athletic event sponsor's interest in protecting the health and safety of participants. Under this model, an athlete receives an individualized evaluation of his or her physical condition and may be legally excluded only "based on reasoned and medically sound judgments."[133] All medically relevant factors relating to the personal health risks created by the athlete's physical impairment such as the nature, duration, probability, and severity of harm, as well as whether reasonable accommodations will effectively eliminate or safely reduce the risk of injury are considered.[134]

Exclusion is permissible only if the court finds the team physician has a reasonable medical basis for determining that athletic competition creates a significant risk of substantial harm to a physically impaired athlete.[135] A court is much better equipped to evaluate whether there is a reasonable basis for medically disqualifying an impaired athlete than to resolve, as a matter of fact, a medical issue when physicians have conflicting opinions. This model creates a presumption favoring the team physician, but it does not establish an irrefutable presumption that the team physician's medical judgment is correct or require a court to defer to it. For example, there may be no reasoned medical basis for excluding athletes with a missing or non-functioning paired organ from a contact sport. In this situation an athlete has the same risk of injury in terms of the probability of personal harm to a paired organ as any other participant.[136] Although the consequences of an injury to a single eye or kidney may be more severe, protective gear or padding probably will effectively reduce this risk. This is the same result that the *Poole*, *Wright*, and *Grube* courts reached while using the athlete informed consent model.[137] Thus, under the team physician model, athletes have a legal right to participate under the Act if there is no valid medical basis for disqualifying them.[138]

The team physician medical judgment model best furthers the legitimate goal of enhancing the quality of sports medicine care rendered to athletes. Although one of the team physician's objectives is to avoid the unnecessary restriction of athletic activity, his or her paramount legal and ethical responsibility is to protect an athlete's health.[139] Judicial recognition of the team physician's legal authority to medically disqualify a physically impaired athlete, without fear of unnecessary second guessing, creates a strong incentive to render high quality care to athletes.

The *Knapp* appellate court held that a team physician may rely on consensus guidelines regarding the advisability of athletic participation when an athlete has physical abnormalities.[140] Such guidelines are particularly helpful to a physician if the medical risks of playing a sport are uncertain.[141] As the *Knapp* appellate court explained, "[S]uch guidelines should not substitute for individualized assessment of an athlete's particular physical condition, [but] the consensus recommendations of several physicians in a certain field do carry weight" in judicial determination of whether there is a reasonable medical basis for disqualifying a physically impaired athlete.[142]

Although use of the team physician medical judgment model may preclude an athlete from engaging in competitive athletics at a particular school, it would not necessarily prevent an athlete from playing elsewhere. As the *Knapp* appellate court observed: "[On] the same facts, another team physician . . . might reasonably decide that Knapp met the physical qualifications for playing on an intercollegiate basketball team."[143] After losing his Rehabilitation Act suit against Northwestern University, Nick Knapp transferred to Northeastern Illinois University and received medical clearance to play college basketball.[144]

The team physician medical judgment model places legitimate communitarian health and safety concerns above an athlete's libertarian personal autonomy interests. If all concerned parties – the athlete, team physician, and school – cannot agree on the acceptability of assuming an enhanced but medically uncertain risk on the playing field, it is better to err on the side of caution.[145]

IV. Physically Impaired Professional Athletes' Potential Claims

A disability discrimination claim brought by a professional athlete most likely would have to be asserted under the ADA because entities and organizations sponsoring professional sports generally do not receive federal funding.[146] Depending upon the particular sport, the ADA's provisions relating to employers,[147] public entities,[148] or places of public accommodation,[149] may apply. For example, a federal magistrate recently held that the Professional Golfers Association Tour is subject to the ADA in a suit brought by a physically impaired golfer seeking to ride in a golf cart in order to play professional golf.[150] Like similar claims brought by amateur athletes under the Rehabilitation Act, the key issues under the ADA are whether a professional athlete is "disabled" and whether exclusion solely because of an enhanced risk of physical harm to one's self is legally valid.

A. Exclusion from Professional Athletics as Substantially Limiting a Major Life Activity

To be protected by the ADA, a professional athlete must have a "disability," which requires proof that his or her physical impairment substantially limits a major life activity, has a record of such an impairment, or is regarded as having such an impairment.[151] The ADA's regulations broadly define "physical impairment," which encompasses a permanent condition such as a missing or non-functioning paired organ (e.g., an eye or kidney), spinal stenosis, or a cardiovascular abnormality.[152] Although these regulations expressly list "working" as a major life activity,[153] courts have held that the exclusion of a physically impaired person from only a particular job for a single employer or a narrow range of jobs does not substantially limit one's ability to work if he or she is eligible for other employment. For example, an individual with a physical abnormality which disqualifies him or her from a particular occupation such as a policeman,[154] or fireman,[155] but does not otherwise substantially limit another major life activity, is not "disabled" under the ADA.

The Equal Employment Opportunity Commission's (hereinafter "EEOC") interpretive guidelines, which accompany the ADA's regulations governing employment, provide that an individual is not substantially limited in working if he or she "is unable to perform a specialized job or profession requiring extraordinary skill, prowess or talent."[156] An illustrative example is "a professional baseball pitcher who develops a bad elbow and can no longer throw a baseball."[157] The baseball player's physical impairment does not substantially limit his ability to engage in most other employment or other major life activities such as "caring for oneself, performing manual tasks, walking, seeing, hearing, speaking, breathing, [or] learning."[158] This illustration suggests that a physically impaired professional athlete is not "disabled" unless he or she proves that the impairment substantially limits a major life activity other than merely working as a professional athlete.

Strict application of the "substantially limits a major life activity" requirement can lead to the result that certain physically impaired professional athletes are covered by the ADA, whereas, others are not. For example, a blind or deaf athlete is "disabled" because either impairment substantially limits, respectively, the major life activity of either seeing or hearing. On the other hand, an athlete with spinal stenosis or a cardiovascular abnormality may not be able to prove that either medical condition substantially limits a major life activity.[159] Yet the blind or deaf athletes are legally entitled to an individualized evaluation of their respective medical conditions, whereas, the other athletes are not. This is despite the fact that all of these athletes have the unique skills needed to play professional sports in spite of their physical impairment and are eligible for other non-athletic employment. There is no principled justification for protecting some physically impaired professional athletes under the ADA, but not others.

Even if a professional athlete's physical impairment does not actually substantially limit a major life activity, he or she should be able to show he or she is regarded as substantially limited in the major life activity of working, which is an alternative means of satisfying the ADA's definition of "disability."[160] In construing the same statutory language under the Rehabilitation Act, the Supreme Court observed that "[C]ongress acknowledged that society's accumulated myths and fears about disability and diseases are as handicapping as are the physical limitations that flow from actual impairment."[161] Therefore, the "disability" requirement is satisfied when a person is regarded as substantially limited in a major life activity, according to the Court, because "[s]uch an impairment might not diminish a person's physical or mental capabilities, but could nevertheless substantially limit that person's ability to work as a result of the negative reactions of others to the impairment."[162]

As a practical matter, a professional athlete is likely to assert an ADA claim only if the governing body for a professional sport, or all of the teams in a professional league, refuse to provide him or her with an opportunity to participate in a sport on the ground that his or her physical impairment is perceived as creating an undue risk of harm to him/herself. If a person is totally excluded from employment as a professional athlete, solely because of a fear that his or her physical impairment exposes him or her to an enhanced risk of personal injury, this effectively and substantially limits his or her ability to work because of all potential employers' negative reactions. Professional athletes train for many years to develop the specialized and unique skills necessary to earn their living.[163] These long years of training and commitment constitute a major life activity for a professional athlete,[164] and exclusion from a professional sport because of a perceived risk of harm to one's self substantially limits this major life activity.

The ADA's central purpose is to ensure that discrimination against a physically impaired person is medically justified based on an individualized evaluation of one's condition, rather than on an unfounded generalization or stereotype about the potential effects of a physical impairment.[165] As a matter of policy, it is appropriate to treat all physically impaired professional athletes the same in determining whether they are protected by the ADA. Each of them should have "the opportunity to have [his or her] condition evaluated in light of medical evidence,"[166] and the federal right to participate in one's chosen profession, namely professional athletes, unless exclusion therefrom is medically justified.

B. "Otherwise Qualified" to Participate in Professional Athletics

The ADA expressly states that a "significant risk to the health and safety of others"[167] is a legitimate basis for excluding a disabled person from employment, but does not state whether a risk of harm to one's self justifies discrimination against a physically impaired employee. However, the EEOC's employment regulations interpreting the ADA provide that "a significant risk of substantial harm to the health or safety *of the individual* or others" justifies exclusion from employment.[168] These regulations adopt the Supreme Court's *Arline* standard under the Rehabilitation Act, which requires an individualized medical assessment of a physically impaired person's condition in making this determination.[169]

Courts are divided as to whether risk of harm to one's self is a legally valid basis for exclusion from employment or other activity under the ADA.[170] *In Devlin v. Arizona Youth Soccer Association*,[171] a federal district court refused to strike a sports organization's affirmative defense that its exclusion of a youth soccer player is justified, because his participation "will pose a substantial risk of harm to him." The court allowed the soccer league to assert this defense and concluded, without elaboration, that there are unresolved issues of law and fact regarding this issue. However, in *Kohnke v Delta Airlines, Inc.*,[172] another federal district court ruled that "potential harm to a disabled person himself" is not a permissible justification for employment discrimination under the ADA. The court held that the EEOC regulation, recognizing this defense, is contrary to the ADA's express language and its legislative history.

A professional sports team or event sponsor has a legitimate interest in protecting the health and safety of all participating athletes. Absent very clear evidence that this furthers congressional intent, the ADA should not be construed to completely disregard this valid interest by refusing to recognize a defense based on a significant risk of substantial personal injury to a professional athlete.[173] The ADA should not be judicially construed to provide an absolute right for a professional athlete to participate in a sport, even if he or she is unable to obtain medical clearance from any competent physician, including the one(s) of his or her choosing.

Unlike an amateur athlete, however, a professional athlete should not be bound by the team physician's medical judgment, regarding whether the athlete's physical impairment creates exposure to a significant risk of substantial personal harm. A professional athlete has a greater interest in pursuing his or her livelihood, with its potential multi-million dollar earning potential, than an amateur athlete does in participating in sports as part of the educational process or for other personal objectives.[174] Even though sponsors of amateur and professional sports both have a legitimate interest in protecting the health and safety of participants, a professional athlete's participation interests are entitled to more weight than those of an amateur athlete. Because exclusion from a professional sport has some significant adverse consequences to an athlete, he or she should be permitted to obtain second opinions regarding the medical risks of participation with his or her impairment.[175]

I propose adopting the athlete informed consent model for professional athletes, which would enable a professional athlete to choose to participate, despite medical disqualification by the team physician, if other competent medical authority clears him or her to play. Under this model, a physically impaired professional athlete has a legal right to choose to participate in a sport only if there is respected medical authority clearing him or her to do so. A professional athlete would not be conclusively bound by the team physician's recommendation that he or she be medically disqualified, but rather may select the physician(s) whose determination of the medical risks of playing a sport with his or her physical impairment would be controlling. For example, although they were precluded from playing intercollegiate sports under the team physician medical judgment model, the ADA would provide Nicholas Knapp and Alani Pahulu with an opportunity to participate in professional sports, under the athlete informed consent model, because respected medical authority cleared them to participate.[176]

Under my proposed athlete informed consent model, a court's role would be to ensure that there is a reasonable medical basis for clearing a physically impaired professional athlete to participate in a sport. The court should not resolve conflicting testimony by medical experts as a matter of fact, but should limit its judicial inquiry to whether medical clearance of a professional athlete is "individualized, reasonably made, and based upon competent evidence as a matter of law."[177] If so, a professional athlete is permitted to participate if he or she chooses to assume the risk of future personal injury resulting from his or her physical impairment while playing the sport. The team or sponsoring entity should be immunized from tort liability for allowing a physically impaired professional athlete to choose to participate under these circumstances.[178]

V. Conclusion

Determining whether a physically impaired athlete has a legal right under the Rehabilitation Act or ADA, to participate in a sport or athletic event, despite an enhanced risk of personal harm requires consideration of both the athlete's libertarian autonomy interest in participating and the athletic event sponsor's communitarian interest in protecting the athlete from an unreasonable risk of injury. Each side's interests are legitimate, but neither side's rights are absolute. I believe that the team physician medical judgment model best balances these respective interests in the context of amateur athletics whereas, the athlete informed consent model most appropriately balances these interests in the context of professional athletics, because professional athletes have a more substantial interest in participating in sports than do amateur athletes.

Notes

1. The term "sponsored athletic competition" refers to organized team athletic events from youth to professional league levels of competition as well as individual sports organized and sponsored by various entities.
2. *See generally* D. Stanley Eitzen & George H. Sage, Sociology of North American Sport 43-55 (6th ed. 1997) (examining the reciprocal relationship between sports and societal values); Drew A. Hyland, Philosophy of Sport 1-32 (1990) (recognizing that values in sports are, in part, a reflection of society's values).
3. 29 U.S.C.A. §§ 701-796 (1985).
4. 42 U.S.C.A. §§ 12101-12213 (1995).
5. Indiana High Sch. Athletic Ass'n, Inc. v. Avant, 650 N.E.2d 1164 (Ind. Ct. App. 1995).
6. Florida High Sch. Activities Ass'n, Inc. v. Bryant, 313 So.2d 57 (Fla. Dist. Ct. App. 1975).
7. Boyd v. Board of Dirs. of McGahee Sch. Dist., 612 F. Supp. 86 (E.D. Ark. 1985).
8. Albach v. Odle, 531 F.2d 983 (10th Cir. 1976); Tiffany v. Arizona Interscholastic Ass'n, Inc., 726 P.2d 231 (Ariz. Ct. App. 1986).
9. Rutledge v. Arizona Bd. of Regents, 660 F.2d 1345, 1352-53 (9th Cir. 1981); Hawkins v. Nat'l Collegiate Athletic Ass'n, 652 F. Supp. 602, 610-11 (C.D. Ill. 1987).
10. Taylor v. Wake Forest Univ., 191 S.E.2d 379-381 (N.C. Ct. App. 1972).
11. Hysaw v. Washburn Univ. of Topeka, 690 F. Supp. 940 (D. Kan. 1987).

12. Harding v. United States Figure Skating Ass'n, 851 F. Supp. 1476 (D. Or. 1994).

13. 36 U.S.C.A. 393 (5), (7) (1997); DeFrantz v. United States Olympic Comm., 492 F. Supp. 1181 (D.C. 1980) (athlete has no constitutional right to participate in Olympics).

14. Vernonia Sch. Dist. v. Acton, 515 U.S. 646, 662 (1995) (public high school has "important" interest in screening for drugs that "pose substantial physical risks" to athlete himself or herself). *Accord* Picou v. Gillum, 874 F.2d 1519, 1521 (11th Cir. 1989) (upholding state law requiring motorcyclists to wear protective headgear and rejecting plaintiff's claim that federal Constitution "forbids enforcement of any statute aimed only at protecting a State's citizens from the consequences of their own foolish behavior and not at protecting others.")

15. Hill v. NCAA, 865 P.2d 633, 637 (Cal. 1994) (finding that private governing body for intercollegiate athletics has valid interest in protecting health and safety of drug-ingesting athletes).

16. Some courts, however, have questioned whether "governmental concern for the health and safety of anyone who knowingly and voluntarily exposes himself or herself to possible injury can ever be an acceptable area of intrusion on individual liberty..." *Hoover v. Meiklejohn*, 430 F. Supp. 164, 169 (D. Colo. 1977).

17. *Picou*, 874 F.2d at 1522; Simon v. Sargent, 346 F. Supp. 277, 279 (D. Mass. 1972); State v. Laitinen, 459 P.2d 789, 791-92 (Wash. 1969).

18. Robotham v. State, 488 N.W.2d 533, 541 (Neb. 1992).

19. In re Winthrop Univ. Hosp., 490 N.Y. S.2d 996 (1985).

20. 960 F. Supp. 1522 (D. Utah 1994).

21. *Id.* at 1526. *See generally* Barbara J. Lorence, *The University's Role Toward Student-Athletes: A Moral or Legal Obligation?*, 29 DUQ. L. REV. 343, 355 (1991) (arguing against "imposing a custodial duty on colleges and universities to protect 'adult' students, even those with known health risks, who decide to participate in school-sponsored athletic events ...").

22. Poole v. South Plainfield Bd. of Educ., 490 F. Supp. 948, 953-54 (D. N.J. 1980).

23. *See generally* Matthew J. Mitten, *Liability of Sports Medicine Providers and Related Entities*, LAW OF PROFESSIONAL AND AMATEUR SPORTS, Chap. 14A, §§ 14A.04[3] and 14A.05 [5] (G.A. Uberstine Ed., vol. 2, 1997).

24. *Id.* at §§ 14A.04[4] & 14A.05[6].

25. *Hysaw*, 690 F. Supp. at 946.

26. Pahulu v. Univ. of Kansas, 897 F. Supp. 1387, 1389 (D. Kan. 1995) (university athletics director acknowledged that university will suffer no foreseeable harm to its reputation if physically impaired player is allowed to continue playing football); Wright v. Columbia Univ., 520 F. Supp. 789, 794 (E.D. Pa. 1981) ("Columbia [University] has never asserted that it would be harmed by plaintiff's intercollegiate football career...").

27. Knapp v. Northwestern Univ., 101 F.3d 473, 478 (7th Cir. 1996).

28. Matthew J. Mitten, *Amateur Athletes With Handicaps or Physical Abnormalities: Who Makes the Participation Decision?*, 71 NEB. L. REV. 987, 1008-09 (1992). Public educational institutions are not immune from suit under the Rehabilitation Act or the ADA. *See* Mayer v. Univ. of Minnesota, 940 F. Supp. 1474 (D. Minn. 1996).

29. *See generally*, Adam A. Milani, *Can I Play?: The Dilemma of the Disabled Athlete in Interscholastic Sports*, 49 ALA. L. REV. 817 (1998).

30. 42 U.S.C.A. §§ 12131 & 12132 (1995).

31. 42 U.S.C.A. § 12181(7)(L) (1995).

32. Anderson v. Little League Baseball, Inc., 794 F. Supp. 342, 344 (D. Ariz. 1992) ("'public accommodation' includes Little League Baseball and its games").

33. The ADA is patterned after the Rehabilitation Act, and courts generally rely on cases construing similar provisions of the Rehabilitation Act in interpreting the ADA. *See generally* Milani, *supra* note 29.

34. 29 U.S.C.A. § 706(8)(B) (1985).

35. *See, e.g., Wright*, 520 F. Supp. at 791 (parties do not dispute that football player with sight in only one eye is handicapped individual covered by the Act).

36. 553 F.2d 296 (2d Cir. 1977).

37. 34 C.F.R. § 104.37(c) & 104.47(a) (1997); 45 C.F.R. § 84.37(c) & 84.47(a) (1997).

38. 553 F.2d at 299.

39. *Id.*

40. *Id.*

41. *Id.* at 300.

42. *Id.*

43. 442 U.S. 397, 414 (1979).

44. *Id.* at 405 and 413.

45. *Id.* at 406, 407 n.7 (emphasis added).

46. 490 F. Supp. 948, 953 (D. N.J. 1980).

47. *Id.* at 953.

48. *Id.* at 954. *See generally* Mitten, *supra* note 28, at 1016-17 (discussing HEW policy interpretation).

49. 490 F. Supp. at 953-54.

50. *Id.* at 952-53.

51. *Id.* at 954.

52. 520 F. Supp. 789, 793 (E.D. Pa. 1981).

53. *Id.* at 793-94.

54. *Id.* at 793.

55. *Id.* (*citing* Southeastern Community College v. Davis, 442 U.S. 397, 413 (1979)).

56. *Id.* at 794.

57. 520 F. Supp. at 794 (*citing Poole*, 490 F. Supp. at 954).

58. *Id.* at 793.

59. 550 F. Supp. 418 (E.D. Pa. 1982).
60. *Id.* at 424.
61. *Id.* at 423-24.
62. *Id.* at 424.
63. *Id.* 424-25.
64. 469 U.S. 287, 300 (1985).
65. 480 U.S. 273, 287 (1987).
66. *Id.* at 285.
67. *Id.* at 288 (citation omitted).
68. *Id.*
69. Partial Transcript of Proceedings, No. C-1-90-619 (S.D. Ohio, filed Aug. 31, 1990) (oral findings of fact and conclusions of law supporting denial of injunctive relief and dismissal of complaint) at 15-16 [hereinafter "Partial Transcript"]. *See generally* Mitten, *supra* note 28, at 1014-16 for a more thorough discussion of this case.
70. Partial Transcript at 16.
71. *Id.* at 11-12.
72. 897 F. Supp. 1387 (D. Kan. 1995).
73. *Id.* at 1390-93.
74. *Id.* at 1393.
75. *Id.* at 1394.
76. 101 F.3d 473 (7th Cir. 1996), cert. denied, 117 U.S. 2454 (1997).
77. *26th Bethesda Conference Recommendations for Determining Eligibility for Competition of Athletes With Cardiovascular Abnormalities,* 24 JOURNAL OF THE AMERICAN COLLEGE OF CARDIOLOGY 845-899 (1984).
78. *Id.* at 477-78.
79. Knapp v. Northwestern Univ., 942 F. Supp. 1191, 1195 (N.D. Ill. 1996).
80. Knapp, 101 F.3d at 480.
81. *Id.* at 481.
82. *Id.* at 482.
83. 942 F. Supp. at 1196.
84. *Id.* at 1196.
85. *Id.* at 1197.
86. *Id.* at 1196-97.
87. *Id.* at 1197-98.
88. 101 F.3d at 482.
89. *Id.* at 483.
90. *Id.* at 484-85 (emphasis in original).
91. *See* 29 U.S.C.A. § 706(8)(B) (1985); 34 C.F.R. § 104.3(j)(2)(ii) (1997); 45 C.F.R. § 84.3(j)(2)(ii) (1997).
92. 29 U.S.C.A. § 706(8)(B) (1985) (emphasis added).
93. *Pahulu,* 897 F. Supp. at 1391; Sandison v. Michigan High Sch. Athletic Ass'n, 863 F. Supp. 483, 488-89 (E.D. Mich. 1994), *rev'd on other grounds,* 64 F.3d 1026 (6th Cir. 1995). *See generally* Milani, *supra* note 29.

94. 863 F. Supp.at 488-89. *See generally* Milani, *supra* note 29.
95. Cohen v. Brown Univ., 991 F.2d 888, 891 (1st Cir. 1993); Kondos v. West Virginia Bd. of Regents, 318 F. Supp. 394, 396 (S.D. W. Va. 1970), *aff'd*, 441 F.2d 1172 (4th Cir. 1971); Harris v. Univ. of Michigan Bd. of Regents, 558 N.W.2d 225, 230 (Mich. Ct. App. 1997); Greenhill v. Carpenter, 718 S.W.2d 268, 271 (Tenn. Ct. App. 1986).
96. *Knapp*, 101 F.3d at 481.
97. Milani, *supra* note 29. In challenging exclusion from amateur athletic sports or events outside of interscholastic or intercollegiate sports, a physically impaired athlete must demonstrate that such exclusion substantially limits a major life activity. The same arguments discussed above can be made regarding the educational benefits of participation in youth sports, although they are somewhat more attenuated outside the context of school-sponsored sports. There is, however, a stronger argument that excluding an elite athlete who has trained for many years for an Olympic sport substantially limits what is for him or her a major life activity.
98. 473 U.S. 432 (1985).
99. *See, e.g.,* Jacobson v. Delta Airlines, Inc., 742 F.2d 1202, 1206 (9th Cir. 1984), *cert. denied*, 471 U.S. 1062 (1985); Pushkin v. Regents of Univ. of Colo., 658 F.2d 1372, 1383 (10th Cir. 1981); Casey v. Lewis, 773 F. Supp. 1365, 1371 (D. Ariz. 1991).
100. *See generally* notes 69-71, and accompanying text.
101. *Davis*, 442 U.S. at 414.
102. *Kampmeier*, 553 F.2d at 299; *Grube*, 550 F. Supp. at 423; *Wright*, 520 F. Supp. at 793; Partial Transcript, No. C-1-90-619, at 16.
103. *See generally* notes 36-90 and accompanying text. Some legal scholars also have advocated that this is the proper standard to apply under the Rehabilitation Act. Cathy J. Jones, *College Athletes: Illness or Injury and the Decision to Return to Play*, 40 BUFF. L. REV. 113, 206 & 212 (1992); Steven K. Derian, *Of Hank Gathers and Mark Seay: Who Decides Which Risks an Athlete Is Allowed to Undertake?*, 5 UCLA J. ED. 1, 15 (Summer 1991). One commentator asserts that, because Congress recognized a threatened harm to others' defense in the ADA's employment provisions [42 U.S.C.A. §§ 12111(3) (1995) and 12113 (1995)] without expressly establishing a threatened harm to self defense, a physically impaired amateur athlete has an absolute right to participate in athletics even if doing so would expose him or her to a significant risk of serious injury. Milani, *supra* note 29. Another commentator argues that the ADA should be construed consistently with the Rehabilitation Act to allow a covered entity to legally exclude an amateur athlete from a sport to prevent exposure to a significant risk of substantial harm to one's self. Jones, *supra* note 103, at 206-07 & 212.
104. The Rehabilitation Act's regulations relating to employment provide that a handicapped person is not "qualified" to perform the essential functions of a position if he or she cannot do so without endangering their

own health and safety. 29 C.F.R. § 1613.702(f) (1997). Mitten, *supra* note 28 at 1019 (collecting cases holding that exclusion from employment to prevent significant risk of substantial harm to one's self is legally valid).

105.*Knapp*, 101 F.3d at 483.

106.942 F. Supp. at 1196-97.

107.*See Poole*, 490 F.Supp. 948; *Wright*, 520 F.Supp. 789; & *Grube*, 550 F.Supp.418; discussed in notes 46-63 and accompanying text.

108.*Poole*, 490 F. Supp. at 953-54.

109.*See Knapp*, 942 F.Supp. 1191 (and text and discussion in notes 83-90); *Kampmeier*, 553 F.Supp.296 (and text and discussion in notes 36-42); & *Pahulu*, 897 F.Supp. 1387 (and text and discussion in note 75).

110.101 F.3d at 484.

111.*See, e.g.*, Wood v. Omaha Sch. Dist., 25 F.3d 667, 669 (8th Cir. 1994); Chiari v. City of League City, 920 F.2d 311, 317 (5th Cir. 1991); Mantolete v. Bolger, 767 F.2d 1416 (9th Cir. 1985); Doe v. New York Univ., 666 F.2d 761, 779 (2d Cir. 1981); Pushkin v. Regents of the Univ. of Colorado, 658 F.2d 1372, 1390 (10th Cir. 1981).

112.442 U.S. at 414.

113.480 U.S. at 285.

114.*Arline*, 480 U.S. at 287, 289.

115."Judges are not trained scientists. They inevitably lack the scientific training that might facilitate the evaluation of scientific claims or the evaluation of expert witnesses who make such claims. They typically are generalists, dealing with cases that may vary widely in respect to substantive subject matter. Their primary objective is usually process-related: That of seeing that a decision is reached fairly and in a timely way." Steven G. Breyer, THE INTERDEPENDENCE OF SCIENCE AND LAW, Address at Annual Meeting of The American Ass'n for the Advancement of Science. Philadelphia, PA, Feb. 16, 1998, at 6.

116.N.Y. Education Law § 3208-a (McKinney Supp. 1997).

117.*Id.* at § 3208-a(2).

118.*Id.* at § 3208-a(3).

119.*Id.* at § 3208-a(4).

120.Kampmeier v. Harris, 411 N.Y.S.2d 744 (1978). *See also* Pace v. Dryden Central Sch. Dist., 574 N.Y.S.2d 142 (1991). *See generally* Milani, *supra* note 29; & Mitten, *supra* note 28 at 1026-28.

121.Kampmeier v. Nyquist, 553 F.2d 296 (2nd Cir. 1978).

122.In *Penny v. Sands*, Case No. H89-280 (D. Conn., filed May 3, 1989), an athlete alleged that a cardiologist was negligent for withholding medical clearance to play college basketball due to his potentially life-threatening heart condition. He claimed economic damages of $1,000,000 because Central Connecticut State University relied on this physician's recommendation to exclude Penny from its basketball program for two years, which allegedly harmed his anticipated future professional basketball career. The university eventually allowed Penny to resume playing intercollegiate after two other cardiologists medically cleared him to do so. Penny voluntarily dismissed this case before the court decided the merits of his claim. He subsequently collapsed and died suddenly while playing in a 1990 professional basketball game in England. *See generally* Matthew J. Mitten, *Team Physicians and Competitive Athletes: Allocating Legal Responsibility For Athletic Injuries*, 55 U. PITT. L. REV. 129 (1993).

123. Mitten, *supra* note 122, at 138-42.

124. Some amateur athletes are willing to take potentially life-threatening risks to participate in competitive sports. *See* Mitten, *supra* note 28, at 993-94. A recent study reveals that college athletes engage in significantly more high risk behaviors then their non-athletic peers. Aurelia Nattiv, *Lifestyles and Health Risks of Collegiate Student-Athletes*, NCAA SPORTS SCIENCES EDUCATION NEWSLETTER, at 2 (Spring 1996). Other athletes, such as Olympic luge racer Duncan Kennedy, who was born with a bleeding brain stem known as arteriovenous malformation, choose not to participate in a sport even with medical clearance. Mike Dodd, *Kennedy Decides to End Luge Run*, USA TODAY, Dec. 15, 1997, at 12C; Bill Sullivan, *One Last Chance – Kennedy Battles Bleeding Brain Stem, Puts Luge Medal in Doubt*, HOU. CHRON., Dec. 14, 1997, at 5B.

125. JOHN STUART MILL, ON LIBERTY (1986).

126. *Id.* at 16 & 19.

127. Mitten, *supra* note 28, at 1016-26.

128. *Id.* at 1023 & 1025-26.

129. Such a liberal individualistic view disregards the communitarian philosophy that we are each other's keepers and have a responsibility to look out for the welfare of others. AMITAI ETZIONI, THE SPIRIT OF COMMUNITY: RIGHTS, RESPONSIBILITIES, AND THE COMMUNITARIAN AGENDA (1993).

130. *See supra* notes 5-12, and accompanying text.

131. *See supra* notes 43-45, and accompanying text.

132. In recent years Boston Celtics basketball player Reggie Lewis and Loyola Marymount University basketball player Hank Gathers, who both had known cardiovascular abnormalities, died while playing basketball. *See* Mitten, *supra* note 122, at 129-31.

133. *Arline*, 480 U.S. at 285.

134. *Knapp*, 101 F.3d at 484-85.

135. *Id.* at 483. *Accord* Daubert v. Merrell Dow Pharmaceuticals, Inc., 509 U.S. 579, 590 (1993) ("Proposed testimony must be supported by appropriate validation - i.e., 'good grounds,' based on what is known. In short, the requirement that an expert's testimony pertain to 'scientific knowledge' establishes a standard of evidentiary reliability.")

136. Greenwood v. State Police Training Center, 606 A.2d 336, 343 (N.J. 1992) (finding that "risk of damage to Greenwood's left eye is as insubstantial as it is to any other trainee.")

137. *See generally* notes 46-63 and accompanying text.
138. The following illustration presents an interesting case under this model. After permitting Danee Mastagni to participate in the university's inter-collegiate swimming program for almost three years, Texas A&M University's team physician medically disqualified her after she passed out in the pool during a race. She has Parkinson-White Syndrome, which is an abnormal electrical conduction pathway in her heart. The American Heart Association says that persons with this syndrome can lead normal lives with no restrictions on their activities, and university medical personnel previously accepted medical clearance recommendations from her treating specialists. Although she may experience fainting spells during strenuous workouts, her condition is not life-threatening. Tom Turbiville, *Diver Down*, AGS ILLUSTRATED, Nov. 8, 1997, at 24. These facts raise the issue of whether there is a reasonable medical basis for excluding her from the University's swimming team.
139. Mitten, *supra* note 122, at 138-42.
140. 101 F.3d at 485. In *Arline*, the Supreme Court held that "courts normally should defer to the reasonable medical judgments of public health officials" in deciding claims under the Rehabilitation Act, but did not consider whether the medical judgments of private physicians should be given deferential weight. 480 U.S. at 287-88.
141. Mitten, *supra* note 122, at 150-52.
142. 101 F.3d at 485. Using guidelines as a means of categorically excluding all athletes with certain physical abnormalities, rather than providing an individualized medical evaluation, would violate the Act. *See, e.g., Bombrys v. City of Toledo*, 849 F. Supp. 1210 (N.D. Ohio 1993). A blanket exclusion of all persons with a particular physical abnormality without an individualized examination of his or her medical condition also violates the ADA. Anderson v Little League Baseball, Inc., 794 F. Supp. 342 (D. Ariz. 1992).
143. 101 F.3d at 485.
144. In November, 1997, his heart defibrillator misread his heart rhythm and activated itself while Knapp was warming up before basketball practice. After reprogramming this device, his cardiologists cleared him to resume playing college basketball. Bill Liesse, *Knapp Step Away From Action*, PEORIA STAR J., 1997 WL 7687563, Dec. 28, 1997; Gene Wojciechowski, *Shocker Is This Player Still Wants the Ball*, CHI. TRIB., 1997 WL 3618045, Dec. 6, 1997.
145. *Hill*, 865 P.2d at 633 (scientific controversy regarding safety risks in connection with athletics participation dictates caution and prudence).
146. Although currently there are no ADA cases considering whether a physically impaired professional athlete may be excluded because of a risk of harm to one's self, a professional hockey player with sight in only one eye relied upon the New York Human Rights Law to successfully challenge a league bylaw that categorically rendered him medically

ineligible to play for any league team. Neeld v. American Hockey League, 439 F. Supp. 459 (W.D.N.Y. 1977).

147. 42 U.S.C.A. § 12111(5)(A) (1995).

148. 42 U.S.C.A. § 12131 & 12132 (1995).

149. 42 U.S.C.A. § 12181(7)(L) (1995).

150. Martin v PGA Tour, Inc., 984 F.Supp. 1320 (D. Or. 1998).

151. 42 U.S.C.A. § 12.102(2) (1995).

152. 29 C.F.R. § 1630.2 (h)(i) (1997).

153. 29 C.F.R. § 1630.2 (I) (1997).

154. Daley v. Koch, 892 F.2d 212, 215 (2d Cir. 1989).

155. Welsh v. City of Tulsa, Oklahoma, 977 F.2d 1415, 1417 (10th Cir. 1992).

156. 29 C.F.R. § 1630, Appendix § 1630.2(j) (1997).

157. *Id.*

158. 29 C.F.R. § 1630 (i) (1997).

159. Courts have held that college athletes with either of these conditions are not "disabled" under the Rehabilitation Act. *See supra* notes 73-74 and 79-82 and accompanying text.

160. 42 U.S.C.A. § 12102(2) (1995).

161. *Arline*, 480 U.S. at 284.

162. *Id.* at 283.

163. Enjoining a professional hockey league from preventing a one-eyed player from participating, one court observed: "The denial to plaintiff of an opportunity to play professional hockey in the AHL will result in the possibility of irreparable harm to plaintiff's professional hockey career. A young athlete's skills diminish and sometimes are irretrievably lost unless he is given an opportunity to practice and refine such skills at a certain level of proficiency." *Neeld*, 439 F. Supp. at 461.

164. One court has held that "intercollegiate athletics can be a major life activity" for a college athlete. *Pahulu*, 897 F. Supp. at 1393. Accordingly, a professional sport is a major life activity for a professional athlete.

165. *Anderson*, 794 F. Supp. at 342.

166. *Arline*, 480 U.S. at 286.

167. 42 U.S.C.A. § 12113(b) and 42 U.S.C.A. § 12111(3) (1995).

168. 29 C.F.R. § 1630.2(r) (1997) (emphasis added).

169. *Id. See supra* notes 65-68 and accompanying text.

170. Legal scholars also disagree whether risk of harm to one's self should legally justify exclusion of a physically impaired athlete from a sport under the ADA. Professor Adam Milani asserts that judicial recognition of a risk of harm to one's self defense is inconsistent with Congress' intended objectives in enacting the ADA. Milani, *supra* note 29. On the other hand, Professor Cathy Jones argues that exclusion of a physically impaired athlete should be legally permitted if necessary to prevent exposure to "a substantial risk of irreversible serious bodily injury or death to the athlete

... which cannot be substantially prevented through 'reasonable accommodation.'" Jones, *supra* note 103, at 206 & 207.

171. 1996 WL 118445, at 4.

172. 932 F. Supp. 1110, 1113 (N.D. Ill. 1996).

173. For a discussion of my arguments against construing the Rehabilitation Act in a similar manner, *see supra* notes 100-104 and accompanying text.

174. A physically impaired amateur athlete with the requisite ability and skills to play a professional sport may have a legal right to choose to participate at the professional level of competition. *See infra* note 176, and accompanying text.

175. In this regard, collective bargaining agreements governing the relationship between a league of professional teams and the players' union already may provide a player with the right to obtain a second medical evaluation of an employment-related injury or illness. *See, e.g.*, Jeffrey S. Moorad, *Negotiating for the Professional Baseball Player*, LAW OF PROFESSIONAL AND AMATEUR SPORTS 5-82, Chap. 5 (G.A. Uberstine, ed., vol. 1, 1997).

176. This model allows a professional athlete to participate despite medical disqualification by the team physician or athletic event sponsor's medical personnel if current consensus guidelines indicate playing a sport with a particular physical abnormality is medically safe.

177. This standard of review is the same as that used by the *Knapp* appellate court in applying the team physician medical judgment model. 101 F.3d at 485.

178. Mitten, *supra* note 28, at 1023-24; Jones, *supra* note 103, at 209-210.

Gender Equity in Athletics: Coming of Age in the 90s*

T. Jesse Wilde

Perhaps no issue has commanded the attention of the administrators of intercollegiate athletics more than the gender equity requirements of Title IX of the Education Amendments of 1972. Enacted more than a quarter century ago, Title IX provided that no person could be excluded from the benefits of an education program or activity receiving federal funds. Given the skeletal nature of women's athletic programs at most universities in 1972, institutions have now spent almost three decades trying to catch up to the statute's requirements.

T. Jesse Wilde's essay reviews the history of Title IX and the complicated legal questions that have arisen in its wake. In addition, Wilde offers a proposal for resolving the classic Title IX dilemma: how to expand athletic opportunities for women in a time of reduced budgets without having to seriously gut longstanding, and popular, men's programs.

Every college or university athletic director dreams of having ample funds to provide sports programs that would satisfy every imaginable interest.[1] The harsh economic realities of college athletics in the 90's, however, are driving athletic administrators in two seemingly irreconcilable directions.[2] On one hand, athletic budgets at many institutions are rapidly shrinking (as part of campus-wide cost cutting measures) leaving athletic administrators with little recourse but to streamline their programs, and ultimately eliminate some sport offerings.[3] On the other hand, there is a growing momentum in favor of enhancing women's athletic programs and eliminating sex discrimination in college sports. As a result of a multitude of factors discussed in this article, public sentiment and

*From Volume 4, Number 2, Spring 1994, pp. 217-258.

attention has finally been focused on equal treatment of the sexes in college athletics, mandating that colleges and universities provide athletic opportunities for male and female students in numbers proportionate to their respective student body enrollments.[4] This equity movement, however, comes at a time when athletic departments can ill afford to pay for new programs. The conflict, therefore, between fiscal restraint and enhancing female athletic opportunities in the name of gender equity is stretching many athletic budgets to the breaking point.[5]

Even though the current gender equity movement in college athletics encompasses a broad spectrum of issues, including equal opportunities for female athletic administrators and equal pay for coaches,[6] this article will focus on the enduring quest for an equitable division of opportunities between male and female students to participate in intercollegiate athletics. Part I will review legal principles relevant to gender equity in athletics. Herein, the article will examine the history and evolution of Title IX[7] and its specific application to college athletics. Thereafter, relevant equal protection principles embodied in federal and state constitutions will be briefly outlined. Part II will consider the impact of Title IX on college athletics. Particular emphasis will be devoted to reviewing recent efforts of student-athletes to litigiously preserve and promote female athletic opportunities, and to examine gender equity initiatives proposed or adopted by colleges and universities and various governing athletic organizations. Part III will consider the future prospects for this gender equity struggle and outline the author's "Three-for-One" gender equity proposal, designed to provide an athletic administrator with an achievable and realistic plan for satisfying the athletic interests and abilities of both sexes on campus.

I. Legal Principles

A. Title IX

1. History

More than twenty years ago, Congress enacted Title IX of the Education Amendments of 1972, which provides in part that: "No person in the United States shall, on the basis of sex, be excluded from participation in, be denied the benefits of, or be subjected to discrimination under any education program or activity receiving federal financial assistance."[8] Even though athletics and athletic programs were not specifically mentioned in Title IX when it first became law, the Act has become the cornerstone[9] of federal statutory protection for female athletes and prospective female athletes in the United States,[10] prohibiting discrimination on the basis of sex in educational programs and activities receiving federal financial assistance, including interscholastic and intercollegiate athletic programs.[11]

2. Scope and Application

The legislative history of Title IX suggests that the Act was originally intended to have limited scope, covering only those educational programs receiving federal financial assistance, and was not directed at imposing gender equity requirements on specific programs, like athletic departments of educational institutions, that received no direct federal funding.[12] The Department of Health, Education and Welfare (HEW), charged with the responsibility of developing regulations and enforcing Title IX requirements, however, broadly construed Title IX as applying to all activities, including athletic programs of educational institutions or agencies, if the institution or agency was in receipt of any federal assistance.[13] In 1975, HEW issued its first set of proposed regulations designed to implement Title IX, specifically incorporating interscholastic and intercollegiate athletics within the scope of Title IX coverage.[14]

Notwithstanding HEW's broad interpretation of Title IX, the threshold issue[15] remained; whether, in law, Title IX applied only to the specific departments receiving direct federal funding (commonly referred to as the "programmatic approach") or extended to any department within an institution that benefits from federal assistance (commonly referred to as the "institutional approach").[16] The resolution of this issue had tremendous significance since few athletic departments or athletic associations receive federal funds.[17] If the statute was interpreted in accordance with the "programmatic approach," to require only the specific programs that receive direct federal assistance to comply with its provisions, Title IX would provide no remedy to redress sex discrimination in most athletic programs. The issue was ultimately decided by the Supreme Court in *Grove City College v. Bell*,[18] wherein the Court favored the programmatic approach, concluding that only those specific programs within an institution receiving direct financial assistance from the federal government should be subject to Title IX requirements and sanctions.[19]

What momentum the gender-equity movement had mustered seemed lost. In 1972, before the enactment of Title IX, only 15% of intercollegiate athletic participants were women. By 1984, that percentage had doubled to 30.8%.[20] In the wake of *Grove City*, however, it appeared that the growth period had ceased since Title IX could no longer be enforced against athletic programs not receiving direct federal financial assistance. As a direct result of *Grove City*, the Department of Education's Office of Civil Rights (OCR),[21] the administering agency for Title IX, suspended all current and pending Title IX compliance investigations of high school and college athletic departments until it could be established that the programs directly received federal funds.[22]

On the heels of *Grove City*, a number of amendments were introduced to legislatively reverse the Supreme Court's programmatic interpretation of Title IX.[23] Such amending legislation failed to gain support until March 1988, when, after overriding a veto by President Ronald Reagan,[24] Congress enacted the Civil Rights Restoration Act of 1987.[25] The Act clarified that entire institutions and agencies are covered by Title IX, and other federal anti-discrimination laws[26] if any program or activity within the organization receives federal aid.[27]

3. Title IX Athletics Requirements

Following the passage of the Civil Rights Restoration Act of 1987, athletic administrators could no longer hide behind the programmatic interpretation to shield their programs from the requirements of Title IX. As such, administrators were compelled to assess departmental compliance under the substantive requirements of the law.

To assist athletic administrators in understanding the requirements of the Title IX and its regulations, and to aid in assessing Title IX compliance, the Department of Education, through the OCR, issued a Title IX Policy Interpretation in December 1979.[28] While the Policy Interpretation does not have the force of law, the document provides the guidelines used by the OCR in assessing Title IX compliance. Therefore, it is useful in clarifying the vague and imprecise requirements of Title IX.

In accordance with its Policy Interpretation, examines three areas in assessing an athletic department's compliance with Title IX: (1) athletic financial assistance;[29] (2) other nonfinancial program areas;[30]

and, (3) the accommodation of athletic interests and abilities of students.[31]

First, Title IX regulations and the Policy Interpretation[32] require institutions to allocate athletic financial assistance in proportion to the number of male and female participants in its athletic program.[33] If the proportion of total scholarship aid given to male and female athletes is substantially equal to the ratio of male and female athletes, or if a disparity is explained by certain nondiscriminatory factors, the institution may be considered in compliance with this requirement.[34] The Policy Interpretation lists two examples of nondiscriminatory factors which would permit disproportionality in favor of one sex: The higher cost of tuition for students from out-of-state and the discretion of an institution to make reasonable professional decisions concerning the scholarship awards most appropriate for team or program development.[35]

Second, for all other nonfinancial athletic program components, Title IX regulations require an institution to provide its athletes with equivalent treatment, benefits and opportunities in ten enumerated areas.[36] Equal athletic expenditures are not required, but an athletics program must exhibit equivalent treatment and distribution of benefits and opportunities in terms of equipment and supplies, games and practice schedules, travel and per diem allowances, coaches and tutors, medical and training services, housing and dining facilities and services, locker rooms, practice and competitive facilities, publicity, support services, and the recruitment of athletes. Identical treatment, benefits, and opportunities, are not required, provided the overall effect of any differences is negligible,[37] or the disparities are the result of recognized nondiscriminatory factors.[38] Examples of such factors outlined in the Policy Interpretation include: the unique aspects of particular sports, such as football, where the rules of play, equipment requirements, rates of participant injury, and facilities requirement for competition may result in an imbalance in favor of men; special circumstances of a temporary nature; spectator management requirements at more popular athletic events; and, differences that have not been remedied but which an institution is voluntarily working to correct.[39]

Third, and perhaps most relevant to the focus of this article, Title IX regulations and the Policy Interpretation require institutions to effectively accommodate the athletic interests and abilities of all students.[40] More specifically, the Policy Interpretation mandates that institutions accommodate effectively the athletic interests and abilities of its female and male students to the extent necessary to provide equal opportunity in the selection of sports and levels of competition available to members of both sexes. In selecting sports offerings, institutions are not required to integrate their teams, nor provide the same choice of sports to men and women.[41] However, where an institution sponsors a team in a particular sport for members of one sex, it may be required either to permit the excluded sex to try out for the team or to sponsor a separate team for the previously excluded sex.[42] In providing athletes of each sex with levels of competition, which equally reflect their interests and abilities, institutions must provide both the opportunity for individuals of each sex to participate in intercollegiate competition, and for these athletes to have competitive team schedules which equally reflect their abilities. Compliance with this two-fold requirement can be satisfied by any one of the following three tests:

(1) whether the institution's intercollegiate level participation opportunities for male and female students are provided in numbers substantially proportionate to their respective enrollments; or

(2) where the members of one sex have been and are under represented among intercollegiate athletes, whether the institution can show a history and continuing practice of program expansion which is demonstrably responsive to the developing interest and abilities of the members of that sex; or

(3) where the members of one sex are underrepresented among intercollegiate athletes, and the institution cannot show a continuing practice of program expansion, whether it can be demonstrated that the interests and abilities[43] of the members of that sex have been fully and effectively accommodated by the present program.[44]

The assessment of whether an institution has satisfied the requirements of Title IX is made on a program-wide basis, focusing on the overall provision of equivalent opportunities in the athletic program in terms of athletic financial assistance, equivalence in other athletic benefits and opportunities, and effective accommodation of student interests and abilities. An investigation may, however, be limited to less than all three of these major areas where unique circumstances justify limiting a particular investigation to one or two of the compliance criteria.[45]

It should also be emphasized that comparisons to determine Title IX compliance are not made on a sport-specific basis, comparing particular sport offerings or specific classes of sports (such as revenue-producing versus non-revenue-producing).[46] The revenue-producing sport of football, for example, is given no separate or special treatment under Title IX.[47] The large number of athletes required for football, however, increases the number of male participants in the overall program, thus increasing the amount of financial aid to be allocated to men under the proportionality test. With respect to other program components, certain special requirements of football are recognized as nondiscriminatory differences justifying departures from equivalency in such areas as medical services, equipment, facilities required for competition, maintenance of those facilities, special event management needs related to crowd size and special publicity requirements.[48] The accommodation of the interests and abilities of both men and women at an institution becomes more problematic when football's large roster size is factored into the equation. Since women do not have a corresponding sport requiring such a large number of athletes, the athletic participation ratio between men and women at most institutions is dramatically skewed in favor of male opportunities. Many argue that when football is factored into the proportional opportunity equation, it becomes practically and economically impossible for an institution to achieve a male to female athletics participation ratio that even closely resembles its student body ratio.[49]

4. Title IX Enforcement

As mentioned above, the Department of Education, through the OCR, is responsible for enforcing compliance with Title IX.[50] The OCR conducts Title IX reviews of schools based on complaints brought by individuals and can also select schools at random for compliance reviews.[51] If the OCR investigation finds the institution in compliance, that finding will be published and the case closed.[52] If violations are found, the OCR may still find the institution in compliance with Title IX if the institution has or agrees to formulate and implement a corrective plan.[53] In this instance, the OCR monitors the progress of the institutional plan; if the institution subsequently fails to implement its plan, it will be found in noncompliance.[54] When an institution is found in non-compliance, and voluntary compliance attempts are unsuccessful, the Department of Education may begin the formal process leading to termination of the institution's federal financial assistance.[55]

In addition to this administrative process, an individual may commence a federal Title IX lawsuit. Even though Title IX does not expressly create a right of action in favor of an individual, courts have held that such a right is implicit in the legislation.[56] It appears that a prospective plaintiff need not first pursue the OCR administrative remedy before commencing an action in a federal district court, since district courts have granted preliminary injunctions without the plaintiff first filing with the OCR.[57] In addition to posing the threat of terminating federal funding, individual plaintiffs may be entitled under Title IX to other remedies against a non-complying institution, including injunctive[58] and declaratory relief,[59] attorneys fees[60] and, in some instances, compensatory damages.[61]

B. Equal Protection

The enactment of Title IX did not remove the issue of sexual discrimination from constitutional concern.[62] In addition to recourse under Title IX, aggrieved individuals may also have a remedy based on the provisions of federal or state constitutions.

1. Federal Constitutional Claims

The equal protection clause of the Fourteenth Amendment guarantees equal protection of the law to all persons found within the United States.[63] This amendment guarantees, in part, that no person be singled out from similarly situated people, or have different benefits bestowed or burdens imposed, unless a constitutionally permissible reason exists for so doing.[64]

The constitution does not bar state actors from creating classifications, or treating groups differently, as long as the differential treatment is constitutionally justifiable under equal protection analysis. When considering the constitutionality of a classification, the court utilizes three different standards of review depending upon the nature of the classification. A "suspect" classification based on race, alienage and national origin, or fundamental rights abridgement, attracts *strict scrutiny*. Under this standard, the classification or infringement will be held unconstitutional unless the state can discharge the heavy burden of establishing that the classification or infringement is supported by a compelling state interest, and there is no less intrusive means by which the same end may be achieved.[65] The constitutionality of all other non-suspect classifications have historically been assessed on the *rational basis* standard. Here, the state need only demonstrate that the classification bears some rational relationship to a legitimate state interest. This is a far simpler onus to discharge. More recently, a third test has been espoused by some courts, set between the two extremes of *strict scrutiny* and *rational basis*. Under this *intermediate* test, "quasi-suspect" classifications may only be justified if the state can demonstrate that the classification is supported by some "important" state interest and there is no less intrusive means by which the same end may be achieved. The difference between "important" under the *intermediate* test and "compelling" under *strict scrutiny* is unclear. However, the onus on the state under the *intermediate* test would certainly be heavier than under the *rational basis* standard.[66]

Under traditional equal protection analysis, gender-based discrimination was considered a non-suspect classification, and, on the *rational basis* standard, could be sustained by the state unless the discrimination was found patently arbitrary or bore no rational relationship to a legitimate governmental interest. Under this light burden, it was relatively easy to justify gender-based rules, or, conversely, difficult for the aggrieved plaintiff to challenge the sex discrimination.[67] More recently, however, gender based classifications have been considered "quasi-suspect" by some courts, requiring the state to discharge a heavier burden of exhibiting that the classification is supported by some "important" state interest and there is no less intrusive means by which the same end may be achieved.[68] As such, this *intermediate* standard of review enhances the prospects for successfully challenging gender-based classifications, such as a state actor disproportionately accommodating the athletic interests and abilities of men over those of women.

2. State Constitutional Claims

In addition to federal and state equal protection claims, some states provide aggrieved plaintiffs with an additional cause of action based on an Equal Rights Amendment (ERA). Depending on the jurisdiction, a plaintiff may be able to take advantage of a heightened level of scrutiny given to gender-based classifications. This may render the discrimination unconstitutional unless the state can discharge the heavy burden of establishing that the classification or infringement is supported by a compelling state interest and there is no less intrusive means by which the same end may be achieved. The imposition of this *strict scrutiny* standard greatly enhances a plaintiff's prospects for success. This remedy, while effective, is limited because all states do not have an ERA.[69] Furthermore, of those that do have an ERA, not all impose the *strict scrutiny* standard to a gender-based classification.[70]

It is obvious that in order to ensure the greatest chance for success in a gender discrimination suit, the wise plaintiff would base the claim on all possible grounds, including Title IX, equal protection, and, if applicable, a state equal rights amendment.

II. Impact of Title IX

A. The First Two Decades

Title IX has been the primary catalyst for the growth of women's intercollegiate athletics since its passage in 1972. Before Title IX, only 15% of the total number of intercollegiate athletic participants were women. By 1984 that percentage had doubled to 30.8%.[71] Additionally, before Title IX, colleges offered an average of 2.5 intercollegiate sports for women;[72] by 1977, that number had risen to approximately 5.61, and to 6.9 by 1984.[73]

After *Grove City*, women continued to find their place in college athletics even though Title IX no longer posed a threat to college athletic administrators. Between 1984 and 1988 approximately 450 new NCAA women's teams were created, raising the average number of women's teams offered by colleges to 7.31 in 1988.[74] While this statistic evidences that college administrators were willing to voluntarily fund women's sports,[75] a more careful examination reveals that the number of female athletes, as a percentage of total intercollegiate athletic participants, remained constant throughout this same period. Even though women accounted for approximately half of all college students, they continued to represent less than one-third of the athletes.[76] In addition, a 1989 NCAA study found that while women comprised approximately 30% of all athletes, women's athletic programs received on average only 18% of athletic department budgets.[77] Clearly, the division of athletic opportunities and resources between the sexes in college athletics was not equitable.

It was expected that the passage of the Civil Rights Restoration Act in 1987[78] would breath new life into Title IX and revitalize the gender equity movement. This, however, was not immediately the case. In fact, figures released by the NCAA in March 1992, as a result of its genderequity study, revealed that in 1991 women accounted for only 30.9% of the total number of intercollegiate athletic participants, virtually identical to the 1984 percentage of 30.8.[79] Further, the NCAA study exposed that Division I women's athletic programs received on average only 23.9% of athletic department budgets, only modestly better than the 18% they received in 1984.[80] After almost twenty years under Title IX, the full assimilation of women in athletics had not been realized.[81]

More recently, however, new and unmistakable momentum has been rekindled in favor of ensuring women an equitable division of college athletic opportunities and resources. The mere publication by the NCAA of statistical information showing that female varsity athletes were no better off in 1991 than in 1984, revealed that some real work had to be done to ensure gender equity. Shortly after the release of the results of its gender-equity study, the NCAA commissioned a Gender Equity Task Force to thoroughly review the issue and provide recommendations.[82] Almost coincidentally with these events, the Supreme Court issued its decision in *Franklin v. Gwinnett County Public Schools*.[83] Although not an athletics case, many have argued that no decision has done more to foster Title IX athletics lawsuits and reprioritize an institution's agenda for gender equity in athletics than *Franklin*.[84]

In *Franklin*, a female high school student brought a Title IX sexual harassment suit against a Georgia school district, alleging that school officials had failed to stop a teacher from forcing unwanted sexual attention on her for more than a year.[85] The Court was presented with the issue of whether compensatory damages may be available under a Title IX cause of action in intentional gender-based discrimination.[86] Overturning an Eleventh Circuit Court of Appeals decision, the Supreme Court unanimously concluded that compensatory damages is an available remedy for victims of deliberate Title IX discrimination.[87]

Franklin expands the remedies for redressing the inequities in athletic programs for women and provides a strong financial incentive for institutions to eradicate discrimination. Previously, the danger in failing to comply with Title IX was the potential loss of federal funding. While significant, this remedy has historically proven to be more of a threat than a reality.[88] *Franklin* has added to this threat, the specter of a monetary damage award for noncompliance, making it more expensive to discriminate than to progress toward equity.[89] Many commentators have predicted that *Franklin* will have considerable impact in advancing the cause of gender equity in college athletics.[90]

B. Post-Franklin Progress

Whether specifically sparked by the result in *Franklin* or not, student-athletes have recently become more disposed to litigiously pursue the preservation and promotion of female athletic opportunities. At the same time, colleges, universities and their governing athletic organizations have become more amenable to considering or adopting gender equity initiatives.

1. Recent Title IX case law

In *Roberts v. Colorado State University*,[91] members of the women's softball team brought an action against CSU, claiming the university violated Title IX when it eliminated their softball program and, thereby, denied women an equivalent opportunity to participate in varsity athletics.[92] The plaintiffs sought injunctive relief to reinstate their varsity softball team and compensation for damages suffered as a result of the cut. The university argued, in defense, that it had not violated Title IX because men's baseball was also eliminated, and that the cuts had, in fact, disproportionately affected males.[93] Prior to the cuts, women accounted for 35.2% of CSU's varsity athletes, and 47.9% of its undergraduate population.[94] After the cuts, the ratio of women participating in athletics improved slightly to 37.7% of all CSU athletes.[95]

The U.S. District Court for the District of Colorado granted the plaintiffs a permanent injunction requiring the university to reinstate the women's softball team. In doing so, the court applied the OCR's three-pronged test set forth in the Title IX Policy Interpretation for assessing an institution's performance in effectively accommodating the athletic interests and abilities of members of both sexes.[96] The court concluded the decision to terminate the softball program violated Title IX when viewed in the context of the university's disproportionate athletic participation rate for women,[97] its failure to demonstrate a history of program expansion for women,[98] and its further failure to satisfy the court that the university was effectively accommodating the athletic interests and abilities of female students.[99]

On appeal, the U.S. Court of Appeals for the Tenth Circuit affirmed,[100] emphasizing that the proportional cutting of men's and women's teams from an already inequitable program was unfair to the underrepresented gender and violative of Title IX.[101] The university sought a further appeal to the United States Supreme Court, but its application was denied without comment.[102]

In *Cohen v. Brown University*,[103] student members of the women's gymnastics and volleyball teams were demoted by the university from full varsity status to intercollegiate club status. They brought a class action suit against the university seeking injunctive relief to restore the two women's teams to varsity status, and to prevent the reduction or elimination of any other women's varsity teams at Brown.

In early 1991, Brown announced that it planned to drop four sports from its intercollegiate varsity athletic roster as an athletics cost-cutting measure: women's volleyball and gymnastics, and men's golf and water polo.[104] The university permitted the teams to continue playing as club teams, a status that allowed them to compete against varsity teams from other colleges, but cut off financial subsidies and support services normally available to varsity teams.[105]

Prior to the cuts, the Brown athletic department supported 31 varsity sports, 16 for men and 15 for women. Women accounted for 36.7% of Brown varsity athletes, and 47.6% of its undergraduate population. As a result of the cuts, Brown's sponsorship of varsity sports was reduced to 27 sports, 14 for men and 13 for women, while the athletic participation ratio remained virtually unchanged with women accounting for 36.6% of Brown varsity athletes.[106]

The plaintiffs contended that the reduction in status of the two women's varsity programs violated Title IX by denying women an equivalent opportunity to participate in varsity athletics. In defense, Brown claimed that it was proportionally accommodating the athletic interests and abilities of both sexes on campus, and that the reduction to club status of the women's volleyball and gymnastics teams was offset by similar treatment of the men's golf and water polo teams.[107]

The federal district court granted the plaintiffs a preliminary injunction mandating the reinstatement of varsity women's gymnastics and volleyball at Brown, and prohibiting the elimination or reduction in status of any existing women's intercollegiate varsity team, pending a full trial on the merits. Following the three-pronged test enunciated in the Title IX Policy Interpretation, the court concluded that Brown, in eliminating the two women's varsity programs, violated Title IX in failing to effectively accommodate the interest and abilities of members of both sexes.[108] Brown gained a stay of the District Court order pending appeal to the First Circuit Court of Appeals.[109]

The district court's order in *Cohen* was affirmed on appeal.[110] In assessing the university's effective accommodation of the athletic interests and abilities of its students, the First Circuit, like the district court, utilized the three-pronged test provided in the Policy Interpretation.[111] In affirming, the court noted first that at no time in Brown's history had athletic participation opportunities between men and women been substantially equivalent, when comparing the percentage of women participating in intercollegiate athletics at Brown to the percentage of women undergraduates.[112] Second, Brown failed to provide any evidence of recent program expansion to demonstrate that the institution was responsive to the developing athletic interests and abilities of women. In fact, Brown had not added a single women's varsity sport since 1982.[113] And third, the court concluded that Brown was not fully and effectively accommodating the athletic interests and abilities of women at the varsity level, since here, the plaintiffs themselves were examples of specific athletic interest and ability and were seeking to forestall the elimination of two healthy varsity teams.[114] Retaining the two women's teams at the club level was, in the court's opinion, insufficient to satisfy the third prong of the test.[115]

The federal district court for the Western District of Pennsylvania was presented with circumstances similar to *Cohen*, in *Favia v. Indiana University of Pennsylvania*.[116] Indiana University of Pennsylvania (IUP) had eliminated school funding for four varsity athletic teams, (women's gymnastics and field hockey, and men's soccer and tennis), and reduced each to club status. As in *Cohen*, the program cuts were made by the athletic department in response to a directive by the university to reduce its departmental budget. The plaintiff class, members of the women's gymnastics and field hockey teams, claimed that the elimination of the two women's varsity programs violated both Title IX and the Fourteenth Amendment by denying women an equivalent opportunity to participate in varsity athletics, and sought a preliminary injunction to restore the two women's teams to varsity status and to prevent the reduction or elimination of any other women's varsity teams at IUP.[117]

The district court in *Favia* granted the preliminary injunction reinstating the two women's teams and prohibited the university from eliminating further women's teams. They applied the three-pronged test outlined in the Title IX Policy Interpretation for assessing an institution's performance in effectively accommodating the athletic interests and abilities of members of both sexes. The court concluded that participation opportunities between the sexes were not substantially proportionate to enrollment and that the university had not met its burden of establishing, under these circumstances, a history and continuing practice of program expansion for female student-athletes, or that the interests and abilities of females had been fully and effectively accommodated.[118] Like *Cohen*, the *Favia* court emphasized that cutting men's and women's teams proportionally from an already inequitable program was unfair and violative of Title IX.

IUP initially elected not to appeal the district court order, but later asked the court for modification of the injunction in order to permit the school to add women's soccer instead of reinstating gymnastics. In denying the IUP application, the district court concluded that the motion was in essence a request for reconsideration of a preliminary injunction that had not been timely appealed. IUP appealed to the U.S. Court of Appeals for the Third Circuit but was unsuccessful. The Third Circuit concluded that, while the proposed substitution of soccer for gymnastics would increase women's participation in athletics at IUP, and thus improve the school's athletics participation ratio, IUP had failed to meet the burden required in a motion to modify a preliminary injunction: demonstrating a significant change in facts from the time the injunction was issued, which would render inequitable the continuation of the order.[119]

Roberts, *Cohen*, and *Favia* represent significant victories for the gender equity movement. A clear message has been sent to college athletic departments mandating that they either provide opportunities for both sexes in proportion to their enrollment, evidence a history and continuing practice of program expansion responsive to the interest and abilities of the members of the underrepresented sex, or demonstrate that the interests and abilities of the underrepresented sex are being fully and effectively accommodated. The central finding of each court reaffirmed the plaintiffs' argument in each case that the proportional cutting of men's and women's teams from an already inequitable program was unfair to women and violative of Title IX. Since many college athletics programs would fail the rigors of the three-pronged test for accommodating the athletic interests and abilities of its students, the result in *Roberts*, *Cohen*, and *Favia* make it virtually impossible for a college to drop any women's sport as part of a general cutback in athletic funding.[120] Ultimately, Title IX requires that women receive "a larger slice of a shrinking athletic-opportunity pie" in times of fiscal restraint.[121]

Unlike the three previous cases cited, *Cook v. Colgate University*[122] does not involve an attempt to reinstate a previously eliminated athletic program. The plaintiffs were all former members of the Colgate women's club ice hockey team. They sought an order directing Colgate to grant varsity status to women's ice hockey, contending that Colgate had violated Title IX in failing to fully and effectively accommodate the athletic interests and abilities of its women's club ice hockey players by repeatedly denying their applications for varsity status.[123]

In 1990, the year the action was commenced, Colgate offered 23 varsity sports, 12 for men and 11 for women. Women accounted for 31% of all varsity athletes and 46.7% of the undergraduate student body. Varsity ice hockey was among the 12 varsity sports offered for men, and the plaintiffs contended that Colgate's failure to provide women with a comparable varsity ice hockey opportunity was violative of Title IX.[124]

In defense, Colgate argued that Title IX only prohibits discrimination in an athletic program as a whole, and that the complaint did not allege, nor did the evidence create a question of fact, that there had been any gender discrimination in the overall athletic opportunities afforded women at Colgate. According to Colgate, Title IX compliance ought to be assessed on a program-wide, rather than sport-specific, basis.[125] The district court, however, did not agree.

In finding for the plaintiffs, the district court ordered Colgate to elevate the women's club ice hockey team to varsity status for the 1993-94 season, and concluded that the university had violated Title IX by failing to provide women's club ice hockey participants with an athletic opportunity equivalent to their male counterparts. After briefly considering the athletic opportunities available to men and women at Colgate, the court embarked on a sport-specific comparison of women's club and men's varsity ice hockey programs. Unlike *Roberts*, *Cohen*, and *Favia*, in which each court examined Title IX compliance in terms of the total number of athletic opportunities in relation to the percentage of men and women in the undergraduate population, the district court, in *Cook*, conducted a sport-specific comparison of a club and a varsity team, which revealed expected inequities.[126] In the court's opinion, none of Colgate's proffered reasons for refusing to provide women with a varsity ice hockey opportunity provided the university with a justifiable excuse.[127]

Colgate appealed. On appeal, the Second Circuit Court of Appeals side-stepped the issue, concluding that the graduation of all named plaintiffs prior to the 1993-94 school year rendered the action moot.[128] Since the plaintiffs were seeking relief in their personal capacities, and not as representatives of a class, the action became moot since none of the plaintiffs could personally benefit from an order requiring equal athletic opportunities for women ice hockey players to take effect after their respective graduations.[129]

In reaction to the Second Circuit's decision, a second lawsuit has been filed against Colgate by five female athletes, seeking the same relief as in the *Cook* action.[130] The issue, therefore, will likely be revisited on appeal to determine whether the district court in *Cook* properly interpreted Title IX in comparing Colgate's treatment of male and female athletes on a sport-by-sport rather than program-wide basis, and by specifically requiring the university to add women's ice hockey. The law seems clear that Title IX and its regulations do not require that women be provided with a replication of men's programs, or that educational institutions allocate equal expenditures to each program offering.[131] Rather, the focus of the law is on the equitable treatment of both sexes in the overall program.[132] In the circumstances of this case, however, it may be argued that the result is correct even though the district court's analysis seems misguided, because participation opportunities between the sexes at Colgate were not substantially proportional to enrollment. Additionally, under these circumstances, the university could not establish a history and continuing practice of program expansion for female student-athletes, or that the interests and abilities of females in ice hockey, for example, had been fully and effectively accommodated.

Even though recent Title IX suits commenced by women have largely been successful in restoring previously cut programs, actions commenced on behalf of male athletes seeking to reinstate programs have not produced similar results. In May 1993, eight members of the University of Illinois men's swim team filed a federal lawsuit to enjoin the school from dropping their program. The plaintiffs claimed they were victims of sex discrimination since the women's team was not also being eliminated. As part of a university-wide cost cutting effort, the athletic department was eliminating men's swimming and diving, fencing and women's diving.[133] A federal district court judge refused to grant the desired relief, ruling that the elimination of men's swimming had not violated Title IX.[134] In similar circumstances, a federal district court judge ruled that Drake University had not violated Title IX when it dropped its wrestling program and denied the request for a temporary injunction by five members of the team who complained that their rights under Title IX were being violated.[135]

2. Title IX Settlements

During the post-*Franklin* period a number of institutions, in reaction to a filed or threatened student-athlete complaint, settled pending Title IX issues by voluntarily adding women's sports, reinstating previously eliminated offerings, or, in one case, eliminating the entire sports program for both men and women.[136]

For example, in June 1993, nine female athletes filed a federal Title IX complaint against Cornell University after the women's gymnastics and fencing teams were eliminated in a cost-savings move.[137] The action came after the plaintiffs had attempted unsuccessfully to reach a compromise with the university to keep their sports, even as club programs. The university had reportedly received legal advice that the cuts would not violate Title IX requirements, because they were cutting more from their men's athletics program than from the women's. However, in December 1993, in light of the U.S. Court of Appeals rulings in *Roberts, Cohen,* and *Favia,*[138] Cornell concluded that the interests of the university and its students would be best served by settling the claim, and reinstating the women's gymnastics and fencing teams, rather than expending its limited resources on a costly court battle.[139]

In August 1993, members of the University of California at Los Angeles (UCLA) women's gymnastics team threatened to file a Title IX lawsuit if the university did not reinstate its program. In early August, UCLA had announced the cancellation of both men's and women's gymnastics due to athletic department financial problems.[140] By late August, UCLA agreed to reinstate the women's program when threatened with legal action.[141]

As part of a university-wide budget reduction, the University of New Hampshire athletic department announced the cancellation of its men's wrestling and women's tennis programs for the 1992-93 academic year. The two sports were selected in part because the participation and funding ratios between men's and women's athletics, after the cuts, would be held constant. Members of the women's tennis team threatened a lawsuit seeking the reinstatement of their sport, contending that since UNH was not providing athletic opportunities for females in numbers substantially proportional to female representation in the student body, the university could not eliminate any women's teams consistent with the dictates of Title IX, (even if a proportional share of men's participation opportunities were concurrently eliminated). In March 1992, prior to the implementation of the cuts, UNH settled the pending claim by reinstating the women's tennis program and assuring full Title IX compliance within five years. In August 1993, a formal plan was adopted by UNH to ensure continued Title IX compliance in athletics. The university committed to increase the athletic opportunities available to female students to ensure that, by the 1997-98 academic year, either the athletic interests and abilities of female students will be fully and effectively accommodated or participation opportunities will be provided in numbers substantially proportionate to the enrollment of male and female students. The plan envisions increasing squad sizes on current women's teams, as well as adding women's golf, crew, volleyball and softball.[142]

In July 1993, the University of Texas at Austin entered into an agreement to settle a class-action lawsuit which alleged that the university had violated Title IX and the Equal Protection Clause of the Fourteenth Amendment by denying varsity intercollegiate athletic opportunities to female students.[143] By agreement, the university committed to increase female participation in varsity sports to 44% by the end of the 1995-96 academic year, to increase to 42% the percentage of athletic scholarships going to women, and to institute women's varsity soccer in the 1993-94 academic year and women's varsity softball not later than the 1995-96 academic year.[144]

In February 1993, members of the women's club soccer team at Auburn University filed an OCR complaint seeking the promotion of their club team to varsity status. This complaint was followed by the filing of a Title IX class-action lawsuit against the university in April 1993 on behalf of all current and future female student-athletes. The plaintiffs sought increased funding for all women's sports.[145] In July 1993, the school entered into a settlement agreement concerning the soccer-related claims filed against Auburn University both with the OCR and in federal district court,[146] wherein the university agreed to elevate women's soccer from club to varsity status, and to support and maintain that program for at least five years, beginning in the fall of 1993. In addition, the university agreed to pay the *Kiechel*[147] plaintiffs $60,000 in compensatory damages, and $80,000 in legal fees.[148]

At the University of Massachusetts, as a component of university-wide budget cuts, the UMass athletic department eliminated five varsity sports over a two-year period between 1990 and 1991, including women's lacrosse, tennis, and volleyball and men's tennis and volleyball. (Men's soccer was also dropped and then brought back as a result of a private cash donation). Prior to the cuts, UMass sponsored 26 sports, 13 for men and 13 for women. Women accounted for 34.5% of UMass varsity athletes, and 51.5% of its undergraduate population. After the elimination of the five varsity sports, the women's participation ratio was slightly reduced to 32.7% of UMass varsity athletes.[149] A Title IX suit was threatened by members of the eliminated women's lacrosse and tennis teams. Ultimately, an October 1992 settlement provided for the immediate reinstatement of the women's tennis, lacrosse, and volleyball teams. UMass also committed to a goal of full Title IX compliance within five years, including the doubling of athletic scholarships available for women.[150]

In January 1992, California State University at Fullerton (CSUF) eliminated school funding for women's volleyball and men's gymnastics. Members of the women's volleyball team commenced an action in California Superior Court against CSUF and the California State University system, seeking injunctive relief to reinstate their program. They claimed that the elimination of women's varsity volleyball was discriminatory and violated the California Education Code as well as the equal protection guarantee under the California Constitution.[151] Prior to the cuts, CSUF sponsored 17 varsity athletic programs, nine for men and eight for women. Women accounted for only 26.6% of CSUF's varsity athletes, but represented 55.6% of its undergraduate population. As a result of the cuts, the ratio of women participating in athletics fell slightly to 24.9% of all CSUF athletes. A temporary restraining order was granted by the California Superior Court in February 1992, followed by the issuance of a preliminary injunction prohibiting CSUF from cutting the women's volleyball program and altering its budget in March. Under the threat of an additional federal lawsuit, alleging CSUF violations of Title IX and the Equal Protection Clause of the Fourteenth Amendment, the university settled the dispute by entering into a consent decree wherein CSUF, in addition to reinstating women's volleyball, agreed to establish a varsity women's soccer program for the 1992-93 season. CSUF pledged to increase the participation ratio of women to 31% in 1992-93, to 40% by 1997-98, and to a number equivalent to the student body ratio by 2002-03 (allowing for a 5% variance in any given year), as well as providing an equivalent percentage allocation of budgetary support. The university also agreed to form a committee which would conduct annual gender equity assessments and survey the athletic interests of female students every three years.[152]

In a further settlement of a class action suit, filed in February 1993 against the entire 20-campus California State University system, university administrators committed to work toward providing male and female students with athletic opportunities and budgetary allocations in amounts proportional to their respective campus enrollments. The settlement requires reasonable progress with a final deadline for compliance by the 1998-99 academic year.[153]

Finally, Brooklyn College announced that it was dropping its entire sports program as part of a college-wide $5.4 million budget cutback in a surprising move in June 1992. A Title IX complaint had been filed with the OCR in 1990 by two Physical Education professors at Brooklyn College, resulting in an OCR finding that the school was not providing male and female athletes with equal opportunities to participate in intercollegiate sports. In response to the findings, the college pledged full compliance by September 1992, but announced the dismantling of its entire athletics program a few months prior to that deadline.[154]

These are but a few of the more publicized settlements that, in addition to the results in *Roberts*, *Cohen*, and *Favia*, have fueled the advance of gender equity in college athletics. They indicate a realization among some college athletic administrators that their programs must inevitably begin to accommodate the athletic interests and abilities of both sexes on campus.

3. Current Gender Equity Initiatives

In spite of recent developments, many institutions continue to turn a blind eye to Title IX non-compliance. Based on recent case law, however, the issue seems unavoidable for most institutions, either through a complaint-initiated process or, more preferably, a self-directed analysis and self-imposed plan for future compliance. Failing any meaningful progress, Congress has also threatened to impose Title IX-related reporting requirements subjecting institutional performance to public scrutiny.[155] Under these circumstances, some institutions and their governing athletic organizations have taken a proactive lead in embracing the cause of gender equity by proposing or establishing plans designed to proportionately increase female participation in college athletics.

Immediately following the release of the results of its gender-equity study in March 1992, revealing that women were indeed second-class citizens in intercollegiate athletics,[156] the NCAA appointed a 16 member task force of men and women with divergent views to thoroughly review the gender equity issue and provide recommendations regarding how the NCAA can better assure that opportunities to participate in athletics are offered without regard to gender.[157] In July 1993, the task force issued its final report in accordance with its charge, wherein it defined gender equity,[158] outlined key principles of gender equity, provided guidelines to attain that goal, endorsed "proportionality" as a measure of equity,[159] identified emerging sports for women, and recommended rule changes to expand scholarship support and participation opportunities for female athletes.[160]

Acting on the recommendations of its Gender-Equity Task Force, the NCAA membership adopted a proposition at the 1994 NCAA Convention designed to add gender equity to the Association's principles for the conduct of intercollegiate athletics[161] and another to establish maximum financial aid limits in emerging sports for women and permit institutions to utilize the emerging sports in order to meet the Association's minimum sports-sponsorship and financial aid award criteria.[162] The legislation, while supportive of Title IX and creating new opportunities for women, fails to identify any penalties for Title IX noncompliance. Perhaps specific penalty provisions will follow at ensuing Conventions. For now, however, gender equity noncompliance may only be penalized by the Association through its new certification program, passed at the 1993 Convention.[163] The certification program requires each member institution to complete an institutional self-study, verified and evaluated through an external peer-review process administered by the Association at least every five years, demonstrating the institution's adherence to prescribed standards, including a commitment to fair and equitable treatment of both men and women in intercollegiate athletics, and the development of a gender equity plan to ensure future adherence to evolving Association standards.[164] Gender equity noncompliance is, therefore, one cause for non-certification, and non-certified schools become ineligible for NCAA championships and related revenue distribution.[165] While these are certainly significant penalties, some may argue that the threat of future non-certification may do little to encourage immediate gender equity compliance. However, the threat of non-certification is not so distant that athletic administrators can afford to delay in devising a gender equity plan and implement measures demonstrating the institution's commitment to fair and equitable treatment of both men and women in intercollegiate athletics.

Certainly, some will be left disappointed with the NCAA's current efforts to promote gender equity. Yet, perhaps the Association's purposes, as a national organization, are best served by establishing general principles and avoiding the temptation to micromanage the issue. Given the heterogeneity of NCAA membership, specific gender equity requirements and resulting penalties for non-compliance may best be left to the conferences. Some conferences, in fact, have already taken the lead in this regard.

In May 1992, for example, the Big Ten became the first college conference to adopt a gender equity plan when conference members voted 10-1 to require that women comprise at least 40% of the participants in intercollegiate athletics at member institutions within five years.[166] When the plan was adopted, women accounted for 30.5% of Big Ten varsity athletes, and approximately 49% of the undergraduate population at Big Ten schools. While praised by some as the first policy of its kind adopted by a college conference, the measure is not without critics who argue that a 60:40 male to female participation ratio over a five-year period is too little over too much time,[167] and that the policy does not outline specific procedures to reach the goal prior to the deadline.[168] The University of Iowa, a Big Ten institution, has gone one step further than its conference office, in committing to provide women, by August 1997, with athletic opportunities in proportion to their representation in the undergraduate student body.[169]

In June 1993, the Southeastern Conference adopted a gender equity proposal requiring its member institutions to provide at least two more women's sports programs than the number of men's sports offered.[170] The proposal, which becomes effective August 1, 1995, requires each conference member to submit a report, based on a Title IX self-evaluation, to the conference office by June 1, 1994, and commits the conference office and member institutions to act affirmatively to increase the quantity and quality of women's athletic opportunities. Specifically, the proposal mandates an equitable distribution of scholarship funding, access to support services, compensation for coaches, and opportunities to participate, coach and administer.[171]

As the administrative agency for Title IX compliance, the OCR has long been criticized for investigating potential Title IX violations only after it receives a complaint, rather than taking a more proactive, aggressive approach to enforcing the law. The complaint process has even been described as an ineffective means of forcing equity.[172] In March 1993, the OCR announced its plans to increase the number of Title IX compliance reviews of intercollegiate athletic programs at randomly selected universities in apparent response to this criticism. During 1993, fourteen programs were targeted for review.[173]

III. The Future?

For institutions that have been dodging the requirements of Title IX for more than twenty years, it appears the day of reckoning has finally arrived. We can only expect the floodgates of Title IX athletics litigation to burst unless universities and their governing organizations take active steps toward gender equity, including providing women with equitable opportunities to participate in intercollegiate athletics. Unfortunately, this day of reckoning has come when institutions and athletic departments around the country can least afford it. In a time of cost-containment, the course many schools will take to improve their female varsity participation ratios will be to cut men's programs, usually non-revenue producing sports, rather than add sports for women.[174] Thus, true or not, the perception is that men's athletic opportunities have become the sacrificial lamb for gender equity. It is not surprising, therefore, that this has become such a heated and polarizing issue.

The key "sticking point" in distributing athletic opportunities proportionally between male and female college athletes is clearly the high- scholarship, high-cost sport of football. In its current big-time form, with 100-man teams and high operating costs, football makes it virtually impossible to balance male and female athletic opportunities. Women quite simply do not have a similar large roster, injury-riddled sport of their own, made up of offensive, defensive and special-team units.[175] The fact that, on average, there are almost as many football players at Division I institutions as there are female athletes,[176] would lead one to reasonably conclude that male participants are always going to outnumber females purely because of football.

It becomes readily apprent under current methods of Title IX analysis, it becomes readily apparent that gender-equity will be difficult to achieve if football is not somehow affected. Yet, even the thought of down-sizing football creates a battle cry among coaches and alumni, arguing that football is the cash cow that supports all college athletic programs, whose profitability will be jeopardized by further budget cuts. Although statistics vary, football unquestionably contributes revenues that provide a financial nucleus for men's and women's intercollegiate programs. That money, along with the revenue earned from the NCAA Division I men's basketball tournament, assists in supporting all of the non-revenue sports, including women's programs.[177]

A gender equity plan that offers practical solutions acceptable to all involved in this polarizing debate becomes almost impossible to formulate. Devising a proposal guaranteeing athletic opportunities for female students based on their proportional representation in the undergraduate student body may be economically unattainable without significantly altering men's sports as we now know them. This attracts predictable opposition from administrators, coaches and participants involved in men's athletics. On the other hand, any plan falling short of a proportional distribution of athletic opportunities between the sexes attracts the wrath of gender equity activists. Can an equitable division of college athletic opportunities between the sexes be realized without significantly affecting programs currently offered to men? In an attempt to respond positively to this question, the author has developed a proposal, the "Three-for-One" plan. It is premised on compromise, seeking some common ground between those interested in promoting female athletic opportunities; and those interested in preserving the quality of programs for men. The plan is formulated in accordance with the three general areas for assessing Title IX compliance, although addressed in reverse order, requiring that: (1) institutions accommodate effectively the athletic interests and abilities of female and male students to the extent necessary to provide equal opportunity in the selection of sports and levels of competition available to members of both sexes;[178] (2) all benefits, opportunities and treatment afforded participants of each sex be equivalent;[179] and (3) scholarship assistance be allocated in proportion to the numbers of male and female participants in intercollegiate athletics.[180]

To effectively accommodate the athletic interests and abilities of both sexes on campus, the "Three-for-One" plan creates two sports program pools: Pool A, comprised of football and a group of sports offered for women only; and, Pool B, encompassing all other varsity sports offerings at the institution. The Pool A grouping is designed to achieve an equitable balance between preserving the flagship sport of football, and enhancing athletic opportunities for women. Since women do not have a high scholarship sport similar to football, the "Three-for-One" plan, in a sense, creates one by grouping together three sports offered by the institution for women only (three-for-one). To qualify as a Pool A for-women-only (FWO) sport, the FWO program must not be offered to men at the institution, and must afford at least twelve participation opportunities. In addition, at least two of the three FWO programs must be team sports. FWO program possibilities will naturally vary regionally and from school to school, but may include such sports as field hockey, volleyball, lacrosse, soccer, or other "emerging sports" recently identified by the NCAA in 1994 Convention legislation.[181] The plan intends that these FWO sports be either added as a new sport offering or identified from current sports offered only to women at an institution, without affecting sports offered to men. In some circumstances, however, economic necessity may require that a FWO sport be created by dropping a matching sport from the men's side. While the distribution of athletics participation opportunities for both sexes in Pool A sports will not necessarily be proportional to the student body ratio, such a grouping is a realistic and practical proposal designed to improve an institution's female athletics participation ratio and comply with the requirements of Title IX, and reaffirm the unique status of football in collegiate athletics.[182]

The Pool B grouping encompasses all other varsity sports not included in Pool A. The plan requires that institutions provide athletic participation opportunities to both sexes in Pool B sports in proportion to their respective undergraduate enrollments or demonstrate that the interests and abilities of members of the underrepresented sex have been fully and effectively accommodated by the overall athletics program. If an institution does not offer football, all sports would be considered Pool B sports, dictating compliance with the above stated test. Here again, the plan intends that women's sports be added to bring the institution into compliance with Pool B's proportionality requirement. However, economic necessity may dictate that compliance be achieved by dropping one or more Pool B sports offered to men.

Under the "Three-for-One" plan, the division of participation opportunities between the sexes will be considered equitable if the institution has complied with the composition requirements of Pools A and B. The overall athletics participation ratio under the plan may favor men's opportunities. Participation ratios will naturally vary depending on the total number of opportunites provided and the FWO sports, selected, yet, on average, institutions following the plan will divide their athletic opportunities 55% to men and 45% to women.[183] While for some, such a ratio may not strictly satisfy the popular proportionality benchmark, the author argues that it will withstand muster under Title IX. The institution will be able to establish that its overall athletics participation ratio is substantially proportional to its undergraduate student body ratio, or exhibit a history and continuing practice of program expansion responsive to the developing interests and abilities of the underrepresented sex, or demonstrate that the athletic interests and abilities of its students of the underrepresented sex have been fully and effectively accommodated.[184] In addition, an athletics program, developed in accordance with the "Three-for-One" plan, might better satisfy the definition for gender equity proffered by the NCAA Gender Equity Task Force. They provide that "an athletics program can be considered gender equitable when the participants in both the men's and women's sports program would accept as fair and equitable the overall program of the other gender."[185]

After defining an equitable division of athletic opportunities between men and women, the "Three-for-One" plan proposes to address the remaining two Title IX compliance requirements in accordance with current practices. Institutions would be required to afford their male and female athletes equivalent treatment, benefits and opportunities in the eleven program areas enumerated in the Title IX Regulations.[186] Equal athletic expenditures would not be required, but an athletics program must exhibit equivalent treatment and distribution of benefits and opportunities in terms of equipment and supplies, games and practice schedules, travel and per diem allowances, coaches and tutors, medical and training services, housing and dining facilities and services, locker rooms, practice and competitive facilities, and publicity. The division of athletic expenditures, excluding scholarships, would be globally assessed for the entire athletic department with women's programs, under the "Three-for-One" plan guaranteed a proportioned share. Furthermore, in accordance with Title IX requirements, scholarship assistance would be allocated in proportion to the number of male and female participants in the entire athletic department.[187]

Since the "Three-for-One" plan envisions the creation of new programs for women, the obvious question is: how will institutions, bent on cost-containment, pay for these new programs? First, to avoid the easy alternative of cutting men's programs to comply with Pool A and B requirements, the plan's success, or indeed any gender equity initiative, requires the involvement and support of the president's office. This involvement would be formulating the institution's plan for compliance and securing adequate university resources for its implementation. The entire institution must internalize and economically commit to the philosophy that the cost of a well-balanced athletic program is worth the positive public perception emanating from a university devoted to providing educational and athletic opportunities to all students regardless of sex.

Second, athletic departments must begin to do a better job of turning their women's sports into revenue producers. Women's athletics is an underrated and undeveloped market. It is generating more spectator interest and is considered by many to be the next frontier for women's intercollegiate athletics.[188] The skill level of female competition has improved tremendously in recent years with better coaching and more girls participating in athletics at younger ages. As a result, women's intercollegiate athletics is developing into a less expensive, entertaining alternative to men's sports as well as one on which athletic departments would do well to focus additional marketing efforts. Women's sports offer the excitement of quality competition, yet currently remain small enough to capitalize on the marketing appeal of direct fan involvement where spectators pay less and sit closer to the action.[189] Additionally, sponsorship might be attracted from various corporations that would like to be associated with and financially support the popular institutional philosophy. As such, the cost of a well-balanced athletic program is worth the positive public perception derived from a university committed to providing educational and athletic opportunities to all students regardless of sex.

Third, since many men's sports in peril of elimination under any gender equity plan are non-revenue producing, Olympics-related programs, the United States Olympic Committee and related national sports governing bodies should become more involved in providing financial support to college athletic programs. Even though the USOC and national sport governing bodies are also suffering from revenue shortages, they do benefit from the collegiate development of Olympic athletes. The cost to develop these same athletes, should colleges continue to cut these non-revenue, Olympics-related programs, would certainly be more than infusing financial support now to help keep them afloat. This extra revenue would allow the current revenue devoted to these programs to be redistributed to existing or new programs for women.[190]

Fourth, while the "Three-for-One" plan does not mandate the reduction of men's sports roster sizes, such a voluntary limitation would allow an athletic department to redistribute cost savings to women's sports, without significantly affecting the quality of programs offered to men.[191] Other cost savings might be achieved through altering current practices, such as further limiting roster or travel squad sizes. Ultimately, however, in the absence of other revenue sources, the elimination of some men's sports may be economically necessary and inevitable.

Finally, in consideration of football's special Pool A classification under the "Three-for-One" plan, the proposal also supports the implementation of a Division I-A football playoff to provide an additional revenue source to indirectly assist in funding women's sports opportunities. This idea has been debated among college football fans for years, but has gained recent support within the decision-making ranks of the NCAA. At the 1993 NCAA Convention, Dick Schultz, then NCAA Executive Director, urged the Association to take a hard look at a playoff in his "State of the NCAA Address."[192] Schultz emphasized that a Division I-A football playoff would be a source of tremendous revenue to sustain existing athletic programs and to support gender equity reforms.

Even though the playoff concept makes sense to college football fans, it will not become a reality until the real power-brokers of college sports — college presidents and chancellors — are serious about such an alternative. Recently, however, college presidents showed some real signs of warming to the idea. A significant step in this direction was taken in December 1993. The powerful NCAA President's Commission appointed a fact-finding task force to consider the pros and cons of a Division I-A football playoff, and to make recommendations to the Commission, the NCAA Council and the Executive Committee.[193] If acted upon, implementing legislation could be put to a membership vote as early as the 1995 convention with playoffs in place for the conclusion of the 1995 college football season.[194] The playoff would answer the college football fan's argument of who is number one, while generating much needed revenue for athletic program enhancement. Proponents of a playoff estimate that a Division I-A championship game could generate revenue as great as $100 million.[195] Based on conservative estimates alone, however, revenues would be sufficient to ease the financial crunch that already has at least two-thirds of Division I programs in the red and scrambling for some way to pay for the additional demands of gender equity.[196] As such, football, long the sticking point in the gender equity debate, may ironically be the revenue generating answer.

IV. CONCLUSION

The cause of gender equity in athletics is about fairness. Certainly, many have and will continue to argue that women will never be able to raise their games to the quality of men's competition, and will never be able to attract the spectators or revenue that men's sports do. These are not the real issues here. Athletic competition at our colleges and universities should, first and foremost, serve an educational purpose, as we teach and instill in these young participants the values of teamwork, courage, commitment and fair play. Do not our young women deserve this educational opportunity as much as our young men?

Through a multitude of factors outlined herein, attitudes toward this issue are changing and legal imperatives are emerging, producing a social consciousness that will no longer tolerate an inequitable division of athletics opportunities favoring one sex over another. Athletic administrators, facing a certain confrontation with gender equity, must act now to determine how their limited financial resources can be fairly apportioned in order to ensure that athletics opportunities are equitably divided and sex discrimination eliminated in intercollegiate sports.

NOTES

1. Bill Byrne, *Funding New Women's Sports Will Stretch Budgets to Breaking Point*, USA TODAY, June 9, 1992, at 10C.
2. Gary Roberts, *Colleges Must Decide on Revenue Questions*, USA TODAY, June 9, 1992, at 10C.
3. Gene Corrigan, *Reaching Gender Equity No Easy Task*, USA TODAY, May 14, 1992, at 14C.
4. Malcolm Moran, *Title IX Is Now an Irresistible Force*, N.Y. TIMES, Jan. 21, 1992, at § L, S1.
5. Byrne, *supra* note 1, at 10C.
6. Equal pay for female coaches, for example, has become a hot issue recently, as a number of women's varsity coaches have commenced actions seeking compensation comparable to what men's coaches receive. In June 1993, Howard University basketball coach, Sanya Tyler, was awarded $1.1 million in her discrimination suit against the university. In August 1993, two other coaches commenced equal-pay suits: Ann Pitts, women's golf coach at Oklahoma State; and, Marianne Stanley, former women's basketball coach at the University of Southern California. At the time of this writing, Pam Bowers, women's basketball coach at Baylor University had also announced her intention to file an equal-pay suit against the university (January 1994). For a discussion of legal principles relevant to sex discrimination in coaching and athletic employment, *see* Glenn M. Wong & Richard J. Ensor, *Sex Discrimination in Athletics: A Review of Two Decades of Accomplishments and Defeats*, 21 GONZAGA L. REV. 345, 385-389 (1985/86).

7. Education Amendments of 1972, Pub. L. No. 92-318, §§ 901-09, 86 Stat. 235 (codified at 20 U.S.C. §§ 1681-1688 (1990)) [hereinafter Title IX].

8. Id.

9. *See* Diane Heckman, *Women & Athletics: A Twenty Year Retrospective on Title IX*, 9 U. MIAMI ENT. & SPORTS L. REV. 1, at 2 (1992). Since the enactment of Title IX in 1972, the number of high schools in the country offering girls' basketball increased from 4000 to 17,000 in 1987. Women's participation in college athletics grew from 66,000 to over 150,000 during that same period.

10. Since female athletes have been historically underrepresented in interscholastic and intercollegiate sports, many associate Title IX with enhancing female athletic opportunities. Title IX, however, has also been successful in creating athletic opportunities for men. *See* Gomes v. Rhode Island Interscholastic League, 469 F. Supp. 659 (D.R.I. 1979), *vacated as moot*, 604 F.2d 733 (1st Cir. 1979) (where the district court required a high school to provide a male student with the chance to play volleyball on the girls' team or to form a boys' team).

11. Wong & Ensor, *supra* note 6, at 359.

12. *See* Janet L. Kuhn, *Title IX: Employment and Athletics are Outside HEW's Jurisdiction*, 65 GEO. L.J. 49, 56-63 (1976). For an examination of the legislative history of Title IX in respect to athletics, *see* Christine Johnson, *The Evolution of Title IX: Prospects for Equality in Intercollegiate Athletics*, 11 GOLDEN GATE U. L. REV. 759 (1981); John Gaal, Louis P. DiLorenzo & Thomas S. Evans, *HEW's Final "Policy Interpretation" of Title IX and Intercollegiate Athletics*, 6 J.C.U.L. 345 (1980); &, Heckman, *supra* note 9.

13. Michael P. Villalobos, *The Civil Rights Restoration Act of 1987*, 1 MARQ. SPORTS L.J. 149, 150 (1990).

14. 45 C.F.R. 86 (1975) (codified at 34 C.F.R. Part 106 (1991)).

15. Heckman, *supra* note 9, at 29.

16. Wong & Ensor, *supra* note 6, at 368. For further discussion of this issue, *see* Gaal, *supra* note 12, at 345; Villalobos, *supra* note 13; Comment, *The Reform of Women's Intercollegiate Athletics: Title IX, Equal Protection, and Supplemental Methods*, 20 CAP. U. L. REV. 691 (1991); Heckman, *supra* note 9; &, Note, *Compensatory Damages are Available in Intentional Sexual Discrimination Cases—Franklin v. Gwinnett County Public Schools*, 3 SETON HALL J. OF SPORT LAW 197 (1993).

17. Heckman, *supra* note 9, at 3.

18. 465 U.S. 555 (1984).

19. *Id.* at 564-577. Grove City College is a private liberal arts college located in Pennsylvania. *Id.* at 559. To maintain its autonomy, the college continually declined to take part in federally and state sponsored direct institutional aid programs, as well as numerous federal student aid programs. *Id.* The school did accept a substantial number of students who

received Basic Educational Opportunity Grants (BEOGs) from the Alternate Disbursement System of the Department of Education. *Id.* In these circumstances, the Department of Education found that the college was a recipient of federal funding requiring the institution to file an Assurance of Compliance with Title IX. *Id.* at 560. When Grove City did not sign the Assurance of Compliance, the college and four of its students filed suit in the District Court of Western Pennsylvania to invalidate the Department of Education's termination of the BEOGs. The district court found that BEOGs received by the students constituted federal aid but that the Department of Education could not terminate the students' aid simply because the school failed to file the Assurance of Compliance. Grove City College v. Harris, 500 F. Supp. 253 (W.D. Pa. 1980).

On appeal, the United States Court of Appeals for the Third Circuit reversed, holding that the Department of Education could terminate aid for failure of the college to execute an Assurance of Compliance. The court also found that indirect as well as direct aid triggered coverage under Title IX, and, although Title IX's language should be given a program-specific interpretation, funds flowing to Grove City through its students were similar to non-earmarked aid, and that in such cases the school itself was the program. Grove City College v. Bell, 687 F.2d 684 (3d Cir. 1982). The United States Supreme Court granted certiorari, 459 U.S. 1199 (1983), and affirmed, 465 U.S. 555 (1984).

20. Villalobos, *supra* note 13, at 151.

21. *See* Wong & Ensor, *supra* note 6, at 359 n.77. Prior to 1984, the Department of Health, Education and Welfare (HEW) was divided into two agencies, the Department of Education and the Department of Health and Human Services. The Office of Civil Rights (OCR) operates under the Department of Education.

22. *Id.* at 370.

23. For a review of attempts to legislatively reverse the Supreme Court's "programmatic" interpretation in favor of the "institutional approach," *see* Villalobos, *supra* note 13, at 149; and, Wong & Ensor, *supra* note 6, at 371 n.135.

24. Heckman, *supra* note 9, at 33.

25. Pub. L. No. 100-259, 102 Stat. 28 (1988).

26. *Id.* The legislation similarly amended Title IV, the Rehabilitation Act, and the Age Discrimination Act.

27. *Id.*

28. 44 Fed. Reg. 71,413 (1979).

29. 45 C.F.R. Pt. 86.37(c) (1975) (codified at 34 C.F.R. § 106.37 (1991)); 44 Fed. Reg. 71,415 (1979).

30. *Id.* at Pt. 86.41(c).

31. *Id.* at Pt. 86.41(c)(1).

32. While the Policy Interpretation does not have the force and effect of law, it does have considerable practical significance since it sets forth the

standards by which the Department of Education assesses compliance with Title IX and its regulations. *See* Villalobos, *supra* note 13, at 155.

33. 45 C.F.R. Part 86.37(c) (1975) (codified at 34 C.F.R. § 106.37 (1991)); 44 Fed. Reg. 71,415 (1979).
34. *Id. See also*, Gaal, *supra* note 12, at 346-347.
35. 44 Fed. Reg. 71,415 (1979).
36. 45 C.F.R. Part 86.41(c) (1975) (codified at 34 C.F.R. § 106.41(c) (1991)). This subsection provides: (c) Equal opportunity. A recipient which operates or sponsors interscholastic, intercollegiate, club or intramural athletics shall provide equal athletic opportunity for members of both sexes. In determining whether equal opportunities are available the Director will consider, among other factors:

(1) Whether the selection of sports and levels of competition effectively accommodate the interests and abilities of members of both sexes;
(2) The provision of equipment and supplies;
(3) Scheduling of games and practice time;
(4) Travel and per diem allowance;
(5) Opportunity to receive coaching and academic tutoring;
(6) Assignment and compensation of coaches and tutors;
(7) Provision of locker rooms, practice and competitive facilities;
(8) Provision of medical and training facilities and services;
(9) Provision of housing and dining facilities and services;
(10) Publicity.

The accommodation of student interests and abilities (34 C.F.R. § 106.41(c) (1991)) is given specific and separate attention in the Policy Interpretation (44 Fed. Reg. 71,418 (1979)). In addition to the remaining nine enumerated areas, subsection 106.41(c) also permits the OCR to consider two other factors in the determination of equal opportunity: the recruitment of athletes and provision of support services.

37. *Id. See also*, Gaal, *supra* note 12, at 347.
38. *Id.*
39. *Id.*
40. 45 C.F.R. Pt. 86.41(c)(1) (1975) (codified at 34 C.F.R. § 106.41(c)(1) (1991)); 44 Fed. Reg. 71,418 (1979).
41. 44 Fed. Reg. 71,418 (1979).
42. *Id.*
43. The Policy Interpretation provides that institutions may determine the athletic interests and abilities of students by nondiscriminatory methods of their choosing provided:
(a) The processes take into account the nationally increasing levels of women's interests and abilities;

(b) The methods of determining interest and ability do not disadvantage the members of an underrepresented sex;

(c) The methods of determining ability take into account team performance records; and

(d) The methods are responsive to the expressed interests of students capable of intercollegiate competition who are members of an underrepresented sex. 44 Fed. Reg. 71,417 (1979).

44. 44 Fed. Reg. 71,418 (1979).

45. TITLE IX ATHLETICS INVESTIGATOR'S MANUAL (April 1990). The MANUAL was issued by the OCR to assist its personnel in conducting Title IX athletic investigations.

46. 44 Fed. Reg. 71,418 (1979).

47. In fact, various amendments, introduced in Congress to exempt revenue- producing sports from the requirements of Title IX, were each defeated. For a discussion of these proposed amendments, including the Tower Amendments (1974 and 1975), the Helms' Amendment (1975), and the McClure Amendment (1976). *See* Heckman, *supra* note 9, at 11. *See also* N. Haven Bd. of Educ. v. Bell, 456 U.S. 512, 532 n.22 & 533 n.24 (1982); &, Haffer v. Temple Univ., 524 F. Supp. 531, 534-35 (E.D. Pa. 1981), aff'd, 688 F.2d 14 (3rd Cir. 1982), *motion for consideration*, 678 F.Supp. 517 (E.D. Pa. 1987).

48. *See supra* notes 38-39 and accompanying text.

49. Roberts, *supra* note 2. *See also* Tom Weir, *All Must Face Cold Facts of Title IX*, USA TODAY, March 13, 1992, at 3C; &, discussion *infra* at notes 175-177, and accompanying text.

50. 34 C.F.R. § 106.41 (1991); 44 Fed. Reg. 71,413 (1979).

51. For further discussion of OCR compliance reviews, *see infra* notes 172-173 and accompanying text. *See also* Heckman, *supra* note 9, at 18-20.

52. 44 Fed. Reg. 71,419 (1979).

53. *Id.*

54. *Id.*

55. *Id.* In the area of athletics, the Department of Education rarely applies the formal administrative process to terminate funds to enforce Title IX. The formal enforcement process is usually avoided because institutions have typically developed voluntary compliance plans acceptable to the OCR. Robert C. Berry and Glenn M. Wong, 2 LAW AND BUSINESS OF THE SPORTS INDUSTRIES 272 (2d ed.) (1993).

56. *See* Cannon v. Univ. of Chicago, 441 U.S. 677 (1979), *on remand*, 605 F.2d 560 (7th Cir. 1979). *See also* Haffer v. Temple Univ., 524 F. Supp. 531 (E.D. Pa. 1981), *aff'd*, 688 F.2d 14 (3rd Cir. 1982), *motion for reconsideration*, 678 F. Supp. 517 (E.D. Pa. 1987).

57. *See* Heckman, *supra* note 9, at 20.

58. For an examination of injunctive relief, *see* Cheryl L. Schubert-Madsen, Arline F. Schubert & George W. Schubert, *Gender Discrimination in Athletics*, 67 N.D. L. Rev. 227 at 237-38 (1991).

59. *See* Yellow Springs Exempted Village School Dist. Bd. of Education v. Ohio High School Athl. Assn., 443 F. Supp. 753 (S.D. Ohio 1978), *rev'd*, 647 F.2d 651 (6th Cir. 1981).

60. Heckman, *supra* note 9, at 21.

61. Franklin v. Gwinnett County Public Schools, 112 S.Ct. 1028 (1992) (compensatory damages may be awarded in a Title IX action when the plaintiff is the victim of the defendant's intentional discrimination). *See infra* notes 83-90 and accompanying text for further discussion of Franklin.

62. Arline F. Schubert, George W. Schubert, and Cheryl L. Schubert-Madsen, *Changes Influenced by Litigation in Women's Intercollegiate Athletics*, 1 Seton Hall J. Sport Law 237, 246 (1991).

63. U.S. Const. amend. XIV, § 1. The Fourteenth Amendment provides that no state shall "deny any person within its jurisdiction the equal protection of the laws." The federal government is held to similar standards under the due process clause of the Fifth Amendment, *See* Berry & Wong, *supra* note 55, at 97.

64. Berry & Wong, *supra* note 55, at 98.

65. *Id.*

66. For further discussion of equal protection analysis, *see* Berry & Wong, *supra* note 55, at 97-102; Wong & Ensor, *supra* note 6, at 354-358; &, Heckman, *supra* note 9, at 7-8 and accompanying notes.

67. Wong & Ensor, *supra* note 6, at 355, 358. For example, health and safety of women have been used as justifications for denying women the opportunity to participate with men in contact sports. *See, e.g.,* Clinton v. Nagy, 411 F. Supp. 1396 (N.D. Ohio 1974).

68. *See* Craig v. Boren, 429 U.S. 190 (1976); *see also* Clark v. Ariz. Interscholastic Assn., 695 F.2d 1126 (9th Cir. 1982).

69. States with equal rights amendments include: Alaska, Colorado, Connecticut, Hawaii, Illinois, Maryland, Massachusetts, Montana, New Hampshire, New Mexico, Pennsylvania, Texas, Utah, Virginia, Washington and Wyoming. *See* Note, *Compensatory Damages are Available in Intentional Sexual Discrimination Cases—Franklin v. Gwinnett County Public Schools*, 3 Seton Hall J. of Sport Law 197, at 142 (1993).

70. Colorado, Hawaii, Illinois, Maryland, Massachusetts, Pennsylvania and Washington apply the strict scrutiny standard of review to their state equal rights amendments. Heckman, *supra* note 9, at 7 n.23.

Some commentators suggest that in non-ERA states, the plaintiff could recharacterize the claim as a violation of the state's due process clause. *See* Comment, *supra* note 16 at 703; and Comment, *Haffer v. Temple University: A Reawakening of Gender Discrimination in Intercollegiate Athletics*, 16 J.C. & U.L. 137, at 143 (1989).

71. *Supra* note 24.
72. Comment, *supra* note 16, at 704.
73. Wong & Ensor, *supra* note 6, at 347.
74. Comment, *supra* note 16, at 704.
75. Villalobos, *supra* note 13, at 151.
76. Comment, *supra* note 16, at 708.
77. *Id* at 707.
78. *See supra* notes 23-27 and accompanying text.
79. GENDER-EQUITY STUDY, NATIONAL COLLEGIATE ATHLETIC ASSOCIATION (March 1992).
80. *Id.*
81. Heckman, *supra* note 9, at 63.
82. PRESS RELEASE, NATIONAL COLLEGIATE ATHLETIC ASSOCIATION (March 11, 1992). *See also supra* notes 157-162 and accompanying text for a review of NCAA gender- equity task force recommendations.
83. 112 S. Ct. 1028 (1992)
84. Peggy Kellers, *Breaking the Silence: Twenty Years of Title IX Litigation*, 11 THE SPORTS LAWYER 1 (Nov./Dec. 1992).
85. *Franklin*, 112 S.Ct. at 1031. Christine Franklin was a student at North Gwinnett High School in Gwinnett County, Georgia between September 1985 and August 1989. *Id.* According to the complaint, Franklin was subjected to continual sexual harassment beginning in the autumn of her tenth grade year (1986) from Hill, a sports coach and teacher employed by the district. *Id.* The complaint further alleges that though teachers and administrators in the district became aware of and investigated Hill's sexual harassment of Franklin and other female students, they took no action to halt it and discouraged Franklin from pressing charges against Hill. *Id.* Faced with mounting pressure, Hill resigned in 1988 on the condition that all matters pending against him be dropped. *Id.*

Prior to bringing her lawsuit, Franklin filed a complaint with the OCR. After investigating these charges for several months, the OCR concluded that the school district had violated Franklin's rights by subjecting her to physical and verbal sexual harassment and by interfering with her right to complain about conduct proscribed by Title IX. The OCR determined, however, that because of Hill's resignation and the school's implementation of a grievance procedure, the district had come into compliance with Title IX. It then terminated its investigation. *Id.* at 1031 n.3.

Thereafter, Franklin commenced a Title IX action in the United States District Court for the Northern District of Georgia, alleging that the school district had intentionally discriminated against her on the basis of sex. The district court dismissed Franklin's complaint on the basis that compensatory damages were not authorized under Title IX. The Court of Appeals for the Eleventh Circuit affirmed. *Franklin*, 911 F.2d 617 (1990).

Approximately six weeks later in *Pfeiffer v. Marion Ctr. Area Sch. Dist.*, the Court of Appeals for the Third Circuit held that compensatory damages were available for certain violations of Title IX., 917 F.2d 779 (3rd Cir. 1990). As a result of the conflict of opinion between the Third and Eleventh Circuits on this issue, the Supreme Court granted certiorari. *Franklin*, 111 S.Ct. 2795 (1991).

86. *Franklin*, 112 S.Ct. at 1032.

87. *Id.* at 1038. Justice White delivered the opinion of the Court and was joined by Justices Blackmun, Stevens, O'Connor, Kennedy and Souter. Justice Scalia filed a concurring opinion, joined by Chief Justice Rehnquist and Justice Thomas.

88. Heckman, *supra* note 9, at 25.

89. Kellers, *supra* note 84, at 6.

90. *See* Heckman, *supra* note 9, at 25; & Kellers, *supra* note 84, at 6.

91. 814 F. Supp. 1507 (D. Colo. 1993), *aff'd*, 998 F.2d 824 (10th Cir. 1993), *cert. denied*, 126 L. Ed. 2d 478 (1993).

92. *Roberts*, 814 F. Supp. at 1509.

93. *Id.* at 1512.

94. *Id.*

95. *Id.*

96. *See supra*, Policy Interpretation discussion at notes 28-49 and accompanying text.

97. *Roberts*, 814 F. Supp. at 1513. The district court focused on CSU's failure under Title IX to effectively accommodate student interests and abilities. In assessing compliance with this requirement, the court referred to the three prong test outlined in the Policy Interpretation, requiring substantial proportionality between athletic participation and undergraduate enrollment, or proof of a history and continuing practice of athletic program expansion for the underrepresented gender, or proof that the athletic interests and abilities of the underrepresented gender are being fully and effectively accommodated. *Id.* at 1510. The court found that a 10.5% disparity between the enrollment of women at CSU and females participating in athletics exhibited CSU's failure to provide athletic opportunities to women "substantially proportional" to their representation in the student body. *Id.* at 1313.

98. *Id.* at 1516.

99. *Id.* at 1518.

100. *Roberts*, 998 F.2d 824. The Court of Appeals for the Tenth Circuit affirmed the district court's use of the Policy Interpretation criteria in determining whether an institution has effectively accommodated the athletic interests and abilities of its students. *Id.* at 829. Substantial proportionality between athletic participation and undergraduate enrollment would provide an institution with a "safe harbor" for compliance with this requirement. However, in the absence of such a gender balance, the institution would be required to show that it has expanded and is

continuing to expand opportunities for athletic participation by the underrepresented gender, or else it must fully and effectively accommodate the interests and abilities among members of the underrepresented gender. *Id.* CSU failed on each prong of the test.

101.*Id.* at 830. Interestingly, the court noted that Title IX does not require financially strapped institutions to expand women's programs to comply with Title IX's effective accommodation requirement. "Expansion" may not be twisted to find compliance under this prong when schools have increased the relative percentages of women participating in athletics by making cuts in both men's and women's sports programs. An institution, however, may bring itself into compliance with this prong by reducing opportunities for the overrepresented gender while keeping opportunities stable for the underrepresented gender (or reducing them to a much lesser extent). *Id.* at 830 n.4.

102.*Roberts*, 126 L. Ed. 2d 478 (1993).

103.809 F. Supp. 978 (D. R.I. 1992), *aff'd*, 991 F.2d 888 (1st Cir. 1993).

104.*Cohen*, 991 F.2d at 892.

105.*Id.*

106.*Id.* at 892.

107.*Id.* at 899. Brown argued that the OCR Policy Interpretation does not comport with Title IX and its regulations. Brown suggested that, to the extent student's interests in athletics are disproportionate by gender, colleges should be allowed to meet those interests incompletely as long as the school's response is in direct proportion to the comparative levels of interest. It contended that an institution satisfactorily accommodates female athletes if it allocates athletic opportunities to women in accordance with the ratio of interested and able women to interested and able men, regardless of the number of unserved women or the percentage of the student body that they comprise. *Id.*

The Court of Appeals disagreed, concluding that the fact that the overrepresented gender is less than fully accommodated will not, in and of itself, excuse a shortfall in the provision of athletic opportunities for the underrepresented gender. *Id.* Rather, the court held that, in the absence of continuing program expansion, schools must either provide athletic opportunities in proportion to the gender composition of the student body, or fully accommodate interested athletes among the underrepresented sex. *Id.*

108.*Cohen*, 809 F. Supp. at 1001.

109.*Cohen*, 991 F.2d at 893.

110.*Id.* at 891.

111.*Id.* at 897. The court characterized the Policy Interpretation as "a proper, permissible rendition of the statute (Title IX)." *Id.* at 900.

112.*Id.* at 903. The court held that a disparity of 10.5% between female students and female athletes did not even closely approach substantial proportionality. *Id.* at 903.

113.*Id.* at 903. *See also Cohen*, 809 F. Supp. at 991.

114.*Id.* at 903-904.

115.*Id.* at 904.

116.Favia v. Indiana University of Pennsylvania, 812 F. Supp. 578 (W.D. Pa. 1993), *motion to modify order denied on appeal*, 7 F.3d 332 (3rd Cir. 1993).

117.*Favia*, 812 F. Supp. 578, at 579. Prior to the cuts, the IUP athletic department supported 18 sports, 9 for men and 9 for women. Women accounted for 37.8% of varsity athletes, and 55.6% of its undergraduate population. As a result of the cuts, IUP's sponsorship of varsity sports was reduced to 14 sports, 7 for men and 7 for women, while the athletic participation ratio for women dropped slightly to 36.5% of IUP varsity athletes. *Id.* at 580.

118.*Id.* at 584-585.

119.*Favia*, 7 F.3d 332 (3rd Cir. 1993).

120.*See Cohen*, 991 F.2d at 905. The *Cohen* court emphasized that the pruning of athletic budgets cannot take place isolated from the legislative and regulatory imperatives of Title IX. *See also* Robert Thomas, Jr., *Ruling for Brown Women to Be Far-Reaching*, N.Y TIMES, April 20, 1993, at B14 column 2.

121.*Id.* at 906.

122.802 F. Supp. 737 (N.D. N.Y. 1992), *dismissed as moot*, 992 F.2d 17 (2nd Cir. 1993).

123.A varsity sport team is the official representative of a school with full-time coaches and specifically designated schedules for competition. Varsity teams are also provided with equipment, practice facilities and travel accommodations. Club teams, on the other hand, are principally run by students, have informal schedules, practices and competitions. Their equipment, facilities and travel are of a make-shift nature. *See* Mel Narol, *The New Title IX Game: Women 2, Colleges 0,* 11 THE SPORTS LAWYER 6, at 6, (Mar.-Apr. 1993). On four different occasions, from 1979 to 1988, members of the women's club ice hockey team had petitioned Colgate's Committee on Athletics for varsity status. Each petition had been denied by the Committee, citing the lack of sufficient competition for women's varsity ice hockey both locally and nationally, the limited interest of students on campus in women's ice hockey, the inability of the current women's club ice hockey team to compete at the varsity level, and the prohibitive expense of promoting the club team to varsity status. *Cook*, 802 F. Supp. 737 at 740.

124.Specifically, the complaint, in comparing men's varsity to women's club ice hockey opportunities, alleged discrimination on the basis of financial support, equipment, locker room facilities, travel, practice time and coaching. *Cook*, 802 F. Supp. 737, at 744.

125.*Id.* at 742.

126.*Id.* at 744.

127. *Id.* at 740. To justify its refusal to promote the team to varsity status, Colgate argued that women's ice hockey was rarely played in public high schools and only at some prep schools, that there was insufficient competition from other schools in the region, that there was no NCAA championship in women's ice hockey, that the sport lacked general student interest, that the women's team lacked the ability to play at the varsity level, and that the school was financially unable to fund a varsity program. *Id.* at 740.

128. *Cook*, 992 F.2d 17, at 20.

129. *Id.* at 20.

130. *Sportsline*, USA TODAY, August 12, 1993, at 1C.

131. *See supra* discussion at notes 45-48 and accompanying text.

132. Heckman, *supra* note 9, at 26.

133. Kelley v. Bd. of Trustees of the Univ. of Ill., 832 F. Supp. 237 (C.D. Ill. 1993).

134. *Id.* at 243-44.

135. Gonyo v. Drake Univ., 837 F. Supp. 989 (S.D. Iowa 1993).

136. Even though this article focuses on post-*Franklin* settlements, institutions involved in noteworthy pre-*Franklin* settlements include: the University of Oklahoma, where the school announced the cut of its women's basketball program, but voluntarily reinstated the program after the threat of a lawsuit (1990); the University of South Carolina, where the school cut softball with the intent to replace it with women's track, but reinstated softball and added women's track under the threat of a lawsuit and after an OCR visit (1991); and, the College of William and Mary, where the school dropped women's basketball, men's and women's swimming and wrestling, but reinstated the programs when faced with a lawsuit from members of the women's basketball team (1991). Information received from the Women's Sports Foundation. The author thanks Mr. Leland Brandt of the WSF for his assistance.

137. *Update*, USA TODAY, June 23, 1993, at 15C.

138. *See supra* notes 91-119 and accompanying text for discussion of the Roberts, Cohen and Favia decisions.

139. Carol Herwig, *Cornell Settlement Will Restore Women's Gymnastics, Fencing*, USA TODAY, Dec. 9, 1993, at 8C.

140. *Sportsline*, USA TODAY, Aug. 20, 1993, at 1C.

141. *Update*, USA TODAY, Aug. 23, 1993, at 9C.

142. The author thanks Ronald R. Rodgers, UNH General Counsel, for providing information relevant to the UNH gender equity dispute and subsequent settlement, including copies of the MEMORANDUM OF AGREEMENT (between UNH and members of the 1992 women's tennis team, dated March 6, 1992) and the PLAN TO ENSURE CONTINUED COMPLIANCE WITH TITLE IX IN ATHLETICS AT THE UNIVERSITY OF NEW HAMPSHIRE (dated July 15, 1993 and formally adopted by the university on August 18, 1993).

143. Sanders v. Univ. of Tex. at Austin, Case No. A-92-CA-405 (W.D. Tex. 1993). The action, similar to *Cook* in some respects, was filed by members of four women's club sports (softball, soccer, crew, and gymnastics) seeking to elevate their programs to varsity status. At the time the action was filed, women accounted for 47% of UT's undergraduate student body, but only 23% of its varsity athletes.

144. *Id.* The author thanks Patricia C. Ohlendorf, Vice Provost of the University of Texas at Austin, for providing information relevant to the UT gender equity dispute and subsequent settlement, including a copy of the court order settling the *Sanders* action.

145. Kiechel v. Auburn Univ., Civil Action File No. 93-V-474-E (M.D. Ala. 1993).

146. *Id.*

147. *Id.*

148. *Id.* The author thanks Lee F. Armstrong, Auburn University General Counsel, for providing information relevant to the university's gender equity dispute and subsequent settlement, including copies of relevant court documents in the *Kiechel* action (SETTLEMENT AGREEMENT AND FINAL ORDER APPROVING CLASS ACTION SETTLEMENT).

149. Edwin Gentzler, *Intercollegiate Sports and Equal Opportunity for Women*, COUNCIL ON THE STATUS OF WOMEN, UNIV. OF MASS. AT AMHERST, Mar. 10, 1992.

150. The author thanks Glenn M. Wong and Carol Barr for providing information relevant to the UMass gender equity dispute and subsequent settlement. At the time of the settlement, Wong served as the UMass Interim Director of Athletics, and Barr as an Assistant Director of Athletics. The author, at the time of the settlement, was an assistant professor in the UMass Sport Management Program.

151. Howlett v. Gordon, Case No. 680299 (Cal. Super. Ct. 1992).

152. *Id.*

153. Carol Herwig, *Gender-Equity Suits Settled, Could Have Far-Reaching Effect*, USA TODAY, Oct. 22, 1993, at 10C.

154. Carol Herwig, *Questions Linger in Wake of Brooklyn's Troubles*, USA TODAY, June 10, 1992, at 2C.

155. In February, 1993, U.S. Representative Cardiss Collins, D-Ill., unveiled a bill entitled the "Equity in Athletics Disclosure Act." If passed, the bill would require all colleges receiving federal financial assistance to reveal their male and female varsity athletic participation ratios and their total expenditures for men's and women's athletics. *See* Carol Herwig, *Compliance with Title IX is Aim of Pending Legislation*, USA TODAY, Feb. 18, 1993, at 13C.

156. NCAA GENDER-EQUITY STUDY, *supra* note 79. While women accounted for approximately 50% of the student body enrollment at Division I institutions, they represented only 30.9% of varsity athletic

participants, and received only 30.4% of scholarship revenue, 22.6% of athletic department operating budgets, and 17.2% of recruiting budgets.

157. *See supra* note 82.

158. FINAL REPORT OF THE NCAA GENDER-EQUITY TASK FORCE, NATIONAL COLLEGIATE ATHLETIC ASSOCIATION, July 26, 1993, at 2. According to the task force report, an "athletics program can be considered gender equitable when the participants in both the men's and women's sports programs would accept as fair and equitable the overall program of the other gender. No individual should be discriminated against on the basis of gender, institutionally or nationally, in intercollegiate athletics."

159. *Id.* at 3. The task force suggested that institutions "should support intercollegiate athletics participation opportunities for males and females in an equitable manner. The ultimate goal for each institution should be that the numbers of male and female athletes are substantially proportionate to their numbers in the institution's undergraduate student population."

160. *Id.* at 2-6.

161. *Gender Equity, Financial Proposals Draw Little Fire,* NCAA NEWS, Jan. 19, 1994, at 27.

162. *Id.* The emerging sports identified by the legislation include: archery, badminton, bowling, crew, ice hockey, squash, synchronized swimming, team handball and water polo. *See* 1994 NCAA CONVENTION OFFICIAL NOTICE, Legislative Proposal No. 12.

163. 1993-94 NCAA MANUAL, Bylaw 23.

164. *Id.* at Bylaw 23.2.4.

165. *Id.* at Bylaw 23.2.3.

166. Carol Herwig, *Big Ten Gives Women's Sports a Boost,* USA TODAY, May 13, 1992, at 1C.

167. *See* Moran, *supra* note 4, at S8. *See also* Evon Asforis, *Big Ten Moves Toward Gender Equity,* THE WOMEN'S SPORTS EXPERIENCE (July-August 1992), at 9 (where Donna Lopiano, executive director of the Women's Sports Foundation is quoted: "The Big Ten should be commended for being the only conference to grapple with gender equity. Its effort, however, falls far short of the requirements of law and common sense.").

168. Even though not officially adopted by the Big Ten Conference, its commissioner, Jim Delaney, has offered some suggestions to achieve the mandated 60:40 male to female participation ratio, including:

•Conducting campaigns to encourage women to join athletic teams even if they do not receive an athletic scholarship.
•Identifying women's sports on each campus that can be upgraded from club status to varsity competition.
•Creating junior varsity teams in the sports that hold the greatest appeal for female athletes, such as basketball and volleyball.

•Establishing limits on the sizes of men's teams, with reductions of 10 percent or more, depending on the size required by the needs of each sport.

See Moran, *supra* note 4, at S8 p.1.

169. PRESS RELEASE, UNIVERSITY OF IOWA SPORTS INFORMATION DEPARTMENT, April 21, 1992.

Christine Grant, women's athletic director and associate professor at the University of Iowa, has offered the following suggestions to assist universities in enhancing female athletic opportunities without necessarily cutting men's programs:

•Putting caps on squad sizes in men's sports. Some sports carry many more participants than are necessary to practice or compete.

•Encouraging the NCAA to increase scholarships (and therefore participation) in existing women's sports. For example, field hockey needs 22 players to scrimmage, but has a scholarship limit of 11.

•Allowing scholarships to be divided in all women's sports to attract more participants.

•Adding one or two women's sports. Almost all universities now offer more sports for men.

•Reforming the system at the national level so expensive and nonessential practices are eliminated.

See Christine Grant, *Universities Must Commit to Achieve Parity*, USA TODAY, May 14, 1992, at 14C.

170. The author thanks Mark Whitworth, of the Southeastern Conference (SEC), for providing a copy of SOUTHEASTERN CONFERENCE PRINCIPLES OF GENDER EQUITY, adopted on June 3, 1993, to be effective after August 1, 1995.

The SEC's current minimum sports offering requirement is seven men's and seven women's programs. This new proposal will increase the women's minimum to nine.

171. *Id.*

172. Kellers, *supra* note 84, at 6.

173. *Sportsline*, USA TODAY, Mar. 24, 1993, at 1C. Included among the schools selected for compliance reviews in 1993 were: Colorado State, Fresno State, Iowa State, Jackson State, Northern Michigan and San Jose State.

174. See Tom Weir, *All Must Face Cold Facts of Title IX*, USA TODAY, Mar. 13, 1992, at 3C.

175. *Id.*

176. According to the NCAA's 1992 Gender-Equity Study, of all Division I athletes, 29.9% are football players and 30.9% are female athletes. The remaining 39.2% represents non-football playing male athletes. See NCAA GENDER-EQUITY STUDY, *supra* note 79, at Table 1.

177. Statistical information examining the financial health of college athletics vary quite remarkably, however, one is lead to the conclusion that the number of Division I sports programs that bring in more revenue than they spend are relatively few, perhaps less than 30%. Even many Division I-A football programs operate at a deficit, however football unquestionably generates more revenue than any other sport, nearly half the revenue in fact, as Division I-A schools. Officials at schools with prominent football traditions fear the wrath of the alumni, boosters and fans if they tamper with what is perceived as the goose that lays the golden egg. *See*, Ben Brown, *Law Gives Women Their Fair Share*, USA TODAY, June 9, 1992, at 2C.

An NCAA study released in August 1994 revealed that men's sports programs under the flagship sport of football, generate an average of 69% of Division I-A athletic department revenue. Women's programs produce an average of 4% of total revenues, with the remaining 27% generated from non-gender specific sources. The study also revealed that 67% of Division I-A football programs are operating in the black, at an average profit in 1993 of $3.9 million. Eighty-five of the 107 Division I-A schools responded to the survey. See, NCAA NEWS, August 31, 1994, at 5.

178. *See supra* notes 40-44 and accompanying text.

179. *See supra* notes 36-39 and accompanying text.

180. *See supra* notes 32-35 and accompanying text.

181. *See supra* note 162. Proposal No. 12 passed at the 1994 NCAA Convention established maximum financial aid limits in emerging sports for women and permits institutions to utilize the emerging sports in order to meet the Association's minimum sports sponsorship and financial aid award criteria. The emerging sports identified by the legislation include: archery, badminton, bowling, crew, ice hockey, squash, synchronized swimming, team handball and water polo.

For purposes of the "Three-for-One" plan, women's softball is considered the equivalent of men's baseball, and is, therefore, ineligible as a FWO program, unless baseball is not offered to men at the particular institution.

182. The following is a representation of the "Three-for-One" plan's implementation at hypothetical university (HU), an NCAA Division I institution. Statistics used are derived from the 1992 NCAA GENDER-EQUITY STUDY, *supra* note 79. The example is intended to depict the average Division I institution, and will describe HU athletics program offerings for men and women both BEFORE and AFTER the implementation of the "Three-for-One" plan.

Men's sports:	8
Women's sports:	7
UGrad student body ratio (M/W):	50/50
Athletics participation ratio (M/W):	69.4/30.6

Men's sports (participants)		Women's sports (participants)	
Football	109	Volleyball	12
Baseball	33	Softball	17
Basketball	15	Basketball	13
Cross country	13	Cross country	11
Swimming	25	Swimming	22
Tennis	10	Tennis	10
Track	38	Track	26
Golf	11		—
	252		111

HU Athletics – After "Three-for-One" Plan

EXAMPLE #1.
Implementation of "Three-for-One" plan WITHOUT cutting a men's sport. Changes high-lighted in **bold**.

Men's sports	8
Women's sports:	**10**
UGrad student body ratio (M/W):	50/50
Athletics participation ratio (M/W):	**56/44**
Pool A participation ratio (M/W):	**63/37**
Pool B participation ratio (M/W):	**54/46**

Men's sports (participants)		Women's sports (participants)	
POOL A		POOL A	
Football*	97	Volleyball**	13
		Soccer	24
	—	**Crew**	20
	97		57
POOL B		POOL B	
Baseball*	28	Softball**	18
Basketball*	13	Basketball**	14
Cross country*	11	Cross country**	12
Swimming*	22	Swimming**	24
Tennis*	9	Tennis**	11
Track*	34	Track**	28
Golf*	10	Golf	11
	142		118
POOLS A+B	224	POOLS A+B	175

* denotes a 10% reduction in men's roster sizes
** denotes a 10% increase in women's roster sizes

> Example #1 adds 64 female athletic opportunities, by creating three new sports (soccer, crew and golf), and increasing preexisting women's roster sizes by 10%. The women's athletic program enhancement is accomplished in part by a 10% reduction in men's roster sizes. Overall athletics opportunites offered by HU have increased, after the implementation of the plan, from 363 to 399.

EXAMPLE #2

Men's sports:	7
Women's sports:	9
UGrad student body ratio (M/W):	50/50
Athletics participation ratio (M/W):	**56/44**
Pool A participation ratio (M/W):	**61/39**
Pool B participation ratio (M/W):	**53/47**

Men's sports (participants)		Women's sports (participants)	
POOL A		POOL A	
Football*	97	Volleyball**	13
		Soccer	24
	—	Swimming**	24
	97		61
POOL B		POOL B	
Baseball*	28	Softball**	18
Basketball*	13	Basketball**	14
Cross country*	11	Cross country**	12
Tennis*	9	Tennis**	11
Track*	34	Track	28
Golf*	10	Golf	11
	105		94
POOLS A+B	202	POOLS A+B	155

* denotes a 10% reduction in men's roster sizes
** denotes a 10% increase in women's roster sizes

> Example #2 adds 44 female athletic opportunities, by creating two new sports (soccer and golf), and increasing preexisting women's roster sizes by 10%. The women's athletic program enhancement is accomplished in part by a 10% reduction in men's roster sizes, and the elimination of the men's swimming program. Since swimming becomes a women's-only sport at HU, it is now eligible for inclusion in Pool A. Overall athletics opportunities offered by HU have actually decreased from 363 to 357.

183.*See* discussion and examples *infra* note 182.

184.*See supra* notes 32-44, and accompanying text.

185.*See supra* note 158, at 2.

186.*See supra* notes 36-39, and accompanying text.

187.*See supra* notes 32-35, and accompanying text.

188.Comment, *supra* note 16, at 715.

189.For further discussion of marketing women's sports *see* Comment, *supra* note 16, at 715-718.

190.The NCAA Gender-Equity Task Force, in its *Final Report*, recommended that the NCAA develop collaborative efforts with, and examine the possibility of obtaining grants and other assistance from, the USOC. *See* FINAL REPORT OF THE NCAA GENDER-EQUITY TASK FORCE, *supra* note 158, at 8.

191.At its 1991 Convention, the NCAA reduced athletic scholarships available for Division I-A football from 95 to 92 for the 1992-93 academic year, to 88 during the 1993-94 academic year, and to 85 for the 1994-95 academic year and thereafter. Athletic scholarships for men's basketball were also reduced from 15 to 14 for the 1992-93 academic year, and to 13 for the 1993-94 academic year and thereafter. *See* 1991-92 NCAA MANUAL, Bylaws 15.5.4 & 15.5.5.

The voluntary limiting of men's roster sizes, in addition to football and basketball, and/or elimination of one or more men's squads, may be necessary to achieve compliance under the "Three-for-One" plan. *See supra* notes 182-183 and accompanying text.

192.Debra Blum, *Schultz Says the NCAA Should Consider a Big-Time Football Championship Game*, THE CHRONICLE OF HIGHER EDUCATION, Jan. 20, 1993, at A45- 46.

193.Steve Wieberg, *NCAA Task Force to Look at Playoff*, USA TODAY, Dec. 8, 1993, at 1C.

194. Numerous two, four, and eight-team playoffs have been proposed, some incorporating the current New Year's Day bowls, others to be played after the bowls. A number of corporations have recently made pitches to the NCAA to promote and sponsor a football playoff, the most noteworthy, perhaps, being Nike and Disney. *See* Steve Wieberg, *Presidents Inch Toward Considering I-A Football Playoff*, USA TODAY, Dec. 8, 1993, at 14C.

The playoff formats currently being preliminarily considered would envision a maximum 14 game schedule, with some combination of 11 regular season games, and three post-season games. This schedule would then equal the 14 game schedule currently being played by Division I-AA, II and III champions. *See* Bryan Burwell, *Playoff Task Force a Small First Step*, USA TODAY, Dec. 8, 1993, at 3C.

195.Wieberg, *supra* note 194, at 14C.

196.*Id.*

Part V

Perspectives

Performing in a Racially Hostile Environment*

Phoebe Weaver Williams

Racial discrimination or harassment in the work place is clearly prohibited by Title VII of the 1964 Civil Rights Act. However, what if the work place is a public arena or stadium and the racial harassment comes in the form of anti black slurs and insults from paying customers? Under those circumstances, can an African-American athlete be disciplined by his employer for "over reacting" to the taunts? Or can the operator of the arena be held accountable for allowing such conditions to occur? In the following essay, Phoebe Williams explores the application of federal anti-discrimination laws to the problem of racially hostile sports environments.

I. Racial Harassment of Black Athletes: Another Paradigm for Understanding African-Americans' Experiences

As I was about to complete this article, I thought I should make it clear to the reader that I acknowledge that there are concerns about exploring this subject. In our society, athletes often receive more positive attention than many other persons who embark on worthwhile endeavors. Some consider athletes as well paid, often catered to, and too often recipients of considerable social deference. When informing some of my friends and relatives that I had decided to write about racial harassment of professional athletes, concerns were raised on more than one occasion that no one really sympathizes very much anymore with the "plight" of the Black professional athlete.[1]

Should other readers share these concerns, I feel obliged to explain why I believe we should continue to care. Initially I should explain that

[1] From Volume 6, Number 2, Spring 1996, pp. 287-314.

I have chosen to focus on the problem of racial harassment of Black professional athletes.[2] Apart from the fact that I am African-American, there are other reasons for my decision. There exists a rich history, along with numerous autobiographical and news accounts, that chronicle the experiences of Black athletes. By focusing on their experiences, I do not mean to suggest that other "outsider" groups have not experienced similar hostilities. On the contrary, as members of immigrant groups, ethnic groups, and persons of different religions entered professional sports, they also encountered racial, ethnic, and religious harassment.[3] However, these individuals eventually blended into the sports terrain so that their unique ethnicity often went unnoticed. Athletes of color, however, have remained visible targets for racial derision.

In particular, I have focused on roles that sports fans or spectators play in creating racially hostile working environments for Black professional athletes. I have chosen to focus on fans because, while a number of constituencies have perpetrated racially hostile working environments for Black athletes, insufficient attention has been given to solving the problem of fans creating racially hostile environments.[4] The legal literature is virtually devoid of academic commentary focusing on this problem.

The fact that Black athletes remain targets of racial abuse from sports fans is perhaps another one of America's racial dilemmas. As a group, Black professional athletes conform to the American meritocratic model. Their successes allegedly affirm the fairness and equality of the American system. They have not only played their sports well, they have excelled at America's game. Their successes "fax" to us America's message: if you are truly talented, work hard, have something of value to offer, and function from an "individualistic" rather than victim perspective, our society will reward you in a "colorblind" fashion.[5] Frustrations surface when Blacks observe that professional athletes and others who have mastered the game are still objects of racial scorn.[6] Another message emerges: no matter what the accomplishment, no matter how appropriate the deportment, for some, African-Americans will remain an objects of racial hostility.

My own frustrations surfaced after reading an article about the fire-bombing of a church in Knoxville, Tennessee. At the time this article was brought to my attention, I had purchased my green and gold "Miracle Man No. 92" t-shirt. Like the rest of the "cheeseheads" in Wisconsin, I was anticipating and awaiting a Green Bay Packer trip to Superbowl XXX, which would come after the victory that weekend over the Dallas Cowboys. As the game approached, I looked forward to putting aside for a few hours the inevitable despair that accompanied this research. My plans for escape were marred after I learned that Reggie White, a defensive lineman for the Packers, is an associate minister of the church at issue. I knew that during the upcoming game I would filter White's performances through the prism of experiences of other African- American athletes who have had to perform at the height of their careers while coping with the severe emotional pain that results from racial violence.[7]

From all accounts, it appears that the church bombing was motivated by racial animosity.[8] Further, while I admit the speculative nature of this contention, it at least appears this violence may have been a deliberately timed attempt to impact White's performance during the Packer playoff game. Prior to the NFC playoff game in San Francisco against the 49ers, Packers' security personnel were informed that a telephone warning had been received which stated that Reggie White's Baptist church would be burned down.[9] The Packers did not "brief" White about this problem until after the game or until after the bombing. The fire-bombing occurred three days after the telephone threat.[10] White and his teammates were required to prepare for the playoffs against the Dallas Cowboys during the wake of investigations about racial violence. White expressed frustration that "the country isn't taking this kind of thing seriously enough."[11] While he was confident that he could block these events out of his mind and not allow them to interfere with his ability to play in the upcoming game, I wondered why, after all these years, he must perform under these circumstances.

Verbal racial abuse and actual racial violence present some complex issues for sports industry employers. To what extent were the Packers required to address racial harassment from unknown parties against their employee? What reasonable measures should sports' employers adopt to prevent and address this type of racial harassment? In Part II, I describe how sports spectators and fans have played a role in creating racially hostile environments for African- American athletes. What reasonable reactions should the Packers expect from White? In Part III, I discuss Title VII of the Civil Rights Act and the legal requirements the Act imposes upon employers, and in Part IV, I contrast the traditional responses of the sports' industry to racial abuse. While White clearly indicated that he would not allow these events to affect his play, what if he had refused to play, or felt unable to play due to the emotional pain resulting from these events? What if he misdirected his frustration while on the field towards the opposing team? Should his play under these circumstances influence whether the NFL fines or sanctions his behavior? I do not plan to specifically address these hypotheses. Their resolution would require consideration of a number of facts and circumstances. I do raise them so that the complexity of the problem of racial harassment in the sports industry may be better appreciated.

Some may consider White's experiences as unique, isolated occurrences. Unfortunately, the history of Black athletes in interracial athletics suggests that they are not. It is against this historical backdrop that we must measure the extent we have progressed in providing an environment free from workplace racial harassment. It is against this backdrop that we should measure contemporary experiences of racial harassment and consider whether the sports industry has done enough to address this problem. In Part V, I conclude that the industry can do more.

When seeking social reforms, African-Americans are reminded that our society rewards merit and excellence. Yet, the experiences of Black athletes, whose merits are meticulously, statistically, and publicly documented,[12] undermine arguments that merit alone rather than race matters in our society.[13] If Black athletes still experience racism, what of other African- Americans whose meritorious performances are not so quantifiable, not so public, and not so clearly extraordinary? If the wealth, the performances, and the economic value African-American athletes bring to our economy do not shield them from racism, then what will shield the rest of us?

II. The Roles Fans Play in Creating a Hostile Working Environment for Professional Athletes

Despite cheers and adulation, fans or spectators have historically played significant roles in creating racially hostile environments for athletes of color. Initially, racial partisanship intensified the emotions of fans to such an extent that when the Black prize fighter, Jack Johnson, faced his white opponent, James Jeffries, on July 4, 1910 in Reno, Nevada, spectators were required to check their guns at the gate.[14] While this early precaution was perhaps one of the first industry responses to potential racial violence and harassment, the fight's promoters could have done more. They could have stopped the band from playing "All Coons Look Alike to Me," a song that only fueled the spectators propensity to greet Johnson with racial slurs.[15]

One might relegate Johnson's experiences to those consistent with racial attitudes of an earlier era--an era when Blacks were often excluded from interracial competition. However, even after penetrating exclusionary barriers to participation, African-Americans were still subjected to racial harassment. Most people know of the racial harassment inflicted upon Jackie Robinson, who during the late 1940s became the first African-American to participate in organized interracial major league baseball competition. Three decades after Johnson, Robinson had to endure racial abuse that was so virulent that his perseverance under these circumstances contributed to the iconic stature he now occupies in history.[16] Again, Robinson's early experiences may be explained as occurrences that were part of the overall pre-Civil Rights era milieu. Yet even after periods of racial progress and improvement in racial relations, there were still the well known and documented experiences of Hank Aaron during the early seventies. During the two years before establishing a new home run record, Aaron received hate mail from fans of Babe Ruth and threats of racial violence directed against himself and members of his family.[17] While racial harassment of athletes by fans may be on the decline, a 1991 survey of professional athletes indicates that thirty-six percent of responding athletes reported having heard racial slurs from whites during games.[18]

During the civil rights era, discrimination against African-Americans became a public issue, and as a result, many expressions of racial animosities were driven underground. Generally, racial bigotry was demonstrated through more subtle behaviors.[19] However, the social controls that ordinarily deterred overt and blatant expressions of racial animosity remained absent from the "workplaces" of professional athletes.[20] Unlike most employment work areas, the athlete's workplace was often a public arena or stadium. Crowds at sporting events produced a type of anonymity for sports customers.[21] Frequently, alcohol was available and consumed by some fans in large quantities.[22] Boisterous or loud behavior became part of the overall milieu that customers expected to enjoy.[23] Recognizing the emotional outlet that sporting events provided their customers, management condoned and encouraged certain forms of aggressive spectator behavior. Within this context, control of fan behavior in general, particularly racially abusive behaviors, was often difficult to achieve.[24]

While there have been some lapses, the United States' sports industry has routinely managed to control levels of fan aggression.[25] Public arenas have employed security staffs whose duties include prevention of fan behavior that interrupts the event, protection of athletes, and protection of spectators. Nevertheless, fans generally have not been sanctioned for verbal racial abuse, and this lack of action has accounted in part for the hostile environment experienced by African-American athletes.[26]

Referring to his early years while playing in the minor leagues at two North Carolina communities, Curt Flood, a Black professional baseball player, recalled as one of his "first and most enduring memories" the verbal racial abuse perpetrated by drunken white fans.[27] For Flood, these incidents were not confined to his early years of competition. During the late sixties, Flood reflected on the hypocrisy of team owners who professed goals of decision making for the "good of the game," but who nevertheless polluted the sport of baseball with racial abuse by actively encouraging unruly, drunken, and obscene fans.[28] Flood's experiences included fans who not only hurled racial epithets, but also pelted him with "groceries" and "flashlight batteries."[29]

More recent accounts of fan abuse suggest that despite the passage of time, fans continue to subject athletes to racially abusive behaviors. During September 1993, Bryan Cox, a professional football player with the Miami Dolphins, was subjected to "an intense barrage of verbal abuse"[30] from several fans attending the game between Miami and Buffalo. This abuse might have gone unnoted but for Cox's response to this scene. At the beginning and during the game, Cox directed two "obscene gestures" towards the Buffalo fans. For these acts, Cox was fined $10,000 by the National Football League (NFL). Cox appealed the fine, and while awaiting the decision he filed a ground-breaking complaint with the Equal Employment Opportunity Commission alleging that the NFL had subjected him to a racially hostile environment. Upon the issuance of a "right to sue" letter, Cox filed an action in the federal court. The NFL reduced his fine to $3,000 and "distributed revised guidelines requiring, among other things, that teams remove from the stadiums fans who take part in 'racial taunts.'"[31]

While the merits of Cox's complaint of a racially hostile environment were not addressed during the federal court litigation, a review of the affidavits of Cox and his teammates suggests that there was strong evidence that Cox was subjected to a racially abusive environment. Some of the Buffalo fans began their harassment with Cox's arrival for the pre-game warm-up at 11:30 a.m. This harassment continued for one and one-half hours before the game and persisted throughout the game.[32] In additional to the racial slurs and epithets, "numerous fans [made] obscene gestures with their hands" towards Cox.[33] Others yelled verbal threats, such as "we will kill you."[34] As if the verbal taunts and threats were not enough, one fan held up a dummy in "blackface" with Cox's number on it. While it was not clear that Cox saw this dummy, the message it sent was clear. Across the chest of the dummy were written the words "Wanted 51 Dead." Tied around the dummy's neck was a noose.

Lynchings in effigy are meant to arouse the type of "demonic terror"[35] white Klansmen inflicted on Blacks decades earlier.[36] The parallel between a "lynching" symbol hoisted in the midst of jeering crowds screaming racial epithets for victory and the scenes of lynch mobs is remarkable. When white fans play these "race cards," African-Americans are reminded of the fragility of their freedoms. Memories are recalled about how political compromises, economic exploitation, or even social "mood swings" provided sufficient justifications for whites to deny African-Americans equal freedoms.[37] Within the context of sporting events, Black athletes are not the only ones harassed. Black fans are similarly reminded that large white crowds filled with persons consuming alcohol may turn "ugly."[38] When white fans are permitted to engage in racially opprobrious conduct towards Black athletes, Black fans are likewise subjected to a racially abusive environment. Ironically, it is an environment for which they have paid to enter.

Threats of racial violence against Black athletes from fans have not been isolated occurrences. Rather, such threats have peppered the careers of athletes performing in a variety of interracial competitions.[39] For some fans, racial harassment becomes one of the arsenal of weapons used to affect a positive outcome for their team.[40] Where racial harassment is used by sports customers as part of a strategy to support their team, one might argue that harassment under these circumstances is simply part of the game. Racism and nationalism have been identified as one of the causes of fan hooliganism at international sporting events.[41] Racially hostile behavior by American sports fans is simply part of the overall deterioration of behavior by sports customers.[42]

Explanations that tend to rationalize, objectify, or justify racially harassing behaviors generally are not effective defenses to claims of a racially hostile work environment under Title VII. Under existing legal paradigms, employers may be sanctioned for permitting race harassment; even harassment which stems from non race based motivations, i.e., the desire to distract an opponent during a game; or harassment from third parties such as customers.

While Cox's complaint represented the first instance where the legal protections provided by Title VII of the Civil Rights Act of 1964 were used to address the racial harassment of Black athletes, the following discussion establishes that sports industry employers, like other employers, are obliged to address racially hostile work environments. Yet, it appears that the industry has only recently taken measures to address this problem. Whether these measures are reasonable is a subject worthy of discussion because for some African-Americans the response of the sports industry to racism becomes a metaphor for the extent the rest of society is willing to provide racial justice. [43]

III. Legal Paradigms for Identifying and Addressing Racially Hostile Work Environments

Title VII of the Civil Rights Act of 1964 forbids discrimination in employment because of an individual's race. This prohibition extends not only to discriminatory treatment that has economic consequences, but also to discrimination that affects non-economic terms and conditions of employment, e.g., the psychological and emotional environment present in the workplace. [44] While Congress, when articulating the Act's prohibitions, did not explicitly mention racial harassment or hostile work environments, courts have consistently recognized that racially abusive work environments may violate the statute. [45] The harassment must be "sufficiently severe or pervasive 'to alter the conditions of employment and create an abusive working environment.'"[46] Where the employer does not commit the harassment, there must be a basis for finding the employer liable for the harassing conduct of third parties, e.g., co-workers and customers. [47]

Recognizing that employees may be subjected to a variety of emotionally abusive behaviors in the workplace, courts have distinguished actionable racial harassment from general harassment by articulating specific criteria. For harassment to violate Title VII, it must be either "racial" harassment or stem from racial "animus." [48] Once the character or motivations for the harassment are demonstrated, the harassment must be "pervasive or severe enough to alter the terms, conditions, or privilege of employment." Of course what is abusive to some workers may be considered part of the routine for others. Therefore, when determining whether the conduct meets a requisite level of severity, courts have applied an objective as well as a subjective standard for scrutinizing the work environment. [49] Further, the employee bringing the action has the burden of proving the existence of each of these criteria. [50]

The Equal Employment Opportunity Commission, the federal agency designated to enforce Title VII, articulates an objective standard that considers "whether a reasonable person in the same or similar circumstances would find the challenged conduct intimidating, hostile or abusive." [51] Recently courts have considered the perspective of the victim of harassment rather than adopting reasonableness standards devoid of the contextual experiences of the particular plaintiff. [52] Some courts are willing to avoid having the white experience become the standard against which Black reaction should be appropriately measured. Rather, courts have considered:

> the nature of the alleged harassment, the background and experience of the plaintiff, her coworkers and supervisors, the totality of the physical environment of the plaintiff's work area, the lexicon of obscenity that pervaded the environment of the workplace both before and after the plaintiff's introduction into its environs, coupled with the reasonable expectations of the plaintiff upon voluntarily entering that environment. [53]

When evaluating the severity of the harassment, some courts have required demonstration of the existence of a pattern of racial insults and/or harassment. These courts ignore the reality that some behaviors even in isolation are so destructive of psychological well being that plaintiffs should not have to demonstrate patterns of behavior. When courts structure their reasoning around a quantitative instead of qualitative assessment of harassment in the work environment, they succumb to a false dichotomy often creating a two part taxonomy for harassing behaviors. Such behaviors are either characterized as involving only "isolated incidents" or "sporadic racial slurs," e.g., non actionable harassment, [54] or characterized as "pervasive" because of evidence of a "steady barrage of opprobrious racial comments," i.e., actionable harassment. [55]

Other courts have declined to consider the severity of harassment along the single dimension of the frequency of events. [56] The Seventh Circuit, for example, has recently explained that when examining the "totality of the circumstances," courts should give proper weight to the "cumulative weight" of several "isolated" racial comments. [57] Agreeing with the reasoning of an opinion of the District Court of Florida, the Seventh Circuit reasoned that a "holistic perspective," which acknowledges that "separate incidents may accumulate, and that the work environment created . . . may exceed the sum of the individual episodes," may be more appropriate than a simple quantitative assessment of harassing behaviors. [58]

Under a subjective standard, a court will give proper weight to an "employee's injury in fact" when determining if the harassment is actionable under Title VII.[59] When applying the subjective standard, courts have "acknowledged the different ways" plaintiffs may initially respond to or cope with harassment.[60] Some employees may quit their employment, while others may "experience a prolonged period of turmoil."[61] Still others may "react angrily to the racial hostility, and may more easily be provoked into arguments or physical altercations with those co-workers responsible for the harassment."[62] Generally, where employees demonstrate that unlawful racial abuse has gradually eroded self-esteem and adversely affected job performance, such showings have been sufficient to discharge the employee's burden under the subjective prong of the test for Title VII racial harassment claims.[63] However, recent statements by the Supreme Court concerning sexual harassment establish that actual demonstrations of psychological injury are not essential for establishing an employee's claim.[64]

The Court reaffirmed that both the objective and subjective standards should be applied when evaluating the severity of the workplace harassment.[65] The Court set forth the the factors appropriate for consideration: "the frequency of the discriminatory conduct; its severity; whether it is physically threatening or humiliating, or a mere offensive utterance; and whether it unreasonably interferes with the employee's work performance."[66]

A final aspect for proving liability under Title VII involves establishing employer responsibility for the racial harassment. Imputing unlawful conduct to an employer becomes a particularly important element of a violation when the harassment stems from co-workers, e.g., teammates, or third parties in the workplace (fans or opposing players). Drawing from principles developed in cases involving sexual harassment claims, courts have rejected theories of strict liability for employer liability. Rather, courts have looked to traditional agency principles to determine employer liability. One such principle requires that the employer must have notice of the harassment. The Eighth Circuit, for example, has recently held that an employer is "liable only for events of which it knows or should have known . . . and with respect to which it fails to take corrective action."[67] When determining if an employer should have known about the racial harassment in the workplace, the courts have imposed a standard of "reasonable care" as a guide for considering whether an employer has exercised appropriate diligence in the workplace. Once notice of the harassment is established, agency concepts of ratification or condonation and/or participation are examined to determine employer liability. Condonation of the harassment occurs if the employer does not take appropriate steps to halt or prevent the harassment. Where courts find that the employer took sufficient and appropriate steps to remedy the harassment, plaintiff's hostile environment claims will not succeed.[68] Participation will provide the requisite link for vicarious liability where the harassment is perpetrated by the employer's supervisors or agents.

IV. Contrasting Traditional and Contemporary Industry Paradigms for Addressing Racially Hostile Environments

Initially, the sports industry's response was to find "model citizen" athletes who would cope with the racially hostile environment. Deference was the only acceptable response. Nevertheless, most athletes adopted the deferential approach as a temporary strategy. As soon as they felt secure in their positions, they began to protest their hostile environments. The industry's response to protest was generally to enforce standards of professionalism. Protesting racial abuse had its costs, including fines, suspensions, bad press, and subsequent lack of endorsement revenues.

A. Model Citizen/Deference Paradigm

Traditionally, athletes have been expected to behave as model citizens, even when confronted with severe racial abuse. Under the model citizen/deference paradigm, athletes of color were expected to demonstrate not only kinesthetic genius; they were expected to display "multiple intelligences."[69] In particular, athletes were required to exhibit a type of intelligence that permitted extraordinary emotional control: control that suppressed retaliatory behaviors; control that left the athlete emotionally and spiritually intact even though experiencing racially abusive environments; control that converted anger and rage into performance enhancing energies; control that transformed assaults on dignity into opportunities that heightened self esteem.[70] While the model citizen/ deference paradigm may have included redemptive and conciliatory nonviolent resistance, it also frequently demanded self-depreciating passivity as the appropriate response to racial harassment.

Perhaps the model citizen/deference paradigm grew out of the earlier strategies imposed on Joe Louis and Jessie Owens. They were devised after white reactions to the reign of Jack Johnson, the first Black heavyweight champion,[71] resulted in complete exclusion of Blacks from interracial competition. Owens[72] and Louis[73] were expected to serve as "race ambassadors" so that Blacks might "win the admiration of the American public."[74] Branch Rickey's use of this strategy when integrating modern professional baseball was not surprising. The following exchange between Rickey and Robinson suggests Rickey knew that he would have to initially demand from Robinson exercise of the more noble and dignified aspects of the model citizen paradigm. During an intense three hour meeting at the beginning of the 1945 season, Rickey, who was known for his ability to coach each player according to his particular problems, offered Robinson passages from Giovanni Papini's The Life of Christ. He exhorted the virtues of nonresistance as a courageous rather than cowardly response to moral wrongdoing.[75] Concluding the exchange, Rickey resorted to physical challenge:

> Rickey turned to Robinson and asked, 'Now, can you do it? I know you are naturally combative. But for three years--three years--you will have to do it the only way it can be done. Three years--can you do it?'
> 'What will you do,' Rickey shouted, 'what will you do when they call you a black son of a bitch? When they not only turn you down for a hotel room but also curse you out?' Rickey was on his feet--pacing and sweating. He sat down then quickly got up again and went over to Robinson. Robinson was tense, his fists clenched. Suddenly Rickey threw his own fist into Robinson's face, 'WHAT DO YOU DO?' he screamed.
> Robinson whispered, 'Mr. Rickey, I've got two cheeks. If you want to take this gamble, I'll promise you there will be no incidents.'[76]

From this exchange it is apparent that when confronted with racial harassment, the only acceptable response for the Black model citizen athlete was the exercise of nonresistance.

The model citizen athletes' strategies were limited.[77] He was neither privileged to retaliate, protest, or resort to self-help. His ability to perform within the confines of this limited strategy was considered evidence of superior intellect.[78] When one considers contemporary theories of emotional intelligence,[79] it becomes apparent that athletes of color have often exhibited exceptional emotional intelligence. While there were isolated attempts to alter the environment, management was generally neither predisposed[80] nor capable of changing the hostile environment. The strategy was to find emotional geniuses who could perform and endure in hostile environments. Years later, complaints from Black athletes would reveal that Robinson was not alone in being required to exercise higher standards of model citizenship than his white counterparts.[81]

At this point it seems important to distinguish between the passivity initially urged upon Black athletes and nonviolent resistance used in later civil rights protests. While some might equate the two, there is a distinction. There is a difference between nonviolent resistance that is protest and passivity induced by fear and coercion. One of the most well known practitioners of nonviolent protest, Dr. Martin Luther King, Jr., has explained that while the latter lowers dignity and self-esteem, leaving an internal violence in its wake, the former redeems human dignity because it protests the evil forces of injustice.[82]

Accounts of Black athletes disclose that they often experienced an internal violence which accompanied their inability to protest.[83] Their only means of reconciling inaction to blatant racial abuse was the belief that they carried on their shoulders the future prospects of an entire race for participation in interracial competition.[84] They carried these loads alone, and the prices they paid were substantial.[85] Accounts of their suffering are not unlike the emotional pain and physical suffering for which Title VII would now compensate victims of unlawful harassment.[86]

B. Professionalism/Protest Paradigm

The concept of professionalism in sports has racially tinged meanings. The "culture of professionalism" that emerged during the late nineteenth-century in America was in part responsible for the exclusion of Black athletes from interracial competition.[87] While current standards of professionalism no longer require racial exclusion, enforcement of professional standards has been used to punish Black athletes for protesting racial injustice. Where African- American athletes are expected to endure and defer to racially hostile environments without protest, standards of professionalism become a metaphor for condoning unlawful racist activity.

The emergence of protest as a response to racial injustice is associated with the Civil Rights movement. Professor Derrick Bell offers a more personal reason than environmental influences. He concludes that "[p]rotest can rescue self-esteem" from the ravages of acts of overt discrimination and unconscious acts which threaten the well being and mental health of Black Americans.[88] While a number of Black athletes adopted protest as their response to racial injustice,[89] Muhammad Ali became a symbol of protest. As one of the first to confront racial injustice, Ali paid a high price.[90] His courage, however, led the way for society to accept protest from other Black athletes.[91]

When one considers the reasons why formerly non-confrontational athletes adopted protest as a means of pursuing racial justice, Professor Bell's explanation provides a means for better understanding the dynamics of hostile environments. Racial abuse by fans injures both dignity and self-esteem.[92] Self-esteem must be redeemed. Where employers have effective systems of complaint or redress for fan racial abuse, then the complaint process becomes an acceptable means of channeling protest energies. Where fans are not reprimanded and abuse is allowed to persist, then self-help becomes the only limited strategy available for protest. Recent accounts indicate that self-help responses often escalate verbal encounters between athletes to physical ones.[93]

Consider how professionalism factored into the National Football League's (NFL) decision to sanction Bryan Cox. Initially, the NFL used professionalism to justify its refusal to even consider Brian Cox's complaints of racial abuse by the Buffalo Bills fans as a mitigating circumstance for his behavior towards the Bills' fans. When responding to Cox's assertions that he was provoked by the Bills' fans, Commissioner Paul Tagliabue stated that "[d]espite what you may consider provocation from Buffalo fans, it is the responsiblity of professionals not to lose their composure in such circumstances."[94] In a letter setting forth his decision, Tagliabue explained to Cox that he had been previously notified that "obscenities and other behavior that [was] considered excessively unprofessional or in extremely bad taste would warrant disciplinary action . . . ."[95] While Cox admitted the impropriety of his behavior, he maintained that the League should have considered the circumstances surrounding his conduct when imposing discipline.[96]

Later, in response to Cox's appeal and after he filed a suit alleging that the NFL condoned the fans' racial harassment, the NFL used standards of professionalism to primarily place responsibility for creating the hostile environment on Cox. Commissioner Tagliabue considered the racial harassment and examined Cox's behavior in "a different and more understandable light," reducing the fine to $3,000.[97] Nevertheless, when doing so he reiterated that Cox's pre-game comments, while not containing racial invectives, provoked the

Buffalo fans. Therefore, "[i]t [was], ultimately, the responsibility of professionals to maintain self-control in difficult and hostile circumstances."[98] Standards of professionalism were again used to shift responsiblity for providing an environment free of racial harassment from the employer to the athlete player. Only after further complaints from Cox did the League require member clubs to take "additional steps . . . to minimize the risk of physical or verbal threats, harassment (including racial taunts) and confrontation between fans and club personnel (especially players and coaches)."[99] The clubs were required to "[t]ake appropriate measures, including removal from the stadium, if any fan engages in physical or extreme verbal abuse of club personnel or game officials (e.g. racial taunts, profane signs or banners, and the throwing of dangerous objects)."[100]

I do not mean to suggest that Title VII's prohibitions against racial harassment prevent employers from disciplining employees for misconduct or privilege employees to respond with misconduct. On the contrary, courts recognize that employers may address employee misconduct even when perpetrated in response to racial harassment.[101] When professionalism instead of sustained, conscientious, and reasonable measures to eliminate racial abuse from sporting events becomes the industry's only response to racial harassment, that approach runs afoul of Title VII.

V. A Racially Hostile Environment Persists and More Can Be Done to Eiminate It

Existing civil rights laws prohibiting discrimination in employment require that employers take reasonable steps to eliminate racial harassment in the workplace. While sports employers, like other employers, are not directly responsible for the behavior of third parties, e.g., fans and spectators, they are nevertheless required to eliminate racial harassment in the workplaces of their professional athletes.[102] In particular policies requiring ejection of fans, seating of fans, revocation of season tickets, controlling consumption of alcohol, and revision of league rules, if necessary, should be explored to improve this environment.

Where the taunts are not obviously racial but disparately based on race, the motivations of third parties will be difficult to establish. Other concerns are raised because frequently white and Black athletes are subject to fan harassment. How can the sports industry determine when or if harassment is motivated by racial animus, behavior on the part of the athlete, or simply fan displeasure with the athlete or the team with which he or she is associated?

While these concerns are legitimate, they can be addressed. Decisions of courts resolving Title VII harassment claims suggest that other employers must address these issues. Courts recognize that the use of race-based strategies to accomplish even non racial goals will nevertheless violate the statutory proscription.[103] Employers are expected to investigate and determine the reasonable inferences which should be drawn about the motivations of perpetrators of neutral but obnoxious behaviors.[104] Likewise, the fact that racial discrimination is provoked by an employee does not cleanse the harassment of its illegality. To suggest that certain behaviors by athletes provoke justifiable racial harassment, particularly from third parties, essentially advocates for employer and societal condonation of racial harassment. However, the law has privileged only certain types of reasonable responses to employee misconduct--racial harassment by third parties has not and should not be one of them.

When assessing the obligations of sports industry employers to address racially harassing behaviors, consideration must be given to the public nature of the harassment. The very public nature of racial harassment by fans "creates a domino effect of anguish and anger" that ripples across communities.[105] When fans are allowed to persist in creating racially hostile environments, their harassment becomes more than simply personal encounters with the athletes. Their insults permeate to entire Black communities. While the public nature of sports employment makes prevention of racially abusive behaviors difficult for the sports industry, the very public nature of the harms caused by racial harassment from sports fans demands even greater degrees of diligence and higher levels of responsiblity.

While employment discrimination laws protect the athlete from racially abusive behaviors in the workplace, racial harassment at sporting events not only harms athletes but also the Black fans who attend sporting events or witness the harassment. Where Black fans have not provoked such behaviors, provocation by the athlete does not even begin to justify their subjection to racial harassment. The sports industry has developed methods for identifying and sanctioning intentional and flagrant fouls, unnecessary roughness, and various types of fan misconduct;[106] the industry can likewise develop a means to clean up racially polluted environments.[107]

NOTES

1. Some commented that considering their contributions to society they were already overpaid, while others felt that too many Black athletes have forgotten "where they came from" and have neglected to "give something back" to Black communities. *See also, The Black Athlete Revisited,* SPORTS ILLUST., Aug. 5, 1991, at 50 (reporting on a thoughtful exchange between ten prominent Black athletes: (1) Buck Williams, a forward for the Portland Trail Blazers remarked that "[p]layers are making a lot of money these days, but I don't think there is the commitment to reach back to their communities."; (2) Henry Aaron, all time home run leader and senior vice-president for the Atlanta Braves, agreed, stating that "[a] lot of black athletes, as soon as they reach a certain status, no longer associate with the black community."; (3) Willie Davis, Pro Football Hall of Fame defensive end and business executive, reacting to complaints about high salaries earned by black athletes remarked that what he hears from comments such as " '[y]ou know, we can't pay schoolteachers enough to teach these black kids, and yet they're paying the athletes this kind of money,' are a form of racism because people "don't talk about white executives' making a lot of money."' *Id.*

2. By focusing on professional athletes I do not intend to suggest that racial harassment is only a problem in the professional sports industry. On the contrary, news accounts demonstrate that racial taunts present problems for college and high school sports programs. (1) college sports: *See, e.g.,* Mike DeCourcy, *Out of Bounds, Tiger fans racially taunted his players, at the Pyramid, UAB's Bartow complains,* COMM. APP., Jan. 26, 1996, at 1A (noting complaints by Bartow, Coach of the University of Alabama-Birmingham's mens basketball team, that students seated behind their bench at the University of Memphis game made racial remarks against three of his players; noting also complaints by Long Beach State coach Seth Greenberg that he heard a racial comment from a student seated near his team's bench in a game at New Mexico State and was affronted that night by an anti-Semitic remark scrawled on the marker board in his team's locker room); NELSON GEORGE, ELEVATING THE GAME: BLACK MEN AND BASKETBALL 212 (1992) (describing how Patrick Ewing was a "chief target" for racist fans while playing basketball for Georgetown University:

> During the 1982-83 season students at Providence College held up 'Ewing Can't Read' signs. At the Meadowlands Seton Hall supporters unfurled a banner that read, 'Think! Ewing! Think!' while in Philadelphia Villanova fans wrote 'Ewing Is a Ape' on placards. T-shirts were sold at the Big East schools declaring, 'Ewing Kan't Read Dis.' Several Georgetown games were inter-

rupted by bananas thrown on the floor. Twice during the 1982-1983 campaign the Hoyas and chief rival St. John's engaged in fistfights partially attributable to the Big East's ultraphysical style--a style Thompson's team helped inspire--as well as the racial slurs from St. John's student body. Far too many of the school's white working-class Catholic student body used Ewing as a sounding board for their own latent racist attitudes. I am a St. John's alumnus, and I saw and heard things from them that brought dishonor on the school. 'Ignorance has no color,' Thompson told Time. 'The point isn't that this season has been degrading to a black man, it has been degrading to any man. On the airplane last week I asked Pat again how he was holding up. He told me, 'I've grown accustomed to it. I got so much of it in high school.' That made me saddest of all.')

(2) high school sports: *See, e.g.,* Candy Hamilton, *Where a Tomahawk Chop Feels Like a Slur,* CHRIST. SCIENCE MONITOR, Oct. 25, 1995, at 3 (discussing derisive caricatures, gestures, and taunts made at nearly every competition between Pine Reservation Native American athletes and whites; noting that in 1994 the South Dakota High School Activities Association adopted policies on racial taunting after slurs directed at a Black player caused a melee at a Black Hills football game). Also, racial harassment from fans is not only a problem for athletes but also for coaches as well. *See, e.g..,* *Racial Taunts At Drake Coach?,* SPORTING NEWS, Feb. 25, 1991, at 15 (noting that Drake Coach Rudy Washington, founder of the Black Coaches Association, stated that he had been subjected to racial slurs repeatedly by fans at Indiana State, Southern Illinois, and Southwest Missouri State); GEORGE, *supra* note 2, at 209 (noting that in response to Thompson's benching of Georgetown's top scorer, Jonathan Smith, and after the loss of six straight games, during the 1974-1975 season "some white students unfurled a banner at a home game that read, 'Thompson, the Nigger Flop, Must Go!'").

3. JACKIE ROBINSON, I NEVER HAD IT MADE 62 (1995) (describing how the manager of the Philadelphia Phillies, Ben Chapman, admitted that his team used ethnic slurs against DiMaggio and Whitey Kurowski as their style of baseball).

4. For accounts of racially harassing behaviors by other constituencies such as: (1) opponents: *See* ARTHUR ASHE, A HARD ROAD TO GLORY 109 (1988) (describing the experiences of Black Drake University running back, Johnny Bright, who during an October 1951 game was knocked unconscious three times by white Oklahoma linemen, but nevertheless the Missouri Valley Conference officials refused to investigate the matter); ROBINSON, *supra* note 3, at 50, 59-62 (describing black cat thrown into the dugout by a Syracuse team and racial insults from the Philadelphia Phillies that were led by Ben Chapman, who had also been accused of shouting anti-Semitic remarks at the Yankees fans); JULES TYGIEL, BASEBALL'S

GREAT EXPERIMENT 309 (1983) (noting that Jackie Robinson and Willie Mays received more than their share of "beanballs"; explaining that shin guards may have been invented by two of the earliest Black players in the International League during the later part of the nineteenth century to keep at bay opponents who deliberately tried to drive their spikes into them); (2) management: *See* CURT FLOOD, THE WAY IT IS 69-70 (1971) (describing racial epithet related by Solly Hemus during a team meeting); MIKE BASS, MARGE SCHOTT: UNLEASHED 239-252 (1993) (chronicling the scandal that emerged after a number of individuals asserted that they heard Marge Schott make racist statements against Blacks and Japanese, anti-Semitic statements against Jews, and pro-Hitler remarks); (3) media: *See* Timothy Davis, *The Myth of the Superspade: The Persistence of Racism in College Athletics*, 22 FORDHAM URB. L.J. 648-650 (1995) (discussing how the media reinforces and perpetuates stereotypical images of Black athletes as having only superior physical instead of intellectual capabilities); GEORGE, *supra* note 2, at 224 (attributing to "black racism" during the eighties the labelling of the Celtics as "a white boy's team").

5. There have been other harbingers of this message: SHELBY STEELE, THE CONTENT OF OUR CHARACTER 29-30 (1990) (proposing that Blacks develop identity based on individual acceptances of personal responsibility rather than on limitations associated with racial identity). But *See*, Jeffrey T. Sammons, *Rebel with a Cause: Muhammad Ali as Sixties Protest Symbol, in* MUHAMMAD ALI, THE PEOPLES CHAMP 158 (ELLIOTT J. GORN ed. 1995) (discussing how "New Blacks" no longer accept that "American" premise); *c.f.* JOEL KOTKIN, TRIBES 34 (1992) (explaining that "group survival, particular in dispersion, relies on ... group self-help, a strong ethnic sense of identity and a powerful ethos of self-preservation").

6. For an account of the frustrations of African-Americans who have "made it" *See generally* ELLIS COSE, THE RAGE OF A PRIVILEGED CLASS (1993).

7. I am clearly not the first to relate victories and defeats of African-American athletes to the African-American experience in the United States. *See* ALLEN GUTTMANN, SPORTS SPECTATORS 119 (1986) (describing how Jack Johnson became a folk hero after defeating James Jeffries, the "Great White Hope"; in North Carolina Blacks sang to the tune of "Amazing Grace," "Amaze an' Grace, how sweet it sounds, Jack Johnson knocked Jim Jeffries down"; after Joe Louis lost to Schmeling, Lena Horne stated: "Joe was one invincible Negro, the one who stood up to the white man and beat him down with his fists.... But this night he was just another Negro getting beaten by a white man.@)

8. Dale Hoffman, *White Tackles Hatred Head On*, MILW. J. SENT., Jan. 12, 1996, at A1, A16 (interviewing White about his reactions to the Monday night firebombing of the Baptist church in Knoxville, Tennes*See* where he is an associate pastor; reporting about White's frustration as he approaches the most important game of his career; noting that "racial graffiti was spray-painted on the back door of the church," and parapher-

nalia discovered pledging to fight against interracial churches, integrated schools, and organizations).

9. Joe Williams, *Warning Preceded Arson*, MILW. J. SENT., Jan. 12, 1996, at A1, A16 (reporting that Jerry Parrins, the corporate security officer for the Packers, stated that the Packers were warned of the bombing).

10. *Id.* at A1.

11. *Id.* at A16 (also expressing frustration over the lack of solving the murder of his stepfather four years earlier and letters stating that the police and fire department were working with the perpetrators of violence).

12. Lawrence M. Kahn, *Discrimination in Professional Sports: A Survey of the Literature*, 45 IND. & LAB. REV. 395-96 (1991) (concluding that because sports data is extensive and publicly available researchers work at a particular advantage when measuring productivity and determining the possiblity of discrimination).

13. *See generally* CORNEL WEST, RACE MATTERS preface (1993)(Professor West expressed how his personal anger and frustration emerged because he was refused service by nine taxi's while in New York; for him that incident conjured up recollections of ugly racial memories--being stopped on fake charges of trafficking cocaine--being stopped for driving too slowly on a street where the speed limit was twenty-five miles per hour); JOE R. FEAGIN & MELVIN P. SIKES, LIVING WITH RACISM: THE BLACK MIDDLE-CLASS EXPERIENCE 16, 17 (1994) (explaining how "discriminatory incidents are freighted with centuries of racial oppression of which the black victims are consciously or unconsciously aware" and that a sharing of these experiences among family and friends creates a "domino effect of anguish and anger rippling across an extended group"; reasoning that "[i]ndividual black Americans soon come to *See* that no amount of hard work or achieved status can protect them from racial oppression across numerous institutional arenas of this society").

14. GUTTMANN, *supra* note 7, at 119 (noting also how racial partisanship intensified the emotions of the fans to such an extent that after Johnson's triumph, there were race riots though the country resulting primarily in murders and injuries of blacks who were assaulted by whites and some whites who were assaulted by blacks).

15. *Id.*

16. Douglas Martin, *History of Brooklyn, Inning by Inning*, N.Y. TIMES, Jan. 5, 1996, at B1, B9 (describing an interactive exhibition, "Play Ball," at the Brooklyn Historical Society which invites visitors to experience what it must have been like for Robinson by having them stand on a plate and grab a bat while hearing the sounds of a roaring crowd with break through voices yelling, "Hey there, big boy," and "What you doin' out there on a white man's field?")(I am indebted to my colleague, Professor Michael Waxman, for bringing this article to my attention). *See also* ROBINSON, *supra* note 3, at 51 (describing fan hostility while playing in the minor

leagues at Louisville as a "torrent of mass hatred from a vicious howling mob that yelled racial remarks).

17. HENRY AARON, IF I HAD A HAMMER 230-238 (1991)(discussing and offering examples of the type of hate mail he received). After publicity about these letters reached the public, Aaron received thousands of letters of encouragement. *Id.* at 242.

18. Williams Oscar Johnson, *A Matter of Black and White*, SPORTS ILLUS., Aug. 5, 1991, at 44 (expressing confidence that the responses to a questionnaire did reflect the thinking of those athletes who participated but noting that due to the low response rate the results did not represent a meaningful statistical measurement of the view of all professional athletes; explaining further how the professional leagues discouraged athletes from participating in the survey).

19. Thomas F. Pettigrew, *New Patterns of Prejudice: The Different Worlds of 1984 and 1964*, *in* RACE AND ETHNIC CONFLICT 53-58 (PINCUS AND EHRLICH eds. 1994) (Developing a thesis based on an extensive body of social psychological research which concludes that severe individual and institutional racism persists, but is "far more subtle, indirect, and ostensibly nonracial," and identifying six features of modern antiblack prejudice:

(1) rejection of gross stereotypes and blatant discrimination; (2) normative compliance without internalization of new behavioral norms of racial acceptance; (3) emotional ambivalence toward black people that stems from early childhood socialization and a sense that blacks are currently violating traditional American values; (4) indirect 'micro-aggressions' against blacks which is expressed in avoidances of face-to-face interaction with blacks and opposition to racial change for ostensibly nonracial reasons; (5) a sense of subjective threat from racial change; and (6) individualistic conceptions of how opportunity and social stratification operate in American society.

Id. at 54.

20. *See generally* Joe R. Feagin, *The Continuing Significance of Race: Antiblack Discrimination in Public Places*, *in* RACE AND ETHNIC CONFLICT, *supra* note 19, at 98-99 (explaining that most workplaces, along with the middle class status of workers, provide some protection against certain categories of discrimination; but this protection weakens when a black person moves from those work settings to large stores and restaurants where contacts are mainly with white strangers).

21. *Cf. id.* at 99 (describing the spatial dimension of discrimination which increases the probability of Blacks and women experiencing racial hostility in unprotected public places such as streets; noting that research has

described women and Blacks as "open persons," i.e. particularly vulnerable targets for harassment that violates rules of public courtesy).

22. Tim Layden, *The 'Vulgar Minority'; Fueled By Alcohol, As Well As Anger And Aggression, A Few Fans Make It Uncomfortable For Many*, NEWSDAY, Feb. 12, 1989, at 9 (concluding that most alcohol is consumed by a minority of the fans attending sporting events).

23. *Id.* (observing that "[t]here are few places in a civilized society where a person can drink to inebriation, curse publicly and get into a fight ... and hope to escape prosecution. Sporting events are one such place.@)

24. Mark Gaughan & Vic Carucci, *More Security This Time Against Miami League Says It Will Be Monitoring Big Game at Rich Stadium Closely*, BUFFALO NEWS, Oct. 6, 1994, at D2 (interviewing Bill Bambach, the Bill's director of security, who indicated that the NFL had met with the Bills and recommended increased security measures; reporting that Charlie Jackson, the head of NFL security, would attend the game at Rich Stadium; observing that the league cannot control the cheering of 80,000 fans in a stadium; nevertheless Bambach offered assurances that "[i]f fans get to the point where they get obnoxious or start making racial remarks, they're going to get ejected or arrested.@)

25. GUTTMANN, *supra* note 7, at 162, 164 (comparing spectator hooliganism in the United States with that abroad and noting that one scholar determined that there had been 312 riots in the U.S. between 1960 and 1972; attributing the irenic atmosphere of most sports events to the institutions of social control such as ticket-takers and policemen and a behavioral code internalized by the majority of modern fans that accepts cheering and jeering but not physical injury).

26. *E.g..*, Affidavit dated Jan. 21, 1994 of Vincent A. Tobia, legal counsel for the Buffalo Bills football team describing the type of security provided at Rich Stadium; stating that fans "who use inappropriate language or act in an inappropriate manner are asked to leave" the stadium and that on the day of the Dolphin game, there were 36 ejections of fans from the stadium; however, "there has never been an ejection from Rich Stadium for racial slurs."

27. Flood, *supra* note 4, at 37-38 (recalling one drunken white fan in particular who made sure that he provided an appropriate example for his four boys who attended the game with him by checking the boys reactions when he yelled racial epithets to Flood; remarking that it did not matter whether they played at home or away in that league, the "stadiums resounded with 'nigger,' 'eight-ball,' 'jigaboo,' and other pleasantries").

28. *Id.* at 57 (offering as an example of the owners cheerful attitude towards hoodlum behavior by fans in the bleachers and the grandstands, the encouragement by the Chicago Cubs during 1969 of drunk and unruly fans known as the "Bleacher Bums").

29. *Id.* at 57 (remarking that each time he took his position in center field he was saluted with "brays of 'black bastard' and 'faggot'").

30. Cox v. National Football League, 889 F. Supp. 118, 119 (S.D.N.Y. 1995) (reciting claims by Cox that he was subjected to an "intense barrage of verbal abuse, much of which was based on race" and which included "[s]houts of 'nigger,' 'monkey,' 'we will kill you,' and a string of racially-based obscenities"; noting that "one fan had rigged up a black dummy with Bryan's number and the words 'wanted dead' on it, and then hung the dummy on a noose").

31. *Id.* (The impetus for the revision of the guidelines was an issue in dispute between the parties with the N.F.L. asserting that they had begun "the process of revising its guidelines soon after it learned of the racial taunts at the January 25 hearing" on Cox's appeal of his fine).

32. Affidavit dated Oct. 22, 1993 of Stuart B. Weinstein, Security Investigator hired by the Miami Dolphins who accompanied Cox onto the football field prior to the pre-game warm-ups for the football game against the Buffalo Bills in Buffalo, New York on Sept. 26, 1993.

33. Affidavit dated Oct. 18, 1993 by Louis Oliver, a professional player employed by the Miami Dolphins who was present during the pre-game warm-ups for the game between the Bills and the Dolphins on September 26, 1993.

34. Affidavit of Troy Vincent, a professional football player with the Miami Dolphins who was present during the pre-game and warm-ups for the Sept. 26, 1993 game between the Bills and the Dolphins.

35. JAMES CAMERON, A TIME OF TERROR 106, 108 (1994). Cameron, a Black man, survived a lynching attempt during 1930 in Indiana. He describes what he calls the "demonic terror" created by the white mobs of men, women, and children who lynched two of his companions and just stopped short of lynching him. His descriptions of those lynchings eerily parallel the spectacles created by racially abusive sports fans: "As far as I could *See*, white faces with open mouths screaming for blood, Black blood, were whooping it up--yelling for my blood. A victory spirit was in the air." He recalled that when some of the mob broke into the jail, the crowd outside "*See*med to yell its approval. They stomped their feet, chanting the way crowds do at a football game for their favorite athlete: 'We want Cameron! We want Cameron! We want Cameron!'"

36. The courts have generally recognized the chilling images that Ku Klux Klan and lynching symbols present to African Americans. *See, e.g..*, Daniels v. Essex Group, Inc., 740 F. Supp. 553, 560 (D.C. Ind. 1990) (commenting that: "The most violent threats to black society are well known to come from that organization [the KKK]. Furthermore, there is no more chilling image than that of a black man being hung by the KKK."); Daniels v. Essex Group, Inc., 937 F.2d 1264 (7th Cir. 1991) (reasoning that the Ku Klux Klan's effect on Blacks is such that only one isolated instance of harassment would be enough to establish the existence of a hostile work environment); Vance v. Southern Bell Tel. & Tel. Co., 863 F.2d 1503 (11th Cir. 1989) (concluding that a Black woman's

repeated experiences of finding a piece of cord over her work station that was fashioned like a noose was sufficient to alter her working conditions).

37. *Cf.* DERRICK BELL, FACES AT THE BOTTOM OF THE WELL 158-194 (1992) (Through the use of science fiction, Bell chronicles how the American public, if offered the proper incentive, could amend the United States Constitution and enact legislation that would strip black Americans of existing protections and permit black enslavement by aliens).

38. ROBINSON, *supra* note 3, at 59 (recalling his feelings about his wife having to sit in the "midst of hostile spectators" who started screaming racial insults that were taken up by the crowd).

39. ASHE, *supra* note 4, at 39 (discussing a threat received by Willie Stargell from a white fan who threatened to "blow his brains out" if he played in a baseball game; noting the experiences of Charlie Sifford, a black golfer who during the 1960 Greater Greensborough Open was harassed by five white men who followed him around the course, threw beer cans, jumped up and down and yelled racial epithets while he attempted to concentrate on a shot (*Id.* at 151); noting also that during the 1967 LPGA tour, Renee Powell, the first Black woman to participate in the tour received racial slurs, hate mail, and threatening letters (*Id.* at 153)).

40. Layden, *supra* note 22, at Sports 9 (describing the "my team" syndrome as a phenomena where fans no longer just witness a team's success of failure but feel that they influence it; also known as the "homecourt" advantage).

41. Phil Hersh, *Soccer Hooliganism Still Plagues Europe*, CHI. TRIB., June 12, 1988, at P1 (reporting about incidents of fan violence at soccer games in Paris and Argentina that stemmed from hard-core hooligans with a "right-wing orientation" against black stars of opposing teams).

42. Layden, *supra* note 22, at 9 (discussing the extent that obscene language, fighting, and beer abuse by a significant minority of sports fans alter the demographics of audiences; observing that during the last two decades there has been an increase in fan violence; chronicling major incidents of fans misbehavior, which have included: (1.) spilling onto the field at Cleveland Municipal Stadium, June 4, 1974; (2.) rioting and overturning several cars at Tiger Stadium in Detroit, Oct. 15, 1984; (3.) after concessionaires accidentally serve full-potency beer instead of the low alcohol variety at Sullivan Stadium and the Patriots clinch a playoff berth, riotous fans tear down the goalpost and while carrying it shock themselves when they touch a high-tension wire, Dec., 22, 1985; (4.) vandalism and destruction of the playing field, Shea Stadium, Sept. 17, 1986; (5.) throwing debris onto the field, Riverfront Stadium, April 30, 1988; (6.) hurling bottles at opposing teams at Candlestick Park, Aug. 10, 1988; (7.) setting fires in the stands at Giants Stadium, Oct. 17, 1988; and (8.) confronting a referee on the ice during a hockey game at Boston Garden, Jan. 28, 1989).

43. For a discussion of sports as a metaphor for racism encountered by African Americans *See* Davis, *supra* note 4, at 618 (proposing that "college sport serves as a metaphor for the racism encountered by African-Americans in our society").

44. In Rogers v. EEOC, 454 F.2d 234, 238 (5th Cir. 1971), the Fifth Circuit, the first court to interpret Title VII as covering hostile environment claims, recognized that "today employment discrimination is a far more complex and pervasive phenomenon, as the nuances and subtleties of discrimination are no longer confined to bread and butter issues."

45. The Supreme Court in Meritor Sav. Bank, FSB v. Vinson, 477 U.S. 57, 65-66 (1986), recognized that hostile environment claims based on race, ethnicity, and gender are actionable under Title VII.

46. *Id.* at 67.

47. Bolden v. PRC Inc., 43 F.3d 545 (10th Cir. 1994) (setting forth three sources of liability for an employer where the harassment stems from coworkers and not the company directly or its supervisors: (1) the harassment was within the scope of the coworkers' employment; (2) the employer either negligently or recklessly refused to recognize or deal with the harassment; and (3) the harassing coworkers acted under apparent authority provided by the employer).

48. *C.f.* Hall v. Gus Constr. Co., 842 F.2d 1010, 1014 (8th Cir. 1988) (concluding that "predicate acts underlying a sexual harassment claim need not be clearly sexual in nature"; "any harassment or other unequal treatment of an employee or group of employees that would not occur but for the sex of the employee or employees may, if sufficiently patterned or pervasive, comprise an illegal condition of employment").

49. Rodgers v. Western-Southern Life Ins. Co., 12 F.3d 668, 674 (7th Cir. 1993) (rejecting a multi-factor test for evaluating Title VII harassment claims and instead evaluating claims against both an objective and subjective standard).

50. Plaintiffs in racial harassment cases have the same burden as those in other types of racial discrimination cases. Plaintiffs have the burden of establishing and proving by the preponderance of the evidence each element of their racial harassment claim. Johnson v. Teamsters Local Union No. 559, 1995 WL 355304 (D. Mass. 1995).

51. 58 Fed. Reg. 51,266, 51,267 (1993).

52. *See, e.g.*., Johnson v. Teamsters Local Union No. 559, 1995 WL 355304, at *4 (D.Mass. 1995) (concluding that the harassment was severe and pervasive and commenting that "when considering the graffiti and the taunting, the Court believes that any reasonable black person in Johnson's situation would have found the work environment hostile or abusive")(emphasis added); Ellison v. Brady, 924 F.2d 872, 878-79 (9th Cir. 1991) (assessing a sexually harassing environment from the perspective of the reasonable woman); Harris v. International Paper Co., 765 F. Supp. 1509, 1515 (D. Me. 1991)("question of whether conduct and

speech rises to the level of harassment, putting aside the question of the employer's knowledge, must be considered only from the employee/victim's perspective").

53. *Rodgers*, 12 F.3d at 674 (citing Daniels v. Essex Group, Inc., 937 F.2d 1264, 1274 (7th Cir. 1991)).

54. Snell v. Suffolk Co., 782 F.2d 1094, 1103 (2d Cir. 1986) (defining actionable harassment as "more than a few isolated incidents of racial enmity"); Hicks v. Gates Rubber Co., 833 F.2d 1406, 1417-18 (10th Cir. 1987) (same).

55. Johnson v. Bunny Bread Co., 646 F.2d 1250, 1257 (8th Cir. 1981) (requiring a steady barrage of opprobrious racial comments); Bolden v. PRC Inc., 43 F.3d 545, 551 (10th Cir. 1994) (considering coworkers threat to plaintiff, "you better be careful because we know people in the Ku Klux Klan," the use of a racial epithet, and one arguably racial cartoon as "only two overtly racial remarks" occurring in eight years and therefore insufficient to be actionable because the comments were not pervasive).

56. Rodgers v. Western-Southern Life Ins. Co., 12 F.3d 668, 674 (7th Cir. 1993) (concluding that when evaluating the totality of the circumstances, "there is neither a threshold 'magic number' of harassing incidents that gives rise, without more, to liability as a matter of law nor a number of incidents below which a plaintiff fails as a matter of law to state a claim").

57. *Id.* at 675.

58. *Id.* (citing Robinson v. Jacksonville Shipyards, Inc. 760 F. Supp. 1486, 1524 (M.D. Fla. 1991))("[A] holistic perspective is necessary, keeping in mind that each successive episode has its predecessors, that the impact of the separate incidents may accumulate, and that the work environment created thereby may exceed the sum of the individual episodes.@)

59. Daniels v. Essex Group, Inc., 937 F.2d 1264, 1272 (7th Cir. 1991).

60. *Rodgers*, 12 F.3d at 676.

61. *Id.* at 677.

62. *Daniels*, 937 F.2d at 1272.

63. *Rodgers*, 12 F.3d at 677.

64. Harris v. Forklift Sys., Inc., 510 S.Ct. 367, 370-71 (1993) (holding that the effect of the harassment on the employee's psychological well-being is relevant but like other factors is not required).

65. *Id.* at 370-71 (Mere utterance of an epithet that "engenders offensive feelings in [an] employee" is insufficient; rather, the work environment must be one that a reasonable person would find hostile or abusive; further, the employee must subjectively perceive the environment as abusive).

66. *Id.* at 371. Some courts enumerate particular elements or factors that plaintiff must demonstrate to prove a racial harassment claim. *See, e.g..*, Johnson v. Teamsters Local Union No. 559, 1995 WL 355304 (D. Mass. 1995) ("[P]laintiff must prove: (i) that he is a member of a protected class; (ii) that he was subject to unwelcome racial harassment; (iii) that the

harassment was based on race; (iv) that the harassment was sufficiently severe or pervasive so as to alter the conditions of plaintiff's employment and create an abusive working environment; and (v) that some basis for employer liability has been established"); Daniels v. Essex Group, Inc., 937 F.2d 1264, 1271 (7th Cir. 1991) (discussing six and five multi-factor articulations by various courts of racial harassment claims).

67. Jeffries v. Metro-Mark, Inc., 45 F.3d 258, 259 (8th Cir. 1995).

68. *Id.* at 261.

69. Daniel Goleman, Emotional Intelligence 38-39 (1995) (citing Howard Gardner, Frames of Mind (1983)) (contrasting the concept of a monolithic IQ view of academic intelligence, which includes verbal and mathematical-logical alacrity, with multiple intelligences, which include also spatial capacity, kinesthetic genius, interpersonal skills and intrapsychic capacity).

70. By assaults on dignity I mean the loss of even an expectation by early athletes that their rights to compete in a sport on an equal basis would be honored. For a discussion of racism's attack on dignity, *See* Bernard R. Boxill, Blacks and Social Justice 186-87 (1984) (quoting A.I. Melden's discussion of dignity: "What we label the dignity of a person is not a matter pertaining to some precious internal quality of his nature as a human being-- his rationality or his autonomy--but that sense he displays of ... the expectation that his rights will be honored.")

71. Othello Harris, *Muhammad Ali and the Revolt of the Black Athlete, in* MUHAMMAD ALI, THE PEOPLE'S CHAMP 56 (ELLIOT J. GORN ed. 1995) (explaining how Johnson's victories over white boxers had so infuriated whites that race riots occurred; how Johnson's betrothal to a white woman resulted in the passage of antimiscegenation laws in some states; and after a white boxer, Willard, regained the title, whites were careful to prevent another African-American like Johnson from regaining the title and, therefore, for two decades barred Black boxers from competing for the title).

72. *Id.* at 56 (explaining how the mayor of Cleveland, Harold H. Burton, declared that at a party in Owens' honor after winning four gold medals in Berlin that by "his high character, his clean living and attention to duty," Owens had brought "credit and honor to his Race.@)

73. *Id.* at 56 (noting that Louis had been instructed that he should not behave like Johnson and citing as an example a letter sent to Louis from the governor of Michigan admonishing him to remember that his "race, at times in the past, has been represented by others who thought they had reached the heights" and that he had in his "strong hands the job of representative-at- large of your people.@)

74. *Id.* at 56 (concluding that "[t]he black athlete of this era was expected to be humble, obsequious, nonthreatening, and tolerant of demeaning stereotypes and characterizations.@)

75. JOHN J. MONTELEONE, BRANCH RICKEY'S LITTLE BLUE BOOK 81 (1995).
    Rickey read the following passage to Robinson:

> You have heard that it hath been said, An eye for an eye and a
> tooth for a tooth: But I say unto you that ye resist not evil: But
> whosoever shall smite thee on the right cheek, turn to him the
> other. . . There are three answers men can make to violence:
> revenge, flight, turning the other cheek. The first is the barbarous
> principle of retaliation. Flight is not better than retaliation. The
> man who takes flight invites pursuit. Turning the other cheek
> means not receiving the second blow. It means cutting the chains
> of the inevitable wrongs at the first link. Your adversary is ready for
> anything but this. . .Every man has an obscure respect for courage
> in others, especially if it is moral courage, the rarest and most
> difficult sort of bravery. It makes the very brute understand that
> this man is more than a man. The results of nonresistance, even if
> they are not always perfect, are certainly superior to resistance or
> flight. To answer blows with blows, evil deed with evil deeds, is to
> meet the attacker on his own ground, to proclaim oneself as low as
> he. Only he who has conquered himself can conquer his enemies.
> *Id.* at 81.

While the sequence of this discussion differs from Jackie Robinson's account
    of the events, which included more elaboration from Rickey regarding the
    type of racial abuse Robinson would face, the substance of the discussion
    is essentially the same. ROBINSON, *supra* note 3, at 31-34.
76. MONTELEONE, *supra* note 75, at 81. Rickey was clearly not the first to use
    Biblical scripture as evidence that African Americans should accept
    without protest racial injustice. FORREST G. WOOD, THE ARROGANCE OF
    FAITH 43-46, 68-69 (1990) (explaining how white southern ministers
    used Biblical scripture to justify slavery; noting that "[i]n 1835, Episcopal
    Bishop Nathaniel Bower circulated a pastoral letter in South Carolina
    that listed ten biblical references 'relating especially to servants' with
    instructions to include them in any service for slaves."; observing that
    northern white ministers also "cited I Timothy 6:1--'Let as many servants
    as are under the yoke count Their own masters worthy of all honor"--as
    'an impregnable demonstration that *slaveholding is not in all cases and
    invariably, sinful.*'")(emphasis in original).
77. ROBINSON, *supra* note 3, at 32 (stating that Rickey informed him that
    they couldn't fight their way through the plan for integration of the major
    leagues; they had no army, no owners, no umpires, and very few
    newspaperman on their side along with many hostile fans: Robinson
    could win only if he could convince the world that he was a great
    ballplayer and a fine gentleman).

78. MONTELONE, *supra* note 75, at 81 (quoting Rickey's requirement for the first Black to integrate baseball).
79. *See generally* GOLEMAN, *supra* note 69, at 43 (defining emotional intelligence along five main domains which include: (1) knowing one's emotions (2) managing emotions (3) motivating oneself (4) recognizing emotions in others and (5) handling relationships).
80. Rickey did not want to be perceived as "holier than thou in the race field." MONTELONE, *supra* note 75, at 80.
81. Professional athletes are not the only ones required to adhere to higher standards. They are also imposed on amateur athletes. Dennis Brackin, *His Play, Not His Race Gets Carter Noticed; MSU Hockey Star Ignores Stereotypes*, STAR TRIB., Nov. 25, 1994, at 1C (noting coach's acknowledgement that a Black player on Michigan State's hockey team heard racial remarks "every so often" but commenting that the player was a " 'pretty realistic young man, a real adult in terms of his behavior. He's just a class kid.'").
82. MARTIN LUTHER KING, JR., A TESTAMENT OF HOPE, THE ESSENTIAL WRITINGS OF MARTIN LUTHER KING, JR. 87-89, 96 (JAMES M. WASHINGTON ed. 1986) (distinguishing nonviolent resistance grounded in faith that "the universe is on the side of justice" from stagnant passivity induced by cowardice; explaining that the former strategy does resist and protest the forces of evil through active mental, emotional, and spiritual aggression).
83. ROBINSON, *supra* note 3, at 79 (explaining how he has stored up a "lot of hostility," was "keyed up because I hadn't been able to speak out when I wanted to," and as a result went home to his wife and child tense and irritable).
84. *Id.* at 60, 63 (describing his disgust with having to cultivate an image that he was a "patient freak" in the face of racial abuse from the Phillies, but regaining his sense of purpose and making a "lonely decision" not to retaliate; describing his feelings after "bowing to humiliations," such as appearing publicly and shaking hands with Chapman, the team manager of the Phillies who encouraged the racial abuse).
85. MONTELONE, *supra* note 75, at 81 (Robinson and other athletes like him were left to "carry the load" and assume the "responsibilities of himself to his race").
86. Jackie Robinson reflected on reactions to taunts, jeers, and ridicule he received in Baltimore, Louisville, and Syracuse during his minor league tour stops:

> The toll that incidents like these took was greater than I realized. I was overestimating my stamina and underestimating the beating I was taking. I couldn't sleep and often I couldn't eat. Rachel was worried, and we sought the advice of a doctor who was afraid I was

going to have a nervous breakdown. He advised me to take a brief
rest.

ROBINSON, *supra* note 3, at 50. *C.f.* Mari J. Matsuda, *Public Response to Racist Speech: Considering the Victim's Story*, 87 MICH. L. REV. 2320, 2340 (1989) (describing "the physiological symptoms of racial harassment to include difficulty in breathing, rapid pulse rate, post-traumatic stress disorder, hypertension, alcoholism and suicide"; describing the "psychological effects ... as includ[ing] headaches, social withdrawal, chronic depression, anxiety neurosis, and displaced aggression.)

87. TYGIEL, *supra* note 4, at 14 (attributing white athletes' antipathy for interracial competition to a "culture of professionalism" that used racial and ethnic barriers to entry into different occupations as a means of defining the "distinctiveness of a given profession").

88. DERRICK BELL, CONFRONTING AUTHORITY: REFLECTIONS OF AN ARDENT PROTESTER x (1994).

89. Kenny Moore, *The Black Athlete Revisited*, SPORTS ILLUS., Aug. 12, 1991, at 60 (describing the protest of Tommie Smith and John Carlos at the 1968 Mexico City Olympics and relating how they not only lost business opportunities but received death threats; noting that while the Black U.S. women were excluded from the men's deliberations over the boycott and the gesture, Wyomia Tyus, nevertheless ignored the slight and dedicated her gold medal to Smith and Carlos); AARON, *supra* note 17, at 187 (describing an interview he gave to a reporter from Jet magazine when he was angry, which protested the "ways in which baseball discriminated against black players--in salary, longevity, managing, the front office, everything"); ROBINSON, *supra* note 3, at 142 (describing the reputation he had developed because of his " 'fiery temper' against violation of [his] personal dignity and the civil rights of [his] people").

90. Harris, *supra* note 71, at 64 (noting that Ali lost his heavyweight title, was expelled for three and one-half years from professional boxing and forfeited a movie, record, and product endorsement contracts).

91. *Id.* at 65, 66 (noting Arthur Ashe's acknowledgement of the influence of Ali's protest on the support given to the 1968 Boycott of the Mexico City Olympics; quoting Kareem Abdul-Jabbar's acknowledgement of the influence of Ali on the public's later acceptance of his conversion to the Nation of Islam).

92. For example, consider the remarks of Bryan Cox revealing the extent his dignity was assaulted by racial abuse from fans during the September 1993 Dolphins-Bills game. " 'I don't care if the fans holler ... or that they hate me,' Cox s*aid*. 'But when you call me racial names you crossed the line and it becomes about my manhood. You can hate me, but you must respect me.'" Gene Warner, *NFL Policy Aims to Curb Verbal Abuse of Players*, BUFFALO NEWS, July 31, 1994, at Local.

93. Bill Campbell, *MSU Player Accuse Two Tigers of Using Racial Slurs*, NEW ORLEANS TIMES-PICAYUNE, Dec. 10, 1995, at D1 (reporting how a Black player, Yakini Allen from Michigan State, accused a white player of using a racial epithet and reacted by grabbing his face mask); *NBA Punishes Maxwell in Excess of $200,000*, PORTLAND OREGONIAN, Feb. 9, 1995, at D1 (reporting how Maxwell received one of the harshest penalties in sports history after he punched a fan during the third quarter of a game; Maxwell arguing that there were mitigating circumstances and asserting that the fan was yelling racial and sexual epithets); Michael A Lutz, *Maxwell to Appeal Suspension, Fine*, PORTLAND OREGONIAN, Feb. 10, 1995, at E06 (reporting that Maxwell claimed that he restrained himself until the fan started making references to his daughter who died in Oct. 1993; Maxwell also stating that "[s]ome reasonable guideline for appropriate fan conduct needs to be adopted"; fan denying directing any racial or profane remarks to Maxwell); Carrie Kirby & Bob Helbig, *Former Packer May Face Charges*, MILW. J. SENT., Oct. 19, 1995, at B1, B4 (Reporting explanation offered by former Green Bay Packer and Black player, Ken Stills, that he kicked a white opponent in the head during a city league football game because he was provoked by a racial remark).

94. Letter from Commissioner Paul Tagliabue to Mr. Bryan Cox dated Sept. 29, 1993 .

95. *Id.* (referring to a training-camp playbook memo sent to all NFL players regarding game-related discipline).

96. Brief in Support of the Appeal of Bryan Cox, Submitted by Michael S. Baird, Attorney for Bryan Cox, at 5 .

97. Letter from Commissioner Paul Tagliabue dated Apr. 15, 1994 .

98. *Id.*

99. Memorandum from Commissioner Tagliabue to Club Presidents & General Managers dated July 28, 1994 (hereinafter Memorandum); Letter from Michael S. Baird to Judge Shira A. Scheindlin dated February 15, 1995 .

100. Memorandum, *supra* note 99, at 2 (Security policy).

101. E.E.O.C. v. Crown Zellerback Corp., 720 F.2d 1009, 1012 (9th Cir. 1983) (concluding that "[u]nreasonably hostile or aggressive" opposition to protected activity may provide a legitimate, nondiscriminatory basis for an employer's decision; opposition to discrimination is unreasonable when it significantly disrupts the workplace or directly hinders employee job performance); Folkerson v. Circus Circus Enter., 68 F.3d 480 (9th Cir. Nev.) (Unpublished Disposition) (reversing summary judgement granted for the defendant employer based on contentions that female employee was engaging in unprotected oppositional conduct when she struck a customer in response to his attempt to sexually harass her).

102. *C.f.* Magnuson v. Peak Technical Serv., Inc., 808 F. Supp. 500, 512-13 (E.D. Va. 1992) (applying EEOC guidelines holding that an employer may be responsible for sexual harassment acts of nonemployees); Powell

v. Las Vegas Hilton Corp., 841 F. Supp. 1024, 1027 (D.C. Nev. 1992)) (holding that an employer may be responsible for the sexual harassment by non-employees when the employer knows or should have known of the conduct and fails to take immediate and appropriate corrective action; noting the EEOC will "consider the extent of the employer's control and any other legal responsiblity the employer may have with respect to conduct of such non-employees").

103. *See, e.g..*, Rodgers v. Western-Southern Life Ins. Co., 12 F.3d 668, 675 (7th Cir. 1993) (rejecting employer's arguments that supervisor's racial insults about the intelligence of all black men should be thought of as a "motivational technique" and concluding that Title VII does not permit "this type of blanket criticism of the intelligence of a racially-defined class of employees as a motivational technique).

104. *Id.* at 676 (upholding district court's conclusion that an otherwise race neutral derogatory statement about people from Arkansas was nevertheless a racial slur; concluding that lower court's characterization was plausible and within permissible views of the evidence).

105. Feagin & Sikes, *supra* note 13, at 16 (explaining how the "cumulative impact on an individual of repeated personal encounters with racial hostility is greater than the sum of these encounters" and the sharing of these accounts "creates a domino effect").

106. Snowball Hurling Fan Says He's A Scapegoat, Charleston Daily Mail, Dec. 29, 1995, at 03B (noting that the Giants and the New Jersey Sports and Exposition Authority offered $1,000 for information leading to the identification of a fan throwing snowballs during the Giants game after his photograph appeared in area papers; also noting that 175 fans were ejected and 15 arrested and the fans nearly caused a game forfeit); Williams F. Nicholson, *Ice-Pelting Controversy Snowballs*, USA TODAY, Dec. 27, 1995, at 1A (reporting that the Giants "*See*k to revoke tickets of the mystery hurler in the widely published photo--and of others they can ID from videotapes and photos*"); Rowdy fans had a snowball's chance; Security tightened, alcohol banned after Giants debacle*, STAR TRIB., Dec. 25, 1995, at 2C (quoting Robert Mulcahy, Chairman of the New Jersey Sports & Exposition Authority, as stating that "[w]e're just not going to take that kind of behavior anymore"; "[w]e have a judge and some lawyers at the stadium and anyone caught will be arrested and arraigned right here"; "no alcohol was sold during the game and security was beefed up").

107. Consider the following suggestions that have been offered to address racial harassment by sports fans: *Stop Racist Behavior--NOW*, WIS. ST. J., Oct. 6, 1994, at 15A (citing to racial incidents at local high school sports events in Texas and Wisconsin that were provoked by name-calling by players and concluding that "forfeiting a game, or attending mandatory sensitivity training does not seem harsh punishment").

RACISM IN SPORTS: A QUESTION OF ETHICS*

Paul M. Anderson

The subject of race and sports has attracted a great deal of attention. As many have noted, the success achieved by African-Americans on the playing fields has not been replicated in other avenues of the sports industry. Although some progress has been made of late, African-Americans have moved into the ranks of head coaches very slowly, and few African-Americans hold meaningful front office positions in sports management. Moreover, as a group male African-American college athletes, particularly those in the big money sports of football and basketball, continue to perform quite poorly on standardized tests and in the college classroom.

In the conclusion to this collection, Paul Anderson accepts the assertion that racism continues to be a problem in American sports. However, he chooses to treat it as an ethical question rather than a sociological one, and argues that sports lawyers have a particular duty to address, and combat, racism and its consequences.

INTRODUCTION

To many people, the sports world is a place in which none of the normal problems of the "real" world could possibly exist. The participants seem to be rich beyond measure, many are educated and well spoken, and though there are disputes, they usually center around money—not trivial problems like poverty and homelessness. Many also believe that the sports world is a model of race relations for the rest of society. Through television and other media coverage, fans see that on the playing field it does not matter whether you are black or white,

*From Volume 6, Number 2, Spring 1996, pp. 357-408.

what matters is your ability. Therefore, sports is often used as a paradigm of how an integrated society should look.

A more sensitive look at the sports world reveals that this idyllic picture is misleading. Although in the major professional sports and college sports today the majority of players are African-American, this does not mean that racism is absent. In college athletics black athletes often deal with racial stereotypes, isolation from the rest of the campus, and the reality that they are in school to play sports, not to get a degree. Furthermore, African-Americans are underrepresented in the coaching and administrative ranks throughout college sports. The professional sports picture shows more integration on the playing field, but few chances for management or other opportunities after a career is over.

This article will analyze the problem of racism in sports. It will propose that sports lawyers can attack the problem from an ethical perspective. The first section will deal with defining racism as a problem in sports. In order to propose any solution to the problem, the analysis must start with an understanding of what the problem is from a sports perspective. This section will also give an overview of the problem of racism in intercollegiate and professional sports. The second section will provide an overview of ethical theory with examples of particular ways of ethical thinking. This section will not seek to promote one way over another; instead, it will seek to develop a basic understanding in the uninitiated of what goes into ethical thinking and the characterization of problems from an ethical perspective. This will be in an effort to show that racism in sports can also be looked at from this ethical perspective. The third section will provide an overview of ways in which lawyers are regulated both professionally and ethically. This will show that sports lawyers already have a duty to act ethically. And finally, the last section will mention some examples of progress in racial relations and ways in which sports lawyers can put a greater emphasis on ethics in their work.[1]

I. Part One: Racism in Sports

A. The Problem in General

Racism can be defined in many ways. For the purposes of this article, the problem of racism can be referred to as "the transformation of race prejudice through the exercise of *power* against a racial group defined as inferior, by individuals and institutions with the intentional or unintentional support of the entire culture."[2] This article will focus on racism as directed to African-American athletes (mostly male) only because these athletes are the most prevalent in the professional team sports world and major revenue producing college sports; therefore, scholarship regarding the problem of racism in sports has often focused on these individuals.[3] Moreover, the problems that black athletes face are unique and extensive.

Today the incidence of overt acts of racism has declined, but this does not necessarily mean that racism has evaporated. What has become prevalent is "unconscious racism." As one author explains, "[r]acism is in large part a product of the unconscious. It is a set of beliefs whereby we irrationally attach significance to something called race."[4] This unconscious racism has become apparent in sports. To most outward perceptions, sports has become a place where racism is no longer a problem, yet as will be explained, the facts do not bear out this conclusion. Today, people who act in ways that result in disparate consequences to racial minorities can claim they did not intend for the negative effects to occur. As unconscious, this racism is not part of cognitive intentional actions. This form of racism is "more insidious because it is for the most part less straightforward, outspoken and 'honest.'"[5]

As will be explained, such actions, even if only expressions of unconscious racism, can be evaluated from an ethical perspective. Such a perspective would look on the action itself, and the consequences of such action on those involved, to help determine the moral significance behind the action.

Any racist actions seem to exact some toll on the actor, as Marge Shott, Jimmy "the Greek" Snider, and Al Campanis found out. Therefore, in the long run racism is "self-defeating."[6] Racism teaches nothing of value and can only breed a hatred or desire to succeed by overcoming the portrayer of the racist action in those it affects. Either way, those who pervade these racist attitudes will be faced with some sort of negative effect.

B. Racism in Society

It seems obvious that "race . . . should be an irrelevant characteristic in interpersonal relations."[7] The reality is that in society, African-Americans are usually worse off than whites. Today, even though the law now outlaws discrimination, "[h]idden cameras . . . reveal that discrimination exists in housing, lending and even retail."[8]

This article will not focus extensively on the legal approaches to combating the discrimination that is faced in parts of society excluding sports. Yet, even though the focus is on the sports world, some statistics can lend validity to this picture of the problem in society as a whole.

African-Americans in the United States face a myriad of problems that can be explained, in part at least, due to past and present racism. These problems or disadvantages include: median incomes that are one-tenth that of white families; at least twice the unemployment rate as white individuals; earning only fifty-nine cents to every dollar earned by whites; thirty percent of African-Americans living in segregated neighborhoods; one-third of African- American children attending public schools where ninety percent of the students are African-American; and one-third of all African-American families earning an income below the poverty line.[9] As a result, whites tend to live an average of ten years longer than blacks, one-fourth of black males between the ages of twenty and twenty-nine are under the jurisdiction of the criminal justice system (either in jail, on parole or on probation), and most black neighborhoods are saturated with crime, drugs, and poor schooling.[10] As a result of the United States long history with racial problems, "successive generations of Blacks and Whites are socialized to accommodate the status quo."[11] The statistics presented are evidence of this *status quo*.

Regardless of the legal remedies, civil rights movement, and lack of overt signs of racism, many African-Americas still do not live in society on an equal footing with whites.[12] Unfortunately, the law and social reform often only recognize the problem of racism in overtly racist acts.[13] As already mentioned, racism today may be more prevalent in its unconscious and hidden form. Professor Harry Edwards put it eloquently when he said:

> The result in both sport and society has been the establishment and perpetuation of what is in effect a *plantation system* of authority arrangements with Whites commanding a virtual monopoly on power and decision-making roles with a negligible proportion of token Blacks in mid-level junior executive positions, and with the masses of Blacks concentrated in lower echelon, relatively power-less production roles.[14]

C. Sport as a Reflection of Society

Most commentators agree that sports is a reflection of society.[15] What this means is that sport often acts as a "microcosm of society" and thus "racial problems in sports have been, and continue to be, brushed away as 'nothing unique.'"[16] It takes outrageous conduct for the reality of racism in sports to come to the forefront.

1. Examples from the Sports World

Three recent and very public examples show how racist beliefs in sports can come to the public forefront, although inadvertently.

In 1987, Al Campanis, then an executive with the Los Angeles Dodgers, was being interviewed on ABC's Nightline regarding the employment of black managers in baseball, among other things. In response to why there were no black managers, Campanis stated that "I truly believe that they may not have some of the necessities to be, let's say, a field manager or perhaps a general manager."[17] Given a chance to correct himself, Campanis instead buried himself (and ended his career with the Dodgers) by saying such things as "why are black men or black people not good swimmers? Because they don't have the buoyancy."[18] Campanis's statements caused an uproar at a time when most Americans thought that society, and especially professional sports, no longer had the problem of pervasive racism. But "Campanis made clear once again that racism cannot be outlawed."[19]

The next public example which made clear that racism was still a problem occurred in 1988. On Martin Luther King day, during an interview Jimmy "The Greek" Snyder, a CBS football commentator at the time, was asked a question regarding the role of blacks in football. Snyder said that "[t]he black is a better athlete to begin with because he's been bred to be that way because of his thigh size and big size."[20] Snyder also said that the reason that there were no blacks in coaching was because "[a]ll the players are black; the only thing that the whites control is the coaching jobs."[21] These comments added to the awareness and uproar caused by Campanis' comments the year before.

A final example that showed the public that racism was still a problem in the sports world was the 1992 fine and suspension of Cincinnati Reds owner Marge Schott for such conduct as calling black players "million-dollar niggers" and saying she would "rather have a trained monkey working for me than a nigger."[22]

These examples showed that racism was still a problem in sports, as many would not admit that it was in society as a whole. Furthermore, beyond these racist comments, statistics show that these comments themselves were merely open commentary on the actual situation in sports.

2. Descriptions

Another public way in which racism is prelevant in society and sports is through the descriptions of the attributes and performance of black athletes. Black athletes are often described in ways that attribute their athletic success to natural ability, whereas white athletes are described as intelligent and hard working. One author notes how in descriptions of two black basketball players (Kenny Anderson and Lee Mayberry) versus that of two white players (Bobby Hurley and Chris Corchiani), the black players were described as "having the tools, but their intellect is questionable. The real praise is reserved for white players because they have managed to prevail despite . . . their modest athletic endowment."[23] One study found that blacks and whites actually agree with these characterizations. In a study that asked respondents to rate blacks and whites in certain categories, black and white respondents ranked white athletes highest for leadership, followed by thinking, instincts, strength and speed; blacks were ranked in the opposite order.[24]

The problem with these descriptions is that this implies that black athletes then are "unthinking, natural performers — born with an advantage;" a characterization that can be "debilitating both to blacks and whites."[25] As Bill Russell explained, black athletes put just as much work into their athletic success as white athletes do. Specifically, Russell stated that "I worked at basketball up to eight hours a day for twenty years — straining, learning, sweating, studying."[26] The perception that black players do not work and that athletics just comes naturally makes black athletes somehow seem less deserving of their success. Implicit in these types of descriptions of black athletes "is that they did not have to exhibit the virtues of hard work and commitment that the white stars did."[27] This also implies that "[w]hites have conceded the physical superiority of blacks because it fits the image: whites still have the brains."[28]

3. Explanations

The descriptions of black athletes just mentioned also lead to another practice that pervades athletics. Since black athletes now make up the majority of the superstars in sports, theorists have attempted to explain why this is so.[29] Explanations for black sport superiority are either sociological — stating that blacks became superior athletes as a way to get out of the ghetto and the poverty and economic distress it may entail, and genetic — as Jimmy "The Greek" explained, that blacks somehow are actually genetically different from whites so that their athletic accomplishments are a reflection of these genetic differences.[30] As to the genetic explanations, years of research (mainly by white researchers) has proven nothing.[31] Still, people "continue to insist on differentiating between human beings based solely on race."[32] In the end, though, "[c]ulture, class, and environment still tell us the most."[33]

Even though such research begins with the admission that black athletes are superior, this superiority "has ironically been turned against them" in implications that they do not possess such virtues as "discipline, commitment, and sustained effort for which white athletes are regularly praised."[34] The real question is why there is the necessity for an explanation in the first place. If it were not for the fact that whites, who dominate almost all other aspects of American life, felt inferior to blacks in certain sports and felt resentment due to this fact, would such questions ever be asked?

4. Culture and Chances

Unfortunately, black culture may add to the problem by promoting athletic success as important for its youth.[35] Black families promote athletic success as a way toward real success in the world without thinking about alternatives if this athletic success fails.[36] Commentators suggest four primary reasons why athletics becomes such a focal point in black culture: 1) racism has kept blacks from the same employment opportunities as whites and so they spend too much time honing their athletic skills; 2) there is a general lack of highly visible black role models in fields other than sports and entertainment; 3) the black family overemphasizes athletic success at an early age; and 4) sports is used as a way for black males to prove their manhood.[37] Studies have shown that regardless of social and demographic factors, blacks are in general more involved in sports.[38]

The media adds to the problem. The African-Americans who are portrayed as success stories in the media are predominantly athletes. Since blacks become more involved in sports and follow sports with such passion, a "[b]lack male's dream of becoming a professional athlete seems far more feasible than envisioning himself as a member of a surgical team at a major hospital."[39] Due to their learnings from culture and the media, many black males believe that "sport is his way out of the ghetto."[40] And due to this belief almost forty-three percent of African-American high school athletes believe that they can reach the promised land of professional sports.[41]

The reality is far different. Of high school basketball, baseball, and football players, "fewer than one in 10,000 succeeds at the professional level."[42] In the end, a black athlete "has a much better chance of becoming a doctor or a lawyer" than of becoming a professional athlete.[43]

D. The Problem in Sport

People argue that sport is a model of racial equality, which facilitates the integration of blacks into society, provides an avenue for upward mobility for blacks, and lacks the segregation and discriminatory problems of society as a whole.[44] Unfortunately, as already explained, sport is a reflection of society and "racism is intertwined in the sports culture."[45] As a result, black athletes face a feeling of double consciousness. On the one hand, they bear pride in their race and its fight against perceptions of black inferiority, while on the other hand, they have had to follow certain standards which are mandated for success in the dominant white society.[46]

1. Intercollegiate Athletics

Numerous articles have been written documenting the problem of racism as felt by African-American student athletes in college sports.[47] Therefore, the many intricacies of the problem will not be repeated here in depth. Instead, this section will focus on an overview of the problem and the types of racism and unethical practices that African-American student-athletes often face in collegiate sports.

a. Statistics

The racism felt by black college athletes often is a "persistent, unconscious racism nourished by fraudulent stereotypes and myths,"[48] but it is real and debilitating just the same. Since their first inclusion in the college sports scheme, African-American athletes have had to be what has been named a "superspade" — or black super athlete.[49] This has meant that blacks usually had to perform at a higher level to become involved in college sports than white student-athletes. Historically, blacks had to be the superstars on their teams in order to get the chance to participate. Although this trend has begun to dissipate in recent years, the myth of the black super athlete has not been eroded completely.[50]

One way this myth is evident is through the existence of stacking in college athletics. Stacking is the "practice of assigning certain racial minorities to some positions and not to others" based on stereotypical perceptions of these individuals.[51] These perceptions are the same type that come out in the descriptions and explanations of the success of black athletes. Research has shown that in basketball, although in the past blacks were restricted to positions based on sheer athletic ability (forward), while whites were put in positions of leadership and intelligence (guard), today blacks dominate all positions except for center.[52] The continued white prominence at center can be explained away merely by the statistical fact that the main requirement for this position is height, not athletic ability or intelligence, and therefore, since there are more whites who are taller (because there are more whites in sheer numbers), the predominance of whites at the center position is not evidence of racism or stacking.[53] In other sports stacking may still be a problem.

The problem is not restricted to the racism that student-athletes are subjected to in a particular sport; the problem extends to the lack of African-American representation in the coaching and administrative ranks throughout college athletics. Several statistics bear out this continuing problem. Of the 5,889 college athletic positions created for athletic programs from 1991 to 1994, only 10.1 percent were filled by African-Americans, giving them a representation of only 8.7 percent of the more than 29,000 positions available in 1994.[54] African-Americans represent only 3.6 percent of college athletic directors and 4.9 percent of associate athletic directors.[55] And, whereas black student-athletes make up sixty-five percent of the athletes in Division I basketball programs, there were only forty-one black head coaches in Division I, or fourteen percent.[56] Also, black males make up some 22.2 percent of all scholarship athletes in Division I representing over sixty percent of men's basketball and forty-three percent of football players, while at the same time approximately 6 percent of all students at these same colleges are black.[57] Finally, only eleven percent of the NCAA's powerful Presidents Commission are African-American.[58]

The problem is that even though black student athletes make up such a high percentage of scholarship athletes, primarily in revenue producing sports, this high percentage is not reflected in the administrative ranks or general student populations at these same schools. Black student-athletes are left playing for the revenue producing sports with the knowledge that there are no racial peers for them to turn to on campus besides their fellow athletes, and there will be few African-Americans in the teaching and administrative ranks for guidance.

b. Academic Situation

Problems such as these lead to the severe academic problems most black student-athletes face. In many cases, colleges take black students who are superior athletes but have no real chance of making it academically in college.[59] Colleges usually show more interest in a black student-athlete than any black students because they can see the possible improvement in their athletic program. This leads to a situation that will "discourage young blacks who are not athletes by suggesting that it's easier to get to college if you play ball."[60]

To many, this acceptance of black athletes who may not be ready for college academically seems to be a positive step. To these individuals, it looks like these athletes are being given a chance to get an education while using their athletic ability to advance in a profession that they may be more able to succeed in. As already mentioned, the chances of this type of success are minuscule, but even black culture promotes athletics as a way to success. This leads to a tremendous amount of pressure being put on student-athletes to succeed athletically because they think that they will be able to "achieve upward social and economic mobility."[61]

This pressure is exacerbated by the fact that these athletes have been admitted with the full knowledge that they probably are not prepared to succeed academically. Through no fault of their own, media coverage glorifies black athletic success, and coaches (predominantly white coaches) overemphasize the importance of success on the playing field at the expense of success in the classroom.[62] The system is a sort of vicious cycle, as black student- athletes are encouraged to focus on athletic success from all sides and are not given proper aid to succeed academically (often being encouraged to take easy courses or having their grades changed, etc.),[63] so that these individuals are unprepared coming in to college to deal with the pressure to succeed in sports and compete academically. They often end up leaving college without attaining a "real" college education to fall back on if athletic success fails.[64]

Part of the problem may be that these black student-athletes allow themselves to be exploited by not taking academics seriously and instead focusing on college as a way to professional athletic success.[65] Unfortunately, these athletes are "throwing away economic and educational opportunities for a dream that is unlikely to be fulfilled."[66]

These athletes also become isolated on campus. As student-athletes, many live in dorms separate from the general student population and are guided in class schedules and course selection by the athletic administration. Their lives become dictated by games and practices. This isolation may insulate them from stronger forms of racism as felt by the general African- American population, but it will also often add to the pressure they feel to succeed because their whole lives are based on athletics.[67]

These athletes also face racist stereotypes throughout their college careers. On the one hand, they are perceived as "dumb jocks" along with athletes of other races.[68] On the other hand, they are perceived as "dumb blacks" who would not have gotten into college except for their athletic ability.[69] And often, they face a third negative perception wherein "fellow students, professors, counselors, and collegiate sports fans assume that the African-American athlete is on campus only for sport participation and not to obtain an education or excel in academics."[70] These perceptions become self-fulfilling as black student-athletes often focus on athletics at the expense of academics, fitting the stereotypes for those who believe in them.

A *USA Today* poll shows the different perceptions blacks and whites have regarding these issues. Approximately sixty percent of blacks and whites agreed that black athletes go to college to play sports, while only around twenty percent thought that black athletes attend college to get an education.[71] Interestingly, seventy-eight percent of blacks felt that black athletes were taken advantage of in college, while only fifty-five percent of whites felt this way.[72] In opposition to this, more blacks and whites thought that white athletes go to college to obtain an education (sixty-eight percent of blacks and forty-six percent of whites), while almost half of blacks and whites agreed (at forty-six percent) that white athletes were also exploited by their universities.[73] This study is at least some evidence that the stereotypical "dumb jock" and "dumb black" perceptions may be more than just academic notions. Although the study proves nothing, it shows that people do perceive the college experience for black and whites differently across racial lines.

In the end, the real problem may be one of a lack of focus regarding the true mission of a university of higher education. As one commentator said, "[i]t should be an embarrassment to predominantly white universities that have a greater proportion of blacks on their intercollegiate football and basketball teams than they have in their general student population."[74] This fact alone makes one wonder if colleges really care about whether black students and student-athletes receive an adequate education at all, or if the colleges' focus is on athletic success and the possible revenue increases that this may entail. Such sacrificing and use of particular individuals for only their athletic prowess while ignoring them as individuals who may need special help to receive an adequate education is unethical and racist, even if unconsciously so. Moreover, the fact that this practice predominantly affects African-American individuals adds to the reality of racism. As no genetic theories have shown that African-Americans are necessarily better athletes, while colleges still focus on them only as such, it seems apparent that at some level many institutions still hold these antiquated beliefs.

2. Professional Sports

Racism in professional sports has not received as much attention,[75] presumably because many of the superstars in the major sports (the National Basketball Association, Major League Baseball and the National Football League) are African-American. However, the Center for the Study of Sport in Society puts out an annual RACIAL REPORT CARD that provides an in depth resource to catalogue the problem within professional sports.[76]

a. Statistics

The Racial Report Cards rank the NBA, NFL, and MLB with a letter grade according to their percentage representations of African-Americans in relation to society.[77] The grades are based on the fact that federal law mandates that a workplace should reflect the percentages of the people of certain races as are found in the general population.[78] Therefore, since recent census figures show that twelve percent of the general population is African-American, a sport would receive a B if it reached this level, an A if it doubled this level, and a C if it had half of this level.[79]

In 1995, all three sports reached peak levels of African-American players — the NBA had eighty-two percent (up from seventy-nine percent in 1994), NFL sixty-eight percent (up from sixty-five percent), and MLB had nineteen percent (up from eighteen percent).[80] However, at the same time there was a decline in the overall number of minority head coaches from fourteen to twelve.[81] Specifically, the African-American representation at the head coach level in the NBA stayed at nineteen percent, in the NFL it stayed at only seven percent, and in MLB it fell from fourteen percent to eleven percent.[82] The number of black assistant coaches reached thirty-nine percent in the NBA, while only ten percent in the NFL.[83] At the league level in 1995, professional staff for the NBA league office who were black declined slightly from twenty percent to nineteen percent, while the NFL held steady at fifteen percent.[84] MLB figures were not available for 1995, but the 1994 percentage was nine percent.[85] At the top management level, only the NBA had a significant amount of African-American representation at fifteen percent, while the NFL was at five percent, and MLB was at six percent.[86]

In regards to stacking in professional sports, the 1995 RACIAL REPORT CARD concluded that "[p]rofessional sports seems to have finally reached the stage where stacking or positional segregation has become a non-issue."[87] The report found no evidence of stacking at any position in professional basketball, significant progress in the NFL at the quarterback position (where blacks represented nine percent of all quarterbacks, the highest level in the NFL's history) and overall progress in minority representation at the pitcher and catcher positions in baseball (although mainly due to the increase in Latino players at these positions).[88]

The final grades for 1995, after averaging percentages from all positions, came out to an A- for the NBA (falling from an A), a B in the NFL, and a B in MLB, both the same as in 1994.[89] Although these grades sound impressive, what the results actually showed were "record-breaking improvements in the area of player opportunities on the field without corresponding improvements in the front offices and coaching ranks. There were actually declining percentages of minorities in front office administration and coaching ranks."[90] The report concluded that sport, "which is America's most integrated workplace for players, is not much better than society in who it hires in font office and decision-making positions."[91]

b. What to Make of the Statistics

Although the Report Cards show that these professional sports do receive unprecedented levels of involvement by African-American athletes, the problem is that this does not often translate into coaching, management, or administrative opportunities. The continued success of black coaches disputes any notion that they can not be successful, and the overwhelming number of players who are black shows that there are many candidates. In 1993-94, Nolan Richardson was named coach of the year in college basketball, Lenny Wilkins was coach of the year in the NBA, and Dusty Baker was named coach of the year in the National League.[92] In 1994-95, Felipe Alou was named Major League Baseball and National League Manager of the year, Lenny Wilkens surpassed Red Auerbach as the winningest coach in NBA history, and Ray Rhodes was named NFL coach of the year.[93] With this evidence, what else but racism or ignorance can account for the continued lack of African-American representation in coaching and management?

At the front office and administrative levels, 1994 saw many African-American individuals such as Stu Jackson, Isiah Thomas, and Magic Johnson being given opportunities.[94] 1995 saw slight increases in these levels in the NBA and MLB, but the overall figures still do not compare to the level of participation by African-Americans in these sports (especially on the playing field).[95] Although there has been progress, the numbers are still inadequate. As Shropshire states, "[i]n all respects there are 'qualified' . . . African-Americans available."[96] With all of the former players who could be counted as qualified, the lack of chances being given to African-Americans is noticeable.

The problem with the numbers provided by the report cards is that the standards are too low. Giving a league a grade of B for having the same amount of African-American representation as the general population does not take into account the fact that the number of African-Americans playing in each league is greater than this twelve percent level. For instance, the fact that eighty-two percent of NBA players are African-American, while only nineteen percent of the head coaches are such, means again that those in charge are white. As one commentator has noted, "our sports hierarchy, an overwhelmingly white domain, has, with notable exceptions, kept its doors shut to people of color. Though these exceptions make sports better than society, it is not by much."[97]

People should not be misled into thinking that these report cards show that sports is an exemplary state of racial affairs. Although professional sports may on a percentage basis achieve higher levels of African-American involvement than society, both society and sports are still lacking. Many athletes admit that they do not feel racist attitudes in professional sports; however, at the same time they think that "whites generally received favored treatment in their sport" and "that blacks were far less likely than whites to be allowed into team management after their playing years."[98] African-Americans seem to be in a similar situation in professional sports as they were in in college. They are paid to play and bring success to ownership and management, the same group that usually will not allow them to continue in administration after their playing careers, as student-athletes are often discarded after their playing careers without academic backgrounds to fall back on.

This perception of African-American success in professional sports is also the direct reason that so many young blacks put their effort into success in sports while possibly ignoring academics and why the black culture promotes athletics as a way out of the ghetto. Numbers like those presented in these report cards, along with media attention on African-American sports success, "conveys a false impression about opportunities for minorities to achieve wealth through sports."[99] Unfortunately, the report cards show that lasting success in management or front offices has not materialized for African-Americans. And even though the percentage of African-Americans who are players is large, these are those lucky ones out of 10,000 who made it. Many more did not.

Again, opinions on why African-Americans may not attain coaching or managing positions differ across race lines. Seventy-three percent of blacks agree that racism is a factor in blacks not getting coaching positions, and seventy-two percent believe that a white individual has a better chance at a coaching job, even if equally qualified.[100] Only thirty-one percent of whites agreed that racism was a problem in hiring and only forty-six percent thought that equally qualified white applicants would have an edge.[101]

E. A Problem of Ethics

The problem is that the issue of race in sports, especially in professional sports, only seems to come to the forefront when comments like those by Al Campanis or Jimmy "The Greek" are made public. Then the unconscious racism that many may still have comes out into the open. Since it is unconscious, many people do not understand that this racism is there or even feel responsible for adding to the problems. The disparate numbers in intercollegiate and professional sports show that something is going on. For some reason, African-Americans are not being given the same chances or being treated in the same way as whites.

This is clearly an ethical problem because a certain group of people is being treated in a different way with extremely harmful effects. Although there are legal solutions to racist and discriminatory conduct,[102] the often unconscious racism that pervades sports is not so easy to regulate. One way to change these practices is to treat the problem as a problem of ethics and morality. Therefore, conduct in sports that hurts African-Americans should not be changed merely because it is illegal, but moreover because it is unethical. As one author states "[f]or questions concerning what to do, the moral point of view just is the ultimately overriding point of view . . . . Doing what is right is just what one should do and indeed must do or at least try to do."[103] Seeking a moral and ethical solution through integration into a system of lawyer regulation can attempt to attack the problem of racism in sports in a new and unique way.

II. ETHICAL THEORY

Lawyers often think of ethics as something that is not of utmost concern as long as they are acting properly within whatever legal rules they are governed by. This type of thinking is wrong. Ethical considerations are important because they are not merely restricted to legal considerations; they are concerned with every action we undertake as human beings. Therefore, in order to understand how to focus on ethics as a solution to the problem of racism in sports, a brief overview of ethical theory is necessary.

A. Overview of Theories

In the modern world, when people come to think of ethics, they tend to believe that it characterizes doing that which makes them feel as if they are doing the right thing and not hurting anyone. Any discussion of ethical or moral theory as a concept, or living an ethical life in any depth, is left to those in academics, specifically philosophers. Since the philosophy world has not agreed on any one ethical theory that they can show as right or true,[104] people dismiss any talk about ethics as something that does not concern them in everyday life, although most people still try to act in a way that could be characterized as ethical.

Even though people think this way and the academic world has not provided one overriding ethical theory that can be proven, ethical thinking is still valuable. Ethical thinking can be understood as "the effort to develop general criteria for distinguishing correct from incorrect moral judgments, within an overall account of moral life and experience."[105] Ethical theory then is a way to characterize how people act as right or wrong, and through this effort, a way to judge people in their actions.[106] Ethics then is a way to systematically look into the reasons why people act in certain ways and determine what the proper standards are to guide these actions. Therefore, "being an ethical person means disciplining oneself to live in accordance with those standards."[107]

For a lawyer, ethics will provide a model for action beyond just what the law entails. Being ethical in certain situations may even advocate not following the law but following some standard of conduct beyond what the law prescribes.

The best way to understand this amorphous concept of ethical thinking and theory is to examine several ethical theories that have been proposed to see what is involved in ethical thinking. Each theory provides a different explanation as to what is right and good and what should be done in acting ethically. These theories attempt to provide an approach to understanding human action in a way which judges whether certain actions should be promoted or not.

B. Two Ways of Thinking

In general, all ethical theories can be characterized under two categories — deontology and consequentialism. Deontological (or nonconsequentialist) theories basically believe that the consequences of a particular action do not count in deciding whether the action is morally right.[108] The moral worth of an action depends on the character of the action itself, especially its adherence to moral rules or principles, and does not focus on consequences. Consequentialist (or teleological) theories of ethics predictably hold that what matters in determining whether an action is right or wrong is the consequences of the particular action.[109] Therefore, in judging the moral worth of an action what is important is only the consequences of the action; the action in and of itself has no moral value. These two categories help to at least provide an overriding method for categorizing particular ethical systems. What follows is a description of three of these systems with a critique of each.

As a warning, what follows may lead some readers to believe that all that is being shown is that each theory can be criticized or challenged and so there cannot possibly be any general ethical theory to follow. Therefore, ethical discussions beyond academic or religious pursuits would seem to have no place in the real world. This conclusion, however, is too simplistic. Although each of the theories proposed can be criticized in some ways, what should be remembered is that they each provides a way to think about actions from a critical ethical perspective. The fact that they can be criticized shows that there are most likely some ethical norms all people follow as a reference to critique these other theories. Therefore, to show that they are wrong, we must have some at least subconscious understandings of what it is to be morally right. And only through discussing ethical ideas such as these can these unconscious moral understandings come to light to better guide our actions.

C. Ethical Theories

1. Utilitarianism

Utilitarianism is an ethical theory based on the view that what is morally right can only be judged by the "principle of utility." This principle states that "the moral goal to be aimed at in all we do is the maximization of the greatest amount of good over evil as a whole."[110] Utilitarianism then is a consequentialist theory because the moral rightness of an action is based on the consequences of that particular action. If an action increases the general happiness of all in a particular society, then the action is morally right.

What really becomes important in utilitarianism is to be able to measure the "utility" in an action. "Utility" can be defined as the "tendency which an action appears to have to augment or diminish the happiness of the party whose interest is in question."[111] In deciding whether to undertake a particular action, utilitarianism calls for a "weighing of all consequences, both good and bad."[112] This weighing is done through what is called the "hedonic calculus" or the "calculus of pleasures."[113] Utilitarians then would have to measure certain factors in each action, such as: the intensity of the pleasure, its likelihood of occurring, and the immediacy of the pleasure, and multiplying these factors by the number of people who would experience this pleasure to determine whether an action should be undertaken.[114] For those who abide by this theory, it becomes a duty to "do the act whose *net* results are a greater good or a lesser evil than that produced by an alternative action."[115]

Utilitarianism seems appealing because it promotes happiness in a moral sense of positively affecting the most people in any action undertaken. Utilitarian theories also promote a sense of equality because each person is treated equally in their pursuit of happiness: no individual pursuit overrides that of the community. And utilitarian theories provide a method for actually measuring particular actions to determine whether they should be undertaken. This undoubtedly would help in situations where the correct course of action is not immediately apparent.

This all too brief explanation of utilitarianism can be criticized in a few important ways. Initially, it becomes apparent that any measuring of what actions promote happiness, and whose happiness is to be promoted, must look to some standard in determining what form of happiness to be promoted. Therefore, someone must determine what standard this is. Not only does utilitarianism avoid providing a definition of what standards to follow, it also fails to explain how it can keep the so called equality among different individuals and their pursuit of happiness without discriminating among particular forms of happiness.[116] If one individual finds happiness in being selfish while one finds happiness in helping others, utilitarianism cannot provide a way to explain why the latter individual's happiness should be promoted at the expense of the former individual.

The next major criticism of utilitarianism is that the overall happiness of the great majority takes precedence over the sacrificing of a small minority. The hedonic calculus would allow innocent individuals to be "sacrificed for the good of the whole."[117] Utilitarian theories promote overall happiness as all important in moral action. The overall happiness, though, is a measure of the value of the combined happiness of all involved. In some situations, then, certain individuals can be left out of the equation if overall happiness is increased, even though for some individuals their happiness is decreased. A classic example is that utilitarianism could allow slavery because its imposition could increase the overall happiness of the majority while sacrificing an innocent minority.

Utilitarianist theories also often avoid taking into account the moral worth of an action itself.[118] Therefore, some actions could be considered morally appropriate due to their consequences, even if they do not seem to be morally correct in and of themselves. For instance, killing an innocent individual to save three other individuals would be morally appropriate in most circumstances because the happiness of the three would outweigh the unhappiness of the one. Although it can be debated whether this action is morally right, utilitarianism provides no way to morally evaluate the killing of the one individual aside from its affect on the combined happiness of the others involved.

Finally, utilitarianism never deals with the reality that we simply cannot know with any degree of certitude what the consequences of our actions are. In fact, we cannot even control many of these consequences. Therefore, to base the morality of an action on these consequences is to base it on something uncertain.

In the end, utilitarianism has suffered criticism by philosophers for these and other reasons and so is often used as an example of the wrong way to think in ethical discourse. However, even though this simplistic explanation of utilitarianism leaves it open to criticism, the theory itself provides a way of thinking about our actions that seems at first blush to be praiseworthy. As a society, we want to do that which would increase happiness for the most people. However, the criticisms of utilitarianism teach that within this "pursuit of happiness" we must also be aware of those who do not receive the happiness we may be pushing toward.[119]

2. Kantianism

Another major theory is explained by Immanuel Kant. His theory is clearly a deontological theory because it bases the ethical validity of an action on how it follows certain standards of action and not on the consequences of the actions themselves. For Kant, the only proper moral intention behind an action is the intention to do your duty, that is, to do the moral thing simply because it is the moral thing to do. For example, Kant would say that a businessman must not cheat, not because it will help his business or that cheating would lead to negative consequences, but because it is simply not the morally right thing to do.

Kant's ethical theory is based on certain universal laws (or maxims) that he believed all people can and should follow in judging how to act. These laws or maxims "describe some sort of general sort of situation, and then propose some form of action for the situation."[120] To act following a maxim "is to commit yourself to acting in the described way whenever the situation arises."[121]

Kant's basic universal law is known as the "categorical imperative," which says that a person should "[a]ct only according to that maxim by which you can at the same time will that it should become a universal law."[122] Although the terminology may seem antiquated, all that this entails is that one should act only in ways that one could accept others acting toward oneself. Therefore, a truly moral person would only undertake actions that follow principles of ethical conduct that they could meaningfully universalize to become standards for everyone to follow in their moral actions.

A good example would be the Christian adage "[d]o unto others as you would have them do unto you."[123] Therefore, if you would not want people to rob you, you should not rob them. And you should be willing to say that nobody should rob anybody. This "universalizability" is key.

The way to judge our actions as moral and immoral is to see whether we could universalize our conduct and accept it from others as the ethically right thing to do. Kant did understand that some maxims that may seem to pass this test still should not be promoted as ethical standards. An example of this would be that "everyone should wake up at six in the morning." Although this could be universalized to all people, the maxim itself has no moral value. This type of failure to be a proper moral maxim could be objective — if the particular conduct could not possibly be universalized as conduct for all people (i.e. everyone should buy whatever they want, though not possible because some people would want the same thing and not be able to get it), or subjective--if, even though the conduct could be universalized, it still would not be desirable to do so (i.e. everyone should not talk to anyone else).[124]

Kant had other ways of expressing the categorical imperative. One formulation was to act in a way that treats others as ends and not merely means.[125] Therefore, Kant recognized a need for respect for persons and not sacrificing them for the goals of an individual or society. Kant recognized that in all our actions "we must recognize the great intrinsic value of human life."[126] Under Kant's theory we have duties then to ourselves and others to act morally in all we do following the maxims and categorical imperative, and we also must always act following a proper moral motive.[127] This motive would again follow the universalized maxims and avoid any subjective determination based on happiness or feelings. All of this is known and understood by individuals through reason again based on these maxims.[128]

There are several problems with Kant's theory even in the oversimplified explanation just provided. For instance, it is apparent that individuals actually act for many reasons, especially past experience and feelings. Acting merely on reason and attempting to universalize all conduct would not only be cumbersome, but it would also ignore the unique reality each individual finds themselves in. The idea of universalizability also does not seem to allow for any exceptions to the rules.[129] For instance, although normally it seems universal that one should not kill, this would not allow for situations involving self-defense. Also, the mere fact that we might believe an action could be universalized does not seem to give the action any moral validity.[130] Again, just because we could say that all people should brush their teeth before going to bed, that does not in itself give this conduct any moral worth. More must be looked at to understand whether something is moral or not. Finally, even though Kant wants to present a theory that avoids basing moral decision making on the consequences of action, the very universalizability necessary for moral action seems based on the consequences of an action being followed or not.[131] How else could an individual judge whether an action should be universalized except for by attempting to understand the consequences of it as a universal law?[132]

In the end, even with its problems, Kant's theory again helps focus ethical decision making on an important goal — the understanding that consideration as to whether particular action should be promoted or followed by others is necessary as a criteria for making an ethical decision and a focus on the intention or motivation behind our actions, which was something utilitarianism ignored. Although Kant may blur the line at times between deontology and consequentialism, he focuses attention on proper respect for others in our own actions.

3. Natural Law Theory

Natural law theory began as an explanation by St. Thomas Aquinas to explain how individuals should act in their lives. Such a theory is usually considered to be deontological because what is important is the way in which we act and not merely the consequences of our actions. Yet there is also a sense in which natural law theory is consequentialist in that the goal of moral action is human fulfillment, the consequence of acting morally. Although the theory has seemed antiquated in the past, recent philosophers have reasserted their interest in it as a basis of ethical action.[133]

Aquinas' natural law theory is embedded in a scheme that recognizes three types of law: eternal, natural, and human. For Aquinas, the eternal law is God's plan, which directs every movement and action in creation.[134] Everything that God creates obeys this eternal law, "and bears the imprint of that law in the form of a natural tendency to pursue whatever behavior and goals are appropriate" to this eternal law. Eternal law is then the beginning of the natural law within us. Aquinas defines the natural law as the way in which "all things partake in the eternal law, in so far as, namely, from its being imprinted on them, they derive their respective inclination to their proper acts and ends."[135] Natural law is a participation by a human being in the eternal law of God. According to Aquinas, since the natural law is imprinted on man's very nature, men cannot be ignorant of it and its general principles, though people may fail to apply the general principles in a particular case.[136] This is very important because, following from this, the natural law is an inclination to the good within all of us, regardless of whether we choose to follow or understand it. This natural law is promulgated by God in that it is imprinted within all human being's minds so as to be known by men naturally and to lead them to human perfection.[137] The natural law then becomes a habit within people because it is the way we are inclined to act from within.[138]

Aquinas then sets out the first principle of natural law, "good is to be done and pursued, and evil is to be avoided."[139] This first principle is the most common and general precept known to all people and is the most general law that human beings must follow in their actions. The secondary principles of natural law are more particular conclusions on how to act.[140]

Human beings come to know the natural law through reason. For Aquinas, moral reasoning begins with premises known by reflecting on our inclinations, and then willing a course of action comes from this natural tendency we have to perfection.[141] Through these types of reason, human beings act toward the goods which are the proper ends of the natural law, therefore, goods for Aquinas are that which man has an inclination to.[142] Then, by looking at our inclinations, we can see the various goods that we naturally seek, and these are then the goods that we should morally seek. These goods would include such things as life, love, friendship, knowledge, etc. By attaining these goods to which we naturally incline, we fulfill our human nature and that is a consequence of a good moral life.

The inclinations and goods that they point to can be understood differently by different individuals in rare occurrences due to a person's acting in accordance with some passion and avoiding the natural tendencies toward the good as provided by the natural law.[143] They may also change in that reasoning may be from false principles based on the first principles, and so in some instances our options in a particular action can be weighed against the first principle.

Another component necessary to an understanding of Aquinas' theory of natural law is his explanation of human law. For Aquinas, law "is an ordinance of reason for the common good, made by him who has care of the community, and promulgated."[144] Human law helps people order their actions toward the goods that are the proper goals of the natural law. A just law conforms to reason and the natural law so that it is binding to conscience, therefore, a human law which does not follow the natural law is no law at all.[145]

One problem with Aquinas' theory comes from his definition of a good as something that man has an inclination to. The problem is that these inclinations can be clouded by desires within individuals, and it is unclear how a person would know which inclination to follow. It is unclear how one could differentiate between an inclination leading to a good and one that only satisfies a desire. Aquinas' explanation of inclinations is hard to understand and reconcile with complicated choices, because it seems that we should just know how to act from within, without an understanding of why we are acting in a particular way.

One distinct positive note concerning natural law theory is that it is rooted in a notion of human nature that should be available for anyone to investigate. Aquinas postulates, perhaps optimistically, that people can find within themselves, in their own inclinations and tendencies, the goods that they should seek in order to live moral lives. By rooting morality in human nature, natural law makes morality something objective, and not simply something subject to the wishes of an individual or society. Natural law theory provides an objective basis for evaluating any and every individual in society since it is rooted in this human nature common to all individuals in all societies.

In the end, natural law theory provides a way to think about ethical decision making that can be helpful. This type of theory explains that, regardless of whether we understand it or not, we are responsible for our moral actions and the consequences of our actions. Contemporary natural law theories allow for diversity in experiences and understanding of how it is to be moral, because individuals have different contexts and ways of reasoning through ethical decisions.[146]

C. Ethics

The three theories discussed are examples of the way in which philosophers attempt to understand the world around them through ethical discussions. Each approach has its shortcomings, but each also adds something to an understanding of ethical decision making that can be valuable. Utilitarianism realizes that people should act in ways that promote the most happiness for all and glaringly shows how a blind approach to this can lead to the sacrificing of innocent minorities; natural law theory presents an explanation of the world following moral norms within each of us, but it fails to show why some people understand these norms and others do not; and Kantianism shows that ethical understandings must be made in a way in which they could actually be promoted for all with a true respect for all individuals, but at the same time it leaves ethical reasoning so inflexible it is hard to account for the variances among individuals and cultures.

These theories were not presented to promote one or the other. Instead, they show that any thorough ethical understanding of the world around us and attempts at acting ethically must be more detailed and comprehensive than merely doing what one thinks is right. Regardless of the system one follows, it must be understood that "it is plainly and unequivocally in our collective interests that we have a morality and that people generally act in accordance with it."[147] For lawyers, ethical decision-making will entail more than merely doing what the law proscribes. Being a good lawyer is one thing; being an ethical person as well as a good lawyer is something far beyond this.

D. Sports Ethics

Several commentators have focused on ethics as it directly relates to sports.[148] Sports in itself can have three types of relationships with ethics. The relationship can be negative — wherein participants learn that to succeed they have to cheat or act immorally in some other way; neutral — where sports itself has no moral significance at all, or is outside of the moral arena entirely; or positive — where there is a connection between playing sports and the development of moral values.[149] This article advocates that the relationship between sports and morality or ethical development should be positive for all of those involved, i.e., players, coaching, management, and agents. The reason is that anyone in sports is constantly faced with the situations where their ethical systems are tested, exhibited, and learned.[150]

Since ethics applies to how people ought to behave, in sports this translates to how all participants should act in the most ethically desirable manner, even if this means possibly sacrificing some sports value (like winning) for a truly ethical reason. A person is never just a sports participant; he is also first and foremost a human being. Unfortunately, athletes are often only held to standards of conduct as necessitated by the rules of the particular sport they play. Similarly, sports lawyers may be only held to the standards of conduct that players associations, the American Bar Association, judicial rules, and specific legislation may mandate. Both "enjoy a remarkable range of freedom to act unethically within the framework of the rules."[151]

One overriding concept that is often promoted as a focus of ethical thought in sports is the idea of sportsmanship. Sportsmanship is an idea that encompasses an adherence to the rules of the particular sport, an acceptance that what is really important is effort and not always the end result, and an appreciation for the effort of all those involved, even the opposition.[152] As the NCAA recently expressed, "[w]ithout sportsmanship, true athletics competition and its important educational value for individuals is sorely compromised."[153] According to the NCAA, sportsmanship is demonstrated by "respect, fairness, civility, honesty and responsibility."[154] The NCAA explained that these values are fundamental to an ethical perspective and ethical conduct because such ethical conduct "reflects a higher standard than law."[155]

Sportsmanship then can provide a touchstone between sports and ethics. If lawyers, players, and coaches can learn to act more sports-manlike in their conduct within the sports world, hopefully the problem of racism in sports would be seen for what it is: a lack of respect and fairness towards those who are affected.

E. Lawyers Ethics

A final area of research that needs to be mentioned is lawyers' ethics. Legal ethics focuses on "what ethical principles and virtues are essential, not to being a good person, but rather to being a good lawyer."[156] Therefore, the study of legal ethics aims to encourage a moral focus within lawyer's responsibility "that is compatible with the social roles and functions that, according to our present legal system, the lawyer is required or expected to fulfill."[157]

Conceptions of legal ethics are embodied in the requirement that all those attempting entry into the legal bar must pass an ethics or moral fitness test. Underlying these tests "is the assumption that to be a good lawyer one must be a morally good person."[158] This conception of legal ethics is also notable in the idea of lawyer professionalism. As ethical considerations deal with the way things ought to be, the notion of professionalism "directs us to what it is that members of the profession believe that we should expect of ourselves."[159] Therefore, within the legal profession, not only is one required to be an ethical entrant into the field, but the very notion of being a professional within the field entails ethical considerations and knowledge that one must have.

As legal ethics should help lawyers realize that ethical considerations must come into legal decision making, they also must realize that "ethics reflects a higher standard than law,"[160] and thus ethical considerations can and should supersede legal considerations in various situations. The law, in itself, cannot provide answers to every situation a lawyer will come into contact with,[161] but still lawyers cannot be expected to be any more knowledgeable about ethical considerations than anyone else. A lawyer can not be expected to know any more about ethical considerations than any reasonable, educated person.[162] This sense of reasonableness should be understandable to lawyers as so much of the law deals with problems from the perspective of the "reasonable" person.

F. Ethics to Responsibility

Taking into account that lawyers do have the responsibility to act ethically and to consider the ethical consequences of their conduct beyond the mere legal answers, it is important now to move to the area of lawyer responsibility and regulation. The focus will be on is the ways in which sports lawyers are regulated, the ways that the leagues and NCAA attempt to also regulate these lawyers, and the specific consideration of sports ethics that lawyers must keep in mind in an effort to deal with racism in sports.

III. Lawyer Responsibility

Lawyers in sports are regulated in many ways, including through players associations, the NCAA, state legislation, and the American Bar Association's professional responsibility rules.[163] Guidance for the ethical regulation of lawyers can also be found in codes of conduct, such as the Association of Representatives of Professional Athletes (ARPA) code of ethics, and other specific codes of conduct.[164]

A. Players Associations

The NBA, NFL, and MLB have developed specific regulations that player agents representing their players must follow.

The National Football League Players Association (NFLPA) has a regulatory scheme wherein agents must become certified with the NFLPA.[165] To become certified, an agent must provide background information regarding such matters as education and past occupations, and the NFLPA may disqualify an agent for past disciplinary problems.[166] Once certified, the agent is subject to many guidelines. They must use a standard form contract; collect a fee limited on a percentage basis; attend annual NFLPA seminars; comply fully with all applicable state and federal law; and not collect a fee until the player has recieved their compensation.[167] The NFLPA rules attempt to provide an obstacle to agents who are not qualified to represent players and will discipline agents who do not follow these rules with fines or revocation of certification.[168]

These rules have several potential problems, including: 1) these regulations do not regulate agents in their contact with athletes signing their first NFL contracts because these athletes are not yet members of the NFLPA — this can lead to significant abuse as the agents may charge exorbitant fees or give bad advice to these new clients; 2) these rules only regulate contract advisors, whereas agents do more than this in providing advice on endorsements and other deals; 3) the rules do not provide specific criteria for judging an agent's qualifications and so most anyone gets certified; and 4) the rules are not particularly enforceable due to the fact that the NFLPA only has the authority to bargain for its members collectively and not individually; therefore, it cannot force agents to become certified.[169]

The NBA Players Association (NBPA) has instituted a program that regulates its agents in a similar manner, while also trying to avoid some of the problems inherent in the NFLPA plan. Within its Collective Bargaining Agreement, the NBA mandates that only those agents who are certified by the Players Association can represent its players.[170] The regulations themselves cover agents who represent players who have not yet signed their first contract with NBA teams, regulates incentive and fee payments to and from players, and regulates agents in their conduct as contract advisors.[171] An agent also must demonstrate their competence through a background disclosure before being certified.[172] Agents are also required to use a standard representation agreement and to comply with compensation limitations as imposed by the NBPA.[173] Agents can receive discipline in the form of fines and revocation of their certification if they do not follow these rules.[174]

Problematically, the NBPA regulations do not provide any objective criteria for measuring the competence and qualifications of its agents, and the plan cannot force agents who represent its players to join the program; therefore, the power of these rules is suspect.[175]

The Major League Baseball Players Association (MLBPA) rules regulating player agents begins with the necessity that agents who want to negotiate contracts for baseball players must be certified by the MLBPA.[176] Unlike the other two systems, the agent must receive a commitment from a player that once the agent becomes certified, the player will retain his services.[177] Furthermore, the MLBPA regulations do not restrict the fees chargeable by agents for their services.[178] In other respects, these rules are similar to the other two leagues with the same basic requirements and restrictions.

B. NCAA

Within its manual, the NCAA provides several rules that in effect attempt to regulate athlete agents.[179] The basic NCAA rule that governs athlete agents is Section 12.3.1, which makes clear that an athlete will lose their remaining eligibility to participate in college athletics if they sign an agreement with an agent to represent them in contract negotiations.[180] Therefore, athletes who sign with an agent will lose their amateur status as seen by the NCAA. Additionally, a college athlete cannot even obtain an agent to be used in future contract negotiations after their eligibility is up,[181] although an athlete can obtain the services of a lawyer if that lawyer does not represent the player in contract negotiations.[182] Also, an agent cannot give any form of benefits to a prospective client who is a student athlete without risking the athlete's college eligibility.[183]

The NCAA has implemented a registration procedure for agents who wish to represent athletes coming out of NCAA schools. Under this system, agents were required to complete the form, agree they would not contact an athlete or coach without first contacting a university's athletic director, and this registration was kept in a listing by the NCAA for athletes and others to view.[184] The aim was that by disclosing the agent's background and qualifications in the registration forms, players and their families would have some resource to evaluate agents they came in contact with.[185] The problem with this registration system is that it is voluntary — the NCAA cannot force agents to participate.[186] And, again, there are no requirements as to general competence that agents must meet to become registered.[187]

A final way the NCAA has attempted to regulate athlete agents is by requiring athletes who will be participating in the Division I basketball tournament or college football bowl games to sign affidavits certifying that they have not signed with an agent.[188] The focus was on these two sports, presumably because they are the two major college revenue producing sports and have been subject to the most frequent agent abuses. A registered agent could be removed from the list if he or she in any way jeopardizes a player's eligibility or fails to contact an athletic director before contacting an athlete or his coach.[189]

The problem with the NCAA's regulations is that all the NCAA can do is regulate its members and student-athletes. And since the agents are not members of the NCAA, the "NCAA has no punitive power over the agent's unscrupulous behavior."[190] Furthermore, the agent registration program is voluntary and many agents just ignore it.[191]

C. State Regulation

Many states have implemented specific statutes that apply to athlete agents.[192] In general, there are two levels of state agent regulation. The first level is under standard criminal and civil laws that may cover misconduct in negotiating and drafting contracts.[193] The second level is actual sports- agent specific statutes which often require agents to register with a state agency.[194] This type of legislation usually attempts to require certification of sports agents, and often the posting of a surety bond or the payment of fees to the state.[195] Early legislation often included provisions for registration, the payment of fees, posting of surety bonds, contract approval by the state, and criminal penalties for agent misconduct.[196] The current trend is legislation that also requires notice to schools and the state before and after the signing of a contract, waiting periods for valid contracts, causes of action by colleges for agent misconduct that damages a school, and less cumbersome registration procedures than the older legislation.[197] In most cases, the states that require registration also provide lists of prohibited activities that can result in punishment.[198] Some states have also begun to incorporate NCAA regulations into their agent regulatory schemes.[199] Therefore, there is a possibility of civil or criminal penalties for agents who violate these rules.

There are many criticisms of these laws. Initially, state laws such as these can lead to confusion resulting from conflicting laws between and among states since there is at present no overriding federal legislation.[200] Therefore, if an agent from Wisconsin signs a player from a school in Illinois who is drafted by a team in Detroit, it is unclear whether the agent must register in all three states. Furthermore, if there is a problem, it is unclear which state law will be controlling.

As a practical matter, for an agent to represent clients in many states, he or she may need to follow extensive registration procedures in each state before having the opportunity to negotiate a contract with a client to recoup money spent on registration.[201] Also, most of the laws do not include any minimum competency requirements that an agent must meet in order to become registered.[202] Therefore, a player cannot be sure if an agent who registers is competent and can represent them properly.

Finally, some commentators suggest that such state regulations may violate the Commerce Clause of the Constitution as improper state regulation of interstate commerce.[203] This is due to the fact that the

Commerce Clause bars states from regulating interstate commerce.[204] Commerce involving an agent in one state and a player in another state may be considered as interstate commerce and regulation of this by state law may be suspect.

D. Federal Regulation

Although there has been a proposal for a Professional Sports Agency Act[205] and Federal Sports-Agent Legislation,[206] there is no current legislation that regulates sports agents at the federal level. The federal Racketeer Influenced and Corrupt Organizations Act (RICO)[207] was used in the famous lawsuit against Norby Walters and Lloyd Bloom involving charges of mismanagement of funds, fraud, and racketeering.[208] Regardless of this example, at present time no federal legislation has been approved that specifically regulates athlete agents.

E. American Bar Association

The American Bar Association has specific Model Rules and a Model Code of Professional Responsibility that regulate athlete agents who are lawyers. Unfortunately, many athlete agents are not lawyers, and so they are not governed by these rules. However, since this article is concerned with sports lawyers, these rules are important.

The Model Rules of Professional Responsibility provide regulations that govern how a lawyer must act in numerous situations. Rules concern matters such as Misconduct,[209] Bar Admission and Disciplinary Matters,[210] Reporting Professional Misconduct of others,[211] Competence,[212] Integrity,[213] Fees,[214] etc.[215] These rules intend to encourage lawyers to act more responsibly in all of their legal activities and mandate review and disciplinary proceedings for violations. Most states have incorporated these rules in some form or another, or developed their own rules of professional responsibility that lawyers within that particular state must follow. As already mentioned, professionalism entails the consideration of the ethical impact of a person's actions and making sure that ethical considerations enter into legal decisions. These rules then implicitly carry a sense that for a lawyer to act responsibly, that lawyer must act ethically. The preamble to these rules specifically mentions that lawyers are responsible for the quality of justice that the legal system provides, and that they must only act with respect for those involved, and for legitimate purposes within the law.[216]

The Model Code of Professional Responsibility entails a similar regulatory scheme with the addition that for each mandate there is a specific "ethical consideration" mentioned that applies to the particular situation. Moreover, the Preamble to the Model Code makes clear that lawyers must consider the ethical impact of their actions when it says that "[n]ot every situation which [a lawyer] may encounter can be foreseen, but fundamental ethical principles are always present to guide him"[217] and that "in the last analysis it is the desire for the respect and confidence of the members of the profession and of the society which he serves that should provide to a lawyer the incentive for the highest possible degree of ethical conduct."[218] Therefore, as a lawyer serves society within his profession, it is a duty of the profession to act with "the highest possible degree of ethical conduct."

The ABA Model Rules and Model Code provide direct evidence that the American Bar Association, in its regulation of all lawyers, expects these lawyers to act ethically in all that they do. Specifically, "[a]ttorneys are held to an ethical standard for every activity in which they practice."[219] These regulations are over and above normal legal responsibilities as mandated by specific laws; they instead mandate the conduct of lawyers regardless of what legal situation they are acting within. Sports lawyers, by the mere reason that they are lawyers, must be aware of these rules and act in ways that appropriately follow them.[220] Also, these rules avoid the shortcomings of the regulations mentioned so far because there is no necessity for registration, all lawyers are regulated by the nature of being admitted to the bar, and competence is specifically delineated and regulated under these rules.

F. Codes of Conduct

Another way to attempt to regulate sports lawyers or agents is through specific codes of conduct. Ethical codes of conduct are attempts to "institutionalize the expectations of the organizations that adopt them, establishing efficient, consistent means of control."[221] Such codes should follow four rules in order to serve their purpose as ethical guidelines. First, they must state expectations concerning how one is to ethically behave.[222] Second, they must clearly indicate the seriousness with which actual ethical considerations should be undertaken within the conduct regulated.[223] Third, they must provide concrete examples of rules of behavior that conform to more abstract ethical principles.[224] Finally, they must be "written, clear, and public."[225] The goal of such a code is to promote ethical conduct in those regulated for the basic reason that "acting ethically is good for its own sake."[226] In other words, acting ethically is just the right thing to do.

With the disparity among different individuals as to what it actually means to act ethically in a particular situation, these codes can serve to help define the range of ethical possibilities. The danger is that "a code of ethics will tend to undermine ethical evaluation"[227] because it takes the individual thought on what is right out of a particular decision, thus making ethical action rigid and formalistic. However, as long as such codes are considered as a possibility for opening up ethical considerations of action in areas where such considerations are not usually explicitly made, they can serve a purpose. Of course, they must be enforced, but their real purpose is to show individuals that whatever conduct they undertake has ethical implications. Therefore, these individuals can hopefully learn to add an ethical perspective to decision making from the beginning.

1. Association of Representatives of Professional Athletes (ARPA)

One example of an organization that attempted to regulate agents was the ARPA, which regulated agents who represented professional athletes through its Code of Ethics.[228] The ARPA's main goals were to promote honesty by sports lawyers through the adherence to a definite ethical code and promote the competence of sports lawyers through continuing professional education.[229] The Code of Ethics itself focused on five main areas: integrity, competence, dignity, management responsibility, and confidentiality in representation.[230] Through its continuing education seminars, the ARPA tried to teach sports lawyers how to become more competent and ethical in their representations of athletes.[231]

The shortcomings of this Code are obvious in that the ARPA was a voluntary organization and could not compel attorneys to join and follow its laudable commitment to ethical development.[232] Furthermore, even if there were violations of the Code, the ARPA had no ability to or mechanism for enforcement or punishment.[233] Finally, in their attempt to not be burdensome to its members, the rules in the Code were too broad to be useful as guides for specific conduct.[234]

2. The American Lawyer's Code of Conduct

The American Lawyer's Code of Conduct was produced in 1982 by a Commission on Professional Responsibility of the Roscoe Pound-American Trial Lawyers Foundation.[235] This code was provided as an alternative to the ABA's Model Code and Model Rules due to perceived shortcomings in these two documents.[236] This code attempted to recognize the "emptiness of some cliches of lawyers' ethics" (such as many of the Model Rules) as mandates that are meaningless in actual context.[237] The code then focused on presenting rules with more substance than the Model Rules and Code, and attempted to strengthen the legal system as "the embodiment of the constitutional values inherent in the administration of justice in the United States."[238]

Looking at the code, however, it seems to be very similar to the Model Rules and Code provided by the ABA. Chapters such as Chapter 1 — "The Client's Trust and Confidences,"[239] Chapter 2 — "Fidelity to the Client's Interests,"[240] and Chapter 3 — "Zealousness on the Client's Behalf,"[241] address the same issues and situations as the Rules and Code. Although not specifically mentioning ethical consideration, the code attempts at least to better delineate all of the considerations that should go into legal decision making and lawyer conduct.

3. Code of Conduct for NFLPA Member Contract Advisors

Another example of a professional code of conduct is the Code of Conduct for NFLPA Member Contract Advisors.[242] This code came about after the NFLPA reformed as a professional association after renouncing its rights to bargain exclusively for the NFL players in 1989.[243] The Code was developed as a necessary step to insure that agents involved with NFL players were actually competent.[244] The Code set out to accomplish this by making sure that agents registered with the NFLPA and provided specific review measures (such as a review period of an initial forty-five days to make sure an applicant met the competency requirements) for which applicants were held.[245] The Code itself specified the types of agreements an advisor could sign, mandates of the type of conduct the advisor must conform to, examples of improper violations of the code, and oversight compliance and arbitration procedures regarding violations of the code.[246]

This code was an effort by the NFLPA to assure that its members received the best representation from their agents that was possible. In providing some explanation of improper conduct and enforcement procedures, this code was a positive step. Unfortunately, although the purpose seemed to be to assure the competence of the agents, there are no specific requirements of background or education mentioned; all that is left is reasons why an applicant would be disqualified.

4. Uniform Code to Regulate Athlete Agents

A final example of a Code is one that was proposed in 1992. Under this proposal, a Uniform Code is needed to regulate all athlete agents and curtail agent abuses. The six basic parts of this proposal included: 1) a broad definition of player and agent to avoid the problems of not regulating agents at all times in their dealings with athletes;[247] 2) a regulatory body for the arbitration of agent-player grievances;[248] 3) qualification and certification requirements developed with the help of leagues and governing bodies and incorporating written tests to prove competence before certification;[249] 4) a bond requirement to provide some security to injured parties;[250] 5) criminal penalties for violations of the code;[251] and 6) the identification of specific prohibited acts that will result in penalties.[252]

The authors who developed this proposal realized that the initiation of a code of this scope would be problematic and could take a long time.[253] However, the code they provide seems to cover all of the problems with the codes and regulatory schemes that have been addressed already. Presumably, this type of code would also act to heighten ethical awareness and responsibility in sports lawyers who would be regulated by it.

G. The Ethical Regulation of Lawyers

Lawyers are clearly expected to act ethically. The ABA, legislation, and various codes of conduct provide ways in which lawyers are already held to ethical standards that may come under the heading of "professional responsibility," but also entail the reality that beyond acting as responsible lawyers, lawyers must be ethical lawyers.

The problem of racism in sports is then a problem of which sports lawyers must be aware. Racism is an evil that sports lawyers must seek to change due to their responsibilities for acting ethically, as part of the responsibilities of their profession. Sports lawyers cannot merely avoid the problem; they must make sure that each action, each deal, and each contract they are involved with does not add to the problem of racism in sports. Furthermore, as ethical individuals and as ethically regulated lawyers, they must realize that they have some responsibility for improving the situation faced by African-Americans in sports.

IV. Proposals for the Future

What does it all mean?

The beginning of this article provided a definition, and evidence, of the continuing problem of racism in sports. The expression of this racism is unethical, even if unconscious, in its lack of respect for others based on nothing else but skin color. A greater focus on ethics can show both that this conduct is wrong and ways in which conduct can be improved to eradicate racism and its negative effects. Ethics does not have to only be encompassed by the various theories proposed by philosophers. Ethics itself can be a way of thought, where someone considers the consequences of his or her actions and adjusts this conduct to attempt to have the least negative effect on others.

Sports ethics and the ideal of sportsmanship can be applied to all those involved in sports, including lawyers. If lawyers learn to act with a notion of sportsmanship, they will not merely represent their client but take an active role, both individually and collectively, in assuring that all those in their particular sport are treated fairly.

Legal ethics and the idea of professionalism shows that lawyers, in all of their pursuits, must keep in mind their ethical responsibilities to themselves and society. The ABA Model Rules and Code are aware of this notion of professionalism and mandate that lawyers should be aware of the ethical consequences of all that they do. As sports lawyers acting within this concept of professionalism, lawyers must bear some responsibility for conduct within leagues wherein racism still is evident.

A. Focus

Sports lawyers must focus on the impact they can have on eradicating racism from sports. Ethics can be practical as mentioned here. Ethical considerations do not need to be and should not be mere academic pursuits. They should be practical, constant, day to day considerations.

For most individuals, they already are. The problem is that many individuals who do not face racism or its negative effects do not see that they too have a responsibility to fight racism as ethical human beings.

Sports lawyers in professional sports may be in the best position to help because they often represent the real money makers, those who are the most in the public eye — the players. Lawyers can not avoid responsibility by claiming they are fulfilling their legal rules and should not be further responsible. Lawyers must realize that as part of their ethical responsibility, they bear responsibility to others beyond mere legal considerations. Furthermore, since sports lawyers are in an industry where the workers (players) are overwhelmingly black, while management is overwhelmingly white, lawyers have an increased responsibility to work for change.

B. Athletes

Lawyers can help African-American athletes by possibly working to incorporate provisions into their contracts that make athletes appear in African-American communities as role models, to make children aware of the problems even these "successful" athletes encounter.[254] Lawyers have a unique position here because they advise their clients on many matters that affect their clients' lives. Players often listen to their lawyers when the public and team disagree with their position. Lawyers are often more educated, and able to see the whole sports picture better than the athletes. They can encourage their players to become involved and find ways to help African-American players receive better chances to attain management positions when their careers are over.

Lawyers who represent star players should especially encourage the players to speak out against racism in sports, possibly to the point of helping set up appearances, commercials, and talks during their playing careers. This is especially necessary due to the lack of leadership in the black community and lack of role models beyond sports and entertainment figures.

Lawyers should also abide by what some have called an "Athletes' Bill of Rights." In following the intent of such documents lawyers should help athletes achieve participation in sports that are free from discrimination by race, and should not jeopardize college athletes' careers by offering improper benefits or getting involved with an athlete before their eligibility is exhausted.[255]

Lawyers should promote and follow these specific ethical considerations in all of their actions as representatives of players: respect for
persons, treating others as ends in themselves and not means for an
end, treating others as you would want them to treat you, and treating
others in a fair and equitable way so they receive the same opportunities as anyone else in their position. These ethical considerations are
not all inclusive, but lawyers must take responsibility for their work in
the sports business, which is an example of equality to so many.

C. Players Associations, Leagues, and Management

Lawyers are also involved in Players Associations, Leagues, and
often representatives of management. As representatives who most
likely must be certified by the Players Associations of a particular
league, lawyers should push for the Associations to adopt a Code of
Conduct similar to the NFLPA Code already discussed, which
specifically mentions that racism in intent or effect is unethical. The
Associations can work together to develop a uniform code that
incorporates a specific provision admitting the problem of racism and
attempting to control such conduct. This code would be based on the
six provisions outlined already[256] and would contain specific provisions making it the responsibility of the agents and associations to do
their part to end the problem of racism in sports. The Associations
should also make it a practice to administer continuing education
programs (like the ARPA), which address such figures as those
presented by the Racial Report Cards and try to develop ways to
further progress.

The leagues can help by incorporating such a code of conduct, as
agreed to through the associations, into their Collective Bargaining
Agreement. Therefore, any agent would be subject to the code, and
the league would have an active role in making sure agent conduct
follows this code.

The 1995 RACIAL REPORT CARD measured the participation in each
Association across racial lines. The report found that the NBA and
NFL possessed strong African-American representation within their
ranks, while MLB was sorely deficient.[257] Many in the administration
of these Associations are African-American and lawyers. These individuals must continue to push for change and demand that the leagues
recognize and publicize the problem of racism in sports as is attempted
through the Racial Report Cards.

At the league level (again where many employees are attorneys), specific awareness and realistic approaches to the problem must be taken. All of these approaches must focus on the fact that it is unethical for these leagues to be made up of high percentages of players who are African-American, while at the same time management is not. The three leagues already have a good number of African-American individuals in high positions.[258] Therefore, these high ranking individuals should take the initiative and act as public role models while heightening awareness of the problem of racism in sports. They should also use their positions to help other qualified African-Americans attain realistic positions within league or team management.

One plan to improve the racial situation within professional sports was the Rainbow Commission on Fairness in Athletics Ten-Point Affirmative Action Plan.[259] Although this plan was presented to MLB, its aim and ideas could apply to all leagues. Particular provisions of this plan pushed for community development programs and youth leagues; purchases of twenty percent of all goods and services from minorities or women; three to five year plans for integration in league posts, marketing, and merchandising; committee formation to seek minority ownership; inclusion of two minority candidates for all executive and managerial positions; diversity and humanities training for owners and executives; and personal development and financial management training for players.[260]

Major League Baseball developed its own plan regarding minority issues, which included similar provisions and also provisions that would seek new minority investors and involvement on their boards of directors; make new efforts to attract minorities as fans; increase community and charitable activities; and mandate sensitivity training for employees.[261] Unfortunately, MLB's plan was less specific in both amount and time frame.

Another proposed plan is the Richardson-Jones plan.[262] This plan suggests the immediate adoption of respect and value of diversity in all employee policies and practices a system-wide planning process "to eliminate racism . . . and other forms of discrimination;" revision of all policies and procedures to reflect multicultural respect; development of team specific Multicultural Advancement plans; development of procedures for recruiting, retaining, and promoting minorities in management positions; the encouragement of managers and players to develop local plans to promote multicultural respect; and the involvement of leaders of minority communities in baseballs financial matters.[263]

These types of plans are examples of what can be done on a league wide basis. Specifically, the Rainbow Commission and Richardson-Jones plans provide comprehensive and specific plans that would move to significant progress. If a plan combining elements from these two and incorporating a code of conduct for agents could be implemented in all three leagues, progress would be likely.

At the commissioner level, both David Stern and Paul Tagliabue have been lobbying within their respective leagues for greater minority hiring.[264] Jerry Reinsdorf, co-chairman of baseball's Equal Opportunity Committee, has also stated that baseball remains committed to equal opportunity for all those involved.[265]

Management and team owners must also be brought into the picture to help reform sports. Without the input of these groups, many of the actual hirings that take place will remain closed to African-American candidates. These groups control the monetary and employment decisions at the player, coach, and often administrative levels. They must be asked to sign on as committed participants to any plan initiated by the leagues.

There must be collaboration between the leagues, players associations, agents, and management in a continued commitment to eradicating racism in sports. Only with collaboration between all parties can progress be made. It is true that sports provides remarkable opportunities for African-Americans, but the figures are misleading; management and administrative positions are still lacking.

D. NCAA

At the collegiate level, although the NCAA cannot work directly to regulate sports agents, an ethical answer can provide a solution. Sports agents, in a focused commitment to ethical conduct, should understand that improper contact with players before their eligibility is up hurts the players and the schools. Furthermore, the majority of players who are involved in scandals due to improper agent relations are African-American due to the fact that the majority of star players in revenue producing sports are African-American.[266] Agents should become educated as to the realities of college for black athletes, including the stereotypes and pressures they must face. Once players continue in the pros, agents should make the effort to help them continue their educations or help them attain possible employment after their careers are over. Often these athletes will not have true college degrees or have the academic background to succeed outside of athletics.

Agents should take it upon him or herself as their moral duty to help the athletes, and not only in their athletic careers. To merely represent them in athletics and do nothing to help them receive an education or not have to bear the problems racism will impose on them is unethical. Again, as lawyers, most agents do have an ethical responsibility in their relations with any client. Even agents who are not lawyers should act ethically as ethical human beings. Any NCAA-wide scheme should take into account these individuals as well.

Agents should also work through the NCAA to develop joint efforts to address the problem of racism in college sports and racism that the athletes may face in professional sports. With greater awareness at this level, athletes may be better able to change things in the future and may have the confidence to take a stand earlier.

E. Code

The overriding code that has been promoted here within professional league sports could also be pushed as federal legislation. This does not mean the literal code itself, but the intent behind it (for example, a federal Sports Agency Code of Conduct). As the code at the league level would create a sense of uniformity among and within the leagues, a federal law would be more effective than the many different state laws that now regulate sports agents. The law could take into account the suggestions of the Uniform Code as already described[267] and the proposals for league reform as already mentioned.[268] The intent here is not to provide the exact wording of such a law, but instead to point out that a federal law of this type would go a long way to mandating a certain type of conduct for those in the sports industry. With the size of the sports industry and amounts of money involved this seems a clear instance of an industry that Congress could regulate through its Commerce Clause powers.

F. Personal Moral Code

Perhaps the most important means by which sports lawyers can attack the problem of racism in sports is through the establishment of their own personal moral code. The ethical theories described earlier all provide a way in which individuals can ethically understand their actions and the world around them. Even though each individual will in the end have a different sense of right and wrong, each person has some ethical guidelines that can at least be understood by others. This type of inner ethical code is important because outside regulation through professional or league wide codes of conduct are "meaningless to persons lacking values and courage to do right."[269] A sports lawyer as a moral human being already understands some sense of what it is to be moral. This inner code then can provide the link between the lawyers acting as a moral human being and the realization that within the profession this same ethical realization is important.

G. Reality

Racism may be something that cannot be totally eradicated. Any solutions to try and attack the problem in sports "must take into account both this permanence and the need for persistence."[270] People will not change without sacrifice and education is necessary to change the racist perceptions that people still hold unconsciously. To really reach a solution there:

> must be a recognition of the existence of racism, discrimination and limited access networks. Next, there must be a successful transition into a period where racial diversity is the standard . . . . As this transition is completed the accomplished goals multi-culturalism--an industry with representation from across American society without racism, discrimination or affirmative action programs.[271]

If progress can be made similar to this, the problem of racism in sports may some day no longer be so prominent. And if sports is still a reflection of society, the problem of racism in society may have also improved.

V. Conclusion

Racism does exist in sports — the numbers from such things as the Racial Report Cards bear this out. Still, many people do not admit this fact until comments such as those by Al Campanis come out into the open. Therefore, the type of racism that still exists in sports is predominantly unconscious. The individuals who take actions that negatively harm African-American individuals may not intend the effects or consciously act in a racist manner. They may merely hire someone they know who also happens to be white. When this type of practice persists, the lack of blacks in management and other positions in sports is not so odd.

However, racism of any kind is unethical. Ethics teaches that as human beings we should never treat others in a way that harms them or devalues them as individuals. The law can fight overt acts of racism and discrimination, but it cannot adequately deal with the unconscious forms of racism. Only through recognition of the problem and commitment to ethical solutions can progress be made.

Sports lawyers have a special role in this because they are involved, for the most part, in sports that are dominated by black players. These lawyers are already mandated to act ethically by the ABA guidelines, Players Associations rules, state laws, and hopefully their own inner ethical consciences. The Uniform Code of Conduct and the Richardson-Jones plan provide laudable guidelines to increase the ethical practice of the law and specifically improve racial policies within sports. In these mandates of ethical conduct, changing systems or practices that add to racist practices is of the utmost ethical concern.

Unfortunately, much of lawyer regulation is self-governance. Therefore, agents can often get away with unethical conduct that may also be illegal. This is not to suggest that agents are intentionally unethical it just suggests that enforcement is lacking. Any effort to change the situation will also be lacking without consistent state or federal legislation because without these guidelines, consistent regulation is not possible.

In the end, the "saddest side of sports is that it serves as a magnet for young African-American males but rejects them when their playing days are over."[272] These are the innocent victims of the problem of racism in sports. The legal bar, specifically sports lawyers, can take an active role in eradicating the problem if they want to. If a lawyer's real role is serving his or her client, then this is what must be done. The only way to ethically serve clients who face the disease of racism is to help them fight to change the situation.

NOTES

1. This article will not provide a rehash of the many laws that deal with discrimination in the workplace and other areas, as these areas have been dealt with by many other authors. Instead this piece will focus on how lawyers can be made to act ethically, even if they are already following the legal rules and responsibilities that they must as lawyers.

2. Carole Oglesby, *Issues of Sport and Racism: Where is the White in the Rainbow Coalition?, in* RACISM IN COLLEGE ATHLETICS 253 (Dana Brooks & Ronald Althouse eds., 1993).

3. This focus on African-American athletes is also warranted due to the history of racist practices directed at this particular group. "Blacks have not simply been treated unfairly; they have been subjected first to decades of slavery, and then to decades of second-class citizenship, widespread legalized discrimination, economic persecution, education deprivation, and cultural stigmatization." Stanley Fish, *Reverse Racism or How the Pot Got to Call the Kettle Black,* ATLANTIC MONTHLY, Nov. 1993, at 130.

4. Charles R. Lawrence III, *The Id, the Ego, and Equal Protection: Reckoning with Unconscious Racism,* 39 STAN. L. REV. 317, 330 (1987).

5. DREW A. HYLAND, PHILOSOPHY OF SPORT 10 (1990). This unconscious racism may also be hard to determine and understand because it is "a persistent and constituent part of our social order, woven into the fabric of society and everyday life." Darryl Brown, *Racism and Race Relations in the University,* 76 VA. L. REV. 295 (1990).

6. FR. CHUCKWUDUM BARNABAS OKOLO, RACISM--A PHILOSOPHIC PROBE (1974).

7. BARRY MCPHERSON ET. AL., THE SOCIAL SIGNIFICANCE OF SPORT 193 (1989).

8. KENNETH L. SHROPSHIRE, IN BLACK AND WHITE: RACE ANDS SPORTS IN AMERICA 18 (forthcoming 1996) (manuscript of August 11, 1995, on file with author).

9. D. Stanley Eitzen, *Racism in College Sports: Prospects for the Year 2000, in* SPORT IN CONTEMPORARY SOCIETY 245-46 (D. Stanley Eitzen ed., 1996).

10. *Id.* at 246.

11. Harry Edwards, *Beyond Symptoms: Unethical Behavior in American Collegiate Sport and the Problem of the Color Line,* 9 J. SPORT & SOC. ISS. 3, 8-9 (1985).

12. Some authors even believe that such an equal footing will never be. Derrick Bell states that "Racial equality is, in fact, not a realistic goal." Derrick Bell, *Racial Realism,* 24 CONN. L. REV. 363 (1992). Although such feelings cannot be diminished, the only way to attempt to deal with the situation is to try to attack the problem and rid society of it. Equality may be an idyllic goal at this point but to slaves, any sense of freedom may have been just as hard to imagine. Without a commitment to rid society of the problem it is hard to understand how improvement that actually seeks to change perceptions can succeed. Unfortunately, for many blacks the "ultimate irony is that the benefits which did accrue from race-specific strategies went to middle-class blacks who had competitive resources such as steady incomes, education, and special talents." Robert L. Woodson, *Race and Economic Opportunity,* 42 VAND. L. REV. 1003, 1019 (1989). Therefore, those most in need have often not received the help they needed.

13. Brown, *supra* note 5, at 307-08.
14. Edwards, *supra* note 11, at 9.
15. *See, e.g.*, RICHARD E. LAPCHICK, FRACTURED FOCUS: SPORT AS A REFLEC-
     TION OF SOCIETY (1986); John C. Gaston, *The Destruction of the Young
     Black Male: The Impact of Popular Culture and Organized Sports*, 16 J.
     BLACK STUDIES 369, 371 (1986).
16. SHROPSHIRE, *supra* note 8, at 39. For an interesting contrast regarding
     the issue of racism in sports *see* Jim Myers, *Racism is a Serious Problem in
     Sports* (133-37) & George Gilder, *Racism in Sports is Exaggerated* (140-42)
     both *in* SPORTS IN AMERICA: OPPOSING VIEWPOINTS (William Dudley ed.,
     1994).
17. SHROPSHIRE, *supra* note 8, at 46.
18. *Id.* at 47.
19. *Id.* at 48.
20. *Id.* at 49.
21. SHROPSHIRE, *supra* note 8, at 50. These comments are reminiscent of
     Edwards' quotation (*see* text accompanying footnote 14) regarding the
     perpetuation of a plantation system for blacks.
22. *Id.* at 51.
23. Othello Harris, *African-American Predominance in Collegiate Sport, in*
     RACISM IN COLLEGE ATHLETICS 62-63 (Dana Brooks & Ronald Althouse
     eds., 1993). Another article which analyzes these differences in descrip-
     tions of athletic performance in more depth is Audrey J. Murrell &
     Edward M. Curtis, *Causal Attributions of Performance for Black and White
     Quarterbacks in the NFL: A Look at the Sports Pages*, 18 J. SPORT & SOC.
     ISSUES 224 (1994).
24. Jim Myers, *Race Still a Player*, USA TODAY, Dec. 16, 1991. As Myers
     says, if applied to society, such views would have disturbing implica-
     tions." *Id.*
25. PHILLIP M. HOOSE, NECESSITIES: RACIAL BARRIERS IN AMERICAN SPORTS
     19 (1989).
26. *Id.* at 8.
27. HYLAND, *supra* note 5, at 10-11.
28. RICHARD E. LAPCHICK, FIVE MINUTES TO MIDNIGHT: RACE AND SPORTS
     IN THE 1990s 235 (1991).
29. Gary A. Sailes, *An Investigation of Campus Stereotypes: The Myth of Black
     Athletic Superiority and the Dumb Jock Stereotype*, 10 SOCIOLOGY OF SPORT
     J. 88, 90 (1993). It is interesting to note that these types of theories were
     never necessary during the 1930s when Jewish players dominated profes-
     sional basketball. Richard E. Lapchick, *Race on the College Campus, in* THE
     RULES OF THE GAME: ETHICS IN COLLEGE SPORT 58-59 (Richard E.
     Lapchick & John Brooks Slaughter eds., 1989). The reason such expla-
     nations are looked to in regards to black athletes seems to be racism.
30. HYLAND, *supra* note 5, at 13.
31. LAPCHICK, *supra* note 28, at 236.

32. David K. Wiggins, *Critical Events Affecting Racism in Athletics, in* RACISM IN COLLEGE ATHLETICS 42 (Dana Brooks & Ronald Althouse eds., 1993).

33. Richard Lapchick, *Race and College Sports: a Long Way to Go, in* SPORTS IN SOCIETY 9 (Richard Lapchick ed., 1995).

34. HYLAND, *supra* note 5, at 15.

35. RICHARD E. LAPCHICK, BROKEN PROMISES: RACISM IN AMERICAN SPORTS 200 (1984); *see also* William Oscar Johnson, *How Far Have We Come*, SPORTS ILLUSTRATED, Aug. 5, 1991, at 40; Douglas Lederman, *Blacks Make Up Large Proportion of Scholarship Athletes, Yet Their Overall Enrollment Lags at Division I Colleges*, 38 CHRON. HIGHER EDUC. A32 (1992); Timothy Davis, *Race and Sports in Intercollegiate Athletics*, 6 FOR THE RECORD 5 (Aug./ Sept. 1995).

36. Gaston, *supra* note 15, at 379.

37. List provided in both Wilbert Marcellus Leonard, II, *The Sports Experience of the Black College Athlete: Exploitation in the Academy*, 21 INT. REV. FOR SOC. OF SPORT 35, 36 (1986) and Elmer Spreitzer & Eldon E. Snyder, *Sports Within the Black Subculture: A Matter of Social Class or a Distinctive Subculture?, in* SPORT SOCIOLOGY: CONTEMPORARY THEMES 308 (4th ed.) (Andrew Yiannakis, Thomas D. McIntyre, & Merrill J. Melnick eds., 1993).

38. Spreitzer and Snyder, *supra* note 37, at 309.

39. Gaston, *supra* note 15, at 377.

40. LAPCHICK, *supra* note 35, at 200.

41. Richard Lapchick, *There is Gold at the End of this Rainbow*, THE SPORTING NEWS, Mar. 15, 1993, at 8.

42. ALLEN GUTTMAN, A WHOLE NEW BALL GAME: AN INTERPRETATION OF AMERICAN SPORTS 137 (1988).

43. Myles Gordon, *Making the Grade*, 124 SCHOLASTIC UPDATE 20, 21 (1992).

44. MCPHERSON ET. AL., *supra* note 7, at 194. Recognizing that people think this way, Richard Lapchick notes that "there is a great deal of evidence that little has changed since Jackie Robinson took that first courageous step. Although America has made numerous promises to its people, the promise of racial equality has been broken many times over." Richard E. Lapchick, *The Promised Land, in* FRACTURED FOCUS: SPORT AS A REFLECTION OF SOCIETY 76 (Richard E. Lapchick ed., 1986).

45. SHROPSHIRE, *supra* note 8, at 64.

46. David K. Wiggins, *The Notion of Double-Consciousness and the Involvement of Black Athletes in American Sports, in* ETHNICITY AND SPORT IN NORTH AMERICAN HISTORY AND CULTURE 133 (George Eisen & David K. Wiggins eds., 1994).

47. The following is a listing of some of the more revealing and interesting articles on the subject of racism, sports, ethics, and African-American participation in intercollegiate athletics-Adolph H. Grundman, *The Image of Intercollegiate Sports and the Civil Rights Movement: A Historian's*

View, in FRACTURED FOCUS: SPORT AS A REFLECTION OF SOCIETY 77 (Richard E. Lapchick ed., 1986); Eitzen, *supra* note 9; RACISM IN COLLEGE ATHLETICS; THE AFRICAN-AMERICAN ATHLETE'S EXPERIENCE (Dana D. Brooks & Ronald C. Althouse, eds., 1993); Donald Siegel, *Higher Education and the Plight of the Black Male Athlete*, 18 J. SPORT & SOC. ISS. 207 (1994); Lederman, *supra* note 35, at A32; Earl Smith, Review Essay, *Race, Sport and the American University*, 17 J. SPORT & SOC. ISS. 206 (1993); Forrest J. Berghorn, et al., *Racial Participation and Integration in Men's and Women's Intercollegiate Basketball: Continuity and Change, 1958-1985, in* SPORT SOCIOLOGY: CONTEMPORARY THEMES 314-326 (4th ed.) (Andrew Yiannakis, Thomas D. McIntyre, & Merrill J. Melnick eds., 1993); Sailes, *supra* note 29; Gregg A. Jones, et al, *Racial Discrimination in College Football*, 68 SOC. SCI. Q. 70 (1987); Edwards, *supra* note 11; Murray Sperber, *Myths About College Sports, in* SPORT IN CONTEMPORARY SOCIETY 220-228 (D. Stanley Eitzen ed., 1996); Norman R. Yetman & Forrest J. Berghorn, *Racial Participation and Integration in Intercollegiate Basketball: a Longitudinal Perspective*, 10 SOCIOLOGY OF SPORT J. 301 (1993); Harris, *supra* note 23; Raymond A. Winbush, *The Furious Passage of the African-American Intercollegiate Athlete*, 11 J. SPORT & SOC. ISS. 97 (1987); THE RULES OF THE GAME: ETHICS IN COLLEGE SPORT (Richard E. Lapchick & Fred Slaughter eds., 1989); LAPCHICK, *supra* note 28; Lapchick, *supra* note 33; Timothy Davis, *supra* note 34; Timothy Davis, *The Myth of the Superspade: The Persistence of Racism in College Athletics*, 23 FORDHAM URBAN L. J. 201 (1994); WALTER BYERS, UNSPORTSMANLIKE CONDUCT: EXPLOITING COLLEGE ATHLETES (1995); Leonard, *supra* note 37.

48. Davis, *supra* note 47, at 202.

49. *Id.* at 215-16.

50. *See* Sailes, *supra* note 29 & the series with Yetman & Berghorn, *supra* note 47.

51. LAWRENCE H. BERLOW, SPORTS ETHICS: A REFERENCE HANDBOOK 38 (1994).

52. Yetman & Berghorn, *supra* note 47, at 305-06.

53. *Id.* at 306.

54. *Blacks Gain in Sports Jobs*, N.Y. TIMES, August 18, 1994, at B18.

55. *Id.*

56. Davis, *supra* note 35, at 5. It bears noting that 1990 census figures put the African-American population in the United States at 12% so that this figure may seem appropriate at higher than the census. With the overwhelming number of players being African-American it bears some consideration as to why so few African-Americans are able to become coaches.

57. Lapchick, *supra* note 33, at 6; Siegel, *supra* note 47, at 207.

58. Richard Lapchick, *Finally, a Small Step in the Right Direction*, THE SPORTING NEWS, Jan. 31, 1994, at 8. Although this is a better percentage then the number of African-American university presidents and athletic

directors it still seems small in proportion to the amount of black student-athletes in the major sports which are the money makers for the NCAA and universities.

59. Robert Lipsyte, *Blacks on the Court; Why Not on Campus?*, N.Y. TIMES, Mar. 27, 1992, at B9.

60. Lederman, *supra* note 35, at A32. In essence, "far too little is expected of the black student-athlete who becomes a commodity serving the financial interests of the institutions for which they compete." Davis, *supra* note 35, at 5. Also, those African-American high school students who have a greater academic potential are often "deprived of the chance of entering a university" because only black student-athletes are actively recruited. Sperber, *supra* note 47, at 226.

61. Siegel, *supra* note 47, at 208-209.

62. *Id.*

63. *See, e.g.,* BYERS, *supra* note 47, for an elaborate discussion of this problem.

64. DONALD CHU, THE CHARACTER OF AMERICAN HIGHER EDUCATION & INTERCOLLEGIATE SPORT 93-99 (1989).

65. Gary A. Sailes, *The Exploitation of the Black Athlete: Some Alternative Solutions*, 55 J. NEGRO EDUC. 439-40 (1985).

66. *Id.* at 440. This is especially problematic because the "current generation of Black males may easily be the most ... intelligent generation ever born in America." Gaston, *supra* note 15, at 376. At the same time, this generation may be the "least productive" yet due to the problems of racism, poverty, and cultural misguidance that have already been discussed. *Id.*

67. William C. Rhoden, *Athletes on Campus: A New Reality*, N.Y. TIMES, Jan. 8, 1990, at A1; Davis, *supra* note 47, at 260.

68. Eitzen, *supra* note 9, at 249; Smith, *supra* note 47, at 210.

69. *Id.*

70. Smith, *supra* note 47, at 210.

71. *Race in Sports: A Black-and White Issue*, USA TODAY, Dec. 18, 1992, at 3C.

72. *Id.*

73. *Id.*

74. Ewald B. Nyquist, *The Immorality of Big-Power Intercollegiate Athletics*, in SPORT IN HIGHER EDUCATION 107 (Donald Chu et. al. eds., 1985).

75. Exceptions to this include articles such as: Murrell & Curtis, *supra* note 23; Wiggins, *supra* note 32; Kenneth L. Shropshire, *Race & Sports: Working Towards Solutions*, 6 FOR THE RECORD 1 (Feb./Mar. 1995); SHROPSHIRE, *supra* note 8; HOOSE, *supra* note 25; Reggie Jackson, *We Have a Serious Problem that isn't Going Away*, SPORTS ILLUSTRATED, May 11, 1987, at 40-48; Sharon Richardson Jones, *Race and Baseball: Getting Beyond Business as Usual*, 17 J. OF SPORT AND SOC. ISS. 67, 70 (1993); Johnson, *supra* 35.

76. What will be used primarily are RICHARD E. LAPCHICK & JEFFREY R. BENEDICT, 1994 RACIAL REPORT CARD (1994); & RICHARD E. LAPCHICK, 1995 RACIAL REPORT CARD (1995). The only reason that the National Hockey League is not discussed here is because to date no major studies have been conducted regarding this sport and racial issues. Information beyond the mere observation that there have never been many African-American players is not available.

77. 1995 RACIAL REPORT CARD, *supra* note 76, at 2.

78. *Id.*

79. *Id.*

80. *Id.* at 3.

81. *Id.*

82. *Id.* at 13.

83. *Id.*

84. *Id.* at 7-8.

85. 1994 RACIAL REPORT CARD, *supra* note 76, at 18.

86. 1995 RACIAL REPORT CARD, *supra* note 76, actual report card (first page of booklet not numbered).

87. *Id.* at 24.

88. *Id.* at 25.

89. *Id.* actual report card (first page of booklet not numbered).

90. *Id.* at 1.

91. *Id.* at 30.

92. 1994 RACIAL REPORT CARD, *supra* note 76, at 3.

93. 1995 RACIAL REPORT CARD, *supra* note 76, at 11.

94. 1994 RACIAL REPORT CARD, *supra* note 76, at 2.

95. 1995 RACIAL REPORT CARD, *supra* note 76, at 4.

96. Shropshire, *supra* note 8, at 3.

97. Lapchick, *supra* note 41, at 8.

98. Johnson, *supra* note 35, at 41.

99. 1994 RACIAL REPORT CARD, *supra* note 76, at 5.

100. *Race in Sports, supra* note 71, at 3C.

101. *Id.*

102. For a thorough overview of the history of the law regarding discriminatory conduct, *see* DERRICK BELL, RACE, RACISM, AND AMERICAN LAW (1992).

103. Kai Nielsen, *Why Should I Be Moral? Revisited, in* CONTEMPORARY ETHICS: SELECTED READINGS (James P. Sterba ed., 1989).

104. ROBERT L. SIMON, SPORTS AND SOCIAL VALUES 10 (1985).

105. Joseph Boyle, *Natural Law and the Ethics of Traditions, in* NATURAL LAW THEORY 3 (Robert George ed., 1992).

106. As Alasdair MacIntyre states, "every moral philosophy offers explicitly or implicitly at least a partial conceptual analysis of the relationship of an agent to his or her reasons, motives, intentions and actions, and in so doing generally presupposes some claim that these concepts are embodied or at least can be in the real social world." ALASDAIR MACINTYRE, AFTER VIRTUE 23 (2d ed. 1984).

107.John Merriman & Jim Hill, *Ethics, Law, and Sport*, 2 J. LEGAL ASPECTS OF SPORT 57 (1992).

108.ROBERT B. ASHMORE, BUILDING A MORAL SYSTEM 93 (1987).

109.*Id.* at 47.

110.Merriman & Hill, *supra* note 107, at 57.

111.CHRISTINA HOFF SOMMERS, RIGHT AND WRONG: BASIC READINGS IN ETHICS 73 (1986).

112.ASHMORE, *supra* note 108, at 74.

113.*Id.*

114.*Id.*

115.*Id.*

116.SOMMERS, *supra* note 111, at 100.

117.Merriman & Hill, *supra* note 107, at 58.

118.ASHMORE, *supra* note 108, at 75.

119.For a more in depth explanation of utilitarianism, *see* ETHEL M. ALBERT ET. AL, GREAT TRADITIONS IN ETHICS 224-249 (4th ed. 1980); FREDERICK COPLESTON, S.J., A HISTORY OF PHILOSOPHY: Volume VIII 1-93 (1985).

120.SOMMERS, *supra* note 111, at 22.

121.*Id*

122.ASHMORE, *supra* note 108, at 95. This is not the exact wording Kant used but there are many ways he expressed this imperative and many ways scholars have expressed it. This delineation is easily understandable and conveys the same concepts Kant expressed.

123.Merriman & Hill, *supra* note 107, at 59.

124.ASHMORE, *supra* note 108, at 95.

125.*Id.* at 95.

126.SOMMERS, *supra* note 111, at 42.

127.ASHMORE, *supra* note 108, at 95-96.

128.*Id.*

129.*Id.* at 97.

130.*Id.*

131.*Id.* at 98.

132.For further reading on Kant, *see* PETER SINGER, A COMPANION TO ETHICS 175-186 (1993); ALBERT, *supra* note 119, at 224-249.

133.For a good overview of contemporary debate over natural law theory please *see* Robert P. George ed., NATURAL LAW THEORY (1992).

134.BASIC WRITINGS OF SAINT THOMAS AQUINAS, Vol. 2, 250 (Anton C. Pegis ed., 1945).

135.*Id.*

136.COPLESTON, *supra* note 119, Volume II, at 408.

137.LLOYD L. WEINROB, NATURAL LAW AND JUSTICE 58 (1987).

138.BASIC WRITINGS, *supra* note 134, at 773.

139.WEINROB, *supra* note 137, at 58.

140.*Id.*

141.ST. THOMAS AQUINAS: SUMMA THEOLOGIAE A CONCISE TRANSLATION 284 (Timothy Mcdermott ed., 1989).

142. COPLESTON, *supra* note 119, at 406.

143. *Id.*

144. WEINROB, *supra* note 137, at 55-56.

145. *Id.*

146. Boyle, *supra* note 105, at 23.

147. Nielsen, *supra* note 103, at 100.

148. *See, e.g.,* Barry C. Pelton, *Moral and Ethical Issues in Sport,* 44 PHYS. EDUCATOR 273 (Late Winter 1986); D. Stanley Eitzen, *Ethical Problems in American Sport,* 12 J. SPORT & SOC. ISS. 17 (1988); DONALD G. JONES, SPORTS ETHICS IN AMERICA: A BIBLIOGRAPHY, 1970-1990 (1991); HYLAND, *supra* note 5; Gary Bauslaugh, *Ethics in Professional Sports,* 46 THE HUMANIST 30 (Nov./Dec. 1986); George Cohen, *Ethics and the Representation of Professional Athletes,* 4 MARQ. SPORTS L. J. 149 (1993); Howard Slusher, *Sport: Morality and Ethics, in* SPORT AND RELIGION (Shirl J. Hoffman ed., 1992); Merriman & Hill, *supra* note 107; John Stieber, *The Behavior of the NCAA: A Question of Ethics,* 10 J. BUS. ETHICS 445 (1991); BERLOW, *supra* note 50; Peter J. Arnold, *Sport and Moral Education,* 23 J. MORAL EDUC. 75 (1994); PETER MCINTOSH, FAIR PLAY: ETHICS IN SPORT AND EDUCATION (1980); LAPCHICK & SLAUGHTER, *supra* note 47; *Part IV: Sport, Religion and Ethics, in* SPORT AND RELIGION 213-217 (Shirl J. Hoffman ed., 1992); WARREN P. FRALEIGH, RIGHT ACTIONS IN SPORTS: ETHICS FOR CONTESTANTS (1984).

149. Arnold, *supra* note 148, at 75.

150. HYLAND, *supra* note 5, at 33.

151. Hoffman, *supra* note 148, at 216.

152. Pelton, *supra* note 148, at 275. *See also* James W. Keating, *Sportsmanship as a Moral Category, in* PHILOSOPHIC INQUIRY IN SPORT (William J. Morgan, & Klaus Meier eds., 1988); Randolph M. Feezell, *Sportsmanship, in* PHILOSOPHIC INQUIRY IN SPORT (William J. Morgan, & Klaus Meier eds., 1988).

153. *Sportsmanship Report Stresses Importance of Association Action,* NCAA NEWS, Oct. 30, 1995, at 1.

154. *Report of Presidents Commission Committee on Sportsmanship and Ethical Conduct in Intercollegiate Athletics,* NCAA NEWS, Oct. 30, 1995, at 10 [hereinafter *Report of Presidents Commission*].

155. *Id.*

156. Susan Wolf, *Ethics, Legal Ethics, and the Ethics of Law, in* THE GOOD LAWYER: LAWYERS' ROLES AND LAWYERS' ETHICS (David Luban ed., 1984). *See also* DAVID LUBAN, LAWYERS AND JUSTICE: AN ETHICAL STUDY (1988); and Robert E. Fraley & F. Russell Harwell, *Ethics and the Sports Lawyer: A Comprehensive Approach,* 13 J. THE LEGAL PROFESSION 9 (1988).

157. *Id.*

158. Frederick A. Elliston, *The Ethics of Ethics Tests for Lawyers, in* ETHICS AND THE LEGAL PROFESSION 58 (Michael Davis & Frederick A. Ellisont eds., 1986).

159.Burnele V. Powell, *Lawyer Professionalism as Ordinary Morality*, 35 S. TEX. L. REV. 275, 280 (1994).

160.*Report of Presidents Commission, supra* note 154, at 10.

161.Marvin W. Berkowitz & William C. Starr, *Ethics, in* REDUCE YOUR RISK: RISK MANAGEMENT FOR HIGH SCHOOL ATHLETIC PROGRAMS 138 (published by the National Sports Law Institute).

162.ETHICS AND THE LEGAL PROFESSION, *supra* note 158, at 23.

163.Three books which give a good general discussion of the responsibility of being a lawyer and being an athlete-agent are ROBERT O'CONNOR, A COMPLETE GUIDE TO SPORTS AGENTS (1990); KENNETH L. SHROPSHIRE, AGENTS OF OPPORTUNITY: SPORTS AGENTS AND CORRUPTION IN COLLE-GIATE SPORTS (1990); and ROBERT RUXIN, AN ATHLETE'S GUIDE TO AGENTS (3d ed., 1993). Also several articles take different approaches to the review of agent regulation, including: Michael A. Weiss, *The Regulation of Sports Agents: Fact or Fiction*, 1 SPORTS LAW. J. 329 (1994); Curtis D. Rypma, *Sports Agents Representing Athletes: The Need For Comprehensive State Legislation*, 24 VAL. U. L. REV. 481 (1990); Gary P. Konn, *Sports Agents Representing Professional Athletes: Being Certified Means Never Having to Say You're Qualified*, 7 ENT. & SPORTS LAW. 1 (Fall 1988)

164.As to perspectives on the ethical regulation of sports agents, *see* Paul T. Dee, *Ethical Aspects of Representing Professional Athletes*, 3 MARQ. SPORTS L.J. 111 (1992) & Cohen, *supra* note 148.

165.David Lawrence Dunn, Note, *Regulation of Sports Agents: Since at First it Hasn't Succeeded, Try Federal Legislation*, 39 HASTINGS L.J. 1031, 1043 (1988). A copy of these regulations, entitled NFLPA REGULATIONS GOVERNING CONTRACT ADVISORS, can be obtained from the NFLPA.

166.*Id.*

167.*Id.* at 1044.

168.*Id.*

169.*Id.* at 1045-46.

170.MARTIN J. GREENBERG, SPORTS LAW PRACTICE 213 (Vol. 1, 1993). For a copy of these rules entitled NBPA REGULATIONS GOVERNING PLAYER AGENTS, *see* GREENBERG (Vol. 2) at 610.

171.Dunn, *supra* note 165, at 1047.

172.*Id.*

173.T. Jesse Wilde, *The Regulation of Athlete-Agents*, 2 J. LEGAL ASPECTS OF SPORT 18, 20 (1992).

174.*Id.*

175.Dunn, *supra* note 165, at 1048.

176.GREENBERG, *supra* note 170, Vol. 1, at 380. For a copy of these regulations entitled MLBPA REGULATIONS GOVERNING PLAYER AGENTS *see* GREENBERG, *supra* note 170, Vol. 2, at 656.

177.GREENBERG, *supra* note 170, Vol. 1, at 380.

178.Wilde, *supra* note 173, at 21.

179.For an overview of this type of regulation *see* Jan Stiglitz, *NCAA-Based Agent Regulation: Who Are We Protecting?* 67 N.D. L. REV. 215 (1991);

Richard J. Evrard, *Common Areas of Agent Liability: "NCAA Rules"*, in SPORTS DOLLARS AND SENSE CONFERENCE MANUAL (published by the National Sports Law Institute, Oct. 1993).

180.1995-96 NCAA MANUAL, Art. 12.3.1.

181.*Id.* at Art. 12.3.1.1.

182.*Id.* at Art. 12.3.2. The NCAA also provides athletes with career counseling panels so that they can evaluate their career possibilities without harming their eligibility. GREENBERG, *supra* note 170, Vol. 1, at 871-73.

183.*Id.* at Art. 12.3.3.1.

184.SHROPSHIRE, *supra* note 163, at 37-38.

185.Wilde, *supra* note 175, at 19.

186.*Id.*

187.*Id.*

188.*Id.*

189.Dunn, *supra* note 165, at 1042.

190.Lori K. Miller et. al., *A Uniform Code to Regulate Athlete Agents*, 16 J. SPORT & SOC. ISS. 93, 95 (1992).

191.Dunn, *supra* note 165, at 1042.

192.For examples of these regulations *see* Kenneth L. Shropshire, *Common Areas of Agent Liability: "Agent Regulations"*, in SPORTS DOLLARS AND SENSE CONFERENCE MANUAL (published by the National Sports Law Institute, Oct. 1993); GREENBERG, *supra* note 163, Vol. 1, at 892-903; GREENBERG, *supra* note 170, at 262-263 (Supp. 1994).

193.SHROPSHIRE, *supra* note 163, at 43.

194.*Id.*

195.*Id.*; *see also* Wilde, *supra* note 175, at 21.

196.Wilde, *supra* note 173, at 22.

197.*Id.* at 22-23.

198.GREENBERG, *supra* note 170, Vol. 1, at 896.

199.SHROPSHIRE, *supra* note 163, at 45.

200.Wilde, *supra*, note 175, at 22.

201.GREENBERG, *supra* note 170, Vol. 1, at 904

202.*Id.* at 905.

203.*Id.* at 904-905; SHROPSHIRE, *supra* note 163, at 92-93.

204.GREENBERG, *supra* note 170, Vol. 1, at 904.

205.This proposal came from the Sports Lawyers Association in 1985. Wilde, *supra* note 173, at 26.

206.*See* DISCUSSION DRAFT OF FEDERAL SPORTS-AGENT LEGISLATION PREPARED BY CONGRESSMAN JOHN BRYANT OF TEXAS, *in* SHROPSHIRE, *supra* note 163, Appendix III, at 131-144.

207.18 U.S.C. 1961 et seq. (1988).

208.United States v. Walters, 711 F.Supp. 1435 (N.D. Ill. 1989).

209.THOMAS D. MORGAN & RONALD D. ROTUNDA, MODEL CODE OF PROFESSIONAL RESPONSIBILITY, MODEL RULES OF PROFESSIONAL CONDUCT,

AND OTHER SELECTED STANDARDS INCLUDING CALIFORNIA RULES ON PROFESSIONAL RESPONSIBILITY, Model Rules, Rule 8.4 (1993).

210.*Id.* at Rule 8.1.

211.*Id.* at Rule 8.3.

212.*Id.* at Rule 1.1.

213.*Id.* at Rule 4.1.

214.*Id.* at Rule 1.5.

215.For an interesting group of articles regarding these rules and their applicability to sports lawyers *see* Daniel L. Shneidman, *Applying the American Bar Association Model Rules Regarding Advertising, Solicitation, Marketing, Specialization and Fees to Lawyers Representing Professional Athletes,* SPORTS DOLLARS AND SENSE CONFERENCE, National Sports Law Institute and Arthur Anderson & Co. (Oct. 22-24, 1992); Daniel L. Shneidman, *Law, Ethics and Professional Responsibility of Attorney Representation in Sports and the Arts,* STATE BAR OF WISCONSIN: 1995 ANNUAL CONVENTION: SPORTS, RECREATION AND ENTERTAINMENT LAW SECTION (June 14, 1995); Daniel L. Shneidman, *Selected Issues of Client Representation By "Sports" Lawyers Under the Model Rules of Professional Conduct,* SECOND ANNUAL SPORTS DOLLARS AND SENSE CONFERENCE, National Sports Law Institute and Arthur Anderson & Co. (Oct. 28-30, 1993); Daniel L. Shneidman, *Selected Issues of Client Representation By "Sports" Lawyers Under the Model Rules of Professional Conduct,* 4 MARQ. SPORTS L.J. 129 (1993).

216.MORGAN & ROTUNDA, *supra* note 209, at 3.

217.*Id.* at 143.

218.*Id.* at 144.

219.GREENBERG, *supra* note 170, Vol. 1, at 924.

220.*See supra* note 215 for specific examples. *See also* Edward Vincent King Jr., *Practical Advice for Attorneys,* 4 MARQ. SPORTS L.J. 89 (1993), for an interesting perspective from a lawyer who prosecutes other lawyers for violations of these types of rules.

221.Steven R. Salbu, *Law, and Conformity, Ethics and Conflict: The Trouble with Law-Based Conceptions of Ethics,* 68 IND. L.J. 101, 103 (1992).

222.Berkowitz & Starr, *supra* note 161, at 160.

223.*Id.*

224.*Id.*

225.*Id.* at 161.

226.*Id.* at 159.

227.Salbu, *supra* note 221, at 106.

228.For a copy of this code *see* SHROPSHIRE, *supra* note 163, at 113-118.

229.GREENBERG, *supra* note 170, Vol. 1, at 891.

230.Dunn, *supra* note 165, at 1040.

231.*Id.*

232.*Id.*

233.*Id.* at 1041.

234.*Id.*

235. MORGAN & ROTUNDA, *supra* note 209, at 238-269.

236. *Id.*

237. *Id.* at 245.

238. *Id.*

239. *Id.* at 246.

240. *Id.* at 250.

241. *Id.* at 252.

242. *See* GREENBERG, *supra* note 170, Vol. 2, at 634-649.

243. *Id.* at 634.

244. *Id.*

245. *Id.* at 636.

246. *Id.* at 638-644.

247. Miller et al., *supra* note 190, at 99.

248. *Id.*

249. *Id.* at 100.

250. *Id.*

251. *Id.*

252. *Id.*

253. *Id.* at 101.

254. This type of provision would be similar to any appearance agreement which is already incorporated into such contracts.

255. *See, e.g.,* BYERS, *supra* note 47, at 374-384; *Athletes' Bill of Rights*, 6 ARENA REV. 58 (May 1982).

256. *See* text accompanying footnotes 247-52.

257. 1995 RACIAL REPORT CARD, *supra* note 76, at 27-28. Specifically, the NBPA and NFLPA received grades of A while the MLBPA received a grade of C-.

258. Specifically, 23% of those in the NBA league office, 21% of those in the NFL office, and 23% of those in the MLB league office were African-American in 1995. *Id.* at actual report card.

259. *Comparison of Baseball Affirmative-Action Plans*, USA TODAY, Mar. 30, 1993, at 5C.

260. *Id.*

261. SHROPSHIRE, *supra* note 163, at 143.

262. Jones, *supra* note 75, at 70.

263. *Id.*

264. 1995 RACIAL REPORT CARD, *supra* note 76, at 6.

265. *Id.* at 8.

266. This is not meant to imply that these individuals somehow cause more scandals. Because African-Americans make up the majority of stars, they end up being involved in these scandals.

267. *See* text accompanying footnotes 247-52; *infra* section IV.C.

268. *See infra* section IV.C.

269. Dee, *supra* note 165, at 114.

270. SHROPSHIRE, *supra* note 163, at 65.

271. *Id.* at 228.

272. SHROPSHIRE, *supra* note 163, at 230.

Index

About the Editors

Paul M. Anderson is the Assistant Director of the National Sports Law Institute and an Adjunct Assistant Professor of Law at Marquette University. He is the author of SPORTS LAW: A DESKTOP HANDBOOK, and his articles have appeared in numerous sports-related publications. His article, "Spoiling a Good Walk: Does the ADA Change the Rules of Sport?" appeared in the inaugural issue of the VIRGINIA JOURNAL OF SPORTS AND THE LAW. He holds both his undergraduate and law degrees from Marquette University and is a former Editor-in-Chief of the MARQUETTE SPORTS LAW JOURNAL.

Joseph Gordon Hylton is Associate Professor of Law and Adjunct Professor of History at Marquette University. From 1997-1999, he served as the Interim Director of the National Sports Law Institute. He is a graduate of Oberlin College and the University of Virginia Law School and holds a Ph.D. in the History of American Civilization from Harvard University. A specialist in the history of sports law, he is also the author of PROFESSIONAL VALUES AND INDIVIDUAL AUTONOMY: THE UNITED STATES SUPREME COURT AND LAWYER ADVERTISING (1998) and PROPERTY LAW AND THE PUBLIC INTEREST (with Callies, Mandelker, and Franzese, 1998).

ABOUT THE CONTRIBUTORS

Paul M. Anderson (see previous page).

W. Kent Davis is a Captain in the Judge Advocate General's Corps, United States Army and currently serves as trial counsel in the Military Law Division at the U.S. Army Reserve Command, Fort McPherson, Georgia. He received his undergraduate degree from Louisiana State University and his J.D. from Georgia State University, where he served as Editor-in-Chief of the GEORGIA STATE UNIVERSITY LAW REVIEW. He has published articles in the GONZAGA LAW REVIEW, SOUTH TEXAS LAW JOURNAL, ARIZONA JOURNAL OF INTERNATIONAL AND COMPARATIVE LAW, VALPARAISO UNIVERSITY LAW REVIEW, GEORGIA STATE UNIVERSITY LAW REVIEW, NAVY TIMES, NAVAL MEDICINE, and the VOICE OF THE DOUBLE EAGLE.

David B. Falk is an attorney, sports agent, and chairman of SFX Entertainment's Sports Group. He is a graduate of Syracuse University and received his law degree from George Washington University. After law school Falk joined ProServ Inc. which he helped expand into the representation of professional basketball players. In 1992, he left ProServ to form Falk Associates Management Enterprises (FAME) which he sold in 1998 to SFX Entertainment. Falk is probably best known as Michael Jordan's agent.

Martin J. Greenberg is an Adjunct Professor at the Marquette University Law School as well as a practicing attorney and Chairman of the Stadium Game Management Group in Milwaukee, Wisconsin. From 1990 to 1997, he was Director of the National Sports Law Institute. He is currently Secretary of the Wisconsin Sports Authority and a member of the Board of the Badger State Games. His books include REAL ESTATE PRACTICE (1969); REAL ESTATE TAX AND ACCELERATED COST RECOVERY SYSTEM (with Sayas and Steiner, 1982); WISCONSIN REAL ESTATE (1982); SPORT$BIZ (with Hoffman, 1989); SPORTS LAW PRACTICE (1993, 2nd ed., with Gray, 1998); and THE STADIUM GAME (with Gray, 1996). He is a graduate of the University of Wisconsin-Madison and the Marquette University Law School.

Bernard P. Maloy is an Associate Professor in the Division of Kinesiology at the University of Michigan where he teaches courses in the legal aspects and management of sport and recreation. Prof. Maloy contributed two chapters to SPORT LAW FOR SPORT MANAGERS (1997) as well as essays published in USA Hockey's Coaching Education Manual (1994) and the handbooks of the Youth Sports Institute at Michigan State University. He is also the author of numerous other articles in the field of sports law. He is a graduate of Wheeling Jesuit College and Notre Dame Law School and holds a masters degree from Ohio University.

Kevin E. Martens is a graduate of Marquette University and Harvard Law School. He currently serves as an Assistant United States Attorney in Milwaukee where he acts as coordinator for the Civil Health Care Fraud, Affirmative Civil Enforcement, and Americans With Disabilities Act divisions of the Milwaukee office. He previously practiced with the Milwaukee law firm of Foley & Lardner.

Matthew J. Mitten is Professor of Law at Marquette University and Director of the National Sports Law Institute. Prof. Mitten currently serves as a consultant for the American Medical Society for Sports Medicine and the Osteopathic Academy for Sports Medicine, and in 1999-2000, he is Chair-Elect of the American Association of Law Schools' Section on Law and Sports. A graduate of Ohio State University and the University of Toledo Law School, he has written extensively in the areas of sports medicine, sport and disability law, and sport and antitrust.

Jan Stiglitz is Professor of Law at the California Western School of Law. He is a former chair of the Sports and Law Section of the Association of American Law Schools and has published extensively in the field of sports law. He is also the host of California Western's Sports Law Symposia. Prof. Stiglitz holds an undergraduate degree from SUNY-Buffalo; a J.D. degree from Albany Law School; and an LL.M. from Harvard.

Gary D. Way heads the Sports Law Practice Group at Nike and is the chief legal advisor to its Sports Marketing Department. Prior to joining Nike, he spent 10 years in the Legal Department of the National Basketball Association, first as a staff attorney in the Commissioner's Office, then as the Assistant General Counsel of NBA Properties. He received his law degree from New York Univer-

sity and his undergraduate degree from Rutgers University where he played varsity football.

T. Jesse Wilde is currently a lawyer in private practice with Huckvale & Co. in Lethbridge, Alberta. He also directs ProGoal Management, a sports administration firm specializing in the representation of athletes. Before entering private practice, he was an Assistant Professor and Director of the Sport Management Program at Rice University, Houston, Texas. Wilde received his undergraduate and law degrees from the University of Alberta and an M.S. Degree from the University of Massachusetts—Amherst.

Phoebe Weaver Williams is an Associate Professor of Law at Marquette University where she received both her undergraduate and law degrees. Her principal areas of teaching and research are labor law, employment discrimination, and civil rights.

John Wunderli is an attorney with Heller, Ehrman, White & McAuliffe, in Washington D.C., where he works as a litigator, with a particular emphasis on antitrust law. Prior to joining his current firm, he worked for the Antitrust Division of the United States Department of Justice. Wunderli is a graduate of the University of Utah and Harvard Law School.

Raymond L. Yasser is a Professor of Law at the University of Tulsa. He is the author of numerous articles in sports law as well as TORTS AND SPORTS: LEGAL LIABILITY IN PROFESSIONAL AND AMATEUR ATHLETICS (1985) and is the co-author of the first sports law casebook, SPORTS LAW: CASES AND MATERIALS (with Gopelrud and McCurdy, 3rd ed. 1997). In recent years he has been involved in several high profile cases involving the rights of female high school athletes under Title IX. He is a graduate of the University of Delaware and Duke Law School.

About the
National Sports
Law Institute

In 1989, in response to the need for a greater understanding of the changing relationship between sports and the law, the Marquette University Law School established the National Sports Law Institute. The Institute was the first, and still the only, law school-affiliated academic center for the study of sport in the United States. From the beginning the Institute's primary mission has been to study the relationship between law and all phases of amateur and professional sports and to provide sports law-related information to students, lawyers, sports industry personnel, and the general public.

The Institute is located in Milwaukee, Wisconsin, on the campus of the Marquette University Law School. Each year it sponsors several conferences devoted to issues of contemporary interest to the sports law community. In November 1998, for example, it hosted, and co-sponsored with the Association of American Law Schools, a conference entitled "Sports Law in the 21st Century" which brought together leading sports law scholars from across the United States. In April 1999, the nation's leading experts on sport and disability law gathered together under Institute sponsorship for "Disability Issues in Sport Law."

Since 1990, the National Sports Law Institute has published, with the assistance of Marquette University law students, the MARQUETTE SPORTS LAW JOURNAL, the first law journal devoted exclusively to sports law. Other National Sports Law Institute publications include FOR THE RECORD (the Institute's bi-monthly newsletter covering Institute news and breaking issues in the field of sports law), FOR THE RECORD ONLINE (an electronic supplement to the newsletter); and YOU MAKE THE CALL. . .(a quarterly newsletter identifying and discussing the significance of recent sports law cases). Books and manuals published by the Institute include SPORTS LAW PRACTICE (1992); REDUCE YOUR RISK: RISK MANAGEMENT FOR HIGH SCHOOL ATHLETIC PROGRAM (1993); THE STADIUM GAME (1996); SPORTS LAW:

A DESKTOP HANDBOOK (1999); and SPORTS LAW AND REGULATION (1999).

The Institute also provides numerous sports law-related opportunities for students enrolled in the sports law program at the Marquette University Law School. These include internships with the Milwaukee Brewers, the Milwaukee Rampage, Conference USA, and Miller Brewing Company; a sports law workshop series that brings speakers from the sports industry to the Marquette campus; a moot court team; and career panels which focus on finding jobs in the sports industry.

For information about the Institute and its various programs contact Paul Anderson, Assistant Director, National Sports Law Institute; Marquette University Law School; 1103 W. Wisconsin Ave.; P.O. Box 1881; Milwaukee, WI 53201-1881; (414) 288-5815; www.mu.edu/law/sports/sports.htm.